Professional Examinations

PART 3

Paper 3.3

Performance Management

ACCA Study Text

ACCA
Official Publisher

ftc
FTC Foulks Lynch
A Kaplan Professional Company

British Library Cataloguing-in-Publication Data

A catalogue record for this book is available from the British Library.

Published by:

FTC Foulks Lynch
Swift House
Market Place
Wokingham
Berkshire
RG40 1AP

ISBN 1 84390 366 0

Printed and bound in Great Britain.

Acknowledgements

We are grateful to the Association of Chartered Certified Accountants, the Chartered Institute of Management Accountants and the Institute of Chartered Accountants in England and Wales for permission to reproduce past examination questions. The answers have been prepared by FTC Foulks Lynch.

Contents

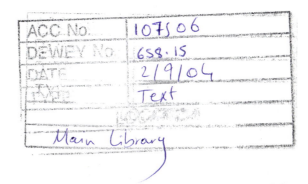

Introduction

This Study Text is the ACCA's official text for Paper 3.3 *Performance Management*, and is part of the ACCA's official series produced for students taking the ACCA examinations.

This new 2004 edition has been produced with direct guidance from the examiner. It covers the syllabus and study guide in great detail, giving appropriate weighting to the various topics. Targeted very closely on the examination, this study text is written in a way that will help you assimilate the information easily. Numerous practice questions and exam type questions at the end of each chapter reinforce your knowledge.

DEFINITION

- **Definitions.** The text defines key words and concepts, placing them in the margin, with a clear heading, as on the left. The purpose of including these definitions is to focus your attention on the point being covered.

KEY POINT

- **Key points**. In the margin you will see key points at regular intervals. The purpose of these is to summarise concisely the key material being covered.

ACTIVITY 1

- **Activities**. The text involves you in the learning process with a series of activities designed to catch your attention and make you concentrate and respond. The feedback to activities is at the end of each chapter.

SELF-TEST QUESTIONS

- **Self-test questions**. At the end of each chapter there is a series of self-test questions. The purpose of these is to help you revise some of the key elements of the chapter. All the answers to these questions can be found in the text.

EXAM-TYPE QUESTIONS

- **End of chapter questions**. At the end of each chapter we include examination-type questions. These will give you a very good idea of the sort of thing the examiner will ask and will test your understanding of what has been covered.

Syllabus and study guide

CONTENTS

Objectives of the study guide

This study guide is designed to help you plan your studies and to provide a more detailed interpretation of the syllabus for ACCA's professional examinations. It contains both the syllabus and a study guide for each paper, which you can follow when preparing for the examination.

The syllabus outlines the content of the paper and how that content is examined. The study guide takes the syllabus content and expands it into study sessions of similar length. These sessions indicate what the examiner expects of candidates for each part of the syllabus, and therefore gives you guidance in the skills you are expected to demonstrate in the examinations.

Syllabus content

1 MANAGEMENT ACCOUNTING FRAMEWORK

a Objectives of management accounting information in relation to:
  - i short-term planning and strategic planning
  - ii control and decision making
  - iii effective use of management accounting techniques.

b The conceptual framework for changes in management accounting
  - i contingency theory
  - iii institutional theory

c Trends and developments in management accounting techniques and methods
  - i evaluation and promotion of change in techniques and methods used
  - ii evaluation of the effect of the rate of change of technology and products on management accounting
  - iii current issues in management accounting principles and their relevance and application
  - iv activity-based management

d Impact of changes in business structures
  - i appraisal of continued use of management accounting techniques (e.g. standard costing)
  - ii impact on management accounting of changes in business processes and management techniques
  - iii changes in business structure and management accounting (e.g. team/project focus).

2 DESIGN OF MANAGEMENT ACCOUNTING SYSTEMS

a System objectives and the uses of information in relation to:
  - i short-term and strategic planning
  - ii control and decision making
  - iii effective use of management accounting techniques.

b Sources of information
  - i from within the organisation
  - ii from suppliers and customers
  - iii by comparison with competitors
  - iv from government and other statistical sources.

c Recording and processing methods
  - i collection and recording of monetary and non-monetary information
  - ii identification of requirements for different purposes
  - iii influence of management accounting principles and techniques
  - iv influence of IT systems
  - v effect of type of business entity.

d Format of reports
  - i analysis and dissemination to relevant individuals/groups
  - ii effect of management structure and style
  - iii frequency, timing and degree of accuracy
  - iv influence of trend, materiality and controllability issues.

3 PERFORMANCE MEASUREMENT

a Performance hierarchy
  - i mission statement and the fulfilment of a vision
  - ii corporate planning and the achievement of strategic objectives
  - iii the accomplishment of operational plans
  - iv the attainment of specific departmental targets.

b The scope of performance measurement
  i financial performance – profitability, liquidity, activity and gearing
  ii non-financial business indicators
  iii performance measurement for non-profit seeking organisations
  iv performance measurement for public sector service provision
  v long and short run performance
  vi performance measurement models such as the balanced scorecard (to improve the range and linkage between performance measures) and the performance pyramid (to relate strategy and operations).

c External considerations
  i economic/market conditions
  ii financial, environmental and service quality regulation from government agencies.

d Management impact on performance measurement
  i accountability issues
  ii benefits and problems of performance measurement
  iii reward schemes and performance measurement
  iv management style and performance measurement.

4 PLANNING AND CONTROL

a Strategic management accounting
  i corporate v operational strategy
  ii life cycle issues
  iii SWOT analysis
  iv benchmarking
  v consideration of risk and uncertainty
  vi strategic management accounting in the context of multinational companies.

b Budgeting and budgetary control
  i the appraisal of alternative approaches to budgeting – incremental, rolling, ABB etc
  ii budgeting as a planning and control device
  iii quantitative aids and risk analysis
  iv behavioural aspects
  v current developments in budgeting.

5 DECISION MAKING

a Pricing strategies and the evaluation of pricing decisions
  i price/demand relationships
  ii relevant costs and pricing decisions
  iii pricing and product life cycles
  iv target costing and pricing
  v transfer pricing and decision making
  vi transfer-pricing in the context of multinational companies

b Information for decision making
  i relevant costs analysis
  ii CVP analysis and profit maximisation
  iii product profitability and limiting factor analysis
  iv customer profitability analysis
  v theory of constraints and throughput accounting
  vi accounting for uncertainty
  vii DCF techniques.

Excluded topics

The syllabus content outlines the areas for assessment. No areas of knowledge are specifically excluded from the syllabus.

Key areas of the syllabus

The key topic areas are as follows:

- the contribution of management accounting systems towards the achievement of corporate objectives
- identifying appropriate performance indicators for particular business situations
- abstracting relevant information from financial reports to assess performance
- identifying and processing costs as an aid to decision making.

Additional information

The Study Guide provides more detailed guidance on the syllabus.

Study guide

1 STRATEGIC PLANNING AND DECISION MAKING

Syllabus reference 1a, Chapter 1

- identify the characteristics of strategic planning and decision making
- contrast strategic planning with short term /operational planning
- identify the areas of management accounting information which are of importance in strategic management
- evaluate the relevance of discounted cash flow principles in information for strategic decision making
- select and analyse costs and revenues relevant to strategic planning and decision making in a range of situations

2 SHORT RUN DECISION MAKING AND CONTROL

Syllabus reference 1a, Chapter 1

- explain the significance of endogenous information sources in relation to short run decision making and control

- identify the characteristics of short term non-strategic activities
- identify the areas of management accounting information appropriate for short term decision making
- explain the differences between management control and operational control in the context of short run decision making and control

3 CHANGES IN MANAGEMENT ACCOUNTING

Syllabus reference 1b, Chapter 4

- explain the contingency theory of management accounting: Otley
- explain how institutional theory presents a framework for understanding changes in, and the implications for, management accounting: Powell and Di Maggio
- explain and demonstrate activity based management

4 TRENDS IN MANAGEMENT ACCOUNTING TECHNIQUES AND METHODS

Syllabus reference 1c, Chapter 4

- discuss the expansion in the scope of management accounting in the last 40 years
- identify and discuss some recently adopted management accounting techniques
- explain how new techniques may be evaluated
- discuss the ways in which management accounting practitioners are made aware of new techniques
- illustrate how an organisation's structure, culture and strategy will influence the adoption of new methods and techniques
- assess the continuing effectiveness of traditional techniques within a rapidly changing business environment

5 TECHNOLOGICAL CHANGE AND MANAGEMENT ACCOUNTING

Syllabus reference 1c, 1d, Chapter 5

- discuss the changing accounting information needs of modern service orientated business compared with the needs of traditional manufacturing industry
- discuss how modern IT systems provide the opportunity for instant access to management accounting data throughout an organisation
- discuss how modern IT systems facilitate the remote input of management accounting data in an acceptable format by non-finance specialists
- explain how modern information systems provide instant access to previously unavailable data that can be used for benchmarking and control purposes
- discuss the need for businesses to continually refine and develop their management accounting systems if they are to prosper in an increasingly competitive and global market

6 CHANGES IN BUSINESS STRUCTURE AND MANAGEMENT ACCOUNTING

Syllabus reference 1d, Chapter 5

- identify the particular information needs of organisations adopting a team /project focus
- discuss the concept of business integration and the linkage between people, operations, strategy and technology
- explain the influence of Business Process Re-engineering on systems development
- identify and discuss the required changes in management accounting systems as a consequence of empowering staff to manage sectors of a business

7 SYSTEM DESIGN AND SYSTEM OBJECTIVES

Syllabus reference 2a, Chapter 2

- identify the accounting information requirements for strategic planning, management control and operational control and decision making
- describe, with reference to management accounting, ways in which the information requirements of a management structure are affected by the features of the structure
- evaluate the objectives of management accounting and management accounting information
- list and explain the attributes and principles of management accounting information
- explain the integration of management accounting information within an overall information system
- define and discuss the merits of, and potential problems with, open and closed systems
- suggest the ways in which contingent (internal and external) factors influence management accounting and its use
- illustrate how anticipated human behaviour will influence the design of a management accounting system
- explain and discuss the impact of responsibility accounting on information requirements

8 INTERNAL SOURCES OF INFORMATION

Syllabus reference 2c, 2d, Chapter 3

- identify the principal internal sources of management accounting information
- illustrate how these principal sources of information might be used for control purposes
- identify the direct data capture and process costs of internally generated management accounting information
- identify the indirect costs of producing internal information
- explain the principal controls required in generating and distributing internal information
- discuss the factors that need to be considered when determining the capacity and development potential of a system
- explain the procedures that may be necessary to ensure security of highly confidential information that is not for external consumption

9 EXTERNAL SOURCES OF INFORMATION

Syllabus reference 2c, 2d, Chapter 3

- identify common external sources of information e.g. suppliers, government, trade associations, customers, database suppliers
- identify the costs associated with these external sources
- discuss the limitations of using externally generated information
- identify the categories of external information that are likely to be a useful addition to an organisation's management accounting system
- illustrate how the information might be used in planning and control activities e.g. benchmarking against similar organisations

10 RECORDING AND PROCESSING INFORMATION

Syllabus reference 2c, 2d, Chapter 3

- identify the stages in the information processing cycle in the context of accounting information
- identify how the collection and analysis of information is influenced by management accounting principles and techniques being used by the organisation
- describe the systems involved in the collection and recording of monetary and non-monetary information
- illustrate how the type of business entity will influence the recording and processing methods
- explain how IT developments e.g. spreadsheets, accountancy software packages and electronic mail may influence recording and processing systems
- discuss the difficulties associated with recording and processing data of a qualitative nature

11 PERFORMANCE HIERARCHY

Syllabus reference 3a, Chapter 9

- discuss the purpose of a mission statement and the pursuit of a vision
- discuss the structure and content of a mission statement
- explain how high level corporate objectives are developed
- identify strategic objectives and how they may be incorporated into the corporate plan
- explain how strategic objectives are cascaded down the organisation via the formulation of subsidiary objectives
- identify any relevant social and ethical obligations that should be considered in the pursuit of corporate objectives
- discuss the concept of the 'planning gap' and alternative strategies to 'fill the gap'
- identify the characteristics of operational performance
- contrast the relative significance of planning as against controlling activities at different levels in the performance hierarchy

12 FINANCIAL PERFORMANCE IN THE PRIVATE SECTOR

Syllabus reference 3b, 3c, Chapter 10

- explain why the primary objective of financial performance should be concerned with the benefits of the shareholders
- discuss the crucial objectives of survival and business growth
- discuss the appropriateness of differing measures of profitability e.g. ROCE, EPS, ROI, sales margin, EBITDA, Residual Income, NPV, IRR
- explain why indicators of liquidity and gearing need to be considered alongside profitability
- compare and contrast short and long run financial performance and the resulting management issues
- contrast the traditional relationship between profits and share value with the long term profit expectations of the stock market and recent financial performance of new technology/communication companies

13 NON-FINANCIAL PERFORMANCE INDICATORS FOR BUSINESS

Syllabus reference 3b, 3c, Chapter 11

- discuss the interaction of NFPIs with financial performance indicators
- discuss the implications of the growing emphasis on NFPIs
- identify and comment on the significance of NFPIs in relation to employees e.g. staff turnover, sickness rates
- identify and comment on the significance of NFPIs in relation to product/service quality e.g. customer satisfaction reports, repeat business ratings, customer loyalty, access and availability
- discuss the difficulties in interpreting data on qualitative issues
- discuss the significance of brand awareness and company profile

14 PERFORMANCE MEASUREMENT FOR NON-PROFIT SEEKING ORGANISATIONS

Syllabus reference 3b, 3c, Chapter 12

- discuss the potential for diversity in objectives depending on organization type
- comment on the need to achieve objectives with limited funds that may not be controllable
- identify and explain ways in which performance may be judged in non-profit seeking organisations
- comment on the difficulty in measuring outputs when performance is not judged in terms of money or an easily quantifiable objective
- explain how the combination of politics and the desire to measure public sector performance may result in undesirable service outcomes
- comment on 'value for money' service as a not-for-profit sector goal

15 PERFORMANCE – A BROAD PERSPECTIVE

Syllabus reference 3c, Chapter 13

- comment on the need to consider the environment in which an organization is operating when assessing its performance e.g. What are the prevailing market conditions? Is funding relatively easy or difficult to secure? Does the strength of the national currency impact on the organisation's performance? Is the prevailing political climate particularly favourable or unfavourable towards the organisation currently? How have these issues changed over time?
- consider the impact of governmental regulation on the performance measurement techniques used and the performance levels achieved (for example, in the case of utility services and former state monopolies)

16 ALTERNATIVE VIEWS OF PERFORMANCE MEASUREMENT

Syllabus reference 3b, Chapter 13

- discuss the 'balanced scorecard' as a way in which to improve the range and linkage of performance measures
- discuss the 'performance pyramid' as a way in which to link strategy and operations
- discuss the work of Fitzgerald and Moon that considers performance measurement in business services using building blocks for dimensions, standards and rewards

17 MANAGEMENT BEHAVIOUR AND PERFORMANCE

Syllabus reference 3d, Chapter 13

- explain the relationship between performance measurement systems and behaviour
- discuss how performance measurement systems can influence behaviour
- consider the accountability issues arising from performance measurement systems
- identify the ways in which performance measurement systems may send the 'wrong signals' and result in undesirable business consequences
- comment on the potential beneficial and adverse consequences of linking reward schemes to performance measurement
- explain how management style needs to be considered when designing an effective performance measurement system

18 STRATEGIC PLANNING AND CONTROL

Syllabus reference 4a, Chapter 17

- compare strategic with operational planning and control
- explain how organisational survival in the long term necessitates consideration of life cycle issues
- identify the role of corporate planning in clarifying corporate objectives, making strategic decisions and checking progress towards the objectives
- explain the structure of corporate planning
- discuss the combining of strategic planning with freewheeling opportunism in a fast changing business environment
- comment on the potential conflict between strategic plans and short term localised decisions
- explain the principles of SWOT analysis
- explain how SWOT analysis may assist in the planning process
- comment on the benefits and difficulties of benchmarking performance with best practice organisations
- explain how risk and uncertainty play an especially important role in long term strategic planning that relies upon forecasts of exogenous variables

19 BUDGETING AND BUDGETARY CONTROL I

Syllabus reference 4b, Chapter 14

- describe the internal and external sources of planning information for an organisation
- list the information used in the preparation of the master budget and in its functional components
- contrast the information used in the operation of zero based budgeting and incremental budgeting
- explain and illustrate the use of budgeting as a planning aid in the coordination of business activity
- explain and illustrate the relevance of budgeting in the coordination of business activities
- explain and quantify the application of positive and negative feedback in the operation of budgetary control
- explain and quantify the application of feed-forward control in the operation of budgeting

20 BUDGETING AND BUDGETARY CONTROL II

Syllabus reference 4b, Chapter 15

- identify quantitative aids which may be used in budgetary planning and control
- discuss and evaluate methods for the analysis of costs into fixed and variable components
- give examples to demonstrate the use of forecasting techniques in the budgetary planning process
- explain the use of forecasting techniques in the budgetary planning process
- describe the use of learning curve theory in budgetary planning and control
- implement learning curve theory
- identify factors which may cause uncertainty in the setting of budgets and in the budgetary control process
- identify the effects of flexible budgeting in reducing uncertainty in budgeting
- illustrate the use of probabilities in budgetary planning and comment on the relevance of the information thus obtained
- explain the use of computer based models in accommodating uncertainty in budgeting and in promoting 'what-if' analysis

21 BUDGETING AND BUDGETARY CONTROL III

Syllabus reference 4b, Chapter 16

- identify the factors which affect human behaviour in budgetary planning and control
- compare and contrast ways in which alternative management styles may affect the operation of budgetary planning and control systems
- explain budgeting as a bargaining process between people
- explain the conflict between personal and corporate aspiration and its impact on budgeting
- explain the application of contingency theory to the budgeting process
- discuss the impact of political, social, economic and technological change on budgeting
- critically review the use of budgetary planning and control
- enumerate and evaluate the strengths and weaknesses of alternative budget models such as fixed and flexible, rolling, activity based, zero based and incremental
- identify the effects on staff and management of the operation of budgetary planning and control
- identify and appraise current developments in budgeting

22 SHORT RUN DECISIONS I

Syllabus reference 5b, Chapter 6

- distinguish between relevant and irrelevant information using appropriate criteria
- identify cost classification(s) in decision making
- explain how quantitative and qualitative information is used in decision making
- evaluate and assess the frequency, timing, format, and degree of accuracy in the provision of decision making information
- describe the basic decision making cycle for business decisions
- classify problems for the purpose of modelling into simple, complex and dynamic problems
- explain the relevance of endogenous and exogenous variables, policies and controls, performance measures and intermediate variables in model building
- explain the nature of CVP analysis and name planning and decision making situations in which it may be used
- compare the accounting and economic models of CVP analysis
- explain the assumptions of linearity and the principle of relevant range in the CVP model
- prepare breakeven charts and profit-volume charts and interpret the information contained within each, including multi-product situations
- comment on the limitations of CVP analysis for planning and decision making including multi-product situations

23 SHORT RUN DECISIONS II

Syllabus reference 5a, 5b, Chapter 6

- explain the use of avoidable cost, incremental cost, marginal cost and variable cost in decision making
- describe the relationship between fixed cost and the time horizon used in a decision situation
- explain how opportunity cost is used in making decisions
- identify and calculate relevant costs for specific decision situations from given data
- explain the meaning of throughput accounting and its use in decision making
- explain and illustrate the impact of limiting factors in decision making
- solve problems involving changes in product mix, discontinuance of products or departments
- implement make or buy decisions using relevant costs
- explain and demonstrate activity-based customer profitability analysis
- make decisions as to whether to further process a product before sale using relevant costs and revenues
- use relevant costs and revenues in decisions relating to the operation of internal service departments or the use of external services

24 PRICING I

Syllabus reference 4a, Chapter 18

- identify and discuss market situations which influence the pricing policy adopted by an organisation
- explain and discuss the variables (including price) which influence demand for a product or service
- explain the price elasticity of demand
- manipulate data in order to determine an optimum price/output level
- calculate prices using full cost and marginal cost as the pricing base
- compare the use of full cost pricing and marginal cost pricing as planning and decision-making aids

25 PRICING II

Syllabus reference 4a, Chapter 19

- calculate prices using activity based costing in the estimation of the cost element
- contrast and discuss the implications of prices using the activity based costing technique with those using volume related methods in assigning costs to products
- take informed pricing decisions in the context of special orders and new products
- discuss pricing policy in the context of skimming, penetration and differential pricing
- explain the problems of pricing in the context of short life products
- explain the operation of target pricing in achieving a desired market share

26 RISK AND UNCERTAINTY

Syllabus reference 5b, Chapter 8

- define and distinguish between uncertainty and risk preference
- explain ways in which uncertainty may be allowed for by using conservatism and worst/most likely/best outcome estimates
- explain the use of sensitivity analysis in decision situations
- explain the use of probability estimates and the calculation of expected value
- explain and illustrate the use of maximin, maximax and minimax regrets techniques in decision making
- describe the structure and use of decision trees
- apply joint probabilities in decision tree analysis
- illustrate the use of decision tree analysis in assessing the range of outcomes and the cumulative probabilities of each outcome

27 TRANSFER PRICING I

Syllabus reference 5a, Chapter 20

- describe the organisation structure in which transfer pricing may be required
- explain divisional autonomy, divisional performance measurement and corporate profit maximization and their link with transfer pricing
- formulate the in general rule for transfer pricing and explain its application
- describe, illustrate and evaluate the use of market price as the transfer price
- assess where an adjusted market price will be appropriate for transfer business
- assess the impact of market price methods on divisional autonomy, performance measurement and corporate profit maximisation
- calculate an appropriate transfer price from given data

28 TRANSFER PRICING II

Syllabus reference 5a, Chapter 21

- describe the alternative cost based approaches to transfer pricing
- identify the circumstances in which marginal cost should be used as the transfer price and determine its impact on divisional autonomy, performance measurement and corporate profit maximisation
- illustrate methods by which a share of fixed costs may be included in the transfer price
- comment on these methods and their impact on divisional autonomy, performance measurement and corporate profit maximisation
- discuss the advantages which may be claimed for the use of standard cost rather than actual cost when setting transfer prices
- explain the relevance of opportunity cost in transfer pricing
- list the information which must be centrally available in order that the profit maximising transfer policy may be implemented between divisions where intermediate products are in short supply
- illustrate the formulation of the quantitative model for a range of limiting factors from which the corporate profit maximising transfer policy may be calculated
- analyse the concept of shadow price in setting transfer prices for intermediate products that are in short supply
- illustrate the corporate maximising transfer policy where a single intermediate resource is in short supply and a limited external source is available and explain the information which must be available centrally in order that the transfer policy may be formulated
- explain and demonstrate issues that require consideration when setting transfer prices in multinational companies

29 LONG TERM DECISIONS

Syllabus reference 5b, Chapter 7

- define and illustrate the concepts of net present value and internal rate of return
- calculate the net present value and internal rate of return in the evaluation of an investment opportunity
- explain the use of DCF techniques for decisions involving cash outlays over long periods
- explain the relationship between net present value and residual income where annuity depreciation is used in the residual income calculations
- compare and contrast net present value with payback and accounting rate of return in the evaluation of investment opportunities.

The examination

CONTENTS

Format of the examination

	Number of marks
Section A: 2 compulsory questions (no single question will exceed 45 marks)	60
Section B: choice of 2 from 3 questions (20 marks each)	40
	100
Total time allowed: 3 hours	

The examination is a three hour paper constructed in two sections. The Section A questions will contain a mix of computational and discursive elements.

Section B questions will comprise at least one question that is purely discursive and other(s) will incorporate both computational and discursive components.

Examination tips

- Spend the first few minutes of the examination **reading the paper**.
- Where you have a **choice of questions**, decide which ones you will do.
- **Divide the time** you spend on questions in proportion to the marks on offer. One suggestion is to allocate 1½ minutes to each mark available, so a 10 mark question should be completed in 15 minutes.
- Unless you know exactly how to answer the question, spend some time **planning** your answer. Stick to the question and **tailor your answer** to what you are asked.
- **Fully explain** all your points but be **concise**. Set out all workings **clearly and neatly**, and state briefly what you are doing. Don't write out the question.
- If you do not understand what a question is asking, **state your assumptions**. Even if you do not answer precisely in the way the examiner hoped, you should be given some credit, if your assumptions are reasonable.
- If you **get completely stuck** with a question, leave space in your answer book and **return to it later.**
- Towards the end of the examination spend the last **five minutes** reading through your answers and **making any additions or corrections**.
- Before you finish, you must fill in the required information on the front of your answer booklet.

Answering the questions

- **Multiple-choice questions**: Read the questions carefully and work through any calculations required. If you don't know the answer, eliminate those options you know are incorrect and see if the answer becomes more obvious. Remember that only one answer to a multiple choice question can be right!
- **Objective test questions** might ask for numerical answers, but could also involve paragraphs of text which require you to fill in a number of missing blanks, or for you to write a definition of a word or phrase, or to enter a formula. Others may give a definition followed by a list of possible key words relating to that description.
- **Essay questions**: Make a quick plan in your answer book and under each main point list all the relevant facts you can think of. Then write out your answer developing each point fully. Your essay should have a clear structure; it should contain a brief introduction, a main section and a conclusion. Be concise. It is better to write a little about a lot of different points than a great deal about one or two points.

- **Case studies**: To write a good case study, first identify the area in which there is a problem, outline the main principles/theories you are going to use to answer the question, and then apply the principles/theories to the case. Include relevant points only and then reach a conclusion and, if asked for, recommendations. If you can, compare the facts to real-life examples – this may gain you additional marks in the exam.

- **Computations**: It is essential to include all your workings in your answers. Many computational questions require the use of a standard format: company profit and loss account, balance sheet and cash flow statement for example. Be sure you know these formats thoroughly before the examination and use the layouts that you see in the answers given in this book and in model answers. If you are asked to comment or make recommendations on a computation, you must do so. There are important marks to be gained here. Even if your computation contains mistakes, you may still gain marks if your reasoning is correct.

- **Reports, memos and other documents**: Some questions ask you to present your answer in the form of a report or a memo or other document. Use the correct format - there could be easy marks to gain here.

Study skills and revision guidance

CONTENTS

This section aims to give guidance on how to study for your ACCA exams and to give ideas on how to improve your existing study techniques.

Preparing to study

Set your objectives

Before starting to study decide what you want to achieve – the type of pass you wish to obtain. This will decide the level of commitment and time you need to dedicate to your studies.

Devise a study plan

- Determine which times of the week you will study.
- Split these times into sessions of at least one hour for study of new material. Any shorter periods could be used for revision or practice.
- Put the times you plan to study onto a study plan for the weeks from now until the exam and set yourself targets for each period of study – in your sessions make sure you cover the course, course assignments and revision.
- If you are studying for more than one paper at a time, try to vary your subjects, this can help you to keep interested and see subjects as part of wider knowledge.
- When working through your course, compare your progress with your plan and, if necessary, re-plan your work (perhaps including extra sessions) or, if you are ahead, do some extra revision/practice questions.

Effective studying

Active reading

You are not expected to learn the text by rote, rather, you must understand what you are reading and be able to use it to pass the exam and develop good practice. A good technique to use is SQ3Rs – Survey, Question, Read, Recall, Review:

1 **Survey** the chapter – look at the headings and read the introduction, summary and objectives, so as to get an overview of what the chapter deals with.

2 **Question** – whilst undertaking the survey, ask yourself the questions that you hope the chapter will answer for you.

3 **Read** through the chapter thoroughly, answering the questions and making sure you can meet the objectives. Attempt the exercises and activities in the text, and work through all the examples.

4 **Recall** – at the end of each section and at the end of the chapter, try to recall the main ideas of the section/chapter without referring to the text. This is best done after a short break of a couple of minutes after the reading stage.

5 **Review** – check that your recall notes are correct.

You may also find it helpful to reread the chapter and try to see the topic(s) it deals with as a whole.

Note-taking

Taking notes is a useful way of learning, but do not simply copy out the text. The notes must:

- be in your own words
- be concise
- cover the key points
- be well-organised
- be modified as you study further chapters in this text or in related ones.

Trying to summarise a chapter without referring to the text can be a useful way of determining which areas you know and which you don't.

Three ways of taking notes:

- **summarise the key points** of a chapter.
- **make linear notes** – a list of headings, divided up with subheadings listing the key points. If you use linear notes, you can use different colours to highlight key points and keep topic areas together. Use plenty of space to make your notes easy to use.
- **try a diagrammatic form** – the most common of which is a mind-map. To make a mind-map, put the main heading in the centre of the paper and put a circle around it. Then draw short lines radiating from this to the main sub-headings, which again have circles around them. Then continue the process from the sub-headings to sub-sub-headings, advantages, disadvantages, etc.

Highlighting and underlining

You may find it useful to underline or highlight key points in your study text – but do be selective. You may also wish to make notes in the margins.

Revision

The best approach to revision is to revise the course as you work through it. Also try to leave four to six weeks before the exam for final revision. Make sure you cover the whole syllabus and pay special attention to those areas where your knowledge is weak. Here are some recommendations:

- **Read through the text and your notes again** and condense your notes into key phrases. It may help to put key revision points onto index cards to look at when you have a few minutes to spare.
- **Review any assignments** you have completed and look at where you lost marks – put more work into those areas where you were weak.
- **Practise exam standard questions** under timed conditions. If you are short of time, list the points that you would cover in your answer and then read the model answer, but do try and complete at least a few questions under exam conditions.
- Also **practise producing answer plans** and comparing them to the model answer.
- If you are stuck on a topic find somebody (a tutor) to explain it to you.
- **Read good newspapers and professional journals**, especially ACCA's *Student Accountant* – this can give you an advantage in the exam.
- Ensure you **know the structure of the exam** – how many questions and of what type you will be expected to answer. During your revision attempt all the different styles of questions you may be asked.

Mathematical tables

Present value table

Present value of 1 i.e. $(1+r)^{-n}$

where r = discount rate

n = number of periods until payment

Periods (n)	1%	2%	3%	4%	5%	6%	7%	8%	9%	10%	
1	0.990	0.980	0.971	0.962	0.952	0.943	0.935	0.926	0.917	0.909	1
2	0.980	0.961	0.943	0.925	0.907	0.890	0.873	0.857	0.842	0.826	2
3	0.971	0.942	0.915	0.889	0.864	0.840	0.816	0.794	0.772	0.751	3
4	0.961	0.924	0.888	0.855	0.823	0.792	0.763	0.735	0.708	0.683	4
5	0.951	0.906	0.863	0.822	0.784	0.747	0.713	0.681	0.650	0.621	5
6	0.942	0.888	0.837	0.790	0.746	0.705	0.666	0.630	0.596	0.564	6
7	0.933	0.871	0.813	0.760	0.711	0.665	0.623	0.583	0.547	0.513	7
8	0.923	0.853	0.789	0.731	0.677	0.627	0.582	0.540	0.502	0.467	8
9	0.914	0.837	0.766	0.703	0.645	0.592	0.544	0.500	0.460	0.424	9
10	0.905	0.820	0.744	0.676	0.614	0.558	0.508	0.463	0.422	0.386	10
11	0.896	0.804	0.722	0.650	0.585	0.527	0.475	0.429	0.388	0.350	11
12	0.887	0.788	0.701	0.625	0.557	0.497	0.444	0.397	0.356	0.319	12
13	0.879	0.773	0.681	0.601	0.530	0.469	0.415	0.368	0.326	0.290	13
14	0.870	0.758	0.661	0.577	0.505	0.442	0.388	0.340	0.299	0.263	14
15	0.861	0.743	0.642	0.555	0.481	0.417	0.362	0.315	0.275	0.239	15

(n)	11%	12%	13%	14%	15%	16%	17%	18%	19%	20%	
1	0.901	0.893	0.885	0.877	0.870	0.862	0.855	0.847	0.840	0.833	1
2	0.812	0.797	0.783	0.769	0.756	0.743	0.731	0.718	0.706	0.694	2
3	0.731	0.712	0.693	0.675	0.658	0.641	0.624	0.609	0.593	0.579	3
4	0.659	0.636	0.613	0.592	0.572	0.552	0.534	0.516	0.499	0.482	4
5	0.593	0.567	0.543	0.519	0.497	0.476	0.456	0.437	0.419	0.402	5
6	0.535	0.507	0.480	0.456	0.432	0.410	0.390	0.370	0.352	0.335	6
7	0.482	0.452	0.425	0.400	0.376	0.354	0.333	0.314	0.296	0.279	7
8	0.434	0.404	0.376	0.351	0.327	0.305	0.285	0.266	0.249	0.233	8
9	0.391	0.361	0.333	0.308	0.284	0.263	0.243	0.225	0.209	0.194	9
10	0.352	0.322	0.295	0.270	0.247	0.227	0.208	0.191	0.176	0.162	10
11	0.317	0.287	0.261	0.237	0.215	0.195	0.178	0.162	0.148	0.135	11
12	0.286	0.257	0.231	0.208	0.187	0.168	0.152	0.137	0.124	0.112	12
13	0.258	0.229	0.204	0.182	0.163	0.145	0.130	0.116	0.104	0.093	13
14	0.232	0.205	0.181	0.160	0.141	0.125	0.111	0.099	0.088	0.078	14
15	0.209	0.183	0.160	0.140	0.123	0.108	0.095	0.084	0.074	0.065	15

Annuity table

Present value of an annuity of 1 i.e. $\frac{1-(1+r)^{-n}}{r}$

where r = discount rate

n = number of periods

Periods (n)	Discount rate (r) 1%	2%	3%	4%	5%	6%	7%	8%	9%	10%	
1	0.990	0.980	0.971	0.962	0.952	0.943	0.935	0.926	0.917	0.909	1
2	1.970	1.942	1.913	1.886	1.859	1.833	1.808	1.783	1.759	1.736	2
3	2.941	2.884	20829	2.775	2.723	2.673	2.624	2.577	2.531	2.487	3
4	3.902	3.808	3.717	3.630	3.546	3.465	3.387	3.312	3.240	3.170	4
5	4.853	4.713	4.580	4.452	4.329	4.212	4.100	3.993	3.890	3.791	5
6	5.795	5.601	5.417	5.242	5.076	4.917	4.767	4.623	4.486	4.355	6
7	6.728	6.472	6.230	6.002	5.786	5.582	5.389	5.206	5.033	4.868	7
8	7.652	7.325	7.020	6.733	6.463	6.210	5.971	5.747	5.535	5.335	8
9	8.566	8.162	7.786	7.435	7.108	6.802	6.515	6.247	5.995	5.759	9
10	9.471	8.983	8.530	8.111	7.722	7.360	7.024	6.710	6.418	6.145	10
11	10.37	9.787	9.253	8.760	8.306	7.887	7.499	7.139	6.805	6.495	11
12	11.26	10.58	9.954	9.385	8.863	8.384	7.943	7.536	7.161	6.814	12
13	12.13	11.35	10.63	9.986	9.394	8.853	8.358	7.904	7.487	7.103	13
14	13.00	12.11	11.30	10.56	9.899	9.295	8.745	8.244	7.786	7.367	14
15	13.87	12.85	11.94	11.12	10.38	9.712	9.108	8.559	8.061	7.606	15

(n)	11%	12%	13%	14%	15%	16%	17%	18%	19%	20%	
1	0.901	0.893	0.885	0.877	0.870	0.862	0.855	0.847	0.840	0.833	1
2	1.713	1.690	1.668	1.647	1.626	1.605	1.585	1.566	1.547	1.528	2
3	2.444	2.402	2.361	2.322	2.283	2.246	2.210	2.174	2.140	2.106	3
4	3.102	3.037	2.974	2.914	2.855	2.798	2.743	2.690	2.639	2.589	4
5	3.696	3.605	3.517	3.433	3.352	3.274	3.199	3.127	3.058	2.991	5
6	4.231	4.111	3.998	3.889	3.784	3.685	3.589	3.498	3.410	3.326	6
7	4.712	4.564	4.423	4.288	4.160	4.039	3.922	3.812	3.706	3.605	7
8	5.146	4.968	4.799	4.639	4.487	4.344	4.207	4.078	3.954	3.837	8
9	5.537	5.328	5.132	4.946	4.772	4.607	4.451	4.303	4.163	4.031	9
10	5.889	5.650	5.426	5.216	5.019	4.833	4.659	4.494	4.339	4.192	10
11	6.207	5.938	5.687	5.453	5.234	5.029	4.836	4.656	4.486	4.327	11
12	6.492	6.194	5.918	5.660	5.421	5.197	4.988	4.793	4.611	4.439	12
13	6.750	6.424	6.122	5.842	5.583	5.342	5.118	4.910	4.715	4.533	13
14	6.982	6.628	6.302	6.002	5.724	5.468	5.229	5.008	4.802	4.611	14
15	7.191	6.811	6.462	6.142	5.847	5.575	5.324	5.092	4.876	4.675	15

Chapter 1
PLANNING, CONTROL AND DECISION-MAKING

CHAPTER CONTENTS

This chapter considers the background to planning, control and decision-making. It also sets them within the context of the management accounting framework. The reader will have encountered these topics already in the course of earlier studies and they will be explored in detail later in the text.

Objectives

When you have studied this chapter you should be able to do the following.

- Identify the characteristics of strategic planning and decision-making
- Contrast strategic planning with short-term /operational planning
- Identify the areas of management accounting information which are of importance in strategic management
- Evaluate the relevance of discounted cash flow principles in information for strategic decision-making
- Select and analyse costs and revenues relevant to strategic planning and decision-making in a range of situations
- Explain the significance of endogenous information sources in relation to short run decision-making and control
- Identify the characteristics of short-term non-strategic activities
- Discuss the significance of brand awareness and company profile
- Identify the areas of management accounting information appropriate for short-term decision-making
- Explain the differences between management control and operational control in the context of short run decision-making and control.

1 Introduction

1.1 Characteristics of strategic decisions

The well-known management writer, Drucker, in his book *Managing for Results*, discusses business strategies and states that whatever a company's programme it must decide:

- what opportunities it wants to pursue and what risks it is willing and able to accept
- its scope and structure, and especially the right balance between specialisation, diversification and integration
- between time and money, between building its own or buying, i.e. using sale of a business, merger, acquisition and joint venture to attain its goals
- on an organisation structure appropriate to its economic realities, its opportunities and its programme for performance.

KEY POINT

There are three kinds of opportunities:

- Additive
- Complementary
- Breakthrough

KEY POINT

Strategic planning:

- is likely to be affected by the scope of an organisation's activities
- involves the matching of the activities of an organisation to its environment and to its resource capability
- must consider the extent to which resources can be obtained, allocated and controlled
- will be affected by the expectations and values of those who have power
- may affect the long-term direction of the organisation.

There are three kinds of opportunities:

- **Additive** – exploitation of existing resources
- **Complementary** – involving structural changes in the company
- **Breakthrough** – changing the fundamental economic characteristics of the business.

Risks can be placed in four categories:

- those that must be accepted
- those that can be afforded
- those that cannot be afforded
- those the company cannot afford to miss.

The right opportunities will not be selected unless the company attempts to maximise opportunities rather than to minimise risk. Quantitative techniques can be used to evaluate the likely outcomes of different decisions.

1.2 Characteristics of strategic planning

In their book, *Exploring Corporate Strategy*, Johnson and Scholes outline the characteristics of strategic planning. They discuss the following areas:

- Strategic planning is likely to be affected by the scope of an organisation's activities, because the scope concerns the way the management conceive the organisation's boundaries. It is to do with what they want the organisation to be like and be about
- Strategy involves the matching of the activities of an organisation to its environment
- Strategy must also match the activities of an organisation to its resource capability. It is not just about being aware of the environmental threats and opportunities but about matching the organisational resources to these threats and opportunities
- Strategies need to be considered in terms of the extent to which resources can be obtained, allocated and controlled to develop a strategy for the future
- Operational decisions will be affected by strategic decisions because they will set off waves of lesser decisions
- As well as the environmental forces and the resource availability, the strategy of an organisation will be affected by the expectations and values of those who have power within and around the organisation
- Strategic decisions are apt to affect the long-term direction of the organisation

Johnson and Scholes argue that what distinguishes strategic management from other aspects of management in an organisation is the complexity. There are several reasons for this including:

- it involves a high degree of uncertainty
- it is likely to require an integrated approach to management
- it may involve major change in the organisation.

1.3 Characteristics of short-term operational planning and decision-making

KEY POINT

Apart from strategic planning, the management of a business has to undertake a regular series of decisions on matters that are purely operational and short-term in character.

Quite apart from strategic planning, the management of a business has to undertake a regular series of decisions on matters that are purely operational and short-term in character. The main features of such decisions are:

- they are usually based on a given set of assets and resources
- they do not usually involve the scope of an organisation's activities
- they rarely involve major change in the organisation
- they are unlikely to involve major elements of uncertainty and the techniques used to help make such decisions often seek to minimise the impact of any uncertainty.

Examples of short-term operational decisions include:

- making or buying-in a component
- accepting or rejecting a customer order
- prioritising products to make the most efficient use of a limited resource
- closing or keeping open a factory site
- setting a profit maximising selling price for a product.

Note that none of these decisions involves anything fundamental about the nature of the business. For example, setting a profit maximising selling price is an exercise based on forecast demand and marginal costs over a coming one-year period. It does not involve asking whether a product should be sold at all, whether its design should be modified or how its selling price should be influenced by the position of the product in its life cycle or the product matrix of the business.

KEY POINT

The techniques used in operational decision-making include cost-volume-profit analysis, limiting factor analysis and linear programming.

The techniques used in operational decision-making are familiar to generations of management accountants. They include cost-volume-profit analysis, limiting factor analysis and linear programming. You should already be familiar with these topics.

2 Decision-making

2.1 The decision-making cycle

Operational decision-making is often considered to work through a cycle.

The following diagram illustrates this decision-making cycle:

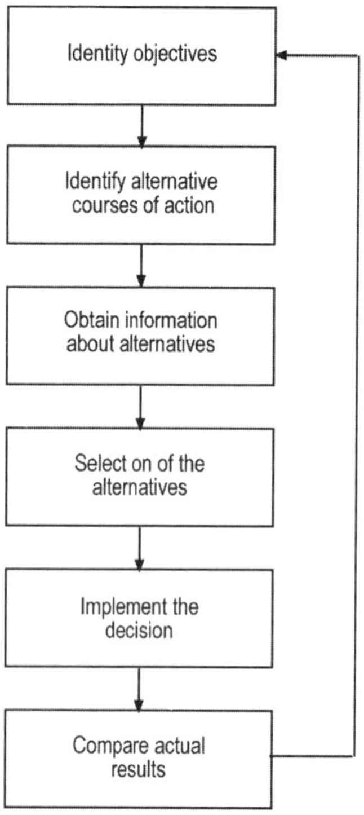

Decision making cycle

The component parts of the decision-making cycle are considered in the following paragraphs.

KEY POINT

The component parts of the decision-making cycle are:

- identify objectives
- alternative courses of action
- implement the decision
- compare actual results.

Identify objectives

The objectives within a decision-making context are likely to be to solve a problem although they may be more of a planning nature to improve profitability. You should appreciate that decision-making is an integral part of the planning process.

Alternative courses of action

Once the objectives have been identified the next stage is to determine the courses of action which may be used to meet those objectives and gather information about them. Such information may be quantitative (both monetary and non-monetary) and qualitative. Once the information has been gathered it must be considered and the best course of action chosen.

Implement the decision

Once the course of action has been chosen the next step is to implement the decision. This may require management to place orders for plant or equipment or other assets, or it may be simply a decision to work overtime or change the product mix. Clearly the timescale in which the decision is implemented will differ depending upon the original objective and the chosen course of action.

Compare actual results

This part of the cycle might be described as a post-implementation review or audit. Before results can be compared they must be collected using both quantitative and qualitative measures. These results are then compared with the original objectives and where necessary a further decision is made to modify the action being taken.

The link between business planning and business control becomes clear at the final stage in the cycle. The process by which actual results are systematically compared with those planned for is the core element in business control.

2.2 Classifying problems for decision-making

KEY POINT

Problems may be classified as being:

- simple
- complex
- dynamic.

Problems may be classified as being:

- simple
- complex
- dynamic.

These may be discussed in turn as follows:

Simple problems

Simple problems are those that have just one or two variables, for example the effects on profit of a single product being sold at differing prices (with the related demand effects). This is a classic short-term decision-making situation and involves a simple algebraic manipulation of figures.

Complex problems

These problems are more complicated because they involve a number of variables, for example a multi-product situation where the selling price of a product affects the demand for that product and for other products with the consequential effects on production of all products. These are usually more complex, but their solution normally still lies within the area of short-term decision-making.

Dynamic problems

These are complex problems where the variables of the problem are constantly changing due to influences such as changes in government policy and technological advance. In dealing with such problems one is likely to be operating within the area of strategic planning.

2.3 The time value of money and strategic planning

A common feature of strategic planning and decision-making is the need to commit funds by purchasing land, buildings, machinery etc or undertaking research and product development in anticipation of being able to earn, in the future, an income greater than the funds committed. This indicates the need for an assessment of the size of the outflows and inflows of funds, the life of the investment, the degree of risk attached (greater risk being justified perhaps by greater returns) and the cost of obtaining funds.

Basic stages in the capital budgeting cycle may be identified as:

Step 1

Needs for expenditure are forecast.

Step 2

Projects to meet those needs are distinguished.

Step 3

Alternatives are appraised.

Step 4

Best alternatives are selected and approved.

Step 5

Expenditure is made and monitored.

Step 6

Deviations from estimates are examined.

KEY POINT

One critical issue in appraising alternative business strategies is allowing for the time value of money.

Step 3 occupies a major place in the theory and practice of management decision-making, and it will be examined later in considerable depth. However, it should be appreciated, at this stage, that one critical issue in appraising alternative business strategies is allowing for the time value of money. When appraising the cash flows associated with alternative strategies, the timing of those cash flows may be as important as their total amount.

A body of technique known as discounted cash flow ('DCF') analysis has been developed to assist in all aspects of business decision-making. The main features of this technique are explored later in this text.

Types of capital project

Reasons for capital expenditure vary widely. Projects may be classified into the following categories:

- **Maintenance** – replacement of worn-out or obsolete assets, safety and security, etc.
- **Profitability** – cost savings, quality improvement, productivity, relocation, etc.
- **Expansion** – new products, new outlets, research and development, etc.
- **Indirect** – office buildings, welfare facilities, etc.

A particular investment project, of course, could combine any or all of the above classifications.

2.4 Methods of appraising capital investment projects

KEY POINT

Time value of money:

'There is a time preference for receiving the same sum of money sooner rather than later. Conversely, there is a time preference for paying the same sum of money later rather than sooner.

An important step in strategic planning is determining whether the benefits from investing large capital sums outweigh the large initial costs of those investments. There are a range of methods that are used in reaching these investment decisions. Broadly speaking they fall into two categories: traditional (non-discounting) methods and DCF methods.

The DCF methods are widely considered to be more satisfactory because they are based on cash flow and use a methodology that recognises the time value of money in a rigorous manner. The traditional alternatives are typically based on subjective accounting concepts of profit and capital employed. Also, those alternatives make, at best, only partial allowance for the time value of money.

The time value of money

A simple method of comparing two investment projects would be to compare the amount of cash generated from each – presumably, the project which generates the greater net cash inflow (taking into account all revenues and expenses) is to be preferred. However, such a simple method would fail to take into account the **time value of money**, the effect of which may be stated as the general rule below:

'There is a time preference for receiving the same sum of money sooner rather than later. Conversely, there is a time preference for paying the same sum of money later rather than sooner.'

Reasons for time preference

The reasons for time preference are threefold:

- **Consumption preference** – money received now can be spent on consumption.
- **Risk preference** – risk diminishes as the period before forecast cash inflows shortens and disappears once cash is received.

- **Investment preference** – money received can be invested in the business, or invested externally.

Strategic decisions have been stated to be long-term decisions that may include a large amount of uncertainty. DCF, in contrast, appears to be a technique that provides clear, accurate answers as to whether or not a particular course of action is worthwhile.

In order to use DCF techniques for strategic decisions it will be necessary to make assumptions; these assumptions must be clearly stated to managers and where possible the effects of errors in these assumptions on the final results should be quantified.

KEY POINT

Strategic decisions are concerned with long-term profitability and survival, which may be obtained at the expense of competitors.

Many aspects of business strategy are therefore guided by concepts of advantage and disadvantage relative to competitors.

3 Costs, revenues and strategy

Strategic decisions are concerned with long-term profitability and survival, which may be obtained at the expense of competitors. It is thus argued that absolute costs and revenues are not as important as relative values.

By measuring costs and revenues relative to those of competitors it is possible to judge the profitability and efficiency of the organisation relative to others. It is relative superiority that will ensure survival and long-term profitability. Many aspects of business strategy are therefore guided by concepts of advantage and disadvantage relative to competitors. We now consider certain aspects of business competition and the associated issues of relative profitability.

3.1 The five forces model

The key text dealing with competitive analysis is Professor Michael Porter's work 'Competitive Strategy: Techniques for Analysing Industries and Competitors' and this provides a useful guide. Porter states that 'competition in an industry is rooted in its underlying economics, and competitive forces exist that go well beyond the established combatants in a particular industry'. The problem for the strategist is to determine which of these forces is relevant, and to what extent. The approach to industry analysis discussed in this section is relatively new, having been developed by Porter in 1980. It is based on the concept of an industry being shaped by five forces. These are illustrated below, and explained in the following subsections:

The five forces model

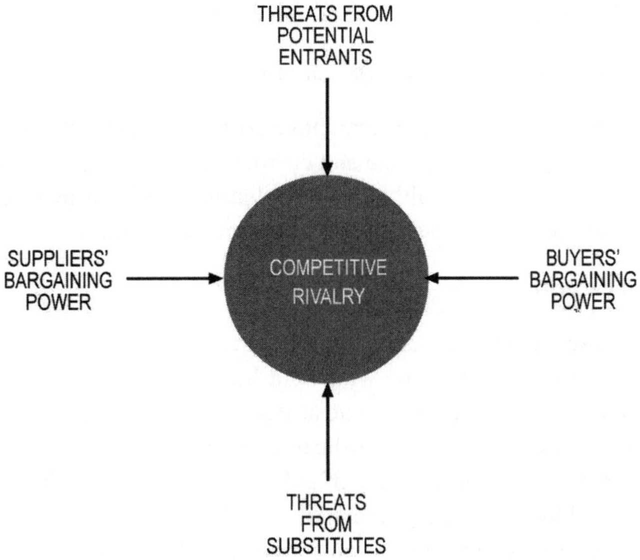

3.2 Threats from potential entrants

By increasing the extent of competition

New competitors to an industry may make it more competitive in three ways:

- expanding capacity without necessarily increasing market demand
- their need to penetrate the market to achieve **critical mass** and then build market share, which may include product and marketing innovations
- increasing costs as they bid for factors of production.

Barriers to entry

It is in the interests of existing competitors to deter new entrants. There are seven main barriers to entry. Several of these are now discussed.

Economies of scale

Many industries, such as cement and chemicals, offer increasing returns in manufacture, and companies benefit by being able to lower unit costs by increasing output volume. Thus potential entrants would be at a considerable cost disadvantage unless they can immediately set up their operations on a scale large enough to reap similar economies. (This scale is termed the 'critical mass'.) In any case, it might take several years and a heavy investment programme to construct and equip the necessary factories to put them on a competitive footing.

Switching costs

These are one-off costs facing a company that switches from one supplier's product to another's. Switching costs may include costs of certification, product redesign, costs and time in assessing a new source, or even the cultural problems of severing a relationship.

For example, in the mid-1970s, FFW-Fokker indicated to British Aerospace (BAe) that it would not tolerate their planned HS-146 aircraft in direct competition against their own existing F28 short-haul jet airliner. Fokker had over 40% of the total cost of both their F-17 and F-28 aircraft supplied by British companies, and indicated that this would be at risk if the HS-146 project continued. BAe correctly considered the threat was not credible since cost shifting (re-design, re-tooling and re-certification for both aircraft using non-British equipment) would be prohibitive to Fokker.

Cost disadvantages independent of scale

Established companies may have costs advantages not available to potential entrants, no matter what their size and cost levels. Critical factors include: proprietary product technology, favourable locations, learning or experience curve, favourable access to sources of raw materials and government subsidies.

Threats from substitutes

These are alternative products that serve the same purpose, e.g. gas central heating systems in competition with solid fuel systems. (One of the starkest examples of substitution, and a rapid one at that, was the way in which gas-fired central heating overtook electrical central-heating after the OPEC oil crisis of 1973/74, one result of which was the insolvency of at least one major British company.) The main threat posed by substitutes, though, is that they limit the price that a company can charge for its products. There is also a danger that the threat of a substitute may not be realised until it is too late to arrest their entry. Substitute products that warrant most attention are those that are:

- subject to an environment improving their price-performance trade-off with the industry's product

- produced by industries earning high profits and who have the resources available to bring them rapidly into play.

For example, in 1978 the producers of fibreglass insulation enjoyed unprecedented demand as the result of high energy costs and severe winter weather in US. But the industry's ability to raise prices was impeded by the plethora of insulation substitutes, including cellulose, rock wool, and styrofoam.

3.3 Branding

Branding is used by cost leaders and differentiators. Branding adds to differentiation, if the values of the brand support it. For example, the Sony brand conveys both innovation and product quality. Consequently, customers are prepared to try a Sony product more willingly than other brands and this allows them to recoup research and development costs before imitators have appeared. Cost leaders also use branding to support and build the volumes upon which their cost leadership depends, although naturally it has be based on different values, such as consistency or appeal to a particular client group. Breweries, for example, launch a range of similar products that cannot usually be told apart, but build volume by branding for particular age and social groups.

3.4 Patents, copyrights and trademarks

Patents, copyrights and trademarks prevent direct copying by legal means. Cost leaders will protect industrial processes – such as Pilkington's extended monopoly of the float glass process it had invented. Differentiators, such as pharmaceutical companies, will use patents to protect innovative products. Innovative marketers, such as Body Shop find it more difficult to legally protect what they do, although they can use laws that prevent imitations that get too close.

It is worth mentioning that firms can rely too much on these legal protections. A small company holding an innovative patent might lack the resources to defend it against encroachment from a larger one. Similarly, many companies have grown rather sloppy behind a legal protect, and are unable to respond when a rival finds a way of creating similar value for the customer using a different process.

3.5 Threats from the bargaining power of buyers

The power used by buyers in an industry may make it more competitive in three ways:

- forcing down prices
- bargaining for higher quality or improved services
- playing competitors against each other.

All three of these are at the expense of industry profitability.

Porter claims that the power of the industry's buyer groups depends on the characteristics of its market situation and of the relative importance of its purchases from the industry compared with its overall business. He suggests that buyers are particularly powerful in seven situations:

- purchasers are large relative to sellers
- purchases represents a significant proportion of the buyers' costs
- purchases are undifferentiated
- buyers earn low profits
- buyers have the potential for backward integration
- the buyer's product is not strongly affected by the quality of the suppliers' product
- the buyer has full information.

3.6 Threats from the power of suppliers

Suppliers can exert bargaining power over companies within an industry in two main ways:

- threatening to raise their prices
- threatening to reduce the quality of their goods and services.

The effect of this power will be to squeeze profitability out of an industry unable to recover cost increases by raising its own prices.

Porter suggests that suppliers are particularly powerful in six situations:

- there are few suppliers
- there are few substitutes for their products
- the industry supplied is not an important customer
- the supplier's product is an important component to the buyer's business
- the supplier's product is differentiated
- suppliers can integrate forward.

3.7 Rivalry and competition among competitors

Conflict among existing competitors takes some form of offensive strategy. Tactics commonly used to implement such strategy include product innovations and improvements, price competitions and increased customer services. Rivalry occurs because one or more companies feels threatened or sees a market opportunity to improve its position, although competitive moves by the initiator company usually results in counter-defensive strategies from its competitors. This interactive pattern of offensive and defensive strategies may not leave the initiating company and the industry better off, and on the contrary may leave all the companies in the industry worse off than before.

Porter suggests that there are seven main determinants relating to the strength of internal competition and rivalry within an industry:

- many equally balanced competitors
- slow rate of industrial growth
- lack of differentiation
- capacity can only be increased by large amounts
- high fixed costs in the industry
- there are many diverse competitors
- there are high exit barriers.

3.8 Competitive analysis

What emerges from the preceding discussion is that for strategic purposes, the costs and revenues of a business operation cannot be considered in isolation. Both are strongly influenced by competitive forces. For example, a producer cannot be considered an efficient producer simply because it appears to have low unit costs. Those costs can only be considered low when measured relative to those of competitors.

The need for a business to incur costs and its ability to extract revenue are strongly influenced by its competitive environment.

The build up of a detailed picture

A detailed profile should be built up on each major competitor. Some competitors span many industries whereas others are part of multi-national organisations, some are concerned almost exclusively with the domestic market while others depend on exports for a high proportion of their sales.

Although it is tempting to evaluate a company's position solely on the basis of whether its products and services are superior to those offered by its competitors, there are a wide range of additional factors that determine competitive success. The objective features of a company's products and services, although important, often form a relatively small part of the competitive picture. In fact, all the elements making up consumer preference, such as product quality, service, price and location are only part of the competitive analysis. The other part involves examining the internal strengths and weaknesses of each major competitor. In the long run a company possessing strong operational assets, with an organisation structure and industrial culture conducive to motivation and innovation, and having ownership of significant financial resources will prove to be a tough, enduring competitor.

The competitive analysis portion of an *'environmental analysis'* for a company will need to focus on four areas of concern:

- identifying the company's major competitors
- establishing on what basis competitive strengths are to be assessed
- comparing the company with its major competitors
- identifying potential new competitors.

Some general rules worth remembering about competitive analysis:

It would be useful, although not always practicable, if every person in the company had ready, visible access to the numbers on market share updated monthly (weekly if possible).

Competitive analysis should be everyone's business – design engineers, manufacturing managers, service staff, sales force, MIS people. The fact is that everyone will hear things – from service and salespeople, from a customer, from a former employee and friend now working with a competitor, from a bank clerk, from a braggart at a professional institute meeting, from tit-bits here and there. Also of course, the benefit of getting every employee to think about competition is the positive effect it has on general readiness to accept change.

The company should be positive rather than negative about competitors' products and should not hesitate to copy if this is legal. ('The best leaders are the best note-takers, the best 'askers', the best learners.')

Benchmarking

Many businesses now adopt performance measurement systems that make use of 'benchmarks'. Critical cost, revenue and quality performance indicators are identified and then these are periodically compared with industry 'best cases'. These comparisons can provide the basis for strategic decisions in a number of areas.

4 Short-term decision-making and control

4.1 The short-term decision and cost volume profit analysis

The characteristics of the short-term decision have already been introduced. Examples include setting profit maximising selling prices, accepting or rejecting customer orders and deciding whether to make or buy in components. These decision-making problems tend to assume a given level of capital investment and often turn around optimising the use of given resources or opportunities from a given market situation.

KEY POINT

The basic management accounting technique involved in short-term decision-making is cost volume profit ('CVP') analysis.

The basic management accounting technique involved in short-term decision-making is cost volume profit ('CVP') analysis – adapted and developed into various forms. You will have encountered the principles of CVP analysis in your earlier studies. CVP is essentially a form of business modelling that seeks to express the relationships between business variables in the form of a series of mathematical equations.

Once decisions have been made and a plan adopted, then the results achieved have to be compared with those planned for. This comparison when carried out on a systematic basis forms a 'control system'.

Both decision-making and control systems have elaborate information requirements. One of the main functions of a management accounting system is to provide this information.

4.2 Relevant and irrelevant information

Decision-making requires both quantitative and qualitative information. Such quantitative information comprises costs and revenues which, to be of use to the decision-maker, must be relevant.

What are relevant costs and revenues?

DEFINITION

Relevant costs and revenues are those which are different as a consequence of the decision made or its recommended course of action being taken.

Relevant costs and revenues are those which are different as a consequence of the decision made or its recommended course of action being taken. Since relevant costs and revenues are those which are different it effectively means costs and revenues which **change** as a result of the decision. Since it is not possible to change the past (because it has already happened), then relevant costs and revenues must be future costs and revenues. Past costs are usually referred to as sunk costs.

Relevant costs and opportunity costs

DEFINITION

Opportunity cost is the value of a benefit sacrificed in favour of an alternative course of action.

An opportunity cost may also be described as the cost of a particular course of action compared to the next best alternative course of action.

Relevant costs may involve incurring a cost or losing a revenue which could be obtained from an alternative course of action. The incurring of costs is sometimes referred to as cash flow costs whereas the loss of revenue is an opportunity cost. Both are relevant for the purposes of decision-making.

Cash flow costs

DEFINITION

Cash flow costs are those arising in cash terms as a consequence of the decision.

Cash flow costs are those arising in cash terms as a consequence of the decision. Such costs can never include past costs or costs arising from past transactions. Costs such as depreciation based on the cost of an asset already acquired can never be relevant, nor can committed costs e.g. lease payments in respect of an asset already leased, nor will re-allocations of total costs ever be relevant to the decision. Only costs which change in total because of the decision are relevant costs.

5 Short-term decision-making

5.1 Cost classification

You should recall from your earlier studies that many different classifications of cost may be used depending upon the purpose of the information. For decision-making purposes one of the most useful forms of classification is by behaviour.

Cost behaviour

DEFINITION

Production cost comprises three elements – materials, wages and expenses; production cost includes both fixed and variable segment elements.

DEFINITION

Cost behaviour is the way in which costs of output are affected by fluctuations in the level of activity.

Production cost comprises three elements – materials, wages and expenses; it can also be noted that production cost includes both fixed and variable segment elements. It is useful to look at the way costs behave in response to changes in production volume.

Example

	Production	
	500 units	*1,000 units*
	£	£
Sales (at £3 per unit)	1,500	3,000
Total costs	1,000	1,500
Profit	500	1,500
Average unit cost	£2.00	£1.50
Average unit profit	£1.00	£1.50

Total costs have increased by only 50% although production has doubled. This is because some costs will not rise in relation to the increase in volume.

Suppose the product is widgets and the only costs are:

(a) rental of a fully equipped factory, £500 pa

(b) raw materials, £1 per widget.

Contribution

If the two types of cost are segregated, then the situation can be presented in a different way:

	Production of widgets		
	1 unit	*500 units*	*1,000 units*
	£	£	£
Sales	3	1,500	3,000
Variable costs – Raw materials	1	500	1,000
Contribution	2	1,000	2,000
Fixed costs – Factory rent	500	500	500
Profit/(loss)	(498)	500	1,500

What we have here is a simple business model. This model can be used to predict the impact of various possible courses of action related to output, unit cost and selling price.

5.2 Decision-making

An understanding of cost and revenue behaviour forms the basis on which many short-term decisions can be made. This topic will be explored more fully later in the text.

The critical thing to appreciate at this stage is that decision-making involves the acquisition and manipulation of information. Providing the information and deploying relevant techniques in interpreting and manipulating that information is a central part of the management accounting function.

6 Information requirements and the entity

6.1 The entity

Entities vary both in size and in their type (manufacturer, service). Each of these differences affects the decision-making information required by the entity.

The effect of size

KEY POINT

The size of an organisation will affect its management structure, and the number and responsibilities of people in decision-making positions.

The size of an organisation will affect its management structure, and the number and responsibilities of people in decision-making positions.

In small organisations many of the decisions will be made by the owners of the business who do not require a formalised information system to tell them what is happening within the entity. They work full-time in the business and are therefore aware of what is happening on a day-to-day basis.

As organisations grow managers are employed and charged with certain responsibilities. As part of this process, these managers are given authority to make decisions within their own area of responsibility. A more formalised information system is required as organisations grow so as to ensure that the effects of decisions on all areas of the business are considered.

In addition, it is unlikely that the owners would delegate responsibility for strategic decisions and so they would require information to assist them in co-ordinating the various aspects of the decision.

KEY POINT

Different types of entity will have different information requirements, e.g. manufacturing v. service industries.

The type of entity and its effect

Different types of entity will have different information requirements. Manufacturers and wholesalers/retailers deal with tangible products to which costs and revenues can be attributed. In these organisations some direct costs will be identifiable to individual product lines, thus enabling the profitability of each to be measured.

In service industries it is more difficult to identify the 'product' and therefore even more difficult to identify direct costs. Instead costs are collected and a measure of activity made, from which an average cost is then calculated.

In service organisations non-monetary quantitative information may be more useful, for example professional practices such as solicitors and accountants record time spent on services for their clients which are used to assess fees.

6.2 Quantitative information

Although often measured in financial terms using costs and revenues measured in monetary units, other forms of quantitative information may be used in a decision-making situation. For example the quantity of resources required (materials, labour, machines), or the effects of the decision on percentage market shares could be useful quantitative information.

KEY POINT

Information can be quantitative, e.g. financial or quantity information, or qualitative, often opinion-based.

6.3 Qualitative information

Qualitative information is often in the form of opinions which show the effects of decisions on people and the community within which the entity operates. Interested groups include:

- **Employees** will be affected by certain decisions which may threaten their continued employment, or cause them to need re-training
- **Customers** will be interested to know about new products, but will want to be assured that service arrangements etc, will continue for existing products
- **Suppliers** will want to be aware of the entity's plans, especially if smart orders are used within a JIT environment

Qualitative factors that need to be considered when making a decision include:

- **The effects on the environment**

  Certain decisions may affect emissions and pollution of the environment. The green issue and the entity's responsibility towards the environment may seriously affect its public image.

- **Legal effects**

  There may be legal implications of a course of action, or a change in law may have been the cause of the decision requirement.

- **Political effects**

  Government policies, both in taxation and other matters may impinge on the decision.

- **Timing of decision**

  The timing of a new product launch may be crucial to its success.

Each of these factors must be considered before making a final decision. Each of these factors is likely to be measured by opinion. Such opinions must be collected and co-ordinated into meaningful information.

6.4 Attributes of information for decision-making and control

KEY POINT

There are four attributes of decision-making information:

- frequency
- timing
- format
- accuracy.

There are four attributes of decision-making information:

- frequency
- timing
- format
- accuracy.

Frequency

Decisions are made daily, weekly, monthly and annually so information is needed to assist managers to make these decisions. Many organisations provide management information on a regular basis, so this may be a source of decision-making information. However, more decision-specific information is likely to be required, and this should be provided whenever a decision is to be made.

Timing

Timeliness is a valuable attribute of any good information system. Information should be provided as soon as possible after the event to which it relates. In this context information is part of the feedback system which is used by management to make decisions to control activities. This is often concerned with tactical decisions. Timeliness of reporting is very important in such situations as the following illustration shows.

It is quite usual for actual outcomes to oscillate about a norm, with management action being used to minimise the fluctuations. Thus the following pattern of outcomes would be quite normal:

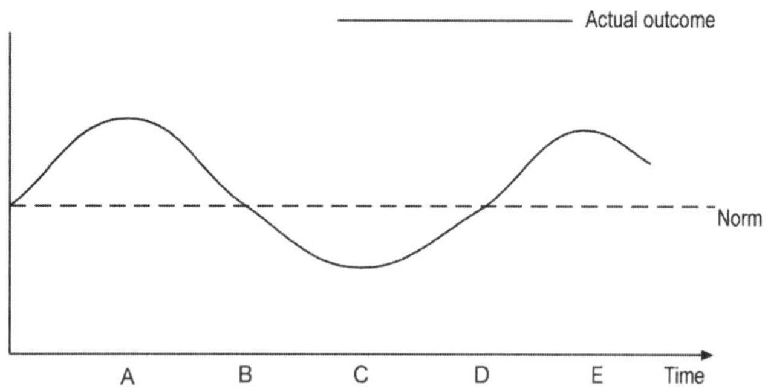

The above diagram shows the oscillating effect where there is no management decision/action being used.

If information is provided to managers earlier than time point A and appropriate action taken the positive and negative oscillations can be reduced:

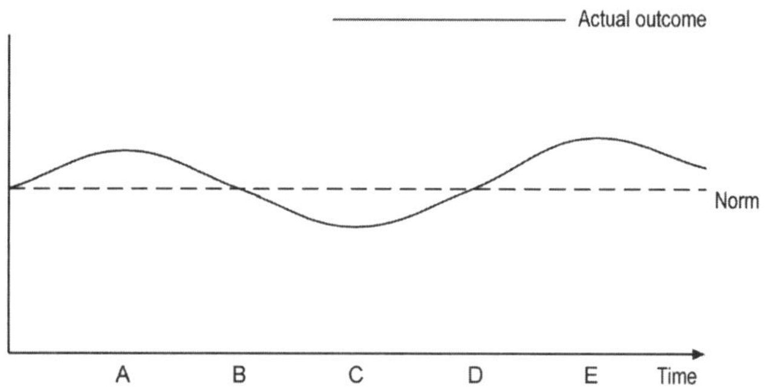

This is known as negative feedback. Managers take decisions and actions to reduce the extent of the oscillation so that when there is positive oscillation there are negative management influences and vice-versa.

However, if the information is delayed so that the initial oscillation effects are not reported until between time points A and B, negative management influences are applied when negative oscillation has already commenced with the following results:

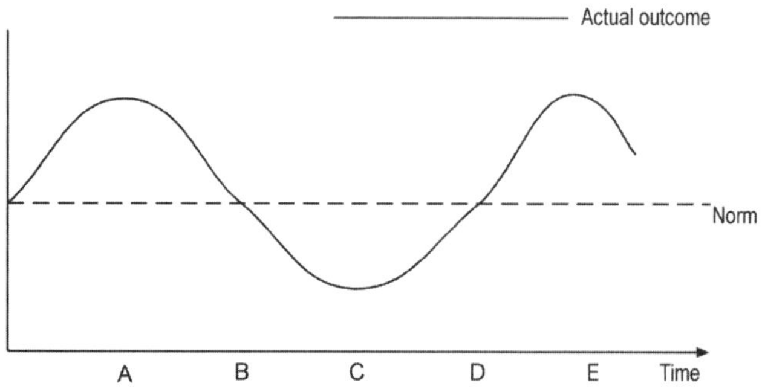

As can be seen, instead of reducing the size of the fluctuations they have been increased. This is caused by the lateness of the information, and as a consequence negative feedback information has been converted into positive feedback information.

Format

The format of the information depends upon the complexity of the decision and the recipient decision-taker.

The information could be presented in the form of a written report, or a presentation which may be supplemented by graphic displays.

Many managers are more comfortable with pictorial representations of information rather than tabulated data. Sometimes the use of charts and diagrams makes it easier to understand the information being presented.

Accuracy

Accuracy and precision have been discussed earlier in this text. In the context of information for decision-making, information should be:

'sufficiently accurate for the purpose for which it is intended.'

It is not always possible or even necessary for information to be 100% accurate. Provided the extent of an error is not sufficient to alter the decision made it does not matter. There is often a conflict between accuracy of information, timeliness of reporting, and the cost of producing the information.

Accuracy of 100% is costly in time as well as money. Such accuracy is often unnecessary. Provided the information is sufficiently accurate timeliness may be more important.

7 Endogenous and exogenous variables

The use of CVP analysis in the manner described above is, essentially, an exercise in business modelling. The financial analyst seeks to express the cost and revenue structures of a business operation in the form of a number of mathematical equations. It should be appreciated that any form of modelling is an attempt to develop a simple and certain representation of a complex and uncertain reality.

KEY POINT

Management have the ability to consider means of altering the relevant values. These are known as endogenous variables.

The equations used in a modelling exercise include those things that originate from within the business operation itself – such as variable cost per unit, fixed cost per period and output. These things are within the control of the management of the business operation. Management have the ability to consider means of altering the relevant values. These are known as endogenous variables and it has been seen that they lie at the core of short-term decision-making practices.

KEY POINT

A business operation is also affected by a range of variables which do not originate from within the business operation itself and are not controllable by the management of the operation. These are known as exogenous variables.

However, a business operation is also affected by a range of variables which do not originate from within the business operation itself and are not controllable by the management of the operation. These are known as exogenous variables. Such variables may include long-term market trends, government policy in areas such as taxation and technological development. The impact of these can be incorporated in CVP analysis and short-term decision-making, but they may be more relevant to long-term, strategic planning.

8 Control

8.1 Management and operational planning and control

The tasks of management are traditionally seen as planning and control. The stages in the planning and control cycle may be represented as follows:

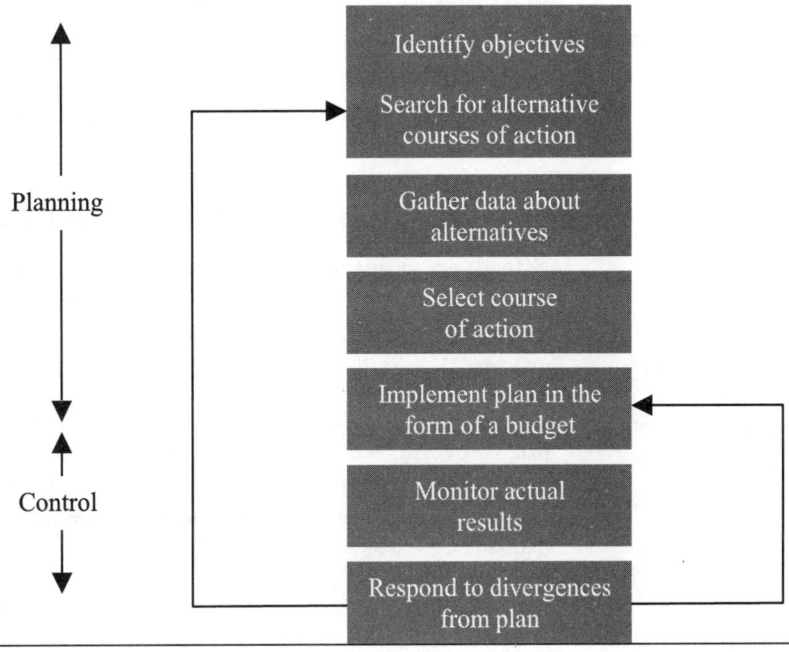

It is instructive to compare this diagram with that used earlier in this chapter to illustrate the decision-making cycle.

8.2 Criticisms of the planning and control model

The view of management planning and control put forward above has been criticised by several writers. For example, RN Anthony argues that, although it is possible to identify the different types of mental activity that are required for planning and control decisions, it is wrong to suggest that the activities are clearly separable in practice. All managers make both planning and control decisions i.e. a foreman who is unhappy with the production figures for his section may revise future forecasts (a planning decision) as well as taking action to motivate his team to perform better in future (a control decision). Where participation is used as a management style, planning and control decisions are bound to be inter-related.

KEY POINT

Anthony identified three types of management activity:

- strategic planning
- management control (or tactical planning)
- operational control.

Anthony identified three types of management activity:

- strategic planning
- management control (or tactical planning)
- operational control.

8.3 Strategic planning and short-term decisions

As we saw earlier, strategic planning involves making decisions about:

- the objectives of the organisation
- changes in these objectives
- the resources used to attain the objectives
- policies governing:
  - (i) acquisition
  - (ii) use
  - (iii) disposition of these resources.

KEY POINT

Strategic decisions involve the formulation of the new objectives and deciding on the manner in which these new objectives will be achieved.

Although strategic planning is concerned with long-term goals it often involves short-term action.

Strategic planning is usually, but not always, concerned with the long-term. For example, a company specialising in production and sale of tobacco products may forecast a declining market for these products and may therefore decide to change its objectives to allow a progressive move into the leisure industry, which it considers to be expanding. Strategic decisions involve the formulation of the new objectives and deciding on the manner in which these new objectives will be achieved i.e., by acquisition of companies which are already established in the industry (external development), or by starting new businesses itself ('organic growth').

Although strategic planning is concerned with long-term goals it often involves short-term action. For example, the acquisition of a new company in the leisure industry is made in order to fulfil a long-term objective but it requires short-term planning and control action, all of which is classified under the heading of strategic planning.

8.4 Management control and tactical planning

DEFINITION

Management controlis the process by which managers ensure that resources are obtained and used **effectively** and **efficiently** in the accomplishment of the organisation's objectives.

Effectively means that resources are used to achieve the desired ends. **Efficiently** means that the optimum (best possible) output is produced from the resources input to the system. Sometimes the word **effectual** is used. **Effectual** means both effective and efficient.

Decisions at the management control, or tactical, level are numerous. They include pricing decisions and other elements of the 'marketing mix', such as advertising, promotion and distribution decisions relating to purchases and suppliers, stock levels and other aspects of working capital management and fixed asset replacement decisions.

Decisions at this level are usually based on financial analysis, money being the common unit of measurement of resources. The control systems are performance reports relating to profit, cost or revenue centres. These reports are a summary of many different operations. The detailed control over each individual operation is exercised at the operational level, which is described below.

8.5 Operational control

DEFINITION

Operational control is the process of ensuring that specific tasks are carried out effectively and efficiently.

As more tasks become automated, the human factor in operational control becomes less important. Many tasks are subject to **programmed control**, that is where the relationship between inputs and outputs is clearly specified. However, where processes are carried out by people, the human factor in operational control will always be important, as people need to be motivated to perform routine tasks to a high standard consistently.

8.6 The pyramid of management decision-making and control

The three levels of management activity described by Anthony can be illustrated by the following diagram:

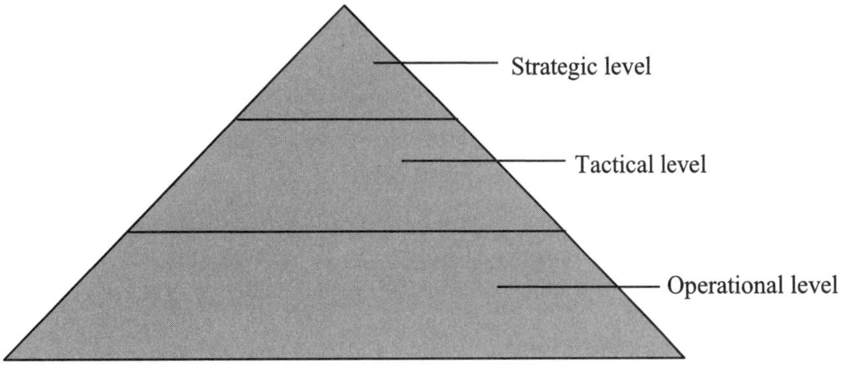

Note that the division into these three levels refers to **types of activity** and does not necessarily refer to divisions of duties between staff. For example, staff involved mainly in tactical level activities may also participate in strategic decisions and may also have certain routine operational level tasks of their own. All three levels involve both planning and control activities. However, at the strategic end, the emphasis is on planning whereas at the operational end it is on control. The diagram can thus be extended as follows:

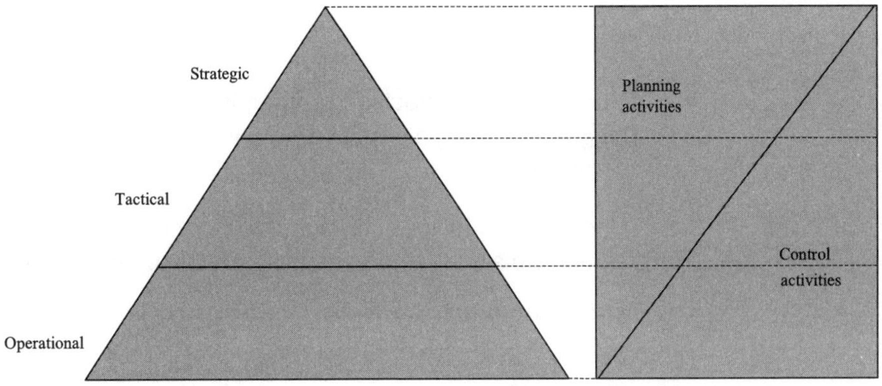

These concepts will be examined later to consider the information needs of management at each level.

8.7 Is management confined to planning and control?

The systems approach to management can sometimes overemphasise the activities of planning and control. In practice, as Mintzberg has shown, managers have many roles. Mintzberg summarises them under the headings of:

- interpersonal (leadership, liaison, etc)
- informational (receiving and giving information, formally and informally)
- decisional (new projects, unusual situations, resource allocation, negotiation).

The working day for most managers is fragmented. Not all routine tasks can be delegated – in practice managers perform a great many of these themselves. Urgent tasks must be finished before time can be set aside for planning. Consequently planning is carried out on a day-to-day basis in the manager's free moments.

Further, most managers prefer to exchange information verbally. Lengthy reports produced by formal information systems may not be regarded as important as information gained from talking to colleagues.

Clearly most managers are far from the efficient processors of information which they are assumed to be by some designers of information systems. Whereas management training (e.g. time management) can improve the effectiveness and efficiency of managers, designers of information systems have to allow for the reality of the manager's situation.

Conclusion

The management of an organisation requires information both to make decisions, which can be strategic, tactical or operational decisions, and for control. The types of information they require will vary depending on the nature of the organisation. Information may come from outside the organisation or from internal sources.

SELF-TEST QUESTIONS

Introduction

1 What are the characteristics of strategic decisions? (1.1)

Costs, revenues and strategy

2 Explain the five forces model. (3.1)

Control

3 Identify the stages of the planning and control cycle. (8.1)

EXAM-TYPE QUESTION

Strategic planning

Your managing director has attended a conference at which a speaker said that long-term strategic planning was obsolete. He is naturally concerned about this comment.

Draft a report to your managing director stressing the benefits of long-term strategic planning and examining the case for its abolition. **(25 marks)**

For the answer to this question, see the 'Answers' section at the end of the book.

Chapter 2
INFORMATION SYSTEM DESIGN AND OPERATION

CHAPTER CONTENTS

This chapter explores conceptual aspects of management information system design and operation.

Objectives

When you have studied this chapter you should be able to do the following.

- Identify the accounting information requirements for strategic planning, management control and operational control and decision-making
- Describe, with reference to management accounting, ways in which the information requirements of a management structure are affected by the features of the structure
- Evaluate the objectives of management accounting and management accounting information
- List and explain the attributes and principles of management accounting information
- Explain the integration of management accounting information within an overall information system
- Define and discuss the merits of, and potential problems with, open and closed systems
- Suggest the ways in which contingent (internal and external) factors influence management accounting and its use
- Illustrate how anticipated human behaviour will influence the design of a management accounting system
- Explain and discuss the impact of responsibility accounting on information requirements.

1 Introduction

1.1 Information for planning, control and decision-making

Anthony's three levels of control were considered in the previous chapter. The levels are:

Strategic planning

'The process of deciding on objectives of the organisation, on changes in these objectives, on the resources used to obtain these objectives and of the policies that are to govern the acquisition, use and disposition of these resources'.

Management control

'The process by which managers ensure that resources are obtained and used effectively and efficiently in the accomplishment of the organisation's objectives.'

Operational control

'The process of assuring that specific tasks are carried out effectively and efficiently'.

The types of information used will traditionally vary according to the level.

Strategic planning

This is concerned with setting a course for the future of the organisation, including how it will cope with the threats and opportunities in its environment:

- information will be predominantly environmental (competitors, market trends, economic data etc)
- strategic planning will take place towards the top of the organisation
- information will consist of long-term forecasts
- the main output at this level of control will be targets and plans
- this will be an ad hoc control system
- information will be imprecise and speculative
- management accounting will not predominate in this form of control except through *Strategic Management Accounting.*

Management control

Concerned with reaching the targets set by strategic planning:

- concerned with the *effective*use of the organisation's resources (i.e. ensuring goals are reached)
- examines the *efficiency* with which goals are reached (i.e. the quantity of resources and time used)
- information used embraces the whole organisation and may involve specific *responsibility centres*
- much of the information may be expressed in financial and volume terms. This gives a key role to management accounting control information.

Information requirements will include:

- productivity measures
- budgetary measures
- labour statistics (manning level, turnover, hours)
- capacity utilisation.

Operational control

Mainly concerned with the day-to-day implementation of the plans of the organisation.

The management accounting controls will be critical here:

- short-term control information (e.g. transactions data)
- very detailed information
- less likely to be summarised financially but rather be in terms of quantity, rates and times.

Management control information is the vital link between Strategic and Managerial decisions because it gets things done.

1.2 Process overview

The processes of planning, control, and decision-making may be inter-connected as is shown by the diagram in the previous chapter. Information is required during each part of the overall process.

Identifying objectives

KEY POINT

In order to identify objectives, information must be obtained concerning the present position of the organisation and of the feasibility of possible strategies.

This is the first stage of the planning process. In order to identify objectives, information must be obtained concerning the present position of the organisation and of the feasibility of possible strategies.

The present position is likely to be known by referring to existing internal information, profit statements, marketing reports etc, but future strategies will require information from external sources. This may include governmental plans and the views of customers, employees etc.

Alternative action plans

DEFINITION

Alternative action plans

This is a 3-stage process which commences when objectives have been determined.

This is a 3-stage process which commences when objectives have been determined. The first stage is to identify the means by which the objectives can be achieved. This is stated as 'Search for alternative courses of action'. Once these alternatives have been identified, then information can be gathered about them, and the course of action selected.

Since there is such a variety of objectives and plans to meet them, each with differing information, an example may be useful.

Example

Suppose the objective is to increase production by 50%.

The following alternative courses of action have been identified to achieve the 50% increase.

- Increase the workforce by 50% and commence a night-shift. Premium wage rates will have to be paid, variable overheads will change proportionately with productive hours. The useful life of the machines will be reduced (on a time basis) from 6 years to 4 years. Machinery servicing and maintenance costs will double.
- Replace the existing machines with higher capacity ones, re-train existing staff in the use of the new machine.

Information must be gathered for each of these alternatives. Some of the information will be financial, the effect on costs per unit of the proposals, the capital expenditure requirement; whereas some will be non-financial e.g. the attitude of the workforce to shift-working, or to using new machines.

All of this information must be gathered and evaluated before the choice can be made between them. This choice is decision-making, and clearly shows how decision-making is implicit within the planning process.

Implement long-term plan

KEY POINT

A long-term plan usually communicates an organisation's objectives and how they are to be achieved over a 5–10 year period.

A long-term plan usually communicates an organisation's objectives and how they are to be achieved over a 5–10 year period. This plan is then broken down into annual targets which are known as budgets. These budgets communicate detailed plans to managers within the organisation.

Plans and budgets are therefore information which is communicated within an organisation.

Monitoring actual results

Before actual results can be monitored by comparing them with the budget (target), data must be collected relating to actual transactions and converted into information. To convert the data into information it must be classified into the same form of analysis used to prepare the budget.

The results obtained by the comparison of actual and budget performance are reported to management as part of the feedback process.

Responses to divergences

The reporting of divergences from the plan to the manager responsible provides information to enable the manager to investigate and take action as appropriate. Managerial involvement in the planning process will encourage a sense of responsibility which may be built upon using responsibility accounting.

2 Responsibility accounting and responsibility centres

2.1 The concept

The traditional structure of a large organisation involves a hierarchy of delegated responsibilities. Typically, an organisation is split into divisions. A division is an organisational unit which is managed by a single identifiable manager. The main divisional structure may be arranged on product, regional or functional lines. A division is responsible for certain defined activities and it usually has some tangible form – a factory site, a regional office, a product group or a machine group. A division itself may be split into further subordinate organisational units.

The performance evaluation and management accounting system has to closely match the structure which has been adopted. For example, a management accounting system which prepared budgets and budget control reports for individual regions would be of little use if the organisation had divisions based on product groups. In such an event, no one manager would be responsible for achieving any of the divisional budgets.

KEY POINT

The concept of responsibility accounting is that the accounting system reports results and performance in a manner that allows the achievements of individual divisions and their managers to be monitored.

The concept of responsibility accounting is that the accounting system reports results and performance in a manner that allows the achievements of individual divisions and their managers to be monitored. It is essential that the accounting system precisely matches the organisational structure. In practice, difficulties are sometimes encountered when small changes are made in an organisation. For example, responsibility for a minor customer or a minor product may be shifted from one division to another. The budget and financial reporting system might not incorporate this change with the result that the accounting system and the organisation do not precisely match one another. In this case the quality of the management accounting system is degraded. The manager of one division will be able to escape responsibility for the reported performance of his division on the grounds that 'there are things in this budget which are nothing to do with me'.

The basic approach described above reflects a traditional, hierarchical approach to management. Some writers have argued that this is based on a Roman legion and that it may be less appropriate for the modern 'flexible' business. Recent years have seen a move to 'flatter' organisation structures and a willingness to 'outsource' many functions which were traditionally carried on in-house. Furthermore, short product life cycles means that many business operations move into a situation where their work is structured in the form of a continuous series of projects. These projects may all involve work with outside consultants and partner companies.

Indeed, one of the main features of BPR (see Chapter 5) down-sizings in the early 1990s was the 'stripping out of layers of management'. Many businesses claim to be moving to flexible management structures where staff teams are constantly formed and re-formed as projects are progressed. Companies such as Microsoft and Apple are often quoted as examples of this. In the case of Microsoft, all professional level staff have their own private offices and there are no rigid 'lines of reporting'. Some junior systems development staff will frequently receive e-mails from Bill Gates in person.

The management accounting system has to try to match this development. The structure of the system may be based on projects and project costs may be reported on a 'life cycle' basis. The need for the management accounting system to be integrated with the organisation and its general information systems is therefore apparent.

However, there are conflicting views on this last point. Academic debate around the general subject of management accounting in the late 1980s turned around 'loss of relevance'. Some people argued that management accounting had become too integrated with other information systems. To give but one example of this, product costing tended to be carried out in a manner needed to meet the requirements of statutory reporting – with its emphasis on full cost stock valuation. Where ABC has been introduced it has often been brought in as a separate and parallel system.

DEFINITION

Responsibility accounting – a system of accounting based upon the identification of individual parts of a business which are the responsibility of a single manager.

That said, we can now consider the more practical aspects of management accounting system design.

2.2 Responsibility accounting

Responsibility accounting is a system of accounting based upon the identification of individual parts of a business which are the responsibility of a single manager.

DEFINITION

Responsibility centre – an individual part of a business headed by a manager having responsibility for its performance.

2.3 Responsibility centre

Responsibility centre is an individual part of a business headed by a manager having responsibility for its performance.

KEY POINT

Budgetary control and responsibility accounting are inseparable.

2.4 Budgetary control and responsibility accounting

Budgetary control and responsibility accounting are inseparable. An organisation chart must be drawn up in order to implement a budgetary control system satisfactorily. It may even be necessary to revise the existing organisation structure before designing the system. The aim is to ensure that each manager has a well-defined area of responsibility and the authority to make decisions within that area, and that no parts of the organisation remain as 'grey' areas where it is uncertain who is responsible for them. This area of responsibility may be simply a **cost centre,** or it may be a **profit centre** (implying that the manager has control over sales revenues as well as costs) or an **investment centre** (implying that the manager is empowered to take decisions about capital investment for his department). Once senior management have set up such a structure, with the degree of delegation implied, some form of responsibility accounting system is needed. Each centre will have its own budget, and the manager will receive control information relevant to that budget centre. Costs (and possibly revenue, assets and liabilities) must be traced to the person primarily responsible for taking the related decisions, and identified with the appropriate department.

Some accountants would go as far as to advocate charging i.e. actually debiting, departments with costs that arise strictly as a result of decisions made by the management of those departments. For example, if the marketing department insists on a special rush order which necessitates overtime working in production departments, then the marketing department and not the production departments should be charged with the overtime premiums incurred. However, there are practical problems with such an approach:

- The rush order itself might actually be produced during normal time because, from a production scheduling angle, it might be more convenient to do it then (e.g. because it would not involve a clean-down of the machines as it was compatible with some other orders currently in production) – normal orders thereby actually being produced during the period of 'overtime'.
- Re-charging costs to other departments can become a common occurrence because managers see it as a way of passing on not only the costs but also the associated responsibility e.g. if the rush order is produced inefficiently in overtime, should the costs of the inefficiency also be charged to the marketing department?

KEY POINT

Most control systems contain within themselves a potential to distort the processes that they are meant to serve.

It is important to appreciate that a control system is rarely 'neutral'. Most control systems contain within themselves a potential to distort the processes that they are meant to serve. In the present context, this may arise when they induce individual managers to do things that are not in the best interests of the business as a whole. For example, the manager of a production line may get his costs back within budget by cutting back on inspection costs – with adverse consequences for the business as a whole when customers report consequent higher numbers of defective units.

Behavioural scientists refer to this phenomenon as 'dysfunctional behaviour'. A control system which is badly designed or which is applied in an insensitive manner may end up doing more harm than it does good.

DEFINITION

Cost centre – a production or service location, function, activity or item of equipment whose costs may be attributed to cost units.

All managers work for the same organisation and, if the costs are shunted around, there is a nil effect on the overall profit of the organisation (except to the extent of any extra costs incurred in operating such a recharging system). Perhaps the effort expended on such a system could be more positively used to increase overall profit.

2.5 The structure of cost, revenue, profit and investment centres

Cost centre

The performance of a manager responsible for a cost centre will be judged on the extent to which cost targets have been achieved. In order to make an appropriate evaluation costs should be classified as being either fixed costs or variable costs. Fixed cost comparisons should be made on a total basis, whereas variable costs should be compared on a per unit basis. An appropriate cost coding and collection system is essential to ensure that the data collected and consequently the information produced from it, is reliable.

DEFINITION

Revenue centre – a centre devoted to raising revenue with no responsibility for the cost of doing so.

Revenue centre

The performance of a manager responsible for a revenue centre is judged based on the revenue raised. Information would need to be collected from sales figures to establish both the total and per unit revenues.

DEFINITION

Profit centre – a part of the business accountable for costs and revenues.

Profit centre

The performance of a manager responsible for a profit centre is measured on profits. The manager must therefore be responsible for both costs and revenues. Such managers therefore have significant authority.

Profit centres are often found in large organisations which have a divisionalised structure. In such structures trading between the divisions gives rise to transfer pricing which is dealt with later in this text.

To operate a profit centre data must be collected relating to both costs and revenues. This data is then used to measure profit trends and to compare actual and target costs and revenues.

DEFINITION

Investment centre – a profit centre whose performance is measured by its return on capital employed.

Investment centre

Managers of investment centres are also responsible for investment decisions, so that their performance can be measured in terms of profit relative to the level of investment. In its simplest form Return on Capital Employed (ROCE) is measured by:

$$\frac{\text{Profit}}{\text{Capital Employed}}$$

To operate an investment centre it is necessary to collect data on costs, revenues and investments. Within this context the principle of controllability is highly important. Whilst controllability refers mainly to costs, it is important to remember that its principles can also apply to revenues and investments.

2.6 Controllable costs

DEFINITION

Controllable costs are costs incurred as a result of a decision or course of action of a manager; or which could be avoided by such a decision or course of action.

Identifying controllable costs

Performance reports should concentrate only on **controllable costs.** Controllable costs are those costs controllable by a particular manager in a given time period. Over a long enough time-span most costs are controllable by someone in the organisation e.g. factory rental may be fixed for a number of years but there may eventually come an opportunity to move to other premises. Such a cost, therefore, is controllable in the long-term by a manager fairly high in the organisation structure.

However, in the short-term it is uncontrollable even by senior managers, and certainly uncontrollable by managers lower down the organisational hierarchy.

There is no clear-cut distinction between controllable and non-controllable costs for a given manager, who may in any case be exercising control jointly with another manager. The aim under a responsibility accounting system will be to assign and report on the cost to the person having **primary** responsibility. The most effective control is thereby achieved, since immediate action can be taken.

Some authorities would favour the alternative idea that reports should include all costs caused by a department, whether controllable or uncontrollable by the departmental manager. The idea here is that, even if he has no direct control, he might influence the manager who does have control. There is the danger of providing the manager with too much information and confusing him but, on the other hand, the uncontrollable element could be regarded as for 'information only', and in this way the manager obtains a fuller picture.

An illustration of the two different approaches is provided by raw materials. The production manager will have control over usage, but not over price, when buying is done by a separate department. For this reason the price and usage variances are separated and, under the first approach, the production manager would be told only about the usage variance, a separate report being made to the purchasing manager about the price variance. The alternative argument is that if the production manager is also told about the price variance, he may attempt to persuade the purchasing manager to try alternative sources of supply.

ACTIVITY 1

What are the potential dangers of including uncontrollable costs in a performance report?

Feedback to this activity is at the end of the chapter.

3 Information and reporting

3.1 Guidelines for reporting

There are several specific problems in relation to reporting which must be identified and dealt with:

Levels of reporting

The problem is how far down the management structure should responsibility centres be identified for reporting purposes? On the one hand, lower reporting levels encourage delegation and identify responsibility closer to the production process. On the other hand, more responsibility centres increase the number of reports and hence the cost of their production. One solution may be to combine small responsibility centres into groups (e.g. departments) for reporting purposes.

Frequency of reports and information to be reported

The frequency of reports should be linked to the purposes for which they are required. This may well mean a variety of reports being produced to different time-scales for different purposes e.g. some control information will be required weekly, or even daily. However, comprehensive budget reports are only likely to be required monthly.

KEY POINT

Generally, as reporting proceeds up the management pyramid, the breadth of the report should increase, and the detail should decrease.

The related problem is the content of such reports. It has been suggested that in computerised information systems the problem is often too much, rather than too little information. Generally, as reporting proceeds up the management pyramid, the breadth of the report should increase, and the detail should decrease. The following series of reports illustrate this principle:

	Budget		*Variance*	
	Current month	*Year to date*	*Current month*	*Year to date*
Managing director				
Factory A				
Factory B				
Administration costs				
Selling costs				
Distribution costs				
R&D costs				
Production director Factory A				
Machining department				
Casting department				
Assembly department				
Inspection and quality control				
Factory manager's office				
Head of machining department				
Direct materials				
Direct labour				
Indirect labour				
Power				
Maintenance				
Other				

The above layout should only be regarded as illustrative, but it does indicate how detail increases as span decreases.

3.2 Degree of summarisation

Even where data is of the correct kind for a particular task, if it is presented in its raw form it will normally be too detailed to be described as information. This is why information usually consists of a large number of data items which have summarised into a smaller number of data items. The degree of summarisation is the comparison between the original number of data items and the number of data items finally presented. For example a report on the sales of 120 individual sales staff summarised into 4 regions is more summarised than a report of the same individuals summarised into 24 sales teams.

Summarisation has the benefit of allowing an individual to gain an overall picture of a situation. However in the process of stepping back to gain this overall view some detail is lost. Therefore the overall reporting procedures should include methods of highlighting individual data items which need management attention. In our sales team example this may include a report which identifies all staff whose total sales were more than 30% above or below the average for the organisation.

3.3 Quantitative and qualitative information

KEY POINT

Information can be classified as being either quantitative or qualitative.

Information can be classified as being either quantitative or qualitative.

Quantitative information

Quantitative information is information that can be expressed in numerical terms; it may therefore be measured in monetary or non-monetary units. Such information may be used to make comparisons between alternatives, for example when choosing between two machines the following quantitative information may be compared:

- capital cost
- running cost per hour
- output per hour
- estimated useful life in hours.

Qualitative information

Qualitative information is information that cannot normally be expressed in numerical terms. It is often opinions which may affect decisions involving the environment and human reaction. For example a decision concerning the closure of a segment of a business may impact on the morale of the workforce which remains, as well as the infrastructure and environment in which the particular segment operates. These factors should be considered in addition to any quantitative information.

3.4 Accuracy of information

As was stated in Chapter 1, information should always be only sufficiently accurate for its intended purpose. Such accuracy of information depends on a number of factors, for example collection and processing techniques.

Accuracy and precision

In order to process data into information it must be appropriately accurate and precise. These two attributes are closely related yet they are distinct.

Precision refers to the detail included in data. This is sometimes referred to as granularity.

Accuracy refers to how close the data is to whatever is being measured.

For example if a decision has been taken that the monthly sales will be reported to the precision of the nearest £1,000 and the sales for a particular month were £24,501 then data which stated £25,000 would be accurate and £24,000 inaccurate. However, if the precision had been decided as the nearest £1 then £25,000 would be inaccurate.

If data is recorded and presented in great precision it can give the impression that the data is accurate, when in fact precision is no indicator of accuracy. Both precision and accuracy can be measured. Precision is relatively easy to measure. In the case of numerical data precision it is stated as the number of significant digits. One measure of accuracy is error rate, this can be expressed as the percentage of data which, after allowing for the specified precision, is not the same as the reality which the data is intended to represent. Inaccuracy can occur due to systematic bias and or error.

Systematic bias is inaccuracy due to a feature of the system used for the collection and processing of data. The raw data in a business system is not normally subject to bias. It is normally the system which collects and presents the data which is biased. Collection bias is in effect distorting reality by withholding certain information. In the case of an information system this would mean that the system had either deliberately or accidentally been designed in such a way that it failed to collect relevant data. Presentation bias occurs when data is presented in a way which only presents one point of view. The axis on graphs can be set in order to bias the presentation of data.

Sometimes collection and presentation bias are used together. An example is a newspaper headline which stated that 25% of chief executives of major companies did not have a university degree or professional qualification, indicating that many unqualified individuals become chief executives. An unbiased presentation would state that 10% of the workforce and 75% of chief executives had degrees or professional qualifications. This data could be further enhanced to state that qualified individuals are seven times more likely to become chief executives than unqualified individuals.

Error in data usually occurs as a result of the inherent variability in the system used to record the data. This should not be confused with random variation in what is being measured. For example measuring devices are normally manufactured to operate within certain limits. A micrometer may be capable of measuring to plus or minus 50 microns. If the device reported measurements larger than whatever is being measured on one occasion and smaller on another then this variation would introduce random error into the data. Conversely if the micrometer was exactly accurate but the parts being measured varied in size then the data would be accurate but would vary randomly (although probably within certain limitations).

Other sources of error are:

- incorrect methods of data collection and measurement
- loss of data
- failure to process some of the data.

3.5 Source

The source of data is the system, person, group or organisation which produced it. Knowing the source helps the user to compensate for systematic bias. If for example the managing director of an organisation receives a sales forecast from the sales director and another from the finance director he will use his knowledge of the two individuals involved to make adjustments to the data. In doing so he would probably consider their personal biases and those placed upon them by their positions within the firm.

KEY POINT

Data may either be formal or informal depending upon its source:

- Formal sources are all sources of data which have authority to make statements on behalf of the organisation.
- Informal sources include all data which is not classified by the company as official.

Data may either be formal or informal depending upon its source:

(a) Formal sources are all sources of data which have authority to make statements on behalf of the organisation. Formal data includes:

- statements from the organisation's officials
- data from the formal systems of the organisation
- published documents
- company advertising.

(b) Informal sources include all data which is not classified by the company as official:

- informal discussions with colleagues
- rumours
- meetings with suppliers or customers
- reports compiled for personal use.

Another classification of source is whether the data is from within the organisation or from outside sources. Most information which is based upon verifiable data is from within the organisation. The vast majority of information produced and consumed in the organisation is from data collected in the organisation.

3.6 Completeness

Completeness refers to the extent to which the data is sufficient for the task. With the exception of a few totally controlled and structured tasks, it is impossible to have complete data. Examination of most decision-making tasks no matter how trivial normally reveals a number of assumptions which have been adopted because of the incompleteness of data. Data which is produced to aid the process of planning will always be incomplete because the future cannot be predicted with certainty.

Data is normally considered complete if the users feel that they have all the data that they can justify for the task or decision. This means that tasks may be carried out with incomplete data - yet additional data is accessible but only at a cost either in money or time which the user feels is not worthwhile. A feature of many managers' jobs is that of making decisions which, due to time pressure, they have to make without data which exists and is available. This will be explored in greater detail shortly under the heading relevance and value.

3.7 Accessibility

KEY POINT

A user of data rarely has complete data.

Data and information have already been discussed in terms of its completeness. A user of data rarely has complete data. One of the factors creating this condition is the time required to gather complete data, which in turn is related to how accessible data is. The factors which affect accessibility are:

- the user's knowledge of what data is available
- the user's skill in locating and retrieving data
- where data is recorded
- the media used to record the data
- the access procedures.

Recording data in computer systems has made a major difference to accessibility of information. A skilled user can usually obtain the data required fairly quickly and cheaply. This contrasts with the situation where the user has physical access to manual records, but because of the quantity involved the cost of manually sifting through many records may effectively render the data inaccessible.

3.8 Relevance and value

In order to be of use data must be relevant. At the beginning of this section information was defined as data which amongst other things is meaningful. Relevance is the attribute of data which allows it to become meaningful in a particular organisational setting. Information systems are conceived to supply information to users of the system. In designing the system planners will define informational requirements and from this relevant data can be identified.

3.9 Accuracy, volume and time

KEY POINT

The accuracy and reliability of information can be significantly affected by changes in operating conditions (i.e. volume changes) and the passage of time.

The accuracy and reliability of information can be significantly affected by changes in operating conditions (i.e. volume changes) and the passage of time.

Accuracy and volume

A significant use of information in management accounting is the prediction of future costs from past information. This is made more difficult when the future predicted level of activity differs from that of the past.

Some costs are affected by changes in activity (variable costs) whilst others are not affected (fixed costs). If these differences are not considered then the predictions made and the information communicated from them will be inaccurate and unreliable.

Age of data

DEFINITION

The **age of the data** is the time that has elapsed since the data was collected.

The age of the data is the time that has elapsed since the data was collected. Establishing the age of the data which is part of a regular reporting system is easy. For example, if monthly accounts are produced in a particular organisation, then a user can assume the stock value included in the latest report is less than one month old. Other data can be much harder to age. This typically occurs where the data originated from an *ad hoc* report.

Associated with the age of the data is its timeliness or the degree to which its age is suitable for the decision or control process it is to be used in. Control processes and decisions differ in their timeliness requirements. For example, the mechanism which controls the stock held on the shelves of a busy supermarket will require data that is only a few hours old.

This is because of two factors. The first is that management will have specified that the shelves should always have some stock on them, the second is that the situation changes very rapidly. An example of a data requirement where the data can be much older would be in long-range company planning. The data used in this process would be part of the information on trends rather than short-term fluctuations, therefore some of the data could refer to a number of years ago.

The duration of data is the period of time that the data spans. For example a set of monthly accounts will span one month and so the data on sales is the aggregation of all individual sales data for the month in question. Where systems produce forecasts the data may refer to some period in the future. The actual duration of the data in the report or forecast can range between hours and years.

3.10 Controlling accuracy

The accuracy of information depends on two factors:

- source reliability
- data capture techniques.

Source reliability

Data may be collected from sources internal and external to the organisation. Internal sources can in many instances be verified, for example a comparison can be made between sales data and finished goods stock records. Such a comparison would prove (or disprove) the accuracy of the data. However other internal sources (e.g. an employee's time sheet) and most external sources do not cross-reference to a second source. Thus information derived from such single sources is dependent on the reliability of the source for its accuracy.

Data capture techniques

On the assumption that the source of the data is reliable and accurate, such data can cause inaccurate information to be provided if the data capture technique is not controlled.

Today, data is typically processed by computer, and to facilitate this data must be entered into the computer system. This may be done manually using a keyboard or by electronic means using scanning devices. Where manual input techniques are used there is a much greater risk of error, due to human involvement. System controls are needed to verify and validate the input. Although this does not guarantee 100% accuracy such controls will minimise the production of inaccurate and meaningless information.

3.11 Management accounting information and uncertainty

KEY POINT

Much of management accounting is concerned with the future and to this extent it relies on predictions based on past data.

Much of management accounting is concerned with the future and to this extent it relies on predictions based on past data. To produce a single set of values based on the past data may therefore give a misleading sense of accuracy. In considering any business situation, the accountant is confronted with a range of contingent factors both internal and external to the organisation. For example, one cannot be sure of the level of customer demand in the following year (it depends on the general state of the economy and actions by competitors). One cannot be sure of unit production cost (it depends on the efficiency of labour and the wage rates that have yet to be negotiated).

To overcome this sensitivity analysis and probabilities are used to give a more balanced view of the future.

Sensitivity analysis

DEFINITION

Sensitivity analysis is a technique which is similar to the 'what-if' facility provided by computer spreadsheet packages.

This is a technique which is similar to the 'what-if' facility provided by computer spreadsheet packages. Initial predictions are produced based on past data. Then each of the variables is changed, usually by the same percentage, and the effect on the final result measured. By using this technique it is possible to establish which variables are more critical than others in achieving a given result. At the same time management may be made aware of the range of outcomes which may occur.

Using probability

Instead of predicting a single value from past data a common technique is to predict three values:

- most likely
- optimistic
- pessimistic

and predict the probability of each occurring. These predictions are made for each variable. It is then possible to combine each of the possible outcomes so as to produce a range of values together with their related probabilities. This again enables management to be made aware of possible outcomes, but the use of probabilities enables the likelihood of each outcome occurring to be shown.

An effective use of sensitivity analysis allows a business plan or budget to be presented in a manner which allows the reader to develop a feel for the expected outcome and the full range of possible outcomes. A business plan which involves a lower expected profit may be preferred to one with a higher expected profit if the former can be shown to involve a narrower range of possible outcomes.

The effective use of spreadsheet modelling facilitates sensitivity analysis.

4 Control systems

4.1 The theory of control system design

We have so far considered practical aspects of system design and related them to management accounting. At this point it is instructive to consider theoretical aspects of control system design.

In order to understand this section it is useful to start with an example of a control system which is in everyday use. General concepts can then be abstracted from this example, developed and applied to business situations.

Thermostat example

All central heating systems contain thermostats to regulate the temperature of the rooms they are heating. The user sets the thermostat to the required temperature on the dial. There is a thermometer in the system which measures the temperature of the rooms. The room temperature is continually compared with the preset temperature on the thermostat dial. If room temperature is above the dial temperature, the power (e.g. gas) is switched off. When room temperature falls below the dial temperature, the power is switched on. This system can be represented diagrammatically as follows:

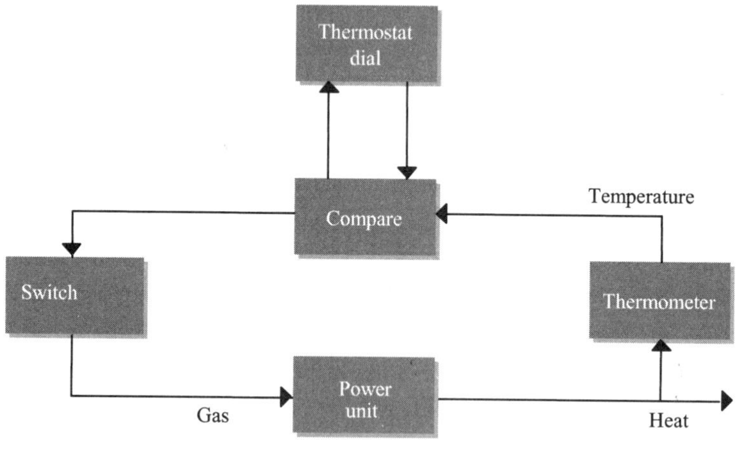

General terms for elements of a control system

The basic gas-burning system is:

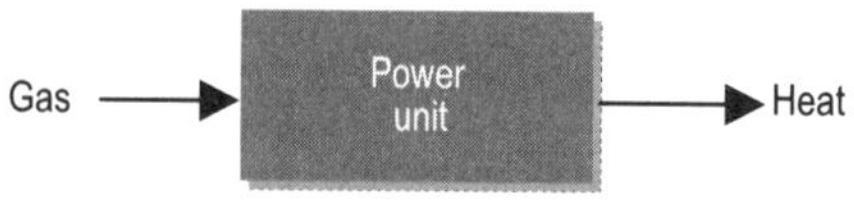

The thermostat system introduces a **controller** which is made up of four elements, a pre-set temperature on the dial, a thermostat, a comparison unit and a switch. The general terms for the elements of a controller are:

- **Standard:** This is what the system is aiming for. In the thermostat system it is the pre-set temperature.

- **Sensor:** (or detector). This measures the output of the system. In the thermostat system it is the thermometer.
- **Comparator:** This compares the information from the standard and the sensor.
- **Effector:** (or activator). This initiates the control action. In the thermostat system it is the switch.

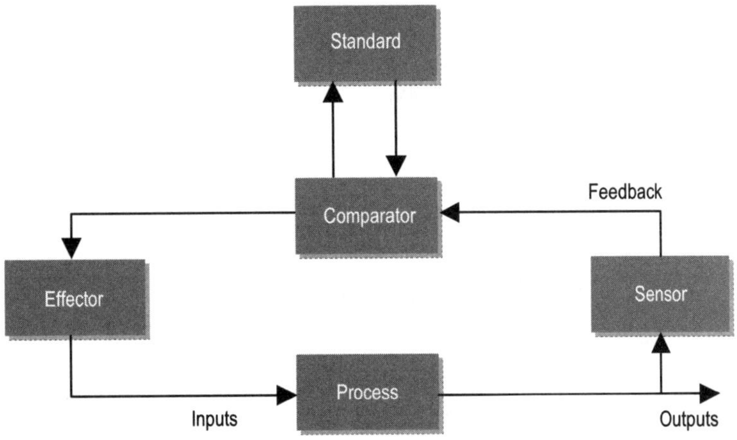

The general term for the information which is taken from the system output and used to adjust the system is **feedback.** In the thermostat example the feedback is the actual room temperature.

Application to an accounting system – budgetary control

In a budgetary control system the financial performance of a department is compared with the budget. Action is then taken to improve the department's performance if possible. The elements of the control system are:

- **standard:** the budget (e.g. standard costs)
- **sensor:** the costing system, which records actual costs
- **feedback:** the actual results for the period, collected by the costing system
- **comparator:** the 'performance report' for the department, comparing actual with budget (e.g. variance analysis)
- **effector:** the manager of the department, in consultation with others, takes action to minimise future adverse variances and to exploit opportunities resulting from favourable variances.

The opportunity may also be taken to adjust the standard (i.e. the budget) if it is seen to be too easy or too difficult to achieve.

A number of complications make this budgetary control system more difficult than it appears at first sight:

- the impact of the environment on the system has not been shown i.e. prices of raw materials may rise uncontrollably or interest rates may increase
- differences between actual and budgeted results may not be controllable directly by the departmental manager i.e. rises in certain input costs may be caused by another department
- the accounting system cannot measure all the output of the department, hence feedback may be incomplete i.e. an investment for longer term profits may have been made at the expense of short-term cost control.

A more complete diagram of the control system would be as follows:

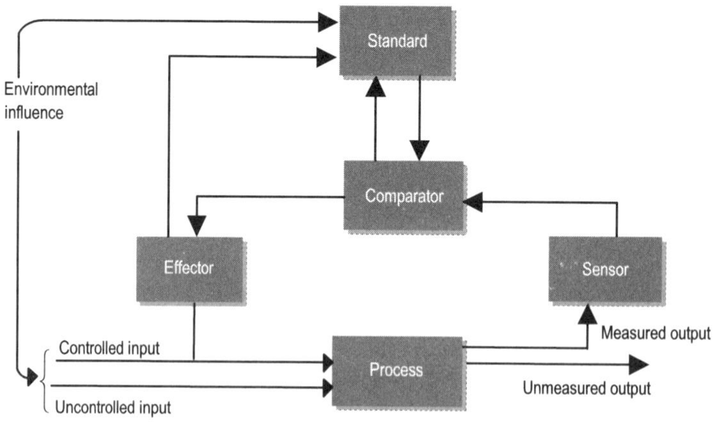

4.2 Open and closed loop systems

KEY POINT

Any systems involving feedback are called **closed loop** systems.

Control systems which do not involve feeding back output information are called **open loop** systems.

The systems described above, and any systems involving feedback are called **closed loop** systems. Associated terms are **feedback loop** and **control cycle**.

Control systems which do not involve feeding back output information are called **open loop** systems. Control is exercised regardless of output.

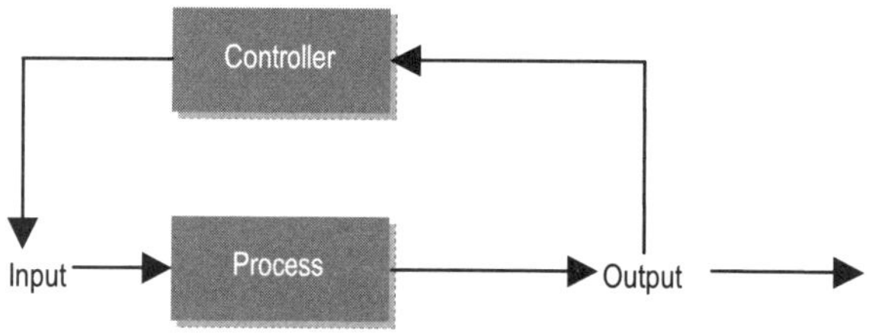

Closed loop system

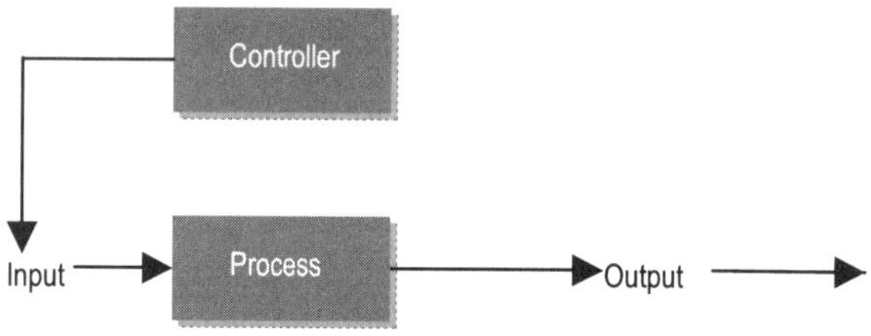

Open loop system

The term **open loop** implies there is a break in the feedback loop. This may arise either because feedback is not produced or because it is not used. For example, in some accounting systems useful cost information is collected but it is 'not reported' to the right people. In other systems the report is given to the right person but it is not read. Both would be examples of open loop systems.

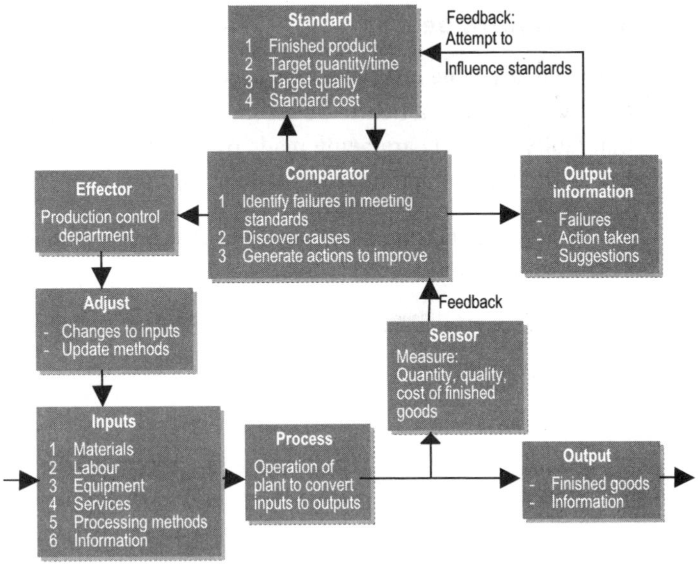

DEFINITION

Feedback makes the difference between open and closed loop systems. Feedback can be defined as:

'modification or control of a process or system by its results or effects, by measuring differences between desired and actual results. Feedback is an element in a feedback system and forms the link between planning and control.'

4.3 Feedback

Double loop feedback

Double loop feedback, or higher level feedback, is when information is transmitted to a higher level in the system. It indicates differences between actual and planned results allowing for control adjustments to be made to the plan itself. Double loop feedback gathers information from both the system output and the environment.

The production system of a firm seen as a double loop feedback control system

DEFINITION

Negative feedback is information which shows that the system is deviating from its planned course in a way which is detrimental to its operation.

4.4 Negative and positive feedback

Negative feedback is information which shows that the system is deviating from its planned course in a way which is detrimental to its operation. Action is needed to return the system to its original course.

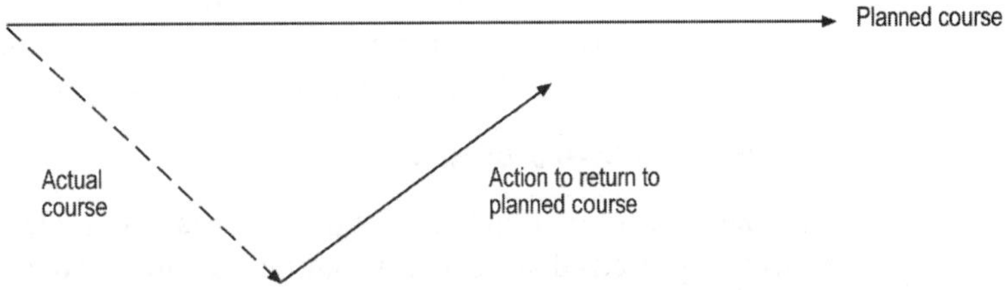

The crash barriers on a motorway provide a graphic example of the action of negative feedback. Most routine management accounting information is used to create negative feedback.

KEY POINT

Positive feedback results in deviations from the plan being continued or increased.

Positive feedback results in deviations from the plan being continued or increased. Sometimes this can be detrimental, leading to a 'vicious circle'. For instance, if sales prices are increased to make up for a shortfall in the sales budget, the result may be a lower sales volume, resulting in a lower sales value and a further attempt to increase sales prices. More often, however, positive feedback results from favourable variances. If sales beat budget, for example, action may be taken to continue this trend.

4.5 Control delay

KEY POINT

For feedback to be effective, it is necessary for the information to be reported quickly and for corrective action to be taken promptly.

For feedback to be effective, it is necessary for the information to be reported quickly and for corrective action to be taken promptly. For example, if an inspection shows that faulty products are being made by a particular machine, the information needs to be reported to the maintenance department immediately and action needs to be swift.

The following diagram shows the proper receipt, and action upon, the feedback in a system at the correct time (X):

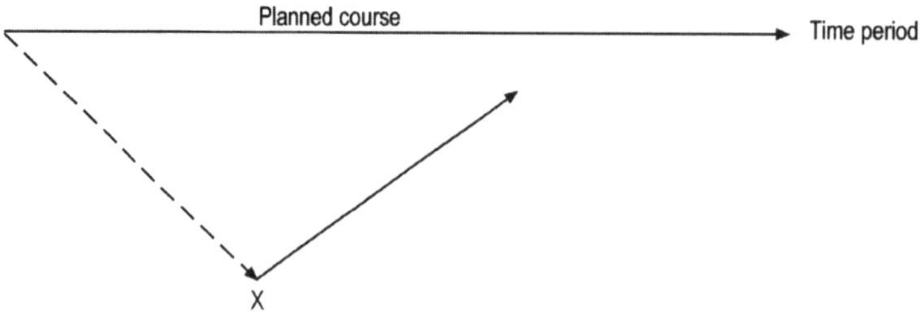

The following diagram shows delays in two places:

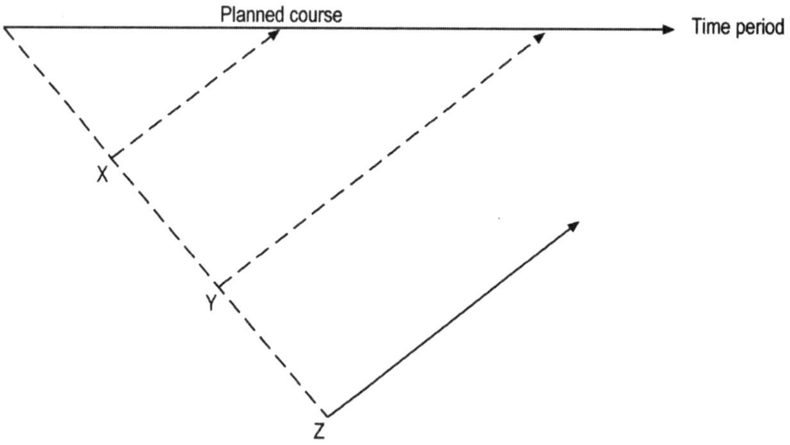

X is the point at which feedback should have been given, and action should have been taken. Y is the point at which feedback was actually given and Z the point at which action was taken. XY represents the reporting delay and YZ the action delay.

It is a general principle of management accounting reports that they should be produced promptly and in a form which is easy for the user to understand. Information which does not satisfy these requirements is of limited use.

4.6 Feedforward control

KEY POINT

Feedback control measures deviation of **actual (historic) data** from control (expected/ desired) data.

KEY POINT

Feedforward control is anticipatory – it measures the deviation of **predicted future results** from the desired future results.

Feedback control measures deviation of **actual (historic) data** from control (expected/desired) data. These deviations are analysed as to their cause and action taken where possible to put the system back on course (if deviations are detrimental).

Feedforward control is anticipatory – it measures the deviation of **predicted future results** from the desired future results i.e. checking where we are likely to be versus where we want to be. Causes of deviations are analysed and action taken where possible to minimise their impact.

For example, in a target costing exercise, a particular required rate of return will be required over the life of a proposed product initiative. If the selling price and demand are assumed to be held constant, a feedforward control exercise may be to ascertain by how much and in what way the product unit cost would have to be reduced from current estimates if the target return is to be achieved.

The information used to predict future results may to some extent arise as a result of the analysis carried out in the feedback control system.

For example, the planning and operational variance analysis (covered in Chapter 21) involves the use of 'ex-post' standards – standards that have been revised in hindsight, once the actual operating and external environment of the period under review are known. Their identification allows traditional variances to be split between amounts caused by inappropriate standard setting (planning variances) and amounts that can fairly be attributed to operations.

The feedback control will then focus on the operational variances, identifying the extent to which these are controllable and thus can be eliminated in future by taking suitable action.

Feedforward control can be aided by the use of the 'ex-post' standards as a basis for predicting future results.

Conclusion

Management accounting information is needed to enable managers to exert control within their area of responsibility. This area may be a cost centre, a revenue centre, a profit centre or an investment centre. The source(s) and accuracy of information must be taken into consideration when using the information to make decisions. Management control is based on feedback and corrective action must be taken promptly if it is to be effective.

SELF-TEST QUESTIONS

Introduction

1 Outline the planning, control and decision-making process. (1.2)

Responsibility accounting and responsibility centres

2 Explain responsibility accounting. (2.1)

3 Distinguish between cost, revenue, profit and investment centres. (2.5)

4 What is a controllable cost? (2.6)

Information and reporting

5 Distinguish between quantitative and qualitative information. (3.3)

6 Distinguish between accuracy and precision. (3.4)

7 Explain the effects of volume on the accuracy of information. (3.9)

8 Discuss difficulties of controlling the accuracy of information. (3.10)

9 Explain two management accounting techniques which are used to deal with uncertainty. (3.11)

Control systems

10 Distinguish between open and closed loop systems. (4.2)

11 Distinguish between negative and positive feedback. (4.4)

12 Explain feedforward control. (4.6)

EXAM-TYPE QUESTION

Management accounting criteria

Management accounting information should comply with a number of criteria including verifiability, objectivity, timeliness, comparability, reliability, understandability and relevance if it is to be useful in planning, control and decision-making.

(a) Explain the meaning of each of the criteria named above and give a specific example to illustrate each. **(14 marks)**

(b) Give a brief explanation of how the criteria detailed in (a) might be in conflict with each other giving examples to illustrate where such conflict might arise.

(3 marks)

(Total: 17 marks)

For the answer to this question, see the 'Answers' section at the end of the book.

FEEDBACK TO ACTIVITY **1**

The dangers of including uncontrollable costs in a performance report are:

(a) Managers might be demotivated if their performance is apparently affected by costs over which they have no influence.

(b) Uncontrollable cost information can divert managers' attention away from what they actually are responsible for.

(c) The manager who **is** responsible for the costs in question might feel that they are not his or her responsibility as they are reported elsewhere.

The problem of dual responsibility

A common problem is that the responsibility for a particular cost or item is shared between two (or more) managers. For example, the responsibility for payroll costs may be shared between the personnel and production departments; material costs between purchasing and production departments; and so on. The reporting system should be designed so that the responsibility for performance achievements (i.e. better or worse than budget) is identified as that of a single manager.

The following guidelines may be applied:

(a) If manager controls quantity **and** price – responsible for all expenditure variances.

(b) If manager controls quantity but **not** price – only responsible for variances due to usage.

(c) If manager controls price but **not** quantity – only responsible for variances due to input prices.

(d) If manager controls **neither** quantity **nor** price – variances uncontrollable from the point of view of that manager.

Chapter 3
GATHERING AND PROCESSING OF INFORMATION

CHAPTER CONTENTS

This chapter explores the gathering, processing and transmission of information within a business management context.

Objectives

When you have studied this chapter you should be able to do the following.

- Identify the principal internal sources of management accounting information.
- Illustrate how these principal sources of information might be used for control purposes.
- Identify the direct data capture and process costs of internally generated management accounting information.
- Identify the indirect costs of producing internal information.
- Explain the principle controls required in generating and distributing internal information.
- Discuss the factors that need be considered when determining the capacity and development potential of a system.
- Explain the procedures that may be necessary to ensure security of highly confidential information that is not for external consumption.
- Identify common external sources of information, e.g. suppliers, government, trade associations, customers, database suppliers.
- Identify the costs associated with these external sources.
- Discuss the limitations of using externally generated information.
- Identify the categories of external information that are likely to be a useful addition to an organisation's management accounting system.
- Illustrate how the information might be used in planning and control activities, e.g. benchmarking against similar organisations.
- Identify the stages in the information processing cycle in the context of accounting information.
- Identify how the collection and analysis of information is influenced by management accounting principles and techniques being used by the organisation.
- Describe the systems involved in the collection and recording of monetary and non-monetary information.
- Illustrate how the type of business entity will influence the recording and processing methods.
- Explain how IT developments, e.g. spreadsheets, accountancy software packages and electronic mail may influence recording and processing systems.
- Discuss the difficulties associated with recording and processing data of a qualitative nature.

1 Introduction

1.1 Data and information

Informationis different from data. Although the two terms are often used interchangeably in everyday language, it is important to make a clear distinction between them, as follows:

DEFINITIONS

Data consists of numbers, letters, symbols, raw facts, events and transactions which have been recorded but not yet processed into a form which is suitable for making decisions.

Informationis data which has been processed in such a way that it has a meaning to the person who receives it, who may then use it to improve the quality of decision-making.

The word **data** means facts.

Data on its own is not generally useful, whereas information is very useful. For example, in cost accounting the accounting system records a large number of facts (data) about materials, times, expenses and other transactions. These facts are then classified and summarised to produce accounts, which are organised into reports designed to help management to plan and control the organisation's activities.

Relationship between data and information

Data processing converts data into information:

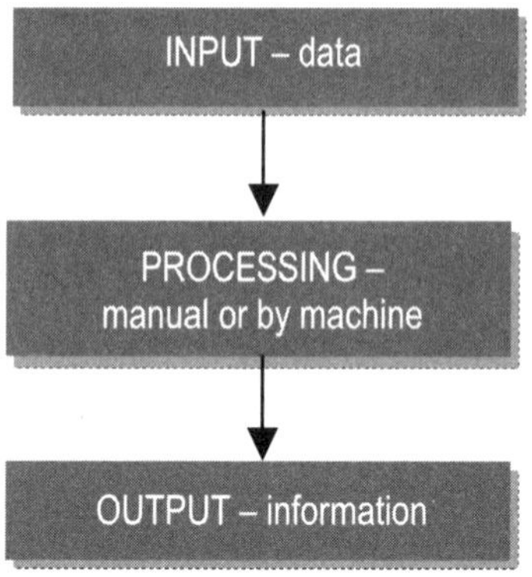

Data processing can be seen as a system, whose interfaces with the environment are data and information. Data is processed into information, perhaps by classifying it or summarising it and producing total figures. For example, a sales ledger system could be required to process data about goods dispatched to satisfy customer orders and:

- produce and send out invoices
- record the invoices sent out in the customers' personal ledgers
- produce a report of the total value of invoices sent out in the day/week etc
- record the total value of invoices sent out in the debtors' control account.

ACTIVITY 1

A typical market research survey employs a number of researchers who interview a sample of the target market and ask them a number of questions relating to the product or service. Several hundred questionnaires may be completed and they will then be processed.

Why does the data need processing and what processing operations will be carried out?

Feedback to this activity is at the end of the chapter.

2 Data capture, reporting, and communicating

2.1 Reporting

The data that an organisation gathers and stores is determined by the information that management needs to control the operations of the organisation. Control will be exercised at several levels in the organisation: operational, tactical, and strategic. Each of these levels requires different information.

KEY POINT

Strategic information is required by the business or entity in order to take a 'long-range' view of how that business is going to perform, over the next *n* years.

- **Strategic information** is required by the business or entity in order to take a 'long-range' view of how that business is going to perform, over the next *n* years. The period of years depends upon the type of business and the ability of the management to scan the planning horizon. Strategic information could relate to the study of overseas markets, the development of new products or to the threats and opportunities in the business environment.

KEY POINT

Tactical information is required for management planning and control.

KEY POINT

Operational information is information which is concerned with a much shorter time scale and relates to more immediate action.

- **Tactical information** is required for management planning and control. It is generally concerned with a shorter time period and is concerned with commitments to particular courses of action. For example, a sales budget for a twelve-month period dedicated to the achievement of an increased sales volume.
- **Operational information** is information which is concerned with a much shorter time scale and relates to more immediate action. Collection of actual sales for comparison with budget or preparing a labour turnover report for a week are both examples of operational information.
- This information is generally supplied in the form of reports. Reports may be produced in a number of forms ranging from periodic printed reports, through to a senior executive producing an individual report on an executive information system.

Typical reports produced in a medium-sized manufacturing company might include the following.

(a) **Production and material control**

- forward loading plans for production cycles
- machine capacity forecast
- departmental operating statements
- stock and work-in-progress reports
- wastage report
- labour utilisation report.

(b) **Marketing, including distribution**

- market surveys
- order reports by product and geographical area
- discount trends
- transport and warehouse cost statements
- salesperson performance
- product service and support costs.

(c) **Personnel**

- numbers employed by category
- overtime hours
- sickness, absence, lateness
- training requirements
- career development plans
- recruitment policy
- job descriptions.

(d) **Financial and management accounting**

- annual statutory accounts
- budgets and forecasts
- sales and contribution analyses
- cash, management and working capital evaluation
- capital project appraisal
- standard cost and variance analysis reports
- returns to government departments e.g. VAT.

From the above list of reports, some assumptions can be drawn:

- information is needed for many different purposes
- the information produced is a mixture of financial and statistical data
- information is needed by different groups of users who work at different levels within the firm
- the information is produced at different times and frequencies in the form of both *ad hoc* and regular reports.

Managers demand a great deal of information to carry out their functions. This raises a question of costs, data capture being the major cost in reporting.

2.2 Methods of data capture

KEY POINT

Design of the data collection methods is an important part of designing a computer system.

Design of the data collection methods is an important part of designing a computer system. The organisation needs to consider its strategic plans in order to assess the future uses of its systems. If it is thought likely that it will be networking with other systems then it will need to ensure that any new equipment purchased will be compatible with the network it wishes to join. When choosing input methods and media, most users are concerned with the following:

- how to economise on the use of manpower
- how to prevent or detect errors in the source data
- how to achieve data capture at the lowest possible cost
- how to achieve input sufficiently quickly
- how data gets into the system.

Input devices can be divided into two main categories:

- those using a keyboard
- those using direct input of the data.

DEFINITION

Communication in business can be defined as the transmission of information so that it is received, understood and leads to action.

KEY POINT

Information is active, relevant and prompts action; data, on the other hand, is passive, may be historical or irrelevant and does not necessarily lead to action.

Information can be classified as 'hard' or 'soft'.

2.3 Key aspects of communication

This definition enables us to understand some of the key aspects of business communication:

(a) Information, and not data, should be communicated. Information is active, relevant and prompts action; data, on the other hand, is passive, may be historical or irrelevant and does not necessarily lead to action.

Information can be classified as 'hard' or 'soft'. Hard information includes documents, reports and facts, whereas soft information covers less tangible information such as feelings, points of view, morale and body language.

(b) Clearly, if information has not been received or is not understood by the receiver, then communication has not taken place.

(c) The communication should lead to action. This action may take the form of a positive decision or may be a change in attitude. If the communication does not lead to any action then, probably, it ought not to have taken place.

Communication means transmitting messages to people in a manner which stimulates response. In some cases, the response will be direct to the sender, as when two people are engaged in debating the merits and demerits of some proposition. In other cases the response will be indirect as when transfer of the information gives rise to some independent action on the part of the recipient or when he or she merely stores it for future reference.

Communication in an organisation supports planning of the objectives of the firm, deciding upon courses of action and measuring performance of the actions taken. In the context of an organisation, communication may be considered as:

- an individual's ability to express himself;
- the method of circulating information within the organisation.

2.4 How data and information are communicated

KEY POINT

Modern communication technologies have changed the nature of how people communicate.

Modern communication technologies have changed the nature of how people communicate. Until the telephone became available people had to communicate with one another at the same place unless they used messengers or the mail. Now it is possible to communicate rapidly with anyone virtually anywhere in the world. This will become increasingly common as networks proliferate and mobile communications become more widespread, and as the cost of the communications falls due to advancing technology and competition.

Data and information may be circulated in a number of ways, for example:

- verbally, as feedback of information such as lunch-time conversations
- as written reports and schedules, for example, monthly accounts
- as data on forms for processing such as goods inwards notes
- as data on graphs, charts and diagrams
- as visual presentations, for example, notices on boards and closed circuit TV.

The two main methods of communicating are still oral and written.

Oral communication can range from **speech without visual contact** – radio, tannoy, personal pager and telephone to **speech with visual contact** – television presentation, television link and face-to-face conversation.

The advantages of oral communication include the following:

- Apart from broadcasting, it is a quick, direct and cheap medium with little time lapse between sending and receiving.
- The meaning of an oral message can be underlined by using stress, timing and pitch.
- It has the potential for informality and the sensitive handling of some communications e.g. bad news, reprimand, sympathy, or encouragement.
- Instant feedback is usually possible, so that misunderstandings can be cleared and messages can be received and acknowledged.
- In speech with visual contact, the meaning can be reinforced by facial expression or gestures.

The disadvantages may include the following.

- Noise can interfere with the message.
- Little time may be allocated to the planning of the communication and this can lead to inferior decisions being made.
- The communication may be distorted because the listener interprets the facial expression or body language wrongly.
- Communications that require memory are better written down than spoken.
- Clash of personalities may be a barrier to conversation.

Written communication can range from permanent hand-written, typed or printed documents, through semi-permanent output such as screen displays to transient outputs such as written information on television screens and electronic bill boards.

Permanent records have:

- **advantages** in avoiding personal contact, assisting with long and complex messages and being able to reach a large audience. They have the potential for formality and their permanence enables them to be used as records.
- **disadvantages** in that their permanence can lead to rigidity. Moreover they demand considerable linguistic skills, are time-consuming to produce, slower to transmit and can be expensive.

2.5 Formal and informal communication systems

All organisations have formal, acknowledged, and often specified communication channels. There will be lists of people who are to attend briefings or meetings, and distribution lists for minutes of meetings or memos. There will be procedures for telling people of decisions or changes, and for circulating information received from outside the organisation.

In addition, an informal 'grapevine' exists in all organisations; people talk about their work, their colleagues, and about the state of their firm, whenever they meet: in corridors, over lunch, after work. They swap rumour, gossip, half-truths and wild speculation.

Communication flows exist within the company in three main directions:

- downwards, or superior-subordinate communication
- upwards or subordinate-initiated communication
- horizontal or lateral.

2.6 Process of communication

Whilst communication flows through channels in organisations, the ultimate success lies in the ability of the individuals to communicate effectively. It is not simply a matter of transmitting the information, care must be taken to ensure that it is relevant and in a usable format for the recipient. Effective communication is a two-way process, or cycle, where signals or messages are sent by the communicator and received by the other party, who sends back some sort of confirmation that the message has been received and understood. This can be a very complicated process, especially in face-to-face communication where the workings of two or more minds and bodies, with nodding and gesturing, add to the difficulty. The diagram below is a model of interpersonal communication, showing the two important parties involved in this process, the sender and the receiver of the information, and each having an important part to play to ensure the effectiveness of the process.

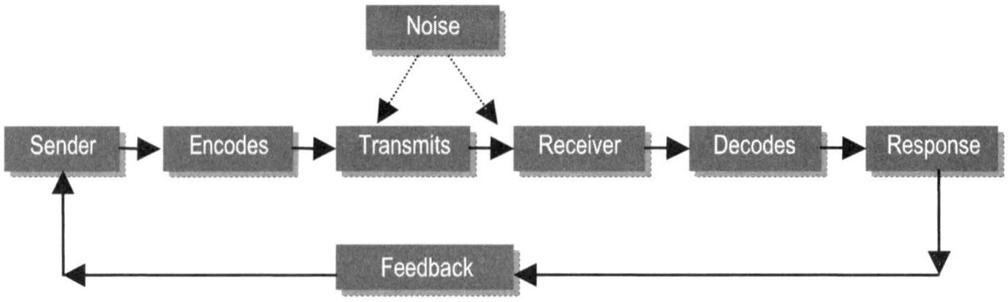

Explanation of stages:

(a) There must be some idea or thought to be conveyed. The sender has to have a message that he or she wishes to transmit to another party. Effective communication depends on the clear identification of the subject of the message. This helps to ensure that the message does not include irrelevant information.

There are endless reasons for interpersonal communication e.g. to inform, to persuade, to instruct and to gain information. It is vital that the sender formulates the communication in an effective way to meet the objective.

Attention should also be paid to the relationship between and the relative status of the sender and the receiver. This will influence both the willingness of the individuals involved to interact and the credence given to the information transmitted.

(b) Next, the message must be encoded and put in a form suitable for transmission. At this point the sender must organise the material of the message into the most coherent and appropriate device. Matters such as whether it should it be written or verbal, whether it needs illustrations or just text, and whether it should be translated into some foreign language, are the sort of issues to be considered at this stage.

(c) The means of transmission has to be decided. Some messages should be conveyed orally because speed is essential and face-to-face feedback is desirable. Other messages will be best suited to the written form e.g. formal announcements for the notice-board.

(d) The message needs to be received by the other party. The receiver needs to be alert and attentive ('tuned-in'), aware that a message has been transmitted and of the need to receive it.

(e) The transmission must be correctly decoded. Receivers have to reconstruct the signs, symbols and language in a form that makes sense to them and which is, hopefully, in line with the intentions of the sender.

Individuals do not passively receive information, rather they are involved in an active process of selection and interpretation known as 'perception'. This is a psychological process in which stimuli are organised into meaningful patterns. Each individual also uses a filtering process known as 'perceptual selectivity', which acts as a barrier when either a large volume of information exceeds the capacity of the brain to deal with it or when the information is deemed irrelevant.

Having allowed the information through the perceptual filter, the receiver must then perceptually organise the information, fitting it into an existing framework known as the 'perceptual set'. This framework enables the receiver to interpret and see the information in the light of past experiences and current needs and interests.

(f) Action should follow. Communication is carried out to bring about a response in the receiver. Sometimes this response involves direct action whilst in other cases it may be a matter of giving information which may or may not involve action at a later date. Even so, registering the new information is to be seen as a form of action resulting from effective communication.

(g) The final element in the process is that of feedback. As illustrated in the diagram above, it is the feedback that makes communication a two-way process rather than a series of send and receive events. It is crucial, though it is sometimes overlooked, for the person sending the communication to get feedback from the receiver. Not only does this confirm that the message was received and understood, it also enables corrective action to be taken in the event of some breakdown of communication. Feedback can take different forms; it can be immediate, as in a conversation or delayed while waiting for the post. It can be simple, as in a yes/no answer or formal, as a reply to a wedding invitation, or computerised, such as the printed receipt that you can request when making a withdrawal from a bank account via the ATM. Ignoring feedback or failing to seek or offer it, is one of the major problems in communication.

(h) From the diagram illustrating the communication process it is also important to note that communication takes place in a specific environment and that a characteristic of most environments is 'noise'. The good communicators will take into account the specific environment adjusting their communication to the demands of the situation. The problem of 'noise' i.e. anything in the environment that impedes the transmission of the message, is significant. Noise can arise from many sources e.g. factors as diverse as loud machinery, status differentials between sender and receiver, distractions of pressure at work or emotional upsets. The effective communicator must ensure that noise does not interfere with successful transmission of the message.

3 Accounting information and reporting

3.1 Internal reporting

KEY POINT

Some managers are responsible for the day-to-day activities whilst others are responsible for long-term planning and decision-making.

Within an organisation there are many different levels of management. Some managers are responsible for the day-to-day activities whilst others are responsible for long-term planning and decision-making. Each of these managers requires information to assist them in carrying out their duties.

It is the responsibilities of the manager which determine the type of information required. Those managers responsible for long-term planning and decisions will require summarised information, including performance reports which compare actual achievements with budgets and forecasts. Those managers responsible for medium-term targets will usually have departmental or functional responsibilities. These managers will receive reports for their responsibility area which, although summarised, are quite detailed. These reports will often include a comparison between actual and target performance, but may also be specific information on a particular aspect of the business e.g. the running cost and activity of a machine. Managers responsible for day-to-day activities are likely to receive information on a daily or even more frequent basis. Much of the information they receive may not be measured in financial terms; for example output units, number of labour hours worked, machine hours lost etc, would be important information for these managers.

3.2 External reporting

The Corporate Report (seminal report published by the ASC in 1975) identified a number of different external user groups:

- suppliers
- customers
- shareholders
- loan creditors
- trade unions and employees
- governmental agencies and departments.

Each of these external user groups will have different information needs, some will primarily be interested in profitability and stability, others will be more interested in liquidity.

Limited companies are required to prepare statutory accounts which summarise the activities of the business and are available at Companies House. However other types of organisation do not have any legal obligation to make their accounts available to the public. Nevertheless there is a flow of information to external user groups in the form of invoices, statements, delivery notes, payslips, newsletters etc. These are in addition to any statutory accounts or formal accounts which may be prepared for government agencies, or loan creditors.

4 Financial and non-financial information

DEFINITION

Financial information is information which measures the cost or revenue of an activity.

4.1 Financial information

Financial information is that usually found to be the dominant feature of reports to middle and senior management, where it is often shown as a profit statement or balance sheet.

DEFINITION

Non-financial information is information which measures activity or non-quantifiable information such as the views of people on a particular course of action.

4.2 Non-financial information

Non-financial information is often found in reports used for lower levels of management i.e. those responsible for day-to-day activities. The type of non-financial information which they would regularly receive would include:

- activity achieved
- machine utilisation and efficiency
- material usage
- labour hours and efficiency.

KEY POINT

At higher levels of management non-financial information is likely to be qualitative rather than quantitative.

At higher levels of management non-financial information is likely to be qualitative rather than quantitative. This has been referred to earlier as soft information. It represents opinions of individuals and user groups and should be considered when determining long-term plans.

5 Using financial accounting records

The financial accounting records of an organisation are a valuable source of data. Some of this data is automatically sorted to provide information by summarising income and costs in various analysis groups. Examples include sales values (possibly by product type), and costs, analysed by type e.g. purchases, wages and salaries, fuel and power, stationery etc. Summaries will be found of assets and liabilities, analysed into groupings suitable for balance sheet presentation. In addition there will be other financial data which could be converted into information. For example invoices will contain details of items bought and sold. If these were analysed, information could be obtained regarding the quantities of each item bought and sold, the profitability of each item, and the percentage that an individual item contributes to the organisation in terms of sales and profits. However, the cost of converting such data into information may be unjustifiable.

In addition there is non-financial data within the accounting records, for example:

- invoice numbers
- cheque numbers
- employee reference numbers and tax codes.

These may be used to produce statistical summaries, for example:

- the percentage of cancelled invoices
- the number and percentage of uncleared cheques
- employees in each part of the business.

6 Sources of information for management accounting

6.1 Internal sources

There are many internal information sources for management accounting, not all of which may be considered to be part of the accounting system. The boundaries of an accounting system are not always clearly defined, particularly in management accounting. There is a grey area between the accounting system and the management information system. The following internal accounting sources may be used:

Source	*Information*
Sales ledger system	Number and value of invoices Volume of sales Value of sales, analysed by customer Value of sales, analysed by product
Purchase ledger system	Number and value of invoices Value of purchases, analysed by supplier
Payroll system	Number of employees Hours worked Output achieved Wages earned Tax deducted
Fixed asset system	Date of purchase Initial cost Location Depreciation method and rate Service history Production capacity

In addition the following internal, non-accounting sources may be used:

Source	*Information*
Production	Machine breakdown times Output achieved Number of rejected units
Sales and marketing	Types of customer Market research results Demand patterns, seasonal variations etc

6.2 The cost of information and system design

An information system can be developed to varying levels of refinement. Specifically:

- Information can be collected and reported with varying levels of frequency. For example, the management accounting system of a manufacturer can report actual production costs on a daily, weekly, monthly or even annual basis.
- Information can be collected and reported at varying levels of detail. For example, in absorbing overheads into product costs one can use a single factory Overhead Absorption Rate or one can operate a complex ABC system. The information requirements of the latter are far more elaborate than those of the former.
- Subtle qualitative factors can be incorporated into information systems at varying levels. For example, information can be rigorously checked for accuracy or a more relaxed approach can be adopted.

Broadly, the more refined the system is (in the terms described above) then the more expensive it is to establish and operate.

In the pre-computer era, management accounting systems were prohibitively expensive for many small and medium sized businesses. In cases where such businesses were required to produce monthly 'operating statements' by banks and/or shareholders then a variety of 'cheap and cheerful' stratagems were adopted.

One practice frequently used was to construct a monthly operating statement by taking the standard production cost of the goods completed from costs incurred in order to arrive at a stock valuation and a gross profit figure. This practice required minimal information and was very similar in concept to the modern 'backflush accounting' associated with JIT and world class manufacturing. However, the use of this practice over 30 years ago frequently gave people unpleasant surprises at the year end. If actual costs had been above standard through the year then this might be concealed by an inflated inventory figure – to be exposed only at the annual year end stock take.

KEY POINT

The design of management information systems should involve a cost benefit analysis.

The design of management information systems should involve a cost benefit analysis. A very refined system offers many benefits, but at a cost. The advent of modern IT systems has reduced that cost significantly. However, skilled staff have to be involved in the operation of information systems and skilled staff can be very expensive to hire.

Let us illustrate this with a simple example. Production costs in a factory can be reported with varying levels of frequency ranging from daily (365 times per year) to annually (1 time per year). Costs of benefits of reporting tend to move as follows in response to increasing frequency of reporting:

- Information has to be gathered, collated and reported in proportion to frequency and costs will move in line with this. Experience suggests some element of diseconomies of scale may set in at high levels of frequency.
- Initially, benefits increase sharply but this increase starts to tail off. A point may come where 'information overload' sets in and benefits actually start to decline and even become negative. If managers are overwhelmed with information then this actually starts to get in the way of the job.

The position may be represented graphically as follows:

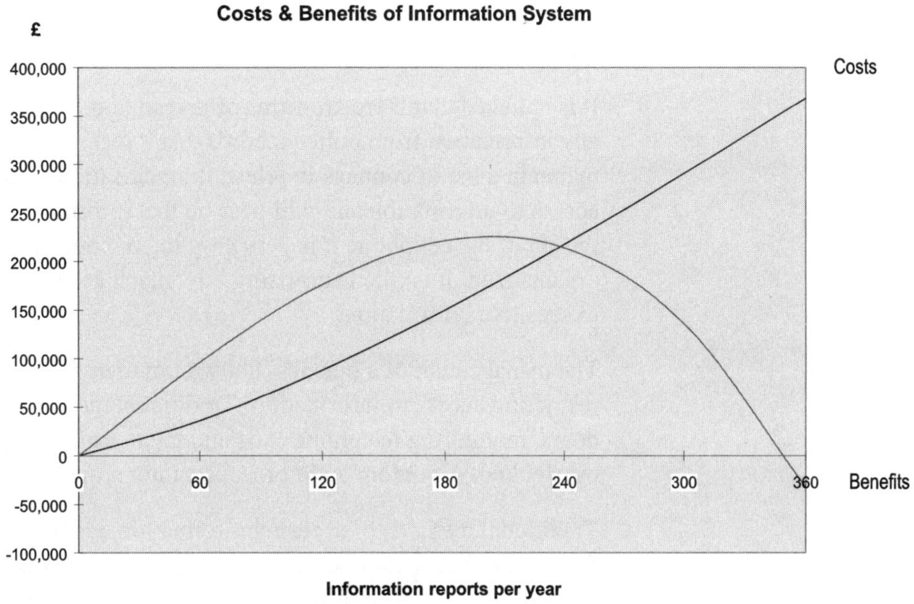

An information system is just like any part of a business operation. It incurs costs and it offers benefits. In designing an information system the accountant has to find some means of comparing the two for different options and determining which option is optimal. In this sense, system design follows the same practices for investment appraisal and decision-making which are explored later in this text.

In the above case it can be seen that net benefits (benefits less costs) are maximised at around 120 reports per year – suggesting an optimal information cycle of about 3 days. The system should be designed to gather, collate and report information at three day intervals. Obviously, this is an over-simplified example but its serves to illustrate a general logic which can be applied to all aspects of information system design.

6.3 Security of information

KEY POINT

One feature of modern information system design is that database material can be readily accessed from remote locations connected to the office network.

One feature of modern information system design is that database material can be readily accessed from remote locations connected to the office network. This ease and immediacy of access offers many advantages to a business operation. For example, a salesman may be able to determine product costs, job resource requirements, resource availability and delivery times using his lap-top computer from the premises of a potential customer. A salesman in this position can offer immediate firm quotes and delivery times to his customer. Such a salesman will always be at an advantage to a competitor using inferior information systems who takes seven days to offer quotes and delivery times.

KEY POINT

Cost and price information is usually commercially sensitive.

However, ease and flexibility of information access carry risks. Cost and price information is usually commercially sensitive. If a competitor is able to access this information then the competitor may be able to use this information to marginally undercut prices quoted on the most attractive jobs. In some sectors (e.g. banking and financial services) customer account information may also be very sensitive.

It is therefore normal to incorporate security features in the design of systems. Certain parts of a database or a website may have access restricted to certain users with passwords.

However, one should be aware that any information system, however sophisticated, is just as secure as the people who operate it. In most organisations there are mildly corrupt people who will provide information to outsiders in exchange for some consideration. The consideration offered may not always be monetary. An individual who has been passed over for promotion may derive some satisfaction from harming his employer. Many people do not perceive the theft of information to be as immoral as the theft of property – and indeed the law tends to follow this perception.

It is believed that there are firms of investigation agents who can readily access almost any information from police records, bank records and company records. Such agents maintain a list of contacts in relevant organisations. These contacts have authorised access to information and will pass on that information upon request from the agent. In the era of the cellphone it is very easy to communicate with a contact in an organisation. It is often surprising how much access certain junior employees may have to sensitive information.

The management of a business should not therefore rely solely on electronic means of restricting access to information. Traditional methods of security (including locked doors, monitoring telephone calls and the use of open plan offices) should not be overlooked. A random audit of information requests from staff may also be productive.

Traditional methods of securing information against the possibility of fire or equipment failure should also not be overlooked. An external back up copy of each database might be made at intervals or after each update. This back up copy should be retained at a different physical location to the main computer.

7 External information

7.1 External sources of information

In addition to the internal information sources referred to above, there is much information to be obtained from external sources as illustrated below:

Source	*Information*
Suppliers	Product prices Product specifications
Newspapers, journals	Share price Information on competitors Technological developments National and Market surveys
Government	Industry statistics Taxation policy Inflation rates Demographic statistics Forecasts for economic growth
Customers	Product requirements Price sensitivity
Employees	Wage demands Working conditions
Banks	Information on potential customers Information on National Markets
Business enquiry agents	Information on competitors Information on customers
Internet	Almost everything via databases (public and private), discussion groups and mailing lists.

Much of this information is free but some comes at a cost. One of the best known business enquiry agents is Dun & Bradstreet. This organisation has 300 offices worldwide and operates on an international basis. It has a substantial database of information concerning businesses, companies, company directors and private business people. This database contains much sensitive information and is continually updated. Much of Dun & Bradstreet's work relates to creditworthiness checks but it is able to provide information with a much wider application. Business enquiry agencies charge fees for work undertaken and in the case of special enquiries these fees can be very high indeed.

Banks and financial journals regularly commission surveys of individual countries and market sectors. These seek to report on recent developments and often provide forecasts of what may happen in the future. These forecasts may relate to market volumes (the number of barrels of oil to be used in the UK during the coming quarter), technology (the capability of computers in 5 years time) and qualitative factors (the level of household adoption of digital television over the next 10 years).

A skilled user of the Internet is able to access information of all sorts from the millions of websites and mailing lists that now exist. Some of this information is completely free but some comes at a price. Many information databases charge a subscription fee.

A visit to www.yahoogroups.com will allow you the opportunity to subscribe to mailing lists, newsletters and discussion groups on almost every conceivable topic. The volume is enormous and much of it is of little worth. The use of the internet is often an exercise in sifting through piles of dross in the search for a few pearls.

A long standing source of information has been central government. The Central Office of Information has traditionally published statistics, forecasts and reports on almost every aspect of the national life.

8 Competitor accounting

8.1 Description

Competitor accounting is a term used by Ward (1992) to refer to the calculation of the relative production costs of competitors. It also explores the likely strategies of competitors and evaluation of their potential effects on the profits of the firm. Aspects of competitor accounting may include the following.

8.2 Evaluation of barriers to entry

Barriers to entry include:

- initial capital costs
- legal and patent protections
- the costs and economies of scale of incumbent firms
- extent of vertical integration
- brand barriers
- scale of investment in R&D
- potential defensive action by incumbent firms (e.g. price cutting).

8.3 Overcoming barriers

Most barriers can be overcome by an outsider providing they are prepared to spend the money e.g.:

- Investing in the capacity, R&D, branding etc.
- Acquiring an incumbent firm
- Riding out the losses caused by high initial costs or competitive retaliation.

8.4 Calculating whether market is defensible

KEY POINT

Competitor accounting must estimate the present value of the costs an entrant will incur to overcome these barriers and compare this with the present value of the returns an entrant could achieve.

Competitor accounting must estimate the present value of the costs an entrant will incur to overcome these barriers and compare this with the present value of the returns an entrant could achieve.

(a) If the costs exceed the revenues then there will be no financial incentive to join and the threat of market entry is low.

(b) If revenues exceed the costs then there is a financial incentive to join. The threat of entry is higher and the incumbent firms must downgrade assessments of the market's attractiveness.

8.5 Entry forestalling behaviour

Where entry is likely the incumbent firm may take *entry forestalling action* by increasing the entry barriers artificially:

- Deliberate adoption of highly capital intensive production techniques
- High R&D spending to increase costs of participation
- High advertising and branding
- Reduction of price to reduce segment attractiveness.

8.6 Competitor accounting should compare

(a) The present value of profits lost through undertaking these pre-emptive strategies *with*

(b) The present value of profits lost as a consequence of market entry

and advise management of whether to resist entry and even whether to invest further in the industry.

8.7 Estimating competitors' costs

Knowing these can help strategic decisions by giving a guide to:

(a) Their likely future pricing behaviour

(b) Their response to strategic action, say price reductions, by our company

(c) Their ability to remain profitable as prices fall and therefore whether they will stay in the market or not

(d) Their potential prices in a tender or sealed bid for a contract.

8.8 Data sources on competitors' costs

- from partnership agreements in a joint venture
- physical analysis of competitors' products
- banks and financial markets
- ex-employees of competitors
- generalisation from own cost base
- industrial experts and consultants
- physical observations (e.g. stand outside, or inside, their factory)
- published financial statements
- competitor press releases
- trade and financial media coverage
- inspection of wage rates for grades of staff in the firm's area
- availability of space for expansion on their present site
- availability and cost of their finance
- the characteristics of the market segment they serve
- the work methods they employ.

9 External information uses

9.1 The use of external information in business planning and operations

KEY POINT

The preparation of any form of business plan or budget involves making forecasts on likely future market conditions.

The preparation of any form of business plan or budget involves making forecasts on likely future market conditions. The use of external information for this purpose is self-evident. A simple business search can often identify a wildly over-optimistic business plan.

For example, the writer of this text was once invited to review a business plan prepared by the promoter of a proposed new business venture. The venture was in the leisure sector and contained a forecast that the business would attract 250,000 customers per year each spending an average of £30. The business plan was presented in the form of a glossy package which had attracted the interest of several financial institutions.

However, a quick search of local businesses revealed that there were several other very similar businesses already operating in the area. None attracted more than 20,000 customers a year and the average existing spend was around £8 per head. It was apparent that the quality of external information used to prepare the business plan was not high.

Information searches via trade directories, the internet etc, can be used in business operations in order to identify new or potential customers. Such searches may be conducted on a worldwide basis and may be very cheap indeed in the era of the internet.

9.2 The use of external information in control and performance management

KEY POINT

The practice of using external information for comparative purposes is known as 'benchmarking'.

The use of external information in business control has been a 'hot topic' in recent years. Traditionally, business control involved comparison between results achieved and internal standards of some sort. The traditional variance analysis report is a reconciliation of budget and actual profit. However, the use of internal standards provides only a limited impression of performance. The practice of using external information for comparative purposes is known as 'benchmarking'.

Among the pioneers in the benchmarking "movement" were Xerox, Motorola, IBM and AT&T. The best known is the Xerox corporation.

Some years ago, Xerox confronted its own unsatisfactory performance in product warehousing and distribution. It did so by identifying the organisation it considered to be the very best at warehousing and distribution, in the hope that "best practices" could be adapted from this model. The business judged to provide a model of best practice in this area was L.L.Bean, a catalogue merchant. Xerox approached Bean with a request that the two engage in a cooperative benchmarking project. The request was granted and the project yielded major insights in inventory arrangement and order processing, resulting in major gains for Xerox when these insights were adapted to its own operations.

The critical observation here is that Xerox did not select another office machine manufacturer as its benchmarking partner. Rather, it selected as its model a business in an entirely unrelated sector. The commonality was in the activities being benchmarked rather than in the output of the operation.

The term benchmark was adopted from surveying. If a surveyor can adopt a known position and altitude as a permanent landmark, then it can serve as a reference point for all the other measurements and points being surveyed.

In business, one can identify the performance gap to be closed between results being achieved and the benchmark that has been adopted.

The basic process of benchmarking involves the following steps:

- decide upon the activity to be benchmarked
- study the activity in your own organisation
- identify suitable benchmarking partners
- analyse the activity of the partners to identify the features that account for their superior performance
- adopt 'best practices'
- monitor and revise.

The practice of benchmarking will usually involve calculating detailed performance benchmarks for each of the main elements in the activity being reviewed. Typically, the performance benchmarks may be arranged in a hierarchy. The features of such a hierarchy may appear as follows:

Strategic benchmarks

- market share
- return on assets
- gross profit margin on sales.

Functional benchmarks

- % deliveries on time
- order costs per order
- order turnaround time
- average stockholding per order.

Operational benchmarks

KEY POINT

An organisation has to understand the benchmarks at the operational level in order to identify the corrective actions needed to close the performance gap.

These are at a level below functional benchmarks. They yield the reasons for a functional performance gap. An organisation has to understand the benchmarks at the operational level in order to identify the corrective actions needed to close the performance gap.

The plans to undertake a benchmarking exercise may have to be tempered by cost, time, value and the incentive for companies to share data.

Critical issues are:

- is the benchmarking partner friendly and willing to share information?
- are the business functions being benchmarked similar enough to allow meaningful comparison?
- is the value of the exercise sufficient to justify its cost?
- what information must be provided to the benchmark partner?

This text returns later to the subject of benchmarking within the general context of performance evaluation.

10 The role of government in the supply of benchmark information

The obvious difficulties in seeking to find partners to participate in a benchmarking scheme may suggest a role for government. Indeed government has co-ordinated a number of benchmarking exercises.

One of these has been in the area of energy (gas and electricity) management. In 1995 the Department of the Environment published "Business Guide to Energy Costs in Buildings". This guide collates energy consumption figures across a wide range of buildings including offices, factories, shops, banks and pubs. Using the guide enables organisations to produce direct comparisons between energy consumption in their own premises and those in other comparable premises.

The guide can be used to derive two benchmarks for a particular building. One is the typical building benchmark. This is the average spend for a building of a specific type in a specific sector. This typical building benchmark gives a figure for what the consumer should be spending on energy. The guide allows the user to prepare a benchmark which incorporates an allowance for floorspace and the part of the country in which the building is situated. For example, a building in Scotland must be expected to require a greater spend than a building in Southern England because of differences in climate.

The other benchmark is a measure for good practice. It is a more exacting measure and is the achievable energy spend for a building using best practices and commonly available technology.

The benchmarks can be calculated both for total spend and spend on particular uses (e.g. 'lighting').

A business can therefore calculate typical building and good practice benchmarks for its own building. Comparison of these benchmarks with its own spend can highlight both deficiencies and opportunities for improvement.

The DoE claims that many businesses may be able to save around 20% of their energy costs by adopting measures suggested through a benchmarking exercise.

For example, the installation of energy efficient lighting systems can cut lighting costs by 60%. The use of natural ventilation systems in place of air conditioning systems can slash total energy bills by up to 50%. Installing thermostats and intelligent time controls in every room can allow temperatures to be maintained in a precise manner and at minimum cost.

One significant observation from this is that valid comparisons can be made between particular types of building. It does not matter what sectors the users of those buildings are engaged in. An office block housing a local authority can be compared to an office block housing a financial services company – and meaningful conclusions drawn.

There have been many benchmarking initiatives in the public sector and these need not be confined to comparing one local authority with another.

11 Information processing

The concept of an information cycle has already been introduced earlier in this text in the context of control system theory and communication theory.

KEY POINT

The information system of an organisation runs in parallel to its production system. Productive activity generates physical output. The parallel information system generates information concerning the resources used in productive activity and the nature of the physical output.

The information system of an organisation runs in parallel to its production system. Productive activity generates physical output. The parallel information system generates information concerning the resources used in productive activity and the nature of the physical output. That information provides input to the information process where it is collated and arranged. It is then used to generate information outputs, usually in the form of financial and information reports.

For example, in the context of a manufacturing operation, information on hours worked is input to the payroll system. The payroll system processes that information and produces information output such as wage slips and BACS payment instructions.

In a management accounting context, the payroll, procurements and payments systems will provide information inputs. The outputs of the information system will include budgetary control reports, product costing statements and variance analysis reports. Many of these outputs will prompt feedback into the manufacturing operation. For example, an adverse wage rate variance may prompt corrective action – such as directing supervisors to use lower grade staff on the jobs.

12 Collecting and recording information

12.1 Structured information systems

Some of the information referred to above is required to be collected and recorded in such a way as to provide information for inclusion in a structured report. This will apply to financial information which is used to prepare accounting reports. Such data must be collected. It may be collected by manual or electronic means, the objective being to minimise the cost of collecting the data whilst trying to ensure its accuracy.

Some organisations, particularly larger ones also have a structured system for some of their management information requirements.

These systems are designed to collect non-financial information alongside the financial information to which it relates. Examples include: units of raw material purchased and used, number of labour hours worked. These are essential pieces of non-financial information if detailed variance reports are to be prepared.

However, management accounting is not a rigid framework, often ad-hoc reporting is required, and the information requirements for these reports are often unknown when the exercise begins. For these a different collection and recording method is required.

12.2 Non-structured information systems

The data and information to be collected and recorded for ad-hoc management reports is extremely varied, and a major problem lies in recognising whether a piece of data is likely to be useful or not in the future.

To collect and record such varied forms of data manually is almost impossible but fortunately electronic devices ease the task.

In the more traditional scenario microfiche may be used to copy the entire contents of newspapers, magazines etc, onto viewing slides which may then be viewed using special equipment at a later date. The disadvantage is that each microfiche must be indexed if many hours are not to be used searching for a particular piece of information. Secondly this method does not allow for any classification or sorting of information.

KEY POINT

The use of scanning devices allows original text and pictures to be stored alongside key descriptions of the information.

A second approach is to use a computer database. This is more sophisticated and with the use of scanning devices allows original text and pictures to be stored alongside key descriptions of the information. These key descriptions may be used to manipulate the data stored, thereby allowing data to be sorted, classified into logical groups. The disadvantage of this technique is the time taken to store the data appropriately together with the storage space required on the computer system. The advantage however is the ease of accessibility to the data once it has been stored.

The relevance of modern IT and the internet cannot be overstated in the present context. A competent PC user with a networked machine has direct access to a mass of internal and external information. For example, an accountant may be interested in some topic – say 'supply chain management'. He or she can access a library database which can give on-line access to electronic versions of almost every newspaper and journal article which has been written on the subject in the last 5 years. The key thing in this case is developing the selectivity needed to isolate only those pieces of information that are strictly relevant to current needs.

12.3 Information for different purposes

Relevance of information

KEY POINT

For information to be useful it must be relevant to the needs of the recipient.

Data is collected and processed into information in many different ways for a variety of different users of information and purposes. For information to be useful it must be relevant to the needs of the recipient. For example a departmental manager would be interested in the results of his department and its effect on the organisation as a whole, but would not be interested in the results of every department.

Each transaction can provide information which is relevant to different people. Consider the purchase of a fixed asset:

- the asset's cost and useful life is needed by the accounts clerk to calculate depreciation
- the operation of the machine is relevant information for the machine operator
- the machine shop supervisor needs details of the service contract and who to contact in the event of a breakdown
- the cashier needs details of the terms of payment for the machine together with details of the supplier, the machine cost, the payment authority and the manager responsible.

There are many transactions in a business, not all of them providing information to so many different people. Much of this depends on the size of an organisation and its structure.

ACTIVITY **2**

Consider the purchase of raw materials. What information is available from such a transaction and to whom is it relevant?

Feedback to this activity is at the end of the chapter.

13 Qualitative information, trend, materiality and controllability

13.1 Qualitative information

Conventional information systems are usually designed to carry quantitative information – costs, revenues, output, material consumption, labour usage and so on. They are sometimes less able to convey qualitative issues – an issue encountered earlier in this text.

The impact of a decreased output requirement on staff morale is something that may be critical but it is not something that an information system would automatically report. The impact of a reduction in product range may have a subtle impact on the image that a business enjoys in the market – again something that an information system may not report.

In both decision-making and control, managers should be aware that an information system may provide a limited or distorted picture of what is actually happening. In many situations, sensitivity has to be used in interpreting the output of an information system.

13.2 Trend

KEY POINT

Often information in respect of a single period is given greater meaning when it is combined with similar information for other periods. When this is done it is possible to identify patterns and trends.

Often information in respect of a single period is given greater meaning when it is combined with similar information for other periods. When this is done it is possible to identify patterns and trends. This may be useful because a minor deviation from a plan may not of itself be significant, but if it reflects a continuing trend management may need to take action.

13.3 Materiality

Materiality is another word for significance. What is significant to one organisation may not be significant to another; it depends on the size of the organisation. To use the earlier example a deviation from a plan may or may not be significant enough to warrant an investigation into its cause. Such an investigation might be costly and if the value to be gained is small it may not be worthwhile.

13.4 Controllability

The term controllability is used in connection with costs and revenues **and** the organisation or individuals within it. Again using the earlier example if the cause of the deviation is not controllable by the organisation then no benefit can be gained by identifying the cause.

KEY POINT

It is a widely held belief that only items controllable by the recipient should be reported to them.

There is also relevance here to reporting and information. It has been noted earlier in this text that information should be relevant to its intended recipient. It is a widely held belief that only items controllable by the recipient should be reported to them.

14 Management accounting and information analysis

14.1 Management accounting in organisations

Management accounting is intended for internal use within organisations and is thus designed to meet the requirements of internal management. As a consequence data is collected and analysed in such a way as to meet those requirements. Whilst every organisation is different there are commonly used management accounting principles which may be identified, for example:

- Marginal costing
- Absorption costing
- Activity Based Costing.

Most organisations will base their management accounting system on one of these principles, though some organisations will analyse data so as to operate several depending upon the use of the information.

The manner in which an accounting database is organised and the coding system used for the records which are being loaded will reflect the accounting systems and principles which the database is being used to support.

For example, if traditional systems are being used then items of cost need only be coded in a manner which allows their nature to be recorded. The accountant is only interested in knowing the total wages, material purchases and overhead costs.

However, if an ABC system is adopted then it is important to know the activity that each item of cost is associated with. So, a rather more complex coding system is required.

14.2 Types of organisation

KEY POINT

The nature of a business will influence the requirements from its information systems at least as much as the accounting principles being used.

The nature of a business will influence the requirements from its information systems at least as much as the accounting principles being used.

A more traditional business which operates in the form of slow and predictable cycles may be able to accept simpler information systems. A farm or a factory which runs a single continuous production line may have relatively simple information requirements. Such businesses will have mainly structured information requirements and may be able to work with a relatively long information cycle. For example, the main management accounting report may be a quarterly cost statement.

A modern 'world-class' manufacturer is likely to operate in an environment where product life cycles are very short and a high degree of flexibility is required to satisfy customer requirements. The items being produced are likely to be large in number and highly customised. The information requirements of such a business are likely to be far less structured. Constant ad-hoc enquiries will be made and the normal information cycle will have to be very short. Furthermore, the more advanced management techniques such as JIT, TQM and ABC will be employed. These issues are explored in Chapter 4.

A world class manufacturer will probably have to invest heavily in 'state of the art' IT and accounting systems if it is to remain competitive.

15 The significance of IT

The role of IT in the development of management accounting systems is explored in Chapter 5. Modern developments in industry and associated changes in the demands made on management accounting systems are discussed in Chapter 4.

Recent years have seen the adoption of far more sophisticated management accounting techniques and the move to a much more rigorous approach in the practice of more traditional techniques. For example, in the pre-computer era, the process of assembling a budget was likely to be a time consuming but essentially simple exercise. In the modern era, budgeting in a large organisation is a much more sophisticated exercise, involving rounds of adjustments, revisions and sensitivity analysis.

The links between changes in the business environment, changes in management accounting practice and the advent of modern IT are not clear cut. It is often difficult to say what is cause and what is effect. It seems likely that modern economies are locked into a self-reinforcing cycle. Economic advances make requirements on information systems in business. These new information systems themselves make possible further economic advances. Obviously, to pursue this debate further is beyond the scope of an accounting course.

Conclusion

Information is data that has been processed so it has meaning to the person who receives it. The production of information should be subject to cost-benefit analysis like any business project. Information may be quantitative or qualitative, financial or non-financial and may be provided for users both within the organisation and outside it. Information is an asset of the company and must be kept securely.

SELF-TEST QUESTIONS

Introduction

1 Distinguish between data and information. (1.1)

Data capture reporting and communicating

2 Distinguish between strategic, tactical and operational information. (2.1)

3 What are the key aspects of communication? (2.3)

Financial and non-financial information

4 Distinguish between financial information and non financial information. (4)

Sources of information for management accounting

5 Explain the main security issues that should be considered in the design of an information system. (6.3)

External information

6 What types of external information might a business use? (7.1)

7 What are the principle sources of external information? (7.1)

8 What types of business information are available on the internet? (7.1)

External information uses

9 Why are a 'typical' benchmark and a 'best practice' benchmark likely to differ? (9.2)

Management accounting and information analysis

10 How are the information requirements of an organisation determined by its type and sector? (14.2)

EXAM-TYPE QUESTIONS

Question 1: AB Ltd

As management accountant of AB Ltd you have been given responsibility for the management and control aspects of the company's new information system. The company has two sites. There are no direct computer links between the sites.

Head Office has 24 PCs linked on an office network. This network is completely self-contained, being without modems or similar external devices. A Subsidiary Office has 6 stand alone PCs.

Required:

Write a report to AB Ltd's Managing Director explaining the main information system controls that are required and their relevance to each site. **(25 marks)**

Question 2: Information for decision-making

The overriding feature of information for decision-making is that it should be relevant for the decision being taken. However, decision-making varies considerably, at different levels within an organisation, thus posing particular difficulties for the management accountant.

Required:

(a) Describe the characteristics of decision-making at different levels within an organisation. **(6 marks)**

(b) Explain how the management accountant must tailor the information provided for the various level. **(5 marks)**

(c) Give an example of a typical management decision, state at what level this would normally be taken and what specific information should be supplied to the decision-maker. **(6 marks)**

(Total: 17 marks)

(***Note:*** in answering this you may care to refer back to the discussion of decision-making in Chapters 1 and 2)

For the answers to these questions, see the 'Answers' section at the end of the book.

FEEDBACK TO ACTIVITY 1

Individually a completed questionnaire would not tell the organisation very much, only the views of one consumer. Once the individual questionnaires have been processed and analysed, the resulting report is information. The company will use the information to make decisions regarding its product.

The processing operations carried out to obtain the results for the reports will include:

- classifying
- calculating
- sorting
- analysing, and
- summarising.

FEEDBACK TO ACTIVITY 2

Information	*User*
Quantity purchased	Storekeeper
Storage conditions	Storekeeper
Price per unit	Buyer
Invoice value	Accountant/Cashier
Payment terms	Cashier

Chapter 4

DEVELOPMENTS IN MANAGEMENT ACCOUNTING

CHAPTER CONTENTS

This chapter explores modern developments in business management practices and considers how they have impacted on the practice of management accounting.

Objectives

When you have studied this chapter you should be able to do the following.

- Discuss the expansion in the scope of management accounting in the last 40 years.
- Identify and discuss some recently adopted management accounting techniques.
- Explain how new techniques may be evaluated.
- Discuss ways in which management accounting practitioners are made aware of new techniques.
- Illustrate how an organisation's structure, culture and strategy will influence the adoption of new methods and techniques.
- Assess the continuing effectiveness of traditional techniques within a rapidly changing business environment.
- Explain the contingency theory of management accounting : Otley.
- Explain how institutional theory presents a framework for understanding changes in and the implications for management accounting: Powell and DiMaggio.
- Explain and demonstrate activity based management .

1 Introduction

The last 40 years have seen dramatic changes in the world manufacturing environment. These changes may be summarised as follows:

KEY POINT

The development of robotics and automation has changed the typical pattern of cost structures.

KEY POINT

Increasingly, products are highly customised and tailored to individual customer requirements.

KEY POINT

The adoption of practices such as value engineering and just-in-time ('JIT') have profound effects on the manner in which businesses operate and the way in which they incur costs.

- The development of robotics and automation at every stage in the manufacturing process has changed the typical pattern of cost structures and the ways in which efficiency is achieved.
- Increasingly, products are highly customised and tailored to individual customer requirements. Product life cycles are short and manufacturers need a customer oriented culture. We have moved from the era of mass production into the era of flexible production.
- A very high proportion of product costs is determined in the design phase of production. Given short product life cycles this implies the need to control costs by looking at products over their whole life, rather than on the basis of costs incurred in short individual periods.
- The advent of world products creates an intensely competitive environment where the design and manufacture of products have to be engineered to deliver maximum value at lowest cost. The adoption of practices such as value engineering and just-in-time ('JIT') have profound effects on the manner in which businesses operate and the way in which they incur costs.

Inevitably, these developments have required the introduction of new management accounting practices and the modification of old ones.

However, it is important to consider new management accounting practices within the context of associated changes in manufacturing.

1.1 World class manufacturing

There is no official definition of 'world class manufacturing'. The first characteristic they identify is a multi-national (or at the very least a multi million pound/dollar organisation) that has adopted total quality control. It is in this context they allude to companies like Toyota but also Asea-Brown Boveri (Sweden/Switzerland) and a number of leading German companies with multinational markets such as BMW. These companies strive to eliminate defects with its resultant impact upon reduced inventory, rejects, rework, waste, scrap, and warranty expense. To achieve such targets, greater consideration had to be given to the manufacture and operation of the product, not just its performance.

World class companies regard the world as their market. In the West, many firms had either tied markets, or operated in a virtual closed system oligopoly. Such a system pervaded in the US automobile market. The classic American gas-guzzler was a model of inefficient manufacturing. However, the faults in Ford were repeated in GM and Chrysler, so there was no real problem. However, when the Japanese began to make inroads into the American market, the quality of the product was a prime selling point. Whatever the jokes about Friday afternoon cars and the inherent poor quality, this did not happen in a Japanese car.

Other features of world class manufacturing companies are alluded to in Bromwich and Bhimani. World class companies invest in R&D where appropriate, they are highly capital intensive and hence highly productive, and have delayered their corporate bureaucracies. Such companies also have a diversity of products, albeit from standard parts and a flexible manufacturing system, high quality, better delivery and aim to satisfy customers at a global level.

This is well seen in companies that have adopted Total Quality Management. Typically, these satisfy their customers through a combination of customer contact, customer training and extensive rapid response customer service. They are highly capital intensive, highly reliant on CAD/CAM technology and export over half their production. There is also an obsession for staying ahead of the competition through continual improvement.

DEFINITION

TQM is defined as 'the continuous improvement in quality, productivity and effectiveness obtained by establishing management responsibility for processes as well as outputs. In this every process has an identified process owner and every person in an entity operates within a process and contributes to its improvement.'

1.2 Total quality management

It is apparent from this rather lengthy definition that it goes beyond the isolated notions of statistical quality control into the whole operating process. This means designing quality manufacturing procedures possibly through the use of CAD/CAM, training all personnel involved with the product/service, continually maintaining equipment to ensure that standards remain up to specification and working with suppliers to eliminate defects. The latter may well involve the use of JIT. It is worth adding that TQM is expected to cross all the company's functional activities, even the accounting function.

2 The modern business environment

2.1 The development of the modern factory

The historical trend in manufacturing progress in the western industrial world was for greater automation and greater economies of scale. The great emphasis in a world of full employment and militant workers was to increase output through more mechanisation. Now, however, faced with intense competition, the emphasis has changed. The successful manufacturer will have to compete by responding rapidly to changing market conditions, tailoring products to meet different tastes and quickly introduce new and innovative products. All this has to be accomplished at much reduced costs in a very much more competitive market place.

One possible solution to the problem is the use of **computer integrated manufacturing (CIM)**. This is defined in Bromwich and Bhimani as 'the use of computers and other advanced manufacturing techniques to monitor and perform manufacturing tasks.' It enables a firm to link all its functions (both offices and shopfloor) to a system of total automation using computers. As a result, firms will be able to manufacture one-of-a-kind products in small batches for specific customers at short notice. This will replace the much criticised mass production of often defective, unsaleable standard items with a job-shop production of high quality unique items. This approach will reduce processing time, cut finished goods inventory, reduce direct labour costs and speed up response times.

2.2 CAD, CAE and CAM

The automated factory has to be capable of performing various functions with the aid of computers including product design, engineering and manufacturing.

DEFINITION

Computer Aided Design (CAD) is defined as 'computer based technology allowing interactive design and testing of a manufacturing component on a visual display terminal'.

(a) **Computer Aided Design (CAD)** is defined as 'computer based technology allowing interactive design and testing of a manufacturing component on a visual display terminal'.

Designers can move pieces of a design around their drawings and manipulate them to see how the shapes change from various angles on their CAD terminals. Such systems are more convenient and economical, especially now that they are run on microcomputer networks. Although there is an initial high cost, the benefits are quickly realised. At Chrysler, a network of over 500 design workstations has reduced the time taken to generate engineering drawings from three months in the 1950s to 15 minutes today.

DEFINITION

Computer Aided Engineering (CAE) enables designers to test whether their design can be manufactured on the available machines and ascertain the cost.

(b) **Computer Aided Engineering (CAE)** enables designers to test whether their design can be manufactured on the available machines and ascertain the cost. This has eliminated much of the effort hitherto carried out by production engineers. Once the CAE system has verified the feasibility of a new design, the necessary information for manufacture can be transmitted to a computer aided manufacturing system (CAM).

DEFINITION

A **CAM system** uses 'computer-based technology to permit the programming and control of production equipment in the manufacturing task'.

(c) A **CAM system** uses 'computer-based technology to permit the programming and control of production equipment in the manufacturing task'. Such a system cuts the time lag between design and manufacturing, and the time taken setting and retooling machines for a new product.

2.3 Flexible manufacturing system (FMS)

DEFINITION

Flexible manufacturing system (FMS) is 'an integrated production system which is computer controlled to produce a family of parts in a flexible manner...a bundle of machines that can be reprogrammed to switch from one production run to another'.

This is 'an integrated production system which is computer controlled to produce a family of parts in a flexible manner...a bundle of machines that can be reprogrammed to switch from one production run to another'. It consists of a cluster of machine tools and a system of conveyor belts that shuttle the work piece from tool to tool in a similar fashion to the traditional transfer line used in mass (large batch) production. Thus the benefits lie in being able to switch quickly from making one product to another.

The major strength of an FMS system is its ability to manufacture not just a family of parts, but a family of products. By using this system, General Electric has been able to produce a range of diesel engines that are of substantially different sizes on the same automated production line, without substantially retooling and time consuming start ups.

Dilts and Russell (*Accounting for the Factory of the Future* 1985) have identified the following benefits:

- More variety of products as compared to conventional automation without the low rate of capacity utilisation of a typical job shop system.

- Better product quality thanks to accuracy and repeatability of the production process.
- Shorter machine set-up times for new production runs which results in reduced lead times to meet customer demands. This, in turn, decreases work-in-progress inventories and plant space.
- Reduced labour costs and the capital costs of human environmental protection. This offers a stability in production even with machine breakdown, because of computer scheduling, which also allows instant responses to changes in demand.

There are risks with implementation. These are:

- FMS may lead to resistance from the labour force who may fear for their jobs.
- There must be an innovative approach to justifying the capital investment since it is likely that conventional appraisal techniques may not yield positive results.
- There may be a lack of qualified engineers and other management systems to support FMS.

2.4 Materials requirements planning

DEFINITION

MRP is a system which maximises the efficiency in the timing of raw material orders through to the manufacture and assembly of the final product.

MRP was first introduced by IBM in 1970 and essentially substitutes excessive inventories for better information systems. MRP schedules the production of jobs through the factory and eliminates the excessive WIP inventory levels required to compensate for job-scheduling problems that arise in decoupled cost or operation centres. MRP releases works orders for parts based upon a master production schedule and the current number and location of parts within the plant.

If there is an order for 100 units of a product, it may be that the economic lot size indicates that 500 should be produced. A Bill of Materials (a specification of the materials and parts required to make the product) is programmed into the computer. The computer will record the number of inventory components required along with time standards for moving, any waiting, setting up and running. This information allows production to be time phased so that the final assembly can begin with all the required components at the ready. The key factor in MRP is that it is demand dependent. Finished products are assembled to order from families of standard components. This is in contrast to traditional systems where components are ordered on the EOQ basis remote from the pattern of final product demand.

MRPII

KEY POINT

MRPII (also written MRP 2) adds the MRP schedule into a capacity planning system and then builds the information into a production schedule.

MRPII (also written MRP 2) adds the MRP schedule into a capacity planning system and then builds the information into a production schedule. It is also seen as a link between strategic planning and manufacturing control. The sequence of events is as follows:

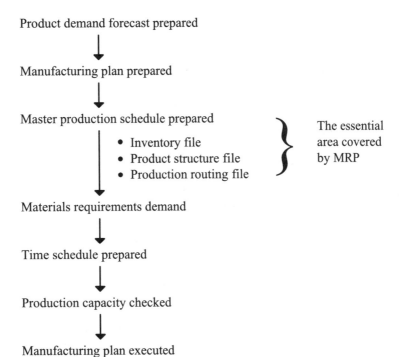

Product demand forecast prepared

↓

Manufacturing plan prepared

↓

Master production schedule prepared

- Inventory file
- Product structure file
- Production routing file

} The essential area covered by MRP

↓

Materials requirements demand

↓

Time schedule prepared

↓

Production capacity checked

↓

Manufacturing plan executed

The student will readily see that MRPII forms a sequence of events that starts with the product demand forecast that is prepared by marketing and approved by management. From that document, a manufacturing plan is developed based upon inputs from purchasing and production. Adjustments may be necessary to allow for production rates, possible inventory levels in seasonal trades and the size of the workforce. The manufacturing plan leads into a detailed master production schedule which is akin to the original philosophy of MRP already outlined.

If correctly applied, MRPII provides a common data base for the different functional units such as manufacturing, purchasing and finance within a firm.

The student should be aware that MRP has not been an unbridled success over the years. While it is beyond the scope of the syllabus to academically discuss the problems encountered, you should be aware that reports of MRP failures were presented by Harrison (1990), Archer (1991) and Maskell (1993).

ERP

MRP (Material Requirements Planning) and MRP2 (Manufacturing Resources Planning) are essentially business planning techniques. They seek to use IT systems to identify the full resource requirements of a given plan of action and then satisfy those requirements in the most cost effective manner.

The 1990s saw a further development along these lines with the advent of Enterprise Resource Planning (ERP). ERP systems involved the preparation of plans for every aspect of the business and was not confined to manufacturing resources. ERP was closely identified with integrated budgeting systems and customer relationship management (CRM) systems.

However, many observers now feel that the elaborate planning concept associated with MRP, MRP2 and ERP has had its day. It is claimed that these systems involve over - elaborate bills of materials, inefficient workflows and excessive data collection. The more modern approach involves the *Lean Enterprise* wherein a business operation is organised in a manner that allows it to respond flexibly to customer demand as it emerges rather than adhere to some plan that may quickly become outdated or irrelevant.

"For the past decade, organizations have spent billions of dollars and countless worker-hours installing huge integrated software packages known as ERP applications. The ERP systems of the 1990s have become a liability for many manufacturers because they perpetuate some of the legendary MRP problems. A new manufacturing model has emerged that is taking the place of the traditional MRP model. It is called Lean, Flow or Demand-Pull.

Lean manufacturing aims at improving efficiency, eliminating product backlogs and synchronizing production to customer demand rather than a long term (often incorrect) forecast."

Bradford, Mayfield and Toney *Does ERP fit in a LEAN World*, Strategic Finance (May 2001)

2.5 Synchronous management/manufacturing

KEY POINT

'The bottleneck factor' is the factor of production which limits the organisation's ability to increase the rate at which sales are achieved.

The profitability of the modern organisation is dependent on a number of factors, not least of which is the rate at which sales are made. Other factors include the reduction of costs and maximisation of efficiency.

Management must identify what is referred to as 'the bottleneck factor'. This is the factor of production which limits the organisation's ability to increase the rate at which sales are achieved. You should recall that this is similar in principle to the limiting factor used in contribution analysis as part of short-term decision-making.

The combination of management policies and practices to improve efficiency and identify and alleviate the bottleneck factor are collectively referred to as synchronous management and manufacturing practices.

2.6 Optimised production technology and synchronous manufacturing

KEY POINT

The OPT technique actively seeks to identify what prevents output and hence productivity from being higher by distinguishing between bottleneck and non-bottleneck resources.

Optimised Production Technology (OPT) has developed out of MRP systems. Like its precursor, MRP, OPT requires detailed information about inventory levels, product structures, routings and the set-up and operation timing for each and every procedure within each product. However, in stark contrast to OPT actively seeks to identify what prevents output and hence productivity from being higher by distinguishing between bottleneck and non-bottleneck resources. A bottleneck might be a machine whose capacity limits the throughput of the whole production process. It might be a key department with highly specialist skills that holds up the process. To avoid large build-ups of inventory, the non-bottleneck areas should be balanced to produce what the bottleneck can absorb in the short-term. Thus, if the bottleneck can only absorb 60% of the output of the non-bottleneck areas, then the output should be scaled down to that level, since any excess over that level is only going to increase the piles of work-in-progress inventory standing about. It has also been suggested that overhead should be absorbed on the basis of throughput based upon the duration of production from the initial input of raw materials and components to the delivery of the finished products. By adopting this approach, management can see how costs can be reduced by cutting the throughput time.

2.7 Synchronous manufacturing

DEFINITION

Synchronous manufacturing is a combination of MRP and OPT and JIT and quality.

This is a combination of MRP and OPT and JIT and quality. The term was coined in 1984, as an attempt to widen the perceived limited scope of OPT. The pioneer behind both techniques is a mathematician, Eli Goldratt. He also prefers the term 'theory of constraints'.

DEFINITION

Resource means materials, components, the direct labour force and machinery and equipment.

The use of the term 'philosophy' is deliberate. OPT is perceived as narrow and very technique based. The use of the term 'Optimised' implied that a theoretical optimum existed and could be achieved. While such a goal might be possible, it implies that a level can be achieved where one can be satisfied, content or even complacent. Such a theoretical level is conceptually contrary to the notions of continuous improvement. Equally, the terms 'Production' and 'Technology' were perceived as failing to encompass the total range of constraints and challenges faced by the firm in trying to achieve its objectives. Markets, logistics, managerial ability, cultural and behavioural problems can all place constraints upon production capacity.

In widening the understanding of terms, it is worth adding that resource is not just confined to materials. Resource means materials, components, the direct labour force and machinery and equipment.

Seven principles are associated with synchronous manufacturing:

- Management should not focus on balancing capacities, but focus on synchronising the flow.
- The marginal value of time at a bottleneck resource is equal to the throughput rate of the products processed by the bottleneck. That is the area of potential savings and improvements.
- The marginal value of time at a non-bottleneck resource is negligible. As we have already seen, lack of synchronisation in these areas merely builds up inventory.
- The level of utilisation of a non-bottleneck resource is controlled by other constraints within the system. (If you cannot get it painted, why build it?)
- Resources must be utilised, not simply activated.
- A transfer batch may not, and many times should not, be equal to a process batch.

  A point of clarification is appropriate here. The transfer batch can only relate to what can be accommodated in the next batch. Thus, it must be lined up with what can be handled. Anything above this will pile up inventory.
- A process batch should be variable both along its route and over time. Thus, batches of work along the line must reflect what can be taken by the next area.

KEY POINT

JIT works upon the principle of continuous improvement.

Synchronous manufacturing purports to be an improvement on JIT based techniques by advocating a more focused approach. JIT works upon the principle of continuous improvement. Such an approach is prone to overlook the capacity constraints upon resources in advance. Rather it waits until the problems occur and disrupt the system. Synchronous manufacturing, by balancing throughput so that there is an even flow and no inventory build up, has to anticipate where the log jams are, accommodate them in the short-term, and then plan for their eventual removal. In addition, JIT works on the approach of improvement right across the business. While this is commendable, the potential for savings at the point of a bottleneck is enormous. Thus it is a better use of resources to focus on the bottlenecks and clear them and thus gain the global improvements.

A further characteristic is that JIT is limited to the final assembly process, and as such, takes no account of the resulting loads at bottleneck work stations. It can also create bottleneck conditions at the final assembly, where tasks have to be done in less than ideal conditions. Thus if throughput is to be improved, and hence output and hence profit, consideration must be given to identifying the bottlenecks and how they may be avoided.

DEFINITION

Synchronous manufacturing also employs a drum-buffer-rope system.

Synchronous manufacturing also employs a drum-buffer-rope system. The drum is a systematic approach to the problem by developing a master production schedule that is consistent with the constraints of the system. It uses a thorough analysis of a plant's capabilities, the manufacturing and hence marketing environment, and identifies these constraints. The 'buffers' are time buffers, designed to protect overall plant performance from any disruption. This is not the universal application of inventory piles such as recently dispensed with by Borg-Warner, but the strategic placing of protective inventory at key locations throughout the plant. The 'rope' is the control process. However, it only controls the schedule release points at the key bottleneck locations to maintain a smooth and timely flow.

3 Value analysis

DEFINITIONS

A **value added activity** is an activity which adds value to the customer's perception of the product. Examples include quality and price.

A **non-value added activity** is an activity which does not add value to a product in the eyes of its customers. Examples include the activities of setting up a production run, purchasing and planning.

3.1 Value added and non-value added activities

Identifying value added

The student should be familiar with the definition of value added: 'sales value less the cost of purchased materials and services. This represents the worth of an alteration in form, location or availability of a product or service.' However, not all costs incurred add value to the basic bought in good or service. Thus **value analysis** has been developed. This is 'a systematic inter-disciplinary examination of factors affecting the cost of a product or service, in order to devise means of achieving the specified purpose most economically at the required standard of quality and reliability'.

The table overleaf illustrates some of the cost categories that could be scrutinised under this form of analysis.

KEY POINT

Value analysis is 'a systematic inter-disciplinary examination of factors affecting the cost of a product or service, in order to devise means of achieving the specified purpose most economically at the required standard of quality and reliability'.

3.2 Value added versus non-value added activities

Activity	*Value added*	*Non-value added*
Purchasing		
Vetting suppliers	X	
Producing orders	X	
Returning goods		X
Correcting orders		X
Customer order processing		
Assessing credit rating		X
Liaising with customer	X	
Expediting delivery		X
Dealing with returns inwards		X
Quality control		
Supplies received		X
In process		X
On completion		X
Material scheduling		
Identifying line needs	X	
Storage		X
Movement from store to line		X

KEY POINT

Quality control ensures that the product is up to customer expectation. It does not add value, but its removal could further add costs.

In theory, all costs that do not add value to the product should be targets for elimination. However, some, such as quality control, are essential to the running of the business in the short-term. Quality control ensures that the product is up to customer expectation. It does not add value, but its removal could further add costs. Some judgement may be seen to be needed in the classification. Expediting delivery could mean ensuring that orders do not fall behind (non-value adding) or saying we can deliver to your schedule but at a premium cost.

A further development in this form of analysis breaks down activities into three components – core, support and discretionary. In the case of sales costs, time spent with customers and potential customers would be core work. That is the essential business of winning orders for the firm. Travelling time would be a support activity while dealing with sales order processing errors would be pure discretionary. Thus effective cost management is about reducing the amount of resources that are being expended on non-core activities. This may mean changing territories to reduce travel time or travel costs, or changing the order process system to minimise errors.

3.3 The mechanics of value analysis

A team approach is the most appropriate and successful. This team should be drawn from:

Design	
Purchasing	(Maximum cost savings are often associated with the bought in goods and services.)
Marketing	(Important in the context of the esteem value of the product. Also marketing costs are now often 30% of the sales price.)
Production	
Maintenance	(Could make the product more user friendly.)
Accounts	

Such an approach is essential since value can be determined at any or all the stages between initial conception, through production to final delivery and after sales care. This also means that everybody gets together to talk about what is being done. Not to do this, argues Tom Peters, **(Liberation Management)** alienates the essential creative workers and induces misunderstandings and dysfunctional competitiveness. The following steps are recommended:

Step 1

Determine the function of the product.

Step 2

Develop alternative designs.

The relative importance placed by the customer upon the following will determine design or redesign objectives:

- function
- appearance
- esteem associated with possession
- intrinsic cost of materials and/or labour
- replacement, exchange or disposal value.

Step 3

Ascertain the costs.

Step 4

Evaluate the alternatives.

For existing products, the following questions will help to identify areas of potential value improvements:

- Which areas appear to offer the largest savings?
- What percentage of total cost is associated with bought out items?
- What percentage of total cost is associated with labour?

  A consideration of labour cost may be relevant here. With the low content of traditional direct labour, scope for savings is limited. However, by identifying 'people cost' the value analysis exercise embraces indirect hourly paid workers such as store-keepers, conversion indirect salaried staff and the whole gamut of non-conversion salaried staff, many of whom add little value to the product or service.
- What percentage of total cost is associated with materials?

  Often the maximum cost saving associated with existing products relates to bought-in parts, materials and services. The value of such purchased parts and materials can be investigated with a view to material or design changes by asking the following questions:

  – How does it contribute to the value of the product?
  – How much does it contribute to the total cost of the product?
  – Are all its features and its specification necessary?
  – Is it similar to any other part?
  – Can a standard part be used?
  – Will an alternative design provide the same function?

  A simple example might be the bumper on a car. Traditionally, these were made of steel, and coated with chrome to give that bright silver finish. No true all-American gas-guzzler was complete without such a bumper to match its whitewall tyres. However, steel was heavy and expensive, so was chrome. Also, the cost of maintenance was high, and there was a tendency for such bumpers to become very shabby. Chrome also wore off causing the steel underneath to rust.

  The idea to replace chrome on cheaper models with black plastic was tried. The effect did not look cheap, but rather sporting. The black contrasted well with the body colours and did not suffer from the drawbacks of chrome and steel. In these days of economy, it was cheaper and also lighter. It also rode collisions better, and was easier and cheaper to replace. Additionally, it did not detract from the value of the car. The result was that most cars now have plastic bumpers.
- What marketing savings can be made?

  Another example from marketing might be useful. A substantial cost of marketing cars is in the dealer network. In the United States, there are still too many of them, poorly managed, with high costs and dubious reputations. With the GM-Saturn range, GM have given dealers territories, made all the dealers look the same, insisted on the same standard of service, and encouraged many of the small family ('mom and pop') outfits to merge. By the year 2000, GM reduced its dealer network to 7,000 from the 14,000 in the 1970s. Those that remain will give a better service, enhance the image of the product and be cheaper to operate. (**Fortune** April 4 1994)

3.4 Implementing value analysis in practice

KEY POINT

There are four steps in the value analysis process (determine the function, develop alternative designs, ascertain costs and evaluate alternatives).

We have seen that there are four steps in the value analysis process (determine the function, develop alternative designs, ascertain costs and evaluate alternatives).

Developing alternative designs and techniques is a vital part of the process, e.g. alternative methods of achieving the required function as illustrated by the fender and dealership examples above. This is the creative aspect of value analysis, and may require 'brainstorming' sessions. No reasonable or even ostensibly unreasonable alternative or suggestion should be rejected during this stage.

The literature suggests that the session should be frenzied, chaotic, energetic, playful, intuitive and structured. It should be possible to come in at any time and at any level. The possibility of a back-to-back brainstormer, whereby employees meet either suppliers or customers should not be eliminated.

Among the objects to be considered at this stage might be:

- eliminate parts or operations
- simplify parts or operations
- use standard parts or materials
- relax manufacturing tolerances. (Is the product being over-engineered for its place in the market?)
- use standard manufacturing methods
- eliminate unnecessary design features
- change design to facilitate easier manufacture or maintenance. (Do we have to remove the dashboard to change a light bulb in the instrument panel?)
- buy in rather than manufacture if it is cheaper
- use prefinished materials
- use prefabricated parts from cheaper specialists
- rationalise product ranges. (Or explore the possibility of putting different products on the same line. The Lexus is made on a standard Toyota production line.)
- introduce low cost manufacturing processes
- rationalise the purchase of parts – single sourcing?
- identify and eliminate material waste.

The above check list emphasises materials. However, what about procedures? Tom Peters illustrates how TIteflex, a US subsidiary of the British TI Group streamlined its procedures and facilitated faster order turn rounds.

4 Just in time (JIT)

4.1 The JIT concept

KEY POINT

JIT has been defined as a 'workflow organisation technique to allow rapid, high quality, flexible production whilst minimising stock levels and manufacturing waste'.

JIT has been defined as a 'workflow organisation technique to allow rapid, high quality, flexible production whilst minimising stock levels and manufacturing waste' (Bromwich & Bhimani).

This system has gained considerable popularity in both the United States and Europe. It has a wide ranging impact upon many of the traditional organisational functions.

In practice, this means producing components only when they are needed and in the quantity that is needed. This shortens lead times and virtually eliminates work in progress and finished goods inventories.

The resultant differences in production are:

- Conventional production

  Provides monthly production schedules to every process including the final assembly line.

  The preceding process supplies the parts to the subsequent process (push through system) which is unable to respond quickly. Each process must adjust their schedule simultaneously requiring back up inventory between processes.

- JIT

  Does not provide simultaneous schedules to every process, only for the final assembly line. Goods are built for the customer, not for stock. The system works on a pull through basis, drawing components through the system. It can respond quickly drawing parts as required. As soon as items are completed in one process, so the next process produces to replace.

Impact on purchasing and production

(a) Under JIT, a buyer can reduce the number of suppliers. GM reduced their suppliers by 50%. Westinghouse has reduced inventories by 45% and plant stockouts by 95%. Warner-Lambert has replaced its costly batch production by a JIT based controlled process. Suppliers are also chosen because of close proximity to the plant. Long-term contracts and single sourcing is advocated to strengthen buyer-supplier relationships and tends to result in a higher quality product. Inventory problems are shifted back onto suppliers, with deliveries being made as required.

(b) **JIT delivery and transportation**

The spread of JIT in the production process inevitably impinges upon those in delivery and transportation. This emphasises to the student who may feel that JIT is too production orientated that it can turn up in the service sector. Ryder has established centres close to its manufacturing plants. These are not warehouses, but rather extensions of the production process. As soon as an order to move material or to call off material is received, the truck moves and delivers. This means smaller more productive loads, more frequently. The use of freight cars and railways fits less well into the JIT pattern, although Union Pacific has developed a system whereby freight can be moved on a JIT basis.

The use of JIT puts new demands on the schedules of the hauliers. Tighter schedules are required, with penalties for non-delivery. The haulier is regarded as almost a partner to the manufacturer.

Does the haulier benefit from JIT? Tom Peters describes Union Pacific, a JIT haulier. As a result of moving to the JIT philosophy, traffic volume is up 18%, revenue 25%, productivity per employee nearly doubled, failure costs reduced to 15% of gross revenue, a saving of $750 million, and locomotive downtime reduced from 13% to 8% a further saving of $150 million. More important, Union Pacific is now regarded by its parent company as an ‘invest and grow’ division.

(c) **Impact on cost systems**

Accounting in an advanced manufacturing environment is dealt with in detail below. Suffice it to say that the traditional short-term approach of the cost accountant is seen as an obstacle to the implementation of JIT. Costing systems need to be simpler and more flexible. However, before making any changes, a thorough review of the costing systems is required.

(d) **Inventory valuation**

The inevitable reduction in inventory levels will reduce the time taken to count inventory and the clerical cost. As for valuing inventory, Hewlett-Packard no longer add conversion costs to inventory, but treat them as period costs.

KEY POINT

Optimal EOQ equals:

$q^* = \sqrt{\frac{2C(1)D}{C(2)}}$ where

C(1) = variable costs of placing a production/ purchase order

D = annual demand for inventory item

C(2) = annual holding costs of one inventory item.

As a final point on JIT, the system also renders the elegant EOQ model virtually useless. The student will recall that the optimal EOQ equals:

$$q^* = \sqrt{\frac{2C(1)D}{C(2)}} \quad \text{where}$$

C(1) = variable costs of placing a production/purchase order

D = annual demand for inventory item

C(2) = annual holding costs of one inventory item.

KEY POINT

JIT causes the ordering cost to decline towards zero and since the model is optimal when holding costs equal ordering costs, the optimum becomes a virtually zero inventory level.

JIT causes the ordering cost to decline towards zero and since the model is optimal when holding costs equal ordering costs, the optimum becomes a virtually zero inventory level.

4.2 The practice of JIT

JIT is a series of manufacturing and supply chain techniques that aim to slash inventory levels and improve customer service by manufacturing not only at the exact time customers require, but also in the exact quantities they need and at competitive prices.

JIT is said to have originated from Toyota's *'Kanban'* system which is named after a card which is passed from workstation to workstation to control the production flow. The card ties production to actual orders effectively pulling orders through the factory. (Compare this with traditional production which is based on maintaining finished goods inventory.)

JIT extends much further than a concentration on inventory levels and also centres around the elimination of **waste**. Waste is defined as any **activity** performed within a manufacturing company which **does not add** value to the product. Example of waste are:

- raw materials inventories
- work-in-progress inventories
- finished goods inventories
- materials handling
- quality problems (rejects and reworks etc)
- queues and delays on the shop-floor
- long raw material lead times
- long customer lead times
- unnecessary clerical and accounting procedures.

JIT attempts to eliminate waste at every stage of the manufacturing process notably by the:

- elimination of WIP by reducing batch sizes (often to one)
- elimination of raw materials inventories by the suppliers delivering direct to the shop floor just in time for use
- elimination of scrap and rework by an emphasis on total quality control of design, of the process, and of the materials
- elimination of finished goods inventories by reducing lead times so that all products are made to order
- elimination of material handling costs by re-design of the shop floor so that goods move directly between adjacent work centres.

The combination of these concepts brings about JIT, which provides a smooth flow of work through the manufacturing plant, a flexible production process which is responsive to the customer's requirements and massive reductions in capital tied up in inventories. The end result of JIT is radical improvements in true productivities. More products of higher quality getting to the customers more quickly at a lower cost.

4.3 The characteristics of an 'ideal' factory layout

Far from 'batching up', JIT manufacturers aim for smaller and smaller batch size (and hence shorter and shorter lead times) in order to become even more reactive to customer demands.

To the traditional manufacturing manager, this sounds like a recipe for disaster, as it removes the slack in the systems that allows things to go wrong without causing immediate disruption. The lengthy customer lead times and large batch sizes tend to cushion the manufacturing if things don't work out the way they were planned.

Only now are such managers beginning to realise that it is often because of these lead times and batch sizes that things go wrong in the first place. JIT works so well precisely because all the conflicts, confusions and soft options that these various safety nets raise have been removed, leaving lean and hungry factories that outperform traditionally managed shop-floors.

Briefly the characteristics of an *ideal* system would seem to be the following:

- It should have a short manufacturing cycle time, to minimise work-in-progress inventory and maximise customer service.
- It should have manufacturing batch sizes identical to customer order quantities (even if this is one), to minimise finished goods inventory and maximise customer responsiveness.
- It should be flexible enough to make products in the same order as the customer wants them, again in order to minimise finished goods inventory and maximise responsiveness.
- It should be able to rapidly trap and cure deviations from quality standards in order to maximise customer service and minimise scrap and rework.
- It should call in raw materials as late as possible in order to minimise raw material inventory.

JIT purchase contracts

KEY POINT

Obtaining the co-operation of suppliers is a vital first step when implementing a JIT system.

Obtaining the co-operation of suppliers is a vital first step when implementing a JIT system. A company is a long way towards JIT if its suppliers will give it shorter lead-times, deliver smaller quantities more often, guarantee a low reject rate and perform quality-assurance inspection at source.

If a company's suppliers make more frequent deliveries of small quantities of material, then it can ensure that each delivery is just enough to meet its immediate production schedule. This will keep its inventory as low as possible.

If suppliers will guarantee the quality of the material they deliver and will inspect it at source, then a company can make enormous savings on both time and labour. Materials handling time will be saved because, as there is no need to move the stock into a store, the goods can be delivered directly to a workstation on the shop floor. Inspection time and costs can be eliminated and the labour required for reworking defective material or returning goods to the supplier can be saved.

In return for this improved service from the supplier, the company can guarantee to give more business to fewer suppliers, place long-term purchase orders and give the suppliers a long-range forecast of its requirements.

The successful JIT manufacturer deliberately sets out to cultivate good relationships with a small number of suppliers and these suppliers will often be situated close to the manufacturing plant. It is usual for a large manufacturer which does not use the JIT approach to have multiple suppliers. When a new part is to be produced, various suppliers will bid for the contract and the business will be given to the two or three most attractive bids. A JIT manufacturer is looking for a single supplier which can provide high quality and reliable deliveries, rather than the lowest price. This supplier will often be located in close proximity to the manufacturing plant.

There is much to be gained by both the company and its suppliers from this mutual dependence. The traditional approach where companies and suppliers regard each other as adversaries has to change because with JIT, the company and the supplier need to work together co-operatively.

In the longer term this can lead to some very fruitful partnerships. For example, co-operation between the company and the supplier can go right back to the design stage.

Example

Jaguar, when it analysed the causes of customer complaints, compiled a list of 150 areas of faults. Some 60 per cent of them turned out to be faulty components from suppliers. One month the company returned 22,000 components to different suppliers. Suppliers were brought on to the multi-disciplinary task forces the company established to tackle each of the common faults. The task force had the simple objective of finding the fault, establishing and testing a cure, and implementing it as fast as possible. Jaguar directors chaired the task forces of the twelve most serious faults, but in one case the task force was chaired by the supplier's representative.

(Source: Goldsmith, W, and Clutterbuck, D, The Winning Streak, Penguin, 1985)

KEY POINT

A SMART contract (systematic material acquisition and review technique) allows for a short lead-time *'call off'* of material from the supplier within the framework of a longer term contract.

Establishment of long-term purchase orders is commonplace among JIT manufacturers. The purpose is to give the supplier an assurance of long-term sales which enables the supplier to plan for the purchase of raw material, specialised machines etc. These long-term purchase orders also create the right environment for the setting up of SMART contracts. A SMART contract (systematic material acquisition and review technique) allows for a short lead-time *'call off'* of material from the supplier within the framework of a longer term contract. Each time material is called off, the company provides the supplier with a detailed schedule of future requirements. This schedule is not a firm commitment but it enables the suppliers to do their own planning well ahead of time and minimise the company's forward commitment of inventory investment.

These SMART or blanket orders are not a new idea but what is different about a JIT manufacturer is the degree to which this type of purchase order is used. The majority of the raw material piece parts and bought-in subassemblies are procured in this way.

There are significant savings to be made within the purchasing department of the company by use of these techniques. It is not necessary for the buyer to negotiate contracts and raise a purchase order on the supplier each time an order is placed. The SMART contract call-off can be done by the material planner, eliminating that additional administrative step and the paperwork associated with it. It is also possible for the MRP computer-run automatically to generate these SMART releases (within certain constraints) and pass them on to the supplier without even the material planner becoming involved. This allows the material planner to concentrate his or her efforts on resolving the problem areas, rather than spending a great deal of time handling the run-of-the-mill requirements.

4.4 Multi-functional workers

KEY POINT

Demarcation of functions must be eliminated and replaced by a team approach where each person is trained in multiple functions and can move quickly within the plant to meet the changing requirements of the customers.

A key element of just-in-time manufacturing is the flexibility of the workforce. Demarcation of functions must be eliminated and replaced by a team approach where each person is trained in multiple functions and can move quickly within the plant to meet the changing requirements of the customers. The same kind of flexible team approach must also be taken by non-direct personnel such as management accountants. Management accountants must be willing to see their role change significantly as the needs of the business change and, in fact, initiate change as part of the continuous improvement concept of just-in-time manufacturing.

There must be a clear and shared understanding of what the critical success factors of the business are. There must be recognition throughout all levels of the organisation of what the overall business objectives are, and how each unit or department can contribute to satisfying these objectives. The management process itself must be integrated in the sense of sharing a common purpose and approach.

In order for the business objectives to be understood and accepted by personnel at all levels, communications and training become increasingly important. Organisations must be slimmer, with fewer levels of management and a removal of traditional barriers. Only by doing this is there a possibility that the top management philosophy and objectives will filter down through the organisation. Equally important, it is the only way that the degree of adherence to these objectives at lower levels will become visible to senior management.

4.5 Dedicated cell layouts

DEFINITION

A **dedicated cell layout** is a team-based approach where flows of material occur around a 'U' shaped production unit.

A dedicated cell layout is a team-based approach where flows of material occur around a 'U' shaped production unit as shown by the following diagram:

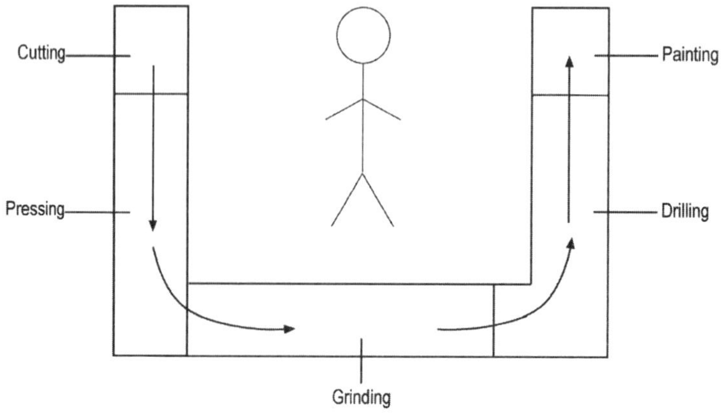

Each operative undertakes several different tasks working with the material around the 'U'. The result is often an increase in quality as operators are responsible for activities within the production process.

5 Accounting in an advanced management techniques environment

5.1 Cost behaviour patterns

KEY POINT

The introduction of computer technicians, software engineers, and programmers replaces traditional direct labour. Most variable costs, other than direct material and energy also disappear. Overheads, both conversion and non-conversion, become an even bigger part of the total cost.

Investment in advanced management techniques and technologies (AMT) dramatically changes cost behaviour patterns. The introduction of computer technicians, software engineers, and programmers replaces traditional direct labour. Most variable costs, other than direct material and energy also disappear. Overheads, both conversion and non-conversion, become an even bigger part of the total cost.

To demonstrate how the accounting may be undertaken, we will illustrate from a real example. Borg-Warner at Ithaca (NY) operates a JIT system producing automotive chain systems in a process system. The operation is completely integrated, the old system of moving piles of work-in-progress having been removed.

Standard transactions

1	Dr	Raw material
	Cr	Account payable

Record material purchases

2	Dr	Conversion costs
	Cr	Raw materials

Issue of raw material to production

3	Dr	Conversion costs at standard
	Cr	Conversion costs payable
	Cr/Dr	Conversion cost variances

Expenses and components committed to work. This entry is made after the components have been inspected and passed for assembly.

4	Cr	Conversion costs
	Dr	Scrap and rejections

Treatment of scrap for both rejected completed items and components.

5	Dr	Finished goods
	Cr	Conversion costs

Charged with conversion costs when the products are finished.

6	Dr	Cost of sales
	Cr	Finished goods

Cost of finished goods charged to profit when goods sold

From this outline, the student should observe:

- Costs are only allowed to accumulate when the product is finished. This directs effort and attention towards output rather than production. There is no WIP account or component stores account – on the basis that components are taken into production at delivery and WIP will be minimal.
- JIT emphasises the elimination of waste. Thus allowances for waste, scrap and rework are removed from the standard costs and detailed reports produced on these items. This means a move to the ideal standard, rather than an achievable standard.
- Output is credited at standard. Thus any difference in input and output is a variance, which can be analysed as either a cost or efficiency variance.

5.2 Cost classification

In a JIT and hence advanced manufacturing environment, cost classifications will change:

	Traditional	*JIT*
Material handling	Indirect	Direct
Repair & maintenance	Largely direct	Direct
Energy	Indirect	Direct
Operating supplies	Indirect	Direct
Supervision	Indirect	Direct
Production support	Indirect	Largely direct
Depreciation	Indirect	Direct

Inevitably many of these costs will be allocated to products on the basis of the cost drivers, hence using activity based costing (see later).

5.3 Overhead absorption

KEY POINT

Where it is necessary to absorb conversion overhead into the cost then the machine hour rate must be favoured.

Where it is necessary to absorb conversion overhead into the cost then the machine hour rate must be favoured. Despite the technical advances, especially in the defence industry, the Howell Report of 1987 found most advanced manufacturers still using a labour hours based system. The predilection for retaining labour hours has resulted in overhead rates in both the UK and the USA well in excess of 1,500% (Innes & Mitchell **Overhead Cost** 1993).

The whole issue of attributing overheads to products becomes more critical in the modern manufacturing environment given that automation increases overheads as a proportion of total costs. Many traditional practices were developed in the manufacturing environment of the early twentieth century where the main components of production costs in many cases were labour and materials.

5.4 Revised performance measures

The introduction of JIT related manufacturing will also change the performance measures.

Traditional	**JIT**
Direct labour (efficiency, utilisation, productivity) Chalos is critical of the excessive focus on a relatively small cost.	Total Head Count productivity (Note the emphasis on 'people' rather than labour)
Machine utilisation	Days of inventory
Stock turnover	Group or cell incentives
Cost variances	Knowledge & capability based promotion
Individual incentives	Ideas generated and implemented
Seniority	Customer complaints

In addition, Chalos (**Managing cost in today's manufacturing environment** 1992) stresses that raw material variances give rise to excess inventories in order to gain discounts, cost centres do not effectively control overhead spends, overhead costs ought to be based upon theoretical capacity rather than the financial accountant's normal capacity to gain an accurate measure of idle facilities and time, and most variances detract from other vital measures of productivity.

5.5 Backflush accounting

DEFINITION

Backflush accounting is a cost accounting system which focuses on the output of an organisation and then works backwards to attribute costs to stock and cost of sales.

This system records the transactions only at the termination of the production and sales cycle. The emphasis is to measure costs at the beginning and at the end with greater emphasis on the end or outputs. Since backflushing is usually employed in parallel with JIT, there is no work-in-progress to consider, nor does work-in-progress materially fluctuate. What is essential, however, is an accurate bill of materials, good measures of yield, generally effective production control and accurate engineering change notices when yields do change.

The principle of a just-in-time system is that production is pulled by customer demand and this in turn pulls the purchasing procedures. Thus, theoretically there are zero stocks of raw materials, work-in-progress and finished goods. For such a situation to exist there needs to be an excellent system of production planning and communications with material suppliers.

The philosophy of traditional cost accounting methods

KEY POINT

Traditional cost accounting methods are based upon the principle that value is obtained by the creation of the asset known as stock.

Traditional cost accounting methods are based upon the principle that value is obtained by the creation of the asset known as stock. As a consequence this value must be measured and cost accumulation systems are used for this purpose. In modern JIT based production, stock does not exist and therefore such cost accumulation techniques are unnecessary. Instead costs are recognised at the point of sale rather than at the point of production.

The variants of backflush accounting

There are a number of variants of the backflush system, each differing as to the 'trigger points' at which costs are recognised within the cost accounts and thus associated with products. All variants, however, have the following common features:

- *the focus is on output* – costs are first associated with output (measured as either sales or completed production) and then allocated between stocks and cost of goods sold by working back.
- *conversion costs (labour and overheads) are never attached to products until they are completed (or even sold)* – thus the traditional WIP account doesn't exist. Materials are recognised at different points according to the variant used, but only to the extent of being either stock of raw materials or part of the cost of stock of finished goods. Again, materials are not attached to WIP.

Two variants of the backflush system are summarised below. Note that in each case, as conversion costs (labour and overheads) are incurred they will be recorded in a conversion cost (CC) account.

Variant 1

This has two trigger points (TP):

TP1 *purchase of raw materials/components*. A 'raw and in process (RIP)' account will be debited with the actual cost of materials purchased, and a creditor credited.

TP2 *completion of good units*. The finished goods (FG) account will be debited with the standard cost of units produced, and the RIP and CC accounts will be credited with the standard costs.

Under this variant, then, there will be two stock accounts:

- raw materials (which may, in fact, be incorporated into WIP)
- finished goods.

Variant 2

This has only one trigger point – *the completion of good units*. The FG account is debited with the standard cost of units produced, with corresponding credits to the CC account and the creditor account.

Thus the cost records exclude:

- raw materials purchased but not yet used for complete production
- the creditor for these materials (and any price variance)

and there is only one stock account, carrying the standard cost of finished goods stock.

Other variants include those using the *sale of complete good units* as a trigger point for the attachment of conversion costs to units – thus there is no finished goods account, just a raw materials stock account, carrying the materials cost of raw materials, WIP and finished goods.

It should be seen that as stocks of raw materials, WIP and finished goods are decreased to minimal levels, as in a 'pure' JIT system, these three variants will give the same basic results.

Backflush accounting – example

The following example will be used to illustrate the first two variants outlined above.

The manufacturing cost information for March for a division of XYZ plc is as follows:

Costs incurred in March	£000
Purchase of raw materials	4,250
Labour	2,800
Overheads	1,640
Activity in March	Units(000)
Finished goods manufactured during the period	180
Sales	145
Standard cost per unit	£
Materials	20
Labour	15
Overheads	9
	44

There were no opening stocks of raw materials, WIP or finished goods. It should be assumed that there are no direct materials variances for the period.

Variant 1

The double entry would be as follows:			*DR*	*CR*
			£000	£000
1	RIP account		4,250	
	Creditor			4,250
2	CC account		4,440	
	Cash			2,800
	Cash/creditor			1,640
3	FG account	(180 × 44)	7,920	
	RIP account	(180 × 20)		3,600
	CC account	(180 × 24)		4,320

4	COGS	(145 × 44)	6,380
	FG account		6,380

The ledger accounts would appear as follows:

Raw and in process materials

	£000		£000
Creditor	4,250	FG	3,600
		Bal c/d	650
	4,250		4,250
Bal b/d	650		

Conversion costs

	£000		£000
Cash/creditor	4,440	FG	4,320
		Bal c/d	120
	4,440		4,440
Bal b/d	120		

Finished goods

	£000		£000
RIP	3,600	COGS	6,380
CC	4,320	Bal c/d	1,540
	7,920		7,920
Bal b/d	1,540		

Cost of goods sold

	£000		£000
FG	6,380		

The stock balances at the end of March would be:

	£000
Raw and in process materials	650
Finished goods	1,540
	2,190

The balance on the conversion costs account would be carried forward and written off at the end of the year.

Variant 2

The accounting entries where there is only one trigger point (on completion of units) would be simpler:

		Dr	*Cr*
		£000	£000
1	CC account	4,440	
	Cash		2,800
	Cash/creditor		1,640

2	FG account	(180 × 44)	7,920	
	Creditors	(180 × 20)		3,600
	CC account	(180 × 24)		4,320
3	COGS	(145 × 44)	6,380	
	FG account			6,380

There would just be one stock balance at the end of March, on the finished goods account, of £1,540,000. The raw materials purchased but not yet attributed to complete production (£650,000) will not have been recorded in the costing system.

This variant is thus only suitable for JIT systems with minimal raw material stocks.

5.6 Suitability of backflush accounting

Both variants illustrated above eliminate the WIP account. If stocks are low in general, a large proportion of manufacturing costs will be attributable to cost of goods sold. The principle of backflush costing is that in these circumstances, the work involved in tracking costs through WIP, COGS and FG is unlikely to be of benefit. As noted above, the stock and cost of goods sold values will be close to those derived from a conventional costing system, with a considerably reduced volume of recorded transactions.

5.7 Throughput accounting (TA)

DEFINITION

Throughput Accounting (TA) is a method of performance measurement which relates production and other costs to throughput. Throughput accounting product costs relate to usage of key resources by various products.

TA is seen as very much in sympathy with the JIT philosophy. It assumes that a manager has a given set of resources available. These comprise the existing buildings, capital equipment and labour force. Using these resources, purchased materials and components must be processed to generate sales revenue. To achieve this, the maximum amount of throughput is required with the financial definition of:

Sales revenue – Direct material cost

The cost of all other factors is deemed at least time related rather than fixed.

Influences on throughput

Throughput is influenced by:

- selling price
- direct purchase price
- usage of direct material
- volume of throughput.

Students should understand that throughput is not production at any price. Rather, throughput is only concerned about output that will effect sales. Stocks are only considered desirable when they can enhance and increase throughput. Such a situation might be maximising output in a seasonal market.

Constraints on throughput might include:

- the existence of an uncompetitive selling price
- the need to deliver on time to particular customers
- the lack of product quality and reliability
- the lack of reliable material supplies
- the existence of shortages of production resources.

It becomes management's task to eliminate these constraints. Shortages of resources are usually termed bottlenecks, and their elimination often only moves a problem from one location to another. Thus the careful planning to minimise and eliminate all bottlenecks becomes very important.

5.8 Throughput reporting

Progress analysed over a range of products can be monitored using a report similar to the one illustrated below.

Product	*A*	*B*	*C*	*D*	*E*	*F*
	£	£	£	£	£	£
Sales						
Direct materials						
Throughput						
Labour						
Other prod. overhead						
Administration						
Selling						
Operating profit						

Costing of any stocks is based upon direct material costs. No conversion costs are added to the inventory valuation whatsoever. The student will recognise that where only materials and components are variable, such a schedule relates very closely to a contribution analysis statement as used for short-term volume decisions.

The principle is that there is no profit and therefore no value in manufacturing for stock unless there is a clear link between increasing stock and future sales (as may occur in seasonal businesses).

Cost classification

DEFINITION

Throughput is defined as sales less material costs.

In a throughput accounting system the only costs which are considered to be variable are material costs. Conversion costs (labour and indirect costs) are classified as being fixed and therefore may be grouped together as 'Total factory costs'. A calculation may be made of the cost per factory hour by relating this cost to the number of hours available on the bottleneck resource.

Return per factory hour

Throughput is defined as sales less material costs. Other costs are considered to be fixed so this is similar in principle to the concept of contribution. The efficiency with which a particular product makes use of the bottleneck resource is calculated by:

$$\frac{\text{Sales} - \text{material costs}}{\text{Usage (in hours) of the bottleneck resource}}$$

You should notice the similarity of this calculation to the contribution per unit of a limiting factor used in short-term decision-making.

KEY POINT

The **throughput accounting ratio** – this is the relationship between the return per factory hour and the cost of each factory hour.

The throughput accounting ratio

This is the relationship between the return per factory hour and the cost of each factory hour. This is found by:

$$\frac{\text{Return per factory hour}}{\text{Cost per factory hour}}$$

Example

A Ltd manufactures a single product which it sells for £10 per unit. The direct material cost of the product is £3 per unit. Other factory costs amount to £50,000 per month. The bottleneck factor is the assembly of the unit which is a labour intensive process. There are 20,000 assembly hours available each month, with each unit taking two hours to assemble.

Calculate the throughput accounting ratio for the product.

Solution

Return per factory hour $= \dfrac{\text{Sales} - \text{material costs}}{\text{Usage of bottleneck resource}}$

$= \dfrac{£10 - £3}{2}$

$=$ **£3.50**

Cost per factory hour $= \dfrac{\text{Total factory costs}}{\text{Bottleneck resource hours available}}$

$= \dfrac{£50{,}000}{20{,}000}$

$=$ **£2.50**

Throughput accounting ratio $= \dfrac{\text{Return per factory hour}}{\text{Cost per factory hour}}$

$= \dfrac{£3.50}{£2.50}$

$=$ **1.4 : 1**

ACTIVITY 1

X Ltd manufactures a product which requires 1.5 hours machining. Due to a lack of machines this has been determined as the bottleneck resource. There are ten machines each of which may be operated for up to 40 hours per week.

The product is sold for £8.50 and has direct material costs of £4.25. Total factory costs are £800 per week.

Calculate the product's:

(i) return per factory hour

(ii) throughput accounting ratio.

Feedback to this activity is at the end of the chapter.

Treatment of bottlenecks

KEY POINT

Bottlenecks can be identified by profiling capacity usage through the system.

Bottlenecks can be identified by profiling capacity usage through the system. Usually they will be areas of most heavy usage. Thus monitoring build ups of inventory and traditional idle time and waiting time will indicate actual or impending bottlenecks.

Traditional efficiency measures will be important in managing bottlenecks. Changes in efficiency will indicate the presence of bottlenecks and the need for a response. This may take the form of creating short-term build-ups of stock to alleviate the problem. Another possible solution might be to prioritise the work at bottlenecks to ensure that throughput is achieved. Measures that highlight throughput per bottleneck capacity measures will need to be developed.

In view of the fact that the JIT philosophy sees all non-value adding activities as potential waste, TA looks for anything that will enhance saleable output. Thus, anything that will reduce costly lead times, set-up times and waiting times will enhance the throughput. Again, these need to be identified and reported on and monitored to see if they are being reduced.

Other factors

All constraints should be considered in the reporting process. If quality is a throughput constraint, then detailed quality cost reports on rework, scrap levels and returns need to be added to the performance measuring process. Equally, if delivery times are crucial, then failure to meet delivery times needs to be reported. The student should begin to see that the essence of throughput accounting is contingent on what is needed and the circumstances that prevail.

Assessment

TA will appear to the student to be going against the trend of emulating Japanese style methods as described by H Thomas Johnson. It is a highly short-term perspective on costs, regarding only material as variable or directly activity-related. It neglects the costs of overhead and people. As a result, there will always be the risk of sub-optimal profit performance. TA will really only work effectively where material remains a high proportion of the cost or selling price. Also, there must be a situation where demand is constant enough or high enough to always put pressure on output and production resources.

It is suggested that TA with its emphasis on direct material is an ideal complement to ABC which can draw attention to the overheads. In that way, a comprehensive cover of costs can be achieved.

6 Activity based costing

6.1 The rationale for ABC

Traditional absorption costing was developed in the early 1900s to cost manufacturing operations at a time when the largest item of expense was direct labour cost. Compared to direct labour costs, overhead costs were fairly low, and the level of overhead expenditure was influenced mainly by direct labour activities. In such circumstances, absorption costing can produce fairly reliable information about product costs.

In an advanced manufacturing technology environment, circumstances are very different. Technology and automation have reduced the need for direct labour substantially so that direct labour costs are proportionately low, and production overhead expenditure is much higher. There have also been large increases in administration and selling and marketing expenses, relative to manufacturing costs.

Within the manufacturing area, significant amounts of expenditure are incurred in 'support functions' or 'service functions', such as set-up costs, production scheduling, inspection costs, the cost of logistics (transportation and storage), despatch, order handling, data processing and customer services.

The work that is done in these support areas is not necessarily related in any way to the volume of production. for example, the costs of setting up machinery for each new batch or production run is likely to vary with the number of batches produced or the number of production runs, in other words with the number of set-ups. The number of set-ups does not necessarily relate directly to the volume of production. For example, if there are 20 production runs of 100 units in each run, set-up costs will be higher than for 10 production runs of 200 units each, even though total production volume would be the same.

In an advanced manufacturing environment, traditional absorption costing information is of little value. Charging overhead costs to units of output (products or services) on the basis of production volume or output level (e.g. on the basis of direct labour hours) cannot provide a meaningful analysis of costs.

Activity-based costing (ABC) was developed to overcome the weaknesses of traditional absorption costing, by trying to charge costs to the products or services that give rise to expenditures.

DEFINITION

Activity Based Costing is the process of cost attribution to cost units on the basis of benefit received from indirect activities, e.g. ordering, setting up, assuring quality.

Bromwich & Bhimani give the following definition using the term 'Activity Based Accounting.'

'Examination of activities across the entire chain of value adding organisational processes underlying causes (drivers) of cost and profit.' The wider definition introduces the important aspect that costs are incurred in selling and distributing a product and the costs of servicing customers are possibly now more important than production.

DEFINITION

A **cost driver** is an activity or factor which generates cost.

Another important definition is the cost driver.

6.2 The origins of activity based costing

ABC first appeared in the 1950s when some US firms made attempts to accurately allocate their selling and distribution overheads. There was a plea in the literature in 1968 when Solomons (Studies in Cost Analysis) explored the need to obtain a reasonably accurate and objective indication of the differing factors driving overhead as a basis for more reliable variance computations. In the 1970s, when zero-based budgeting came into vogue, some of the analysis was based upon activity. However, it was the work of Robin Cooper and R S Kaplan that eventually codified ABC into a coherent framework and disseminated it among academics, consultants and practitioners.

KEY POINT

ABC is most appropriate where overhead is a relatively important cost element and there is a diversity of product lines and possibly markets.

ABC is most appropriate where overhead is a relatively important cost element and there is a diversity of product lines and possibly markets. Essentially, it requires pooling the overhead spend and allocating it out over activities. Note the use of the term 'allocate' indicating an objective cost driven charge rather than a subjective apportionment.

6.3 The mechanics of ABC

To implement ABC, an organisation must first of all look at all its overhead costs, and try to *identify the main activities* that result in costs being incurred. These are the activities that use up resources. There are no standard rules as to what these major activities should be and they will differ in each organisation. The activities identified in this way need not be confined to a single department, but might be carried out in a number of different departments.

Examples of resource-consuming activities might be the cost of processing a customer order, procurement costs, the cost of quality inspection, set-up costs, despatch costs, warehousing costs, and so on.

Instead of collecting overhead costs for a service department or an overhead cost centre, an organisation collects the overhead costs for **activity pools** or **cost pools**. There is a separate activity pool for each major resource-consuming activity. For each activity pool, there should be a **cost driver**. A cost driver is a unit of activity that results in the consumption of resources, and so leads to costs being incurred.

Examples of cost drivers might be the number of orders handled for despatch costs and order processing costs, the number of purchase orders for purchasing costs, the number of stores requisitions for materials handling costs, the number of batches for set-up costs, and so on.

There are no established rules about what the cost driver should be for any particular activity, and the selected cost driver should be one that seems most appropriate for each particular activity pool. Cost drivers might be production-oriented, such as the production cycle time, the number of orders, the number of production runs or batches of output, the number of machine hours operated or the number of inspections. Alternatively, cost drivers might be related to the cost of providing service to customers, such as the number of changes to order specifications or the characteristics of a customer's order.

For each activity pool or cost pool, a *cost per unit of cost driver* is then calculated. The costs in an activity pool are then assigned to products and services on the basis of:

Units of cost driver × Cost per unit of cost driver.

This is similar to the absorption of overheads, using an absorption rate, in traditional costing. However, the cost driver represents the factor that results in costs in the activity pool. For example, if a particular product accounts for 40% of all sales orders and there is a cost pool for order handling costs, the product should attract 40% of the total costs of order handling.

Suppose for example that there is a cost pool for handling sales orders, and that the cost driver for this activity is the number of orders processed. The total costs for the cost pool might be £300,000, and the company might process 1,000 orders in the year. The cost of order processing would therefore be £300 per order. A product for which there are 200 orders in a year would be charged £60,000 for order processing costs.

6.4 Illustrative example

Oceanides has four departments who make use of the procurement function. The total cost of the function is £10,000,000 per annum. The four departments use the function in the following way:

Department	*No of orders*	*Cost allocation*
		£
A	200,000	6,666,667
B	50,000	1,666,667
C	40,000	1,333,333
D	10,000	333,333
	300,000	10,000,000

Simply dividing the total cost by the cost driver we get:

$$\frac{£10,000,000}{300,000} = £33.33 \text{ per order}$$

ACTIVITY 2

Pelleas has the following indirect costs:

	£	*No. of cost drivers*
Quality control	90,000	450 inspections
Process set-up	135,000	450 set-ups
Purchasing	105,000	1,000 purchase orders
Customer order processing	120,000	2,000 customers
Occupancy costs	150,000	75,000 machine hours
	600,000	

Calculate the charge out rates for each of the activities.

Feedback to this activity is at the end of the chapter.

Example

Pelleas, (the company in the above activity), makes a standard product called the Melisande.

The cost details are as follows:

Unit material cost	£0.50
Unit labour cost	£0.40
Total production for the coming year	1,000,000 units
No. of production runs	50
No. of purchase orders required	50
No. of customer orders	10
Unit machine time	3 minutes

The product run is inspected once at the end of each production run.

You are required to calculate the standard cost of a Melisande.

Solution

We need to draw up a grid for the overheads.

Function	*Rate × Usage*		£
Quality control	£200 × 50	=	10,000
Process set-up	£300 × 50	=	15,000
Purchasing	£105 × 50	=	5,250
Customer orders	£60 × 10	=	600
Occupancy	£2 × 50,000	=	100,000
			130,850

Dividing the total overhead cost by the number of units produced we get:

$$\frac{130,850}{1,000,000} = £0.1385 \text{ (say £0.14)}$$

Thus the standard unit cost for a Mclisandc is:

	£
Material	0.50
Labour	0.40
Overhead	0.14
	1.04

The typical examination question that has appeared thus far has required the student to compute overhead rates in the traditional manner and using the ABC method and compare the results over two or more products, one like the Melisande, (standard and with long runs), and others which are likely to be non-standard with short runs.

6.5 Selecting the cost drivers

In the main, the cost driver will be measured in terms of volume of transactions. However, ABC also tries to identify costs that are not contributing to the value of the product/service so the following questions are relevant:

- What services does this activity provide?
- Who receives the services?
- Why do you require so many people?
- What might cause you to require more/less staff?
- Why does over/idle time exist?

KEY POINT

Three types of cost driver have emerged:

- Pure activity output volume
- Activity/output volume/complexity
- Situation

Three types of cost driver have emerged.

(a) **Pure activity output volume** – where the basic transactions of the activity are identical in terms of their resource demands such as the purchasing of raw materials or a similar range of items.

(b) **Activity/output volume/complexity** – where the basic transactions differ in terms of their resource demands as when purchases are made from different overseas suppliers.

(c) **Situation** – where an underlying factor can be identified as driving the workload of an activity such as the number of suppliers when supplier vetting and liaison were vital components of the cost pool.

6.6 Examples of cost drivers

The following are examples of cost drivers.

Activity	*Cost driver*
Material procurement	No. of purchase orders
Material handling	No. of movements
Quality control	No. of inspections
Engineering services	No. of change orders
Maintenance	No. of break-downs
Line set-up	No. of set-ups

For the service sector the following taken from the field of Health Care may serve as an example. The cost drivers form the basis of costs charged to patients.

Activity	*Cost driver*
Patient movement	No. of in-patients
Booking appointments	No. of patients
Patient reception	No. of patients
X-ray:	
Equipment preparation	Time taken
Patient preparation	Time taken
Patient aftercare	Time taken
Film processing	No. of images
Film reporting	No. of images

From Kirton 'ABC at Luton & Dunstable Hospital' 1992.

6.7 The merits of ABC

An improved more accurate product cost may enable a company to concentrate on a more profitable mix of products or customers. ABC has been effectively used in identifying customers who are unprofitable to service.

It is argued that traditional overhead apportionment leads to an arbitrary attribution of overhead costs to individual products.

KEY POINT

ABC helps identify value added and non-value added costs so that the non-value added items can be appraised effectively with a view to elimination.

ABC extends the variable cost rationale to both short and long-term costs by quantitatively addressing the cost behaviour patterns in terms of both short run volume changes as well as long-term cost trends.

It helps identify value added and non-value added costs so that the non-value added items can be appraised effectively with a view to elimination. As such it forces managers and supervisors to consider the drivers that effect costs and what these drivers contribute to the final product.

Thus the managers will have a better understanding of the economics of production and the economics of the activities performed by the company.

A warning

Ahmed and Scapens (**Cost allocation: theory and practice 1991**) warned that ABC was unlikely to relate all overheads to specific activities. It also ignores the potential for conflict, especially where there is more than one potential cost driver.

More recently, the warning has been reiterated by emphasising that there is no such thing as a 100% accurate cost. At best, ABC will only improve the quality of cost information. The student should perhaps note Brimson's 1991 definition of product cost – 'a summation of the cost of all traceable activities to design, procure material, manufacture and distribute a product'.

Perhaps the key word in that definition is traceable, whether or not a cost can be traced objectively to the production/delivery of a good/service.

ACTIVITY **3**

A business manufactures a range of products, including Product X and product Y. Product X is made in standard batch sizes of 300 units, and Product Y is made in standard batch sizes of 100 units. Cost information is as follows:

	Product X	*Product Y*
Production run (size)	400 units	150 units
Direct materials cost per unit	£20	£30
Direct labour cost per hour	£8	£8
Direct labour time per unit	0.25 hours	0.5 hours
Number of set-ups per batch	6	2
Machine hours per unit	0.5 hours	0.5 hours

Overhead costs are as follows:

	Total annual costs	*Annual volume of activity*
Set-up costs	£1,200,000	3,000 set-ups
Handling costs	£1,350,000	1,500 batches (production runs)
Other production overheads	£1,800,000	100,000 machine hours

Activity Based Costing is used. Set-up costs are charged to products on the basis of a cost per set-up, and handling costs are charged on the basis of a cost per batch/production run. Other production overheads are absorbed on a machine hour basis.

Required:

Using ABC, calculate the cost per unit of Product X and the cost per unit of Product Y.

Feedback to this activity is at the end of the chapter.

6.8 Activity based management (ABM)

The terms ABC and ABM have been used interchangeably in the past. This is not always appropriate since ABC is a specific technique concerned with determining what it costs to undertake certain activities and what it costs to produce the outputs that those activities relate to.

ABM is a rather wider concept. ABM may involve the use of ABC information in the management of a business. Typically a range of activity based techniques (ABTs) are elements in the practice of ABM. Businesses that practice ABTs are likely to have a good understanding of their own cost structures but ABM relates to the application of that understanding in general performance management and the making of management decisions.

Some writers have claimed that the adoption of ABTs has produced disappointing results in terms of profitability improvement for many organisations. Academic and professional researchers have invested time and resources in considering why this should be so. One key finding is that the information generated by ABTs (such as ABC systems) has to be used effectively in order to achieve the expected results.

"An ABC implementation failure could be defined as the inability of a company to move from simply generating ABC information towards actually using that information".

Roberts & Silvester, "Why ABC failed and why it may yet succeed", JCM 1996

Roberts & Silvester suggested that organisations sometimes contain structural and cultural barriers that make it difficult to progress from ABC to ABM. In any event, the design and installation of complex management information systems is pointless if the output of those systems is not effectively used.

Let us consider some features of ABM in operation.

Cost visibility

The activity based approach brings costs out into the open and helps management see what they get for the commitment of resources. For example, the buying department ties up people, equipment (office space, desks, filing cabinets) and uses stationery, telephones etc, and produces purchase orders. Ignoring the classic cynical view of R C Townsend, the effectiveness of the department can be monitored in terms of delays, reductions in lead times and errors. This would enable the purchasing function to be monitored effectively and improved upon. A purchasing department is not just concerned with buying. It will have input from the design area, perhaps being told to find standard parts for specialist products, it will obviously buy and track prices, it may be responsible for receiving and it will pass invoices to accounting. The speed and effectiveness with which it performs these tasks can be used to monitor performance and control costs.

It is suggested that ABC is perhaps most useful in monitoring how effectively the traditional overhead departments operate. Since a factory needs material, it follows that it needs buyers. It is tempting to say that they are indispensable and not track the cost. What ABC does do is enable management to really ask whether or not any department is as cost effective as it could be. One way of doing this is to create cost profiles to measure resource consumption.

Activity cost profile

This is not a new idea. Students should already be familiar with traditional overhead reporting statements which show last year's figures as a comparison. The profile is merely a different approach.

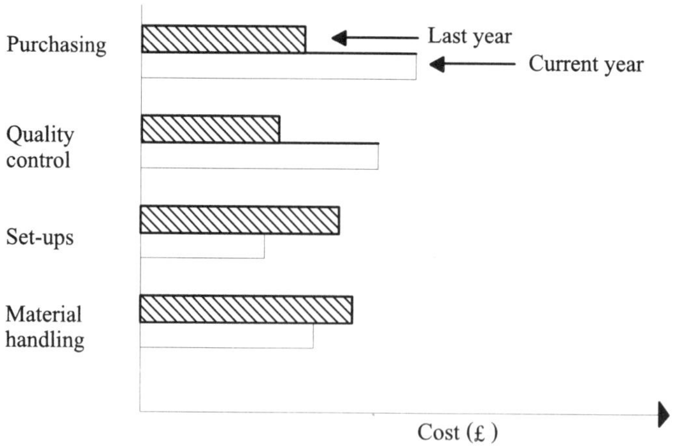

The activity cost profile

From the profile, it can be asked, 'Why has purchasing gone up?' This could be because of increased volume, diversity of products, change in mix of production runs etc.

The dramatic increase in quality control may be offset by fewer external failures, fewer warranty claims and fewer recalls. It may be due to the changing expectation of the customer, demanding a higher quality product. Similar analyses can be performed on set-up and material handling costs.

6.9 Cost behaviour patterns

The student should be familiar with the traditional narrow view of cost behaviour patterns. In essence a linear assumption is made that is based upon one variable, production or possibly sales volume. Common sense indicates that not all costs vary in a direct linear relationship with activity. One obvious example is the telephone. It may actually be used far more if activity is slack in order to drum up more business.

Fixed costs have increased in proportion to the total but have also not remained unchanged. More resources are being committed to elements of the fixed cost structure. What is required is an analysis of what is driving these increases. One approach to investigating and exploring ways of reducing these costs is to establish a hierarchy which classifies types of activity and identifies how costs are driven.

ABC based cost hierarchy

Level 1	Unit basis	Costs depend on the volume of production, e.g. machine power.
Level 2	Batch basis	Costs depend upon the number of batches, e.g. set-up and monitoring.
Level 3	Process level	Costs depend upon the existence of the process, e.g. quality control and supervision.
Level 4	Product level	Costs depend upon the existence of a group or line, e.g. product management and parts administration.
Level 5	Facility level	Costs depend on the existence of a facility of plant, e.g. rent, rates, general management.

This approach highlights the pattern of costs as one moves further away from the product. It also highlights the position in the hierarchy of decision-making. The fixed set-up cost can be reduced by longer runs, but at the expense of increased storage if there is no immediate demand. Further up the hierarchy, consideration can be given to reducing the number of processes, merging lines and changing facility capacity.

Such an approach requires a different view of costs which traditional analysis does not give. Traditional analysis with its subjective apportionments assumes that the product drives all the costs. By definition, fixed costs cannot be product driven and what is required is to find out how they are driven and if they add value to the product. It also provides an attention directing signal that highlights the cost of resources consumed by a product in order to gain a particular market price. Such a signal enables consideration of future strategies towards volumes and product development.

6.10 Customer driven costs

This is an area that has been traditionally neglected. All the emphasis has been upon manufacturing costs with over emphasis on direct labour. It may come as a salutary shock to the student that the labour cost content of a $18,000 (£12,000) car is about $840 (£560) while the selling and distribution cost is about 30% of the showroom price i.e. $5,400 (£3,600) (*Fortune* April 4 1994). Major potential cost savings can be achieved in this hitherto almost sacred area.

The following customer driven costs have been identified:

- **Supply and delivery patterns**

  Influenced by the frequency of delivery – a JIT system will need more but smaller deliveries compared with a customer who maintains high buffer inventories.

- **Customer location**

  Distribution, communication and contact costs are all influenced by distance.

- **Quality provided**

  Different customers may require different standards, both of supply and product. A JIT customer will demand a higher quality of service.

- **Provision of after sales service**

  This will have been negotiated with the individual customer. Obviously, the customer who wants 24 hours support for his PCs is going to pay a premium over the customer who is happy to buy the cheapest 'box' from a specialist supermarket.

- **Required documentation**

  This may be determined by the needs of the customer.

- **Sales and promotion effort**

  This again may be geared to different types of customers, who may be attracted to different attributes of the product on offer.

- **Discounts given**

  Repeat business, special relationships, offers or promptness of paying can all differ among customers.

Customer Profitability Analysis (CPA) is one example of ABM in practice. CPA is about determining the costs and revenues associated with servicing particular customers or customer groups.

Say we have two customers – A and B. Both generate about the same annual revenue, both pay invoices on time and both have the same growth potential. On the face of things we might consider that the two customers are worth the same to us.

However, upon investigation we might find that A has been a customer for years, gives us most of his business, refers other customers to us, pays his bills electronically and requires little by way of special service. However B has recently been re-acquired as a customer for the fourth time in six years by offering him major price concessions. B buys low margin items in a complex mix, varies orders at the last moment, requires a great deal of special service and pays by cheque.

It is fairly apparent that A is a more valuable customer than B. But this is not something that a conventional cost accounting system can be relied upon to report. The relative performance of A and B as customers can only be determined through a careful ABC exercise distributing customer driven costs between customers using appropriate cost drivers. The use of the appreciation of A and B's relative performance is an exercise in ABM.

CPA exercises often disclose that a small numbers of customers generate a high proportion of the profits of a business – 20% of customers giving 80% of profit is a finding reported by Bellis-Jones in 1989 (Customer Profitability Analysis – Management Accounting, June 1989). Such a finding might induce appropriate management action. For example, less profitable customer accounts might be priced upwards, reallocated to an agent or even closed.

However, caution should be exercised in this regard. Modern strategic thinking indicates that a business may well find that its current cash flow is sustained by a number of cash cows which, while being mature products, are not ones which may have a long term future. A business has to accept products and customers on the basis of future potential rather than present value. This issue is explored further in Chapter 17.

6.11 Illustrative example

Diomed manufactures a single product with a production cost of £40 per unit which is sold to three customers. The details are:

Sales pattern:	Customer	X	10,000 units per annum
		Y	10,000 units per annum
		Z	10,000 units per annum

All sales are made at £75 per unit.

Non-production overhead is:

	£
Delivery	220,000
Quality inspection	200,000
Salesmen	80,000
After sales service	100,000
	600,000

This is currently apportioned on the basis of a rate on the production cost. The MD is unhappy about this and asks for an analysis based upon ABC methods.

The following period activity volumes have been identified.

Customer	*X*	*Y*	*Z*
No. of deliveries	2,500	50	12
No. of inspections	10,000	500	0
No. of salesmen visits	200	24	6
After sales visits	200	100	50

Solution

Cost driver rates:

Delivery $\frac{£220{,}000}{2{,}562}$ = £85.87 per delivery

Inspection $\frac{£200{,}000}{10{,}500}$ = £19.05 per inspection

Salesmen $\frac{£80{,}000}{230}$ = £347.83 per visit

After sales $\frac{£100{,}000}{350}$ = £285.71 per after sales visit

Analysing these costs:

Customer			*X*	*Y*	*Z*
			£	£	£
No. of deliveries	2,500 @	85.87	214,675		
	50 @	85.87		4,294	
	12 @	85.87			1,030
Inspection	10,000 @	19.05	190,500		
	500 @	19.05		9,525	
Salesmen visits	200 @	347.83	69,566		
	24 @	347.83		8,348	
	6 @	347.83			2,087
After sales visits	200 @	285.71	57,142		
	100 @	285.71		28,571	
	50 @	285.71			14,286
			531,883	50,738	17,403

Final unit cost analysis:

	Production cost	*Non-production cost*	*Total cost*	*Selling price*	*Profit (loss)*
	£	£	£	£	£
Customer X	40	53.19	93.19	75.00	(18.19)
Customer Y	40	5.07	45.07	75.00	29.93
Customer Z	40	1.74	41.74	75.00	33.26

Thus the MD's misgivings were justified. The high cost of serving customer X effectively wipes out the profit being made on producing and selling the product and some consideration has to be given to the quality of service offered for the price charged.

6.12 Activity based budgeting (ABB)

KEY POINT

Activity based budgeting extends the use of ABC from individual product costing, for pricing and output decisions, to the overall planning and control system of the business.

Activity based budgeting extends the use of ABC from individual product costing, for pricing and output decisions, to the overall planning and control system of the business.

The basic principle of ABB is that the work of each department for which a budget is to be prepared is analysed by its major activities, for which cost drivers may be identified. The budgeted cost of resources used by each activity is determined (from recent historical data) and, where appropriate, cost per unit of activity calculated.

Future costs can then be budgeted by deciding on future activity levels and working back to the required resource input.

6.13 ABB – example

The following 'activity matrix' shows the resources used (rows) and major functions/activities (columns) of the stores department of a manufacturing business.

The total current annual costs of each resource consumed by the department are shown in the final column; they have then been spread back over the various activities to establish the cost pools. The allocation of resource costs between activities will, to some extent, be subjective.

Each of the first four activities has an identifiable cost driver, and the total resource cost driver rates can be determined (cost per unit of activity).

The last two activities that occur within the department are non-volume related, and are sometimes referred to as 'sustaining costs'. They are necessary functions and should not be ignored in the budgeting process; however, they should not be attributed to particular cost drivers, as this would not reflect their true cost behaviour and would result in inappropriate budgets being set.

Activity cost matrix for stores department

Activity:	*Goods inwards*	*Goods out*	*Stock orders*	*Monthly stock counting*	*Records*	*Supervision*	*Total*
Cost driver:	Deliveries	Stores requisitions	Orders	Counts	–	–	
Resource	£000	£000	£000	£000	£000	£000	£000
Management salary	–	–	–	1.5	3.5	25	30
Storekeepers' wages	50	30	10	4	20	–	114
Overtime	15	–	–	5	5	–	25
Stationery, etc	1	2	2	1	3	–	9
Other	6	4	2	1	2	4	19
Total	72	36	14	12.5	33.5	29	197
Volume of activity	450	375	100	12	–	–	
Cost per activity unit	£160	£96	£140	£1,042	£33,500	£29,000	

The budget for the stores department for next year will be set by deciding upon the expected number of deliveries, stores requisitions, orders etc, and costing these accordingly. Sustaining costs will effectively be treated as fixed costs.

Advantages of ABB

- The costs of activities are identified. Each delivery of goods costs £160 to process. This should be taken into account when determining optimum order sizes etc. Is it necessary to have monthly stock counts at a cost of £1,042 each? To what extent can the stock records be relied upon if counts are reduced?
- It takes into account the impact of activity levels on resource costs, of assistance in cost reduction programmes and in setting realistic cost targets
- Activity unit costs allow easier analysis of cost trends over time and intra-departmental comparisons
- Resource allocation decisions are assisted by the activity related cost information
- ABB links directly to a TQM programme by relating the cost of an activity to the level of service provided (e.g. stores requisitions processed) – do the user departments feel they are getting a cost-effective service?

7 The continuing relevance of traditional accounting techniques

Some observers have suggested that developments in manufacturing and associated accounting practices have rendered many traditional techniques redundant. For example, traditional standard costing and variance analysis place an emphasis on reporting costs incurred in given short periods and matching these with predetermined standards. This has been one of the main elements in traditional budgetary control.

This approach seems to cut right across modern developments in management. Concepts of continuous improvement and target costing are ignored by an approach which adopts an inherently passive approach to cost determination. A standard is set, and if the production operation achieves that standard then the operation is deemed to be efficient.

Variance analysis considers only what has happened in one short period. This may be meaningless in an environment where most costs are determined in the design phase and efficiency is determined by flexibility.

All that said, standard costing and variance analysis remain widely used, even though they may be less central to the modern thrust of management than was the case in earlier years.

8 Contingency theory in the practice of management accounting

It has been seen that a variety of different approaches are possible in regard to the design of management accounting systems and associated performance management practices. Several theorists have sought to develop some unifying theory to demonstrate how particular approaches are appropriate to given circumstances. The thrust of this is that the style of management accounting appropriate to a given organisation depends on its environment, its strategy and its structure.

"The contingency approach to management accounting is based on the premise that there is no universally appropriate accounting system applicable to all organisations in all circumstances. Rather a contingency theory attempts to identify specific aspects of an accounting system with certain defined circumstances and to demonstrate an appropriate matching"

D.T. Otley, *The contingency theory of management accounting: achievement & prognosis,* - Accounting, Organisations and Society, 1980

The advocates of contingency theory have identified five sets of contingent variables that impact on the character of management accounting in an organisation:

(1) The external environment – degree of certainty, change and complexity

(2) Competitive strategy – relative importance of unit cost and product differentiation

(3) Technology – whether small batch or mass production

(4) Business unit – organisation size, diversification and structure

(5) Knowledge and observability – the extent to which performance is measurable

A full exploration of each of these topics would be beyond the scope of this text, so what follows is a very summarised account. Let us consider each of the five groups of contingent variables in turn and consider how they impact of management accounting in organisations. The following discussion a conceptual underpinning for a number of the topics (such as performance measurement and budgeting) that follow later in this text.

The external environment

The external environment of a business can range from being certain, static and calm to being uncertain, dynamic and turbulent. It is widely considered those businesses in the certain/static end of the range are most amenable to a formula based approach to performance evaluation. Where market conditions are well known in advance then it is possible to produce budgets and standards that provide meaningful targets. Compliance with such targets provides a reliable measure of performance.

Conversely, at the uncertain/dynamic end of the range, market conditions are very difficult to predict and pre-determined budgets and standards may be meaningless. An attempt to rely on budgetary control in this sort of environment is likely to produce dysfunctional behaviour of various kinds. In an uncertain environment a more sophisticated approach to performance evaluation is needed, relying on a range of financial and non-financial indicators.

Competitive strategy

This issue has already been touched on in an earlier consideration of Porter's five competitive forces (Chapter 1). Where a business follows a low cost strategy, that is producing an undifferentiated product and competing mainly on unit cost, then it may be appropriate to adopt management control systems that seek to standardise operating procedures in order to maximise production efficiency. Reliance on a traditional standard costing and variance analysis may work well in such a case.

Conversely, where a business produces a differentiated product and constantly seeks to introduce new products or constantly seeks to enter new markets – then a more comprehensive management information/performance evaluation system may be required. Success in such an environment depends on initiative and innovation. Sole reliance on a simple standard costing system is entirely inadequate in such a case.

Technology

Business units can range from being independent through to having pooled, sequential or reciprocal interdependencies with other business units. To the extent that a business unit is interdependent with others, it shares pooled resources and is constantly confronted with the need to share pooled costs on an appropriate basis with the other units.

The treatment of pooled resources can involve the design of sophisticated accounting systems for the treatment of overheads. To the extent that sequential or reciprocal interdependencies exist then business units inside the same business supply one another with goods and services. Appropriate transfer pricing systems have to be devised to account for such supplies.

Business unit

Many studies have supported the contention that the larger and more complex a business is, the more sophisticated its management accounting system is likely to be. There are various reasons for this, but one traditional factor has always been that the design, implementation and operation of a management accounting system is a high fixed cost. Such a cost may be prohibitive to the smaller business. Another point is that the benefits of sophisticated information may be relatively low to a simple business.

Where a business is pursuing a related diversification strategy which involves a high level of commonality between business units, then reliance on some traditional management accounting systems such as budgeting may help to maintain communication between managers. Such communication may promote co-ordination between the business units and help to promote synergies.

Conversely, where a business follows an unrelated diversification strategy it involves its business units in different areas and the scope for co-ordination and synergies may be limited. A degree of information asymmetry may develop whereby group management may find it difficult to maintain control of individual business units. In this case a degree of devolution is likely to occur with the units taking on the role of profit and investment centres. This in turn can lead to a heavy reliance on financial controls.

Knowledge and observability

In a factory that produces widgets on a continuous basis, it is not difficult to know what the production process involves and observe what inputs it uses and what outputs it achieves. The management accounting system will be built around this high degree of knowledge and observability.

However, the situation may be much more opaque in a research laboratory or in a sales office. In such cases, there may be limited knowledge of what actually happens in the production process and it may be very difficult to observe what the outputs of the process are. One writer advocates the use of clan controls in the context of a drug company's research laboratory. Performance is monitored and evaluated by reporting number of seminars attended by researchers, number of articles published and number of breakthroughs that will lead to new marketable products.

The key point to note is that there are many circumstances when performance cannot be measured by reliance on wholly accounting or financial controls. This is a point that we will return to again and again as we proceed through this text.

9 Other behavioural theory relevant to management accounting

Other academic theory has been advanced to explore or explain aspects of management accounting. One of these is institutional theory which considers the link between organisational and administrative behaviour. Two leading academic writers in this area are Paul J. DiMaggio and Walter W. Powell. Institutional theory traces the adoption of distinctive forms, processes and strategies as they emerge from patterns of organisational interaction and adaptation. Such patterns may be understood as responses to both internal and external environments.

One central thrust that emerges from this thinking turns around the concept of 'isomorphism' – the process of change tending to result in things becoming equal. In the context of business management, organisations become increasingly similar in character and adopt similar control systems as a result of institutional forces. This move towards institutional norms takes place as a result of internal and external pressures of various kinds. DiMaggio and Powell describe these pressures as being mimetic (following a model in response to uncertainty), normative (the adoption of accepted standards) and coercive (legal or regulatory). The recent widespread adoption of benchmarking as a method of performance evaluation is stated to be a product of mimetic process.

Several studies have been undertaken which support this contention. For example, David Deephouse in Does isomorphism legitimate? (Academy of Management Journal, August 1996), tests a central proposition of institutional theory, that organisational isomorphism increases organisational legitimacy within the context of commercial banks. Results show that isomorphism in the strategies of commercial banks is related to legitimacy conferred by bank regulators and the media, even in the presence of differences in organisational age, size, and performance. Various pressures force different organisations to harmonise their strategy and systems.

"Organizations tend to model themselves after similar organizations in their field that they perceive to be more legitimate or successful. The ubiquity of certain kinds of structural arrangements can more likely be credited to the universality of mimetic processes than to concrete evidence that the adopted models enhance efficiency."

(DiMaggio and Powell, 'The new institutionalism in organisational analysis, 1991).

This particular aspect of institutional theory runs counter to the contingency theory that was explored earlier in the chapter. Contingency theory tends to embrace the idea of diversity – whereby systems and practices are developed to match individual circumstances on a rational basis. Institutional theory suggests ubiquity – whereby standard systems and practice evolve which are adopted by all players regardless of individual circumstances.

"The formal structure of an organization cannot be understood as a rational system for co-ordinating activities, nor can it be accounted for by a logic of transaction costs. Rather, the formal structure is institutionalized from without as well as from within, and it reflects prevailing concepts of how work should be organized. Formal structures dramatically reflect the myths of their institutional environments instead of the demands of their work activities. Furthermore, the more an organization's structure is derived from institutionalized myths, the more it maintains elaborate displays of confidence, satisfaction, and good faith, internally and externally. Myths are complemented by routine procedures, such as rationalized rituals of inspection and evaluation."

Meyer, John W., and Brian Rowan , *'Institutionalized organizations: formal structure as myth and ceremony.'* 1991 (DiMaggio and Powell, eds.)

The implication of this is that a management accounting system may be understood as a rationalised ritual which seeks to support the myth and ceremony of a community. This is not an idea that many management accountants will immediately accept, but on reflection they may perceive that there is more than a grain of truth in it.

The topic is an interesting one, but it is unlikely to feature prominently in ACCA examinations at a theoretical level.

10 The dissemination of modern management accounting practices

The dissemination of modern management techniques has generated an industry which provides well paid employment for an army of management consultants, business writers and 'management gurus'. Some techniques have been developed by consultancy practices as a vehicle for the marketing of their own services. Some individuals have become rich by inventing a new technique and then popularising it. The reference to mimetic, normative and coercive processes of change in our earlier discussion of institutional theory is relevant in this context.

An exploration of the role of management consultants goes beyond the scope of this text. However, the reader may care to note that the main means through which new ideas are disseminated include:

- Articles published in professional journals and the financial press
- Studies published in specialised journals (e.g. 'Management Accounting Research'), often based on work funded by various research foundations
- Documentary series broadcast on television
- In-house and public seminars organised by professional accounting bodies
- The marketing and promotional literature of professional consultancy practices
- Books

The reader should be aware that some observers have claimed that the development of many new management techniques in recent years is, at least partly, a social phenomenon. Again, exploring this proposition in any depth is beyond the scope of this text.

Conclusion

The increasing use of automated production has changed traditional cost structures. New management accounting techniques are needed to support modern business practices such as JIT, TQM, CAD, CAM, CAE and FMS. Throughput accounting, value analysis, backflush accounting and activity based costing are some of the techniques used.

The term 'strategic management accounting' has come into common use in recent years. It refers to the full range of management accounting practices used to provide a guide to the strategic direction of an organisation. Some of these have been explored in this chapter, and we will encounter others as we proceed through the text. Most particularly, strategic management accounting places an emphasis on using information from a wide variety of internal and external sources in order to evaluate performance, appraise proposed projects and make decisions.

SELF-TEST QUESTIONS

The modern business environment

1 Explain the role of computers in an automated factory. (2.2)

2 What is a flexible manufacturing system? (2.3)

3 Explain Materials Requirements Planning (MRP). (2.4)

Just in time (JIT)

4 Explain Just In Time. (4.1)

Accounting in an advanced management techniques environment

5 Explain the key features of a backflush accounting system. (5.5)

Activity based costing

6 What is Activity Based Costing? (6)

7 What is a cost driver? (6.3)

8 State the advantages of Activity Based Costing as identified by its supporters. (6.7)

9 Explain Activity Based Management. (6.8)

10 What is an activity cost profile? (6.8)

EXAM-TYPE QUESTIONS

Question 1: Limitation of traditional management accounting

The new manufacturing environment is characterised by more flexibility, a readiness to meet customers' requirements, smaller batches, continuous improvements and an emphasis on quality. In such circumstances, traditional management accounting performance measures are, at best, irrelevant and, at worst, misleading.

Required:

(a) Discuss the above statement, citing specific examples to support or refute the views expressed. **(10 marks)**

(b) Explain in what ways management accountants can adapt the services they provide to the new environment. **(7 marks)**

(Total: 17 marks)

Question 2: ABC terms

(a) In the context of activity based costing (ABC), it was stated in **Management Accounting – Evolution not Revolution** by Bromwich and Bhimani, that

'Cost drivers attempt to link costs to the scope of output rather than the scale of output thereby generating less arbitrary product costs for decision-making.'

Required: Explain the terms 'activity based costing' and 'cost drivers'.

(8 marks)

(b) XYZ plc manufactures four products, namely A, B, C and D, using the same plant and processes.

The following information relates to a production period:

Product	*Volume*	*Material cost per unit*	*Direct labour per unit*	*Machine time per unit*	*Labour cost per unit*
A	500	£5	½ hour	¼ hour	£3
B	5,000	£5	½ hour	¼ hour	£3
C	600	£16	2 hours	1 hour	£12
D	7,000	£17	1½ hours	1½ hours	£9

Total production overhead recorded by the cost accounting system is analysed under the following headings:

- Factory overhead applicable to machine-oriented activity is £37,424.
- Set-up costs are £4,355.
- The cost of ordering materials is £1,920.
- Handling materials – £7,580.
- Administration for spare parts – £8,600.

These overhead costs are absorbed by products on a machine hour rate of £4.80 per hour, giving an overhead cost per product of:

A = £1.20 B = £1.20 C = £4.80 D = £7.20

However, investigation into the production overhead activities for the period reveals the following totals:

Product	*Number of set-ups*	*Number of material orders*	*Number of times material was handled*	*Number of spare parts*
A	1	1	2	2
B	6	4	10	5
C	2	1	3	1
D	8	4	12	4

Required:

(i) Compute an overhead cost per product using activity based costing, tracing overheads to production units by means of cost drivers. **(6 marks)**

(ii) Comment briefly on the differences disclosed between overheads traced by the present system and those traced by activity based costing. **(3 marks)**

(Total: 17 marks)

For the answers these questions, see the 'Answers' section at the end of the book.

FEEDBACK TO ACTIVITY 1

(i) $\frac{£8.50 - £4.25}{1.5\text{ hours}} = £2.83$

(ii) $\frac{£2.83}{£2} = 1.42 : 1$

FEEDBACK TO ACTIVITY 2

Quality control	90,000	÷ 450	=	£200 per inspection
Process set-up	135,000	÷ 450	=	£300 per set-up
Purchasing	105,000	÷ 1,000	=	£105 per order
Customer order processing	120,000	÷ 2,000	=	£60 per customer
Occupancy costs	150,000	÷ 75,000	=	£2 per machine hour

Note that occupancy cost has been allocated on traditional machine hours. The cost driver there is time, and as such, a conventional ABC method is not applicable. The student should remember that ABC will never cater 100% for all overheads.

FEEDBACK TO ACTIVITY 3

Cost item	*Annual cost*	*Activity level*	*Recovery rate*
Set-up costs	£1,200,000	3,000 set-ups	£400 per set-up
Handling costs	£1,350,000	1,500 batches	£900 per batch
Other	£1,800,000	100,000 machine hours	£18 per machine hour

		X		
Batch size		400 units		150 units
		£		£
Direct materials	(400 x £20)	8,000	(150 x £30)	4,500
Direct labour	(400 x 0.25 x £8)	800	(150 x 0.5 x £8)	600
Set-up cost	(6 x £400)	2,400	(2 x £400)	800
Handling cost		900		900
Other overheads	(400 x 0.5 x £18)	3,600	(150 x 0.5 x £18)	**1,350**
Full production cost		15,700		**8,150**
Cost per unit		£39.25		**£54.33**

Chapter 5
DEVELOPMENTS IN BUSINESS STRUCTURE AND IT

CHAPTER CONTENTS

This chapter explores the management information needs of a modern business operation and the role that IT plays in satisfying those needs. In particular it explores how developments in business economics, manufacturing practices, management accounting techniques and information technology relate to one another.

Objectives

When you have studied this chapter you should be able to do the following.

- Discuss the changing accounting information needs of a modern service orientated business compared with the needs of a traditional manufacturing industry.
- Discuss how modern IT systems provide the opportunity for instant access to management accounting data throughout an organisation.
- Discuss how modern IT systems facilitate the remote input of management accounting data in an acceptable format by non-finance specialists.
- Explain how modern information systems provide instant access to previously unavailable data that can be used for benchmarking and control purposes.
- Discuss the need for businesses to continually refine and develop their management accounting systems if they are to prosper in an increasingly competitive and global market.
- Identify the particular information needs of organisations adopting a team/project focus.
- Discuss the concept of business integration and the linkage between people, operations, strategy and technology.
- Explain the influence of Business Process Re-engineering on systems development.
- Identify and discuss the required changes in management accounting systems as a consequence of empowering staff to manage sectors of a business.

1 Introduction

In the previous chapter, changes in manufacturing practices were related to new developments in management accounting. In particular, it was seen that as we enter the era of flexible manufacturing with its emphasis on customised service then a range of new management information needs arise. In general, more information is needed and that information needs to be accessed more immediately than was formerly the case. Also, the processing of data to provide management information requires a greater sophistication of technique.

These developments all bring us to the role that IT plays in management accounting.

The use of automated data processing in management information systems has a history which goes back many years. Early forms of mechanical data processing using punched cards were used as early as the 1920s. However, since the 1960s information has been increasingly processed by electronic means.

The most recent developments in computing for management information purposes include the following:

- Improvements in the technology of hardware used. Machines of ever increasing power have become ever cheaper to acquire and easier to use. Telephone modems and network systems are now standard features of office IT. The desk top PC is now a standard feature of any office work station.
- Improvements in the power and user-friendliness of systems available. Word processing, spreadsheet, graphics and database systems are now available which can be used by any educated person with minimal training. Standardisation in systems allows information to be exchanged easily between work stations around the world.
- The advent of satellite telecommunication, the Internet and e-mail allows a mass of external and internal information to be instantly accessed from a work station anywhere in the world.
- The culture of management information has changed. Almost all office workers are now highly computer literate and the desk top PC is now a standard work tool.
- Developments in the economic environment and manufacturing practices (discussed in Chapter 4) create demands for more management information and for that information to be available on a highly flexible basis at all levels in the organisation. The era of stable mass production has given way to the era of flexible production where new products and services are constantly having to be tailored to the individual requirements of the customer.

2 Management information processing

2.1 The three stages of information processing

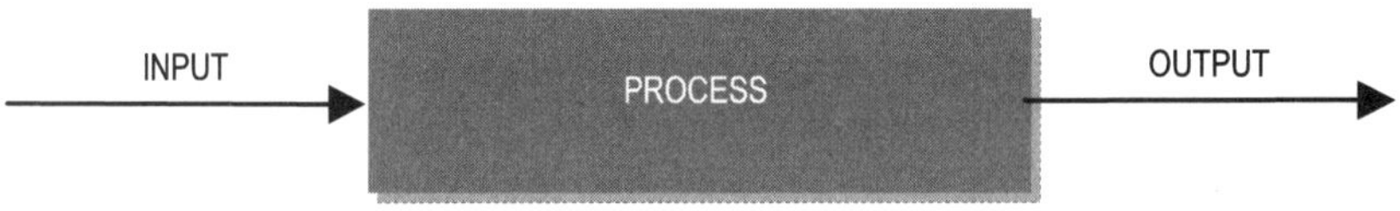

KEY POINT

The processing of information has traditionally been divided into three stages: input, processing, and output.

The processing of information has traditionally been divided into three stages: input, processing, and output. These are often illustrated by a simple diagram:

It is the process activity which converts input data into information which is output to users. All systems follow this principle whether they are computerised or manual systems.

Processing accounting information

The processing of accounting information adheres to the above principle of input, process, output. For example, if we consider a payroll system the three stages would involve:

INPUT	– wage rates	
	– number of hours	
	– PAYE codes	for each employee
	– Tax and NI tables	
PROCESS	– calculate gross pay	
	– calculate deductions	
	– calculate net pay	
OUTPUT	– wage slips (for each employee)	
	– bank/cash analysis	
	– nominal ledger analysis	

2.2 Information levels

KEY POINT

Transaction processing is the information level below that of operational needs. It comprises the most fundamental, routine transactions.

Transaction processing is the information level below that of operational needs. It comprises the most fundamental, routine transactions. Every organisation perceives, documents, and controls such transactions in order to undertake necessary tasks or to assist management in their decision-making. Examples are: invoices and receipts, sales and purchase orders.

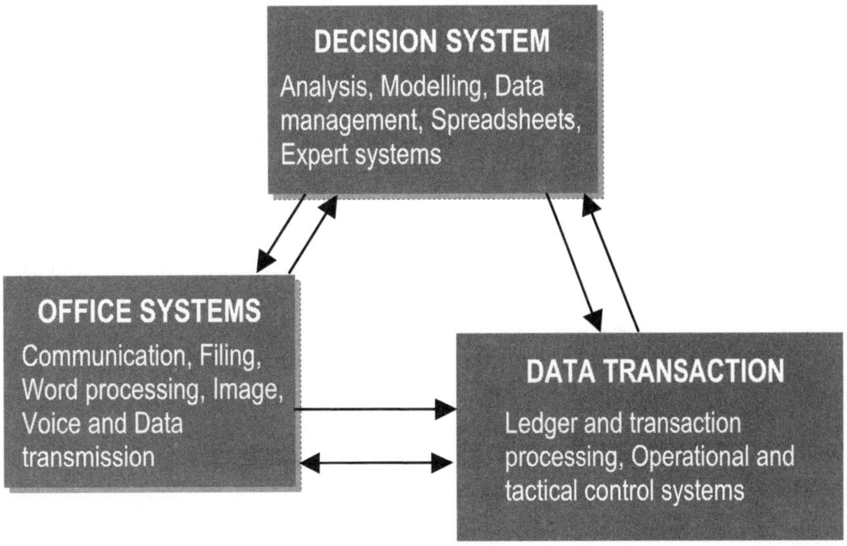

Data is input to the system during the transaction, for example, to amend existing records. In a supermarket, for instance, transaction processing would entail recording the sale and the sum involved, maintaining a continuing total of incoming payments and updating stock levels.

2.3 IT system options

A system may adopt different processing approaches. These include:

- batch processing
- demand processing
- batch-demand processing mix
- on-line.

The approach chosen depends firstly on management requirements. These may be:

- Routine recording of accounts data e.g. purchase ledger, sales ledger, payroll.
- Preparation of regular 'packages' of management information e.g. monthly reports.
- Fact retrieval for decision-making e.g. can customer Y exceed its credit limit? This will also include facts for strategy evolution.

The processing system must also take into account:

- input volumes
- management priorities
- the purpose of the information processed
- response-time (i.e. the time between the collection of the source data and the processing of results).

2.4 Batch processing mode

This is the traditional mode in which data is input to a system for management information purposes. A group of similar (routine) transactions is processed in the same processing-run. Input data could be entered into the system over a period of time, or at the same time. But the actual processing of the data commences only when the transactions data collection is complete and is held in a **transactions file**.

A classic example of batch processing is an organisation's payroll. Typically, the wages section segments transaction records into small batches (e.g. one per department). In this way, most input data is in smaller collections.

The data may accumulate over a given time resulting in a delay before it is all processed at once, for example, when purchase invoices are processed and paid on a monthly basis.

This mode was formerly the major form of processing. It is still the most logical method of dealing with large transaction volumes at a specific time.

Advantages

- Error detection is simpler (facilitated by the nature of the single processing run).
- No special hardware/software is needed (all computer systems should be able to adopt this).
- It contributes to large-scale economies due to bulk processing.
- System design is simple.
- If necessary, part may be processed now and the remainder later.

Disadvantages

- The system is 'time-driven' and so is not geared to rapid action.
- The system provides bulk information and so is not selective.
- Preparing batches results in duplication of effort.

The method of input is usually by disk or tape for the encoding of transactions. This is also the transactions file input medium.

Demand processing mode

This is undertaken when a transaction must be processed straightaway, and delay through batch processing cannot be allowed. It is often referred to as **transaction-processing**. Here, the user literally processes 'on demand'.

This may arise due to:

- a request for information from transaction files (e.g. the amount owed by a customer)
- the decision to pay a large account immediately (e.g. if previously delayed because of an error)
- recording of an infrequent or special activity.

Batch-demand processing 'mix'

Various combinations of batch and demand processing can occur. The 'mixes' are:

- batch input/processing of all transactions (including such activities as file enquiries and updating activity)
- batch input/processing of all transactions, plus file enquiries on-line

DEFINITION

RJE is the transmission of user data for processing from an on-line terminal.

- remote job entry (RJE) plus batch processing and on-line file enquiry (RJE is the transmission of user data for processing from an on-line terminal)
- on-line (including real-time (OLRT) updating) and on-line enquiry, allowing data input from remote terminals, the updating of the relevant master file on an immediate basis, and *ad hoc* file enquiries as necessary.

The next section will clarify the 'on-line' and 'OLRT' references.

2.5 On-line mode

KEY POINT

A system is referred to as 'on-line' when the data is input directly to the computer from the point of origination, and where the output is transmitted to the user's location.

An on-line system which processes the input immediately is said to be operating in **real time**.

The **response time** is the period within which the computer is able to carry out the input instruction transmitted from the terminal.

A system is referred to as 'on-line' when the data is input directly to the computer from the point of origination, and where the output is transmitted to the user's location. This involves **data communications**.

An on-line system may be **batch-based**. This permits input to be held in backing storage so that processing may be subsequently carried out during an off-peak period. An on-line system which processes the input immediately is said to be operating in **real time**.

The **response time** is the period within which the computer is able to carry out the input instruction transmitted from the terminal. This usually includes transmitting the result back to the terminal.

Good examples of such a system are ground-to-air missile control, or a bank's cashpoint dispenser.

Advantages of the real-time system

- A higher level of customer satisfaction is achieved (e.g. the real-time banking system).
- Information needed is obtained by adopting very simple procedures.
- Prompt and early information assists in improving and maintaining the quality of management decisions.

Disadvantages

- The system is relatively high-cost (in terms of hardware and software required, installation, and essential storage).
- A high level of security is required (e.g. the OLRT bank cash dispenser).
- To avoid loss should the system fail ('go down'), duplicate processors and files are needed.
- System failure could cause great organisational problems.

The advent of computer networks which connect many terminals at remote locations probably makes on-line and real-time systems more attractive. There may be little point in operating an on-line system until access to data in the system is widely available.

At the same time, customer service demands have changed. The need to respond to customer needs promptly, in both manufacturing and service environments, has also been associated with a move to on-line systems.

ACTIVITY 1

When deciding on the type of processing to use, what considerations would you take account of?

Feedback to this activity is at the end of the chapter.

3 Accounting systems

3.1 Management accounting information and software packages

KEY POINT

Software packages may be specially written or they may be purchased 'off the shelf.'

Software packages may be specially written or they may be purchased 'off the shelf.' The difference between these is that those purchased 'off the shelf' are designed so as to be useful to many different businesses and they have the advantage of being thoroughly tested before being sold. Specialist software packages are very expensive in comparison because they are written for a single user who will be heavily involved in the testing of the package.

Using standard systems (such as the ubiquitous Microsoft Office or Sage Accounting suites) also allows easy exchange of information between different entities and organisations. The flexible economy has created a situation where management work of all sorts is 'contracted out' to small specialist firms. Such contracting is made much easier by widespread use of common office systems. This is but one illustration of the link between technology and culture.

Program suites

Most packages are written in modules which may be thought of as sub-systems within the overall package. These modules link together to produce a comprehensive accounting system from which management reports may be obtained. The modules which are most commonly found in such systems include:

- sales accounting
- purchases
- cash/bank
- fixed assets
- nominal ledger.

The next two paragraphs consider the sales and purchases systems in more detail.

3.2 A sales accounting system

Scope

This system is designed to deal with:

- order processing
- preparation of daily invoices and despatch notes
- cash-posting
- preparation of sales analysis reports
- monthly ledger balancing and statements preparation.

In addition the system will provide various error and exception reports. Some of these will be available by screen display only. Others will be in the form of printouts. For example, a system might be configured as follows:

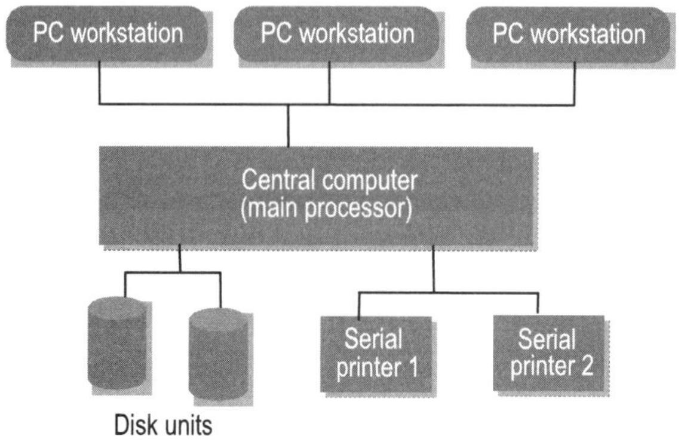

The main processor will also provide a server which allows Internet access from the PC workstations if required. One feature in the design of modern management accounting systems is that data can be loaded locally by staff who have no IT expertise. The use of forms and coding systems allows transactions to be posted correctly. Aspects of information security were discussed in Chapter 2.

Files

The example system is based on two **master files** – a customer master file and a product master file. The files are designed to provide direct access, and the data items associated with each file are as follows:

Customer		*Product*	
Description	*Number of characters*	*Description*	*Number of characters*
Account no.	8	Part no.	8
Name	20	Description	12
Address	20	Made in/bought out indicator	2
Credit limit	6	Main supplier code	8
Agent no.	5	Standard cost per unit	8
Sales, year to date	10	Standard price per unit	8
Balance	10	Maximum quantity	8
Balance × 30 days	10	Minimum quantity	8
Balance × 60 days	10	Reorder quantity	8
Balance × 90 days	10	Balance in hand	10
Date last paid	8	Total receipts this period	15
Bad debt indicator	2	Total issues this period	15
Overdue a/c indicator	2	Date of last issue	8

Processes

(a) **Order** – All orders whether for cash or credit are input and validated for:

- correct stock code
- stock availability
- account on order (credit items only).

The operator performs the relevant operation via a menu and appropriate screen dialogues (see Figure below). From the main sales ledger menu the user can key '1' in order to get to the Order Processing screen.

SALES LEDGER SYSTEM	
1	Order processing
2	Cash payments
3	Journals
4	New/amended account details
5	Account display
6	Month-end routines
Select option number 1 - 6	

Screen menu

ORDER PROCESSING	
Order number	
Date	
Cash/credit	
Customer number	
Stock number	
Quantity	
Correct Y/N	'Y'
Press 9 to continue Q to end	'Q'

Screen dialogue

When the order details have been entered and stored, the fields are cleared to permit the operator to enter the next order.

Once the order is complete, the program evaluates it by multiplying quantities by prices and summing for all the products. VAT is computed as appropriate. If the resulting transaction value is greater than that permitted by the customer's credit limit then the order is rejected. A printout of rejected orders is generated for follow-up by sales staff.

If the order is accepted, an invoice/despatch note record is created on a file which is periodically printed out. This may be shown on a **systems overview chart.**

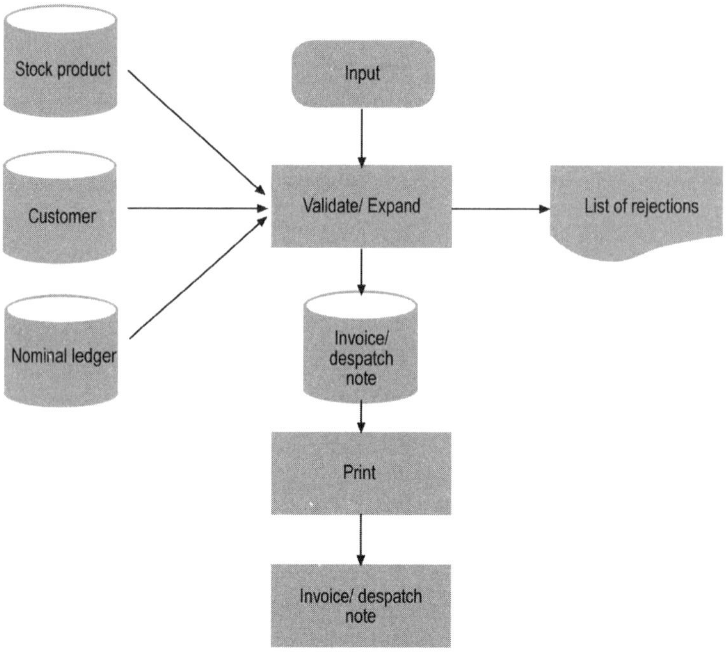

Each time an order is processed the stock file and debtor (customer) file are **updated**. The nominal ledger containing the sales account and the ledger control account is also updated. The invoice file can be used by various **report-writing** routines to generate:

- a VAT extract for the VAT return
- a sales analysis for month-end reporting
- a cost of sales reconciliation for monthly stock control.

(b) **Cash** – is identified with orders (if we are dealing with cash transactions) or with account numbers (if we are dealing with credit customers). Most commercial companies maintain their ledger files on an **open-item** system, in which sub-files are maintained of all open or uncleared items i.e. there is no opening balance.

If an open-item system is kept, all cash transactions have also to be identified with individual transactions or the system 'throws them out' as unallocated. This affects the ability of the program logic to 'age' the ledger balances when producing a monthly statement.

(c) **Journals** – The system has a facility for entering journal items. These are used for:

- making transfers between accounts (in the event of mis-coding a cash payment)
- adjusting for discounts or write-offs.

Outputs

The typical outputs from the system are:

(a) **Invoices** – These are produced on a printer to give near-letter quality (NLQ) results. The system provides continuous numbering (to avoid the problems of sequential control of pre-printed paper).

(b) **Statements/remittance advice** – The statement/remittance advice is a turnaround document. The open-item ledger allows all debits and credits to be itemised on the remittance advice as well as on the statement. The remittance advice can then be utilised as a source document for cash-posting purposes when it is returned by the customer.

(c) **Sales reports and audit trail reports** – The system produces:

(i) daily listings and totals of invoices
(ii) daily cash-posting reports
(iii) monthly sales analysis reports
(iv) monthly reconciliation of the debtors' ledger comprising:

- opening balance
- invoices
- cash
- journals
- closing balance.

3.3 Using spreadsheets and databases in management accounting

KEY POINT

Spreadsheets and databases are both systems which may be used to store, sort, retrieve and manipulate data.

Spreadsheets and databases are both systems which may be used to store, sort, retrieve and manipulate data.

3.4 What is a spreadsheet?

The computer spreadsheet is now such a ubiquitous feature of the modern business world that the reader is assumed to have a reasonable familiarity with it. You are well advised at this point to inspect the spreadsheet system which will almost certainly be installed on your PC at work or at home.

3.5 Advantages and disadvantages of spreadsheets

KEY POINT

The advantages of spreadsheets include:

- data is easily manipulated
- the data can be formatted and printed to suit the needs of the user
- the user may identify different outcome possibilities by using the 'what-if' facility.

This is a heading that has traditionally appeared in many accounting texts and manuals. It relates to an era when the computer spreadsheet was a new development that was compared with the pencil and paper approaches that preceded it. On this basis, the advantages of spreadsheets include:

- data is easily manipulated, changes in one item of data being quickly recalculated throughout the spreadsheet
- the data can be formatted and printed to suit the needs of the user. This may be in the form of reports, tables of values, or graphs which may be linked together
- the user may identify different outcome possibilities by using the 'what-if' facility. This would often be too time consuming to be done manually, thus the spreadsheet brings computer modelling to the data user.

Of course, these advantages are all relative to manual preparation of information. There are other alternatives where the advantages are less clear cut.

KEY POINT

The following disadvantages can be identified:

- data can be accidentally changed
- errors in design, particularly in the use of formulae, can produce invalid output
- the manipulation of the data using such a mathematical approach may lead to the loss of the original concepts.

There are some apparent disadvantages to the use of spreadsheets. Spreadsheets take time to develop and it is important to ensure that this is to be time well spent. There is no benefit in taking many hours to develop a spreadsheet which is then only used occasionally to complete a task which could easily be done efficiently using a manual method. In addition, the following disadvantages can be identified:

(a) data can be accidentally changed (or deleted) without the user being aware of this occurring

(b) errors in design, particularly in the use of formulae, can produce invalid output. Due to the complexity of the model, these design errors may be difficult to locate

(c) the manipulation of the data using such a mathematical approach may lead to the loss of the original concepts, these being replaced with a seemingly accurate set of output reports. In the context of budgets and forecasts it must be remembered that such output is based on data which are estimates and which may therefore be incorrect.

The critical thing to understand about a spreadsheet is that it is a personal productivity tool. Problems in the use of spreadsheets often arise when people try to do things with them for which they are not well suited. For example, the production of a budget in a large, complex organisation may be undertaken using a family of linked spreadsheets – the individual spreadsheets being maintained by different individuals in the organisation. Such an arrangement is 'user-friendly' and easy to set up. But it may cause a variety of problems, which are discussed below.

3.6 What is a database?

KEY POINT

A database consists of a number of files, each containing information on a similar topic. Each file comprises a number of records which individually contain fields which hold data relating to a specific item within the file.

A database consists of a number of files, each containing information on a similar topic. Each file comprises a number of records which individually contain fields which hold data relating to a specific item within the file. For example a vehicle maintenance/service organisation may use a database for the work it provides. There could be two files:

- for jobs which are completed
- for jobs which are in progress.

There would be a record for each job which would be uniquely identified by a job number. The record would contain fields for:

- vehicle registration number
- description of work
- date work started
- date job completed
- number of hours
- details of parts used
- cost incurred.

In practice this would be much more detailed than the outline example above but this should enable you to understand the relationship between files, records and fields within a database.

The database is the essential component of an accounting system. Each entry in the system is a record. Typically, each record will be coded and then the codes are used to sort records to produce information in the manner required.

ACTIVITY 2

Obtain access to a database system (such as Microsoft Access) on your own PC. Construct a database to store the names, addresses, telephone numbers and e-mail addresses of your friends.

There is no feedback to this activity.

3.7 Advantages and disadvantages of databases

KEY POINT

The advantage of databases is their ability to manipulate data.

The advantage of databases is their ability to manipulate data; many people would suggest that they are more powerful than spreadsheets. Mathematical functions may be carried out on values contained within fields, and searching/sorting of data may be used to produce meaningful reports. For example, in the context of the vehicle maintenance/service organisation referred to above, the files could be searched to produce a report showing the details of all work carried out on a particular vehicle between specified dates.

KEY POINT

The disadvantages of databases are that they are often very complex, and there is a large amount of time required to structure them appropriately.

The disadvantages of databases are that they are often very complex, and there is a large amount of time required to structure them appropriately. Often once the structure has been defined, it is very difficult to modify it, without losing some of the data previously stored.

Database systems are presently being developed which take the place of spreadsheets in some tasks. Budgeting is one of these. Until recently, many large organisations conducted budgeting using complex spreadsheet based systems. Each budget centre would have its own budget spreadsheet linked into other spreadsheets. An update in one spreadsheet would automatically update the others. Problems with this approach are:

- it is often difficult to detect where updates have been made and who has entered the updates
- the logic involved in linking layers of spreadsheets is notoriously complex and error prone
- while 'bottom up' adjustments are easy to accommodate, 'top down' adjustments may be more difficult; this may make sensitivity and 'what if?' analysis (key elements in modern budgeting) very tricky.

In short, it is very easy for a complex spreadsheet based system to turn into a "dog's breakfast".

One of the fastest growing areas in accounting software supply in recent years has been in budgeting systems. Database systems such as Hyperion Pillar and Comshare Budget Commander have been designed to provide a comprehensive answer to the budgeting problems of the large organisation. The records used to input data are coded in a manner that allows both master budget and profit centre budgets to be extracted. The coding also identifies the source of the entry. The centralised nature of the database allows both top down and bottom up adjustments to be made with ease.

The central database holding the budget can be accessed from remote locations but appropriate security coding can be arranged for some categories of item (e.g. 'management salaries'). Modern budget systems allow data to be inserted and information extracted easily by all potential users. Further, the means of data input and information output are user friendly. No specialised IT skill is needed to work with them.

One of the traditional advantages claimed for the spreadsheet is that it is simple for the user to input data without any special training – and the output of the system is almost self evident. The output is achieved simply by inspecting the spreadsheet.

However, modern developments in database systems almost eliminate these advantages. The budget systems referred to above allow data to be input in a simple tabular form and retrieved in the same way.

4 The impact of IT on modern management accounting

It is widely accepted that IT has greatly influenced the way in which businesses are run. Databases, networks and the Internet all make it possible to directly access and manipulate information from both internal and external sources. In the modern business environment (see Chapter 4), managers are constantly having to receive customer enquiries concerning product availability and price. Instant access to cost and resource availability information is therefore crucial to providing a customer centred service.

Many of the more modern forms of management accounting have been developed in conjunction with IT systems. For example a traditional overhead costing system, using a labour hour overhead absorption base, may make few information demands. However, a more sophisticated ABC system makes much more elaborate information demands. It might be difficult to run a meaningful ABC system without IT support.

KEY POINT

'E-commerce' is a form of business which provides a great deal of power to the customer. It is easy for the customer to conduct a web based search for alternative suppliers, so only the supplier who meets world standards will survive in the long run.

Not only have IT systems changed the way in which businesses are run, but they have changed the nature of the business. 'E-commerce' is a form of business which provides a great deal of power to the customer. It is easy for the customer to conduct a web based search for alternative suppliers, so only the supplier who meets world standards will survive in the long run. World standards implies not only low costs but also a fast and full response to customer needs. In order to survive a business needs to be constantly updating its information systems and developing the IT capabilities of its staff.

For both decision-making and control purposes the management may draw on external information databases. To explore a few examples of these, you may care to visit the following free web sites:

Yahoo! (full records on 9,000 quoted US companies)

www.yahoo.com

Enter the main Yahoo! website, then go to Yahoo Finance. This provides a mass of financial information including an Annual Report Service. It allows the annual financial reports of many US companies to be instantly downloaded, free of charge, in pdf format. This sort of information can be used both to compare the performance of your own business with that of others (benchmarking) and to provide information on the market for decision-making purposes.

FindArticles (search facilities on a large number of professional and academic journals)

www.findarticles.com

Entering the FindArticles website allows you to undertake subject, author or keyword searches on articles from a large number of published sources. It provides a good starting point for research into any area.

Most newspapers have search facilities on their websites which allows the visitor to seek articles on particular topics. Typically, such search facilities are free but some newspapers (e.g. the Financial Times) require a paid subscription for unrestricted access. Large business libraries (mostly attached to universities) will have access to electronic databases of journals and newspapers. Such libraries usually restrict free membership to students, staff and alumni, but will provide access to professional people either upon application and/or on payment of a small fee.

www.companieshouse.gov.uk

Companies House in the UK provides full on-line details for all limited companies including annual financial reports. Some of this material is provided free but some is provided only on payment of a fee for each request.

5 The impact of structure and culture on information needs

5.1 Use made of management accounting information

KEY POINT

The management accounting information system is a structured formal information system, and concentrates its attention on the regular quantifiable parts of the management process.

The management accounting information system is a structured formal information system, and concentrates its attention on the regular quantifiable parts of the management process. The analysis above indicates that these activities are only parts of the management process; informal information is at least as important. A study by Dew and Gee (1973) of 85 managers indicated the following use of budgets:

	No.
Full use	12
Limited use	35
No use	38
Total	85

Thus the largest group made no use at all of the budgets, and only 12 made full use of the budgets.

A further study by Mintzberg (1975) revealed a significant difference in the perception of the purpose of cost information by senior and middle manager, respectively. Whilst senior managers saw its prime purpose as a control tool for managers, middle managers saw cost information as a measure of personal (i.e. their) efficiency.

This led Mintzberg to the conclusion that four major factors reduced the effectiveness of formal information systems:

- Too limited - weak on external information, ignores non-quantitative and non-economic information.
- Too aggregated - data is summarised and aggregated to the point where essential detail is often missing.
- Too late - often the information arrives too late to be useful.
- Unreliable - often numbers are put in to represent information that is essentially qualitative.

Given these problems, Mintzberg makes certain recommendations about formal information:

- Broad based - independent of the computer (remember this was written in 1975 when computer output used to be large quantities of badly designed output; this is hardly a realistic recommendation today).
- Filtering systems - these should be more sophisticated than merely aggregating data, so as to leave in important detail and remove irrelevant detail.
- Channels of information should be capable of in-depth searching, and should encourage alternative, conflicting sources of information.

These conclusions on the design of accounting information systems are best summarised by Emmanuel and Otley:

'(The designer) must be aware of the organisational and environmental situation in which he is designing the information system, and its inter-relationships with other mechanisms of integration and control. He must also be responsive to the political process in which accounting information plays a role, for the accounting system will inevitably be moulded by such pressures.'

5.2 Information for management

Information should be provided to managers at all levels in order to assist them with planning and controlling the activities for which they are responsible. Information will be gathered from all relevant sources (internal and external) in order to help managers make timely and effective decisions.

It is very difficult to generalise further on the principles of presenting information to managers. There are many influencing factors, including:

- The objectives of the organisation.
- The size and diversity of its operations.
- Management structure.
- Management style e.g.

  (i) Centralised or decentralised
  (ii) Authoritarian or participative
- The types of decisions which are made.
- The degree to which the organisation is an open system and interacts with its environment.

The general thrust of this is that the provision of management accounting information is linked to the culture and structure of the organisation.

KEY POINT

Two of the most significant developments in organisation and management structure are Total Quality Management ('TQM') and Business Process Re-engineering ('BPR').

Two of the most significant developments in organisation and management structure are Total Quality Management (TQM) and Business Process Re-engineering (BPR). These two approaches are closely linked – involving the analysis of method, organisation and technology used in business in order to provide maximum possible value to customers. They also both involve the idea of empowering individual workers and groups of workers. They also both involve a move to a team or project work orientation.

TQM is also closely linked to JIT (see Chapter 4). High levels of quality assurance are implicit in JIT. It is impossible to operate with low levels of stock without high quality standards. High stock levels are often used to compensate for poor quality.

The two recurring themes that run through the literature of the 'TQM movement' are teams and empowerment. The team approach is in such descriptions of TQM as it being a ballet rather than a hockey game. TQM is also closely associated with employee empowerment through the ability to make decisions being widely distributed through the organisation regardless of rank.

This approach impacts on the supply of management accounting information.

6 Total quality management

6.1 Quality as strategic variable

In recent times a great deal of attention has been devoted to quality issues. Although there has always been a general awareness of the need to ensure the satisfaction of the customer, it is the worldwide nature of competition that has focused attention on the need to act. Competitor pressure has often come from the Japanese, whose basic premise is that poor quality is unacceptable.

The term 'quality' is difficult to define because it has a wide range of meanings, covering a large and complex area of businesses and processes. Quality is also a matter of perception and relative measure. For example, if you asked a group of people to each nominate a 'quality sound system', it could be that you would get a different suggestion from each of them.

The Japanese have shown, with their highly competitive products, that high quality does not always mean high cost. The response in the West to improve quality is still really in its infancy.

6.2 Quality equals profit

The evidence of the value that customers place on quality is all around us. For many years, both in the UK and the US, every survey of car quality showed Japanese producers way ahead. For ten years after establishing the PIMS database, the researchers argued that market share was the best way to achieve profits. But a re-analysis of the data showed that, while high market share does bring profit, sustainable market share comes from leadership in perceived product or service quality. The PIMS researchers now call relative quality i.e. vis-à-vis competitors, the most important single factor affecting a business unit's long-term performance.

One feature of traditional management accounting is that it may not report the cost of quality failure. Poor quality work results in costs, but those costs may be 'buried' at several points in the management accounting system and thus not be specifically reported. The costs of quality failure may include:

- internally rejected and test failed units
- compensation/replacement for units rejected and returned by customers
- rectification costs
- compensation for units failed in service with customers
- loss of customer goodwill and market reputation.

KEY POINT

The adoption of a TQM approach is likely to require the provision of cost of quality control reports.

The adoption of a TQM approach is likely to require the provision of cost of quality control reports. This involves identifying the costs of quality failure and collecting them together for management information and reporting purposes. It is only when the costs of quality are known that the measures needed to achieve and maintain high quality can be justified.

6.3 Quality management

Quality management suggests a concern that the organisation's products or services meet their planned level of quality and perform to specifications. Management has a duty to ensure that all tasks are completed consistently to a standard which meets the needs of the business. To achieve this they need to:

- set clear standards
- plan how to meet those standards
- track the quality achieved
- take action to improve quality where necessary.

Setting standards

To manage quality everyone in the organisation needs to have a clear and shared understanding of the standards required. These standards will be set after taking account of:

- the quality expected by the customers
- the costs and benefits of delivering different degrees of quality
- the impact of different degrees of quality on:
  - (i) the customers and their needs
  - (ii) contribution to departmental objectives

(iii) employee attitude and motivation.

Having decided on the standards these must be communicated to everyone concerned to ensure that the right standards are achieved. Documentation of the standards must be clear, specific, measurable and comprehensive.

Meeting the standards

Having decided on appropriate quality standards management should then:

- agree and document procedures and methods to meet the standards
- agree and document controls to ensure that the standards will be met
- agree and document responsibilities via job descriptions and terms of reference
- prepare and implement training plans for employees to ensure they are familiar with the standards, procedures, controls and their responsibilities.

Tracking the quality

After the process to achieve quality has been set up, an information system to monitor the quality should be set up. This is called quality control.

When a good system to track the quality has been achieved, it can be used constructively to improve quality and work on problem areas.

Employees within the organisation have a huge influence on the quality of their work and to gain their commitment and support the management should:

- publish the quality being achieved
- meet regularly with the staff involved to discuss the quality being achieved as well as the vulnerabilities and priorities as they see them and also agree specific issues and action points for them to work on to improve quality
- encourage ideas from the staff about improvements and consider introducing short-term suggestion schemes.

6.4 Quality revolution

Tom Peters in his book *Thriving on Chaos*, concentrates on the twelve attributes of a quality revolution:

- Management obsessed with quality
- A guiding system or ideology
- Quality is measured
- Reward for quality
- Training in technologies for assessing qualities
- Teams involving multiple functions or systems are used
- Concentration on small improvements
- Constant stimulation
- Creation of a shadow or parallel organisation structure devoted to quality improvement
- Everyone is involved. Suppliers especially, but distributors and customers too, must be a part of the organisation's quality process
- Quality improvement is the primary source of cost reduction
- Quality improvement is a never-ending journey.

These are traits which companies like IBM, Ford and Federal Express share in their quality improvement programs.

Peters argues that most quality programs fail for one of two reasons: they have a system without passion, or passion without a system. The type of system to follow, and the results obtained, causes some controversy. There are many ideologies used in quality processes. Let us just consider one of them, its leading 'guru' being Deming.

6.5 W Edwards Deming

In the 1920s and 1930s in America, statistical quality control methods were used to monitor and control the quality of output in flow line production processes.

These methods, the origins of modern quality management, were introduced into Japan by American consultants like Deming, who were involved in the aid program to rejuvenate the industry in Japan after the war.

Some companies (and governments) blame unions for having a negative impact on worker productivity. Deming insists that management is 90% of the problem. Organisations need to address the problems of the quality of direction being given to the workforce, the resources available to get the job done efficiently and the opportunities for workers to contribute ideas about how to do the job better.

Deming, in his book *Quality, Productivity and Competitive Position*, suggests that improving quality leads to improved productivity, reduced costs, more satisfied customers and increased profitability. His system for management to improve quality and competitiveness covers the following main areas:

- The organisation should have a constant purpose of improving their product or service.
- Quality objectives should be agreed and action taken to accomplish them.
- Systems for production and service delivery should be improved, eliminating all waste.
- Consideration of quality and reliability should be just as important as price when choosing a supplier.
- Attention must be paid to training people so they are better at their jobs and understand how to optimise production.
- Mass inspection of goods ties up resources and does not improve quality.
- Education and self improvement should be encouraged in all members of the organisation. Management should enable staff to take a pride in their work.
- Barriers between staff areas should be broken down.

6.6 The difference between quality control and quality assurance

Quality control is the title given to the more traditional view of quality. It may be defined as the process of:

- establishing standards of quality for a product or service
- establishing procedures or production methods which ought to ensure that these required standards of quality are met in a suitably high proportion of cases
- monitoring actual quality
- taking control action when actual quality falls below standard.

Quality assurance, however, is the term used where a supplier guarantees the quality of goods supplied and allows the customer access while the goods are being manufactured. This is usually done through supplier quality assurance (SQA) officers, who control the specification of the goods supplied.

Some companies follow Japanese practice and use supervisors, work people or quality circles to control suppliers' quality. These representatives or the SQA officer may enter the supplier's plant, to verify that production is to the correct specification, working tolerances, material and labour standards. For example, the Ministry of Defence would reserve the right to ensure that defence contractors produce to specification, since defective work could mean the failure of a multi-million pound aircraft, loss of trained pilots and possibly ground crew as well as damage to civilian life and property. Likewise, a weapons system failure could have disastrous consequences.

One great advantage of SQA is that it may render possible reduction of the in-house quality control headcount, since there will be no need to check incoming materials or sub-assemblies or components.

6.7 Quality control

DEFINITION

Quality control is concerned with maintaining quality standards.

Quality control is concerned with maintaining quality standards. There are usually procedures to check quality of bought-in materials, work-in-progress and finished goods. Sometimes one or all of these functions is the responsibility of the research and development department on the premise that production should not self-regulate its own quality.

Statistical quality control through sampling techniques is commonly used to reduce costs and production interruptions. On some occasions, where quality assurance has been given, customers have the contractual right to visit a manufacturer unannounced and carry out quality checks. This is normal practice with Sainsbury's and Tesco's contracts with manufacturers producing 'own label' goods (e.g. Tesco Baked Beans).

In the past, failure to screen quality successfully has resulted in rejections, re-work and scrap, all of which add to manufacturing costs. Modern trends in industry of competition, mass production and increasing standards of quality requirements have resulted in a thorough reappraisal of the problem and two important points have emerged:

- It is necessary to single out and remove the causes for poor quality goods before production instead of waiting for the end result. Many companies have instigated 'zero defects' programmes following the Japanese practice of eradicating poor quality as early in the chain as possible and insisting on strict quality adherence at every stage – as Crosby points out in his book *Quality is Free*, this is cost effective since customer complaints etc, reduce dramatically.
- The co-ordination of all activities from the preparation of the specification, through to the purchasing and inspection functions and right up to the function of delivery of the finished product, is essential.

It is accepted that it is not possible to achieve perfection in products because of the variations in raw material quality, operating skills, different types of machines used, wear and tear etc, but quality control attempts to ascertain the amount of variation from perfect that can be expected in any operation. If this variation is acceptable according to engineering requirements, then production must be established within controlled limits and if the variation is too great then corrective action must be taken to bring it within acceptable limits.

6.8 Approaches to TQM

KEY POINT

Total quality management (TQM) is the name given to programmes which seek to ensure that goods are produced and services are supplied of the highest quality.

Total quality management (TQM) is the name given to programmes which seek to ensure that goods are produced and services are supplied of the highest quality. Its origin lies primarily in Japanese organisations and it is argued that TQM has been a significant factor in Japanese global business success. The basic principle of TQM is that costs of prevention (getting things right first time) are less than the costs of correction.

KEY POINT

The basic principle of TQM is that costs of prevention (getting things right first time) are less than the costs of correction.

This contrasts with the 'traditional' UK approach that less than 100% quality is acceptable as the costs of improvement from say 90% to 100% outweigh the benefits. Thus in the analysis of quality related costs there may be a trade-off between a lowering of failure (internal and external) at the expense of increased prevention and appraisal costs.

Which view is correct is a matter of debate but the advocates of TQM would argue that in addition to the cost analysis above the impact of less than 100% quality in terms of lost potential for future sales also has to be taken into account.

6.9 Features of TQM

The philosophy of TQM is based on the idea of a series of quality chains which may be broken at any point by one person or service not meeting the requirements of the customer.

The key to TQM is for everyone in the organisation to have well-defined customers - an extension of the word, beyond the customers of the company, to anyone to whom an individual provides a service. Thus the 'Paint shop' staff would be customers of the 'Assembly shop' staff who would themselves be the customers of the 'Machine shop' staff. The idea is that the supplier-customer relationships would form a chain extending from the company's original suppliers through to its ultimate consumers. Areas of responsibility would need to be identified and a manager allocated to each, and then the customer/supplier chain established. True to the principle outlined above the quality requirements of each 'customer' within the chain would be assessed, and meeting these would then become the responsibility of the 'suppliers' who form the preceding link in the chain.

Quality has to be managed – it will not just happen. To meet the requirements of TQM a company will probably need to recruit more staff and may also need to change the level of services on offer to its customers, which includes 'internal' customers. This would probably entail costs in terms of the redesign of systems, recruitment and training of staff, and the purchase of appropriate equipment.

Thackray indicated the following features of companies which follow TQM:

- There is absolute commitment by the chief executive and all senior managers to doing what is needed to change the culture.
- People are not afraid to try new things.
- Communication is excellent and multi-way.
- There is a real commitment to continuous improvement in all processes.
- Attention is focused first on the process and second on the results.
- There is an absence of strict control systems.

The last two points may appear to go against the central thrust of traditional UK management accounting. The point being made is that concentrating on getting a process right will result in an improved result. A process is a detailed step in the overall system of producing and delivering goods to a customer. Improving a process without worrying about the short-term effects will encourage the search for improvement to take place, the improvement will more likely be permanent, and will lead to further improvements. A concentration on results and control generally means attaching blame to someone if things go wrong. Therefore employees would not have an incentive to pick up and correct errors but rather would be encouraged to try and conceal them.

6.10 Analysis and restructuring of resources

DEFINITION

Discretionary activities are activities such as checking, chasing and other tasks related to product failures.

In many businesses, employees' time is used up in **discretionary activities**. Discretionary activities are activities such as checking, chasing and other tasks related to product failures. Some/most of this time may be capable of being redeployed into the two other categories of work:

- Core activities
- Support activities.

KEY POINT

Core activities add direct value to the business. They use the specific skills of the particular employees being examined and are the reason for their employment. Support activities are those activities which clearly support core activities and are thus necessary to allow core activities to add value.

Core activities add direct value to the business. They use the specific skills of the particular employees being examined and are the reason for their employment. Support activities are those activities which clearly support core activities and are thus necessary to allow core activities to add value. The importance of this analysis can be seen in a quote from a US Chief Executive some years ago: 'The only things you really need to run a business are materials, machines, workers and salesmen. Nobody else is justified unless he's helping the worker produce more product or the salesman sell more product.'

One of the principal features of BPR (discussed below) is the rearrangement of working practices to concentrate resources on value adding activities in a business.

Analysis of employees' time will provide a clearer view of the costs of poor quality and whether efforts in other departments could reduce the amount of time spent by a department further down the product chain on discretionary activities. For example, suppose there are seven processes from purchasing of raw materials through various stages of production to delivery of the product to the customer. If each process is 90% effective then there will be only a 48% success rate at the end of the seventh stage (90% × 90% × 90% etc). What happens in practice however may be that personnel employed in stage 4 of the process spend a lot of their time on discretionary activities trying to remedy the effect of defects at earlier stages. It is suggested that it would be more sensible for departments in the earlier stages to get things right the first time.

An example has been quoted of an office equipment supplier which analysed employees' time into core, support and discretionary activities. It was found that half of the salesmen's face-to-face selling time with customers consisted of listening to their complaints about poor customer service.

6.11 Quality circles

Quality circles consist of about ten employees possessing relevant levels of skill, ranging from the shop-floor through to management. They meet regularly to discuss the major aspect of quality, but other areas such as safety and productivity will also be dealt with.

The main aim is to be able to offer management:

- ideas connected with improvement and recommendation
- possible solutions and suggestions
- organising the implementation of the above.

KEY POINT

The development of Quality circles allows the process of decision-making to start at shop floor level, with the ordinary worker encouraged to comment and make suggestions, as well as being allowed to put them into practice.

The development of Quality circles allows the process of decision-making to start at shop floor level, with the ordinary worker encouraged to comment and make suggestions, as well as being allowed to put them into practice. Circle members experience the responsibility for ensuring quality, and have the power to exercise verbal complaint. Quality circles may be applied at any level of organisational activity, being used to cover all aspects and could conceivably involve all employees.

Jaguar, the established motor company, has used this system effectively resulting in the involvement of ten percent of the workforce. A notable point here is that in one decade the number of quality inspectors required has been roughly halved. Clearly, quality circles are a practical means of gaining employee participation, they are not mainly for reducing costs although this aspect will be a major topic for discussion. Other benefits are increased awareness of shop-floor problems, members gain confidence over problem solving etc, greater output, improved quality and shop-floor participation.

Equally, putting this system into practice can prove difficult. The well established system of hierarchical management is difficult to penetrate, and to some organisations it would present extreme changes. Some systems may not be able to accommodate such change e.g. the armed forces or Police Force where a powerful hierarchy has developed.

6.12 A total quality programme

The characteristics of a total quality programme should include the following:

- Everyone in the organisation is involved in continually improving the processes and systems under their control and each person is responsible for his or her own quality assurance.
- A commitment to the satisfaction of every customer.
- Employee involvement is practised and the active participation of everyone in the organisation is encouraged.
- There is an investment in training and education to realise individual potential.
- Teamwork is used in a number of forms e.g. quality circles.
- Suppliers and customers form an integrated part of the process of improvement.
- Process re-design is used to simplify processes, systems, procedures and the organisation itself.

6.13 Performance measurement in a TQM environment

Inputs may be in the form of materials from suppliers and skills and efficiency from the employees of the organisation.

KEY POINT

Targets or benchmarks must be set against which the performance of suppliers can be measured.

Outputs too must be measured for quality against pre-determined targets.

Customer reaction may be measured by number of customer complaints, the percentage of returned goods and similar factors.

Targets or benchmarks must be set against which the performance of suppliers can be measured. These may include delivery times, rejection rates, the percentage of incorrect/short deliveries and similar measures.

Outputs too must be measured for quality against pre-determined targets. Such targets may be based on the number of rejects as a result of internal inspection procedures, but customer reaction is also important. Customer reaction may be measured by number of customer complaints, the percentage of returned goods and similar factors.

Use of control charts

An example of a control chart is shown below:

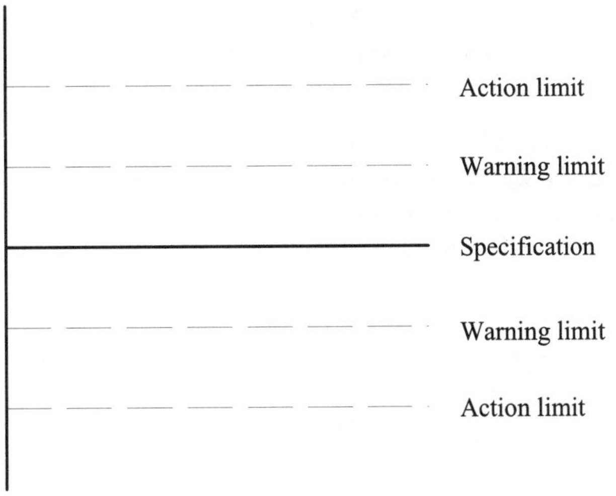

The specification or target shows what is expected in respect of the particular performance measure which is measured along the vertical (y) axis. The horizontal (x) axis is normally used to represent time. Individual values are plotted on the control chart and provided the points lie within the upper and lower warning limits, the performance is acceptable. Outside these tolerances it is not acceptable but the cost of action is likely to exceed its rewards. Only when the individual values exceed the upper or lower action limits is management action required.

6.14 Training for quality

As mentioned above, one of the inputs to a product is the skills and efficiency of the employees. Training can improve these employee skills and efficiencies provided the employee also perceives the benefits of such training.

Training can occur both inside and outside the workplace. Internal training could be in the ideas of team working and quality discussion groups which are known as quality circles (see earlier in this chapter). Quality attitudes are important, for no amount of discussion or training are likely to have the desired effect unless employees understand and accept the benefits of quality.

6.15 Designing for quality

When a product is designed, its specification should consider factors which will minimise future rectification costs. Production methods should be as simple as possible and use the skills and resources existing within the sphere of knowledge of the organisation and its employees. It is significant that in the modern environment, it is often found that 90% of the production costs of a given product are determined in its design phase. Effective performance management therefore involves monitoring costs and results over the whole life-cycle of a product. Just considering production costs over a 1 month period (in the from of traditional standard costing and variance analysis) may therefore be of marginal relevance. Ensuring that quality factors have been correctly engineered into the design of products may therefore only be apparent when costs are reported on a 'life cycle' basis.

6.16 Quality information systems

KEY POINT

An information system is needed to provide feedback on the success or otherwise of quality procedures. Such systems should attempt to measure both monetary and non-monetary factors.

An information system is needed to provide feedback on the success or otherwise of quality procedures. Such systems should attempt to measure both monetary and non-monetary factors.

Quality can be measured in terms of its effect on profit via costs and revenues, and also in non-monetary terms. An example of a monetary measure would be the costs of rectification whereas non-monetary measures may include the percentage of wastage or the number of customer complaints.

Care must be taken with regard to traditional performance reports such as variance analysis, which can operate in opposition to quality. For example favourable price variances can arise because of using poorer quality resources. These poorer quality inputs may lead to a reduction in the quality of outputs.

6.17 Measuring and reporting the cost of quality

DEFINITIONS

Quality related costs – cost of ensuring and assuring quality, as well as loss incurred when quality is not achieved. Quality costs are classified as prevention cost, appraisal cost, internal failure cost and external failure cost.

Prevention costs – the cost incurred to reduce appraisal cost to a minimum.

Appraisal costs – the cost incurred, such as for inspection and testing, in initially ascertaining and ensuring conformance of the product to quality requirements.

Internal failure costs – the cost arising from inadequate quality before the transfer of ownership from supplier to purchaser.

External failure costs – the cost arising from inadequate quality discovered after the transfer of ownership from supplier to purchaser such as complaints, warranty claims and recall cost.

These activities are central to the operation of a TQM philosophy. The full costs of quality have to be identified and reported regularly. Furthermore, relevant performance indicators have to be developed based on the cost of quality and these may be used as a basis for staff remuneration.

The concept of empowerment means that relevant information has to be supplied to all levels in the organisation.

There are costs associated with quality which may be divided into costs of ensuring quality and costs of quality failure.

A report *'The effectiveness of the corporate overhead in British business'* Develin & Partners, estimates that the average cost of waste and mistakes in the UK represents 20% of controllable corporate overhead.

Quality related costs – cost of ensuring and assuring quality, as well as loss incurred when quality is not achieved. Quality costs are classified as prevention cost, appraisal cost, internal failure cost and external failure cost.

Prevention costs – the cost incurred to reduce appraisal cost to a minimum.

Appraisal costs – the cost incurred, such as for inspection and testing, in initially ascertaining and ensuring conformance of the product to quality requirements.

Internal failure costs – the cost arising from inadequate quality before the transfer of ownership from supplier to purchaser.

External failure costs – the cost arising from inadequate quality discovered after the transfer of ownership from supplier to purchaser such as complaints, warranty claims and recall cost.

Calculating quality costs

Quality costs may be measured both in terms of costs incurred in assuring quality and rectifying units, and also in the opportunity cost of lost sales. Each item must be analysed and individually considered and where possible a cost benefit approach applied to a quality control programme.

Example

The following question is based upon a past exam question:

Boatbits Ltd moulds fibre glass sheets into body parts for leisure cruise boat manufacturers. Its main products are parts X215 and Y54. The company is planning a TQM programme at a cost of £320,000. The following information relates to the costs incurred by Boatbits Ltd both before and after the implementation of the programme.

Fibre glass sheets

The sheets cost £25 each. On average 5% of the sheets received are returned to the supplier as scrap because of deterioration in stores. The supplier allows a credit of £5 per sheet for such returns. In addition, specification conformity checks carried out in stores on receipt of a delivery cost a total of £24,000 per annum.

A move to a just-in-time purchasing system will eliminate the holding of stocks of fibre glass sheets. This has been negotiated with the supplier who will deliver sheets of guaranteed quality specification for £28 each, eliminating all stockholding costs.

Moulding process

Upon receipt of a stores requisition, the sheets are issued to the moulding process which has variable conversion costs of £15 per sheet. Losses of 8% of process input arise through poor process temperature control, which can be sold as scrap at £8 per unit.

The TQM programme will improve the temperature control and reduce losses to 1% of input.

Each sheet input into the process produces two basic parts, X2 and Y5, each with the same cost structure.

Finishing process

The finishing process has a bank of machines which perform additional operations on basic parts X2 and Y5 in order to convert them to the finished parts X215 and Y54 respectively. The variable conversion costs for this process are £10 and £18 per unit of X215 and Y54 respectively. At the end of the finishing process, 10% of the units are found to be defective, and can be sold as scrap for £12 per unit (for either part).

The TQM programme will convert the finishing process into two dedicated cells, one for each part, with variable costs per unit of £7 and £16 for X215 and Y54 respectively. Defective units are expected to fall to 1% of input to each cell, and will be sold as scrap as at present.

Finished goods

A finished goods buffer stock of parts X215 and Y54 of 400 and 600 units respectively is held throughout the year in order to allow for variability in customer demand and replacement of faulty parts returned by customers. Customer returns are currently 4% of sales. Variable stock holding costs are £3 per part per annum for both products.

The revised "cell" format of the finishing process will reduce the stockholding requirement to that required for one month's replacement of faulty parts, estimated at 15 and 20 units for parts X215 and Y54 respectively. Variable stockholding costs will be unaffected.

Quantitative data

Some calculations have already been made of the number of units of fibre glass sheets, basic parts X2 and Y5 and finished parts X215 and Y54 required before and after the implementation of the TQM programme, based upon the projected sales and information above. The figures are summarised below:

	Current position		**Post TQM position**	
	Part X2/215 (units)	*Part Y5/54 (units)*	*Part X2/215 (units)*	*Part Y5/54 (units)*
Sales	20,000	24,000	20,000	24,000
Customer returns	800	960	180	240
Parts delivered	20,800	24,960	20,180	24,240
Finishing proc. losses	2,311	2,773	204	245
Input to fin. proc.	23,111	27,733	20,384	24,485
	50,844		44,869	
Moulding losses	4,421		453	
Input to moulding	55,265		45,322	
Returns to supplier	2,909		-	
Purchases of fibre glass sheets	58,174		45,322	

You are required to evaluate and present a statement showing the net financial benefit or loss per annum of implementing the TQM programme.

Solution

It is important to lay out your answer clearly, including any necessary workings. The logical approach would be to work through the manufacturing stages in order. Don't forget one of the biggest savings - the reduced volume of purchases necessary under the TQM system (reduced by the increased purchase price for guaranteed quality).

Financial (costs)/savings of proposed TQM programme

	£
Purchase cost savings 58,174 × £25 – 45,322 × £28	185,334
Move to JIT system - purchasing	
Deteriorated stock savings (2,909 × £(25 – 5))	58,180
Specification check savings	24,000
Improved temperature control - moulding	
Conversion cost savings (55,265 – 45,322) × £15	149,145
Reduced scrap proceeds (4,421 – 453) × £8	(31,744)
Cell format production - finishing	
Conversion cost savings	
(23,111 × £10 + 27,733 × £18 – (20,384 × £7 + 24,485 × £16))	195,856
Reduced scrap proceeds ((2,311 + 2,773) – (204 + 245)) × £12	(55,620)
Reduction of stockholding requirements - finished goods	
Holding cost savings ((400 + 600) – (15 + 20)) × £3	2,895
	528,046
Less: cost of TQM programme	(320,000)
Net financial benefit of implementation of TQM programme	208,046

Note: it would appear that the cost of implementation of the TQM programme (£320,000) is a one-off cost, whereas the net savings before this cost are per annum. Thus the overall benefit will be much greater than shown above.

7 Business process re-engineering

7.1 Background

KEY POINT

BPR involves examining business processes and making substantial changes to the way in which an organisation operates. It involves the redesign of how work is done through activities.

BPR involves examining business processes and making substantial changes to the way in which an organisation operates. It involves the redesign of how work is done through activities. A business process is a series of activities that are linked together in order to achieve given objectives. For example, material handling might be classed as a business process in which the separate activities are scheduling production, storing materials, processing purchase orders, inspecting materials and paying suppliers.

The aim of BPR is to improve the key business process by focusing on simplification, improved quality, enhanced customer satisfaction and cost reduction.

In the case of material handling, the activity of processing purchase orders might be re-engineered by integrating the production planning system with that of the supplier (an exercise in 'supply chain management' (or 'SCM')) and thus sending purchase orders direct to the supplier without any intermediate administrative activity. Joint quality control procedures might be agreed thus avoiding the need to check incoming materials. In this manner, the cost of material procurement, receiving, holding and handling is reduced.

The practical result of this exercise is that a lot of non-value adding activities are eliminated and cost reductions are achieved. It can be seen how closely linked BPR is to TQM, JIT, SCM and ABC.

7.2 The practice of BPR

BPR was one of the leading management 'fads' of the early 1990s. In practice, BPR programmes were exercises in introducing elements of all the techniques listed in the preceding paragraph. Unfortunately, BPR gained a rather unfortunate reputation through being too closely associated with corporate down-sizings which were widespread throughout the recession of that period. The practitioners of BPR (mostly firms of consultants associated with the larger firms of Chartered Accountants) often saw their job as being to implement waves of brutal sackings in their client companies. The climate of the time was such that brutal sackings were often seen as a necessity in order to ensure corporate survival. However, as the economic and political climate changed in the late 1990s, BPR attracted a certain revulsion. As one writer commented

'If you do something badly often enough, then it gets a bad name'

'Management by Messing Around' by Tim Falconer (CA Magazine 11/96).

An article in a 1995 edition of the *Financial Times* reported favourably on a BPR programme at the Leicester Health Trust which had allowed 50 nurses to be sacked although it did add that this had caused 'some bitterness'. The BPR programme had been implemented by a large team of management consultants who had been on site for over a year. One wonders what fees were paid to those consultants? Such a programme would be far less acceptable today than was the case in 1995.

That said, the concepts and ideas which BPR embodies are still perfectly valid. It is the term itself that has gone out of fashion.

One of the principal accounting developments associated with the management techniques discussed above is ABC. The previous discussion of BPR and TQM demonstrates the importance of determining and reporting the costs of activities. That is, the emphasis is on the outputs of the operation rather than on the inputs. People are more concerned with what the costs achieve rather than with how they are made up.

KEY POINT

Many organisations now use cost driver rates (see Chapter 4) in order to measure efficiency.

Many organisations now use cost driver rates (see Chapter 4) in order to measure efficiency. Elaborate ABC systems are needed to provide the depth and style of information that modern management operations need. SCM is the current 'hot topic' in the area of management ideas. It involves an integration of the information systems of different companies on the supply chain. A full exploration of the implications of this for management and information systems is beyond the scope of this text - however, those implications are obviously considerable.

Conclusion

Information can now be provided on a flexible basis due to developments in information technology such as spreadsheets and databases. This information is needed to support changes in business structures. Two of the most significant developments are Total Quality Management and Business Process Re-engineering.

SELF-TEST QUESTIONS

Management information processing

1 What are the three stages of information processing? (2.1)

2 Explain 'batch processing'. (2.4)

3 Explain 'demand processing'. (2.4)

Accounting systems

4 What is a database? (3.6)

The impact of IT on modern management accounting

5 Explain the relevance of modern developments in IT to management accounting. (4)

Total quality management

6 Explain the difference between quality control and quality assurance. (6.6)

7 Explain what a quality circle is. (6.11)

8 Explain the use of cost of quality reports. (6.17)

Business process re-engineering

9 Explain BPR and its link with JIT, TQM, SCM and ABC. (7)

EXAM-TYPE QUESTIONS

Question 1: IT

'Computerised financial planning packages have revolutionised the process of budget preparation.'

Describe the main features of such packages and give your views on the quotation.

(Total: 25 marks)

Question 2: Quality assurance

You have just been informed by the MD that 'something drastic has to be done about quality'. In his view, quality is the responsibility of your department and he has suggested that you take a tougher line with those responsible for quality problems, raise quality standards, increase inspection rates, and give greater authority to quality control inspectors.

Required:

(a) Evaluate the suggestions made by the MD. **(10 marks)**

(b) State what additional or alternative proposals you would offer. **(15 marks)**

(Total: 25 marks)

For the answers to these questions, see the 'Answers' section at the end of the book.

FEEDBACK TO ACTIVITY 1

The decision depends firstly on management requirements for:

– routine recording of accounting data

– packages of reports

– information for decision-making.

The processing system must also take account of:

– input volumes

– management priorities

– the purpose of the information processed

– response time.

Chapter 6
SHORT-TERM DECISION-MAKING

CHAPTER CONTENTS

This chapter explores short-term decision-making. In doing so it makes extensive use of conventional Cost Volume Profit Analysis.

Objectives

When you have studied this chapter you should be able to do the following.

- Distinguish between relevant and irrelevant information using appropriate criteria.
- Identify cost classification(s) in decision-making.
- Explain how quantitative and qualitative information is used in decision-making.
- Evaluate and assess the frequency, timing, format and degree of accuracy in the provision of decision-making information.
- Describe the basic decision-making cycle for business decisions.
- Classify problems for the purpose of modelling into simple, complex and dynamic problems.
- Explain the relevance of endogenous and exogenous variables, policies and controls, performance measures and intermediate variables in model building.
- Explain the nature of CVP analysis and name planning and decision-making situations in which it may be used.
- Compare the accounting and economic models of CVP analysis.
- Explain the assumptions of linearity and the principle of relevant range in the CVP model.
- Prepare breakeven charts and profit-volume charts and interpret the information contained within each including multi-product situations.
- Comment on the limitations of CVP analysis for planning and decision-making including multi-product situations.
- Explain the use of avoidable cost, incremental cost, marginal cost and variable cost in decision-making.
- Describe the relationship between fixed cost and time horizon used in a decision situation.
- Explain how opportunity cost is used in making decisions.
- Identify and calculate relevant costs for specific decision situations from given data.
- Explain the meaning of throughput accounting and its use in decision-making.
- Explain and illustrate the impact of limiting factors in decision-making.
- Solve problems involving changes in product mix, discontinuance of products or departments.
- Implement make or buy decisions using relevant costs.
- Make decisions as to whether to further process a product before sale using relevant costs and revenues.
- Use relevant costs and revenues in decisions relating to the operation of internal service departments or the use of external services.

1 Decisions and relevant costs

The characteristics of short-term decisions were introduced in earlier chapters. Examples include setting profit-maximising selling prices, accepting or rejecting customer orders and deciding whether to make or buy in components. These decisions tend to assume a given level of capital investment and often turn around optimising the use of given resources or opportunities from a given market situation.

Short-term decisions are decisions whose costs will be incurred and whose benefits will be obtained in the short-term. Since costs and benefits are all short-term, the financial appraisal of decisions does not have to consider the time value of money.

KEY POINT

The financial evaluation of decision options should consider only relevant costs and revenues. A relevant cost is a future cash flow arising as a direct consequence of the decision.

Taking a decision means making a choice between two or more possible courses of action. These might be a choice between option A and option B. Alternatively, it might be a choice between doing something and doing nothing. Yet another type of decision is what to make and sell in order to maximise profits.

Accountants can help managers to reach decisions that will maximise profitability, by providing information about the likely costs and benefits of various decision options.

Accounting for short-term decision-making is based on common sense.

- It starts from the position that whatever a manager decides to do now, the decision cannot affect what has already happened in the past. It can only affect the future.
- It also takes the position that the only costs and revenues that are relevant to a decision are the extra costs incurred, or the costs saved, or the revenue gained or lost as a result of making the decision. Costs that will be incurred anyway, or revenues that will be earned anyway cannot be relevant to a decision.
- Thirdly, it is also recognised that the relevant consequences of a decision are those that result in higher or lower cash spending, or higher or lower cash income. Cash flows are what matter in business, not 'accounting profit'. Non-cash items are irrelevant for decision-making: these include depreciation charges and absorbed fixed overheads.

The **only** costs to be taken into consideration in the financial evaluation of decisions are therefore **relevant costs**. A relevant cost is a future cash flow arising as a direct consequence of the decision that is taken.

2 Short-term decision and cost volume profit analysis

2.1 Cost/revenue behaviour and structures

In many cases, a short-term decision deals with identifying the profit-maximising level of production and sales, or the additional costs of doing extra volumes of work. In such cases, costs might simply be analysed into fixed costs and variable costs. Fixed costs are irrelevant to a decision if they will be the same regardless of what decision is taken. On the other hand, variable costs are relevant, provided they are cash flow items of expenditure, because they will be affected by the volume of output or sales

It is often necessary to look at the way costs behave in response to changes in production volume.

DEFINITION

Cost behaviour is the way in which costs of output are affected by fluctuations in the level of activity.

Example

	Production	
	600 units	*1,000 units*
	£	£
Sales (at £3 per unit)	1,800	3,000
Total costs	1,100	1,500
Profit	700	1,500
Average unit cost	£1.83	£1.50
Average unit profit	£1.17	£1.50

You should be able to deduce from the above information that:

- The variable cost per unit is £1
- The fixed cost per period is £500
- The break-even point is 250 units
- The Contribution to Sales (C/S) ratio is 66.66%.

The variable cost per unit and fixed costs can be estimated using the **high-low method.** This takes total costs at two different levels of activity or output. Here, we have total costs of £1,000 at 500 units of output and £1,500 at 1,000 units of output.

We assume that costs consist of fixed costs plus variable costs, fixed costs per period are the same regardless of the activity level and unit variable costs are a constant amount at all levels of activity. It therefore follows that since fixed costs are the same at all activity levels, the difference in total costs at two different activity levels must consist of variable costs only. In the example above:

	£
Total cost of 1,000 units	1,500
Total cost of 600 units	1,100
Variable cost of 400 units	400
Variable cost per unit (£400/400)	£1

Substituting

	£
Total cost of 1,000 units	1,500
Variable cost of 1,000 units (x £1)	1,000
Fixed costs	500

You should be familiar with basic concepts of costs behaviour including semi-fixed costs, semi-variable costs, stepped costs and margins of safety. You should also be familiar with the Cost-Volume-Profit chart (or 'break-even chart) and the Profit-Volume chart. This familiarity is assumed in what follows.

2.2 The relevance of variable costs

Variable costs are those costs which change in proportion to changes in the level of activity. Thus whenever a business decision involves increases or decreases in activity it is almost certain that variable costs will be affected and therefore will be relevant to the decision.

2.3 The relevance of fixed costs

KEY POINT

Fixed costs are generally regarded as those costs which are **not** affected by changes in the level of activity.

Fixed costs are generally regarded as those costs which are **not** affected by changes in the level of activity. However a variation on the basic fixed cost, known as a stepped fixed may be depicted as follows:

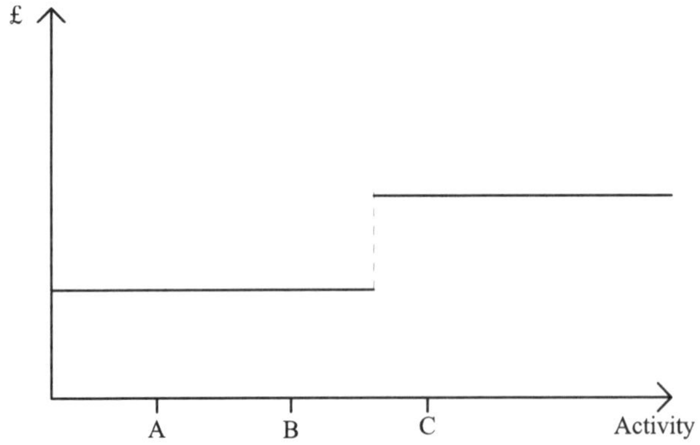

A change in activity from point A to point B does not affect the level of **total** fixed costs because both activity levels lie on the same fixed cost step. For such a decision the fixed cost is irrelevant because it is not changing. However a change in activity from point B to point C does affect the level of total fixed costs. Thus such a decision causes the total fixed costs to change and in such circumstances they are relevant. When fixed costs become relevant to a decision by changing in this way the extra fixed cost is usually referred to as the **incremental fixed cost**.

Few costs are truly fixed in the long-term. However, in the short-term, many costs really are fixed.

2.4 The relevance of semi-variable costs

KEY POINT

Semi-variable costs are those costs which comprise both a fixed and variable element.

Semi-variable costs are those costs which comprise both a fixed and variable element. The variable element is relevant to decision-making using the same reasoning as was applied to variable costs. The fixed element is irrelevant unless it is a step fixed cost element as described above. It is therefore necessary to separate the fixed and variable components of semi-variablc costs to isolate the relevant and non-relevant parts of the cost. The high-low method will usually be the most suitable method to apply, because if its simplicity.

3 Developing CVP analysis

3.1 The CVP analysis concept

In its simplest form, CVP analysis makes the following assumptions:

- the selling price is constant per unit irrespective of the number of units to be sold
- fixed costs in each period are constant in total, and are unaffected by the level of output or activity in the period
- variable costs are constant per unit irrespective of the number of units produced.

This simple form of revenue and cost analysis may is shown in an 'accountant's break-even chart':

Accountant's break-even chart

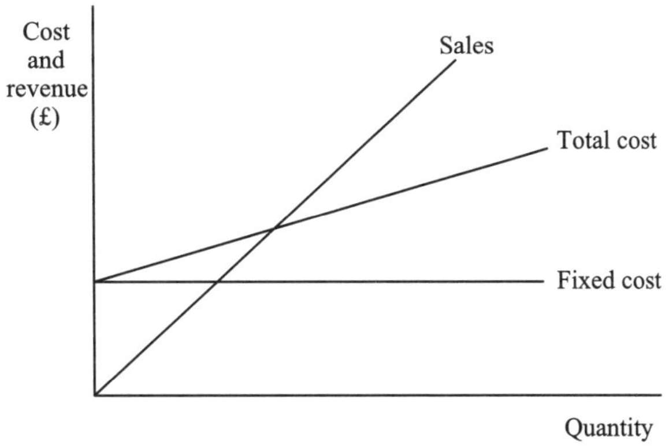

An alternative set of assumptions can be described in terms of the 'economist's' break even chart:

- It is unlikely that as the volume of sales rises, the sales price per unit can be kept unchanged. In general, prices have to be reduced in order to sell more.
- Unit costs of materials and labour rise as the output volume increases .The beneficial effect of quantity discounts on materials is offset by higher labour costs due to less efficient production and overtime rates or having to take on less-skilled labour employees to do the additional work.

The CVP chart then becomes nearer to the economist's concept having two break-even points:

Economist's break-even chart

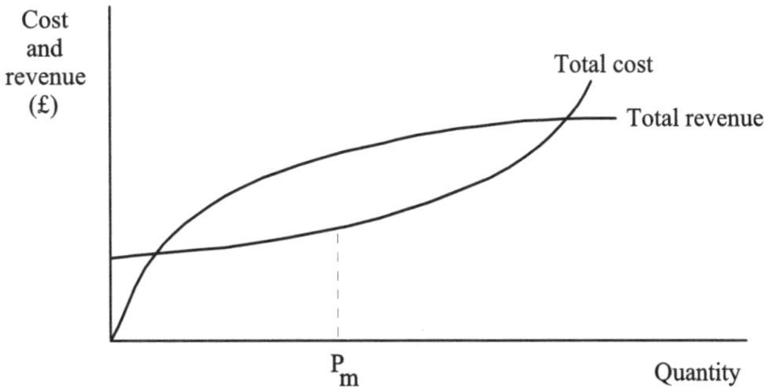

Profit is maximised at the level of output P_m where there is the greatest vertical difference between the total cost and total revenue curves.

The assumption of constant unit selling price at all levels of output (contained in the accountant's break-even chart) applies to those markets where there is a going world price – such as oil, grain and minerals. One individual supplier can sell as much or as little as he can produce at that price.

Some observers have suggested that the development of world products in many classes of manufactured good may have extended the concept of a going world price into many new areas of the economy in recent years.

3.2 Revenue curves

KEY POINT

The economist's model of revenue behaviour is based on the principle that in order to sell more units demand must be increased, and to do this the price must be reduced.

The economist's model of revenue behaviour is based on the principle that in order to sell more units demand must be increased, and to do this the price must be reduced. On this basis sales revenue may be depicted thus:

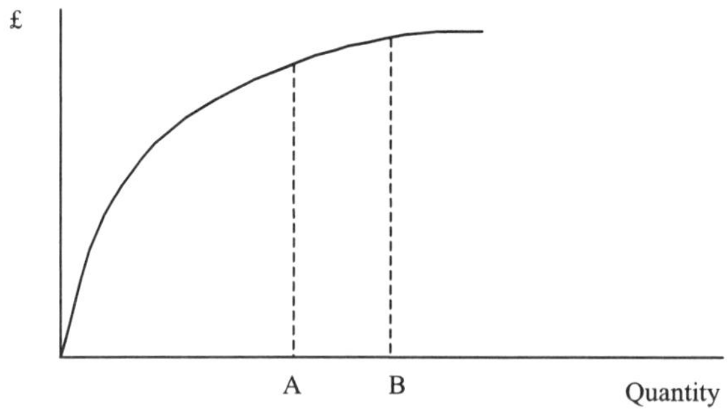

It may be that to push quantity sold beyond a certain point, unit selling prices must be reduced to a point where the revenue curve actually starts to fall.

However, this chart assumes that the range of activity levels under review range from zero to maximum and this is unlikely to be appropriate in reality. It is more likely that the range of activity will lie between points A and B. It can be seen that between these points the revenue curve is virtually a straight line.

3.3 Curvi-linear variable costs

A similar principle applies to variable costs where it could be argued that the effects of quantity discounts on materials, and overtime/inefficiencies on labour costs cause these to be depicted as curves:

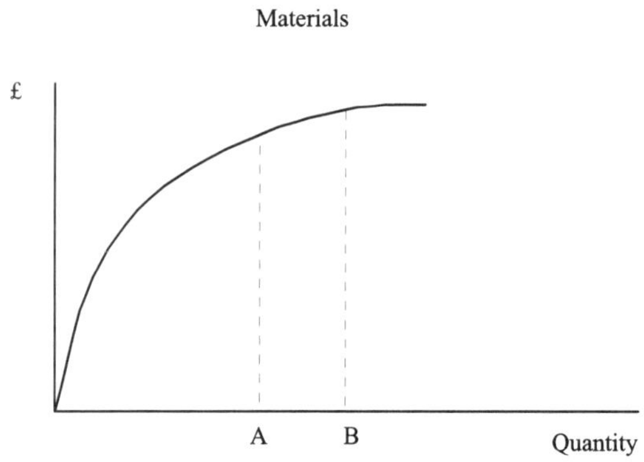

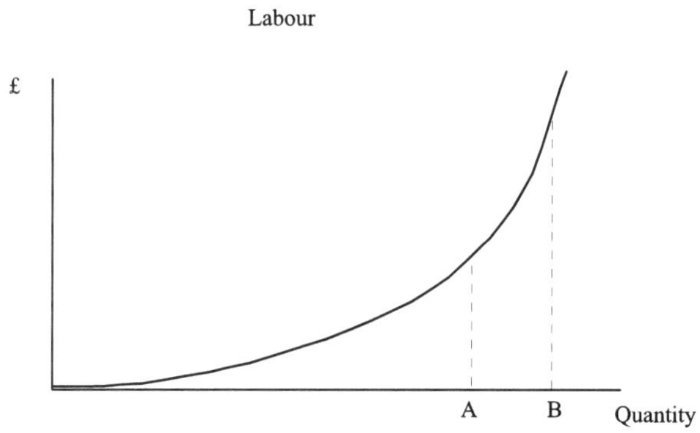

However, two arguments exist to support the accountant's linear model in respect of these costs:

- If each of these types of cost is added together, their total will approximate to a straight-line.
- Within a likely range of activity the curves themselves are virtually linear.

Thus, business decisions may often be made with very limited parameters. One may be considering the relative merits of two alternative levels of output which are quite close together. Within the limited range of output levels under review, a cost function may be treated as being linear.

3.4 Multi-product profit-volume chart

A further complication in CVP analysis arises when a firm sells more than one product. To calculate the break-even point, an assumption has to be made about the proportions in which the products will be sold. The issues involved are best illustrated with a simple example.

Example

Budgeted data:

	Sales	*Contribution*
	£	£
Product A	10,000	2,000
Product B	14,000	7,000
Product C	8,000	2,400
Total	32,000	11,400

Total annual fixed costs £8,000.

Either of two approaches may be adopted:

(a) Assume a constant sales mix.

(b) Assume, somewhat unrealistically, that products are sold in descending order of contribution/sales ratios.

A profit-volume chart can be drawn that incorporates both assumptions.

Data needed for graph:

Start by putting the products in descending order of C/S ratios.

Contribution sales ratios ($\frac{\text{Contribution}}{\text{Sales}} \times 100$)

Product A	$\frac{2,000}{10,000} \times 100 = 20\%$	3rd
Product B	$\frac{7,000}{14,000} \times 100 = 50\%$	1st
Product C	$\frac{2,400}{8,000} \times 100 = 30\%$	2nd

The order of sale and cumulative profit figures will be assumed to be as follows:

		Total sales	*Total contribution*	*Fixed costs*	*Profit/(loss)*
		£	£	£	£
1st	Product B	14,000	7,000	8,000	(1,000)
2nd	Product C	8,000	2,400		
		22,000	9,400	8,000	1,400
3rd	Product A	10,000	2,000		
		32,000	11,400	8,000	3,400

The multi-product profit-volume chart can be drawn as follows:

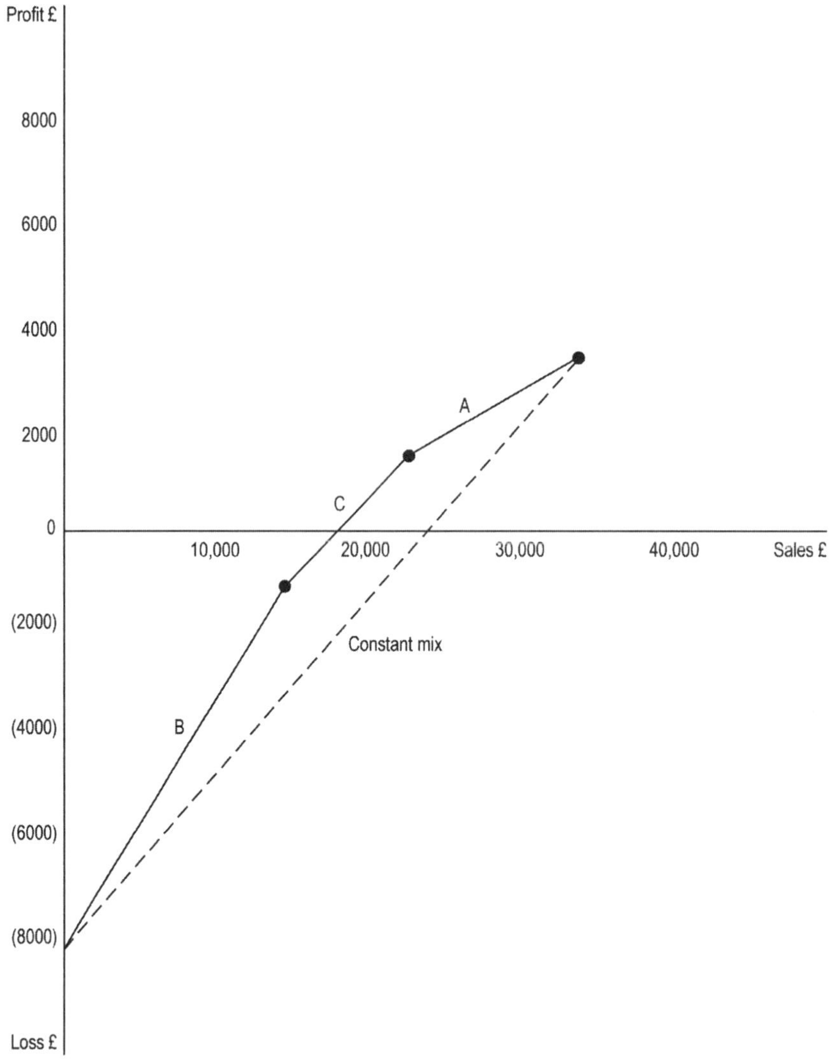

Total sales of the three products are expected to be £32,000 and total contribution will be £11,400, so the weighted average contribution/sales ratio for the period is (11,400/32,000) 0.35625 or 35.625%.

The breakeven point, assuming that the three products are sold in their budgeted proportions, can be calculated in revenue terms as:

Contribution required to break even/Contribution/sales ratio

= Fixed costs/Contribution/sales ratio.

In this example, the breakeven point in sales revenue is £8,000/0.35625 = £22,456.

4 Information requirements of CVP analysis model

CVP analysis is useful insofar as it either meets or approximates to the information requirements of the model. These requirements are:

- Cost behaviour is known and individual cost components can be classified as either fixed or variable.
- Over the time scale and activity range under review, unit variable costs remain constant and total fixed costs remain constant.
- Unit selling prices are known and remain constant over the range under review.

In practice, these information requirements may make quite formidable demands on the financial analyst. Despite the obvious limitations these requirements impose, CVP analysis is of great practical importance. This is not just for itself, but because of the understanding it gives of cost behaviour patterns for decision purposes, considered further below.

The information requirements of the basic model referred to above, may limit the usefulness of CVP analysis for planning and decision-making under certain circumstances. In particular its usefulness is limited in multi-product situations and where uncertainty of input values exists.

When an organisation sells more than one product there is always difficulty in identifying the fixed costs relating to a specific product, and inevitably there will be some fixed costs which are not product specific. Consequently a particular sales mix has to be assumed in order to use the model, and then the break-even point can only be quantified in terms of sales values.

The model is over-simplistic by assuming that variable costs are constant per unit and fixed costs are constant in total. In reality there will be economies and diseconomies of scale which occur, although it is uncertain as to the level of activity which causes them, and the extent to which the costs will be affected. The CVP model cannot be manipulated to deal with these and other forms of uncertainty.

5 Decision-making

CVP analysis can be used in fairly straightforward planning situations, where the aim is to formulate a profit-maximising plan, or a plan where there is a good prospect of doing better than break even.

Information could be required in more unusual or 'one off' situations, when a simple analysis of fixed and variable costs is insufficient. Concepts such as sunk costs, avoidable costs, incremental costs and opportunity costs have to be applied.

DEFINITION

An **opportunity cost** is a benefit forgone as a result of following some course of action.

DEFINITION

A **sunk cost** is one which has been incurred in the past and is therefore no longer 'decision relevant'.

An **opportunity cost** is a benefit forgone as a result of following some course of action. If we undertake job A instead of job B (the two being mutually exclusive) then the contribution we forgo on job B is an opportunity cost of job A.

A **sunk cost** is one which has been incurred in the past and is therefore no longer 'decision-relevant'. If we have already acquired materials for which we have no alternative use other than on Job A – then that materials cost is a sunk cost and need not be considered in our decision on whether or not to accept Job A.

Example

A company employs two grades of labour, skilled and unskilled. Skilled labour is paid £8 per hour and unskilled labour is paid £6 per hour. Labour costs are treated as a variable cost, although the work force is fixed in size and employees are paid for a 38 hour week

The company produces a single product, which takes 4 hours of skilled labour and 3 hours of unskilled labour to make. The contribution earned is £20 per unit.

A customer has asked for a delivery of a special batch of products, manufactured to order. These would have a materials cost of £500, and would require 12 hours of skilled labour and 9 hours of unskilled labour to produce. The skilled employees are currently fully utilised on making the standard product, but there is sufficient unskilled labour time to do the work.

What is the minimum price the company should charge for the work?

Solution

The minimum price to charge is one that leaves the company no worse off by doing the customer's order. The problem here is that if the order is undertaken, production of the standard product will fall by 3 units, and the contribution from these will be lost. This is because skilled labour is being fully utilised already. There is an opportunity cost, which is the loss of contribution from doing the order for the customer instead of making and selling the standard product. The opportunity cost is generally measured as a contribution per unit of scarce resource. Here it is (£20/4) £5 per skilled labour hour.

A pitfall to watch out for is that contribution is measured after deducting variable costs, which in this case includes labour costs. So contribution from the standard product is measured after deducting the costs of skilled and unskilled labour. The sales price charged to the customer for the special order must be sufficient to cover these labour costs too.

The minimum price to charge is therefore:

	£
Materials (incremental cost)	500
Skilled labour cost (12 hours × £8)	96
Unskilled labour cost (9 hours × £6)	54
Opportunity cost (12 hours × £5)	60
Minimum price	710

To understand the concept of relevant costs and opportunity costs, it helps to study relevant costs in a variety of different decision situations.

6 Avoidable and incremental costs

6.1 Avoidable cost

DEFINITION

An **avoidable cost** is a cost which will not be incurred if a particular decision is made. It is usually used in the context of a fixed cost.

An avoidable cost is a cost which will not be incurred if a particular decision is made. It is usually used in the context of a fixed cost. For example if a fixed cost can be identified to the production of a single product, and the production of that product is stopped, then the fixed cost would not be incurred: it is therefore avoided because of the decision.

6.2 Incremental cost

DEFINITION

An **incremental cost** is the extra cost incurred as a result of a decision.

KEY POINT

A relevant cost in a decision-making situation is one that is likely to change as a result of the decision made. An irrelevant cost is one which will not change as a result of the decision made.

An incremental cost is the extra cost incurred as a result of a decision. Thus if a decision is made to increase production and to do so an additional machine is to be leased, then the lease cost of the additional machine is an incremental cost.

A wide range of short-term decision-making situations involve determining the 'marginal' effect of particular courses of action. Such a determination involves identifying avoidable and incremental costs. The terms 'relevant'and irrelevant'costs are commonly used in the same contexts. A relevant cost in a decision-making situation is one that is likely to change as a result of the decision made. An irrelevant cost is one which will not change as a result of the decision made. A cost is said to be "decision relevant" if it is one that is influenced by the decision that is being made. One issue in the design of management accounting systems is that it may or may not report costs in a manner that allows decision relevant costs to be clearly identified.

Circumstances may arise where any relevant or incremental cost is an 'opportunity cost' rather than a straight cash outflow. If taking action A involves loss of contribution from some other area in the business then that loss is an opportunity cost of taking action A and should be considered in the evaluation of action A.

A comprehensive example will be used to illustrate the principles. Study it carefully.

Example

Accept or reject decision analysis

Spartan plc manufactures a wide range of soft toys. The managers of the business are considering whether to add a new type of toy animal, the Wimble, to the product range. A recent market research survey, undertaken at a cost of £2,000, has indicated that demand for the Wimble would last for only one year, during which time 100,000 of these could be sold at £6 each.

It is assumed that production and sales of the Wimble would take place evenly throughout the year. Manufacturing cost data is available as below.

Raw materials

Each Wimble would require three types of raw material, A, B and C. Material A is used regularly in the business and stocks are replaced as necessary. Material B is currently being held as surplus stock as a result of over-ordering on an earlier contract. This material is not used regularly by Spartan plc and would be sold if not required for the manufacture of the Wimble. Material C would have to be bought in specially for the Wimble, since stocks of this item are not normally held.

Current stock levels and costs of each raw material are shown below:

Raw material	*Amount required per Wimble* (m)	*Current stock level* (m)	*Original cost* (£/m)	*Replacement cost* (£/m)	*Realisable value* (£/m)
A	0.8	200,000	1.05	1.25	0.90
B	0.4	30,000	1.65	1.20	0.55
C	0.1	0	-	2.75	2.50

Labour

In producing one Wimble, half an hour of skilled labour and a quarter of an hour of unskilled labour would be required, at wage rates of £3 per hour and £2 per hour respectively. One supervisor would be required full-time at an annual salary of £7,000.

Skilled labour for the production of Wimbles would have to be recruited specially, whilst 25,000 surplus unskilled labour hours are expected to be available during the coming year if Wimbles are not manufactured. However, company policy dictates that no unskilled worker will be made redundant in the foreseeable future.

The supervisor has agreed to delay immediate retirement for one year, and to waive his annual pension of £4,000 in return for his annual salary during this period.

Machinery

Two machines, X and Y, would be required to manufacture Wimbles, details of which are as below:

	X	*Y*
Original cost	£35,000	£25,000
Accumulated depreciation	£24,000	£18,000
Written down value	£11,000	£7,000
Age	4 years	6 years
Estimated remaining useful life	1 year	2 years
Estimated value at end of useful life	£5,000	£1,000

Details are also available of cash values relating to the two machines at the start and end of the year during which Wimbles would be produced.

		Start of the year £	*End of year* £
Machine X:	Replacement cost	40,000	45,000
	Resale value	7,000	5,000
Machine Y:	Replacement cost	30,000	33,000
	Resale value	4,000	3,000

If machine X is not used for the manufacture of Wimbles then it would be used to manufacture existing products, the sale of which would result in an estimated £50,000 net receipts.

Machine X is one of a number of identical machine types used regularly on various products by Spartan plc. Each of this type of machine is replaced as soon as it reaches the end of its useful life.

Machine Y is the only one of its type within the firm and if not used in the manufacture of Wimbles would be sold immediately.

Overheads

Variable overhead costs attributable to Wimbles are estimated at £1.50 per item produced. Production fixed overheads are allocated by Spartan plc to products on the basis of labour hours, and the rate for the coming year has been established at £2.50 per labour hour. The manufacture of Wimbles will not result in any additional fixed costs being incurred.

We can now turn our attention to assessing whether, on the basis of the information given the manufacture and sale of Wimbles represents a profitable opportunity to Spartan plc. In doing so, the relevant cost of using each resource required to produce Wimbles must be identified. For each resource, a comparison is required showing the cash flows associated with manufacture and those associated with non-manufacture. The difference between the two represents the incremental cost of applying each resource to the production of Wimbles.

Cash flows (explanations follow)

	Manufacture	*Non-manufacture*	*Incremental cost of manufacture*
	£	£	£
Raw materials			
A	(100,000)	0	(100,000)
B	(12,000)	16,500	(28,500)
C	(27,500)	0	(27,500)
			(156,000)
Labour			
Skilled	(150,000)	0	(150,000)
Unskilled	(50,000)	(50,000)	0
Supervisor	(7,000)	(4,000)	(3,000)
			(153,000)
Machinery			
X	(35,000)	(40,000)	5,000
Y	3,000	4,000	(1,000)
			4,000
Overheads			
Variable	(150,000)	0	(150,000)
Fixed	-	-	-
			(150,000)
Total incremental cost			(455,000)
Total sales revenue			600,000
Net cash inflow (contribution)			145,000

Thus, £455,000 is the relevant cost to Spartan plc for producing 100,000 Wimbles during the forthcoming year. Taking the cash generated from sales into consideration a net cash inflow of £145,000 would result from this trading opportunity. At this stage you are advised to review critically the build-up of incremental cost shown above before reading further, in order to establish whether or not the principle of relevance has been fully understood. The basis for establishing the relevant cost of each resource is examined below.

Notes and discussion

Raw materials

A: since this material is used regularly within the business and stocks are replaced as used, the 80,000 metres required would be replaced for subsequent use on other jobs at the current replacement cost of £1.25 per metre.

B: if Wimbles are manufactured a further 10,000 metres would have to be purchased at £1.20 per metre. The historic cost of the 30,000 metres already in stock is a sunk cost and is therefore not relevant. If Wimbles are not manufactured, the existing stock would be sold off at the realisable value of £0.55 per metre.

C: the only cash flow arising here is that relating to the special purchase of 10,000 metres at £2.75 per metre if Wimbles are produced.

To summarise, the relevant cost of raw materials is identified as being their current replacement cost, unless the material in question is not to be replaced, in which case the relevant cost becomes the higher of current resale value or the value if applied to another product (economic value).

Labour

Skilled: in manufacturing Wimbles additional wage payments of £150,000 would be made i.e. 50,000 hours @ £3 per hour. These payments relate to specifically recruited labour.

Unskilled: the cost of 25,000 hours of unskilled labour will be incurred by Spartan plc regardless of whether Wimbles are produced. Company policy has effectively turned this unskilled labour wages element into a fixed cost which cannot be adjusted in the short-term and is therefore not relevant to the decision at hand.

Supervisor: the relevant cost of the supervisor is the difference between the wages paid if Wimbles are produced, and the pension cost that would be avoided in this situation.

In assessing the relevant cost of labour the avoidable costs of production have been identified i.e. those which will not be incurred unless Wimbles are produced. If any element of the labour resource could be used for some other profitable purpose, then the opportunity cost representing the income forgone would have to be included in the analysis.

Machine X

Using the machine to manufacture Wimbles.

Start of year	cash outflow from purchasing another machine X	(£40,000)
End of year	cash inflow from selling machine X at the end of its useful life	£5,000

Decision not to manufacture Wimbles.

Start of year	no cash movement	
End of year	cash outflow from buying new machine X	(£45,000)
	cash inflow from selling machine X	£5,000

This is summarised as:

	Manufacture	*Non-manufacture*	*Increment*
	£	£	£
Start of year	(40,000)	0	(40,000)
End of year	5,000	(45,000)	45,000
		5,000	
	(35,000)	(40,000)	5,000

Thus the net effect of manufacturing the Wimble is to accelerate the purchase of machine X by 1 year to the start of the year, thereby saving £5,000 due to the lower cost of machine X at the start of the year.

Y: the manufacture of Wimbles would delay the sale of machine Y by one year, during which time the resale value of the machine would have been reduced by £1,000 as shown in the table of machine values above.

In determining the relevant costs associated with the use of plant and machinery, similar considerations apply as to those identified in respect of raw materials. If plant and equipment is to be replaced at the end of its useful life, or would be immediately replaced should the business be deprived of the use of an asset, then current replacement cost is the relevant cost. If the asset is not to be replaced, then the relevant cost becomes the higher of resale value or associated net receipts arising from use of the asset (economic value).

In this analysis of relevant cost, the assumption is made that the use of machine X is profitable for the company. If a situation arises in which an asset is not generating sufficient net receipts to meet a target rate of return the replacement of the asset would presumably not be encouraged since its use is uneconomic, and thus replacement cost is not relevant since it would not represent a viable option.

You should note however, that correctly identifying the true cost of using a particular asset may be difficult in practice, since economic values are not easily identified.

Overheads

Variable costs of £1.50 per Wimble are avoidable, being incurred only if Wimbles are produced. In contrast, fixed overhead may be assumed to be fixed regardless of the product being produced and the level of activity over a given range. Since fixed overhead is unaffected by the opportunity being considered, any apportionment of fixed cost is meaningless and would serve only to distort the profitability of the project.

For decision purposes, only those costs that will vary as a result of the decision taken are relevant.

A form of statement similar to that shown above for the analysis of differential cash flows could be used for presentation to management. In addition, supplementary information should be provided in order to disclose the principles adopted in evaluating the cost of use of each resource. Attention should be drawn to the fact that the surplus cash figure of £100,000 is the anticipated increase in Spartan plc's cash reserves arising from the manufacture of Wimbles rather than applying the required resources to their best alternative use.

Thus from a purely financial viewpoint the production and sale of Wimbles appears to be worthwhile. However, as was noted earlier, there may be other factors of interest to the decision-maker. Non-quantifiable qualitative factors such as the effect on longer- term marketing strategy, customer reaction, competitor reaction etc, should be identified and incorporated into the analysis so that a balanced judgement may be made.

Conclusion

In the above analysis the principle of relevance was applied in the evaluation of the financial factors surrounding the manufacture of Wimbles. At no time was historic cost suggested as being an appropriate measure of the relevant cost of a resource.

This presents a practical problem since conventional cost accounting records deal with costs already incurred i.e. historic cost. It may therefore be difficult to extract replacement costs or opportunity costs from the organisation's information system. Moreover, if the relevant cost approach is to be adopted, the accountant is faced with the task of educating managers, if the correct interpretation is to be placed on the figures presented.

However, despite these obstacles to adopting the correct approach to decision-making, the alternative route of applying conventional cost accounting principles is likely to lead to sub-optimal decisions. The dangers inherent in the historic cost accounting approach are discussed below.

Generally, the conventional cost accounting approach involves the identification of the historical or estimated costs of the resources actually used on a project, and these are then related to the revenues arising. The costs as identified often include fixed costs which are assigned on a subjective basis and do not therefore directly relate to the project under consideration. As a result, the worthiness of the particular opportunity may well be under or over-estimated.

Consider the conventional profitability statement set out below in relation to the manufacture of Wimbles:

Trading statement: Wimbles

	£	£	£
Sales			600,000
Less: Costs:			
Raw materials			
A (80,000m @ £1.05)	84,000		
B (30,000m @ £1.65 + 10,000m @ £1.20)	61,500		
C (10,000m @ £2.75)	27,500		
		173,000	
Labour			
Skilled (50,000 hours @ £3)	150,000		
Unskilled (25,000 hours @ £2)	50,000		
Supervisor	7,000		
		207,000	
Depreciation of machinery			
X [(11,000 - 5,000) ÷ 1]	6,000		
Y [(7,000 - 1,000) ÷ 2]	3,000		
		9,000	
Overheads			
Market research survey	2,000		
Variable (100,000 @ £1.50)	150,000		
Fixed (75,000 @ £2.50)	187,500		
		339,500	
Total costs			728,500
Trading loss			(128,500)

In applying conventional cost accounting practice, some specific resources are charged to a project at their original cost. Consider, for example, the costs of raw materials applied to the trading statement above. However, the inclusion of historic cost is incorrect for decision analysis. The crucial question to be answered in evaluating a course of action is: how will the cash flows of the business be affected? Thus, in the case of raw materials in our example, only the costs of the extra 10,000 metres of B and the 10,000 metres of additional material C are relevant costs. The historic costs are not, since they do not have any impact on future cash flows.

A second major difference of approach lies in the treatment of depreciation of assets. The traditional accounting methods of depreciation, such as those on a straight line or reducing balance basis, are an extension of the practice of matching or recovering past costs. Yet for decision purposes what is required is an evaluation of the sacrifice involved in using the asset on the project under consideration.

The third area of difference concerns fixed costs. In the example above, there are unskilled labour wages and fixed overhead costs in respect of the decision to manufacture Wimbles since they cannot be affected by it. Nevertheless, fixed costs such as these are often assigned to available project opportunities under conventional accounting practice.

It has been shown that the differences between conventional accounting practice and differential cash flow analysis may give rise to alarming discrepancies. In our example a conventional trading 'loss' of £128,500 is in fact an incremental cash flow surplus of £100,000. It is therefore not difficult to envisage sub-optimal decisions being taken as a result of advice which is based on conventional accounting practice. The notion of 'different costs for different purposes' should be borne in mind when providing financial information for managers.

7 Issues in decision-making

Decision-making may be applied to solve short-term operating problems or be part of the longer-term planning process. In this way decision-making may be stated to be short-term or long-term.

7.1 Short-term decision-making

KEY POINT

Short-term decision-making assumes that decisions previously made concerning fixed plant and equipment cannot be altered. Thus such decisions often involve making the best use of existing resources.

Short-term decision-making assumes that decisions previously made concerning fixed plant and equipment cannot be altered. Thus such decisions often involve making the best use of existing resources.

7.2 Long-term decision-making

KEY POINT

In the longer-term earlier decisions may be altered, new investment in plant and equipment may be considered.

Specifically, costs which may be considered 'fixed' in the short-term (and hence not decision relevant) may become variable and/or decision relevant if the situation demands that we take a longer time horizon.

In the longer-term earlier decisions may be altered, new investment in plant and equipment may be considered, and so such decisions have more variables and are more complex.

Specifically, costs which may be considered 'fixed' in the short-term (and hence not decision relevant) may become variable and/or decision relevant if the situation demands that we take a longer time horizon. Thus, if one is considering whether to accept Job A or Job B next week then the cost of equipment (hire, depreciation and maintenance) to be used on the jobs is probably fixed and not decision relevant.

However, if one is considering whether or not to produce Product A or Product B over the next five years then the decision will almost certainly impact on the amount and type of equipment that is needed. Hence the 'fixed' costs associated with equipment are decision relevant.

Long-term decisions require more assumptions about the future and must consider the opportunity cost of investing for a future reward. These aspects of uncertainty and the time value of money are considered later in this text.

7.3 Qualitative factors

Not all aspects of decision-making are amenable to a strictly quantitative analysis. The following factors (interested groups) may be affected by a decision:

- employees. Any decision which affects working practices will have a morale effect on employees. Some decisions, such as to close a department, will have a greater effect than others, for example an increase in production, but both will affect employees.
- customers. Customers will be affected by any decision which changes the finished product or its availability. For example, the deletion of a product will force customers to choose an alternative item.
- suppliers. Suppliers will be affected by changes to production which require different raw materials or delivery schedules. For example an increase in production may cause the supplier to increase their production of the raw material.
- competitors. Any decision to change product specification or pricing will affect competitors who will then choose whether or not to respond.
- scarce resource management. A change in production as a result of the decision may alter the demand for individual resources and the result of the decision may alter availability.
- social and environmental effects of a particular objective.
- the opinions of customers and employees.

KEY POINT

In most business situations only a limited number of business opportunities may be undertaken. Some factor will limit the ability to undertake all the alternatives. This factor is referred to as the **limiting factor.**

8 Limiting factors

In most business situations only a limited number of business opportunities may be undertaken. Some factor will limit the ability to undertake all the alternatives. This factor is referred to as the **limiting factor**.

8.1 Production scheduling with one limiting factor

Consider the situation where there is one factor limiting operations and two or more possible products. The management accountant must advise management on how to schedule production so as to maximise profits subject to the constraint.

The essential elements of the problem are as follows:

- The object is to maximise profits. Therefore only costs and revenues that vary according to the decision are considered. Since fixed costs do not, they are irrelevant and may be ignored.
- This leaves revenue and variable costs, which together specify the contribution of each product line. The aim is to maximise the total contribution.
- The real cost of producing Product 1 rather than Product 2 is the contribution of Product 2 forgone – the opportunity cost. It must be ensured that the total contribution of Product 1 gained exceeds that of Product 2 lost.
- Total contribution is given by units multiplied by contribution per unit. The number of units is limited by the limiting factor. In the evaluation of alternative products consideration must be given not only to contribution per unit, but also to the number of units that can be produced, subject to the limiting factor.
- To take both of these factors together, total contribution is maximised by concentrating on that product which yields the highest contribution per unit of limiting factor.

Example

A company makes and sells two products – X and Y. It has a shortage of labour, which is limited to 200,000 hours pa. This is insufficient to satisfy the full demand for both products. The unit costs, contributions and labour hours used are as follows:

	Product X	*Product Y*
Labour hours per unit of output	5	10
	£	£
Selling price	80	100
Variable cost	50	50
Contribution per unit	30	50

There are two ways in which the production scheduling problem can be solved.

(a) Calculate total contribution if each is produced in turn:

	Total contribution
Product X units = $\frac{200,000}{5}$ = 40,000	
Contribution × units = £30 × 40,000	£1,200,000
Product Y units = $\frac{200,000}{10}$ = 20,000	
Contribution × units = £50 × 20,000	£1,000,000

Thus, Product X would be produced since it maximises total contribution.

(b) A quicker approach is to find which product has the higher contribution per unit of limiting factor i.e. per labour hour:

	Contribution per labour hour
Product X = $\frac{£30}{5}$ =	£6
Product Y= $\frac{£50}{10}$ =	£5

This is of course merely a way of short-cutting the calculations in (a) above, and exactly the same conclusion is reached: production should concentrate on Product X.

8.2 Other considerations in the limiting factor situation

KEY POINT

In the long run management must seek to remove the limiting factor.

- In the long run management must seek to remove the limiting factor. In the above example management should be recruiting and training additional labour. Thus, any one limiting factor should only be a short-term problem. However, as soon as it is removed it will be replaced by another limiting factor.
- Even in the short run management may be able to find ways round the bottleneck e.g. overtime working, temporary staff and sub-contracting might all be solutions to the situation described.
- Nor may it always be easy to identify the limiting factor. In practice several limiting factors may operate simultaneously. However, even in examination questions, where there is only one limiting factor, it may be necessary to identify between several possible limiting factors.

- It is also possible that there may be other parameters setting minimum production levels e.g. there may be a contract to supply Y so that certain minimum quantities must be produced.

Example

X Ltd makes three products, A, B and C, of which unit costs, machine hours and selling prices are as follows:

	Product A	*Product B*	*Product C*
Machine hours	10	12	14
	£	£	£
Direct materials @ 50p per lb	7 (14 lbs)	6 (12 lbs)	5 (10 lbs)
Direct wages @ 75p per hour	9 (12 hours)	6 (8 hours)	3 (4 hours)
Variable overheads	3	3	3
Marginal cost	19	15	11
Selling price	25	20	15
Contribution	6	5	4

Sales demand for the period is limited as follows:

Product A	4,000
Product B	6,000
Product C	6,000

As a matter of company policy it is decided to produce a minimum of 1,000 units of Product A. The supply of materials in the period is unlimited, but machine hours are limited to 200,000 and direct labour hours to 50,000.

Indicate the production levels that should be adopted for the three products in order to maximise profitability, and state the maximum contribution.

Solution

First determine which is the limiting factor. At potential sales level:

	Sales potential units	*Total machine hours*	*Total labour hours*
Product A	4,000	40,000	48,000
Product B	6,000	72,000	48,000
Product C	6,000	84,000	24,000
		196,000	120,000

Thus, labour hours is the limiting factor. The next stage is to calculate contribution per labour hour:

Product A $\frac{£6}{12} = £0.500$

Product B $\frac{£5}{8} = £0.625$

Product C $\frac{£4}{4} = £1.000$

Thus production should be concentrated on C, up to the maximum available sales, then B, and finally A.

However, a minimum of 1,000 units of A must be produced. Taking these factors into account, the production schedule becomes:

	Units produced	*Labour hours*	*Cumulative labour hours*	*Limiting factor*
Product A	1,000	12,000	12,000	Policy to produce 1,000 units
Product C	6,000	24,000	36,000	Sales
Product B	1,750	14,000	50,000	Labour hours

9 Throughput accounting

We have encountered this technique earlier in the text in the context of modern developments in management accounting.

KEY POINT

OPT works on the principle that profits can be maximised by making the most productive use of 'bottleneck resources' in a plant and concentrating on means to relieve those bottlenecks.

One of the management ideas introduced in the 1980s was "optimised production technology" (or OPT).OPT works on the principle that profits can be maximised by making the most productive use of 'bottleneck resources' in a plant and concentrating on means to relieve those bottlenecks.

The idea is that managers should seek to identify those resources in a plant which constrain production – known as bottleneck resources. Profit is only maximised when production is scheduled in such a way that the bottleneck resources are both fully utilised and utilised in a manner which makes the most efficient use of them. A system of management accounting which reports on products in terms of the contribution per unit of the bottleneck resources that they generate will assist in decision-making and production scheduling. Essentially, limiting factor analysis is built into the management accounting system. The bottleneck resources are the limiting factors. Long-term action can be directed to investing in new resources, redesigning products or altering work methods in order remove the bottleneck resource/activity/factor. Of course, when you remove one bottleneck factor, then another one will immediately emerge and the process has to be repeated again.

KEY POINT

The TA ratio amounts to the contribution per unit of the limiting factor of each product.

The term throughput accounting was first promoted in 1988 by the academic accountants Galloway and Waldron. They devised a performance measure called the 'throughput accounting ratio'. The TA ratio amounts to the contribution per unit of the limiting factor of each product. In calculating the TA ratio it may be assumed that, in the very short run, all costs other than material costs are fixed. Hence contribution is taken to be sales price less material costs.

The theory of throughput accounting very closely follows limiting factor analysis. Throughput accounting has never been widely adopted in UK industry and one of its principle early advocates (Galloway) now rejects its use. Instead, he advocates the wider use of TOC (Theory of Constraints) concepts. These concepts include limiting factor analysis (discussed above) and linear programming (an OR technique, not explored in this text).

10 Problems involving product mix and discontinuance/shutdown

KEY POINT

The term contribution describes the amount which a product provides or contributes towards a fund out of which fixed overhead may be paid, the balance being net profit.

It is considered more informative to present comparison statements on a contribution basis. The term contribution describes the amount which a product provides or contributes towards a fund out of which fixed overhead may be paid, the balance being net profit. Where two or more products are manufactured in a factory and share all production facilities, the fixed overhead can only be apportioned on an arbitrary basis.

Example

A factory manufactures three components – X, Y and Z – and the budgeted production for the year is 1,000 units, 1,500 units and 2,000 units respectively. Fixed overhead amounts to £6,750 and has been apportioned on the basis of budgeted units: £1,500 to X, £2,250 to Y and £3,000 to Z. Sales and variable costs are as follows:

	Component X	*Component Y*	*Component Z*
Selling price	£4	£6	£5
Variable cost	£1	£4	£4

The budgeted profit and loss account based on the above is as follows:

	Component X		*Component Y*		*Component Z*		*Total*	
Sales units		1,000		1,500		2,000		4,500
	£	£	£	£	£	£	£	£
Sales value		4,000		9,000		10,000		23,000
Variable cost	1,000		6,000		8,000		15,000	
Fixed overhead	1,500		2,250		3,000		6,750	
		2,500		8,250		11,000		21,750
Net profit/(loss)		1,500		750		(1,000)		1,250

Clearly there is little value in comparing products in this way. If the fixed overhead is common to all three products, there is no point in apportioning it. A better presentation is as follows:

	Component X	*Component Y*	*Component Z*	*Total*
Sales units	1,000	1,500	2,000	4,500
	£	£	£	£
Sales value	4,000	9,000	10,000	23,000
Variable cost	1,000	6,000	8,000	15,000
Contribution	3,000	3,000	2,000	8,000
Fixed cost				6,750
Net profit				1,250

Analysis may show, however, that certain fixed costs may be associated with a specific product and the statement can be amended to differentiate specific fixed costs (under products) from general fixed costs (under total).

10.1 Closure of a business segment

Part of a business may appear to be unprofitable. The segment may, for example, be a product, a department or a channel of distribution. In evaluating closure the cost accountant should identify:

- loss of contribution from the segment
- savings in specific fixed costs from closure
- penalties e.g. redundancy, compensation to customers etc
- alternative use for resources released
- non-quantifiable effects.

Example

Harolds department store comprises three departments - Menswear, Ladies' Wear and Unisex. The store budget is as follows:

	Mens	*Ladies*	*Unisex*	*Total*
	£	£	£	£
Sales	40,000	60,000	20,000	120,000
Direct cost of sales	20,000	36,000	15,000	71,000
Department costs	5,000	10,000	3,000	18,000
Apportioned store costs	5,000	5,000	5,000	15,000
Profit/(loss)	10,000	9,000	(3,000)	16,000

It is suggested that Unisex be closed to increase the size of Mens and Ladies.

What information is relevant or required?

Solution

Possible answers are:

- Unisex earns £2,000 net contribution (store costs will be re-apportioned to Mens/Ladies).
- Possible increase in Mens/Ladies sales volume.
- Will Unisex staff be dismissed or transferred to Mens/Ladies?
- Reorganisation costs e.g. repartitioning, stock disposal.
- Loss of custom because Unisex attracts certain types of customer who will not buy in Mens/Ladies.

10.2 Comparing segment profitability

When presenting information for comparing results or plans for different products, departments etc, it is useful to show gross and net contribution for each segment. The information in the example above would be presented in the following form.

	Mens Wear £000	*Ladies Wear* £000	*Unisex* £000	*Total* £000
Sales	40	60	20	120
Direct cost of sales	20	36	15	71
Gross contribution	20	24	5	49
Department costs	5	10	3	18
Net contribution	15	14	2	31

Note that the store costs if shown would only appear in the total column. In addition, the statement should include performance indicators relevant to the type of operation. For a department store, such indicators would include:

- C/S ratios (based on **gross** contribution)
- gross and net contribution per unit of floor space
- gross and net contribution per employee.

For a manufacturing company, more relevant indicators would include:

- contribution per labour/machine hour
- added value/conversion cost per hour
- added/value conversion cost per employee.

10.3 Temporary shut-down

When a business has experienced trading difficulties which do not appear likely to improve in the immediate future, consideration may be given to closing down operations temporarily. Factors other than cost which will influence the decision are:

- suspending production and sales of products will result in their **leaving the public eye**
- dismissal of the labour force will entail bad feeling and possible difficulty in recruitment when operations are restarted
- danger of plant obsolescence
- difficulty and cost of closing down and restarting operations in certain industries, e.g. a blast furnace.

The temporary closure of a business will result in additional expenditure e.g. plant will require protective coverings, services will be disconnected. In the same way, additional expenditure will be incurred when the business restarts.

On the other hand, a temporary closure may enable the business to reorganise efficiently to take full advantage of improved trading conditions when they return.

In the short-term a business can continue to operate while marginal contribution equals fixed expenses. In periods of trading difficulty, as long as some contribution is made towards fixed expenses, it will generally be worthwhile continuing operations.

Example

A company is operating at 40% capacity and is considering closing down its factory for one year, after which time the demand for its product is expected to increase substantially. The following data applies:

	£
Sales value at 40% capacity	60,000
Marginal costs of sales at 40% capacity	40,000
Fixed costs	50,000

Fixed costs which will remain if the factory is closed amount to £20,000. The cost of closing down operations will amount to £4,000.

Prepare a statement to show the best course of action.

Solution

Statement of profit or loss

Continuing operation	£	*Temporary closure*	£
Sales	60,000	Fixed expenses	20,000
Marginal cost of sales	40,000	Closing down costs	4,000
Contribution to fixed costs	20,000		
Fixed costs	50,000		
Net loss	(30,000)		(24,000)

Ignoring non-cost considerations, the company will minimise its losses by closing down for one year.

Students should note that the marginal contribution of £20,000 does not cover the difference between existing fixed costs and those that remain on closure (i.e. £(50,000 – 24,000) = £26,000 compared to £20,000).

10.4 An approach to shutdown problems

If you are asked in an examination to advise on the merits or otherwise of shutting down a department, an operation or a product line, you might find it useful to present the financial implications in a table that distinguishes between avoidable and unavoidable costs. A proforma table is suggested below, with illustrative figures.

Product X/Department Y	£
Sales	800,000
Variable cost of sales	500,000
Contribution earned by the product	300,000
Avoidable fixed costs, not yet committed	120,000
Net cash flow lost in the short term by shutting down	180,000
Fixed costs committed for this year, avoidable longer-term	220,000
Net cash flow saved in the longer term by shutting down	(40,000)
Unavoidable fixed costs	(80,000)
Share of general company-wide overhead	(140,000)
Budgeted loss for the product/department	(260,000)

Fixed costs are avoidable or unavoidable, but avoidable fixed costs might have been committed in the short term, for example by a one-year contract that has already been signed. In the longer term, these costs too could be avoided. A shutdown decision might therefore need to consider what to do in both the immediate term and the longer-term.

11 Divestment

A company may have to drop existing product-market areas as well as develop new ones. For instance, a product might be nearing the end of its life cycle and it might be better to 'kill it off' once sales have fallen below a certain level rather than let it decline to zero. Advertising expenditure to boost the sale of a declining product is often not worthwhile in terms of the return achieved.

The precise timing of a decision to drop a certain line (or cease selling it in a particular market) is admittedly difficult, but most companies probably tend to leave it too late. Some of the reasons for the reluctance to drop products are:

The company might have invested large sums of money in the project and does not want to abandon it. Management accountants will recognise that this is a quite erroneous standpoint – the money already spent is a sunk cost and it is the future not the past which is important. Companies should be prepared to 'cut their losses' – it is no good throwing good money after bad.

- Perhaps the person who designed the product is still with the firm. He and probably many others are 'attached' to the product and want to keep it going. In addition, the marketing director might be an optimist who thinks that sales of the product will suddenly turn up again. This can happen, but is unlikely unless the cause of the fall in demand is the general economic climate – but we are really talking about products which have a history of continuously falling demand.
- Attention is directed towards new products and no-one thinks what should happen to the old ones (until resources are scarce and there is a search for economies).
- There is a feeling that customers should be kept happy and a fear that they will be lost to the firm if the particular product is withdrawn. This fear need have no foundation if a new product is launched as the old one is withdrawn. Anyway, does it matter if some old customers are lost, as long as more new ones are gained?
- A very real problem exists of what to do with the work force who have been running an existing production line if it is suddenly shut down. It may be easier to absorb the work force into other areas if production is run down gradually. There are, however, arguments against this:
  - (i) Morale among those remaining on the product may fall if they know that their job is eventually going to go and they do not know when, or where they will be moved. If this loss of morale is reflected in their work the product may become even more uneconomic.
  - (ii) A sensible programme of retraining can ensure that workers released from an old line will be available for a new process.
  - (iii) It may prove more costly to keep the workers employed on the old process than to pay them for doing nothing until their services are again required elsewhere.

The detailed programming of divestment is of course a matter for the administrative and operating plans, but at the strategic level it is important to emphasise that this is one area for examination.

12 Make or buy decisions

12.1 Types of make or buy decisions

Occasionally a business may have the opportunity to purchase, from another company, a component part or assembly which it currently produces from its own resources. In examining the choice, management must first consider the following questions:

- Is the alternative source of supply available only temporarily or for the foreseeable future?
- Is there spare production capacity available now and/or in the future?

12.2 Spare capacity

If the business is operating below maximum capacity, production resources will be idle if the component is purchased from outside. The fixed costs of those resources are irrelevant to the decision in the short-term as they will be incurred whether the component is made or purchased. Purchase would be recommended, therefore, only if the buying price were less than the variable costs of internal manufacture.

In the long-term, however, the business may dispense with or transfer some of its resources and may purchase from outside if it thereby saves more than the extra cost of purchasing.

Example

A company manufactures an assembly used in the production of one of its product lines. The department in which the assembly is produced incurs fixed costs of £24,000 pa. The variable costs of production are £2.55 per unit. The assembly could be bought outside at a cost of £2.65 per unit.

The current annual requirement is for 80,000 assemblies per year. Should the company continue to manufacture the assembly, or should it be purchased from the outside suppliers?

Solution

A decision to purchase outside would cost the company £(2.65 - 2.55) = 10p per unit, which for 80,000 assemblies would amount to £8,000 pa. Thus, the fixed costs of £24,000 will require analysis to determine if more than £8,000 would actually be saved if production of the assembly were discontinued.

12.3 Other considerations affecting the decision

Management would need to consider other factors before reaching a decision. Some would be quantifiable and some not:

- **Continuity and control of supply.** Can the outside company be relied upon to meet the requirements in terms of quantity, quality, delivery dates and price stability?
- **Alternative use of resources.** Can the resources used to make this article be transferred to another activity which will save cost or increase revenue?
- **Social/legal.** Will the decision affect contractual or ethical obligations to employees or business connections?

12.4 Capacity exhausted

If a business cannot fulfil orders because it has used up all available capacity, it may be forced to purchase from outside in the short-term (unless it is cheaper to refuse sales). In the longer term management may look to other alternatives, such as capital expenditure.

It may be, however, that a variety of components is produced from common resources and management would try to arrange manufacture or purchase to use its available capacity most profitably. In such a situation the limiting factor concept makes it easier to formulate the optimum plans. Priority for purchase would be indicated by ranking components in relation to the excess purchasing cost per unit of limiting factor.

Example

Fidgets Ltd manufactures three components used in its finished product. The component workshop is currently unable to meet the demand for components and the possibility of sub-contracting part of the requirement is being investigated on the basis of the following data:

	Component A	*Component B*	*Component C*
	£	£	£
Variable costs of production	3.00	4.00	7.00
Outside purchase price	2.50	6.00	13.00
Excess cost per unit	(0.50)	2.00	6.00
Machine hours per unit	1	0.5	2
Labour hours per unit	2	2	4

You are required:

(a) to decide which component should be bought out if the company is operating at full capacity;

(b) to decide which component should be bought out if production is limited to 4,000 machine hours per week;

(c) to decide which component should be bought out if production is limited to 4,000 labour hours per week.

Solution

(a) Component A should always be bought out regardless of any limiting factors, as its variable cost of production is higher than the outside purchase price.

(b) If machine hours are limited to 4,000 hours:

	Component B	*Component C*
Excess cost	£2	£6
Machine hours per unit	0.5	2
Excess cost per machine hour	£4	£3

Component C has the lowest excess cost per limiting factor and should, therefore, be bought out.

Proof:

	Component B	*Component C*
Units produced in 4,000 hours	8,000	2,000
	£	£
Production costs	32,000	14,000
Purchase costs	48,000	26,000
Excess cost of purchase	16,000	12,000

(c) If labour hours are limited to 4,000 hours:

	Component B	*Component C*
Excess cost	£2	£6
Labour hours	2	4
Excess cost per labour hour	£1	£1.50

Therefore, component B has the lowest excess cost per limiting factor and should be bought out.

Proof:

	Component B	*Component C*
Units produced in 4,000 hours	2,000	1,000
	£	£
Production costs	8,000	7,000
Purchase costs	12,000	13,000
Excess cost of purchase	4,000	6,000

13 Evaluating proposals

13.1 Volume and cost structure changes

KEY POINT

Management will require information to evaluate proposals aimed to increase profit by changing operating strategy.

Management will require information to evaluate proposals aimed to increase profit by changing operating strategy. The cost accountant will need to show clearly the effect of the proposals on profit by pin-pointing the changes in costs and revenues and by quantifying the margin of error which will cause the proposal to be unviable.

Example

A company produces and sells one product and its forecast for the next financial year is as follows:

	£000	£000
Sales 100,000 units @ £8		800
Variable costs:		
Material	300	
Labour	200	
		500
Contribution (£3 per unit)		300
Fixed costs		150
Net profit		150

As an attempt to increase net profit, two proposals have been put forward:

(a) to launch an advertising campaign costing £14,000. This will increase the sales to 150,000 units, although the price will have to be reduced to £7;

(b) to produce some components at present purchased from suppliers. This will reduce material costs by 20% but will increase fixed costs by £72,000.

Proposal (a) will increase the sales revenue but the increase in costs will be greater:

	£000
Sales 150,000 × £7	1,050
Variable costs	750
	300
Fixed costs plus advertising	164
Net profit	136

Solution

Proposal (a) is therefore of no value and sales must be increased by a further 7,000 units to maintain net profit:

Advertising cost	=	£14,000
Contribution per unit	=	£2
∴ Additional volume required	=	7,000 units

Proposal (b) reduces variable costs by £60,000 but increases fixed costs by £72,000 and is therefore not to be recommended unless the total volume increases as a result of the policy (e.g. if the supply of the components were previously a limiting factor).

The increase in sales needed to maintain profit at £150,000 (assuming the price remains at £8) would be:

Reduced profits at 100,000 units	=	£12,000
Revised contribution per unit	=	£3.60
∴ Additional volume required	=	3,333 units

13.2 Utilisation of spare capacity

Where production is below capacity, opportunities may arise for sales at a specially reduced price, for example, export orders or manufacturing under another brand name (e.g. 'St Michael'). Such opportunities are worthwhile if the answer to two key questions is 'Yes':

- Is spare capacity available?
- Does additional revenue (Units × Price) exceed additional costs (Units × Variable cost)?

However, the evaluation should also consider:

- Is there an alternative more profitable way of utilising spare capacity (e.g. sales promotion, making an alternative product)?
- Will fixed costs be unchanged if the order is accepted?
- Will accepting one order at below normal selling price lead other customers to ask for price cuts?

The longer the time period in question, the more important are these other factors.

Example

At a production level of 8,000 units per month, which is 80% of capacity, the budget of Export Ltd is:

	Per unit	*8,000 units*
	£	£
Sales	5.00	40,000
Variable costs:		
Direct labour	1.00	8,000
Raw materials	1.50	12,000
Variable overheads	0.50	4,000
	3.00	24,000
Fixed costs	1.50	12,000
Total	4.50	36,000
Budgeted profit	0.50	4,000

An opportunity arises to export 1,000 units per month at a price of £4 per unit.

Should the contract be accepted?

Solution

(a) Is spare capacity available? Yes

			£
(b)	Additional revenue	1,000 × £4	4,000
	Additional costs	1,000 × £3	3,000
			1,000

Increased profitability

Therefore, the contract should be accepted.

Note that fixed costs are not relevant to the decision and are therefore ignored.

13.3 Special contract pricing

A business which produces to customer's order may be working to full capacity. Any additional orders must be considered on the basis of the following questions:

- What price must be quoted to make the contract profitable?
- Can other orders be fulfilled if this contract is accepted?

Note that if other orders cannot be fulfilled if this contract is accepted, then the contribution that has to be thereby foregone is an opportunity cost of the contract.

KEY POINT

The limiting factor needs to be recognised so that the contract price quoted will at least maintain the existing rate of contribution per unit of limiting factor.

In such a situation the limiting factor needs to be recognised so that the contract price quoted will at least maintain the existing rate of contribution per unit of limiting factor.

Example

Oddjobs Ltd manufactures special purpose gauges to customers' specifications. The highly skilled labour force is always working to full capacity and the budget for the next year shows:

	£	£
Sales		40,000
Direct materials	4,000	
Direct wages 3,200 hours @ £5	16,000	
Fixed overhead	10,000	
		30,000
Profit		10,000

An enquiry is received from XY Ltd for a gauge which would use £60 of direct materials and 40 labour hours.

(a) What is the minimum price to quote to XY Ltd?

(b) Would the minimum price be different if spare capacity were available but materials were subject to a quota of £4,000 per year?

Solution

(a) The limiting factor is 3,200 labour hours and the budgeted contribution per hour is £20,000 ÷ 3,200 hours = £6.25 per hour. Minimum price is therefore:

	£
Materials	60
Wages 40 hours @ £5	200
	260
Add: Contribution 40 hours @ £6.25	250
Contract price	510

At the above price the contract will maintain the budgeted contribution (check by calculating the effect of devoting the whole 3,200 hours to XY Ltd.)

Note, however, that the budget probably represents a mixture of orders, some of which earn more than £6.25 per hour and some less. Acceptance of the XY order must displace other contracts, so the contribution rate of contracts displaced should be checked.

(b) If the limiting factor is materials, budgeted contribution per £ of materials is £20,000 ÷ 4,000 = £5 per £1.

Minimum price is therefore:

	£
Materials/wages (as above)	260
Contribution £60 × 5	300
Contract price	560

Because materials are scarce, Oddjobs must aim to earn the maximum profit from its limited supply.

14 Further processing decisions

In processing operations, particularly those involving more than one product, there is often a choice to be made between selling a product in an unfinished state (to another manufacturer) or to further process it into a finished product for sale to the consumer.

14.1 Relevant costs and revenues of further processing decisions

KEY POINT

Relevant costs are those which are incurred as a consequence of the decision to further process the item.

KEY POINT

Relevant revenues are the extra revenues earned from selling the product in its further processed state instead of selling it in its semi-processed state.

Relevant costs are those which are incurred as a consequence of the decision to further process the item. Thus common costs incurred already, for example pre-separation costs, should always be ignored.

Relevant revenues are the extra revenues earned from selling the product in its further processed state instead of selling it in its semi-processed state.

Example

PST Ltd produces three products from a common process which costs £104,000 per month to operate. Typical monthly outputs are:

Product	*Output (litres)*
P	10,000
S	5,000
T	8,000

Each of the products may be further processed. Selling prices and further processing costs per litre are as follows:

		Product	
Cost/Revenues/litre	*P*	*S*	*T*
	£	£	£
Further processing	5.00	3.00	9.00
Selling price:			
Before further processing	11.00	14.00	13.00
After further processing	15.00	19.00	20.00

Advise PST Ltd whether it should further process any of its products.

Solution

The common cost is irrelevant, only the incremental costs and revenues should be considered:

	P	S	T
	£	£	£
Selling price:			
Before further processing	11.00	14.00	13.00
After further processing	15.00	19.00	20.00
Incremental revenue	4.00	5.00	7.00
Further processing cost	(5.00)	(3.00)	(9.00)
Incremental contribution	(1.00)	2.00	(2.00)

The above table, based on values per litre, shows that the further processing of product S is the only further processing activity which leads to an increase in contribution.

Therefore, PST Ltd should further process product S, but should sell products P and T without further processing them.

ACTIVITY 1

Z Ltd operates a process which produces three products: X, Y, and Z. Each of these may be sold without further processing or refined and sold as higher quality products. The following costs/revenues have been determined:

	X	Y	Z
Refining cost/litre (£)	3.00	2.50	3.50
Selling prices/litre (£):			
Refined	6.00	5.50	7.00
Unrefined	2.50	2.75	4.00

On the basis of the above, which products, if any, should Z Ltd refine?

Feedback to this activity is at the end of the chapter.

15 The choice between internal service departments and external services

Typically these decision choices are concerned with the administration function of a business, though it is possible to make these choices in other areas, for example in selling a choice may be made between using selling agents or company employees.

Relevant costs

The decision is very similar to that described earlier as make or buy, the difference being that it is likely that if internal service departments are to be used there will be a significant amount of fixed costs incurred whereas if external services are used the cost may be significantly variable.

Example

KRS Ltd is considering whether to administer its own purchase ledger or to use an external accounting service. It has obtained the following cost estimates for each option:

Internal service department:

Purchase computer cost	£1,000
Purchase computer software	£600
Hardware/software maintenance	£750 per annum
Accounting stationery	£500 per annum
Part-time accounts clerk	£6,000 per annum

External services:

Processing of invoices/credit notes	£0.50 per document
Processing of cheque payments	£0.50 per cheque
Reconciling supplier accounts	£2.00 per supplier per month

KRS Ltd would have to assess the forecast volumes of transactions involved before making its decision.

15.1 Qualitative factors

Such decisions will also involve qualitative factors, such as:

- the reliability of supply
- the quality of supply
- security of information.

Conclusion

Basic management accounting techniques for short term decision-making are cost volume profit analysis and relevant cost analysis. The concept of relevant costs is quite straightforward, but applying the concept can sometimes be a bit tricky. It certainly helps to study relevant costs by working on examples. We recommend that you attempt the questions at the end of this chapter, and study the solutions carefully.

SELF-TEST QUESTIONS

Issues in decision-making

1 List the qualitative factors that may be relevant in short-term decision-making. (7.3)

Limiting factors

2 What is a limiting factor? (8)

Throughput accounting

3 What is throughput accounting? (9)

Problems involving product mix and discontinuance/shutdown

4 What information is relevant in the decision to close a segment of a business? (10.1)

EXAM-TYPE QUESTIONS

Question 1: JK Ltd

JK Ltd has prepared a budget for the next 12 months when it intends to make and sell four products, details of which are shown below:

Product	*Sales in units* (thousands)	*Selling price per unit*	*Variable cost per unit*
		£	£
J	10	20	14.00
K	10	40	8.00
L	50	4	4.20
M	20	10	7.00

Budgeted fixed costs are £240,000 per annum and total assets employed are £570,000.

Required:

(a) Calculate the total contribution earned by each product and their combined total contributions. **(2 marks)**

(b) Plot the data of your answer to (a) above in the form of a contribution to sales graph; (sometimes referred to as a profit-volume graph). **(6 marks)**

(c) Explain your graph to management, to comment on the results shown and to state the break-even point. **(4 marks)**

(d) Describe briefly three ways in which the overall contribution to sales ratio could be improved. **(3 marks)**

(Total: 15 marks)

Question 2: A company

The annual flexible budget of a company is as follows:

Production capacity	*40%*	*60%*	*80%*	*100%*
Costs:	£	£	£	£
Direct labour	16,000	24,000	32,000	40,000
Direct material	12,000	18,000	24,000	30,000
Production overhead	11,400	12,600	13,800	15,000
Administration overhead	5,800	6,200	6,600	7,000
Selling and distribution overhead	6,200	6,800	7,400	8,000
	51,400	67,600	83,800	100,000

Owing to trading difficulties the company is operating at 50% capacity. Selling prices have had to be lowered to what the directors maintain is an uneconomic level and they are considering whether or not their single factory should be closed down until the trade recession has passed.

A market research consultant has advised that in about twelve months' time there is every indication that sales will increase to about 75% of normal capacity and that the revenue to be produced in the second year will amount to £90,000. The present revenue from sales at 50% capacity would amount to only £49,500 for a complete year.

If the directors decide to close down the factory for a year it is estimated that:

(a) the present fixed costs would be reduced to £11,000 per annum;

(b) closing down costs (redundancy payments etc) would amount to £7,500;

(c) necessary maintenance of plant would cost £1,000 per annum; and

(d) on re-opening the factory, the cost of overhauling plant, training and engagement of new personnel would amount to £4,000.

Prepare a statement for the directors, presenting the information in such a way as to indicate whether or not it is desirable to close the factory. **(15 marks)**

Question 3: Choice of contracts

A company in the civil engineering industry with headquarters located 22 miles from London undertakes contracts anywhere in the United Kingdom.

The company has had its tender for a job in north-east England accepted at £288,000 and work is due to begin in March 20X3. However, the company has also been asked to undertake a contract on the south coast of England. The price offered for this contract is £352,000. Both of the contracts cannot be taken simultaneously because of constraints on staff site management personnel and on plant available. An escape clause enables the company to withdraw from the contract in the north-east, provided notice is given before the end of November and an agreed penalty of £28,000 is paid.

The following estimates have been submitted by the company's quantity surveyor:

Cost estimates

	North-east	*South coast*
	£	£
Materials:		
In stock at original cost, Material X	21,600	
In stock at original cost, Material Y		24,800
Firm orders placed at original cost, Material X	30,400	
Not yet ordered - current cost, Material X	60,000	
Not yet ordered - current cost, Material Z		71,200
Labour - hired locally	86,000	110,000
Site management	34,000	34,000
Staff accommodation and travel for site management	6,800	5,600
Plant on site - depreciation	9,600	12,800
Interest on capital, 8%	5,120	6,400
Total local contract costs	253,520	264,800
Headquarters costs allocated at rate of 5% on total		
Contract costs	12,676	13,240
	266,196	278,040
Contract price	288,000	352,000
Estimated profit	21,804	73,960

Notes

(1) X, Y and Z are three building materials. Material X is not in common use and would not realise much money if re-sold; however, it could be used on other contracts but only as a substitute for another material currently quoted at 10% less than the original cost of X. The price of Y, a material in common use, has doubled since it was purchased; its net realisable value if re-sold would be its new price less 15% to cover disposal costs. Alternatively it could be kept for use on other contracts in the following financial year.

(2) With the construction industry not yet recovered from the recent recession, the company is confident that manual labour, both skilled and unskilled, could be hired locally on a sub-contracting basis to meet the needs of each of the contracts.

(3) The plant which would be needed for the south coast contract has been owned for some years and £12,800 is the year's depreciation on a straight-line basis. If the north-east contract is undertaken, less plant will be required but the surplus plant will be hired out for the period of the contract at a rental of £6,000.

(4) It is the company's policy to charge all contracts with notional interest at 8% on estimated working capital involved in contracts. Progress payments would be receivable from the contractee.

(5) Salaries and general costs of operating the small headquarters amount to about £108,000 each year. There are usually ten contracts being supervised at the same time.

(6) Each of the two contracts is expected to last from March 20X3 to February 20X4 which, coincidentally, is the company's financial year.

(7) Site management is treated as a fixed cost.

Required:

As the management accountant to the company,

(a) Present comparative statements to show the net benefit to the company of undertaking the more advantageous of the two contracts; **(12 marks)**

(b) Explain the reasoning behind the inclusion in (or omission from) your comparative financial statements, of each item given in the cost estimates and the notes relating thereto. **(13 marks)**

(Total: 25 marks)

For the answers to these questions, see the 'Answers' section at the end of the book.

FEEDBACK TO ACTIVITY **1**

		Product	
	X	*Y*	*Z*
	£	£	£
Incremental revenue/litre (£)	3.50	2.75	3.00
Incremental cost/litre (£)	(3.00)	(2.50)	(3.50)
	0.50	0.25	(0.50)

Products X and Y should be refined.

Chapter 7
LONG-TERM DECISION-MAKING

CHAPTER CONTENTS

This chapter explores long-term decision-making with particular reference to the use of DCF analysis.

Objectives

When you have studied this chapter you should be able to do the following.

- Define and illustrate the concepts of net present value and internal rate of return.
- Calculate the net present value and internal rate of return in the evaluation of an investment opportunity.
- Explain the use of DCF techniques for decisions involving cash outlays over long periods.
- Explain the relationship between net present value and residual income where annuity depreciation is used in the residual income calculations.
- Compare and contrast net present value with payback and accounting rate of return in the evaluation of investment opportunities.

1 Introduction

This chapter explores a variety of concepts and techniques that are used in long-term decision-making. You should have encountered many of these techniques earlier in your studies.

2 Long-term decision-making techniques

2.1 Net present value

KEY POINT

DCF analysis is one of the most powerful analytical techniques available to the management accountant and it is widely used in almost every area of accounting, finance and economics.

Net Present Value (NPV) is a performance measure based on Discounted Cash Flow (DCF) analysis. DCF analysis is one of the most powerful analytical techniques available to the management accountant and it is widely used in almost every area of accounting, finance and economics.

To illustrate how it works, let us consider the following simple case.

Today (year 0) is your birthday and a relative has promised to give you £1 for your next birthday (year 1), £1 on your birthday the following year (year 2) and £1 on your birthday the year after that (year 3). You are therefore assured of an annual cash inflow of £1 starting at year 1 and continuing until year 3.

You wish to realise this cash flow now (at year 0). To do this, you approach a bank manager and make following proposition: "If I give you the £1 receivable at year 1 when I receive it, how much will you give me now?" The answer to this question will depend on the interest rate. If the interest rate is 10% then the amount given (or rather 'loaned') will be:

£1 / 1.10 = £0.90909

The 'present value' of £1 receivable at year 1 is £0.90909. If 10% interest is added to that amount at year 1, then £1 will be precisely the amount required to discharge the debt with interest added.

The same logic may be applied for the £1 receivable at year 2, except that 10% annual interest has to be applied twice. The present value of £1 receivable at year 2 if the annual interest rate is 10% will be:

£1 / 1.10 / 1.10 = £0.82645

The present value of £1 receivable at year 3 with a 10% interest rate is:

£1 / 1.10 / 1.10 / 1.10 = £0.75131

So, the present value of the whole year 1 to year 3 cash stream is:

Year 1	0.90909
Year 2	0.82645
Year 3	0.75131
Total	2.48685

At this point, you should refer to the mathematical tables in the preliminary pages of this book. The annual discount rates can be identified in the 10% column of the present value table. The total of these (or the cumulative discount rate) can be identified in the 3 year row on the 10% column of the annuity table. The purpose of these Tables is self-evident.

Note that the higher the applicable interest rate then the lower the relevant present values. The present value of future cash receipts is reduced if interest rates are increased.

This basic logic can be applied to the appraisal of a long-term investment. Let us consider the case of an investment that involves a present (year 0) purchase of £100 worth of equipment and generates a £30 annual cash inflow (year 1 to year 5). The 'net present value' of this project may be calculated as follows.

	c/f	Rate	PV
Year 0	–100	1.00000	–100.00
1	30	0.90909	27.27
2	30	0.82645	24.79
3	30	0.75131	22.54
4	30	0.68301	20.49
5	30	0.62092	18.63
		NPV	13.72

The net present value of the project is £13.72. This figure can also be calculated using the annuity table. The 5 year cumulative 10% discount factor is 3.79079. Therefore, the present value of the five-year stream of cash inflows is £113.72 (that is, £30 x 3.79079). This last figure less the initial (year 0) capital outlay of £100 gives an NPV of £13.72.

KEY POINT

The prime decision rule concerning NPV is that any project that generates a positive NPV is viable.

The prime decision rule concerning NPV is that any project that generates a positive NPV is viable. One secondary rule is that where two mutually exclusive projects are being considered (you can only do one of them), the one with the highest NPV is preferred.

NPV is an absolute measure of performance. Therefore, it does not easily allow two projects of very different scales to be compared. An alternative relative measure of performance based on DCF analysis has to be introduced.

2.2 Internal rate of return (IRR)

KEY POINT

IRR is the interest rate that when applied to the cash flows associated with a project gives a nil NPV.

IRR is the interest rate that when applied to the cash flows associated with a project gives a nil NPV. Let us illustrate this by returning to our earlier project and applying interest rates of 10%, 12%, 14% and 16% in turn to the cash flows. The results are:

rate	npv
	£
10%	13.72
12%	8.14
14%	2.99
16%	–1.77

The position may be represented graphically as follows:

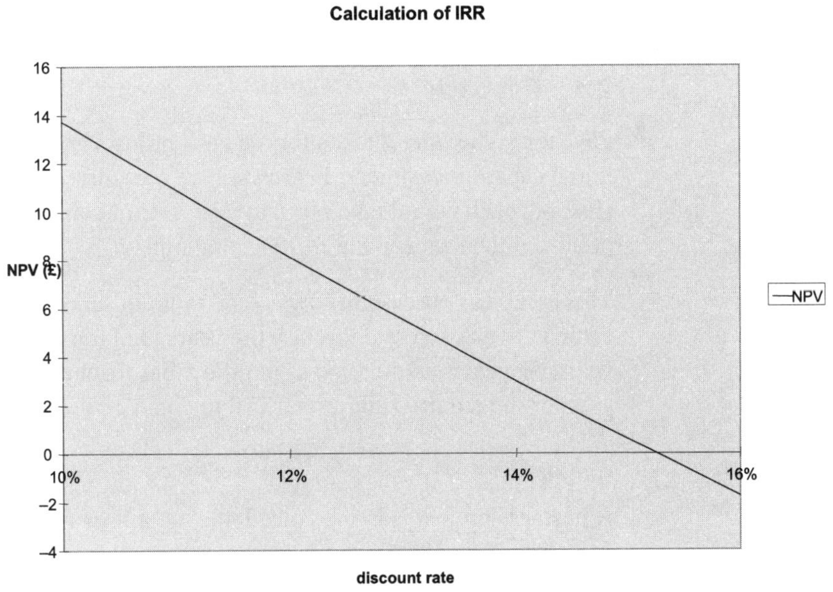

It can be seen that the IRR is near 15%. Accurate graphics or spreadsheet modelling can pin this figure down a little more tightly.

Alternatively, provided the annual cash inflows are all the same then one can calculate IRR using the annuity table. The cumulative discount factor required to reduce the PV of the £30 annual cash inflows to £100 (and thus give a nil NPV) is:

100/30 = 3.33333

If you go to the 5 year row on the annuity table and work along it from left to right you eventually come to 3.352 – which is the nearest you can get to 3.33333. The 3.352 appears under the 15% column. Hence, IRR is near 15%.

IRR is a relative measure. A hamburger bar might have an IRR of 18% and an oil refinery might have an IRR of 14%. Even though these projects are very different in scale, one can compare the return they make.

KEY POINT

The basic IRR decision rule is that any project whose IRR exceeds the current interest rate (or 'cost of money') is viable.

Mutually exclusive projects cannot be ranked using IRR.

The basic IRR decision rule is that any project whose IRR exceeds the current interest rate (or 'cost of money') is viable. This is entirely consistent with the corresponding NPV decision rule.

However, mutually exclusive projects cannot be ranked using IRR. A very small project may yield a very high IRR – but a larger project that yields a lower IRR but a higher NPV will be preferred. The logic behind this is self-evident.

2.3 ROCE, ARR and RI

These are alternative performance measures that can be used for the purpose of investment appraisal. They are based on accounting values which you will have encountered earlier in your studies.

KEY POINT

ROCE (Return on Capital Employed) is accounting profit divided by the book value of net assets.

KEY POINT

RI (Residual Income) is the accounting profit less the finance cost of net assets (net assets x an interest rate).

KEY POINT

ARR (Accounting Rate of Return) is the average annual accounting profit divided by the average book value of net assets.

KEY POINT

Payback is the time it takes for the cash inflows associated with a project to recover the initial capital investment.

ROCE (Return on Capital Employed) is accounting profit divided by the book value of net assets. RI (Residual Income) is the accounting profit less the finance cost of net assets (net assets x an interest rate). When one is considering a project, the ROCE will vary over the life that project, so ARR (Accounting Rate of Return) is the average annual accounting profit divided by the average book value of net assets.

2.4 Payback

Payback is the time it takes for the cash inflows associated with a project to recover the initial capital investment. In the case we considered above in the context of NPV and IRR, payback would take place at year 4. Cumulative cash inflows reach £120 at that point and then exceed the £100 capital outlay.

This assumes that cash inflows come in lump sums at the year-ends. However, if they come in at an even rate through the years then it might be said that payback is 3.333 years. At year 3 cumulative cash inflow has reached £90 and it will take one third of a year for the required additional £10 to come in.

Example

A business project is being considered, details as follows:

Initial capital investment in equipment - £100,000

Annual sales, year 1 to year 5 - 5,000 Units at £10 per Unit

Variable costs (labour and material) - £3 per Unit

Life of project – 5 years, with equipment having nil residual value

All sales and costs are on 'cash' terms. That is, there are no debtors or creditors. You may assume that all cash flows take place on the final day of the year in which they occur with the exception of the initial capital investment, which takes place at the very start of the project. All surplus cash is paid out as dividends. Equipment is depreciated on a straight-line basis.

Required:

(a) calculate the profit earned each year of the project;

(b) calculate the capital employed at the end of each year of the project;

(c) calculate the ROCE generated each year of the project;

(d) calculate the ARR of the project;

(e) calculate the payback period of the project;

(f) calculate the NPV of the project using a 10% discount rate

(g) calculate the IRR of the project.

You are now told that all sales are to be on six months' credit terms. That is, at the end of each year, 6 months' sales will be outstanding in the form of debtors.

Required:

(h) calculate the profit earned each year of the project

(i) calculate the capital employed at the end of each year of the project

(j) calculate the ROCE generated each year of the project

(k) calculate the ARR of the project

(l) calculate the payback period of the project

(m) calculate the NPV of the project using a 10% discount rate

(n) calculate the IRR of the project.

Solution

NO DEBTORS

	Profit (a)	**Capital (b)**	**ROCE (c)**	**Cash flow**	**Discount**	**PV**
Year 0				–100000	1	–100000
1	15000	80000	18.75%	35000	0.909	31818
2	15000	60000	25.00%	35000	0.826	28926
3	15000	40000	37.50%	35000	0.751	26296
4	15000	20000	75.00%	35000	0.683	23905
5	15000	0	infinite	35000	0.621	21732
					NPV (f)	32678
					p.back (e)	year 3

Discount rate	**NPV**
16%	14600
18%	9451
20%	4671
22%	227
24%	–3912

IRR (g) near 22%

ARR (d) 30%

(15000/50000)

WITH DEBTORS

	Profit (h)	Capital (i)	ROCE (j)	Cash flow	Discount	PV
Year 0				–100000	1.000	–100000
1	15000	105000	14%	10000	0.909	9091
2	15000	85000	18%	35000	0.826	28926
3	15000	65000	23%	35000	0.751	26296
4	15000	45000	33%	35000	0.683	23905
5	15000	25000	60%	35000	0.621	21732
6				25000	0.564	14112
					NPV (m)	24062
					p.back (l)	year 4

	NPV
16%	3310
18%	–2475
20%	–7789
22%	–12682
24%	–17196

IRR (n) near 17%

ARR (k) 20%

(15000/(50000+25000))

One critical point to note here is that according to all the performance indicators used, performance deteriorates when cash flows are delayed.

3 Project performance indicators compared

Discussing the relative merits of the different performance indicators attracts pages of discussion in accounting textbooks and many of these issues will be explored further in the context of performance evaluation in Chapter 10. So, what follows is only a summarised exploration of the topic.

It is generally considered that the DCF based measures are superior to the alternatives for the following reasons:

- ROCE, ARR and RI are all based on accounting figures. These are very subjective and vulnerable to one's choice of accounting policy on such matters as depreciation and stock valuation
- ARR is based on annual 'averages' over the life of a project. It takes no account of the precise timing at which profit is earned. Using ARR, profit at year 1 is the same as profit at year 5
- ROCE and RI move with the equipment replacement cycle. This gives the spurious impression that performance improves as equipment ages (but see discussion on annuity depreciation below).
- Payback ignores what happens after the payback date and takes no account of the timing at which cash inflows arrive inside the payback period. A cash inflow at year 1 is considered the same as a cash inflow at year 2.

For these reasons, DCF analysis is almost universally accepted as the appropriate technique for use in making long-term investment decisions. There is however one qualification to this. Payback focuses on one narrow aspect of performance – the time it takes to recover the initial investment. This may be narrow but it is also a very critical consideration in many cases for basic behavioural reasons. Academic accountants may be "too clever by half" when they dismiss payback. It is often found that sophisticated appraisals of proposed investments incorporate payback calculations 'as an aside' to the main analysis.

4 Annuity depreciation

4.1 Background

KEY POINT

As equipment ages, ROCE and RI automatically rise if straight-line depreciation or something similar is applied.

One of the problems identified with ROCE and RI above is that they move with the equipment replacement cycle. As equipment ages, ROCE and RI automatically rise if straight-line depreciation or something similar is applied. This may induce managers to defer or avoid acquisition of new equipment if their performance is monitored using these measures.

One approach to dealing with this is the adoption of the annuity depreciation method. This incorporates an element of DCF technique. The following simple example illustrates a possible approach to the use of annuity depreciation in the context of investment appraisal.

Example

Say, we plan to acquire a piece of equipment at a cost of £634,000. The equipment has a life of 4 years, nil residual value and is expected to generate an annual cash inflow of £200,000.

The IRR of this project (the interest rate required to give a nil NPV) is calculated as follows using the annuity tables:

Required discount factor is 634/200 = 3.170

Running along the four-year row on the annuity table from left to right we find 3.170 under the 10% column. The project has a 10% IRR.

So, let us say that:

- We are going to claim a profit each year calculated to give a 10% ROCE
- The difference between cash inflow and profit is taken to be depreciation
- ROCE is calculated on start year book value
- RI interest is calculated at an 8% interest rate on start year book value

The results are as follows:

	Capital	*Profit*	*Depreciation*	*ROCE*	*RI*
Year 1	634.0000	63.4000	136.6000	10%	12.6800
2	497.4000	49.7400	150.2600	10%	9.9480
3	347.1400	34.7140	165.2860	10%	6.9428
4	181.8540	18.1854	181.8146	10%	3.6371
					29.5708

The most notable feature here is that ROCE is smoothed out. ROCE does not vary with the stage in the equipment replacement cycle. The pattern of depreciation that emerges from this almost (but not quite) fully depreciates away the value of the equipment.

It is instructive to compare these figures with the NPV calculation for the project using an 8% discount rate:

	c/f	*Discount*	*PV*
Year 0	-634	1.00000	-634.0000
1	200	0.92593	185.1852
2	200	0.85734	171.4678
3	200	0.79383	158.7664
4	200	0.73503	147.0060
		NPV	28.4254

The most notable feature here is that total RI is very close to NPV.

The general idea of this approach is that some attempt is made to reconcile accounting measures of performance with DCF measures. The reader will form his/her own opinion on whether this is of practical use or simply an interesting theoretical digression.

In any event, DCF methods are considered superior to accounting methods on several grounds listed earlier in this discussion. The use of annuity depreciation may offer some relief on only one of those grounds.

Conclusion

The basic management accounting technique involved in long-term decision-making is Discounted Cash Flow analysis. This may be used to evaluate projects by means of NPV, IRR, ROCE, RI, payback or ARR analysis.

SELF-TEST QUESTIONS

Long-term decision-making techniques

1 Explain what NPV is. (2.1)

2 Explain what IRR is. (2.2)

3 Explain what payback is. (2.4)

Project performance indicators compared

4 List the advantages of DCF over accounting performance measures. (3)

EXAM-TYPE QUESTION

Ski runs

(***Note***: the currency unit in this question is the Euro, denoted '€')

A property company in Scotland is considering the development of new ski runs down the side of a mountain. Two alternative strategies for this development are being considered, details as follows:

Low investment

Building a series of 'tows' to pull skiers to the summit. Associated capital costs are € 440,000 (year 0) and € 20,000 (years 4 and 8). The variable cost per skier is € 3 and fixed costs (excluding depreciation) are € 40,000 per year.

High investment

Building a cable car system to carry skiers to the summit. Associated capital costs are € 850,000 (year 0) and € 60,000 (years 4 and 8). The variable cost per skier is € 1 and fixed costs (excluding depreciation) are € 10,000 per year.

The number of skiers using the runs is dependant on weather conditions. In a year with good snow cover, the season lasts longer and more runs can be kept open.

It is known that in any ten season cycle, the quality of the seasons is:

	skiers	*number*
good season	60,000	3
moderate season	25,000	4
poor season	4,000	3

The standard fee charged to skiers using such facilities (either investment strategy) is €8.

You are engaged in preparing an independent appraisal of the project to be used in raising funds. The Chief Executive of the property company has commented as follows:

"It is easy enough to work out the expected number of skiers using the runs in a typical year. Just use this figure as the annual level of demand."

But a local business adviser has commented as follows:

"In an average season, skiing conditions in Scotland are as good as any in Europe. However, the problem with winter sports in Scotland is the variability and unpredictability of snow cover. In a poor season there is almost no snow and hence almost no skiing. If your first three seasons are poor then this could have a devastating impact on project viability. It might be wise to minimise investment in this project."

The company appraises investments using a ten-year time horizon and a 12% discount factor.

Required:

(a) calculate the NPV of the Low investment strategy using the methodology advocated by the Chief Executive; **(5 marks)**

(b) calculate the NPV of the High investment strategy using the methodology advocated by the Chief Executive; having regard to your answers to (a) and (b) only, state which of the two alternative strategies is optimal; **(5 marks)**

(c) identify a "worst case scenario" in regard to the outcome of the project and calculate the NPV of both strategies in this case; **(5 marks)**

(d) identify a "best case scenario" in regard to the outcome of the project and calculate the NPV of both strategies in this case; **(5 marks)**

(e) construct a diagram to illustrate the sensitivity of both strategies to the sequence of weather conditions over the life of the project (making use of your answers to requirements (c) and (d)); **(5 marks)**

(f) having regard to this sensitivity analysis, state which of the two alternative strategies is optimal. **(5 marks)**

(Total: 30 marks)

For the answer this question, see the 'Answers' section at the end of the book.

Chapter 8
ACCOUNTING FOR RISK AND UNCERTAINTY

CHAPTER CONTENTS

This chapter explores aids to decision-making that may be deployed in conditions of risk and uncertainty. These practices may be used in the context of budgeting or operational and strategic decision-making.

Objectives

When you have studied this chapter you should be able to do the following.

- Define and distinguish between uncertainty and risk preference.
- Explain ways in which uncertainty may be allowed for by using conservatism and worst/most likely/best outcome estimates.
- Explain the use of sensitivity analysis in decision situations.
- Explain the use of probability estimates and the calculation of expected values.
- Explain and illustrate the use of maximin, maximax, and minimax regrets techniques in decision-making.
- Describe the structure and use of decision trees.
- Apply joint probabilities in decision tree analysis.
- Illustrate the use of decision tree analysis in assessing the range of outcomes and the cumulative probabilities of each outcome.

1 Introduction

KEY POINT

It is the uncertainty of the outcome that creates risk for the investor.

Uncertainty exists in virtually all decision-making situations, however in some scenarios the extent of the uncertainty is less significant than others. It is the uncertainty of the outcome that creates risk for the investor. If the outcome is certain, there is no risk.

2 Uncertainty and risk preference

2.1 Risk preference

KEY POINT

Risk preference is the term used to describe an investor/decision-maker's attitude to risk.

Decision-makers are often classified into one of three groups:

- Risk seekers
- Risk neutral
- Risk averse

Risk preference is the term used to describe an investor/decision-maker's attitude to risk. There is a relationship between risk and required reward, though individuals have different risk/reward profiles.

Decision-makers are often classified into one of three groups:

(a) Risk seekers

– people who will take risks to achieve the best outcome no matter how small is the chance of it occurring.

(b) Risk neutral

– people who only consider the most likely outcome

(c) Risk averse

– people who make decisions based on the worst possible outcome.

These classifications are not universally accepted and there are alternative ways of looking at things.

2.2 Techniques to appraise uncertainty

The most commonly used techniques to appraise uncertainty and provide information to the decision-maker are:

- the pay-off matrix
- decision trees.

KEY POINT

The pay-off matrix is often used for single decisions, whereas decision trees are used for more complex situations where there are a number of interconnected decisions required.

The pay-off matrix is often used for single decisions, whereas decision trees are used for more complex situations where there are a number of interconnected decisions required.

In a business decision-making situation where the manager is confronted with uncertainty, outcomes include the following:

- the best case, where all variables combine to produce the most favourable possible outcome
- the worst case, where all variables combine to produce the least favourable possible outcome
- the expected case, where all variables combine to produce an outcome based on the weighted average of their probabilities

Calculation of the expected case is based on probability theory explored below. Suffice it to say that the expected case may itself be an impossible outcome. For example, if you throw a dice 1,000 times, you will find that the average of all the scores you achieve will be very close to 3½. However, it is impossible to get the dice to give a score of 3½ on one throw – for obvious reasons.

KEY POINT

Some form of sensitivity analysis is often carried out to demonstrate how outcomes respond to changes in a key variable.

In evaluating alternative business options, it is common to present those options in the form of three scenarios – best case, worst case and expected case. Some form of sensitivity analysis is often carried out to demonstrate how outcomes respond to changes in a key variable. We have already encountered this general approach in the contexts of both spreadsheet modelling and long-term decision-making.

3 Single decisions

3.1 The pay-off matrix

The pay-off matrix is a tabular layout specifying the result (pay-off) of each combination of decision and the 'state of the world', over which the decision-maker has no control.

Example

A company has three new products A, B and C of which it can introduce only one. The level of demand for *each* course of action might be low, medium or high. If the company decides to introduce product A, the net income that would result from the levels of demand possible are estimated at £20, £40 and £50 respectively. Similarly, if product B is chosen, net income is estimated at £80, £70 and –£10, and for product C, £10, £100 and £40 respectively.

Construct a pay-off matrix to present this information concisely.

Solution

	Decision (action to introduce)		
Level of demand	*A* £	*B* £	*C* £
Low	20	80	10
Medium	40	70	100
High	50	(10)	40

Tutorial note: a realistic assumption might be that the company is obliged to meet whatever level of demand arises (for fear of incurring customer *bad will* and thus fewer sales of its other products).

This would justify the fall in net income at higher levels of demand in the case of product B in particular, where it appears that there may be considerable cost diseconomies of scale.

ACTIVITY 1

The Zeta company has estimated that the demand for one of its products is either 100, 200 or 300 units in a month. The product is sold for £15/item and total variable costs amount to £7/item. If demand is less than supply the surplus product may be sold off cheaply for £5 per item. There is no penalty cost for not meeting demand.

Considering only production levels of 100, 200 and 300, draw up a pay-off table for this situation.

Feedback to this activity is at the end of the chapter.

3.2 Decision-making criteria

In the A,B,C example given above it is by no means clear which decision is going to produce the most satisfactory result, since each product gives the most desirable outcome at one level of demand.

Three possible criteria for choosing between A, B and C in this situation are:

- maximin rule
- minimax regret rule
- maximisation of expected values.

It is important to appreciate that no one criteria can be 'right or wrong'. They are alternatives and the one that is adopted in any given situation depends on circumstances and the attitude to risk of the decision-maker.

KEY POINT

Maximin rule
Select the alternative that maximises the minimum pay-off achievable.

This pessimistic approach seeks to achieve the best results if the worst happens.

3.3 Maximin rule

Select the alternative that maximises the minimum pay-off achievable.

Note that this pessimistic approach seeks to achieve the best results if the worst happens. The logic here follows the 'sod's law' principle. If a bad outcome can happen, then (no matter how unlikely the combination of circumstances required to make it happen) it will happen.

Example

Apply the *maximin rule* to the example in the A,B,C case above to select a course of action.

Demand	*Action*		
	A	*B*	*C*
	£	£	£
Low	20	80	10
Medium	40	70	100
High	50	(10)	40
Minimum Pay-off	20	(10)	10

Thus, introducing product A will ensure the maximum pay-off if the worst result were to happen in each case.

If the worst result in each strategy is a loss, then this criterion amounts to choosing the strategy that has the lowest loss i.e. which *mini*mises the *maxi*mum loss. Hence, it is also called the *minimax* rule. This should not be confused with the *minimax regret* criterion described below.

KEY POINT

Minimax regret rule

'Regret' in this context is defined as the opportunity loss through having made the wrong decision.

3.4 Minimax regret rule

'Regret' in this context is defined as the opportunity loss through having made the wrong decision.

In the pay-off matrix above, if the market state had been low, the correct decision would have been B (net income £80). If A had been chosen instead, the company would have been out of pocket by £60 (i.e. 80–20) and if C had been chosen, it would have been out of pocket by £70 (i.e. 80–10). The opportunity loss associated with each product is A = 60, B = 0, C = 70.

It will be seen that the opportunity losses for a given market state are obtained by subtracting each value in the row from the highest value in that row.

The opportunity loss table is therefore:

State	*Decision*		
	A	*B*	*C*
Low	60	0	70
Medium	60	30	0
High	0	60	10
Maximum regret	60	60	70

KEY POINT

The minimax regret strategy is the one that minimises the maximum regret.

KEY POINT

A decision rule which seeks to maximise the maximum possible gain may be described as a maximax rule.

The minimax regret strategy is the one that minimises the maximum regret.

The maximum regret value for:

A = 60
B = 60
C = 70

The minimum value of these is 60, hence the minimax regret strategy would be either A or B. B would probably be adopted because its second highest regret outcome (30) is lower than the second highest for A (60).

Permutations on these two basic decision rules are possible and various terms are encountered in the description of these. A decision rule which seeks to maximise the maximum possible gain (C in the case used above) may be described as a maximax rule.

4 Expected values

4.1 Probabilities

The fundamental weakness of the above rules is that they take no account of the relative likelihood of each of the possible outcomes occurring.

For instance, in the example above if there were a 98% chance that demand would be medium and only a 2% chance of it being low or high, there would be a very strong temptation to choose product C (pay off £100 when outcome is medium demand).

In order to have a *rational* basis for decision-making it is therefore necessary to have some estimate of the probabilities of the various outcomes and then to use them in the decision criterion. Thus, the third possible criterion is the *maximisation of expected value.*

KEY POINT

The expected value of a particular action is defined as the *sum of the values of the possible outcomes, each multiplied by their respective probabilities.*

The expected value of a particular action is defined as the *sum of the values of the possible outcomes, each multiplied by their respective probabilities.*

Example

Using the same data as above which we reproduce here, apply the criteria of maximisation of expected value to decide the best course of action for the company, assuming the following probabilities:

P (Low demand)	0.1
P (Medium demand)	0.6
P (High demand)	0.3
	1.0

A company has three new products A, B and C of which it can introduce only one. The level of demand for *each* course of action might be low, medium or high. If the company decides to introduce product A, the net income that would result from the levels of demand possible are estimated at £20, £40 and £50 respectively. Similarly, if product B is chosen, net income is estimated at £80, £70 and –£10, and for product C, £10, £100 and £40 respectively.

Solution

The expected value of the decision to introduce product A is given by the following summation:

$0.1 \times 20 + 0.6 \times 40 + 0.3 \times 50 =$ £41

On 10% of all occasions demand will be low and net income £20, on 60% of all occasions will be medium and net income £40 and on 30% of all occasions demand will be high and net income £50. Thus on average, net income will be the weighted average of all three net incomes, weighted by their respective probabilities.

The expected value of all the products may be calculated by use of a table, as shown below.

The table shows us that, if the criterion is to maximise the expected value, it means that the product with the highest expected value will be chosen, in this case product C, unless, of course, all products have negative expected value, in which case none should be chosen.

Table of expected values

Level of demand	*Prob of demand*	*Product*					
		A		*B*		*C*	
		Income £	*Income × Prob.* £	*Income* £	*Income × Prob.* £	*Income* £	*Income × Prob.* £
Low	0.1	20	2	80	8	10	1
Medium	0.6	40	24	70	42	100	60
High	0.3	50	15	(10)	(3)	40	12
Total	1.0		41		47		73

KEY POINT

When dealing with a situation which repeats frequently, the law of large numbers means that the average outcome and the expected outcome are going to be virtually identical.

We could base our decision on the value of expected outcomes, on that basis we would select C since it gives the highest expected outcome. If we were being confronted with a choice between A, B and C on a regular basis, then the law of large numbers would mean that the average outcome from each product would be the expected outcome. We should always choose C. The position may be more ambiguous if the decision is a unique 'one-off' and in that case reference to maximin and minimax rules might be appropriate, since these allow for behavioural issues relevant to risk preference.

ACTIVITY 2

(a) Determine the Maximin and Minimax regret solutions to the pay-off table determined in the activity in the Zeta company case above.

(b) If the probabilities of demands are as follows:

Demand	100	200	300
Probability	0.3	0.6	0.1

determine the optimal solution using expected values.

Feedback to this activity is at the end of the chapter.

4.2 Applicability of expected values

Reliance on expected value as the criterion for decision making is only valid where the decision being made is either:

- one that is repeated regularly over a period of time
- a one-off decision, but where its size is fairly small in relation to the total assets of the firm and it is one of many, in terms of the sums of money involved, that face the firm over a period of time.

In other words, the *law of averages* will apply in the long run, but clearly the result of any single action must, by definition, be one of the specified outcomes. Thus, while the expected value of introducing product C is £73, each actual outcome will result in either £10, £100 or £40 net income, and it is only if a whole series of product introductions were involved that the *average* over a period of time would approach £73, so long as the expected value criterion was applied consistently to all the decisions.

KEY POINT

It is acceptable to adopt expected value as the decision making criterion so long at the decision is one which relates to a situation which frequently repeats itself.

Therefore, it is quite acceptable to adopt the expected value as the decision-making criterion for the company, so long as it has several other products and the same sort of marketing decision arises fairly regularly.

To illustrate the distinction being made, consider a man insuring his house against fire damage for a year. Suppose the house is worth £50,000 and the probability of the house being burnt down is 0.0001 (the only other outcome being that the house is not burnt down with a probability of 0.9999). The man would be quite prepared to pay, say, £15 pa to insure his house even though the expected value of the insurance is only $0.0001 \times £50{,}000 + 0.9999 \times 0 = £5$. The man cannot afford to pay £50,000 out more than once in his lifetime and therefore cannot afford to *play the averages* by using expected value as his decision criterion (if so he would refuse to pay a premium greater than £5).

However, to the insurance company, £50,000 is not a large sum, most of their transactions being for similar or greater amounts and therefore expected value would be appropriate as a decision criterion for them. In fact, the expected value of the insurance company's decision to insure the house at £15 pa is:

$$0.0001 \times (-£49{,}985) + 0.9999 \times £15$$

or $-£4.9985 + £14.9985 = £10$

and any positive expected value would, in theory, have made it worth their while to insure.

4.3 Development of the laws of probability

There is a substantial amount of theory under the heading of 'the law of probability'. This involves an appreciation of event exclusivity, event dependency, complementary probability, contingent probability and so on. It is unlikely that these will ever be tested at a theoretical level in the Performance Management examination.

However, it is appropriate to develop an appreciation of expected values in several areas. For example, let us say that we are confronted with a situation in which there are two variables, each with distinct outcomes and associated probabilities.

Example

The sale of cans of soft drink depends on weather conditions. The weather conditions have two relevant characteristics:

- windy (0.3 probability) or still (0.7 probability), and
- wet (0.4 probability) or dry (0.6 probability)

Sales of cans are as follows in the different possible weather conditions:

- windy and wet – 100 cans, windy and dry – 140 cans
- still and wet – 110 cans, still and dry – 200 cans

Required:

Calculate the expected sales of cans.

Solution

The probabilities of the four possible outcomes can be determined as follows:

Windy and wet	$0.3 \times 0.4 =$	0.12
Windy and dry	$0.3 \times 0.6 =$	0.18
Still and wet	$0.7 \times 0.4 =$	0.28
Still and dry	$0.7 \times 0.6 =$	0.42
Total		1.00

KEY POINT

The joint probability of two uncertain and unrelated events happening can be determined by multiplying their two respective probabilities.

The probability of the conjunction of two unrelated and uncertain events can be determined by multiplying their respective probabilities together.

Weighting the four alternative possible outcomes by their associated probabilities gives the following expected outcome:

Windy and wet	0.12×100	=	12.0
Windy and dry	0.18×140	=	25.2
Still and wet	0.28×110	=	30.8
Still and dry	0.42×200	=	84.0
Expected sales (cans)			152.0

Let us consider another illustrative example.

Example

40% of the output of a factory is produced in workshop A and 60% in workshop B. Fourteen out of every 1,000 components from A are defective and six out of every 1,000 components from B are defective. After the outputs from A and B have been thoroughly mixed, a component drawn at random is found to be defective.

Calculate the probability that it came from workshop B.

Solution

Consider 10,000 components, we know that of these 4,000 are from workshop A and 6,000 from workshop B. Of the 4,000 from workshop A, 1.4%, that is 56 will be defective, and from workshop B 0.6%, that is 36, will be defective. A table can therefore be completed as follows:

	Workshop		
	A	*B*	*Total*
Defective	56	36	92
Non-defective	3,944	5,964	9,908
Total	4,000	6,000	10,000

The above presentation of the problem may be described as a 'contingency table'. The problem may now be solved. Given that our one particular component is defective, we know that we are dealing with one of the ninety-two components in the top row of the table. We can see that of these ninety-two components, thirty-six come from workshop B.

$$\text{The probability that the component came from workshop B} = \frac{36}{92} = 0.39$$

ACTIVITY 3

30% of the new cars of a particular model are supplied from a factory X, the other 70% from factory Y. 10% of factory X's production has a major fault, 12% of factory Y's production has such a fault.

A purchaser's new car has a major fault. What is the probability that it was made at factory Y?

Feedback to this activity is at the end of the chapter.

5 Decision trees

5.1 The technique

KEY POINT

A *decision tree* is a way of applying the expected value criterion to situations where a number of decisions are made sequentially.

So far only a single decision has had to be made. However, many managerial problems consist of a rather long, drawn-out structure involving a whole sequence of actions and outcomes. Where a number of decisions have to be made sequentially the complexity of the decision-making process increases considerably. By using *decision trees,* however, highly complex problems can be broken down into a series of simpler ones while providing, at the same time, opportunity for the decision-maker to obtain specialist advice in relation to each stage of his problem.

A *decision tree* is a way of applying the expected value criterion to situations where a number of decisions are made sequentially.

It is so called because the decision alternatives are represented as *branches* in a *tree* diagram.

Example

A retailer must decide whether to sell a product loose or packaged. In either case, the product may sell, or not sell.

The decision facing the retailer can be represented by a tree diagram:

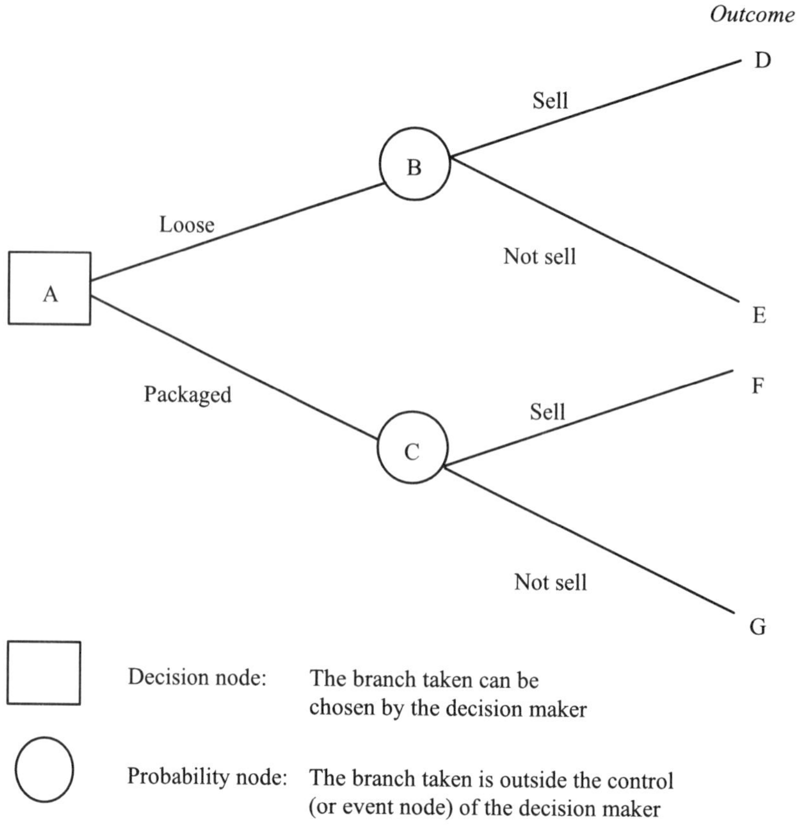

In this example, say the profitability of selling packaged products is £10, loose products £15. The loss through not selling is £5 in either case. The probability of the product being sold is 0.7 for packaged products, 0.5 for loose products.

You are required to evaluate the expected values of each decision alternative.

Solution

The decision tree is evaluated working back from right to left. At each probability node the expected value of the possible outcomes is computed. At each decision node it is assumed, initially, that the decision-maker will choose the route with the highest EV. All other branches from such a node are therefore eliminated.

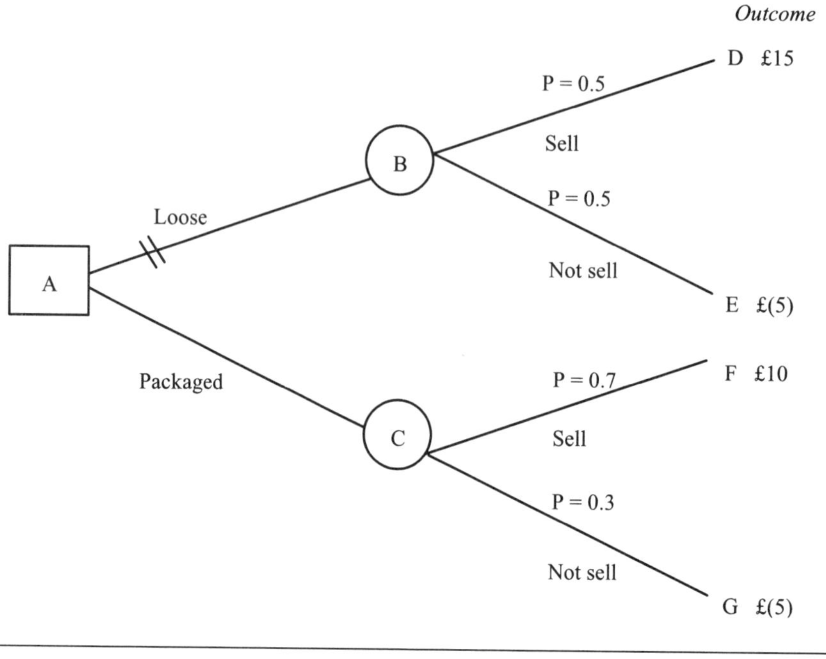

The diagram is then evaluated as follows (using obvious notation):

$EV_B = (0.5 \times EV_D) + (0.5 \times EV_E)$

$= (0.5 \times 15) + (0.5 \times (-5))$

$= 5$

$EV_C = (0.7 \times EV_F) + (0.3 \times EV_G)$

$= (0.7 \times 10) + (0.3 \times (-5))$

$= 5.5$

∴ at node A the retailer will choose to go towards node C as this has the higher EV. The discarded routes are sometimes indicated by drawing two short parallel lines across that particular path.

Therefore the decision to sell a packaged product has the higher expected value.

ACTIVITY 4

The Janus company is considering expanding its activities either in the UK, or in Europe or in Asia. It can at this time only expand in one region.

If it expands in the UK, there is a probability of 0.3 that contribution will increase by £200,000 or 0.7 that it will increase by £800,000.

If it expands in Europe, there is a probability of 0.4 that contribution will increase by £100,000 or 0.6 that it will increase by £1,000,000.

If it expands in Asia, there is a probability of 0.6 that contribution will decrease by £1,000,000 or 0.4 that it will increase by £2,500,000.

(a) Draw a decision tree and determine whether the company should expand and if so where?

(b) What important aspect does this analysis ignore?

Feedback to this activity is at the end of the chapter.

5.2 Decision trees – a comprehensive example

The last problem could have been solved without a tree diagram, but the technique comes into its own in a more complex situation, as illustrated by the next example.

Plant example

The manager of a newly-formed specialist machinery manufacturing subsidiary has to decide whether to build a small plant or a large plant for manufacturing a new piece of machinery with an expected market life of ten years. One of the major factors influencing his decision is the size of the market that the company can obtain for its product.

Demand may be high during the first two years, but if initial users are unhappy with the product, demand may then fall to a low level for the remaining eight years. If users are happy then demand will be maintained at its high level. Conversely, caution by prospective buyers may mean only a low level of demand for the first two years but again, depending on how satisfied these few buyers are, demand may then either remain low or rise to a high level.

If the company initially builds a large plant, it must live with it for the whole ten years, regardless of the market demand. If it builds a small plant, it also has the option after two years of expanding the plant but this expansion would cost more overall, when taken with the initial cost of building small, than starting by building a large plant.

Various pieces of information have been collected, or estimated by the marketing manager, the production manager and the finance department.

(a) **Marketing information**

The probabilities of the outcomes have been assessed as follows:

Outcome	*First two years*	*Next eight years given first two years were:* *High*	*Low*
High	0.8	0.75	0.25
Low	0.2	0.25	0.75

(b) **Annual income estimate**

(i) A large plant with high market demand would yield £1m pa, for each of ten years.

(ii) A large plant with low market demand would yield only £0.1m pa because of high fixed costs and inefficiencies.

(iii) A small plant with low demand would yield £0.4m pa.

(iv) If demand was high, a small plant during an initial period of high demand would yield £0.45m pa for the first two years but this would drop to £0.25m pa for the next eight years, because of increasing competition from other manufacturers.

(v) If the initially small plant were expanded after two years and demand was high in the last eight years, it would yield £0.7m pa i.e. being less efficient than one that was initially large.

(vi) If the small plant were expanded after two years but demand was low for the cight year period, then it would yield £0.05m pa.

(c) **Capital costs**

(i) Initial cost of building a large plant £3m

(ii) Initial cost of building a small plant £1.3m

(iii) Additional cost of expanding a small plant £2.2m

Using expected value as the decision criterion, advise the manager on what choice of plant to make.

Ignore the time value of money and taxation.

Solution

The first stage in solving a problem of this nature, which involves more than one decision being made over a period of time, is to construct a decision tree to demonstrate the structure of the decisions that have to be made.

□ Decision node.

○ Outcome or probability node.

Each path represents a different series of events and outcomes, for example path A.C.F.H.

Low represents an initial decision to build a small plant, demand for the first two years turns out be high, whereupon a further decision is taken to expand the plant, but unfortunately demand for the next eight years falls to a low level.

Each of the twelve possible monetary outcomes has a certain chance of occurring, depending on which decisions are made, and since expected value is the criterion to be used in making the decisions, the expected value of building the large plant must be compared with the expected value of building the small plant (whichever gives the higher value being chosen). This is done by a process known as *roll-back.*

Method

Insert relevant cash flows and probabilities on each branch. Starting from the right-hand side, work back towards the left-hand side. At each probability (outcome) node, calculate the expected monetary value (EMV) for events leading out from the node, and insert this value in the circle. At each decision node, after subtracting any decision costs from the EMVs, accept the decision with the highest net EMV and reject the others at that point by placing a barrier (a double line) across them. Insert this maximum net EMV in the square and use this value in subsequent EMV calculations. Continue working back in this way to the initial decision node. The calculations are shown in the diagram, where cash flows are in £m.

Calculations

The cash inflows are the yields per annum multiplied by the number of years. These are inserted on each line. The cash outflows are put in brackets and treated as negative inflows. The probabilities are also inserted on each line where appropriate.

At node D, EMV $= (8.0 \times 0.75) + (0.8 \times 0.25) = 6.2$

At node E, EMV $= (8.0 \times 0.25) + (0.8 \times 0.75) = 2.6$

The total cash inflows from B are: $6.2 + 2.0 = 8.2$ (high) and $2.6 + 0.2 = 2.8$ (low)

At node B, EMV $= (8.2 \times 0.8) + (2.8 \times 0.2) = 7.12$

At node H, EMV $= (5.6 \times 0.75) + (0.4 \times 0.25) = 4.3$

At node I, EMV $= (2.0 \times 0.75) + (3.2 \times 0.25) = 2.3$

From F, expanding will yield an EMV of $4.3 - 2.2 = 2.1$
not expanding will yield an EMV of 2.3

It is better not to expand, so a barrier is put across the expansion line and the EMV at F is then 2.3.

At node J, EMV $= (5.6 \times 0.25) + (0.4 \times 0.75) = 1.7$

At node K, EMV $= (2.0 \times 0.25) + (3.2 \times 0.75) = 2.9$

From G, expanding will yield an EMV of $1.7 - 2.2 = 0.5$ (a loss)
not expanding will yield an EMV of 2.9

It is better not to expand, so a barrier is put across the expansion line from G and the EMV at G is then 2.9.

The total cash inflows from C are: 2.3 + 0.9 = 3.2 (high) and 2.9 + 0.8 = 3.7 (low)

At node C,	EMV = $(3.2 \times 0.8) + (3.7 \times 0.2)$	=	3.3
At node A,	building big has a net EMV of 7.12 – 3.0	=	4.12
	building small has a net EMV of 3.3 – 1.3	=	2.0

Hence, it is better to build big, so a barrier is put across the build small line and the EMV of the optimum policy of building big is inserted in the square.

Diagram 1

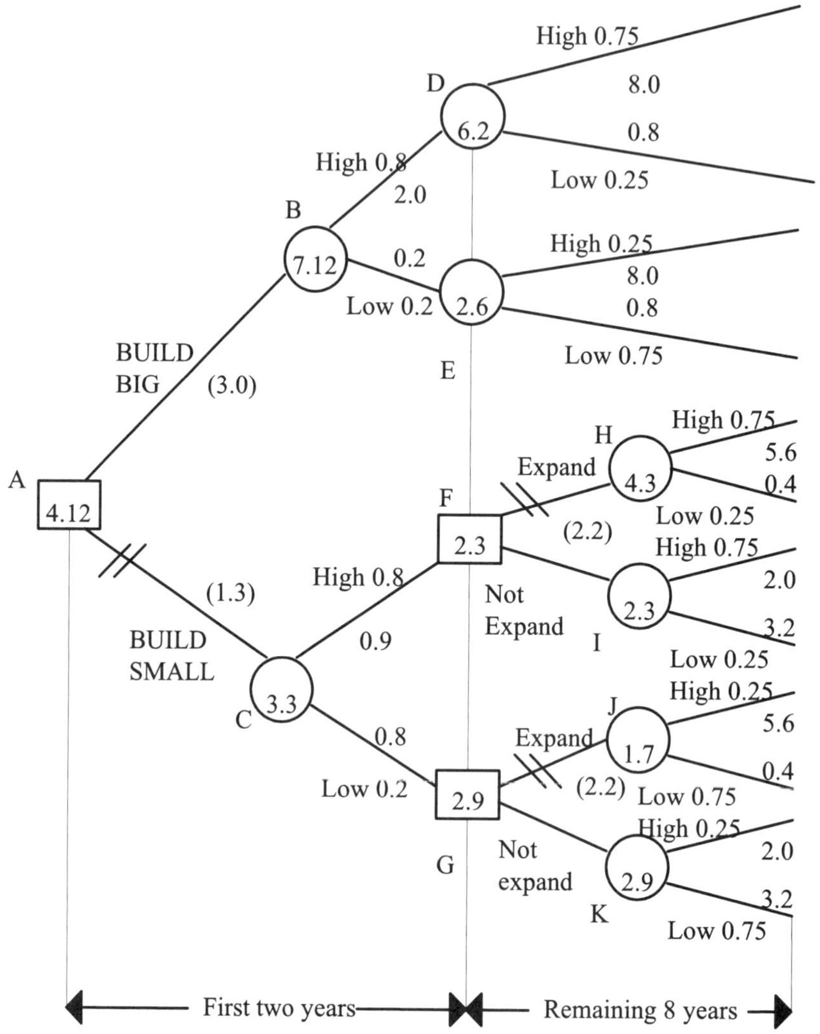

Tutorial notes:

(1) In practice, only one diagram is used and all data and results are inserted on the one tree.

(2) Do not eliminate branches from a probability node. The decision-maker has no control over which of these branches will be taken and all outcomes must therefore be considered.

(3) When stating the optimum policy, the route to be taken at each decision node must be specified. For example, if building small had been the best initial policy, the decision whether or not to expand at F and G should also have been stated.

(4) No account has been taken in this example of the timing of cash flows i.e. discounting has not taken place. This was omitted deliberately to keep the example simple. In practice, however, cash flows must not be added or subtracted unless they have been discounted to the same point in time. The simplest method of doing this is to discount all cash flows to their present values.

However, it should be borne in mind that decisions are often based on the cash flow occurring at the time when the decision is made. If, for example, an investor is considering aborting an investment after one year if it yields less than a specified amount of £x in the first year, then his decision would depend on the value of the cash flow at the end of the first year, not on its present value. In such cases, cash flows should be discounted to the point in time when the decision is to be made.

5.3 The value of information and/or reduced uncertainty

The basic models we have been working with can be developed into a variety of practical areas and applications. One commonly encountered is the use of probability theory to determine the value of information which is able to completely eliminate uncertainty. This may be illustrated by the following simple example.

Example

The launch of a new product is being considered and two possible alternative strategies are available to carry out the launch. The market may be weak (0.4 probability) or strong (0.6 probability) and the outcome of each strategy depends on the market. Outcomes are:

- Strategy 1 – weak market gives –30k and strong market gives +120k
- Strategy 2 – weak market gives +20k and strong market gives +80k

The expected outcomes of the two alternative strategies are:

- Strategy 1 +60k (that is, (–30k × 0.4) plus (+120k × 0.6))
- Strategy 2 +56k (that is, (+20k × 0.4) plus (+80k × 0.6))

So, solely on the basis of expected outcomes, strategy 1 would be selected.

Required:

Calculate the value of a market forecast that would inform us in advance of whether the market would be weak or strong.

Solution

If the forecast is for a weak market (probability 0.4) then we will adopt strategy 2 with a certain outcome of +20k. If the forecast is for a strong market (probability 0.6) then we will adopt strategy 1 with a certain outcome of +120k. The expected outcome in this situation is +80k (that is, (+20k × 0.4) plus (+120k × 0.6)). Our expected outcome is therefore 20k higher with a forecast than without one. 20k is what the forecast is worth to us and that is the maximum amount we would be prepared to pay for it. That 20k is the value of information.

In the above case we considered the compete elimination of uncertainty. We can also consider the reduction of uncertainty. This may be illustrated by the following simple example:

Example

A proposed project is being considered, the outcome of which is dependent on whether the market is strong (probability 0.75 with outcome +500k) or weak (probability 0.25 with outcome –180k).

A consultant offers to provide a forecast on whether the market will be weak or strong. The consultant requests a fee of 15k and it is known that she has a 90% chance of correctly forecasting a strong market and a 95% chance of correctly forecasting a weak market.

Required:

Determine whether or not the forecast should be commissioned.

Solution

The expected outcome of proceeding without a forecast is +330k (that is, (+500k ×0.75) plus (–180k × 0.25)).

The expected outcome of proceeding with a forecast involves calculation of probabilities of four possible result scenarios:

(1) Strong forecast, strong market	0.6750 (that is, 0.75 × 0.9)
(2) Strong forecast, weak market	0.0125 (that is , 0.25 × 0.05)
(3) Weak forecast, weak market	0.2375 (that is, 0.25 × 0.95)
(4) Weak forecast, strong market	0.0750 (that is, 0.75 ×0.10)
Total	1.0000

Logic:

- the probability of a strong market happening multiplied by the probability of the consultant forecasting it correctly
- the probability of a weak market happening multiplied by the probability of the consultant failing to forecast it correctly
- the probability of a weak market happening multiplied by the probability of the consultant forecasting it correctly
- the probability of a strong market happening multiplied by the probability of the consultant failing to forecast it correctly

The expected outcome of proceeding with the project after a weak forecast is –5.25k (that is (+500k × 0.0750) plus (–180k × 0.2375)). Therefore, the project should be rejected if there is a weak forecast (scenarios (3) and (4) above) – giving a nil expected outcome.

That leaves only scenarios (1) and (2) influencing the overall expected outcome, giving an expected outcome of +335.25k (that is, (+500k × 0.6750) plus (–180k × 0.0125)).

Therefore, the expected value of the forecast may be disclosed as follows:

Expected outcome from proceeding without a forecast	+330k
Expected outcome from proceeding with a forecast	+335.25k

The value of the forecast is 5.25k and this is not enough to justify the required fee of 15k.

The basic logic we have used here may be represented as a decision tree:

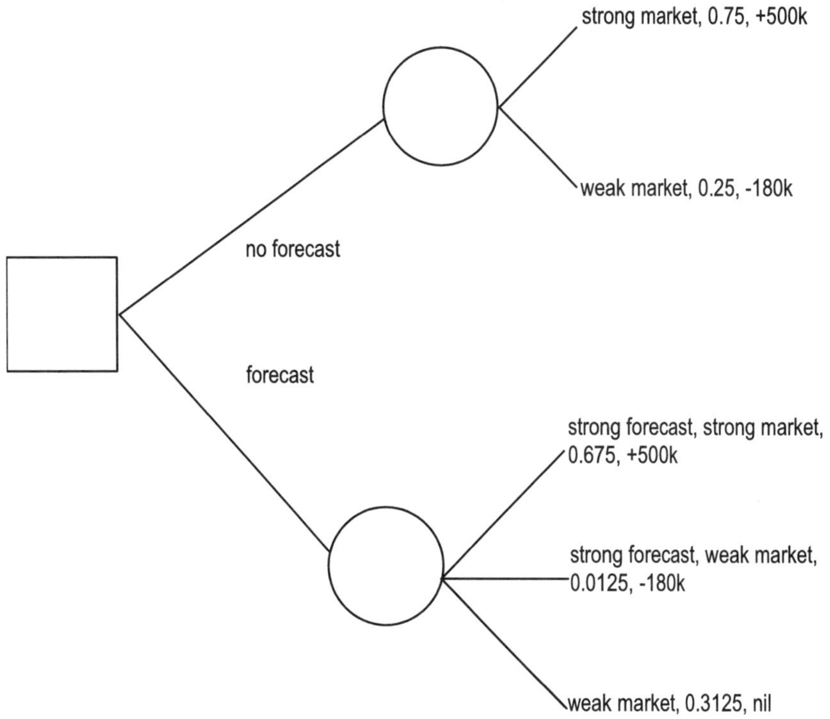

6 Sensitivity analysis

KEY POINT

Sensitivity analysis involves testing outcomes for changes in key underlying variables. It can be carried out and reported in many different ways and the management accountant has to decide on the approach that gives the most meaningful results in any given case.

There is always a significant degree of uncertainty over the many elements in a budget, business plan or project evaluation. The management accountant is often required to report on or represent this uncertainty in some way. One approach commonly encountered is 'sensitivity analysis'. This is a topic that has been encountered several times earlier in this text in a variety of different contexts. The full example of sensitivity analysis in Chapter 7 is probably the most practical application of sensitivity analysis and the one that the accountant is most likely to encounter.

Sensitivity analysis is an approach that can be used for various purposes and at varying levels of refinement. Let us illustrate the approach using a simple example.

Example

A proposed project to make and sell Units over a three year period has the following details:

Initial capital cost	£4,000
Annual Unit sales	100
Selling price per Unit	£61
Variable cost per Unit	£36
Fixed costs per year	£900

The management accountant would normally evaluate this project using DCF technique (see Chapter 7) at an appropriate discount rate, say 6%. This gives the following result:

		Cash flow	Discount	PV
Year	**0**	-4,000	1.000	-4,000
	1	1,600	0.943	1,509
	2	1,600	0.890	1,424
	3	1,600	0.840	1,343
			NPV	277

This appears to be viable project with a positive NPV. However, the information used to construct this evaluation will include numerous uncertainties. The various figures listed above are typically mean or most likely outcomes from a range of possibilities

For example, the 100 Unit sales per year is a forecast and actual sales in any one year could differ significantly from that figure. The common assumption made is that there is a mean or most likely outcome (in this case, 100 Units per year) and a range of alternative possible outcomes above and below that. A sensitivity analysis would seek to give an impression of what the overall outcome of the project is in a range of alternatives annual Unit sales scenarios. For example, it might be judged that a worse case scenario would be annual sales of 90 Units and a best case scenario would be annual sales of 110 Units. The three alternatives outcomes would be:

Cases	Unit sales	NPV
Worst	90	-391
Expected	100	277
Best	110	945

The sensitivity of the project to annual Unit sales may be represented graphically, as follows:

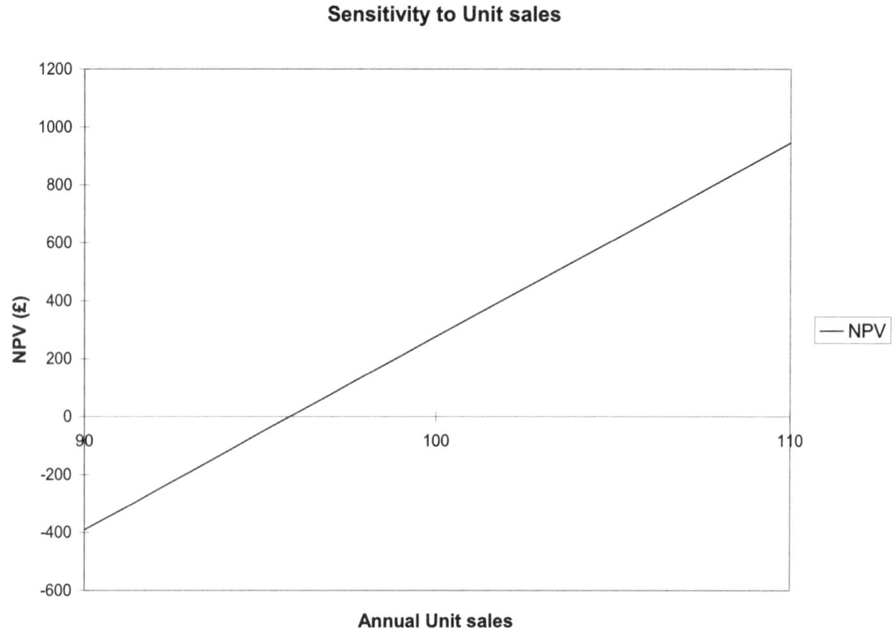

This diagram is an obvious oversimplification but it offers the following additional insights:

- Approximately 70% of possible outcomes in the range 90 to 110 annual Unit sales give a positive NPV
- Annual sales of 96 Units or over are required to give a positive NPV

Presenting the sensitivity analysis in this way gives an impression of the dynamics of the situation. However, it is probably an imperfect impression. One consideration is that it is unlikely that annual Unit sales is the only element of uncertainty.

It is possible that all elements contained in the project are uncertain. A sensitivity analysis might be undertaken to give an impression of which of the elements gives rise to the greatest uncertainty in the overall project outcome. For example, one might consider the impact on project NPV of a 2.5% adverse variance in each of the elements in turn. NPV is re-calculated with a selling price per Unit of £58.50 (that is, £60 × 0.975) with all other factors held constant and so on. The result is:

	NPV £	**% change**
Base case	277	
2.5% adverse variance		
Capital cost, £4,100	177	-36.10%
Selling price per unit, £59.47	-131	-147.29%
Variable cost per unit, £36.90	36	-87.00%
Fixed cost per year, £922.50	217	-21.66%
Units sold per year, 97.5	110	-60.29%

This analysis gives the following further insights:

- A relatively small proportional change in any one of the variables produces a much larger proportional change in the overall project outcome. Small uncertainties in key project variables commonly produce large uncertainties for project outcome and viability.
- The viability of the project is more vulnerable to some key variables than others. The project NPV appears particularly sensitive to Unit selling price, given that a 2.5% adverse variance in price causes a 147% adverse variance in NPV

The business manager is not always in a position of making only go/no-go decisions on proposed projects. It may be possible to re-engineer a project in some way in order to alter its risk-return profile. For example, customers might be prepared to contract for £60.50 as a fixed selling price with an assured take up of 100 Units. In this event the expected project NPV would be reduced from £277 (original base case) to £143.

The expected return from the project would be reduced but a major source of uncertainty affecting project viability would be eliminated. Such a modification to the project might be judged acceptable. Indeed, the move might convert the project from being non-viable to being viable. The sensitivity analysis approach would provide a valuable aid to the manager having regard to the basic engineering of the project.

The general thrust behind the sensitivity analysis approach is that it is possible to present the vulnerability of a project, business plan or budget to movement in the values of key variables. An appreciation of this vulnerability might guide decision makers in various aspects of the decision making and planning processes.

Conclusion

The future is uncertain and this creates risk when evaluating projects, preparing plans, preparing budgets and making decisions. Techniques such as probability analysis, sensitivity analysis and decision trees can help to represent uncertainty and quantify it.

Be aware that these techniques do not eliminate or reduce uncertainty, they just make uncertainty more manageable.

SELF-TEST QUESTIONS

Single decisions

1 What is the maximin rule? (3.3)

2 What is the minimax regret rule? (3.4)

Expected values

3 In probability theory, what is an 'expected outcome'? (4.1)

4 What is a contingency table used for? (4.3)

Decision trees

5 Do the probabilities on a decision tree occur after a decision node or after an event node? (5.1)

6 What is the expected value of information? (5.3)

Sensitivity analysis

7 What is sensitivity analysis? (6)

EXAM-TYPE QUESTIONS

Question 1: Homeworker Ltd

Homeworker Ltd is a small company that manufactures a lathe attachment for the DIY market called the 'Homelathe'.

The data for manufacturing the attachment are as follows:

		For each batch of 10 Homelathes				
			Components			*Total*
	A	*B*	*C*	*D*	*E*	
Machine hours	10	14	12			36
Labour hours				2	1	3
	£	£	£	£	£	£
Variable cost	32	54	58	12	4	160
Fixed cost (apportioned)	48	102	116	24	26	316
Total component costs	80	156	174	36	30	476

Assembly costs (all variable) £40 per 10
Selling price £600 per 10

General-purpose machinery is used to make components A, B and C and is already working to the maximum capability of 4,752 hours and there is no possibility of increasing the machine capacity in the next period. There is labour available for making components D and E and for assembling the product.

The marketing department advises that there will be a 50% increase in demand next period so the company has decided to buy one of the machine-made components from an outside supplier in order to release production capacity and thus help to satisfy demand.

A quotation has been received from General Machines Ltd for the components but, because this company has not made the components before, it has not been able to give single figure prices. Its quotation is as follows:

Pessimistic		*Most likely*		*Optimistic*		
	Price	*Probability*	*Price*	*Probability*	*Price*	*Probability*
	£	£	£	£		
Component A	96	0.25	85	0.5	54	0.25
Component B	176	0.25	158	0.5	148	0.25
Component C	149	0.25	127	0.5	97	0.25

It has been agreed between the two companies that audited figures would be used to determine which one of the three prices would be charged for whatever component is bought out.

As management accountant of Homeworker Ltd, it is your responsibility to analyse the financial and production capacity effects of the proposed component purchase and **you are required** to:

(a) show in percentage form the maximum increased production availability from the three alternatives i.e. buying A or B or C **(4 marks)**

(b) analyse the financial implications of the purchase and, assuming a risk neutral attitude, recommend which component to buy out, noting that the production availability will be limited to a 50% increase **(6 marks)**

(c) prepare a profit statement for the period assuming that the component chosen in (b) is bought out and that the extra production is made and sold (show your workings) **(6 marks)**

(d) state **three** other factors you would consider if you were advised that management had decided to avoid risk as much as possible when buying out a component. (Calculations are not required for this section.) **(4 marks)**

(Total: 20 marks)

Question 2: Test marketing

A company has the opportunity of marketing a new package of computer games. It has two possible courses of action: to test market on a limited scale or to give up the project completely. A test market would cost £160,000 and current evidence suggests that consumer reaction is equally likely to be 'positive' or 'negative'. If the reaction to the test marketing were to be 'positive' the company could either market the computer games nationally or still give up the project completely. Research suggests that a national launch might result in the following sales:

Sales	*Contribution* *£m*	*Probability*
High	1.20	0.25
Average	0.30	0.50
Low	–0.24	0.25

If the test marketing were to yield 'negative' results the company would give up the project. Giving up the project at any point would result in a contribution of £60,000 from the sale of copyright etc, to another manufacturer. All contributions have been discounted to present values.

Required:

(a) Draw a decision tree to represent this situation, including all relevant probabilities and financial values **(8 marks)**

(b) Recommend a course of action for the company on the basis of expected values. **(8 marks)**

(c) Explain any limitations of this method of analysis. **(4 marks)**

(Total: 20 marks)

For the answers to these questions, see the 'Answers' section at the end of the book.

FEEDBACK TO ACTIVITY 1

Production level

		100	200	300
Possible demands	100	800	600	400
	200	800	1,600	1,400
	300	800	1,600	2,400

Note on workings.

When supply equals demand the contribution = £15 – 7 = £8. So, in the first cell, demand = supply = 100 and total contribution = 100 × £8 = £800. Similarly if demand exceeds supply, the same contribution applies.

e.g. Supply = 100, demand = 300, still only 100 sold giving £800.

If supply exceeds demand then the surplus will be sold off at a loss of £(7–5) = £2/item

e.g. Supply = 300, demand = 100

Contribution for the 100 supplied	= £800
Less loss on 200 @ £2	= £400
	£400

FEEDBACK TO ACTIVITY 2

(a) **Maximin solution**

Production level

		100	200	300
Possible demands	100	800	600	400
	200	800	1,600	1,400
	300	800	1,600	2,400
	Min	800	600	400

The maximum of the minimums is 800 from the 100 column, therefore produce only 100 items.

Minimax regret solution

Minimax regret table

Production level

		100	200	300
Possible Demands	100	0	200	400
	200	800	0	200
	300	1,600	800	0
	Max	1,600	800	400

Note on calculations of regrets:

For each row subtract the values in the row from the maximum value in the row. The minimum of the maximum regrets is 400 in the 300 column. Hence produce 300 items.

(b) **Expected value**

			100	200	300
Possible Demands	100	0.3	800	600	400
	200	0.6	800	1,600	1,400
	300	0.1	800	1,600	2,400
Expected Values			800	1,300	1,200

Working: e.g. Expected value for last column:

$400 \times 0.3 + 1{,}400 \times 0.6 + 2{,}400 \times 0.1 = 1{,}200$

Maximum expected value is 1,300 in the 200 column, hence produce 200 items only.

FEEDBACK TO ACTIVITY **3**

Using 1,000 as a suitable multiple i.e. considering 1,000 cars are manufactured, the contingency table is:

Made at factory

	X	*Y*	*Total*
Has major fault	30	84	114
No major fault	270	616	886
Total	300	700	1,000

Hence P(made at factory Y/major fault exists) $= \frac{84}{114}$

$= 0.737$

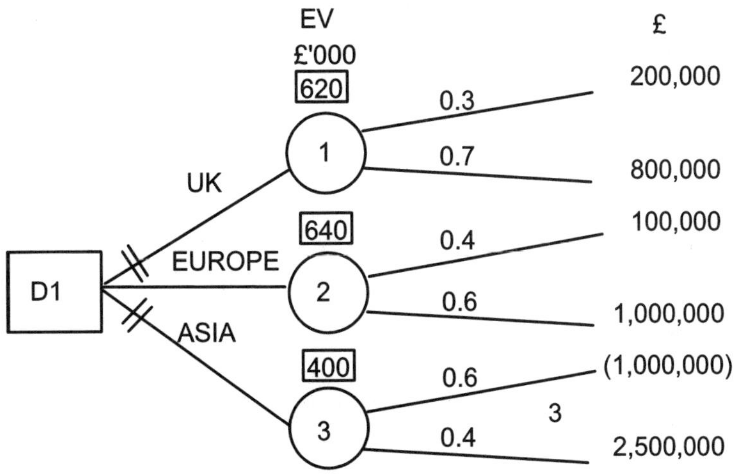

FEEDBACK TO ACTIVITY **4**

(a)

EV = Expected value

EV (Node 1) = 0.3 × 200,000 + 0.7 × 800,000 = £620,000

EV (Node 2) = 0.4 × 100,000 + 0.6 × 1,000,000 = £640,000 maximum

EV (Node 3) = 0.6 × (1,000,000) + 0.4 × 2,500,000 = £400,000

Maximum expected value is the Europe option at £640,000. Therefore reject UK and Asia (shown by scissor cuts on tree after D1) and accept expansion in Europe.

(b) The expected value approach ignores risk. If the Asia option had worked out to give the highest expected value, and the Asia option had been adopted there would be a risk that a loss of £1,000,000 of contribution could occur.

Chapter 9
BUSINESS OBJECTIVES AND GOALS

CHAPTER CONTENTS

This chapter provides an introduction to performance evaluation by exploring how objectives, goals and targets are formulated within an organisation.

Objectives

When you have studied this chapter you should be able to do the following.

- Discuss the purpose of a mission statement and the pursuit of a vision.
- Discuss the structure and content of a mission statement.
- Explain how high level corporate objectives are developed.
- Identify strategic objectives and how they may be incorporated into the corporate plan.
- Explain how strategic objectives are cascaded down the organisation via the formulation of subsidiary objectives.
- Identify any relevant social and ethical obligations that should be considered in the pursuit of corporate objectives.
- Discuss the concept of the 'planning gap' and alternative strategies to 'fill the gap'.
- Identify the characteristics of operational performance.
- Contrast the relative significance of planning as against controlling activities at different levels in the performance hierarchy.

1 Introduction

1.1 An organisational perspective

KEY POINT

Every organisation needs to be clear about its goals. As the environment changes and presents new challenges, organisations need to review and reassess their goals.

Every organisation needs to be clear about its goals. As the environment changes and presents new challenges, organisations need to review and reassess their goals. Some organisations will discover that their goals are no longer relevant and they are drifting. Others will find that their goals are clear, relevant, and effective. Still others will discover that their goals are no longer even clear and that they have no firm direction. The purpose of developing a clear set of goals for an organisation is to prevent it from drifting into an uncertain future.

The issue of setting an organisation's goals breaks into two distinct steps: first determining what the current goals are, and second deciding what the goals should be. Even the image of current goals will differ from person to person, and group to group in, or associated with, the organisation.

Objectives in general are likely to be shaped by the needs of different coalitions of interest, including those of the strategic decision-makers themselves, and how they, the decision-makers, see the power structure in the organisation. Such coalitions of interest, as we have already seen in a previous chapter, are sometimes referred to as stakeholders.

Objectives are normally formulated within a hierarchical structure, with each level in the hierarchy deriving its objectives from the next level above, all therefore emanating from the organisation's overall mission or vision. Objectives therefore cascade downwards in the sequence: mission - goals - objectives - strategies - tactics -

operational plans. The hierarchy of objectives suggests, for example, that strategy is planned to achieve objectives, but that in turn it provides targets for the planning of tactics.

1.2 Organisation goals and objectives

Organisations are created to carry out activities that cannot be achieved by individuals alone. Such activities can be technical, benefiting from economies of scale and specialisation, or they can be social and satisfy human need for companionship.

Considerable confusion exists over the use of the terms goals and objectives. The *Oxford English Dictionary* includes the following definitions:

(a) Goal - *'object of effort or ambition'*.

(b) Objective - *'the point aimed at'*.

The similarity of these terms causes some writers to use them interchangeably whilst others refer to them as two specific concepts - one related to intermediate issues (*means*) and the other to ultimate purposes (*ends*). Unfortunately, there is no consistency as to which term refers to which concept. We will discuss this dilemma in more depth later.

In this text short-term objectives stemming from the practical needs of a particular situation will be distinguished from longer-term goals which relate value systems of individuals and the way they perceive things - their *'weltanschauung'* or world view. Goals are, therefore, much more subjective in their nature than objectives.

Example

Take your own position. It is probable that your own long-term **goal** is to achieve career success as a professionally qualified management accountant. Your immediate short-term **objective** is to pass the ACCA examinations. But passing the examinations will be only one part of achieving your overall and ultimate goal.

Confusion also arises in that goals and objectives are primarily ways of referring to the purposes of human beings - the application of these concepts to organisations and the relationship between organisational goals and objectives to those of the individual members is highly complex.

A further complication is the existence of both official and operative goals. As pointed out by Perrow:

- **Official goals** are the general purposes of the organisation as put forth in the charter, annual reports, public statements by key executives and other authoritative pronouncements ... Official goals are purposely vague and general ...
- **Operative goals** designate the ends sought through the actual operating policies of the organisation; they tell us what the organisation is actually trying to do ...

The divergence between official and operating goals at every level within an organisation and the fact that, as they are independent, both have to be considered, means that the situation may become very complex with a potential for contradictions and dysfunctional behaviour.

However, Paton does stress:

'The formulation of clear objectives and goals is important for those in senior positions in organisations because they provide the reference points for ensuring the appropriateness and consistency of decisions, policies and practices in different areas and levels of the organisation, and also the basic criteria for the assessment of performance.'

2 Mission statements

2.1 Hierarchy of objectives

Most writers agree with the idea that there is a hierarchy of objectives, just as there is a hierarchy of managers. At each higher level in the hierarchy the objectives are more relevant to a greater proportion of the organisation's activities so that the objectives at the top of the hierarchy are relevant to every aspect of the organisation. The following diagram illustrates the hierarchical relationship of mission, goals, objectives, strategy, tactics and operational plans.

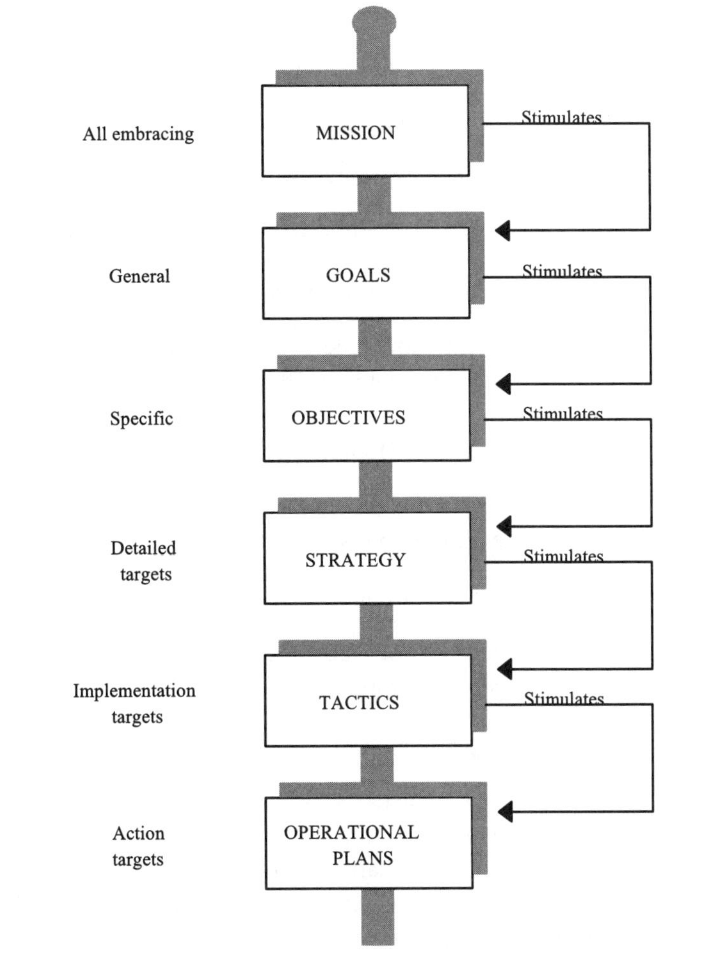

Hierarchy of objectives

The topmost statement of organisational objectives is usually termed 'the mission'. This is where we start.

2.2 The importance of the mission statement

Mission – the *raison d'être* of an organisation which is central and overriding. If it is subject to change there can be considerable disturbances within the organisation. It is normally very general and visionary. It should be viewed as where the organisation is conceived to be throughout time rather than where it currently is or where it wants to get to at any one moment in time.

DEFINITION

The **mission statement** is a statement in writing that describes the basic purpose of an organisation, that is, what it is trying to accomplish.

2.3 Characteristics of a good mission statement

A mission statement can be viewed as a statement primarily directed towards the employees of an organisation which should assist in the attainment of the objectives of the organisation. In short, a 'Mission statement' will have some or all of the following characteristics:

- It is usually a brief statement of no more than a page in length. (Some companies have produced very effective mission statements comprising a single sentence, although there are also successful company credos that extend into several pages, for example the statement written by William Hewlett for Hewlett-Packard, What is the HP Way?, which is relatively lengthy.)
- It is a very general statement of entity culture.
- It states the aims (or purposes) of the organisation.
- It states the business areas in which the organisation intends to operate.
- It is open-ended (not stated in quantifiable terms).
- It does not include commercial terms, such as **profit**.
- It is not time-assigned. (For example, the credo of JC Penny Company, The Penny Idea was formulated in 1913; that of Johnson and Johnson, Our Credo in the 1940s; and some missions are carved on stone or etched on plaque, such as that found at Lever House.)
- It forms a basis of communication to the people inside the organisation and to people outside the organisation.
- It is used to formulate goal statements, objectives and short-term targets.
- It therefore guides the direction of the entity's strategy and as such is part of management information.

Example: ICI plc

'The chemical industry is a major force for the improvement of the quality of life across the world. ICI aims to be the world's leading chemical company, serving customers internationally through the innovative and responsible application of chemistry and related sciences. Through achievement of our aim, we will enhance the wealth and well-being of our shareholders, our employees, our customers and the communities which we serve and in which we operate.'

2.4 Mission statements with an external orientation

KEY POINT

A mission's goals do not have to be 'internal'.

A mission's goals do not have to be 'internal'. Some of the most effective are directed outside the company, on customers, or competitors. Federal Express Corporation's US operation has a short but powerful mission statement: Absolutely, Positively Overnight! Everyone in the company knows what that statement means. Almost nothing more has to be said to ensure that every action of every person is aimed at total customer satisfaction. Another short credo that says it all belongs to PepsiCo. PepsiCo's mission has long been simply to Beat Coke, a mission it has yet to achieve. Honda, faced with the prospect of Yamaha dethroning it as the world's leading motorcycle maker, penned the memorable mission, We will crush, squash, slaughter Yamaha! It did! But like that of Federal Express most mission statements place an emphasis on serving the customer. Here is another example of such:

The mission of our company, as William Hesketh Lever saw it, is to make cleanliness commonplace, to lessen work for women, to foster health and to contribute to personal attractiveness so that life may be more enjoyable for the people who use our products.

Plaque: Lever House

2.5 The search for a mission

According to Peter Drucker there are a number of fundamental questions that an organisation will need to address in its search for purpose. These are:

- What is our business?
- What is value to the customer?
- What will our business be?
- What should our business be?

KEY POINT

The mission of an organisation is generally influenced by five key elements:

- The history of the organisation.
- The current preferences of the organisation's management and owners.
- The environmental factors influencing the organisation.
- The organisation's resources.
- The organisation's distinctive competence.

Although seemingly simple these questions are among the most difficult the strategist will need to solve. Successful planners will raise these questions and seek to answer them correctly and thoroughly. The mission of an organisation is generally influenced by five key elements:

- The history of the organisation.
- The current preferences of the organisation's management and owners.
- The environmental factors influencing the organisation.
- The organisation's resources.
- The organisation's distinctive competence.

Producing a formal mission statement is not an easy task. It will relate to a lot of factors and people, including in many cases, shareholders, customers, employees and the public. The organisation's mission acts as an 'invisible hand' that guides widely dispersed management to work independently, and yet collectively towards the achievement of the organisational goal.

To summarise these points, a 'Mission Statement' for an organisation should incorporate a number of different factors. These include:

- The business domain in which the organisation will operate.
- The organisation's raison d'être (or reason for existence).
- The stakeholder groups the organisation will serve.

The top level of management should be responsible for the preparation of a statement of corporate mission. Consequently, the mission statement should incorporate the broad aims of the executive management.

2.6 The relevance of a mission for strategic planning

A statement of corporate mission is inextricably linked with the organisation's goals and objectives, although it is important to draw a distinction between these three aspects of the strategic planning process.

Whilst the organisational objectives comprise the specific targets of the company and the goals comprise its broad aims, the mission encapsulates the reason that the entity exists in terms of the service and utility provided to meet specific needs of society. Refer back to the diagram which illustrates the hierarchy of objectives in an organisation and you will see this relationship again.

Before setting about the preparation of a strategic plan the management should consider the mission of an organisation. Many commentators have suggested that consideration and determination of the mission and its articulation into a statement of corporate mission constitutes the first stage in the strategic planning process and that therefore it is central to the whole planning process.

Johnson and Scholes have suggested that 'the mission of an organisation is the most generalised type of objective and can be thought of as an expression of its raison d'être'. On the other hand, some commentators believe that the mission statement is the end product of the process of strategic planning and this illustrates the confusion which often exists between the organisation's mission and its goals and objectives.

2.7 Effect on employees

A statement of corporate mission will provide all managers involved in the decision-making process within the organisation with a clear indication as to what constitutes the raison d'être of the organisation. The existence of a mission statement should assist those responsible for the formulation of strategic plans since it will focus upon critical issues which will help to ensure that strategic plans are prepared in accordance with desired norms within the organisation.

Mission statements can provide motivation to the employees of the organisation in the sense that they tell people what is important from the standpoint of executive management. A mission statement will clearly specify the business domain in which the company is to operate thereby facilitating planning activities. Decision-making processes within an organisation should be improved as a result of the clarification of the overall direction of the company which is contained within a corporate mission statement.

A mission statement will also aid staff, both existing and newly appointed, in their appreciation of the company's philosophies as well as providing a clear indication as to the expectations and attitudes which exist within the company.

ACTIVITY 1

Think about the organisation you are currently employed in, or one that you have been employed in, or one that you know of, and then draft a 'mission statement' that would be appropriate for it.

There is no feedback to this activity.

3 Goals and objectives

3.1 Goal statements

Characteristics

DEFINITION

Goals are long-run, open-ended attributes or ends a person or organisation seeks and are sufficient for the satisfaction of the organisation's mission.

In short, goals will have all or some of the following characteristics:

- They are mainly narrative statements derived from the mission.
- More than one goal statement is required to satisfy the organisation's mission.
- Goal statements are set in advance of the objectives. (They decouple the organisation's mission from the detailed, time-assigned objectives.)
- They are open-ended (not stated in quantifiable terms).
- In the main they have no time-assigned basis.

The distinction between goals, objectives and targets is a common cause of confusion. Some writers assign different meanings to the same terms, others use them interchangeably and almost all disagree on their relative values and significance. For example, the terms 'strategic objective' and 'goal' are often taken to be the same thing. One example will serve to exemplify the distinction.

Lorange, P. 'Corporate Planning, An Executive Viewpoint'

'Objectives, as referred to in this book, are more general statements about a direction in which the firm intends to go, without stating specific targets to be reached at particular points in time. A goal, on the other hand, is much more specific, indicating where one intends to be at a given point in time. A goal thus is an operational transformation of an objective; typically a general objective often gets transformed into one or more specific goals.'

KEY POINT

We categorise objectives into five components:

- mission
- goals
- corporate objectives
- strategic targets
- standards of performance.

However as mentioned previously, in this text we adhere to the view that goals will be a narrative transformation of the mission statement (or mission), and typically a goal will be transformed into one or more specific objectives. Thus we categorise objectives into five components:

- **Mission**, the primary raison d'être set in advance of strategy.
- **Goals**, the secondary and mainly narrative objectives derived from the mission and also set in advance of strategy.
- **Corporate objectives,** which are time-assigned aims derived from the goals and also set in advance of strategy.
- **Strategic targets** which are time-assigned and derived from the strategy.
- **Standards of performance** (often identical with targets) assigned to particular individuals.

3.2 Objectives

Characteristics

DEFINITION

Objectives are time-assigned targets derived from the goals, and are set in advance of strategy.

In short, objectives have all or some of the following characteristics:

- They are mainly statements expressed in quantitative terms ('closed') derived from the goals.
- More than one objective may be required to satisfy a goal.
- Objectives are set in advance of strategy.
- They are time-assigned.

One thing which is clear is that objectives must be capable of being quantified, otherwise progress towards them cannot be measured. For a local authority, for instance, to state a goal as 'to improve the welfare of old age pensioners in the Borough' is not precise enough. The goal needs to be translated into objectives which state how it is going to measure the achievement - in terms perhaps of the number of places made available in old people's homes by *x* date, the number of meals-on-wheels served in *x* period, the number of patients treated in geriatric wards - so that several targets may make up its overall objective.

KEY POINT

For objectives to be of use in practice, they must have three components:

- attribute chosen to be measured
- scale by which it is to be measured
- target.

In other words, for objectives to be of use in practice, they must have three components:

- Attribute chosen to be measured e.g., profit, return on capital, output.
- Scale by which it is to be measured e.g., £, %, tonnes.
- Target i.e. the level on the scale which it is hoped to achieve e.g., £1m, 12%, 350,000 tonnes.

As well as being **explicit,** objectives need to be realistic and attainable. Ideally, existing performance statistics should be used to measure objectives, for if a new system of data collection or processing has to be instituted in order to measure progress towards objectives, extra cost will be incurred.

Example

Let us take a hypothetical example for a private-sector company and use it to see the hierarchical structure at work.

Mission Statement (extract)

.... and we will enhance the wealth and well-being of our shareholders, ...

Goal Statements

1 We will provide our shareholders with a return on their investment which is commensurate with their expectations.

2 We will protect the security of our shareholders' investments.

3 We will endeavour to increase the capital value of our shareholders' investment.

Objectives

- **Goal 1: Shareholders' return on investment**
  - To realise a return on investment of 25% during the next *x* years.
  - To achieve a growth in sales turnover of x % in *y* years.
  - To maintain net profit margins.
  - That the return to shareholders should grow in line with the growth in net profit. .....
- **Goal 2: Security of shareholders' investments**
  - To maintain the quality of existing assets by investing not less than 8% of sales annually for the next *x* years, and to make new investment at rates of return applicable to the risk involved to meet the company's targeted return on capital employed.
  - To ensure that loans should not exceed 45% of capital employed unless required for exceptional circumstances of a short-term nature.
  - To maintain a match between foreign currency assets and liabilities. .....
- **Goal 3: Growth in shareholders' investments**
  - To achieve a price-earnings multiple of *x* by *y* date. .....

It is the achievement of the subsidiary objectives that forms the basis for performance evaluation. This general area is explored further in the following chapters.

3.3 The purposes of objectives

It is generally agreed that objectives serve several purposes in the strategic planning and control processes:

- Objectives provide the target or benchmark against which plans can be evaluated, investments appraised and the viability of ideas tested. For example, we have already seen that an objective could be stated in terms of a return on investment measure, and this could be used as a hurdle-rate for justifying an investment envisaged in a proposed strategy.
- The participation of managers in the setting of objectives might provide a basis for communication within the management group, motivation of the managers concerned to achieve agreed results, commitment of the managers to the changes involved, and the setting and monitoring of clear and specific management responsibility and accountability.

- Detailed operational objectives in the form of revenue and spend budgets, and non-financial targets provide essential yardsticks for use in cybernetic feedforward/feedback control systems. The data obtained at this level can also feed into the strategic model and be aggregated and thus help to monitor the implementation of the strategy.
- Objectives are a useful way of ensuring that all the different activities in the organisation remain in harmony, or that goal congruence is achieved.
- It is built into the approach of many organisations to inform external groupings, such as the shareholders' group and the loan group of their intentions, to ensure as wide a base as possible both for the grounds of the objectives, and for ulterior motives, such as obtaining funds.

KEY POINT

Operational performance is frequently defined by consideration of how far objectives have been achieved.

Operational performance is therefore frequently defined by consideration of how far objectives have been achieved. In subsequent chapters we will consider how appropriate performance measures can be designed to indicate meaningfully how far objectives have been achieved.

4 The planning gap

Manufacturing development can be viewed as subsidiary to product-market development. A manufacturing strategy is concerned with methods to make products, e.g.

- control of costs and productivity
- location of plant
- procurement of raw materials.

Due to the close inter-relationship between the product and the market for that product, strategic planners refer to a **product-market strategy**. The term merely describes the strategy(ies) used to develop products and markets. You should note, however, that most writers do not use the term to restrict an organisation to its **existing** products and markets. **New** products and markets may be developed. For example, the tobacco companies BAT and (before they were taken over) Imperial had a product-market strategy of developing their interests in non-tobacco products and markets. Eventually about 50% of their profits came from non-tobacco sources.

Before deciding which products and which markets to develop, the organisation should undertake an analysis of its performance in **existing** products and markets to determine whether there is a gap between its objectives (its desired performance) and expected performance. Product-market development can then be decided. This chapter and the next two chapters consider how gaps can be closed.

Clearly, forecasts must be taken far enough ahead to reveal any significant gap, indeed that there is a gap on which corrective action needs to be taken now. How far ahead a company must plan for this depends on the lead time for corrective action to take effect, which in turn depends on the nature of the business and on the type of action required.

KEY POINT

The possible ways of closing a gap are:

- internal efficiency improvement
- expansion within the present industry
- diversification into new fields.

The possible ways of closing a gap are:

- internal efficiency improvement (which we will look at in this chapter)
- expansion within the present industry, which may involve market penetration, product development or market development (which we deal with in the next chapter)
- diversification into new fields (which is covered later).

The components of the total gap are shown in the diagram below. The tendency will be for the lead time to be longer for diversification than for expansion (which means growth within the existing product-market sphere), and efficiency can usually be improved most quickly of all.

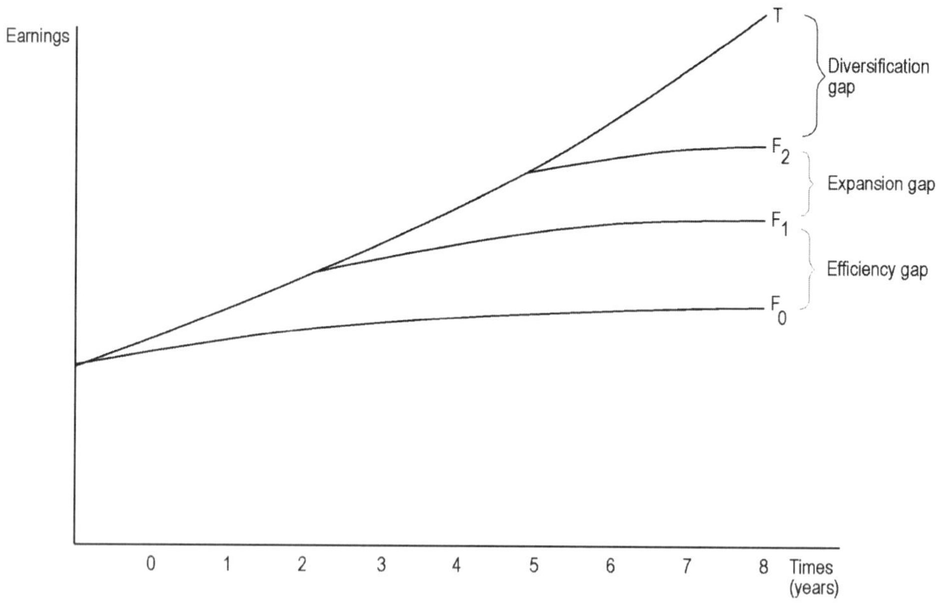

In the diagram showing the gap:

T = target

F_0 = initial forecast

F_1 = forecast adjusted for improvements in internal efficiency

F_2 = forecast adjusted for product-market expansion

Analysis of the gap reveals that in this instance the objectives cannot be achieved beyond year 4 without diversification. This gap is significant if the lead time for diversifying exceeds 4 years.

The existence of the gap may or may not lead to the revision of objectives. (There are after all two ways of closing a gap - revising objectives or taking action to improve performance expectations.) Objectives would be revised upwards if the forecasts showed that performance could be expected to exceed objectives: in this case the objectives might also be raised if forecasts showed that the gap was considerably more marked for one objective than for another. For instance, suppose the ROI target is 10% and increased flexibility is also desired. The forecast shows that the ROI target can be achieved but that little increase in flexibility can be expected. In this case the flexibility objective might be given greater emphasis.

5 The link between planning and control

This chapter has explored the role of planning in determining the objectives of an organisation. It has also been seen that control and performance measurement in the organisation are based on those objectives. The objectives form the benchmarks against which performance is measured. Performance measurement at levels in the organisation are a key element in the control of the organisation.

The concept of a hierarchy of objectives was introduced early in this chapter. Goals or strategic objectives may be cascaded down through successive layers in the organisation with subsidiary objectives. It might be argued that planning activities have more significance than controlling activities the higher in the hierarchy one considers. This, however, implies a rather top down approach to management that not everyone would be comfortable with in the modern era.

Conclusion

Organisations need to review their objectives as the business environment changes. The five components of business objectives are mission, goals, corporate objectives, strategic targets and standards of performance.

SELF-TEST QUESTIONS

Introduction

1 Explain the term 'goal' in the context of business planning. (1)

2 Explain the term 'objective' in the context of business planning. (1)

Goals and objectives

3 Explain the link between objectives and performance measurement. (3)

The planning gap

4 Explain what 'gap analysis' is and how the gap might be filled. (4)

EXAM-TYPE QUESTION

Corporate mission

The managing director of TDM plc has recently returned from a conference entitled 'Strategic planning beyond the 90's'. Whilst at the conference, she attended a session on 'corporate mission statements'. She found the session very interesting but it was rather short and she has asked the following questions:

(a) 'What does corporate mission mean? I don't see how it fits in with our strategic planning process.'

(b) 'Where does our mission come from and what areas of corporate life should it cover?'

(c) 'Even if we were to develop one of these mission statements, what benefits would the company get from it?'

Prepare a report which answers the managing director's questions. **(25 marks)**

For the answer to this question, see the 'Answers' section at the end of the book.

Chapter 10
FINANCIAL PERFORMANCE IN THE PRIVATE SECTOR

CHAPTER CONTENTS

This chapter considers the means that are used to measure business performance in the context of a private sector operation.

Objectives

When you have studied this chapter you should be able to do the following:

- Explain why the primary objective of financial performance should be concerned with the benefits of shareholders.
- Discuss the crucial objectives of survival and business growth.
- Discuss the appropriateness of differing measures of performance e.g. ROCE, EPS, ROI, sales margin, EBITDA, Residual Income, NPV, IRR.
- Explain why indicators of liquidity and gearing need to be considered alongside profitability.
- Compare and contrast short and long run financial performance and the resulting management issues.
- Contrast the traditional relationship between profits and share value with the long-term profit expectations of the stock market and recent financial performance of new technology/communication companies.

1 Introduction

1.1 The measurement of business performance

- A central area in management accounting is the measurement of how well or how badly a business is performing. This general theme can be extended in several directions:
- It is necessary to measure the performance of whole businesses, sectors within businesses, functions within businesses and business projects.
- Business performance may be measured in terms which are both relative and absolute. For example, profit divided by capital employed is a relative measure whereas profit less cost of capital is an absolute measure.
- Business performance measures may be used for a variety of purposes including decision-making, financial control and executive remuneration. A measurement of business performance may influence the way in which the business behaves.
- Business performance is a multi-faceted thing. It takes into account both 'short and long-term' and 'quantitative and qualitative' factors. One may have to find several different measures in order to develop a full impression of performance in a given situation.

KEY POINT

Business performance may be measured in terms which are both relative and absolute.

KEY POINT

The most traditional measure of business performance is Return on Capital Employed (ROCE). This is calculated by dividing operating profit through by the book value of fixed assets.

The most traditional measure of business performance is Return on Capital Employed (ROCE) or Return on Investment (ROI). This is calculated by dividing operating profit through by the book value of fixed assets – both figures taken from financial reports. However, there are many problems with this measure. For one thing, ROCE tends to rise as the book value of equipment diminishes through depreciation. ROCE tends to move with a firm's equipment replacement cycle. When new equipment is acquired, ROCE falls. As that equipment ages, then ROCE rises.

Consequently, if ROCE is used as a basis of management remuneration then managers may be reluctant to undertake new investments since the immediate impact of those investments may be a decline in current year ROCE. In fact, the use of ROCE as the key performance indicator may induce business contraction.

In the 1980s an insurance company was bought by a bank. The bank installed a management bonus system linked to ROCE. Writing new life insurance business involves a major initial investment whereas returns come much later. So, the insurance company practically stopped writing new business. Performance (as measured by ROCE) and management salary bonuses soared – but the company shrank. After five years the company was worth less than half the price paid for it. The new owner of the company had effectively paid its management to destroy it.

This kind of phenomenon is usually described as 'dysfunctional behaviour' or 'failure of goal congruence'. A control system is distorting the process it is meant to serve. Ultimately, a performance measure should induce behaviour calculated to maximise the wealth of shareholders.

The value of a business to its shareholders is linked to growth and growth prospects. Hence, in recent years a whole body of new 'metrics' has been developed to measure business performance. These new measures are broadly grouped under the topic headings 'economic value added' and 'shareholder value analysis'.

2 Performance criteria

2.1 Measurement and control systems

KEY POINT

Performance criteria enable the measurement and evaluation of performance.

Performance criteria enable the measurement and evaluation of performance.

Tom Peters in his book *Thriving on Chaos*, states that our fixation with financial measurement leads us to downplay or ignore less tangible non-financial measures, such as product quality, customer satisfaction, order lead time, factory flexibility, the time it takes to launch a new product and the accumulation of skills by labour over time.

The management writer Drucker argued that the objectives set by the organisation should be supported by appropriate measures which could be used to continually monitor the organisation's performance against objectives. Since Drucker's work there have been many more authors identifying a range of performance areas which organisations have to control and measure. These cover areas such as profitability, cost control, competitiveness, product leadership, productivity, quality of service, quality of working life, delivery performance, innovation and flexibility.

2.2 Design of the system

KEY POINT

The managers of every organisation will need to develop their own set of performance measures to help them gain and retain competitive advantage.

The managers of every organisation will need to develop their own set of performance measures to help them gain and retain competitive advantage. The set of measures they adopt will be affected by the interaction of three contingent variables:

- the competitive environment they face
- their chosen strategy e.g. cost leadership or product differentiation
- the type of business they are running.

The design of the system is linked to these variables. The three steps are as follows:

- The first stage is to determine the competitive environment that the organisation faces. If it is relatively turbulent and competitive (dynamic) the managers will need to build an interactive information system (by exception), focusing on strategic threats and uncertainties. Regular dialogue between top management and operating staff will facilitate organisational learning. If the conditions are stable, management can rely on delegated control of day-to-day operations to ensure sustained competitive success.
- What is measured depends on strategic intentions. Where an organisation decides to differentiate itself in the market on the basis of service quality, then it should design measures to monitor and control the quality of the service. If the strategy is based on technology and innovation, then it should be measuring its performance in these areas relative to its competitors.
- The third stage is to decide what type of business you are dealing with. Some measures may be feasible in one sector of the business, but not in others. Even when the strategy and what should be measured are known, it may not be that easy to see how to measure it.

The performance dimensions that are used also fall into distinct categories. Financial performance and competitiveness are set to measure the results of the organisation's strategy. All companies will wish to measure the results of their strategy. Innovation, quality measurements, resource utilisation and flexibility are measures of factors which determine competitive success and will vary between companies.

ACTIVITY 1

If an organisation is following a cost leadership strategy, what will their performance measurement focus on?

Feedback to this activity is at the end of the chapter.

2.3 Areas that require performance measures

Each area of a business will have differing requirements for operational planning and control and thus will use different performance measurements. The following paragraphs illustrate these differences.

2.4 Sales/marketing

This department has to analyse sales statistics and salesforce returns in order to build up a file of customer characteristics for each type of customer, and for each product in each market. These statistics will be needed to analyse demand trends over time and to predict latent and incipient demand as an aid to strategic decisions.

The department will be responsible for conducting market research exercises to ascertain customer reaction to new products. Such exercises need to be carefully controlled in order to ensure that an unbiased sample is selected.

It will have to decide on advertising campaigns - which media to use, how long to run the campaign etc. It will have to try and assess the effectiveness of different media to provide for planning future campaigns. For instance, if advertisements are placed in magazines with enquiry slips which the reader may complete, these should be coded so that the company can tell which magazine brings the best response.

In order to control selling activities, good communications are needed between head office, regional sales offices, and salespeople as they travel around. Data links connecting regional sales offices to a central computer can be very useful - by interrogating the central data bank, each regional office can obtain precise up-to-date information on availability of each product. Others can also be transmitted over such a link.

Example

In 1990 Market Solutions added the Distributed Database module to its SaleMaker Plus range of software. The module allows SaleMaker Plus client records to be distributed between corporate users in up to 999 remote locations. Any time a record on the user company's central database is added to, deleted or updated, the DDB changes the record in the remote locations. Two-way contact can be made by modem at night to take advantage of off-peak call rates, and special monitoring routines are said to guarantee error-free transmission during the process.

2.5 Credit control

The credit control department needs to analyse overall credit, on a year by year basis, to see if customers are beginning to take longer to pay and therefore whether credit arrangements need to be revised.

In addition, they will have to analyse credit on a product by product basis, on a customer type by customer type basis, and on a credit type basis, in order to see if there is any particular type of customer who is a bad risk, any type of credit which should be discontinued, or any products which should be sold only for cash. The statistics collected by the sales department will be useful in this analysis.

2.6 Production

The problem of the production department will depend on whether production is on a batch or continuous flow system. Production scheduling will be a particular problem if products are made to customers' specific order. The aim will be to minimise setting-up time and setting-up costs, to minimise machine idle time, to work as near as possible to economic batch quantities, to avoid production bottlenecks or hold-ups. Network analysis will help in scheduling.

When an order is placed, the production department will have to fit it into the production schedule in the optimum manner which allows the delivery date to be met, decide on the materials (type and quantity) to be used, and requisition the stores for same, decide on any overtime necessary to meet the delivery date, finally carry out the work in the most efficient manner possible. On all jobs, the department will have to ensure that material wastage is minimised, that overtime is kept to a reasonable level, and that optimum machine utilisation is obtained.

There will have to be some form of inspection to ensure the quality of the finished product - for instance Quality Control, which is a statistical method for sampling products for inspection and for deciding whether any deviations in quality are random only or are due to a defect in the process which should be investigated. This is a very cost-effective method of controlling quality: it provides the best assurance of quality possible short of inspecting every item, which is usually not feasible.

The production department also has to decide on maintenance methods - should maintenance be primarily on a preventive basis, or only when the machines actually break down? This will depend on the cost of maintenance, the cost of lost production if there is a machine breakdown, and the likelihood of machine breakdown. Again, this problem can be solved by statistical techniques. Indeed, the production department provides several very good examples of programmable control. Normally however companies opt for preventive maintenance.

The department should keep records which will form the basis of longer term decisions such as the need for capital investment. Records will be needed of the amount of overtime worked or the extent of idle time, machine utilisation (measured by capacity ratio), and deterioration in quality of output over time, wastage of materials etc.

2.7 Personnel

This department will be responsible for specific industrial relations issues such as negotiating wage settlements. It is responsible for ensuring that the company complies with such legislation as the Health and Safety at Work Act, equal opportunities and race relations legislation, and other relevant labour legislation.

In addition the department plays an important part in helping to plan and operate the company's manpower plan, and is responsible for activities such as advertising vacancies, making arrangements for interviews (probably in conjunction with the relevant functional manager), arranging training, seeing that the staff appraisal exercise is properly conducted etc.

This is not an area which is easily susceptible to programmable control.

2.8 Accounting

This department is of course responsible for seeing that accounts are prepared for audit in accordance with statutory requirements, for seeing that budgets are properly prepared and approved in accordance with the agreed timetable, and for seeing that management accounting information is extracted.

2.9 Purchasing and stores

This department will receive requisitions for stores from the production department and must ensure that the company receives the materials at the time required. Orders must be placed with suppliers in accordance with pre-determined re-order levels and economic order quantities which should be periodically reviewed. This department will be responsible for buying policy - whether to buy in large quantities to obtain discounts, whether to buy from several suppliers to retain flexibility etc. They will have to decide, in conjunction with the production departments, which items to stock as standard and which to order only when required.

3 Determining business objectives

3.1 Profit maximisation

Many of the theoretical models used for decision-making assume an objective of profit maximisation. Whilst this is a useful starting point such an objective is only one of the objectives pursued by organisations today.

Organisations are responsible for employee relations and have social responsibilities both of which incur costs which therefore reduce profits. Many of these responsibility areas are now considered extremely important if the business is to succeed. These are known as critical success factors.

3.2 Critical success factors (CSFs

DEFINITION

Critical success factors are the limited number of areas in which results, if they are satisfactory, will ensure successful competitive performance for the business. They are the vital areas where 'things must go right' for the business to flourish.

Critical success factors are defined as the limited number of areas in which results, if they are satisfactory, will ensure successful competitive performance for the business. They are the vital areas where 'things must go right' for the business to flourish.

They were developed by John Rockart, at the Sloan School of Management at MIT, as an attempt to identify the real information needs of management, mainly chief executives.

The areas referred to in the definition include core activities, new markets and new products. For example, one of the critical success factors to run a mail order service is speedy delivery.

3.3 Sources of CSF

KEY POINT

Rockart claims that there are four sources for the CSFs:

- the industry that the business is in
- the company itself and its situation within the industry
- the environment
- temporal organisational factors.

Rockart claims that there are four sources for the CSFs:

- the industry that the business is in. Each has CSFs that are relevant to any company within it.
- the company itself and its situation within the industry. Actions taken by a few large dominant companies in an industry will provide one or more CSFs for small companies in that industry.
- the environment e.g. the economy, the political factors and consumer trends in the country or countries that the organisation operates in. An example use by Rockart is that, before 1973, virtually no chief executive in the USA would have stated 'energy supply availability' as a critical success factor. However, following the oil embargo many executives monitored this factor closely.
- temporal organisational factors, which are areas of company activity that are unusually causing concern because they are unacceptable and need attention. Cases of too little or too much inventory might classify as a CSF for a short time.

Examples of CSFs will include 'develop new products', 'market success' and 'support field sales representatives'.

Some CSFs are industry-specific, as wc noted above. For example, one of the car industry's is 'Compliance with the Department of Transport's pollution requirements with respect to car exhaust gases'.

Rockart identified two types of CSF:

- monitoring – keeping abreast of ongoing operations
- building – tracking progress of the 'programs for change' initiated by the executive.

CSFs vary between organisations, periods and managers. The higher an executive is in the organisation, the more building CSFs they have to deal with.

3.4 Critical success factors and performance indicators

KEY POINT

The organisation will identify its CSFs by first determining its goals and objectives.

The organisation will identify its CSFs by first determining its goals and objectives.

Goals represent the aspiration of the organisation, the direction in which it will focus its effort. Objectives are measurable targets that an organisation sets to meet its goals. Each set of objectives will support one goal. There may be many or few objectives supporting one goal.

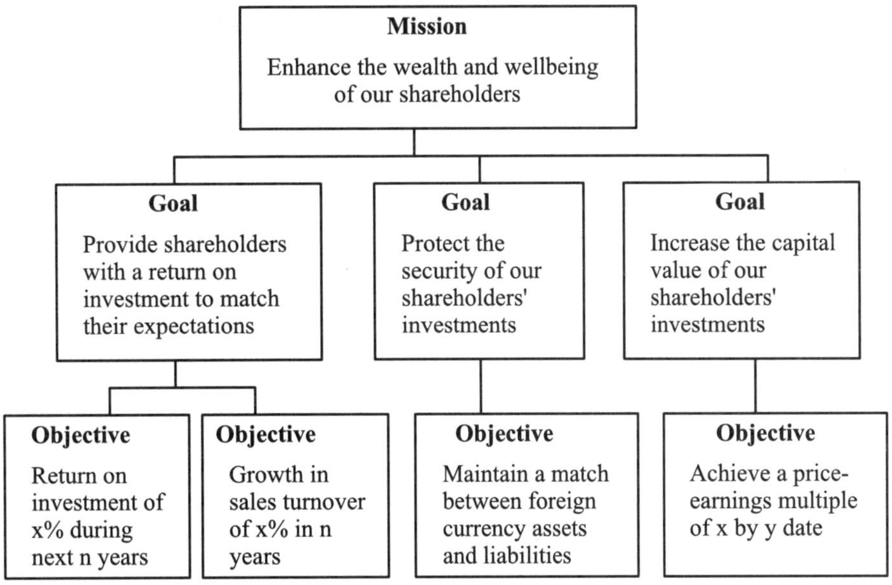

This general area was explored fully in the previous chapter.

Once the objectives are identified, they can be used to determine which factors are critical for accomplishing the objective. The performance measure for the CSF is a characteristic of its associated objective. Knowing the units of measurement for each objective makes it easy to identify the information required. Once the critical factors have been determined, two or three prime measures for each factor are found. Some measures use hard, factual data and these are the easiest to identify. Other measures are 'softer', such as opinions, perceptions and hunches and take more analysis to uncover their appropriate source.

KEY POINT

All CSFs should have a performance measure. It is this measure which is used to monitor the actual success of each factor and information will need to be supplied to managers in a form that they can use.

All CSFs should have a performance measure. It is this measure which is used to monitor the actual success of each factor and information will need to be supplied to managers in a form that they can use.

CSFs provide a way of achieving a clear definition of the information that is needed, limiting the costly collection of more data than is necessary. For example, where the CSF is to achieve market success, the information needs may be identified as the changes in market share over the last 12 months and the growth in the market over the same period.

4 Management performance measures

4.1 ROCE and RI

At the start of this chapter it was stated that some techniques of performance measurement draw on information reported through the accounting system. Clearly, performance can be measured by comparing actual ROCE to target ROCE.

Such targets are often set in the context of organisational objectives but many organisations use the same targets to appraise managers.

KEY POINT

The measures used to appraise a manager should be independent of the performance of the unit being managed.

The measures used to appraise a manager should be independent of the performance of the unit being managed. This is because not all units present the same degree of managerial problems and thus any manager comparisons based on unit performance are inappropriate.

Most management performance measures are qualitative though sometimes Residual Income is used.

4.2 What is residual income?

KEY POINT

Residual income is the profit of the unit for which the manager is responsible less a notional interest charge based on the value of the assets used by the unit to generate its income.

Residual income is the profit of the unit for which the manager is responsible less a notional interest charge based on the value of the assets used by the unit to generate its income. This is a quantitative measure, but it is based on the unit's performance.

In modern management argot, Residual Income is often known as "Economic Value Added". It represents the return generated from a business less the cost of the capital engaged in it.

4.3 Qualitative management performance measures

In small to medium-sized organisations such measures will be in the form of internal judgement by senior managers of their subordinates and by staff of their manager.

The first of these requires a detailed knowledge of the problems faced by the subordinate manager and the techniques used to solve them. The appraisal by staff requires that there is a very good working relationship between the staff and their manager.

In large organisations it may be possible for such judgements to be made by outsiders, perhaps from other divisions or subsidiaries. Where this is possible the performance evaluation is likely to be impartial.

5 Divisional assessment

5.1 The concept

A main feature in modern business management is the practice of splitting a business into 'divisions'. A division is a sector within a business which has its own designated management. A business may be split into divisions on geographical, product or functional lines. The critical thing is that the management of a division is given a measure of authority over how that division is run. The management may have control over its production, sales, investment and strategy.

The management of a division are normally remunerated on a basis linked to the performance they achieve. Typically, they are given performance targets and only if they achieve those targets do they get a salary bonus.

The central idea is that the manager of a division is in the same position as an independent entrepreneur. If he experiences the risks and rewards of business ownership then he/she will act in a manner calculated to maximise the value of the division – or that is the theory. The modern variation on this theme is to give management 'share options' –the right to buy shares at a given price. If the share price performs well (and the stock market is a good judge of business performance) then the manager benefits. The theory is that this promotes goal congruence between managers and shareholders.

Having decentralised, it is essential that senior management monitors and controls the performance of the divisions and those with direct responsibility for those divisions. An accounting information system (a management control system) must be in place to allow for divisional assessment. The system used must have a close bearing on divisional goals and must recognise that some costs of a division will be controllable by its managers and some will not.

5.2 Methods

A range of methods are available for assessing divisional performance, the two most common being:

- Return on investment (ROI)
- Residual income (RI).

The term ROI is almost interchangeable with ROCE, but ROI is more commonly used in the context of project appraisal or business sector performance appraisal. ROCE is more commonly used in the context of whole business performance appraisal.

These are discussed fully in the next two sections of this chapter. However other methods exist.

- **Variance analysis** – is a standard means of monitoring and controlling performance. Care must be taken in identifying the controllability of and responsibility for each variance.
- **Ratio analysis** – there are several profitability and liquidity measures that can be applied to divisional performance reports.
- **Other management ratios** – under this heading would come contribution per key factor and sales per employee or square foot as well as industry specific ratios such as transport costs per mile, brewing costs per barrel, overheads per chargeable hour etc.
- **Other information** – such as staff turnover, market share, new customers gained, innovative products or services developed.

KEY POINT

Whilst it is common to focus on one key measure of performance, it is important to keep an eye on, and stress the relevance of, a range of measures in order that performance in its widest sense is assessed.

Whilst it is common to focus on one key measure of performance, it is important to keep an eye on, and stress the relevance of, a range of measures in order that performance in its widest sense is assessed.

5.3 Points on performance measures

The information system and reports that a company produces on divisional performance should follow three simple principles:

- **Timeliness** – any report should be produced sufficiently quickly after the end of an accounting period (week, month, quarter) to allow corrective action to be taken on any unsatisfactory performance. There is a balance to maintain here between the speed with which information is produced, the accuracy of that information and the cost of producing the figures.
- **Goal congruence** – the performance measures used, the assessment criteria, should not encourage divisional managers to make decisions which shows their divisions performing well against the criteria set, but adopting strategies which are against the well-being of the company as a whole. An example might be a sales department that is judged on total volume of sales made irrespective of the price charged or the credit worthiness of the customers.
- **Controllability** – the important measure of divisional performance will be linked to profit but care has to be taken in deciding how that profit is calculated. Much is written on this aspect of divisional assessment and five factors to consider are:
  - **Definition of controllable or managed cost** – a controllable cost is defined as a cost which can be influenced by its budget holder. It is not always possible to pre-determine responsibility, because the reason for deviation from expected performance may only become evident later.
  - **Division or manager** – the measure of profit will depend upon whether it is the performance of the division or its manager that is being assessed as discussed below.

- **Short-term v long-term** – few costs are controllable in the short-term and it is only in the longer term that action can be taken to control most costs. For instance, if the rent on premises is deemed to be too high, moving an office or a factory cannot happen at a week's notice. This means that short-term performance reports should concentrate on those costs controllable in the short-term.
- **Absorption v marginal format** – it is often suggested that a marginal costing format for profit statements and performance reports is more appropriate for management purposes. In divisional assessment there is an argument in favour of a marginal format to assess divisional managers since many fixed costs with which a division may be charged are unlikely to be under the control of the manager. However some fixed costs will be controllable at divisional level. It is suggested that a use of absorption costing information may, on the one hand, be demotivating (in view of uncontrollable costs it contains); on the other hand, it might encourage divisional managers (and therefore senior management) to question the wisdom of using certain central services whose costs are apportioned out to divisions.
- **Interdependence** – whilst it is a desirable aim in a divisionalised organisation that the actions of one division cannot affect the performance of another, in most cases it is unrealistic. When assessing divisional performance, care has to be taken in deciding the true cause of any adverse performance by a division.

5.4 Divisional v managerial performance

The main board of a decentralised company will wish to assess two aspects of performance:

- the personal performance of the divisional manager
- the economic performance of the manager's divisions.

The type of measures used and the way in which they are evaluated will vary according to who or what is being assessed.

It is quite possible that the best manager within an organisation produces the worst divisional profit, because that manager is operating in the toughest or newest market, but is still doing well under the circumstances. By the same token good divisional performance might not indicate a well-run division and a competent manager, but rather a controllable business environment. This raises the issue of performance targets. An organisation will compare the performance of divisions and set targets for managers, but this will have to be done with caution.

Targets set should take into account:

- the difficulty of the economic environment in which a division is operating
- the motivational value of tough or lenient targets for the divisional manager concerned.

KEY POINT

Targets set should take into account:

- the difficulty of the economic environment in which a division is operating
- the motivational value of tough or lenient targets for the divisional manager concerned.

Added to the difficulty or leniency of targets, the question must be asked of profit-based measures, 'which profit to use?' To answer this question the pro-forma below shows a profit and loss account (section of a performance report) for a division.

	£000	£000
Outside sales		X
Internal transfers		X
		X

Variable cost of goods sold and transferred	(X)	
Other variable divisional costs	(X)	
	—	(X)
		—
Contribution		X
Depreciation on controllable fixed assets	(X)	
Other controllable fixed costs	(X)	
	—	
		(X)
		—
Controllable operating profit (1)		X
Interest on controllable investment		(X)
		—
Controllable residual income before tax (2)		X
Non controllable divisional fixed costs	(X)	
Apportioned head office costs	(X)	
Interest on non-controllable investment	(X)	
	—	
		(X)
		—
Net residual income before tax (3)		X
		—

The features of this statement are:

- **absence of tax charges** – it is generally felt that the tax charge of a company cannot be controlled at divisional level and therefore any profit-based measures should be pre-tax.
- **inclusion of interest charges** – this is a contentious issue and is discussed further when explaining the two main measures ROI and RI.
- **which profit?** – a divisional manager's performance should be assessed by reference to figures (1) or (2) whereas the division, which received the benefits from head-office costs and other non-controllable elements even if the manager cannot influence them, should be assessed by reference to figure (3).

5.5 Return on investment (ROI)

Return on investment (ROI), or return on capital employed (ROCE) or return on net assets (RONA), is calculated for a division or investment centre for a particular period as follows:

KEY POINT

ROI =

$$\frac{\text{Earnings before interest and tax}}{\text{Capital employed}} \times 100$$

$$\text{ROI} = \frac{\text{Earnings before interest and tax}}{\text{Capital employed}} \times 100$$

If assessing the performance of a manager the earnings figure should be controllable operating profit and capital employed should be controllable investment. When assessing a division's performance costs and assets that are not controllable at divisional level could be included, although all interest costs are usually excluded. This is very similar to the return on capital employed (ROCE) traditionally used to analyse capital investment projects. The only difference is that here the profits from all projects for a single year are compared to the book value of all investments, whereas in investment appraisal the profits of a single investment project over the several years of that investment's life are compared to the book value of that one single investment.

The return on investment is widely used by external analysts of company performance when the primary ratio is broken down into its two secondary ratios.

$$\text{ROI} = \frac{\text{Earnings}}{\text{Capital employed}} \times 100 = \frac{\text{Sales}}{\text{Capital employed}} \times \frac{\text{Earnings}}{\text{Sales}} \times 100$$

On the right, the first term is the asset turnover ratio and the second is the net profit percentage.

KEY POINT

ROI =

$$\frac{\text{Earnings}}{\text{Capital employed}} \times 100 = \frac{\text{Sales}}{\text{Capital employed}} \times \frac{\text{Earnings}}{\text{Sales}} \times 100$$

5.6 Advantages of ROI

The return on investment is regarded as inferior to the residual income for several reasons. Nevertheless it is widely used and has several good features.

- As a **relative measure** it enables comparisons to be made with divisions or companies of different sizes. It could be argued that it is particularly appropriate for profit centres rather than investment centres since the former are not in a position to increase overall profit by undertaking further capital investments.
- It is **used externally** and is well understood by users of accounts.
- The primary ratio **splits down** into secondary ratios for more detailed analysis as mentioned above and discussed further later.
- ROI forces managers to **make good use** of existing capital resources and focuses attention on them, particularly when funds for further investment are limited.
- The nature of the measure is such that it can clearly be improved not just by increasing profit but by reducing capital employed. It therefore encourages **reduction in** the level of **assets** such as obsolete equipment and excessive working capital.

KEY POINT

Advantages of ROI:

- As a **relative measure** it enables comparisons to be made with divisions or companies of different sizes.
- It is **used externally** and is well understood by users of accounts
- The primary ratio **splits down** into secondary ratios for more detailed analysis
- ROI forces managers to **make good use** of existing capital resources
- It encourages **reduction in** the level of **assets** such as obsolete equipment and excessive working capital.

5.7 Disadvantages of ROI

The disadvantages fall into two categories: those that are problems common to **both** ROI and RI; and those that are **specific** to ROI.

Specific disadvantages

- **Disincentive to invest** – a divisional manager will not wish to make an investment which provides an adequate return as far as the overall company is concerned if it reduces the division's current ROI. By the same token existing assets may be sold if, by doing so, ROI is improved even though those assets are generating a reasonable profit.
- **ROI improves with age** – on the other side of the coin most conventional depreciation methods will result in ROI improving with the age of an asset, being unsatisfactory initially then improving as the net book value of assets improves. This might encourage divisions hanging on to old assets and again deter them from investing in new ones. Alternatively a division may try to improve its ROI still further by **leasing** its assets. It is suggested that gross book value or even replacement cost should be used when evaluating performance. Also complex depreciation calculations are recommended by academics to overcome some of these difficulties.
- **Corporate objectives** of maximising total shareholders' wealth or the total profit of the company are not achieved by making decisions on the basis of ROI. In this way, as a relative measure, it can be compared to the internal rate of return whose use is also dysfunctional.

KEY POINT

Disadvantages of ROI:

- Disincentive to invest
- ROI improves with age
- Corporate objectives of maximising total shareholders' wealth or the total profit of the company are not achieved by making decisions on the basis of ROI.

5.8 General problems

Whether it be ROI or RI that are used, there are certain problems common to both measures.

- **Calculation of profit** – apart from issues such as its controllability mentioned earlier there is some scope, even within the strictures of a group accounting policy, for some variation in treatment of depreciation. Also the need to increase profit may lead to cutting down on discretionary costs such as training, advertising and maintenance which, whilst improving short-term profit figures, will jeopardise the long-term future of a business. Standards for these should be set and monitored.
- **Asset measurement** – again group policies should ensure a consistent treatment, but comparison is difficult when some divisions buy and some lease assets. Thought has to be given to the treatment of permanent bank overdrafts. Are these current liabilities or a source of finance?
- **Conflict with investment decisions** – the performance of a division will be influenced by investment decisions that it makes. However those decisions should be made on the basis of NPV calculations, whereas the subsequent performance of the division is assessed by a different criterion. Clearly there is likely to be a problem when a long-term investment decision is accepted, but the short-term effect on profit is detrimental. Some academics have recommend adopting depreciation methods such that the ROI or RI calculation is consistent with DCF calculations. This possibility was considered in the context of long-term decision-making in Chapter 7.

An alternative approach, where the actual cash flows associated with an investment that has been made can be identified, suggests that the performance of a division should be carried out by comparing those actual cash flows with the budgeted figures used when the initial investment decision was made.

ACTIVITY **2**

The Arca division of Botten Ltd currently has an investment base of £2.4m and annual profits of £0.48m. It is considering the following three investments, funds for which will be supplied by the company.

Project	*A*	*B*	*C*
Initial outlay (£000)	1,400	600	400
Annual earnings (£000)	350	200	88

You are required to find the current ROI of the Arca division, the ROI of each investment and the ROI of Arcadia with each of the three additional investments added to current earnings in turn.

Feedback to this activity is at the end of the chapter.

ACTIVITY **3**

McKinnon Ltd sets up a new division in Blair Atholl investing £800,000 in fixed assets with an anticipated useful life of 10 years and no scrap value. Annual profits before depreciation are expected to be a steady £200,000.

You are required to calculate the division's ROI for its first three years by expressing annual (post depreciation) profits as a percentage of the book value of assets at the start of each year.

Feedback to this activity is at the end of the chapter.

5.9 Residual income (RI)

KEY POINT

The modern variant on RI is Economic Value Added (EVA).
RI = Controllable profit – Imputed interest charge on controllable divisional investment

As indicated above, the modern variant on RI is Economic Value Added (EVA). Many commentators would consider that, for our present purposes, RI and EVA may be considered to be the same thing.

In view of the disadvantages of ROI, particularly its tendency to induce under-investment, most management authors recommend that the performance of investment centres is assessed by calculating an absolute measure of profitability, residual income as follows:

$$\text{RI} = \text{Controllable profit} - \text{Imputed interest charge on controllable divisional investment}$$

The two figures shown in the earlier profit and loss account were residual income figures, one (with controllable profit and controllable investment) being used to assess a manager's performance, the other (with all costs included) being used to assess the performance of the division. The rate at which interest is charged on assets is open to debate. Various possibilities exist:

- **Group cost of capital** – commonly used although it reflects the risk of the group as a whole and not the individual divisions.
- **Current group ROI** – again the specific circumstances of the division are overlooked.
- **Different rates** – either of the above might be starting points for an interest rate but it is then adjusted for the specific circumstances of the group: the business environment, the type of investments being made and the motivational requirements for the divisional manager. It may be necessary to use different interest rates for different types of asset.

5.10 Advantages of RI

KEY POINT

Advantages of RI:

- It **reduces the problem of under investing**
- It is more consistent with the objective of **maximising** the **total profitability** of the group
- It is possible to use **different rates** of interest for different types of asset
- The **cost of financing** a division is brought home to divisional managers.

Residual income overcomes many of the disadvantages of ROI, specifically:

- It **reduces thc problem of under investing** or failing to accept projects with ROI's greater than the group target but less than the division's current ROI. Any project which generates a positive RI contributes to measured performance.
- As a consequence it is more consistent with the objective of **maximising** the **total profitability** of the group.
- It is possible to use **different rates** of interest for different types of asset.
- The **cost of financing** a division is brought home to divisional managers.

However, it will suffer from the same problems associated with profit and asset measurement, and potential conflict with NPV investment decisions, as the ROI.

Despite these advantages, and that there are few significant disadvantages that are specific to RI apart from the difficulty of comparison with different sized enterprises, it is not as widely used as ROI. In one of the more recent surveys on the subject, albeit with transatlantic origins, the methods used amongst a sample of 459 companies were:

	%
ROI only	65
Both ROI and RI	28
RI only	2
Other criteria	4
No response	1
	100

ACTIVITY 4

Division Z has the following financial performance:

Operating profit	£40,000
Operating assets	£150,000
Cost of borrowing	10%

Would the division wish to accept a new possible investment costing £10,000 which would earn profit of £2,000 pa if the evaluation was on the basis of

(a) ROI

(b) Residual income?

Feedback to this activity is at the end of the chapter.

5.11 Net present value and internal rate of return

Cash flows payable and receivable in the future can be expressed in terms of their present value – being what they are worth to you now having regard to the current interest rate. £1 receivable 1 year from now is worth £0.9091 to you now if the current interest rate is 10%. You could borrow £0.9091 now at 10% and use your £1 to repay that amount with interest at Year 1.

DEFINITION

Cash Flow Return on Investment (CFROI) is a business performance measure which expresses the return a business generates as the present value of its sustainable cash flow.

Cash Flow Return on Investment (CFROI) is a business performance measure which expresses the return a business generates as the present value of its sustainable cash flow. It can be expressed as either an absolute of money (a 'net present value' or a yield rate (an 'internal rate of return').

CFROI is a cash flow based approach which is not vulnerable to the accounting policies adopted or to manipulations relating to off-balance sheet finance and similar devices.

DEFINITION

CFROI is a cash flow based approach which is not vulnerable to the accounting policies adopted or to manipulations relating to off-balance sheet finance and similar devices.

5.12 Divisional project evaluation – ROI, RI and NPV

The potential for inappropriate investment decisions.

It has already been identified that a potential problem with the use of ROI or RI as a short-term management performance measure is the possibility that this will encourage long-term investment decisions that are not in the company's best interest. Specifically, a project with a positive net present value (NPV) at the company's cost of capital may show poor ROI or RI results in early years, leading to its rejection by the divisional manager.

Example 1 – equal annual cash flows

Division X of ABC plc, currently generating an ROI of 12%, is considering a new project. This requires an investment of £1.4 million and is expected to yield net cash inflows of £460,000 per annum for the next four years. None of the initial investment will be recoverable at the end of the project.

ABC plc has a cost of capital of 8%. Annual accounting profits are to be assumed to equal annual net cash inflows less depreciation, and tax is to be ignored.

NPV of project at 8%

This can be computed using the annuity discount factor for four years at 8%:

NPV = £460,000 × 3.312 - £1,400,000 = £123,520

It can be seen that a £1.4 millions initial investment gives later cash inflows which have a present value of £1.523 millions.

The project is therefore worthwhile accepting from the company's point of view.

(note: DCF analysis is explored fully in Chapter 7)

ROI and RI using straight line depreciation

Annual depreciation on a straight-line basis will be £1.4m/4 = £350,000 per annum.

ROI and RI computations will be as follows:

	Year 1	*Year 2*	*Year 3*	*Year 4*
	£000	£000	£000	£000
NBV at start of year	1,400	1,050	700	350
Net cash inflow	460	460	460	460
Depreciation	350	350	350	350
Profit	110	110	110	110
Interest on capital @8%	112	84	56	28
RI	(2)	26	54	82
ROI on NBV	7.9%	10.5%	15.7%	31.4%

If the manager's performance is measured (and rewarded) on the basis of RI or ROI he is unlikely to accept the project. The first year's RI is negative, and the ROI does not exceed the company's cost of capital until year 2, or that currently being earned until year 3. Divisional managers will tend to take a short-term view. More immediate returns are more certain, and by year 3 he may have moved jobs.

ROI and RI using annuity depreciation at 8% (company's cost of capital)

A compatibility between RI and NPV may be achieved by using an alternative form of depreciation. This is calculated as follows:

- the equivalent annual cost (EAC) of the initial investment at the cost of capital is calculated:

$$\frac{\text{Initial investment}}{\text{cum. disc. factor at 8\%}} = \frac{£1.4\text{m}}{3.312} = £422,705$$

- annual depreciation is then computed such that depreciation + imputed interest on capital = EAC, i.e. Depreciation = EAC - interest on opening NBV
- So for the first year of Division X's project, depreciation = 422.7 - 112 = 310.7

The results for the project over its life will now be as follows:

	Year 1	Year 2	Year 3	Year 4
	£000	£000	£000	£000
NBV at start of year	1,400	1,089.3	753.7	391.3
Net cash inflow	460	460	460	460
Depreciation	310.7	335.6	362.4	391.4
Profit	149.3	124.4	97.6	68.6
Interest on capital @8%	112	87.1	60.3	31.3
RI	37.3	37.3	37.3	37.3
ROI on NBV	10.7%	11.4%	12.9%	17.5%

The project now has an equal, positive, RI over its life, which will encourage the manager to invest, a decision compatible with that using NPV. This consistency will always be achieved because the method ensures that discounting RI for each year at the cost of capital gives the NPV - thus provided the first year's RI is positive, so will be the NPV, and vice versa.

However, there is still a problem if ROI is used as the performance measure, in that the short-term low rate of return may not encourage investment in what is, in fact, a worthwhile project. A way round this is to use annuity depreciation at a different rate that will ensure a level ROI over the project life. The rate to be used will be the IRR of the project.

ROI and RI using annuity depreciation at the project IRR

The IRR of the project, which has equal annual cash flows, is estimated from the IRR annuity factor:

$$\frac{\text{Initial investment}}{\text{Annual NCI}} = \frac{£1.4\text{m}}{£460{,}000} = 3.043$$

Using annuity (cumulative) factor tables, the IRR is identified as approximately 12%.

What this means is that if the current interest rate is 12% then the present value of all the cash inflows and outflows associated with the project is nil. This 12% figure is a form of yield known as the internal rate of return of the project.

12% is now used instead of 8% in computing both the EAC of the investment (which will simply revert to being the annual NCI), and the interest on capital, yielding the following results:

	Year 1	Year 2	Year 3	Year 4
	£000	£ 000	£000	£000
NBV at start of year	1,400	1,108	781	414.7
Net cash inflow	460	460	460	460
Depreciation	292	327	366.3	410.2
Profit	168	133	93.7	49.8
Interest on capital @12%	168	133	93.7	49.8
RI	–	–	–	–
ROI on NBV	12%	12%	12%	12%

The ROI (and the RI) is now level over the project life, ensuring a consistent decision whether the short or long-term view is taken. Using 12% as an appraisal rate for the project yields consistent results under all three methods (NPV, ROI and RI) i.e. the project is at break-even.

This somewhat contrived approach is probably less useful than the one above – i.e. using RI with annuity depreciation at the company's cost of capital as a management performance measure, which will ensure compatibility with a DCF approach to project appraisal.

Example 2 – uneven cash flows

The use of annuity depreciation as illustrated above does not produce helpful results when cash flows are uneven.

Suppose Division X was considering an alternative project requiring an initial investment of £1m with annual cash flows of £380,000/£350,000/£320,000/£290,000 over the four years of its life respectively.

The NPV of this project at 8% = £119,063

The RI/ROI results, using annuity depreciation at 8%, are as follows:

- the equivalent annual cost (EAC) of the initial investment at the cost of capital is calculated:

$$\frac{\text{Initial investment}}{\text{Cum. disc. factor at 8\%}} = \frac{£1.0\text{m}}{3.312} = £301,932$$

- the results for the alternative project would be as follows:

	Year 1	*Year 2*	*Year 3*	*Year 4*
	£000	£000	£000	£000
NBV at start of year	1,000	778.1	538.4	279.6
Net cash inflow	380	350	320	290
Depreciation	221.9	239.7	258.8	279.5
Profit	158.1	110.3	61.2	10.5
Interest on capital @8%	80	62.2	43.1	22.4
RI	78.1	48.1	18.1	(11.9)
ROI on NBV	15.8%	14.2%	11.4%	3.8%

Consistency with the NPV using either ROI or RI is not guaranteed with uneven cash flows. If the pattern of cash flows had been increasing, it is easy to see that the RI in the first year could be negative, and the ROI low, discouraging investment in this worthwhile project.

Furthermore, comparing the results above with those for the original project in the early years (under the same depreciation method), early years RI and ROI measures look far superior, and thus, if a choice were to be made, the manager of Division X would be encouraged to accept the alternative project over the original. This is contrary to the DCF evaluation, which shows the alternative as having a lower NPV than the original.

KEY POINT

The *adjusted RI approach* calculates annual depreciation by deducting interest on capital from the annual *net cash inflow.*

There is an approach that can overcome this – the *adjusted RI approach* – which calculates annual depreciation by deducting interest on capital from the annual *net cash inflow* (rather than the EAC of the initial investment).

However, this results in depreciation charges that can increase and decrease according to the pattern of the cash flows, and although it makes comparisons between projects with uneven cash flows easier, it does not guarantee investment decisions compatible with NPV evaluations.

6 Ratio analysis

6.1 Ratio pyramid

KEY POINT

The starting point for ratio analysis is the primary ratio ROI which then splits down into the asset turnover ratio and net profit percentage.

One important means of assessing performance both of companies by outside observers and of divisions by senior management is by the use of assorted accounting ratios. The reason for this is the difficulty of getting a true picture of performance by just using one figure. The starting point for ratio analysis is the primary ratio ROI which then splits down into the asset turnover ratio and net profit percentage. The first of these, asset turnover, then leads on to various liquidity ratios whilst the net profit percentage can be investigated further by calculating additional profitability measures. The whole process is best shown as a ratio pyramid or ratio tree.

Ratio pyramid

The initial split of ROI into secondary ratios has been mentioned before.

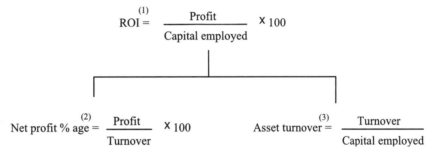

$$\text{ROI} \overset{(1)}{=} \frac{\text{Profit}}{\text{Capital employed}} \times 100$$

$$\text{Net profit \% age} \overset{(2)}{=} \frac{\text{Profit}}{\text{Turnover}} \times 100 \qquad \text{Asset turnover} \overset{(3)}{=} \frac{\text{Turnover}}{\text{Capital employed}}$$

They are linked since (1) = (2) × (3). After this there is no clear relationship although the Net profit percentage can be investigated by finding:

$$\text{Gross profit percentage} = \frac{\text{Gross profit}}{\text{Turnover}} \times 100$$

and

$$\text{Operating ratios} = \frac{\text{Various expenses}}{\text{Turnover}} \times 100$$

Asset turnover can be investigated by finding:

$$\frac{\text{Turnover}}{\text{Fixed assets}} \text{ and } \frac{\text{Turnover}}{\text{Net current assets}}$$

The first pair of ratios (or group of ratios) would require careful study if the net profit percentage indicated problems over profitability to determine whether this was due to an unduly low margin or poor control of overheads. The second pair of ratios would indicate whether s

Sufficient sales were being generated and whether working capital was being sufficiently well controlled. If a problem was detected in this last area then various liquidity ratios would be found:

$$\text{Current ratio} = \frac{\text{current assets}}{\text{current liabilites}}$$

$$\text{Quick ratio (Acid test ratio)} = \frac{\text{quick assets (CAs - stock)}}{\text{current assets}}$$

$$\text{Debtors period} = \frac{\text{debtors}}{\text{daily credit sales}}$$

$$\text{Stock period} = \frac{\text{stock}}{\text{daily cost of sales}}$$

$$\text{Creditors period} = \frac{\text{creditors}}{\text{daily credit purchases}}$$

KEY POINT

Comparison would be made with group standards, other divisions, other periods and other firms in the same business.

These ratios could be found using year end figures or average figures. In some divisionalised companies some of these liquidity ratios are less important since the assets are managed centrally. Comparison would be made with group standards, other divisions, other periods and other firms in the same business.

Even using accounting figures, it is important to appreciate the multi-faceted nature of business performance. Particular ratios can be used to measure the performance of particular functions within a business. Obviously, the debtors period is a comment on the performance of the credit control department.

Example

The example which follows shows an evaluation of the production, commercial and financial management of a company using key ratios. The following information relates to a company manufacturing consumable goods.

	Actual		*Budget*
	20X5/6	*20X6/7*	*20X7/8*
	£000	£000	£000
Sales	215	236	276
Less: Production costs:			
Material	79	82	96
Labour – direct	34	33	37
Labour – indirect	35	39	44
Other costs	26	29	36
	174	183	213
Administration	21	26	33
Selling	6	7	7
Distribution	3	3	4
	204	219	257
Net profit before tax	11	17	19

Balance sheet (at year end)

	Actual		*Budget*
	20X5/6	*20X6/7*	*20X7/8*
	£000	£000	£000
Fixed assets at cost	120	155	175
Less: Depreciation	(65)	(65)	(80)
	55	90	95
Stocks and work-in-progress	55	62	68
Debtors	35	32	34
Bank	4	4	3
	94	98	105
Less: Current liabilities	(17)	(13)	(15)
	77	85	90
	132	175	185

	Actual		*Budget*
	20X5/6	*20X6/7*	*20X7/8*
Number of people employed:			
Average during year:			
Direct	43	41	47
Works indirect	31	35	40
Administration	30	37	36
Sales	6	7	7
	110	120	130
Floor space occupied (square feet)	30,000	30,000	32,000

Give your interpretation of the production, commercial and financial management of the company over the period shown illustrating your conclusion with selected key ratios through the period.

Solution

Evaluation of performance:

	Actual		*Budget*
	20X5/6	*20X6/7*	*20X7/8*
Profitability			
Profit: Capital employed	8.3%	9.7%	10.3%
Profit: Sales	5.1%	7.2%	6.9%
Sales: Capital employed	1.63 times	1.35 times	1.49 times
Production costs			
% of works cost	%	%	%
Materials	45.4	44.9	45.0
Direct labour	19.5	18.0	17.4
Indirect labour	20.1	21.3	20.7
Other costs	15.0	15.8	16.9
	100.0	100.0	100.0

Labour			
Indirect/Direct			
Monetary values (£)	1.03	1.18	1.19
Numbers	0.72	0.85	0.85
£ per employee per annum:			
Direct	£791	£804	£787
Indirect	£1,129	£1,114	£1,100
Profit:			
Per direct worker	£256	£415	£404
Per indirect worker	£354	£485	£475
Sales			
Selling costs/Sales	2.8%	3.0%	2.5%
Sales per sales employee	£35,833	£33,714	£39,429
Profit per sales employee	£1,833	£2,428	£2,714

	Actual		*Budget*
	20X5/6	*20X6/7*	*20X7/8*
Financial control			
Stock period			
Stock and WIP : Production cost	115 days	124 days	117 days
Debtors period			
Debtors: Sales	59 days	49 days	45 days
Creditors period			
Current liabilities: Materials	78 days	58 days	57 days
Current ratio			
Current assets/Current liabilities	5.5	7.5	7.0
Acid test			
(Debtors + Bank)/Current liabilities	2.3	2.8	2.5

Interpretation

(a) *Profitability*

The profit increase from £11,000 to £17,000 represented an increase of more than 50% from a sales volume increase of only 10%. The ROCE improved whilst sales as a percentage of capital employed declined, indicating increased efficiency but lower utilisation. This has been recognised in the higher sales to capital employed set for the next budget. Although budgeted sales are much higher for 19X7/8 the target profit to sales figures is reduced suggesting effort to increase volume at the expense of price.

(b) *Production*

Material content as a proportion of total cost remains constant whilst direct labour is declining. Other costs have shown an increase in proportion suggesting a change in production methods. This is supported by the increased ratio and cost of indirect compared with direct employees. Profit per worker of both categories has risen whilst earnings have remained constant suggesting improved productivity as a result of plant and methods rather than labour. Selling costs to sales did not change significantly the addition to staff being represented by higher volume of turnover. Since no increase is planned in staff numbers to achieve the substantially higher sales budgeted for 20X7/8 there is still some capacity available in the existing sales force.

(c) *Balance sheet*

Plant has increased this year and a further increase is planned for the coming year. The higher stock relates to the increased turnover budgeted but maintenance of the debtors figure suggests a quicker turnover confirmed by the debtors turnover rate. All working capital ratios are better than standard supporting interpretation of effective financial control. The current year indicates investment in new equipment reflected in higher productivity from labour. The budget forecasts the intention to continue this trend through the next period.

7 EBITDA

EBITDA is a financial performance measure that has appeared relatively recently. It stands for 'earnings before interest, taxes, depreciation and amortisation' and is particularly popular with high tech start up businesses. However, a report from Moody's Investors Service in New York describes it as 'an accounting gimmick' used to make a company's financial picture look rosier than it really is and to deflect investor's attention away from bad news. It is spoken of as a substitute for cash flow, based on depreciation and amortisation being non-cash expenses, and used to support requests for additional debt funding. In reality, there are significant difficulties with this performance measure:

- It ignores changes in working capital and their impact on cash flow
- It fails to consider the amount of fixed asset replacement needed by their businesses
- It can easily be manipulated by aggressive accounting policies related to income recognition and capitalisation of expenses.

8 Business performance and share value

KEY POINT

The thrust of modern developments in business performance management was the development of metrics which related to shareholder value.

At the start of this chapter, it was stated that the thrust of modern developments in business performance management was the development of metrics which related to shareholder value. The idea is to identify those factors in a business which drive shareholder value and relate the measurement of performance to these.

The insensitive use of simple metrics such as RI and ROCE can induce dysfunctional behaviour. Managers are induced to do things in order to maximise short-term performance as measured by these metrics and these things are not always to the best long-term advantage of shareholders.

The modern move has been towards a more comprehensive approach to performance measurement linked to key value drivers (see the Balanced Scorecard, discussed later in this text). At the same time, management remuneration may be linked to share value through the use of share options. The stock market values shares taking into account what it considers to be important. Typically, the stock market takes into account long-term growth prospects and strategic issues. The market appreciates that a major new investment will not yield immediate financial returns. Managers will not therefore be dissuaded from undertaking a new investment by a short-term adverse impact on ROCE.

From time to time, certain sectors in the stock market experience spectacular bubbles. This happened in the 1980s with biotechnology and in the late 1990s with the Internet. When this happens, share prices in certain companies rise beyond what any common valuation model or performance metric would suggest they are worth.

Some observers then suggest that existing models and metrics are all obsolete and that some totally new philosophy is needed in order to appreciate and recognise the drivers of shareholder value. However bubbles always burst, sooner or later. The recent collapse in Internet company share prices is just the latest example of this phenomenon.

Conclusion

Business performance measures in the private sector may be used for a variety of purposes including decision-making, financial control and executive remuneration. All critical success factors should have a performance measure associated with them. Traditional performance measures relate to the generation of value to shareholders.

SELF-TEST QUESTIONS

Introduction

1 Identify at least five different areas of performance measures relevant to a business. (1)

Determining business objectives

2 What are critical success factors? (3.2)

Divisional assessment

3 What are the advantages of ROI as a means of divisional appraisal? (5.6)

4 How do you calculate residual income? (5.9)

5 What are the advantages of RI as means of divisional appraisal? (5.10)

EXAM-TYPE QUESTIONS

Question 1: Theta Ltd

Theta Ltd compares the performance of its subsidiaries by return on investment (ROI) using the following formula:

Profit: Depreciation is calculated on a straight-line basis.

Losses on sale of assets are charged against profit in the year of the sale.

Capital employed: Net current assets, at the average value throughout the year.

Fixed assets, at original cost less accumulated depreciation as at the end of the year.

Theta Ltd, whose cost of capital is 14% per annum, is considering acquiring Alpha Ltd whose performance has been calculated on a similar basis to that shown above except that fixed assets are valued at original cost.

During the past year, apart from normal trading, Alpha Ltd was involved in the following separate transactions:

(A) It bought equipment on 1 November 20X4 (the start of its financial year) at a cost of £120,000. Resulting savings were £35,000 for the year. These are expected to continue at that level throughout the six years' expected life of the asset after which it will have no scrap value.

(B) On 1 November 20X4 it sold a piece of equipment that had cost £200,000 when bought exactly three years earlier. The expected life was four years, with no scrap value. This equipment had been making a contribution to profit of £30,000 per annum before depreciation and realised £20,000 on sale.

(C) It negotiated a bank overdraft of £20,000 for the year to take advantage of quick payment discounts offered by creditors. This reduced costs by £4,000 per annum.

(D) To improve liquidity, it reduced stocks by an average of £25,000 throughout the year. This resulted in reduced sales with a reduction of £6,000 per annum contribution.

The financial position of Alpha Ltd for the year from 1 November 20X4 to 31 October 20X5, **excluding the outcomes of transactions (A) to (D) above**, was:

	£000
Profit for the year	225
Fixed assets:	
Original cost	1,000
Accumulated depreciation	475
Net current assets (average for the year)	250

Required:

(a) Calculate the ROI of Alpha Ltd using its present basis of calculation:

(i) if none of the transactions (A) to (D) had taken place;
(ii) if transaction (A) had taken place but not (B), (C) or (D)
(iii) if transaction (B) had taken place but not (A), (C) or (D)
(iv) if transaction (C) had taken place but not (A), (B) or (D)
(v) if transaction (D) had taken place but not (A), (B) or (C).

(b) Calculate the ROI as in (a)(i) to (a)(v) above using Theta Ltd's basis of calculation.

(c) Explain briefly whether there would have been any lack of goal congruence as between Theta Ltd and the management of Alpha Ltd (assuming that Alpha Ltd had been acquired by Theta Ltd on 1 November 20X4 and that Theta Ltd's basis of calculation was used) in respect of:

(i) transaction (A)
(ii) transaction (B).

Taxation is to be ignored. **(25 marks)**

Question 2: Hawlit Ltd

Hawlit Ltd, a transport company, is planning its future investment strategy. Hawlit's best projections of profit outcome are dependent upon the cost of diesel fuel.

	Annual net income at following costs per gallon:				
Annual investment level	£1.20	£1.25	£1.30	£1.40	£1.50
(£000)	(£000)	(£000)	(£000)	(£000)	(£000)
350	55	52	46	40	30
400	60	58	52	46	35
450	68	63	55	47	35
500	72	68	58	49	34
550	74	67	56	43	30
600	75	64	53	40	25
Estimated probability of outcome	0.1	0.1	0.4	0.3	0.1

The company's minimum required rate of return is 10% pa.

Required:

(a) Compute, for each level of investment, the return on investment (ROI) and the residual income. **(10 marks)**

(b) Calculate the optimal investment level, stating your reasons. **(3 marks)**

(c) Evaluate the merits of residual income and return on investment as measures of performance. **(12 marks)**

(Total: 25 marks)

For the answers to these questions, see the 'Answers' section at the end of the book.

FEEDBACK TO ACTIVITY **1**

Cost leaders will tend to focus on measuring their resource utilisation and controlling costs along the value chain.

FEEDBACK TO ACTIVITY **2**

Return on investment, ROI = $\frac{\text{Earnings}}{\text{Capital investment}} \times 100$

(a) Current position

ROI = $\frac{480}{2,400} \times 100$ = 20%

(b) Additional investments

A: ROI = $\frac{350}{1,400} \times 100$ = 25%

B: ROI = $\frac{200}{600} \times 100$ = $33^1/_3$%

C: ROI = $\frac{88}{400} \times 100$ = 22%

(c) Potential position

Arca + A: ROI = $\frac{830}{3,800} \times 100$ = 21.8%

Arca + B: ROI = $\frac{680}{3,000} \times 100$ = 22.7%

Arca + C: ROI = $\frac{568}{2,800} \times 100$ = 20.3%

Note that although all three projects have returns that are greater then the current 20%, once project B is accepted the ROI rises to 22.7% making C look less attractive. It would be worth Arca's while accepting projects A and B, if this were possible since this would raise its ROI to: 1,030 ÷ 4,400 = 23.4%.

FEEDBACK TO ACTIVITY **3**

$$\text{ROI} = \frac{\text{Earnings before interest and tax (but after depreciation)}}{\text{Capital employed (book value at start of year}} \times 100$$

Year	*Opening book value of assets* £000	*Annual depreciation* £000	*Closing book value of assets* £000	*Pre-dep'n profits* £000	*Post-dep'n profits* £000	*ROI* %
1	800	80	720	200	120	$\frac{120}{800}$ = 15%
2	720	80	640	200	120	$\frac{120}{720}$ = 17%
3	640	80	560	200	120	$\frac{120}{640}$ = 19%

Note that ROI increases, despite no increase in annual profits, merely as a result of the book value of assets falling. It might be more appropriate to use the average book value of assets (see discussion of ARR in Chapter 7), although the use of opening book values is common.

FEEDBACK TO ACTIVITY **4**

(a) Current ROI = $\frac{£40,000}{£150,000}$ = 26.7%

If the investment is accepted, revised ROI

= $\frac{£42,000}{£160,000}$ = *26.3%*

i.e. REJECT the project

(b) Current RI = £40,000 – (10% × £150,000) = £25,000

Revised RI = £42,000 – (10% × £160,000) = £26,000

i.e. ACCEPT the project

Note here is a classic example of ROI giving the wrong conclusion in that a project that was worthwhile as far as the company was concerned is rejected since it reduces the division's current ROI.

Chapter 11
NON-FINANCIAL PERFORMANCE MEASURES

CHAPTER CONTENTS

This chapter considers the full range of non-financial performance measures that might be used to develop a more complete impression of business performance.

Objectives

When you have studied this chapter you should be able to do the following.

- Discuss the interaction of NFPIs with financial performance indicators.
- Discuss the implications of the growing emphasis on NFPIs.
- Identify and comment on the significance of NFPIs in relation to employees, e.g. staff turnover, sickness rates.
- Identify and comment on the significance of NFPIs in relation to product/service quality e.g. customer satisfaction reports, repeat business ratings, customer loyalty, access and availability.
- Discuss the difficulties in interpreting data on qualitative issues.

1 Introduction

In the preceding chapter we explored the nature and use of business performance indicators. Most attention was given to the use of simple financial metrics such as ROCE and RI. It was seen that modern thinking on business performance is that these simple metrics provide only a very limited impression of performance. For one thing, they report only on what has happened over a short period in the immediate past and give very little indication on what might happen in the future. For another thing, they are very subjective measures which are vulnerable to choice of accounting policies and position in the equipment replacement cycle.

So, a wide range of alternative performance measures have been developed.

2 The full range of performance measures

2.1 Classifications

There are a large number of business performance measures which may be used. These may be classified into various groups:

- **Quantitative and qualitative measures**

  Quantitative measures are those which may be expressed in numerical terms; examples include profit and market share.

  Qualitative measures are those which cannot be expressed in numerical terms, but which may be supported by numerical data. For example quality may be evidenced by the number of complaints.

- **Financial and non-financial measures**

  Another classification distinguishes between financial and non-financial performance measures. Financial performance measures include turnover, profit, and return on capital employed.

KEY POINT

There are a large number of business performance measures which may be used. These may be classified into various groups:

- **Quantitative and qualitative measures** Quantitative measures are those which may be expressed in numerical terms; examples include profit and market share.

Qualitative measures are those which cannot be expressed in numerical terms, but which may be supported by numerical data.

- **Financial and non-financial measures**

Financial performance measures include turnover, profit, and return on capital employed.

Non-monetary performance measures include market share, capacity utilisation, labour turnover etc.

KEY POINT

Tom Peters has argued that 'what gets measured gets done'.

Non-monetary performance measures include market share, capacity utilisation, labour turnover etc.

Performance measures may be expressed either in absolute terms or relative to other measures. Index numbers may also be used to show trends over a period of time.

The areas of performance criteria, as we have already discussed, will vary. Some of the criteria, and the control and measurement used, are as follows:

Financial performance	• cost • profitability • liquidity • budget variance analysis • capital structure • market ratios • level of bad debts • return on capital employed
Competitiveness	• sales growth by product or service • measures of customer base • relative market share and position
Activity	• sales units • labour/machine hours • number of passengers carried • number of material requisitions serviced • number of accounts reconciled Whichever measurement is used it may be compared against a pre-set target.
Productivity	• efficiency measurements of resources planned against consumed • measurements of resources available against those used • productivity measurements such as production per person or per hour or per shift
Quality of service	• quality measures in every unit • evaluate suppliers on the basis of quality • number of customer complaints received • number of new accounts lost or gained • rejections as a percentage of production or sales
Customer satisfaction	• speed of response to customer needs • informal listening by calling a certain number of customers each week • number of customer visits to the factory or workplace • number of factory and non-factory manager visits to customers
Quality of working life	• days absence • labour turnover • overtime • measures of job satisfaction
Innovation	• proportion of new products and services to old ones • new product or service sales levels

The well known management writer Tom Peters has argued that 'what gets measured gets done'. If something cannot be measured it cannot be improved. However, there are criteria which are more difficult to measure and control such as responsiveness, quality, flexibility, efficiency and effectiveness.

The critical thing being that if performance is measured only on the basis of a narrow range of simple metrics then the behaviour of the business may be distorted in order to improve the performance as measured by those metrics – but at the expense of the long-term prospects of the business as a whole.

Various aspects of non-financial performance measurement are now considered.

2.2 Responsiveness

KEY POINT

The World Class Manufacturing concept underscores the importance of measuring responsiveness to customer requirements, in terms of lead time.

The World Class Manufacturing concept underscores the importance of measuring responsiveness to customer requirements, in terms of lead time. It has been claimed that 'the number of believers in zero lead time as a primary target is still small but growing fast'. Many companies are coming to the conclusion that reducing lead time is a simple, powerful measurement of how well they are doing. Lead time is a sure and truthful measure, because a plant can only reduce it by addressing the problems that cause delays. If these problems are solved the lead times drop. They include:

- order entry delays and errors
- wrong blueprints or specifications
- long setup times and large lots
- high defect counts
- machines that break down
- operators who are not well trained
- supervisors who do not co-ordinate schedules
- suppliers that are not dependable
- long waits for inspectors or repair people
- long transport distances
- multiple handling steps
- stock record inaccuracies.

2.3 Quality

Quality is difficult to measure and control. In most companies, poor quality cost includes such items as manufacturing (or any other function's) rework, warranty costs, cost of repair or return of goods from suppliers and inspection costs. In service industries the quality of service is measured by customers' letters of complaint. This is not a very good measurement as it only measures those customers prepared to write and many customers either remain silent or take their custom elsewhere.

The traditional view of quality costs may be illustrated by the following diagram:

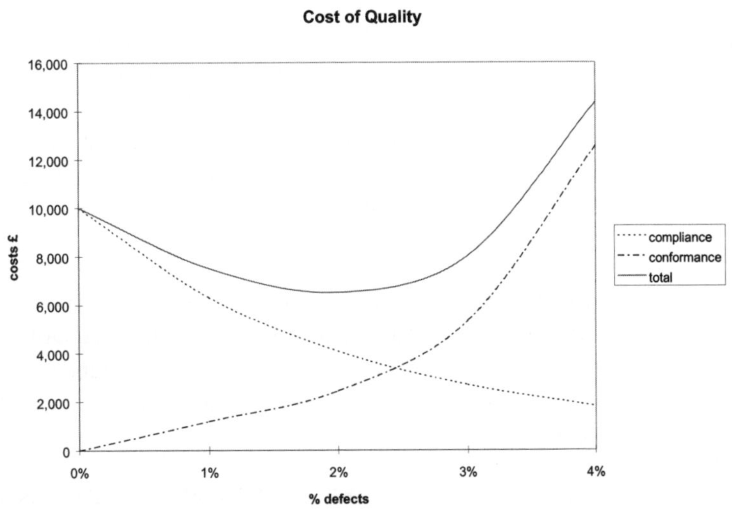

In order to achieve 0% defects, compliance costs (testing and inspection) costs must be high but these can be reduced as higher levels of defects are accepted. At 0% defects, conformance costs (rejections, reworking and replacement) are nil but these rise as higher levels of defects are accepted. In theory, there is an optimum level of acceptable defects – which in this case is at 2%. This occurs at the point where total quality costs (compliance and conformance) are minimised.

The immediate costs of poor quality are dispersed through the costing system of the whole operation and their total may not be apparent. Furthermore, the long-term implications of poor quality in terms of customer response are not immediately quantifiable. The role of quality in the modern business environment was discussed in Chapters 4 and 5 in regard to the Total Quality movement.

KEY POINT

The proponents of Total Quality tend to reject the traditional concept of an acceptable level of defects.

The proponents of Total Quality tend to reject the traditional concept of an acceptable level of defects. At a recent management seminar, the writer of this text was told that in a Total Quality environment there are few compliance costs as such since quality is rooted in the whole culture of the operation. Hence the acceptable level of defects is 0%.

One modern innovation is the Cost of Quality Report. This seeks to identify all the costs associated with maintaining quality and the costs of failing to maintain quality. These costs can be matched against targets to provide a performance measure. Measures taken to maintain quality may extend to locating technical specialists at the factory site of suppliers.

Regular surveys of customer appreciation can be used to measure the less quantifiable aspects of quality performance.

Rewards based on quality are a good measurement of success as everyone becomes involved in the measurement and control process. 'Empowerment' is a central element in the TQ movement. One of IBM's cable suppliers paid a premium for 0.0 to 0.2 percent defects; for a 0.21 to 0.3 percent defect level they knocked $2 off the price of a cable; for 0.31 percent and over, there was a $4 reduction. With the system in place, a defect rate that had averaged 0.11 percent for years rapidly dropped to 0.04 in 60 days – and stayed there.

2.4 Flexibility

KEY POINT

Flexibility concerns the organisation's ability to react quickly to changing customer demands and the external environment.

Flexibility concerns the organisation's ability to react quickly to changing customer demands and the external environment. Robert Reich, in his book *The Next American Frontier*, argues that rapid changes in the technology of products and production necessitate the development of 'flexible production systems' to sustain competitive advantage. Global market segmentation, better informed consumers, increasingly complex products and the rapid change in tastes and fashions mean that speed and flexibility of response are essential organisational characteristics. As international competition increases and companies are having to respond more quickly to market demands, they are seeking to increase their ability to re-deploy employees between different tasks (functional flexibility), to increase and decrease the number of their employees to match peaks and troughs of work (numerical flexibility), and to have the freedom to pay rates which reflect market conditions and not be constrained by pay differentials (financial flexibility).

It is commonly found that customers do not judge potential suppliers only on the basis of unit prices. They are also concerned with a range of factors linked to flexibility. A supplier who responds quickly to customer demands in terms of delivery times, product design and technical assistance will always be preferred to one who does not respond quickly.

It may be argued that 'world class manufacturing' status is not achieved merely by purchasing the latest equipment, and that the roles and skills of operators in equipment set up, maintenance and quality control, need to be re-combined. Companies want employees who are able to change jobs and develop skills as the products and production process develop. They want them to be able to deal with manufacturing problems on their own initiative, without management intervention and effectively operate expensive equipment and identify and fix expected faults.

The long-term competitiveness of a business therefore depends on its flexibility, and that flexibility has been both internal and external dimensions. It relates both to the manner in which the business conducts its internal affairs and the manner in which it relates to customers.

Some ways of measuring and controlling flexibility as a criteria can include measuring:

- product/service introduction time
- product/service mix flexibility
- internal set up times – the time taken to switch production from one product to another
- delivery response time – the time taken to meet customer delivery requests.

Flexibility in a service industry such as a travel agency could include measures of the average time taken for one assistant to respond to a customer's service request. If a customer enters a travel agent with a request to buy a ticket to fly from London to Helsinki then the customer will rate the service highly if:

- The assistant is able to advise on flight availability and fares on the required dates using information concerning all airlines
- The assistant is able to make a seat booking on the spot
- The assistant is able to provide a range of ancillary services such as insurance, car hire, currency, hotel bookings and local train times.

These are the elements of a flexible response. The customer enters the shop and is provided with a service package tailored to his/her precise needs and with immediate delivery. Clearly these elements are only amenable to non-financial performance indicators.

KEY POINT

The factors that contribute to achieving a flexible response include systems and personnel.

The factors that contribute to achieving a flexible response include systems and personnel. Obviously, the use of appropriate network systems and electronic communication facilities are needed. However, the human element is also important. A knowledgeable and well motivated member of staff is needed to make the system work. Thus, if a customer walks into the shop with his request for a flight to Helsinki and is greeted with a response along the lines of "it is only Jenny who deals with these things and she will be out at lunch for the next two hours" then the customer will probably go elsewhere.

The writer of this text once booked a flight to Helsinki and asked the travel agent about whether the flight would arrive in time to allow onward rail travel to a provincial town in Finland on the same day. The agent had no idea how to answer this question and directed the writer to Railtrack. In fact, train times are given on the English language website of Finnish Railways – which a good travel agent should be able to access instantly.

The sort of performance indicators that might be useful to the travel agency in monitoring the flexibility of its operation might include:

- Staff turnover rates
- Staff sickness rates
- Proportion of staff trained in all booking systems.

If staff turnover or sickness rates starts to rise, or staff training levels and morale start to fall – then this is an indication of potential poor performance. Temporary or new staff are unlikely to be as able as experienced and long-serving staff. The poor performance so identified may not have an immediate financial result (e.g. a decline in the ROCE of the operation over the past three months) but will have a long-term strategic consequence.

Flexibility means ensuring that every option is covered and it must be accepted that this has an immediate cost.

2.5 Efficiency and effectiveness

The essential principles of the classical management theory concerned the issue of how to allocate tasks, control the work being done and motivate and reward those doing it. The essence of the theory is the 'logic of efficiency', which stressed:

- bureaucratic forms of control
- narrow supervisory span
- closely prescribed roles
- clear and formal definition of procedures, areas of specialisation and hierarchical relationships.

The management activities which are carried out in order to achieve this efficiency have generally been grouped in terms of planning, organising, motivating and controlling. However, this approach focuses on the **actions** (inputs) of managers rather than on **results** (outputs). One particularly influential writer on the subject of management effectiveness, Professor Bill Reddin, considers it essential for management to be judged on output, rather than input, and by achievements rather than by activities. In his book, he writes that there is a tendency to confuse efficiency with effectiveness.

DEFINITION

Efficiency is the ratio of output to input.

However, this ratio allows for 100% efficiency to be achieved by high output in relation to high input but the same result can be obtained where both input and output are low.

DEFINITION

Effectiveness according to Reddin, is:

'the extent to which a manager achieves the output requirements of his or her position'.

This assumes that the outputs have been identified and made measurable.

Examples of differences between 'effective' managers and 'efficient' managers, are that efficient managers seek to solve problems and reduce costs, whereas effective managers seek to produce creative alternatives and increase profits. On this basis, the management activities of planning, organising, motivating and controlling are more concerned with efficiency rather than effectiveness.

Because organisations are social arrangements in which people strive to achieve control over the use of resources to produce goods and services efficiently, some individuals (managers) hold positions from which they control and co-ordinate the activities of others. Members who have little or no influence must comply or leave. The concern with performance leads to work that is simple and monotonous and to strict rules and procedures which employees are expected to follow. These features may contribute to the efficiency with which collective activity can be carried out because they simplify the tasks of planning, organising, co-ordinating and controlling the efforts of large numbers of people. The need for efficiency, however, conflicts with human values such as individual freedom, creativity and development. It is difficult to design organisations that are efficient both in using resources and in developing human potential.

In terms of measuring performance one therefore has to consider both inputs and outputs. This is particularly difficult when one is dealing with a sector in a business which is not normally a profit centre (e.g. a maintenance department) or a non-profit making organisation. We will return to this topic in Chapter 12.

3 Measures of quality of service in service industries

3.1 BAA plc

BAA (the former state owned British Airports Authority) uses regular customer surveys for measuring customer perceptions of a wide variety of service quality attributes, including, for example, the cleanliness of its facilities, the helpfulness of its staff and the ease of finding one's way around the airport. Public correspondence is also analysed in detail, and comment cards are available in the terminals so that passengers can comment voluntarily on service levels received. Duty terminal managers also sample the services and goods offered by outlets in the terminals, assessing them from a customer perspective.

They check the cleanliness and condition of service facilities and complete detailed checklists which are submitted daily to senior terminal managers. The company has also a wealth of internal monitoring systems that record equipment faults and failures, and report equipment and staff availability. These systems are supported by the terminal managers who circulate the terminals on a full-time basis, helping customers as necessary, reporting any equipment faults observed and making routine assessments of the level of service provided by BAA and its concessionaires.

Examples of service quality measures and mechanisms at BAA plc are shown below:

Quality	Measures	Mechanisms
Access	Walking distance/ease of finding way around	surveys/operational data
Aesthetics	Staff appearance/airport appearance/quality of catering	surveys/inspection
Availability	equipment availability	internal fault monitors
Cleanliness	environment and equipment	surveys/inspection
Comfort	Crowdedness	surveys/inspection
Communication	information clarity/clarity of labelling and pricing	surveys/inspection
Competence	staff efficiency	management inspection
Courtesy	courtesy of staff	surveys/inspection
Friendliness	staff attitude	surveys/inspection
Reliability	equipment faults	surveys/inspection
Responsiveness	staff responsiveness	surveys/inspection
Security	efficiency of security checks/ number of urgent safety reports	surveys/internal data

It is factors of this kind which contribute to favourable brand awareness and positive company profile. The Virgin group has been active in many sectors ranging from condoms to air travel. Its company profile is high and it is critical that brand awareness is entirely positive. Measures of the kind listed above therefore report on issues that contribute to the long-term strategic development of the Virgin group.

3.2 Internal quality measurement in service industries

Inspection and monitoring of the inputs to the service process is important for all organisations. The quality of the solicitors in a practice or the number and grades of staff available in a consultancy organisation are crucial to the provision of service quality. Multibroadcast (a retailer) measure the number of shop refits per month and BAA monitor the availability and condition of equipment and facilities.

KEY POINT

Many service companies use internal mechanisms to measure service quality during the process of service delivery.

Many service companies use internal mechanisms to measure service quality during the process of service delivery. Multibroadcast uses managers to formally inspect the premises, goods and service provided by the staff using detailed checklists covering, for example, the correct pricing of items, correct layout of displays and attitude of staff to the customers. BAA have advanced systems to monitor equipment faults and the terminal managers are expected to report any problems they see.

The quality of the service may be measured after the event, that is by measuring the results by outputs of the service. For example, Multibroadcast measure the number of service calls they have to make for each of their products, in order to assess product reliability.

3.3 Service quality measures – key points

KEY POINT

There are twelve factors of service quality: reliability, responsiveness, aesthetics/ appearance, cleanliness/ tidiness, comfort, friendliness, communication, courtesy, competence, access, availability and security.

- Providing high level of service quality may be a source of competitive advantage.
- Achieving high service quality means ensuring all the factors of the service package meet customer requirements.
- There are twelve factors of service quality: reliability, responsiveness, aesthetics/appearance, cleanliness/tidiness, comfort, friendliness, communication, courtesy, competence, access, availability and security.
- The relative importance of the factors will vary from company to company and between customers.
- Service quality can be measured using external customer satisfaction measures and internal organisational quality systems at different stages of the service process.
- Both internal and external measures of the service quality factors are required to facilitate target setting, the tracking of the costs of changing quality targets and the linking of pay to quality performance.
- Quality control systems vary between professional, service shop and mass service organisations.

KEY POINT

Modern thinking indicates that a whole range of performance indicators is needed (financial and non-financial, qualitative and quantitative) to provide a full impression of how well or badly a business is doing.

3.4 The balanced scorecard

This topic will be explored in depth in Chapter 13. At this stage it is only important to be aware that modern thinking indicates that a whole range of performance indicators is needed (financial and non-financial, qualitative and quantitative) to provide a full impression of how well or badly a business is doing.

Conclusion

Business performance can be evaluated using both quantitative and qualitative, financial and non-financial measures. Quality and flexibility are important areas for performance measurement.

SELF-TEST QUESTIONS

The full range of performance measures

1 Distinguish between financial and non-financial performance indicators. (2.1)

2 Distinguish between qualitative and quantitative performance indicators. (2.1)

3 State performance indicators that might be used to measure responsiveness. (2.2)

4 State performance indicators that might be used to measure flexibility. (2.4)

6 Explain the difference between efficiency and effectiveness in management. (2.5)

Measures of quality of service in service industries

7 State performance indicators that might be used to measure quality in a service operation. (3)

EXAM-TYPE QUESTION

New manufacturing environment

The new manufacturing environment is characterised by more flexibility, a readiness to meet customers' requirements, smaller batches, continuous improvements and an emphasis on quality. In such circumstances, traditional management accounting performance measures are, at best, irrelevant and, at worst, misleading.

Required:

(a) Discuss the above statement, citing specific examples to support or refute the views expressed. **(10 marks)**

(b) Explain in what ways management accountants can adapt the services they provide to the new environment. **(10 marks)**

(Total: 20 marks)

For the answer to this question, see the 'Answers' section at the end of the book.

Chapter 12
PERFORMANCE IN THE NOT-FOR-PROFIT SECTOR

CHAPTER CONTENTS

This chapter explores performance measurement within the context of public, charitable and voluntary sector organisations.

Objectives

When you have studied this chapter you should be able to do the following.

- Discuss the potential for diversity in objectives depending on organisation type.
- Comment on the need to achieve objectives with limited funds that may not be controllable.
- Identify and explain ways in which performance may be judged in non-profit seeking organisations.
- Comment on the difficulty in measuring outputs when performance is not judged in terms of money or an easily quantifiable objective.
- Explain how the combination of politics and the desire to measure public sector performance may result in undesirable service outcomes.
- Comment on 'value for money' service as a not-for-profit sector goal.

1 Introduction

The not-for-profit sector incorporates a diverse range of operations including national government, local government, charities, executive agencies, trusts and so on. The critical thing about such operations is that they are not motivated by a desire to maximise profit.

KEY POINT

The prime objective of commercial businesses is to maximise profit.

The prime objective of commercial businesses is to maximise profit. Such a businesses may take a short or long-term view of the manner in which they wish to do this. There are often different routes available which are capable of achieving this objective and management has to choose between them. However, there is a clear and identifiable objective.

In a manufacturing operation, the means of achieving that objective may also be clear and well defined. If one is in the business of manufacturing widgets then one can only do this using the current technology and available production methods. However, as has been seen in earlier Chapters, the position becomes a little more complicated in the modern era of flexible manufacturing.

2 Management in the not-for-profit sector

2.1 Objectives

KEY POINT

Not-for-profit organisations have a variety of different objectives. Those objectives may be partly legislated for, partly constitutional and partly political.

Not-for-profit organisations have a variety of different objectives. Those objectives may be partly legislated for, partly constitutional and partly political.

For example, the Driver and Vehicle Licensing Agency (based at Swansea, UK) is charged with keeping records of vehicle registration and issuing driving licenses and road tax disks to motorists. This is a legal obligation. Oxfam (a British Charity) has an obligation to act in order to prevent and relieve famine written into its constitution.

Newcastle City Council has an obligation to run local schools – but has a wide measure of discretion over how it does this. It can organise the schools along selective or comprehensive lines. It can spend money on salaries for teachers or it can switch some of that money into acquiring IT systems and making greater use of Computer Assisted Learning. The various choices the Council makes are determined by a political process. Parties contesting local elections will indicate their spending proposals in party manifestos and the public will choose between them.

One assumes that the party offering the most popular public spending plan will be elected to office – and, in this way, 'the will of the people' emerges.

However, the general problem of management in the not-for-profit sector is that:

- objectives may be diverse and ill-defined
- objectives may change regularly through the political process
- there are often different means of achieving given objectives.

A further consideration is that the distinction between 'objectives' and 'means' is often misunderstood. For example one public objective is 'to contain crime within reasonable limits'. One means of achieving that objective is to have police officers patrolling the streets on foot. In fact, police foot patrols are a very inefficient method of containing crime. The use of video surveillance cameras and police response units using fast cars is much more cost effective.

However many political parties will advocate the need to 'have more bobbies on the beat'. They like the means – and they seem to lose sight of the objective.

2.2 Efficiency and effectiveness in the not-for-profit sector

KEY POINT

Much of the debate over performance management in the NFP sector has turned around how to achieve efficiency and effectiveness in the public sector.

Much of the debate over performance management in the NFP sector has turned around how to achieve efficiency and effectiveness in the public sector. We encountered these concepts in Chapter 11 while considering NFPIs. It is useful to consider aspects of them at this point.

2.3 Efficiency

KEY POINT

Efficiency turns around making the maximum possible use of a given set of resources.

Efficiency turns around making the maximum possible use of a given set of resources. That is, it involves a straight comparison of output and input.

Many UK local authorities in the 1970s were judged to be making an inefficient use of the resources available to them. They undertook most of their activities (e.g. council house maintenance, road repairs, maintenance of parks and gardens etc) using large numbers of direct council employees. It was often found that the use of obsolete equipment and inefficient working practices (strict job demarcation was widespread) resulted in the operation involving excessive costs.

Financial management initiatives in the 1980s required local authorities to put much of their activities 'out to tender'. Private contractors may submit bids in order to undertake programmes of work for the local authorities. If the councils retain a direct works department, then that department has to bid in competition with private contractors for most available work.

The advent of Executive Agencies in national government is another example of this approach. Government has devolved some of its functions to agencies (e.g. the DVLC at Swansea) which are run on semi-commercial lines. The performance of these agencies is monitored using target performance indicators (e.g. the average time it takes to issue a new driving licence or the average time it takes to respond to a police enquiry concerning a vehicle).

Experience over the last twenty years suggests that this process has considerably improved efficiency in local authorities. This means that the public obtain greater 'value for money '.

As will be seen below, a variety of performance indicators can be used to monitor efficiency in local authorities and similar public sector bodies.

2.4 Effectiveness

KEY POINT

Effectiveness turns around finding the cheapest combination of means to achieve a given objective.

Effectiveness turns around finding the cheapest combination of means to achieve a given objective.

This concept is a little more difficult to handle than efficiency. An NFP organisation will normally have a number of stated objectives. For example, a local authority may have 'maintaining an acceptable quality of life for elderly residents' as one of its objectives. It has several means by which it may achieve this objective, including:

- providing 'meals on wheels' (Social Services Department)
- providing a mobile library (Libraries Department)
- maintaining access to and facilities in local parks (Parks Department)
- providing police support to the elderly at home (Police Department)
- providing nursing homes (Housing Department).

All of these departmental activities contribute to achievement of the objective. The problem is to find the optimum combination of spending for each of the Departments.

Many elderly people continue to live in their own homes, but are just on the threshold of requiring accommodation in a nursing home. One may find that a small cut back in spending in one area (e.g. the withdrawal of a mobile library) may push a lot of elderly people over that threshold. There is then an enormous demand for extra spending by the Housing Department. Nursing home accommodation is an expensive last resort in caring for the elderly.

It works the other way. An occasional visit by a care worker or a police officer may enable many elderly people to stay in their own homes for much longer than would otherwise be the case. The key to effectiveness is in finding an optimum pattern of spending to achieve a given objective. We will return to this topic when we consider zero based budgeting in Chapter 14.

In the 1980s, a city on the North East coast of England developed a considerable problem with car thefts. It became known as 'the car crime capital of the North'. There was considerable public pressure to spend more money on policing in order to deter or arrest the car thieves.

Investigation showed that much of the problem was caused by youths leaving pubs and clubs in the early hours of the morning. They were often in a rather excited state and had to travel several miles to their homes in the estates and villages around the city. The city council would not support bus services after 11pm on the grounds that everyone should be in bed after that time – so what were the youths to do? Not surprisingly, stealing a car was the common response.

KEY POINT

Effectiveness is, by its very nature, rather more difficult to measure than efficiency. Performance in an NFP organisation is a function of both efficiency and effectiveness.

The introduction of a few late night bus services was a low cost action which did much to relieve the problem. This was an action in promoting effectiveness.

Effectiveness is, by its very nature, rather more difficult to measure than efficiency. However it should be appreciated that performance in an NFP organisation is a function of both efficiency and effectiveness. Performance measurement has to take account of this.

3 Performance measures in non-profit making organisations

Let us take an example.

3.1 Performance measures in education

Education is an example of a non-profit making organisation whose objectives include the provision of a value for money service.

The costs of the service must be compared against budgets but other performance indicators may be used in total for the establishment and within each faculty/department. These measures include:

Overall:

- Numbers of students
- Amount of research funding received
- Proportion of successful students (by grade)
- Quality of teaching – as measured by student and inspector assessments
- Number of publications by staff.

Faculty:

- Cost per student
- Cost per examination pass
- Staff / Student ratios
- Students per class
- Number of teaching hours per member of staff
- Availability of learning resources e.g. number of PCs per student
- Number of library books per student
- Average age of library books.

It requires only a little imagination to develop a similar range of performance indicators for other NFP operations.

3.2 Behavioural implications of performance measures

Both profit making and non-profit making organisations now use measures to evaluate performance. There are consequences of this which are outlined below.

3.3 Measuring staff performance

The purpose of providing targets and measuring performance is often intended to motivate staff to achieve those targets, but this will only be achieved through involvement and the development of goal congruence. Staff may well see the measurement of performance as a policing device particularly if it is used to assess their personal performance rather than that of the unit they manage.

It must be remembered that managerial performance depends on a number of factors. Sometimes good results will occur despite poor management whereas in other areas average results will only occur due to very good management.

4 One approach – benchmarking in the public sector

4.1 The concept

Probably the most important recent development in measuring performance in NFPs has been in the area of benchmarking.

A great deal of attention has been devoted in recent years to the concept of managing for results in the public sector and to finding appropriate means by which performance can be measured. Performance measurement and related management initiatives in the UK have been encouraged for many years. The Financial Management Initiatives of the early 1980s were merely an early stage in this development.

In the 1970s and early 1980s, it was difficult to generate much interest in performance comparison of two or more local government units, although it was widely accepted that many public sector operations made an inefficient use of resources at their disposal. Typically, many public sector managers claimed that the units they were responsible for were unique in some way and that performance could not be measured by comparison with other units.

KEY POINT

Local authorities themselves are more receptive to performance comparisons, if they are done properly.

However local authorities themselves are more receptive to performance comparisons, if they are done properly. Reasons for this new found acceptance of performance measurement are not sure, but various explanations are plausible. One possible explanation lies in the institutional theory explored in Chapter 4. The widespread adoption of benchmarking and associated concepts of value for money have gradually permeated many areas of economic activity through a 'mimetic' process. Public bodies have to accept a degree of measurement and inspection if they are to legitimise themselves.

Another explanation is that the increased adoption of 'contracting out' brought private and public sectors into a much closer degree of contact than was previously the case. Where private contractors are undertaking programmes of work for public bodies then means of performance management including performance measures and targets must be written into the relevant contracts. Once this approach is adopted for dealings with private contractors, it seems logical to extend it to areas where the public sector is still doing work on a direct basis.

Media pressure may also be relevant. Politicians and investigative journalists often highlight simple expenditure comparisons, witness the comparison of refuse disposal costs per head of population in the 1980s between socialist Lambeth and conservative Wandsworth (neighbouring London Boroughs). Such comparisons are crude and may be highly misleading – so many local authorities have sought to carry out performance measurement on a sophisticated and meaningful basis.

4.2 The practice

Local authorities are exchanging management lessons with the private sector and adapting systems and strategies from the private sector. In many cases, they are competing with the private sector for the privilege of producing public services.

The FMIs of the 1980s involved requiring local authorities to put programmes of public work out to tender . The PFIs (Private Finance Initiatives) of the 2000s involve capital projects being undertaken by the private sector with the use of relevant facilities (schools, leisure centres etc) being leased on to the public sector.

There is therefore a considerable degree of competition between public sector managers and the private sector. In the case of contracted out programmes of work, there have been many cases in the UK where a direct labour organisation has lost a programme to the private sector, learned lessons from this and then won the programme back again the next time tenders are invited. Recent history has shown that public sector operations can be surprisingly resilient when challenged.

However, there remain many areas of government where public sector operations are not directly challenged by the private sector. It is therefore necessary to develop meaningful performance measures for such areas and then tie such measures into the associated management systems. Managers should be required to achieve appropriate performance targets, however those targets are arrived at – with career advancement and remuneration depending on it. Where performance measures merely serve as attachments to the budget documents then they are not likely to be very effective.

4.3 Meaningful performance measures

An NFP organisation can measure performance on many aspects of its operation. For example:

- cost per km of road maintained
- cost per child in school
- cost per square metre of pavement swept
- cost per library book maintained
- cost per tonne of sewage disposed of.

KEY POINT

Almost every aspect of an NFP's operation can be measured

KEY POINT

Performance indicators have to reflect both quality and cost.

The list is limitless. Almost every aspect of an NFP's operation can be measured . One caveat is that information has to be gathered and maintained in a consistent manner. If two organisations classify costs differently then it may be difficult to compare ratios. Also, one has to consider qualitative differences.

Town A's cost of sewage disposed of may be £250 per tonne whereas that of town B might be £400. Are we to conclude that A is more efficient than B and B should try to learn from A? Maybe not. If A just pumps its sewage untreated into the sea whereas B adopts a more refined approach then we are not comparing likes. Performance indicators have to reflect both quality and cost.

Having taken the time and trouble to calculate such measures on a meaningful basis, the manager and/or public stakeholder now has to decide whether or not the relevant numbers indicate good, bad or indifferent performance.

"OK, I have done as you suggested," the manager reported. "Our result for this measure is 7.2 and our result for that measure is 84 percent. Are these results good?"

In the absence of some external reference point, that question could be very difficult to answer. The comparison of this year's result with results for earlier years might give some feel for what is happening. A steady increase in cost per tonne of sewage processed might indicate some decline in efficiency. But equally it might not – if the cost rise was caused by (a) a phased investment in new equipment, or (b) by a general increase across the market in resource costs.

4.4 The implementation of benchmarking

What is required is the systematic comparison of performance measures with meaningful internal or external reference points – that is benchmarking. The problem is to develop an appropriate framework for making benchmarking comparisons and then making use of the insights that those comparisons yields. Benchmarking in public sector and NFP organisations can be carried out in several ways. The simplest of these is using the standard approach associated with corporate benchmarking:

(a) Study processes in the organisation and decide what to benchmark

(b) Identify appropriate benchmark partners

(c) Analyse comparative figures and processes from benchmark partners

(d) Adopt and implement 'best practices'.

It is important to note that a benchmark partner need not necessarily be another local authority. For example, in Chapter 3 we encountered a UK government sponsored benchmarking scheme seeking to promote energy efficiency in commercial buildings. If the activity being benchmarked is office costs then an insurance company might provide an excellent benchmark partner for a local authority. However, this approach to benchmarking is more likely to contribute to efficiency than effectiveness because of its focus on individual processes and activities.

Other more profound approaches to benchmarking are possible. For example, we encountered the concept of effectiveness leading to 'value for money' earlier in this chapter. A variety of different public sector activities can contribute to the achievement of a given public objective. For example, youth crime can be contained by a combination of spending on police, education, social services and recreation. The issue is to find the optimum pattern of spending. A local authority may run an efficient police service, but if too little is being spent on education then this may be an ineffective means of containing youth crime. A small amount spent on running vocational courses at schools and deploying a schools attendance officer may avoid the need to spend very large sums on police services needed to deal with truants.

Different local authorities can compare their different spending strategies adopted to achieve the same public objectives – and best practice may be identified.

Various studies have been undertaken to determine the results achieved by benchmarking where it has been undertaken. A 1999 study reported in the journal of the ASPA (American Society of Public Administration) indicated significant benefits from a programme of benchmarking between local authorities in South Carolina.

Benchmarking is not so much a specific technique as a concept of intelligent management. The basic idea behind benchmarking – a constant quest for best practice – should just be common sense. But the complexity of a large organisation often makes the application of common sense difficult.

Conclusion

Not-for-profit organisations have a variety of objectives. Performance in this sector is a function of both efficiency and effectiveness. Organisations may use benchmarking with other similar organisations to evaluate performance.

SELF-TEST QUESTIONS

Management in the not-for-profit sector

1 Distinguish between objectives and means in an NFP operation. (2.1)

2 Explain efficiency in an NFP operation. (2.3)

3 Explain effectiveness in an NFP operation. (2.4)

Performance measures in non-profit making organisations

4 State the role of performance measures in an NFP operation. (3)

One approach – benchmarking in the public sector

5 Explain the role of benchmarking in a local authority. (4)

6 List some performance indicators that might be used for benchmarking by a local authority. (4.4)

EXAM-TYPE QUESTION

A college

A college offers a range of degree courses. The college organisation structure consists of three faculties each with a number of teaching departments. In addition, there is a polytechnic administrative/management function and a central services function.

The following cost information is available for the year ended 30 June 20X7:

(i) **Occupancy costs**

Total £1,500,000.

Such costs are apportioned on the basis of area used which is:

	Square feet
Faculties	7,500
Teaching departments	20,000
Administration/management	7,000
Central services	3,000

(ii) **Administration/management costs**

Direct costs: £1,775,000

Indirect costs: an apportionment of occupancy costs.

Direct and indirect costs are charged to degree courses on a percentage basis.

(iii) **Faculty costs**

Direct costs: £700,000.

Indirect costs: an apportionment of occupancy costs and central service costs.

Direct and indirect costs are charged to teaching departments.

(iv) **Teaching departments**

Direct costs: £5,525,000.

Indirect costs: an apportionment of occupancy costs and central service costs plus all faculty costs.

Direct and indirect costs are charged to degree courses on a percentage basis.

(v) **Central services**

Direct costs: £1,000,000.

Indirect costs: an apportionment of occupancy costs.

Direct and indirect costs of central services have in previous years been charged to users on a percentage basis. A study has now been completed which has estimated what user areas would have paid external suppliers for the same services on an individual basis. For the year ended 30 June 20X7, the apportionment of the central services cost is to be recalculated in a manner which recognises the cost savings achieved by using the central services facilities instead of using external service companies. This is to be done by apportioning the overall savings to user areas in proportion to their share of the estimated external costs.

The estimated external costs of service provision are as follows:

	£000
Faculties	240
Teaching departments	800
Degree courses:	
Business studies	32
Mechanical engineering	48
Catering studies	32
All other degrees	448
	1,600

(vi) Additional data relating to the degree courses is as follows:

	Degree course		
	Business Studies	*Mechanical Engineering*	*Catering Studies*
Number of graduates	80	50	120
Apportioned costs (as % of totals)			
Teaching departments	3%	2.5%	7%
Administration/management	2.5%	5%	4%

Central services are to be apportioned as detailed in (v) above.

The total number of graduates from the College in the year to 30 June 20X7 was 2,500.

Required:

(a) Prepare a flow diagram which shows the apportionment of costs to user areas. No values need be shown. **(3 marks)**

(b) Calculate the average cost per graduate, for the year ended 30 June 20X7, for the College and for each of the degrees in business studies, mechanical engineering and catering studies, showing all relevant cost analysis. **(14 marks)**

(c) Suggest reasons for any differences in the average cost per graduate from one degree to another, and discuss briefly the relevance of such information to the College management. **(5 marks)**

(Total: 22 marks)

For the answer to this question, see the 'Answers' section at the end of the book.

Chapter 13
ASPECTS OF PERFORMANCE MEASUREMENT

CHAPTER CONTENTS

This chapter considers various general aspects of performance evaluation and the manner in which the regulatory environment may influence reported performance in some sectors. In particular it considers performance evaluation in a service environment and behavioural issues in business performance measurement.

Objectives

When you have studied this chapter you should be able to do the following.

- Comment on the need to consider the environment in which an organisation is operating when assessing its performance e.g. What are the prevailing market conditions? Is funding relatively easy or difficult to secure? Does the strength of the national currency impact on the organisation's perfromance? Is the prevailing political climate particularly favourable or unfavourable towards the organisation currently? How have these issues changed over time?
- Consider the impact of governmental regulation on the performance measurement techniques used and the performance levels achieved (for example, in the case of utility services and former state monopolies).
- Discuss the 'balanced scorecard' as a way in which to improve the range and linkage of performance measures.
- Discuss the 'performance pyramid' as a way in which to link strategy and operations.
- Discuss the work of Fitzgerald and Moon that considers performance measurement in business services using building blocks for dimensions, standards and rewards.
- Explain the relationship between performance measurement systems and behaviour.
- Discuss how performance measurement systems can influence behaviour.
- Consider the accountability issues arising from performance measurement systems.
- Identify the ways in which performance measurement systems may send the 'wrong signals' and result in undesirable business consequences.
- Comment on the potential beneficial and adverse consequences of linking reward schemes to performance measurement.
- Explain how management style needs to be considered when designing an effective performance management system.

1 Introduction

In the previous three chapters we explored general aspects of business performance measurement and saw that performance might be measured under various headings including the following:

- financial performance
- competitiveness
- resource utilisation
- quality of service
- customer satisfaction
- innovation

- flexibility.

The types of measures that may be used under each of these headings were discussed in general terms. In this chapter we will consider performance measures within the context of specific sectors, different types of business and particular sets of circumstances.

- manufacturing (including specific order and process environments)
- service
- the statutory and regulatory situation.

2 Performance measures in manufacturing

KEY POINT

The performance measures used in manufacturing may be either qualitative or quantitative and will be different for various parts of the business, and for differing manufacturing environments.

The performance measures used in manufacturing may be either qualitative or quantitative and will be different for various parts of the business, and for differing manufacturing environments. Some specific measures for these areas are discussed in the following paragraphs.

2.1 Performance measures and sales

Sales may be measured in absolute terms and compared with targets, but other measures may also be used to identify the success of the selling activity.

These include:

- profitability by customer
- market share
- customer satisfaction
- orders as a percentage of quotations.

Each of these may be supported by numerical values which can be compared against targets and trends may be established from one period to another.

Each of these performance measures offers insights into some aspect of business performance. For example, it is often found that 80% of the profit earned by a business is generated from sales to 20% of its customers. Customer profitability analysis (CPA) often throws up some surprising results.

Cases have been reported where CPA exercises have shown that sales to 50% of the customers of a given business were actually loss-making. Of course, there are reasons why you might wish to continue unprofitable sales. Nevertheless, a finding of this kind should certainly prompt some thought.

2.2 Performance measures and materials

In respect of performance there are three aspects to materials:

- purchase
- storage
- usage.

Each of these aspects must be monitored.

Purchasing performance may be measured using price variances, especially if planning and operating causes are separated.

Storage performance may be measured by considering:

- average stock levels

- stock losses
- number of stockouts.

Usage of materials performance may be monitored using:

- usage variances, analysed into planning and operating causes
- wastage rates
- rejection rates.

2.3 Performance measures and labour

KEY POINT

Traditional variance analysis may be used to identify performance against a target in terms of rate and efficiency variances, especially if planning and operating causes are separated.

Traditional variance analysis may be used to identify performance against a target in terms of rate and efficiency variances, especially if planning and operating causes are separated.

In addition idle time and absenteeism should be measured. These may be indicators of employee morale which could also be measured qualitatively by management.

Labour turnover is another performance measure which should be used. Comparisons can be made on a trend basis. Where possible the reasons for leaving should be identified and analysed.

2.4 Performance measures and overhead

Many of the overhead costs incurred are fixed in nature, so the use of variances merely places an accounting value on the underlying cause.

KEY POINT

It is important to measure the utilisation of assets, relative to the available capacity and to identify the cause of any differences.

It is important to measure the utilisation of assets, relative to the available capacity and to identify the cause of any differences e.g. machine breakdown.

Performance measurement in specific order environments

Specific order environments include job, batch, and contract situations where items are made to specific customer requirements using common skills. However each item/job is different in its finished form because it is customer specific.

The measures used may vary slightly between job/batch/contract environments but the general principles are the same.

Costs will be compared with estimates and any significant differences investigated to identify their cause. Where common tasks can be identified they may be the subject of standard times and costs which will allow traditional variance analysis to be used.

Time taken may also be compared with estimates and for more complex work (e.g., contracts) the use of network analysis may be appropriate.

Suppliers' performances on delivery, quality of supply and price should also be monitored as failures by suppliers may be a cause of any differences in cost/time performance of the organisation.

3 Performance measures in process environments

KEY POINT

Process environments are those where homogeneous items are made and later sold from stock to customers who may not be identifiable at the time of production.

Process environments are those where homogeneous items are made and later sold from stock to customers who may not be identifiable at the time of production. Typically there are a limited number of items which are made, often from a continuous process.

It is easy in such environments to set targets against which actual performance can be measured because the output may be clearly defined.

Cost may be controlled against a standard using traditional variance analysis.

Activity and the quality of output may be measured using:

- output per input unit (yield)
- output per shift
- wastage per good output unit.

4 Service operations

4.1 Performance measures in service environments

KEY POINT

The four key differences between the products of service industries and those of manufacturing businesses are:

- Intangibility
- Heterogeneity
- Simultaneity of production and consumption
- Perishability.

Service environments exist to provide a service to a variety of customers. The four key differences between the products of service industries and those of manufacturing businesses are:

- **Intangibility** - the output being a performance rather than tangible goods
- **Heterogeneity** - the variability in standard of output performance due to the heavy reliance on human input and also the heterogeneity of customer requirements (e.g. the need for customised services and/or support)
- **Simultaneity of production and consumption** - precluding advance verification of specification or quality
- **Perishability** - the inability to carry stocks of the product to cover unexpectedly high demand

These differences pose problems in measuring and controlling performance. A matrix of performance measures used by the British Airports Authority was explored in Chapter 11 in the context of NFPIs. You may care to refer back to this now.

The following paragraphs describe measures that may be used in some examples of service business, each of which will suffer to varying extents from problems caused by the four characteristics summarised above.

A comprehensive example for a particular service business, based upon a past exam question, then follows.

4.2 Performance measures in professional services

Accountancy and law are two examples of professional services. Such services tend to be specific to a client's needs, though the service provided is based on common skills and knowledge.

Whilst perishability may not be quite so relevant to professional services (work loads are generally known reasonably well in advance and can be scheduled) the other three service characteristics will pose problems. The success of such a business can depend upon the performances of a few key personnel, the ultimate measurement of which will be customer satisfaction, which will directly impact upon financial performance. However, control systems should operate such that poor performance is identified prior to the point of losing important clients!

Performance may be measured in quantitative terms by considering chargeable time as a proportion of time available.

Qualitative measures centre around client satisfaction and the ability to adapt to clients' needs.

4.3 Performance measures in retail services

Retail services sell products to the general public. Their performance should therefore be measured in terms of profitability and customer satisfaction.

It is a business that could perhaps be said to be between manufacturing and pure service. It deals with tangible goods, the quality of which can be checked in advance and which can be stocked. However, the success of a retail business may also depend upon the service provided by the personnel involved (cashiers, shop assistants, store managers etc).

The balance of emphasis between goods and service related performance measures should be dictated by the relative importance placed upon these by the customer. For example, the quality of service provided by individual employees is unlikely to have the same impact on customer spending in large supermarkets as it would in the smaller, more personal shops.

Profitability can be measured in total, per product line, and per square metre of floor space. These may be compared with industry averages and as trends over time.

Customer satisfaction can be measured by monitoring the number of customer complaints and returns. Returns may be caused by poor stock control.

Stock control should be monitored by the rate of stock turnover, and the value and volume of stock losses. These losses should be analysed between perished and obsolete (out-of-date) stocks.

4.4 Performance measures in transport operations

Transport operations provide a service to convey goods or passengers from one place to another.

To some extent, the service output of a transport business is more easily standardised and tangibly measured than other service businesses. The objective is clear - to get the goods or passengers intact from A to B within a given time at minimum cost.

Cost measures will inevitably play a large part in the performance measure system, along with timing targets (particularly for public transport systems - the introduction of 'Passenger Charters' directly penalised operations that failed to meet specified timetable criteria).

The service provided by personnel will probably be more important to passenger transport services than those relating to goods, although the customers may, in fact, have less choice between suppliers and thus be less able to reflect their satisfaction or otherwise in financial performance.

Costs may be analysed into standing (fixed) costs and running (variable) costs and those may be compared with pre-set targets. Costs per unit may also be calculated and trends established over time.

Other measures which may be used include the frequency of late arrival and the extent of the lateness involved. These factors will impact on customer satisfaction.

At the time of writing issues such as number of crashes and passenger fatalities may also be considered important performance measures.

Example

FL Ltd provides training on financial subjects to staff of small and medium-sized businesses. Training is at one of two levels - for clerical staff, instructing them on how to use simple financial accounting computer packages, and for management, on management accounting and financial management issues.

Training consists of tutorial assistance, in the form of workshops or lectures, and the provision of related material - software, texts and printed notes.

Tuition days may be of standard format and content, or designed to meet the client's particular specifications. All courses are run on client premises and, in the case of clerical training courses, are limited to 8 participants per course.

FL Ltd has recently introduced a 'helpline' service, which allows course participants to phone in with any problems or queries arising after course attendance. This is offered free of charge.

FL Ltd employs administrative and management staff. Course lecturers are hired as required, although a small core of technical staff is employed on a part-time basis by FL Ltd to prepare customer specific course material and to man the helpline. Material for standard courses is bought in from a group company, who also print up the customer-specific course material.

Additional information for the year ended 31 March 20X6 is as follows:

(i) Clients are charged at £400 per half day for tuition time and course set-up time (customer specific courses). Course material is sold at standard cost (excluding set-up time) plus 120%.

(ii) Extracts from management accounts:

Summary profit and loss account for the year ended 31 March 20X6

	Budget		*Actual*	
	½ days	£'000	½ days	£'000
Income				
Fees				
– Clerical tuition	360	144	520	208
– Management tuition	250	100	180	72
– Course set-up	80	32	110	44
	690	276	810	324
Material		185		240
		461		564
Costs				
Lecturer hire		171		204
Technical staff salaries		30		39
Material		84		136
Other operating costs		38		45
		323		424
Net profit		138		140

	Budget	Actual
Financial ratios		
Net profit margin on sales	29.9%	24.8%
Net profit on capital employed	42.7%	39.8%
Operating statistics		
Technical staff: non-chargeable time		
– help-line (days)	25	37
– other (days)	10	6
Tuition time analysis		
– standard	80%	68%
– customer specific	20%	32%
Client complaints received(prev yr =10)		16
New course proposals		
– existing clients	6	5
– new clients	8	10
New courses undertaken		
– existing	3	2
– new clients	3	5

For each of the performance criteria measured below, comment on the performance of FL Ltd using the data given above to illustrate your answer:

- financial performance
- competitiveness
- quality of service
- flexibility
- resource utilisation
- innovation.

Outline solution

The following summarises the computations and comments that could be made under each heading:

Financial performance

- Fees 17.4% up on budgeted, material sales up 29.7%, costs up 31.3%, net profit up 1.4%
- No fee increases, thus increase in fees all due to increase in chargeable time
- Outside lecturer cost up 19.3% - investigate why rates are higher than budget (or perhaps not all time invoiced by lecturers has been re-charged to clients)

In-house technical time/cost analysis:

		% on budget
• chargeable time:	course set-up	+37.5
• non-chargeable:	help-line	+48
• other		–40
• total		+22.9
• overall time		+33
• cost		+30

The increase in set-up time ties in with the increased proportion of customer-specific tuition time.

Cost per day of technical staff appears to have fallen.

- Material costs are 61.9% higher than budgeted, against increased sales of 29.7% - the budgeted mark-out system is not being fully applied - check that stock is not being over-ordered and that clients are being re-charged properly
- Overall, financial performance up on budget in absolute terms, but down in relative terms (net profit ratios): costs have increased out of line with income

Competitiveness

- Usually measured in terms of market share or sales growth
- Limited information given here; sales up on budget - but need to look in terms of longer-term trend
- Success rate on proposals: budgeted to win 50% of new courses proposed for existing clients and 37.5% of those for new clients; actual success rates were 40% and 50%. In absolute terms, the number of new course proposals and wins were both down by 1

It would appear that FL are good at marketing to new clients, but not so good at expanding sales to existing clients. This may be tied in with quality.

Quality

- Lower than budgeted success rate in winning proposals for new business from existing clients may be indicative of a quality problem
- Help-line use was 48% higher than expected - this may tie into tuition quality, but will also be affected by standard of course participants, basis on which budget (for a new service) was prepared, problems with computers etc.
- Number of customer complaints up from 10 last year to 16 this

Flexibility

- Relates to ability to cope with changes in volume and content of service
- Actual tuition time was 700 half days compared to a budget of 610; the use of freelance lecturers assists cost-effective flexibility here, although this will to some extent depend upon the amount of notice they need
- The level of course proportions moved from a budgeted ratio of 360 clerical to 250 management tuition half days to one of 520 to 180. Again, access to a bank of lecturers with varying skills will help to respond to such demand changes
- The employment of some technical staff allows speedy response to additional demands for help and new course development, although the actual margin of "spare time" is now quite small and the trend in demands upon their time must be monitored to ensure sufficient room for flexibility in the future
- The mix of standard courses and customer-specific courses changed from a budgeted 80/20 ratio to an actual 68/32. This indicates the ability to be flexible in response to market demands - the design of the standard courses may be in the form of modules, that can be modified and combined to form the basis for customer-specific courses

Resource utilisation

- Use of freelance lecturers is an efficient use of resources, with 100% chargeable time
- There is a trade-off between resource utilisation, flexibility and innovation. Full resource utilisation restricts flexibility, and non-chargeable time invested in innovative schemes can impact on longer-term results

Innovation

- The introduction of the new help-line service must be assessed in terms of its impact on the previous five performance criteria, in both the long and short-term
- Currently it is not having an obvious direct impact on immediate financial performance, as its resource needs can be met from technical staff availability, although alternative uses of this time need to be identified and evaluated in comparison
- It is hoped that its longer term impact will be to increase the proportion of new proposals won, by increasing the competitiveness of the quality of the product offered and
- Use of technical staff time on this non-chargeable activity may limit the flexibility to respond to future new course development demand

Consideration should perhaps be given to limitation of the amount of help-line time available for each course.

4.5 Current thinking on performance in the service sector

A striking feature of the UK economy in recent years has been the growth in service industries in a highly competitive environment. Banks, airlines, transport companies, consultancy firms and service shops such as those that retail and/or rent consumer durables all function with an awareness of the need to demonstrate flexibility, competitive edge and quality. These are the critical success factors in the service sector. Two leading writers in this area are Fitzgerald and Moon.

The importance of the topic is recognised by a research report written by Fitzgerald, Silvestro et al. As a result the designers of information systems are investing considerable effort in setting up systems for performance measurement and evaluation. The measurement and appreciation of service businesses covers both financial and non-financial issues in seeking ways to inform management on how best to plan control and make decisions in order to achieve corporate goals.

Service industries are those included in Sections 6 to 9 of the Standard Industry Classification (SCI).

"In 1989 services accounted for 64 per cent of UK gross domestic product (CSO 89) and this proportion is growing. Since the mid-1970's services have grown at twice the rate of the rest of the UK economy, and this expansion has been mirrored elsewhere in the developed world. Some services such as tourism increasingly support the UK's declining visible balance of payments. In an interdependent economy the growth of the service sector underpins the health of the rest of the economy by providing a competent workforce to manufacturing industry and a demand for its products. 'It is an inescapable fact that services are a critical cost dimension to the nation's manufacturing competitiveness'." (Fitzgerald, Silvestro *et al.*)

4.6 Suggested approach to developing controls for service activities

(a) **Identify the key outputs required from the service**

- often stated verbally in terms of what the various users and other stakeholders require may be incorporated into a mission statement for the service

KEY POINT

Effective control follows the rationale of QA rather than QC by focusing on the inputs and processes as well as the eventual outputs.

(b) **Identify the key processes in providing the outputs**

Effective control follows the rationale of QA rather than QC by focusing on the inputs and processes as well as the eventual outputs.

This will be accomplished by:

- discussions with management and staff involved in providing the service
- observation and 'walk-through' of the process
- investigation into instances of service breakdown
- examination of background to decisions and structures of authorisation.

(c) **Identify the interfaces of the service provider**

These are the outside persons or other processes which the service provider relies on to do their work. This will include suppliers, customers and co-workers in other processes. The quality of this interface may have an impact on the service quality

For example

- how good is the relationship?
- how timely are the information exchanges?
- is the relationship managed and reviewed periodically?

(d) **Develop performance indicators for the key processes**

Fitzgerald et al. (CIMA 1991) identify six areas which are controlled by service industries

Financial performance

- cash flows
- profitability
- EPS and investor ratios

Competitiveness

- relative cost
- market share
- popularity in eyes of target customers

Resource utilisation

- ratio of outputs to inputs
- capacity utilisation

Quality of service

- reliability
- courtesy
- competence
- access
- availability

- friendliness
- comfort
- security
- aesthetics/appearance
- communication
- cleanliness
- responsiveness

Innovation

- proportion of old to new products
- time taken from conception to final production

Flexibility

- speed of changeover between products/services
- extent of multi-skilling in staff and machinery
- diversity in product range

(e) **Identify data sources for measures**

These will obviously vary enormously according to what is being measured. Many will not be readily quantifiable. The following may be useful to guide your thoughts:

Physical input/output

For example

- staff/customer ratios
- time to output measures
- space to staff/customer ratios
- chargeable time to slack time ratios

Attitudinal

e.g.

- customer satisfaction surveys
- client retention, repeat business and client turnover rates
- staff turnover and attitude measures
- peer group ratings
- expert ratings
- market standing ratings

Compliance

These measure whether the systems are being adhered to

For example

- achievement of key deadlines (delivery, keeping appointments, answering phones, processing orders)
- attendance on necessary training courses
- accuracy of documentation and fullness of its completion
- data security
- review of process of decision taking

Competence

For example

- quality and training of staff in key positions
- appropriateness of capital equipment and information available
- abilities of management in controlling the service

These are likely to lead to *subjective scoring* by the assessor

Comparators

Performance measures may be used:

- through time to look for improvement or deterioration (time-series)
- across firms or divisions to look for best practice and poor practice (cross-sectional)

Suitable comparators are important in both uses (e.g. benchmarking)

(f) **Develop reporting system**

This will depend on the management style and systems being used. A TQM approach would have different information requirements from a more management led one.

Issues will include:

- development of reporting media (electronic, paper-based, oral)
- instruction of end user in interpreting the data

(g) **Review effectiveness of the control system**

Initial control systems will have faults. Therefore

- pilot the system on a limited scale before a 'big bang' introduction
- record the improvements to KPIs through time
- review the adequacy of the system as the work of the firm changes

5 The statutory and regulatory environment

5.1 Influence on performance

KEY POINT

The performance of many business operations is influenced very strongly by statutory and regulatory environment.

The performance of many business operations is influenced very strongly by statutory and regulatory environment. There is nothing new about this although the privatisation of UK public utilities and the railway network has tended to raise the profile of the issue.

The capital engaged in some business operations is a direct function of relations with government. Let us consider an extreme example of this.

The UK Independent Television regional franchises were last 'auctioned' in the early 1990s. The system is that the Independent Televsion Authority (or ITA - a public body) owns the transmitter network but franchises the right to broadcast programmes (and advertising) from regional centres every 10 years. Organisations interested in obtaining a franchise were required to submit sealed bids prior to certain dates. Those bids stated (among other things) the amount that the applicant was prepared to pay for the franchise.

Some of the franchises were keenly contested – particularly some of the more attractive ones in London and the South East. Several well resourced consortia offered substantial nine figure sums for the London franchises.

One organisation, Central Television, was preparing a bid for the Birmingham franchise. Through discrete enquiries it found that no other bids were going to be made for the franchise. So, it submitted a bid for £2,000 – which the ITA had to accept. A rich franchise, worth millions, was thereby acquired without any significant capital outlay.

The performance of Central Television on the basis of ROCE would have been phenomenal – but this had nothing to do with commercial success or efficiency. It was just an accident of the way that the industry is regulated.

One can find many similar cases to this in the history of UK North Sea oil and gas exploration.

5.2 The public utilities

When the public utilities (water, gas and electricity) and the railways were privatised they remained subject to elaborate regulatory regimes. Train operating companies can be fined for poor performance (as measured by frequency of journey delays and cancellations) and water companies can be required to invest in new facilities in order to improve services. The performance of the operations involved is monitored and measured using various indicators. Some have been required to reduce prices charged to customers if the relevant industry regulator thought they were too high.

After the recent (September 2000) Hatfield rail crash, the Secretary of State for the Environment was effectively able to demand the resignation of Railtrack's Chief Executive and insist on an enormous nationwide programme of track refurbishment. In 2001, the Secretary of State appointed administrators to Railtrack and is in the process of returning Railtrack to a form of public ownership.

In the case of one utility (Yorkshire Water), the company running it decided that the nature of recent regulatory action to minimise leaks from pipes and to contain charges to customers was such that the business had no commercial basis. They attempted to transfer the business to a voluntary trust. The water industry regulator resisted this.

Many businesses that are not vulnerable to statutory regulation are nevertheless vulnerable to things which are normally considered to lie within the domain of government. For example, some business operations are sensitive to movements in currency exchange rates.

5.3 Exchange rates

During the late 1990s, the pound sterling floated freely against other major currency blocs. During this time the £ tended to weaken against the $US but strengthen against the €. It was claimed that these developments had a devastating impact on the performance of businesses in the manufacturing sector. It was claimed that many such businesses bought materials and components in $US and sold to customers in the € zone. Hence, profit margins were squeezed by rising costs and declining revenues.

Many sectors, including haulage and farming claim to have suffered in recent years because of the UK's greater involvement in the EU. Not all observers accept this argument. The business environment changes over time and people must adapt to change. Some people are unable or unwilling to adapt and they blame the problems they suffer as a result of this on Government policy.

6 The Balanced Scorecard

6.1 Background

The need to codify an approach to performance measurement leads to the development of 'The Balanced Scorecard'. The term was used by two academic accountants, Kaplan and Norton in a seminal 1992 article in the Harvard Business Review titled 'The Balanced Scorecard – Measures that Drive Performance'. This article has prompted a minor industry of academic writing and business consulting.

KEY POINT

At the core of the Balanced Scorecard is the idea that performance has to be measured from four different perspectives:

- How do customers view the business?
- What skills and processes must we excel at?
- How can we improve and increase value?
- How do shareholders view the business?

At the core of the Balanced Scorecard is the idea that performance has to be measured from four different perspectives:

- **A customer perspective.** How do customers view the business?
- **An internal perspective.** What skills and processes must we excel at?
- **A learning and growth perspective.** How can we improve and increase value?
- **A financial perspective.** How do shareholders view the business?

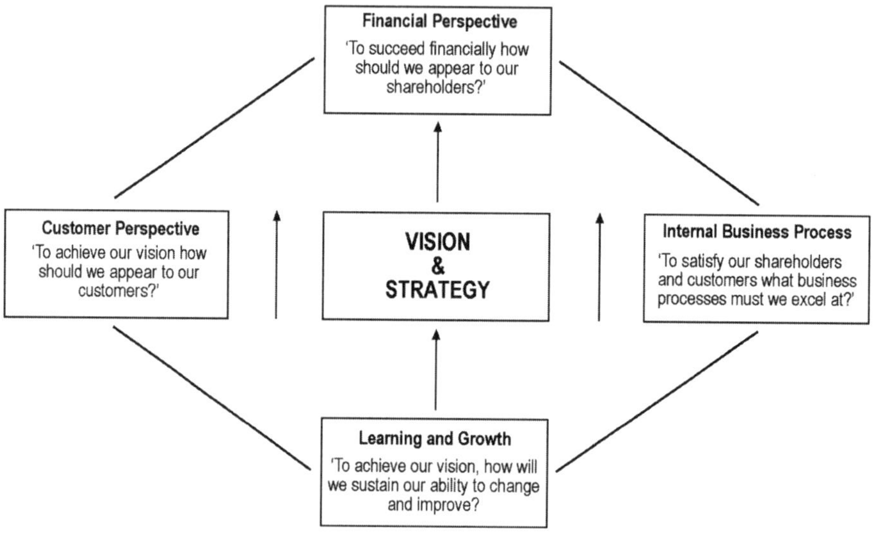

The idea is that the business develops a comprehensive framework for translating a company's strategic objectives (emerging from answers to the four questions asked above) into a coherent set of goals and performance measures. The goals and measures should be clear and limited in number.

Each organisation will have different strategic objectives and hence each will require a customised Scorecard. In their 1992 article, Kaplan and Norton consider the case of Electronic Circuits Inc ('ECI'). The balanced scorecard they create for ECI may be summarised as follows:

Customer perspective

Goals	*Measures*
new products	percentage of sales from new products
responsive service	percentage on-time delivery (as defined by customer)
preferred supplier	customer ranking
partnership ventures	number of cooperative operations

Internal perspective

Goals	*Measures*
manufacturing excellence	production cycle time, unit cost
design productivity	engineering and material efficiency
new product development	introduction times, actual v plan

Learning and growth perspective

Goals	*Measures*
time to market	introduction times, actual v competition
product focus	% of products giving 80% of sales
manufacturing learning	process time to maturity
technology leadership	time to develop next generation products

Financial perspective

Goals	*Measures*
survival	cash flow
success	quarterly sales growth and operating income
prosperity	increase in market share and ROE

The critical thing in all this is that the business has to identify those strategic factors that will determine the long-term fortunes of the business. The goals that are adopted should be based on those factors. The measures that are adopted to identify success or failure have to be meaningful given the goals.

6.2 The use of the Balanced Scorecard

The Balanced Scorecard is essentially a management tool that links strategy with performance evaluation through use of a mix of financial and non-financial performance indicators. The general thrust that emerges from this is that performance is measured using a indicators that report on both what has happened in the immediate past and what is likely to happen in the future.

But the balanced scorecard, in common with all performance measurement systems, has to be applied sensitively if it is not to induce dysfunctional behaviour. If inappropriate indicators are selected then firms may be induced to do things in order to satisfy those indicators but which are not in the best interests of the firm. For example, a firm might minimise its inventory holding in order to meet some inventory holding target – but at the expense of total operating costs.

KEY POINT

There are four essential activities that have to be executed rigorously and diligently if the implementation is to be a success:

- make the strategy explicit
- choose the measures
- define and refine
- deal with people.

Experience has shown that there are four essential activities that have to be executed rigorously if the implementation is to succeed.

- **Make the strategy explicit**: The organisation's strategy must be made explicit and made to form the basis for the scorecard.
- **Choose the measures:** The performance measures must be aligned with the strategy and the relationships between the measures must be clearly understood.
- **Define and refine:** Performance measures must be put into place so that the scorecard becomes the language of the company.
- **Deal with people:** Above all, people and change management must be properly managed.

Each of these steps is critical and requires the deployment of different skills. The task of implementing a balanced scorecard may therefore best be charged to a multi-skilled team.

6.3 Make the strategy explicit

The starting point in producing a balanced scorecard is identifying the strategic requirements for success in the firm. The determination of strategy is discussed further in Chapter 17. Typically, those strategic requirements will relate to products, markets, growth and resources (human, intellectual and capital).

For example, businesses such as Compaq or Dell may want to be low-cost producers achieving competitive advantage from selling undifferentiated products at lower prices than those of competitors, or a business may have a product development strategy to become a leader in technology and command a premium like Apple. Their strategy may also be to develop and maintain market share, like Microsoft, or their strategy may be to occupy the number-one or number-two position in their lines of business.

6.4 Choose the measures

Performance measures have to be selected that clearly relate to the achievement of the strategies identified in the earlier process. As has been seen throughout the discussion of performance measures in this text, the selection of appropriate indicators and measures is critical. The selected measures form the goals that management communicates to staff as being important. Those goals are what staff will strive to achieve. If the wrong goals are selected then the firm may find itself doing the wrong things.

"performance measures have one purpose – to induce the parts to do what is good for the whole."

Eliyahu Goldratt, from The Goal [1993]

The general problem is that performance measures that relate to limited parts of the business can be very prone to inducing dysfunctional behaviour. The writer once encountered the case of a manufacturer which experienced surges in completions towards the end of each month and could not understand why this was happening. Investigation showed that management performance was measured by the achievement of monthly completion targets. Accordingly, production was arranged in a manner best calculated by managers to achieve this.

A batch that might best be produced as one whole over two periods might be split into two in order to maximise completions in the first period. The manufacture thus adopted a production system working on a monthly cycle induced by its own control systems. This did not minimise costs or advance customer satisfaction. Features such as this can be found over whole industries and not just in individual firms.

6.5 Define and refine

KEY POINT

Systems and procedures need to be set up to track and report the measures regularly.

Management reporting systems and procedures need to be set up to track and report the measures regularly. This involves all the issues relating to the processing of data and the reporting of information discussed earlier in this text.

The precise requirements of reporting associated with the use of the balanced scorecard will make demands on both the management accounting and IT systems in an organisation. Fully satisfying those demands has a cost and sometimes compromises may have to be made in order to contain that cost.

All sorts of practical problems may be encountered in reporting on an indicator. For example, when reporting on revenue:

- How is revenue calculated and when is it recorded?
- Should it include the non-core business activity?
- Should revenue be reported under product, region or customer headings?
- How should inter-divisional transactions be reported?

Operating the management accounting system associated with the balanced scorecard requires that the things being reported should be defined and periodically refined.

6.6 Deal with people

The balanced scorecard is an exercise in modifying human behaviour. It is its interaction with people that determines whether or not it will work.

"Show me what you will measure and I will show you what I will do. Confuse me as to what you will measure, and even I do not know what I will do."

Eliyahu Goldratt, from The Goal [1993]

Balanced scorecards can easily become a confusing mass of measures, some of which even contradict each other. There may be too many measures and action to achieve some of them may contribute to failure to achieve others. The measures may not always be prioritised.

To be effective, the measures contained in the scorecard should be limited in number, reasonably consistent and ranked in some order of priority. Further, performance measures should be aligned with the management structure. Career progression and remuneration should be appropriately linked to scorecard measure linked performance. Organisations which adopt a balanced scorecard but continue to reward managers on the basis of a narrow range of traditional financial measures are likely to be disappointed by the results.

6.7 Illustrative example

One example reported in management literature of how the balanced scorecard might be applied is the US case of Analog Devices (a semi-conductor manufacturer) in the preparation of its five-year strategic plan for 1988–1992.

Analog Devices had as its main corporate objective

'Achieving our goals for growth, profits, market share and quality creates the environment and economic means to satisfy the needs of our employees, stockholders, customers and others associated with the firm. Our success depends on people who understand the interdependence and congruence of their personal goals with those of the company and who are thus motivated to contribute towards the achievement of those goals.'

Three basic strategic objectives identified by the company were market leadership, sales growth and profitability.

The company adopted targets as follows:

Customer perspective

- Percentage of orders delivered on time. A target was set for the five-year period to increase the percentage of on-time deliveries from 85% to at least 99.8%.
- Outgoing defect levels. The target was to reduce the number of defects in product items delivered to customers, from 500 per month to less than 10 per month.
- Order lead time. A target was set to reduce the time between receiving a customer order to delivery from 10 weeks to less than three weeks.

Internal perspective

- Manufacturing cycle time. To reduce this from 15 weeks to 4 to 5 weeks over the five-year planning period.
- Defective items in production. To reduce defects in production from 5,000 per month to less than 10 per month.

Learning and innovation perspective

- Having products rated 'number one' by at least 50% of customers, based on their attitudes to whether the company was making the right products, performance, price, reliability, quality, delivery, lead time, customer support, responsiveness, willingness to co-operate and willingness to form partnerships.
- The number of new products introduced to the market
- Sales revenue from new products
- The new product sales ratio. This was the percentage of total sales achieved by products introduced to the market within the previous six quarters.
- Average annual revenues for new products in their third year.
- Reducing the average time to bring new product ideas to market.

Financial targets were set for revenue, revenue growth, profit and return on assets. But the idea was that the financial targets would flow from achieving the other targets stated above.

Analog Devices sought to adopt financial and non-financial performance measures within a single system, in which the various targets were consistent with each other and were in no way incompatible.

7 The performance pyramid

This was developed by Coopers and Lybrand (now called PriceWaterhouseCoopers) in their consultancy practice to help organisations improve their information provision.

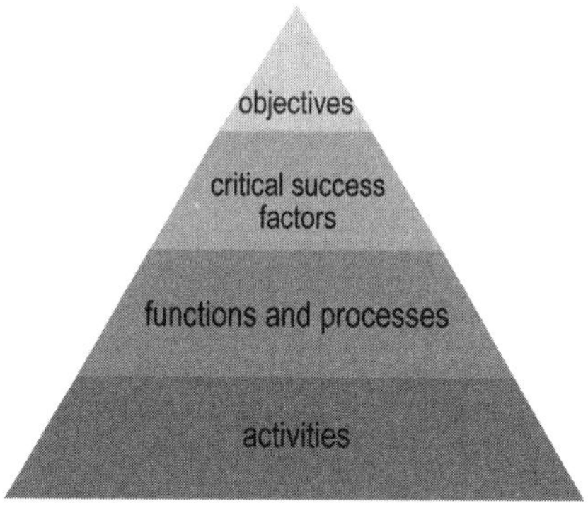

Critical success factors (CSF) have been defined in an earlier chapter and relate to how these objectives can be attained.

Functions and processes refer to KPI which help to measure the achievement of CSF.

Activities refer to the day to day functions that drive the organisation and the need to do these with excellence.

This model is similar in concept to the balanced scorecard in that it aims to overcome the drawbacks of traditional financial based reporting and provide a balanced view of the factors that create sustainable competitive advantage in a dynamic organisation.

The apex defines the objectives for the organisation.

- Improve shareholder wealth
- Improve ROI
- Improve EPS
- Improve market position
- Develop innovation
- Identify environmental issues
- Objectives for good corporate citizenship.

The whole of this appraisal process demonstrates a commitment to **strategic business information**.

8 Behavioural aspects of performance measurement

8.1 Control of organisations

To control an organisation and ensure it attains its goals we must pose and answer the following questions.

- what do we intend to happen?
- what has happened?
- who is responsible for what has happened?
- how does what has happened compare with what we intended?
- what action is necessary?

To answer these questions each organisation needs:

- a responsibility accounting system
- an internal control system
- a selection of performance measures.

As we have seen in earlier chapters, performance measures are commonly incorporated in the design of business control systems. The adoption of a responsibility accounting system means that the performance of individual managers is measured and reported on.

8.2 Responsibility accounting

KEY POINT

The aim of responsibility accounting is to ensure that each manager has a well-defined area of responsibility and the authority to make decisions within that area, and that no parts of the organisation remain as 'grey' areas where it is uncertain who is responsible for them.

The basic concept of responsibility accounting was introduced in Chapter 2. The aim of responsibility accounting is to ensure that each manager has a well-defined area of responsibility and the authority to make decisions within that area, and that no parts of the organisation remain as 'grey' areas where it is uncertain who is responsible for them. This area of responsibility may be simply a **cost centre,** or it may be a **profit centre** (implying that the manager has control over sales revenues as well as costs) or an **investment centre** (implying that the manager is empowered to also take decisions about capital investment for his department). Once senior management have set up such a structure, with the degree of delegation implied, some form of responsibility accounting system is needed. Each centre will have its own budget, and the manager will receive control information relevant to that budget centre. Costs (and if relevant, revenue, assets and liabilities) must be traced to the person primarily responsible for taking the related decisions, and identified with the appropriate department.

8.3 The factors to be considered when designing a responsibility accounting system

Controllable and uncontrollable costs

It Chapter 2 it was suggested that performance reports in the context of a responsibility accounting system should focus mainly on controllable costs. However, considerable caution should be exercises in this regard, since what constitutes a controllable cost may depend very much on detailed circumstances.

Some accountants would go as far as to advocate charging i.e. actually debiting, departments with costs that arise strictly as a result of decisions made by the management of those departments. For example, if the marketing department insists on a special rush order which necessitates overtime working in production departments, then the marketing department and not the production departments should be charged with the overtime premiums incurred. However, there are practical problems with such an approach:

(a) The rush order itself might actually be produced during normal time because, from a production scheduling angle, it might be more convenient to do it then (e.g. because it would not involve a clean-down of the machines as it was compatible with some other orders currently in production) - meaning 'normal' orders are produced during the period of 'overtime'.

(b) Re-charging costs to other departments can become a common occurrence because managers see it as a way of passing on not only the costs but also the associated responsibility e.g. if the rush order is produced inefficiently in overtime, should the costs of the inefficiency also be charged to the marketing department?

All managers work for the same organisation and, if the costs are shunted around, there is a nil effect on the overall profit of the organisation (except to the extent of any extra costs incurred in operating such a recharging system). Perhaps the effort expended on such a system could be more positively used to increase overall profit.

ACTIVITY 1

What are the potential dangers of including uncontrollable costs in a performance report?

Feedback to this activity is at the end of the chapter.

8.4 The problem of dual responsibility

KEY POINT

A common problem is that the responsibility for a particular cost or item is shared between two (or more) managers.

A common problem is that the responsibility for a particular cost or item is shared between two (or more) managers. For example, the responsibility for payroll costs may be shared between the personnel and production departments; material costs between purchasing and production departments; and so on. The reporting system should be designed so that the responsibility for performance achievements (i.e., better or worse than budget) is identified as that of a single manager.

The following guidelines may be applied:

(a) If manager controls quantity and price – responsible for all expenditure variances.

(b) If manager controls quantity but not price – only responsible for variances due to usage.

(c) If manager controls price but not quantity – only responsible for variances due to input prices.

(d) If manager controls neither quantity nor price – variances uncontrollable from the point of view of that manager.

8.5 Guidelines for reporting

There are several specific problems in relation to reporting which must be identified and dealt with:

- **Levels of reporting**

  The problem is how far down the management structure should responsibility centres be identified for reporting purposes? On the one hand, lower reporting levels encourage delegation and identify responsibility closer to the production process.

  On the other hand, more responsibility centres increase the number of reports and hence the cost of their production. One solution may be to combine small responsibility centres into groups (e.g. departments) for reporting purposes.

- **Frequency of reports and information to be reported**

  The frequency of reports should be linked to the purposes for which they are required. This may well mean a variety of reports being produced to different time-scales for different purposes e.g. some control information will be required weekly, or even daily. However, comprehensive budget reports are only likely to be required monthly.

KEY POINT

As reporting proceeds up the management pyramid, the breadth of the report should increase, and the detail should decrease.

The related problem is the content of such reports. It has been suggested that in computerised information systems the problem is often too much, rather than too little information. Generally, as reporting proceeds up the management pyramid, the breadth of the report should increase, and the detail should decrease.

9 Goal congruence and possible failure thereof

KEY POINT

A business may be harmed if the controls it uses motivates its employees to indulge in behaviour that is not organisationally desirable.

9.1 Dysfunctional behaviour

We have noted at several points in earlier Chapters that a business may be harmed if the controls it uses motivates its employees to indulge in behaviour that is not organisationally desirable. In this situation, the control system leads to a failure of goal congruence – otherwise known as dysfunctional behaviour.

Results controls based on performance measurement are a common cause of dysfunctional behaviour. Here, there is a danger that employees will concentrate only on what is measured – regardless of other issues that may be far more important to the well being of the organisation. In other words, they seek to maximise individual performance according to the performance metric being used regardless of whether or not this contributes to achievement of the organisation's objectives.

For example, if the performance of police officers is measured on the basis of the number of arrests they make (and perhaps a bonus is paid if they achieve more than 100 arrests per week), then you may be sure that the arrest rate will soar. Police officers will arrest people for the most trivial offences. However, it is highly unlikely that this will contribute to efficiency and effectiveness in policing the community. The police will concentrate on making 'easy' arrests (e.g. children riding bicycles on the footpath, motorists driving without wearing seat belts etc.) while giving a lower priority to crime which is more difficult to detect (e.g. fraud, murder etc).

The whole thrust of the discussion in preceding chapters has been on the need to adopt a sensitive and full approach to performance measurement. There is no need to go over this again. However, there are a number of additional issues that may be considered.

9.2 Manipulation of data

Data manipulation occurs where individuals distort data in order to improve measured performance. Employees may attempt to negotiate lower (and hence more easily attainable) performance targets in later periods by deliberately underperforming in the current period. Employees may attempt to improve reported performance by wrongly classifying items of cost and revenue.

Clearly, this kind of behaviour is not to the advantage of the organisation.

9.3 Social alienation

Where performance measures and targets are insensitively used, employees may develop very negative attitudes towards their job. An employee who is suffering job related stress, job conflict and poor working relationships is unlikely to perform effectively.

In the area of marketing, salesman performance measures related to customer call numbers, customer orders and order values are all commonly used. These can be a source of great worry to many salesmen. Even the best salesmen have lean patches and the volume of business in many sectors is often subject to cyclical variations. That apart, time invested in cultivating a new client does not always produce immediate orders.

A good salesman takes the long view in dealing with customers and always conveys a relaxed manner. A salesman who is pressured by short-term performance targets may be unable to take a long view and is not likely to be relaxed. This is all a question of management style. Some managements make a rigid use of performance targets and link a high profile scheme of employee rewards and sanctions to achievement of those targets. In some environments, this may produce satisfactory results.

Performance measures have been introduced in recent years for many areas of the public sector including policing and healthcare – and these have been discussed in Chapter 12 in the context of benchmarking. It should be noted that many senior police officers and healthcare workers feel that such measures are demeaning, particularly when they are linked to remuneration.

9.4 Social or cultural controls

Having regard to the problem of results based performance measurement discussed above, some behavioural scientists have advocated a greater use of social or cultural controls in business. It is claimed that these work well, without formal rules, where one is dealing with skilled and highly motivated workers. The key thing is to develop a working environment where people feel that their efforts are valued by colleagues and superiors.

This approach is entirely consistent with the TQM movement. This movement incorporates features such as empowerment and job enrichment.

9.5 Performance related pay

Central to the ideas of responsibility accounting and performance measurement is that managers should be rewarded according to the results they achieve.

KEY POINT

When valuing shares, the market takes into account a range of qualitative and strategic issues – and hence share price may serve as proxy for a balanced scorecard.

It was stated in Chapter 10 that the ultimate measure of performance is shareholder value. When valuing shares, the market takes into account a range of qualitative and strategic issues – and hence share price may serve as proxy for a balanced scorecard. So, share options are a common way of rewarding senior managers in quoted companies. If a manager has an option to buy shares at a price of £5 at a certain time in the future then he has a powerful incentive to do things that ensure that the market price is above £5 at that date.

Obviously, managers in unquoted companies cannot normally receive PRP in this way.

KEY POINT

Performance related pay has recently been extended into many areas of the public sector, with senior managers being paid bonuses according to those performance measures which are judged most appropriate.

Performance related pay has recently been extended into many areas of the public sector, with senior managers being paid bonuses according to those performance measures which are judged most appropriate.

PRP offers many theoretical advantages, but all the problems relating to choice of performance measure, manipulation of data and alienation are encountered.

For example, the UK government is anxious to reduce numbers on NHS hospital waiting lists in order to meet targets that it set itself at the time of the 1997 election. Performance targets have been set for hospital managers on the basis of waiting list numbers and, in some cases, PRP is linked to achievement of these targets.

However, many observers claim that this approach distorts the pattern of healthcare. Hospitals will give priority to patients suffering from minor complaints since they can be treated quickly and cleared off the waiting list without undue expense. Patients suffering from more serious illnesses may find that their treatment is delayed and their stay on the waiting list is extended. Is this a good thing? On the one hand, 90% of people on hospital waiting lists are suffering from only minor conditions and this group will perceive that service standards have improved. But, one must worry about the experience of the other 10% who may need treatment more urgently.

Conclusion

Organisational objectives and appropriate performance measures will vary between business sectors. The statutory and regulatory environment may also influence performance. The Balanced Scorecard is a management tool designed to deploy and monitor a strategy by using an appropriate mix of financial and non-financial performance measures. Performance measures should encourage goal congruence among employees.

SELF-TEST QUESTIONS

Introduction

1 What are the main headings under which business performance may be measured? (1)

Performance measures in manufacturing

2 Explain what customer profitability analysis is. (2.1)

Performance measures in process environments

3 State the main performance measures that might be used in a manufacturing concern. (3)

Service operations

4 State the main performance measures that might be used in a transport operation. (4.4)

5 State some of the performance measures that might be used in the regulation of a railway operating company. (4)

The statutory and regulatory environment

6 State some of the ways in which the statutory and regulatory framework might influence the performance of a business in the UK. (5.1)

The Balanced Scorecard

7 State the activities that need to be carried out in preparing a balanced scorecard. (6)

Goal congruence and possible failure thereof

8 Explain what ‘failure of goal congruence’ is. (9)

9 What are the advantages and disadvantages of PRP? (9.5)

EXAM-TYPE QUESTIONS

Scenario (Common to Questions 1 and 2)

Frantisek Precision Engineering plc (FPE) is an engineering company which makes tools and equipment for a wide range of applications. FPE has twelve operating divisions each of which is responsible for a particular product group. In the past divisional performance has been assessed on the basis of Residual Income (RI) - with an annual finance charge (at bank base + 2%) on net assets (excluding cash) being made to each division at the end of the year.

Rapier Management consultants have recently been engaged to review the management accounting systems of FPE. In regard to the performance evaluation system, Rapier have reported:

"RI is a very partial and imperfect performance indicator. What you need is a more comprehensive system which reflects the mission, strategy and technology of each individual division. Further, executives should each be paid a performance bonus linked to an indicator which relates to their own personal contribution."

FPE's directors provisionally accepted the Rapier recommendation and have carried out a pilot scheme in the diving equipment ('DE') division. DE division manufactures assorted equipment used by sport and industrial divers. Safety is a critical factor in this sector. Customers are deeply conservative and will not readily accept new products, design features and technologies - many of which remain unexploited.

At the start of 20X8, Rapier designed a performance evaluation system for DE division as follows:

Factor	**Calculated**
Return on Capital Employed (ROCE)	operating profit for the year divided by book value of net assets (excluding cash) at the end of the year
Cash conversion period (CCP)	number of days debtors plus days stock minus days creditors outstanding at the end of the year
Strategy (innovations)	number of new products and major design features successfully brought to market

Under the terms of DE's new performance evaluation system annual salary bonuses are paid to individual divisional managers as follows:

ROCE over 10%	–	chief executive, production manager, sales manager
CCP less than 40 days	–	accountant, office manager
More than 4 innovations	–	chief executive, design manager

Question 1: FPE 1

In early December 20X8 DE's accountant forecasts that DE's results for 20X8 will be as follows:

	20X8		**end 20X8**
sales	£6,900,000	stock	£530,000
purchases	£2,920,000	debtors	£1,035,000
operating profit	£450,000	creditors	£320,000
innovations number	4	net assets	£4,800,000

The accountant further forecasts that, in the absence of some change in policy or new investment, corresponding figures for 20X9 and end 20X9 will be the same as those shown above for 20X8. Upon receiving this forecast, DE division's chief executive convenes a meeting of his managers to discuss strategy for the rest of 20X8 and for 20X9. Several proposals are made including:

from the office manager - "I propose that we immediately dispose of £160,000 of stock at cost and defer a creditor payment of £180,000 due 16 December 20X8 until 2 January 20X9. The first measure will reduce profit by £16,500 a year from 20X9 onwards and the second measure will incur an immediate £2,000 penalty."

from the production manager - "I recommend we invest £400,000 in new equipment. This will increase operating profit by £25,000 per year for eight years and the equipment will have a residual value of £40,000 at the end of its life."

from the design manager - "I propose we introduce a new electronic digital depth gauge to the market. This will involve an initial investment of £100,000 in new equipment having a life of at least ten years and sales will have to be on 6 months' 'buy or return' credit in order to overcome market resistance. I forecast that the new depth gauge will generate £20,000 extra operating profit per year with purchases, sales, stock and creditors all increasing in proportion.

Required:

(a) Explain the impact of each proposal on the reported performance of DE division in 20X8 and 20X9 and state whether or not each proposal is likely to be acceptable to members of DE management. **(15 marks)**

(b) State your views (supported by financial evaluation) on the inherent merits of each proposal having regard to factors you consider relevant. **(10 marks)**

Note: where relevant you may assume that depreciation is on a straight line basis and DCF evaluation is carried out using an 8% discount rate and 10 year time horizon. **(Total: 25 marks)**

Question 2: FPE 2

"There is nothing inherently wrong with business financial performance indicators. The problem is what those indicators are used for - in particular their use as a basis for management remuneration. For one thing, almost any indicator is highly vulnerable to manipulation. For another thing, they can seriously distort business decision-making."

Required:

Having regard to this statement:

(a) Explain the relative strengths and weaknesses of RI and ROCE as business performance indicators as far as FPE is concerned. **(8 marks)**

(b) Explain the relative strengths and weaknesses of financial and non-financial performance indicators as far as FPE is concerned and state what you consider the proper use of business performance indicators to be. **(8 marks)**

(Total: 16 marks)

For the answers to these questions, see the 'Answers' section at the end of the book

FEEDBACK TO ACTIVITY 1

The dangers of including uncontrollable costs in a performance report are:

(a) Managers might be demotivated if their performance is apparently affected by costs over which they have no influence.

(b) Uncontrollable cost information can divert managers' attention away from what they actually are responsible for.

(c) The manager who is responsible for the costs in question might feel that they are not his or her responsibility as they are reported elsewhere.

Chapter 14
THEORY AND PRACTICE OF BUDGETING

CHAPTER CONTENTS

This chapter provides an introduction to the practice of budgeting and the role that budgeting plays in the control of business operations.

Objectives

When you have studied this chapter you should be able to do the following.

- Describe the internal and external sources of planning information for an organisation.
- List the information used in the preparation of the master budget and in its functional components.
- Contrast the information used in the operation of zero-based budgeting and incremental information.
- Explain and illustrate the use of budgeting as a planning aid in the coordination of business activity.
- Explain and illustrate the relevance of budgeting in the coordination of business activities.
- Explain and quantify the application of positive and negative feedback in the operation of budgetary control.
- Explain and quantify the application of feedforward control in the operation of budgeting.

1 Introduction

KEY POINT

A budget is a plan of action, relating to activities during a defined time period, normally expressed in financial terms.

A budget is a plan of action, relating to activities during a defined time period, normally expressed in financial terms. Occasionally, one finds plans expressed in quantitative (but non-financial terms) described as budgets. However, this last practice is strictly a misuse of the term.

2 Budgeting as a concept

2.1 Preparing and using a budget

The process of preparing a budget is usually a part of the planning function within the organisation. An organisation has a mission which it translates into objectives. The activities needed to achieve those objectives are expressed in the form of plans which may cover periods of 1 year (a short-term plan), 5 years (a medium term plan) and 10 years (a long-term plan). These plans will cover capital costs, revenue costs and revenues.

The plans (particularly the 1 year plan) may then be converted into budgets. A budget is usually a detailed expression of the plan which contains all the costs and revenues that are associated with the execution of the plan. In preparing its plans and budgets, the organisation will have regard to all strategic considerations, market forecasts, an appraisal of available resources and will make use of a variety of quantitative techniques.

KEY POINT

Once the budget exists, it may be used as an instrument of business control. The preparation of periodic budgetary control reports is the 'bread and butter' work of management accounting.

Once the budget exists, it may be used as an instrument of business control. The results that are achieved may be continuously compared with those which were budgeted for. The preparation of periodic budgetary control reports is the 'bread and butter' work of management accounting.

Typically, a one year budget will be split into twelve monthly components. That is, the budget is constructed with a one month budget interval. This makes possible the construction of monthly control reports comparing actual to budget for the month immediately past and the year to date.

The budget control report for May will appear in early June. It will contain four sets of cost and revenue figures – May (actual), May (budget), beginning of financial year to May (actual) and beginning of financial year to May (budget). The control report will normally arrange these sets of figures in neat columns which allow easy comparison.

The budget will provide a benchmark against which actual performance can be measured. The budget may contain figures for sales, costs, profit, stock, debtors and so on. Performance ratios can be calculated from these. These budget figures and performance ratios form targets against which actual results achieved can be measured. If the actual results are better than those budgeted for then we conclude that the business is performing well and vice versa.

DEFINITION

"**Budget conformance**" is the central performance measure when using a budgetary control system.

All the issues that were explored in earlier chapters concerning performance measurement are relevant in the context of budgetary control. The critical thing is that 'budget conformance' is the central performance measure when using a budgetary control system. If a manager, department or business performs at a level below that budgeted for, then (in the absence of other considerations) performance is judged to be poor. Corrective action may be prompted.

DEFINITION

A **flexible budget** is one which is revised while it is current to take account of changing circumstances

A flexible budget is one which is revised while it is current to take account of changing circumstances – typically price levels and output levels. Thus in a given quarter, comparison of actual results with a flexed budget allows comparison of likes through the exclusion of what might be termed 'planning variances'. Divergences from a flexed budget thus reflect only operational efficiencies and inefficiencies – or that is the theory.

Critics of flexible budgets sometimes argue that it is an approach which allows managers to revise targets after the event to ensure that those targets have been met. It thus degrades the budget as an instrument of control.

2.2 Budgeting in the context of control system theory

KEY POINT

A control system consists of a Sensor which reports information (a monthly operating statement), a Comparator which measures performance (comparison of actual with budget and identification of variances) and an Effector (management action to correct identified deficiencies or opportunities).

Various aspects of control system theory and the role that management information plays in it have been explored in the earlier chapters of this text. At this point we can set budgetary planning and control within the context of control system theory.

A control system consists of a Sensor which reports information (a monthly operating statement), a Comparator which measures performance (comparison of actual with budget and identification of variances) and an Effector (management action to correct identified deficiencies or opportunities).

The whole information control process by which information flows and analysis initiates corrective action is known as a feedback loop. 'Negative' feedback is a feature which seeks to normalise activity around some plan or standard. For example, if actual unit costs are rising above budget unit costs then action may be automatically taken to reverse this.

'Positive' feedback works the other way – when action is taken to reinforce some divergence from plan. For example, if sales volumes are found to be rising above budget then action may be automatically taken to increase production above budget.

One of the features of a budgetary control system is that it involves operating on a fixed period time cycle (typically monthly) and information is reported at the end of given time periods. Corrective action is then prompted on the feedback principle described above. This may not always be satisfactory because of the time delay involved – and feedforward elements may therefore be built into the system.

A feedforward element may be a requirement for a manager to seek approval before taking some action that will create a variance from budget. This attention is focused on a problem or opportunity before it has actually had an impact.

3 Planning information

3.1 Position audit

A company's operational environment is composed of those dimensions which directly or indirectly influence corporate success or failure. Most external factors are beyond the control of the company, whereas internal dimensions are generally within its management ambit. The essential purpose of a strategic position audit is to collect and analyse all the relevant and available information about the company and its current operations which will provide strategic planners with information on:

- The competitive strengths and weaknesses of the company's current strategic position
- The consequences of the company continuing its present strategy
- The internal resources which are available for implementing any strategic change that may be required.

KEY POINT

The essential purpose of a strategic position audit is to collect and analyse all the relevant and available information about the company and its current operations which will provide strategic planners with information on:

- Competitive strengths and weaknesses
- Consequences of the company continuing its present strategy
- Internal resources which are available for implementing any strategic change.

The sources of information available to management during the budgeting process were explored earlier in this text and the theory of strategy formulation is explored later, in Chapter 17.

3.2 The detailed audit

It is not possible to provide a definitive list of the aspects that should be analysed in a strategic position audit. This must depend on the particular situation, circumstances and forces at work in the operational environment of a given organisation. However, the analytical audit approach should utilise a systematic set of questions that takes the auditor into the main areas of a company's structure and operations.

3.3 Macro-economic statistics

Statistics are produced for all macro-economic variables such as:

- inflation
- balance of payments
- terms of trade
- exchange rates
- interest rates - domestic and international
- money supply
- growth of GDP.

Again, these are useful indicators of the country's overall economic position, but are of limited value to an individual company that is trying to assess its performance.

The figures will tell the company if the economy is pulling out of recession, or if factory gate prices or unit labour costs across the whole economy are increasing. But they will not tell the company anything of detail about its own performance compared to those of its immediate competitors in the same industry.

The company's own cost records will provide a great deal of information concerning the cost structure of its operation – the manner in which its costs will vary with the level and structure of output.

3.4 Interfirm comparison schemes

KEY POINT

There are a number of schemes set up by agencies such as the Centre for Interfirm Comparisons, or by various trade associations. These attempt to produce information about the relative performance of companies that contribute to the scheme.

There are a number of schemes set up by agencies such as the Centre for Interfirm Comparisons, or by various trade associations. These attempt to produce information about the relative performance of companies that contribute to the scheme.

The difficulties of such schemes are:

- Information supplied by different companies may not be based on the same accounting policies and will have to be adjusted.
- Companies may be reluctant to divulge information that will be used by the competition for reasons of confidentiality.

The problems are not insurmountable and the data provided does have benefit for participating companies. This form of benchmarking may indicate what actions may be needed to strengthen the cost structure of a business. Reliance only on past experience in a firm to predict the cost outcome of given actions is an inherently passive approach.

4 The practice of budgeting

4.1 How to budget – the seven steps

Preparation of the budget involves seven steps. These are illustrated diagrammatically on the next page:

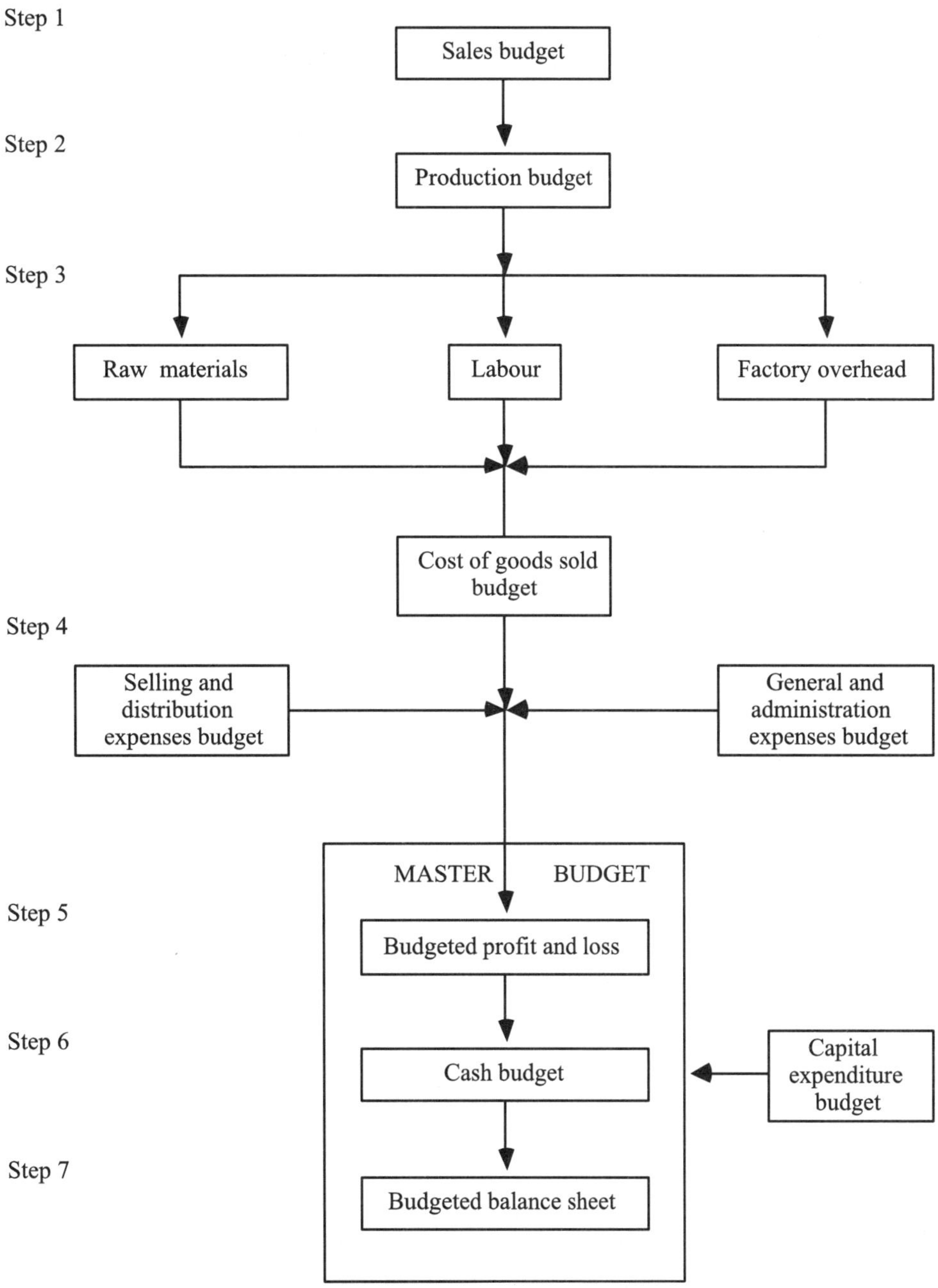

KEY POINT

The master budget is the full budget for the whole organisation.

The master budget is the full budget for the whole organisation and this is normally divided into a series of subordinate budgets. The budgeting process can be carried out on a top-down or bottom-up basis. The organisation can start with the master budget and then divide that into subordinate budgets for functions and departments – or it can prepare the subordinate budgets first and summarise them into the master budget.

The merits of alternative approaches depend on circumstances and management style.

4.2 Principal budget factor

KEY POINT

The limiting factor must be identified at the first stage of the budgeting process, since it will determine all the other budgets. In this context the limiting factor is referred to as the principal budget factor.

The sales budget is shown in the diagram because this is the pattern in most businesses, where it is the volume of the demand for the product which limits the scale of operation. It is possible, however, for there to be some other limiting factor e.g. labour, material, cash or machinery. The limiting factor must be identified at the first stage of the budgeting process, since it will determine all the other budgets. In this context the limiting factor is referred to as the principal budget factor.

DEFINITION

ZBB is a method of budgeting whereby all activities are re-evaluated each time a budget is set. Discrete levels of each activity are valued and a combination chosen to match funds available.

4.3 Zero-based budgeting (ZBB)

ZBB requires the budgeting of every part of an organisation from 'scratch' or 'base'. The technique forces managers to consider all the costs of an operation, consider the level of service provided and the costs of providing that service. Often the 'zero-option' is not feasible, nor desired, but different levels of operation are considered.

The costs of providing each level of service will be assessed against the level of service provided and the most appropriate chosen.

4.4 The technique of zero-based budgeting

The first requirement in a ZBB process which is most effective in controlling service department budgets is the development of a *decision package.*

This has been defined by its first proponent Peter A Pyhrr of Texas Instruments as:

'A document that identifies and describes a specific activity in such a manner that senior management can:

(a) evaluate it and rank it against other activities competing for limited resources
(b) decide whether to approve or disapprove it.'

KEY POINT

Decision packages are developed by managers for their particular areas of responsibility.

Decision packages are developed by managers for their particular areas of responsibility.

Decision packages will contain information such as:

- the function of the department
- a performance measure for the department
- costs and benefits of operating a department at a range of different levels of funding
- consequences of not operating at those levels.

The second requirement is the actual ranking of the decision packages, using cost/benefit analysis.

The result is a list of ranked projects or activities which senior management can use to evaluate needs and priorities in making budget approvals. The resources available to the organisation for the forthcoming budget period are thus allocated accordingly.

This in practice may be a formidable task, particularly with the interrelationships that exist within an organisation, and probably no organisation can afford to take the time to examine every activity in the necessary depth every year. A review cycle covering each activity once every three or four years may be more practical. ZBB is said to be particularly useful in local government. It may be easier to apply in that situation because it is possible to segregate and assess the benefits of each activity (e.g., refuse collection, schools, road maintenance) and the complicated links often found in industry are minimal. In the private sector its most productive use would seem to be in the area of non-manufacturing costs. In this area efficiency standards are difficult to develop and costs often tend to mushroom.

4.5 Benefits of zero-based budgeting

Despite considerable practical problems associated with applying ZBB throughout the organisation, some important benefits are envisaged in its rationale:

- it helps to create an organisational environment where change is accepted
- it helps management to focus on company objectives and goals

- it concentrates the attention of management on the future rather than on the past
- it helps to identify inefficient and obsolete operations within the organisation
- it provides a framework to ensure the optimum utilisation of resources by establishing priorities in relation to operational activity
- it should lead to a more logical and beneficial allocation of resources available to an organisation
- it can assist motivation of management at all levels
- it provides a plan to follow when more financial resources become available
- it establishes minimum requirements from departments
- it can be done piecemeal.

It does have some disadvantages namely:

- it takes more management time than conventional systems, in part because managers need to learn what is required of them
- there is a temptation to concentrate on short-term cost savings at the expense of longer-term benefits
- it takes time to show the real benefits of implementing such a system.

Example

ZBB Ltd has two service departments - material handling and maintenance, which are in competition for budget funds which must not exceed £925,000 in the coming year. A zero base budgeting approach will be used whereby each department is to be treated as a decision package and will submit a number of levels of operation showing the minimum level at which its service could be offered and two additional levels which would improve the quality of the service from the minimum level.

The following data have been prepared for each department showing the three possible operating levels for each:

Material handling department

Level 1. A squad of 30 labourers would work 40 hours per week for 48 weeks of the year. Each labourer would be paid a basic rate of £4 per hour for a 35 hour week. Overtime hours would attract a premium of 50% on the basic rate per hour. In addition, the company anticipates payments of 20% of gross wages in respect of employee benefits. Directly attributable variable overheads would be incurred at the rate of 12p per man hour. The squad would move 600,000 kilos per week to a warehouse at the end of the production process.

Level 2. In addition to the level 1 operation, the company would lease 10 fork lift trucks at a cost of £2,000 per truck per annum. This would provide a better service by enabling the same volume of output as for level 1 to be moved to a customer collection point which would be 400 metres closer to the main factory gate. Each truck would be manned by a driver working a 48 week year. Each driver would receive a fixed weekly wage of £155.

Directly attributable overheads of £150 per truck per week would be incurred.

Level 3. A computer could be leased to plan the work of the squad of labourers in order to reduce their total work hours. The main benefit would be improvement in safety through reduction in the time that work-in-progress would lie unattended. The computer leasing costs would be £20,000 for the first quarter (3 months), reducing by 10% per quarter cumulatively thereafter.

The computer data would result in a 10% reduction in labourer hours, half of this reduction being a saving in overtime hours.

Maintenance department

Level 1. Two engineers would each be paid a salary of £18,000 per annum and would arrange for repairs to be carried out by outside contractors at an annual cost of £250,000.

Level 2. The company would employ a squad of 10 fitters who would carry out breakdown repairs and routine maintenance as required by the engineers. The fitters would each be paid a salary of £11,000 per annum.

Maintenance materials would cost £48,000 per annum and would be used at a constant rate throughout the year. The purchases could be made in batches of £4,000, £8,000, £12,000 or £16,000. Ordering costs would be £100 per order irrespective of order size and stock holding costs would be 15% per annum. **The minimum cost order size would be implemented**.

Overheads directly related to the maintenance operation would be a fixed amount of £50,000 per annum.

In addition to the maintenance squad it is estimated that £160,000 of outside contractor work would still have to be paid for.

Level 3. The company could increase its maintenance squad to 16 fitters which would enable the service to be extended to include a series of major overhauls of machinery. The additional fitters would be paid at the same salary as the existing squad members.

Maintenance materials would now cost £96,000 per annum and would be used at a constant rate throughout the year. Purchases could be made in batches of £8,000, £12,000 or £16,000. Ordering costs would be £100 per order (irrespective of order size) and stock holding costs would now be 13.33% per annum. In addition, suppliers would now offer discounts of 2% of purchase price for orders of £16,000. The minimum cost order size would be implemented.

Overheads directly related to the maintenance operation would increase by £20,000 from the level 2 figure.

It is estimated that £90,000 of outside contractor work would still have to be paid for.

Required:

(a) Determine the incremental cost for each of levels 1, 2 and 3 in each department. **(16 marks)**

(b) In order to choose which of the incremental levels of operation should be allocated to the limited budgeted funds available, management have estimated a 'desirability factor' which should be applied to each increment. The ranking of the increments is then based on the 'incremental cost × desirability factor' score, whereby a high score is deemed more desirable than a low score. The desirability factors are estimated as:

	Material handling	*Maintenance*
Level 1	1.00	1.00
Level 2 (incremental)	0.60	0.80
Level 3 (incremental)	0.50	0.20

Use the above ranking process to calculate which of the levels of operation should be implemented in order that the budget of £925,000 is not exceeded. **(3 marks)**

(Total: 19 marks)

Solution

(a) **Material handling department**

Level 1:

		£	£
Wages cost	30 × 40 hours × 48 weeks × £4		230,400
	30 × 5 hours × 48 weeks × £2		14,400
			244,800
Employee benefits	20% × £244,800		48,960
Variable overhead	30 × 40 hours × 48 weeks × 12p		6,912
Incremental cost			**300,672**

Level 2:

Leasing	10 trucks @ £2,000		20,000
Drivers' wages	10 drivers × 48 weeks × £155		74,400
Overhead	10 trucks × 48 weeks × £150		72,000
Incremental cost			**166,400**

Level 3:

Leasing	(£20,000 + £18,000 + £16,200 + £14,580)		68,780
Savings			
(30 men × 40 hours × 48 weeks × 10% = 5,760 hours)			
Wages cost	5,760 hours × £4	23,040	
	2,880 hours × £2	5,760	
		28,800	
Employee benefits	20% × £28,800	5,760	
Variable overhead	5,760 hours × 12p	691	
			(35,251)
Incremental cost			**33,529**

Maintenance department

Level 1:

		£
Engineers' salaries	2 × £18,000	36,000
Outside contractors		250,000
Incremental cost		**286,000**

Level 2:

Engineers' salaries	2 × £18,000	36,000
Fitters' salaries	10 × £11,000	110,000
Materials		48,000
Ordering costs (W1)		600
Stockholding costs (W1)		600
Overheads		50,000
Outside contractors		160,000
		405,200
Less level one costs		(286,000)
Incremental cost		**119,200**

Level 3:

Engineers' salaries	2 × £18,000	36,000
Fitters' salaries	16 × £11,000	176,000
Materials		96,000
Ordering costs (W2)		600
Stockholding costs (W2)		1,045
Discount		(1,920)
Overheads		70,000
Outside contractors		90,000
		467,725
Less level two costs		(405,200)
Incremental cost		**62,525**

(b) **Factor scores:**

		Material handling		*Maintenance*
Level 1:	(£300,672 × 1.00)	300,672	(£286,000 × 1.00)	286,000
Level 2:	(£166,400 × 0.60)	99,840	(£119,200 × 0.80)	95,360
Level 3:	(£33,529 × 0.50)	16,765	(£62,525 × 0.20)	12,505

The budget will be spent as follows:

			£
Material handling	-	Level 3 (£300,672 + £166,400 + £33,529)	500,601
Maintenance	-	Level 2 (£286,000 + £119,200)	405,200
			905,801

Workings

(W1)

Order size	*No. of orders*	*Average stock*	*Ordering cost*	*Holding cost*	*Total cost*
£4,000	12	£2,000	£1,200	£300	£1,500
£8,000	6	£4,000	£600	£600	£1,200
£12,000	4	£6,000	£400	£900	£1,300
£16,000	3	£8,000	£300	£1,200	£1,500

(W2)

Order size	*No. of orders*	*Average stock*	*Ordering cost*	*Holding cost*	*Total cost*
£8,000	12	£4,000	£1,200	£533.20	£1,733.20
£12,000	8	£6,000	£800	£799.80	£1,599.80
£16,000	6	£8,000	£600	£1,066.40	£1,666.40

The discount of 2% is worth (2% × £96,000) = £1,920 per annum. Therefore net cost if orders are placed for £16,000 each time is negative, orders will be placed at this level.

As stock is thereby reduced by 2% the stock-holding cost is also reduced by 2% to £1,045.07.

4.6 Incremental budgeting

DEFINITION

Incremental budgeting is a system of budgeting based on previous budgets and actual results. Data from past years is adjusted by adding or subtracting a percentage so as to adjust the values for known changes in activity and price effects.

KEY POINT

The incremental approach does not identify obsolete techniques or inefficiencies.

Benefits of incremental budgeting

Incremental budgeting is a simple process which can easily be automated using spreadsheet models. Very little management intervention is required and as a consequence the method is not costly to operate.

Disadvantages of incremental budgeting

The incremental approach does not identify obsolete techniques or inefficiencies. In effect they are continued into the future and become built in to the target so that they may not be identified in the future.

Example

Narud plc is nearing the end of year 7 and has prepared summary profit and loss account data for year 6 (actual) and year 7 (projected actual) as shown in **Table 1. Table 1** also shows the bank overdraft at the end of year 6 and the projected bank overdraft at the end of year 7. Sales and production mix may be taken as constant from year 6 to year 9, with all production being sold in the year of production.

Budgeted direct material cost is variable with output volume but budgeted direct labour cost contains a fixed element of £50,000 in year 6 with the remainder varying with production volume and used in the calculation of the labour efficiency index in **Table 2.**

Production overhead contains a fixed element of £150,000 (at year 6 price levels). Included within this fixed element is a depreciation provision of £30,000 which will remain unaltered irrespective of price level changes.

Variable production overhead varies in proportion to units produced.

Budgeted administration/selling overhead is wholly fixed, whilst distribution expense should vary with sales volume.

The financial charges figure for each year is calculated as the average borrowing for the year times the borrowing rate (taken as 20%).

i.e. Financial charges per year = ((2x – y) × 0.20)/2

where x = previous year end overdraft and
y = net profit for current year before financial charges and depreciation.

Narud plc are concerned about the level of borrowing and high financial charges. A number of changes are planned in order to attempt to eliminate the overdraft by the end of year 9 e.g.

(i) change the type of material used from year 8 onwards as a means of reducing scrap and hence improving efficiency.

(ii) it is anticipated that the material change per (i) above together with extra training of operatives in each of years 8 and 9 will improve labour efficiency.

(iii) selling prices will be cut in years 8 and 9 in order to stimulate demand.

Tables 2 and 3 show cost indices for performance and price respectively which show the projected changes from a year 6 base of 100. The performance indices show the cost effect of performance changes e.g. material usage in year 8 indicates a 5% cost reduction from the base year level because of the reduced scrap level of material per product unit referred to in (i) above.

Table 4 shows the sales volume and price movements from a year 6 base of 100.

Required:

(a) Give detailed working calculations which show how the year 7 projected figures (per Table 1) have been arrived at for (i) labour cost (ii) production overhead and (iii) financial charges, using the year 6 data per Table 1 as the starting point and using indices from Tables 2, 3 and 4 as necessary.

(b) Prepare forecast profit and loss accounts for years 8 and 9 and calculate the forecast bank balance or overdraft at the end of years 8 and 9, assuming that the overdraft is affected only by net profit adjusted for the non-cash effect of the depreciation charge.

Table 1

Narud plc – Summary Profit and Loss Account

	Year 6	*Year 7*
	£	£
Sales revenue	2,000,000	2,310,000
Less: Cost of sales:		
Direct material cost	1,000,000	1,201,200
Direct labour cost	150,000	163,300
Production overhead	310,000	350,124
Admin/selling overhead	100,000	115,500
Distribution overhead	140,000	158,466
Financial charges	130,000	124,859
	1,830,000	2,113,449
Net profit	170,000	196,551
Bank overdraft	800,000	573,449

Table 2

Indices reflecting the cost effect of changes in performance level from year 6

Year	*Material usage*	*Labour efficiency*	*Production overhead utilisation (fixed and variable)*	*Admin/ selling overhead utilisation*	*Distribution overhead utilisation*
6	100	100	100	100	100
7	104	103	103	110	98
8	95	99	99	105	95
9	85	97	97	100	95

Note: utilisation indices monitor the cost effect of a change in the quantity of a cost item used (a) other than changes due to a change in the number of units produced and (b) even where the cost is defined as fixed by the company.

Table 3

Indices reflecting the cost effect of price level changes from year 6

Year	*Material price*	*Labour rate*	*All overheads expenditure*
6	100	100	100
7	105	100	105
8	120	110	112
9	125	115	118

Table 4

Indices for sales/production volume changes and sales price changes from year 6

Year	*Sales volume*	*Sales price*
6	100	100
7	110	105
8	120	103
9	130	101

Solution

(a) (i) **Labour cost**

	Fixed £	*Variable* £
Yr 6 = £150,000	50,000	100,000
Volume + 10%	-	10,000
	50,000	110,000
Efficiency + 3%	-	3,300
Yr 7 = £163,300	50,000	113,300

(ii) **Production overhead**

	Dep'n	*Fixed*	*Variable*
	£	£	£
Yr 6 = £310,000	30,000	120,000	160,000
Volume + 10%	-	-	16,000
	30,000	120,000	176,000
Eff'y + 3%	-	3,600	5,280
	30,000	123,600	181,280
Price + 5%	-	6,180	9,064
Yr 7 £350,124	30,000	129,780	190,344

(iii) Finance charges

$$\frac{(((2 \times 800{,}000) - 351{,}410) \times 0.2)}{2} = £124{,}859$$

(b) **Year 8**

	£	£
Sales (2m × 1.2 × 1.03)		2,472,000
Mat'ls (1m × 1.2 × 0.95 × 1.2)		1,368,000
Labour - F (50,000 × 1.1)	55,000	
- V (100,000 × 1.2 × 0.99 × 1.1)	130,680	185,680
Prod Ohd - D	30,000	
- F (120,000 × 0.99 × 1.12)	133,056	
- V (160,000 × 1.2 × 0.99 × 1.12)	212,890	375,946
Admin/Selling (100,000 × 1.05 × 1.12)		117,600
Dist (140,000 × 1.2 × 0.95 × 1.12)		178,752
Finance chgs (W1): $\frac{(((2 \times 573{,}449) - 276{,}022) \times 0.2)}{2}$		87,088
PROFIT		158,934
Overdraft (573,449) + 158,934 + 30,000		(384,515)

Year 9

		£	£
Sales (2m × 1.3 × 1.01)			2,626,000
Materials (1m × 1.3 × 0.85 × 1.25)			1,381,250
Labour	- F (50,000 × 1.15)	57,500	
	- V (100,000 × 1.3 × 0.97 × 1.15)	145,015	202,515
Prod Ohd	- D	30,000	
	- F (120,000 × 0.97 × 1.18)	137,352	
	- V (160,000 × 1.3 × 0.97 × 1.18)	238,077	405,429
Admin/Selling (100,000 × 1.00 × 1.18)			118,000
Distribution (140,000 × 1.3 × 0.95 × 1.18)			204,022
Finance charges (W2): $\frac{((2 \times 384,515) - 344,784) \times 0.2}{2}$			42,425
PROFIT			272,359
Overdraft (384,515) + 272,359 + 30,000			(82,156)

Workings

(W1) The value of £276,022 is the profit before depreciation and finance charges

(W2) The value of £344,784 is the profit before depreciation and finance charges.

4.7 Information for zero-based budgeting and incremental budgeting

Zero-based budgeting

ZBB requires that each activity be justified and be considered on a cost/benefit basis. Thus information is required as to the nature of the organisation and its products and their alternative methods of provision. For each of the alternatives costs/revenues and other technical estimates are required so that relevant cost/benefit analysis may be carried out.

Incremental budgeting

Managers require details of the previous period, and must be aware of any activity changes which are expected during the budget period. Forecasts of changing price levels are then applied to previous prices to value the resources expected to be consumed. Basic cost behaviour analysis will be useful when adjusting for changes in the level of activity.

4.8 Importance of long-range planning for successful budgeting

The nature and role of long-range planning are explored fully in Chapter 17.

No doubt some managers would argue that because long-range forecasting can never be completely accurate, it is pointless. However, a system of budgetary control introduced in isolation without any form of corporate or long-range planning is unlikely to yield its full potential benefit, and it is important to understand the reasons for this.

KEY POINT

A forecast is a statement of what is expected to happen; a budget is a statement of what it is reasonable to believe can be made to happen.

Firstly, a budget is not (or should not be) the same as a forecast. A forecast is a statement of what is expected to happen; a budget is a statement of what it is reasonable to believe can be made to happen. An organisation without a long-range plan probably starts with the sales forecast and perhaps tries to improve the expected results slightly by increasing the advertising budget. This modified sales forecast then becomes the budget on which the other budgets are based. However, this approach has several limitations, some of which are listed below:

- In the absence of specified long-term objectives, there are no criteria against which to evaluate possible courses of action. Managers do not know what they should be trying to achieve.
- Performance evaluation can only be on a superficial 'better/worse than last year' basis: no one has assessed the *potential* of the business.
- Many decisions e.g. capital expenditure decisions or the decision to introduce a new product, can only be taken on a long-term basis. Long-term forecasts may be inaccurate, but they are better than no forecast at all. A company with no long-range forecasting would be in dire straits when, sooner or later, sales of its existing products decline.
- There is a limit to the influence a company can exert over events in the short-term (e.g., by increased advertising). If it wishes to improve its position markedly, it must think long-term.
- Eventually some factor other than sales may become the limiting factor e.g. shortage of materials or labour. If the company has not anticipated the situation, it may simply have to live with the problem. With adequate long-range planning it might be able to avoid or overcome it.

4.9 What does management hope to get out of budgeting?

The principal advantages relate to:

- planning and co-ordination
- authorising and delegating
- evaluating performance
- discerning trends
- communicating and motivating
- control.

Planning and co-ordination

Success in business is closely related to success in planning for the future. In this context the budget serves three functions:

- It provides a formal planning framework that ensures planning does take place.
- It co-ordinates the various separate aspects of the business by providing a master plan (the *master budget)* for the business as a whole (this is particularly important in a large organisation engaged in making several different products, where otherwise it is too easy for individual managers to concentrate on their own aspects of the business).
- Though not all decisions can be anticipated, the budget provides a framework of reference within which later operating decisions can be taken.

KEY POINT

Adoption of a budget by management explicitly authorises the decisions made within it.

Authorising and delegating

Adoption of a budget by management explicitly authorises the decisions made within it. This serves two functions:

- the need continuously to ask for top management decisions is reduced;
- the responsibility for carrying out the decisions is delegated to individual managers.

Evaluating performance

One of the functions of accounting information is that it provides a basis for the measurement of managerial performance. By setting targets for each manager to achieve, the budget provides a benchmark, against which his actual performance can be assessed objectively.

Note, however, that before a budget can successfully be used for this purpose, it must be accepted as reasonable by the individual manager whose area of responsibility it covers and whose performance is to be evaluated.

The effect of budgeting and performance appraisal on people is discussed in detail later.

Discerning trends

It is important that management should be made aware as soon as possible of any new trends, whether in relation to production or marketing. The budget, by providing specific expectations with which actual performance is continuously compared, supplies a mechanism for the early detection of any unexpected trend.

Communicating and motivating

The application of budgeting within an organisation should lead to a good communications structure. Managers involved in the setting of budgets for their own responsibility need to have agreed strategies and policies communicated down to them. A good system of downwards communication should itself encourage good upwards and sideways communication in the organisation. Budgets that have been agreed by managers should provide some motivation towards their achievement.

Control

When the goals have been set for the organisation, the management uses the budgetary system to control the running of the business to evaluate the extent to which those goals are achieved. By a continuous comparison of actual performance with planned results, deviations or variances are quickly identified and appropriate action initiated. This is a fundamental aspect of the whole process: if targets were set but little or no attempt were made to measure the extent to which they were achieved, then the advantages of budgeting would be severely curtailed.

There is, however, a danger in adhering to the budget too inflexibly. Circumstances may change, and the budget should change accordingly or the control system should identify separately the variances arising due to the changed conditions. Organisations operate within a dynamic environment, and the control systems need to be appropriately flexible.

5 Inflation

5.1 Coping with inflation

Inflation was once a very conspicuous feature in the UK economy. At several points in the 1970s and 1980s inflation touched 25% per year. This had a profound impact on all aspects of accounting and it attracted a great deal of attention from practitioners, the professional bodies, academics and government.

As an issue, inflation (and its opposite, deflation) attracts little interest these days. For one thing, general price inflation has been below 3% for almost ten years. For another thing, the prices of many goods are actually falling because of advances in technology.

So, it is highly unlikely that inflation will feature prominently in any accounting examinations. The next few paragraphs just provide an overview of the topic which you need only skim read.

5.2 Inflation and price changes

DEFINITION

Inflation may be defined alternatively as:

(a) a general increase in prices; or

(b) a fall in the value of money.

The effect is that money will buy less goods or, to put it another way, the same quantity of goods will cost more money.

Effect on budgets

In inflationary conditions budgeting is made more difficult because a prediction has to be made not only of future income and expenditure in real terms, but also an estimate of the level of inflation in order to arrive at a satisfactory value of the money which must be spent.

Example

LFC bought 500 tons of material for its production process last year at a cost of £2 per ton. It expects production levels to increase by 20% next year and inflation of 5% is expected to prevail. How much should LFC budget in respect of material?

Current situation	*Increase due to production*	*Budget in real terms*	*Inflation*	*Budget in money terms*
500 tons @ £2/ton = £1,000	20% × £1,000 = £200	£1,200	5% × £1,200 = £60	£1,260

Thus, if the price level remained constant LFC could expect to spend £1,200 on material. Because of inflation, however, an additional £60 must be budgeted, resulting in a total of £1,260.

Effect on control

Inflation will lead to changes in prices, as illustrated above. Because inflation is so difficult to predict, however, it is unlikely that estimates will in fact be met. Thus there is, almost inevitably, certain to be a price variance which is due to inflation - a situation outside the control of the company. It would be possible to isolate the effects of this inflation variance, but the cost of doing so may be prohibitive. Nevertheless, without such isolation the control function becomes much more difficult.

Effect on decisions

Decisions may become clouded in inflationary conditions for two reasons:

- the problem of estimating: costs associated with different options may be wrongly adjusted for inflation
- different factors may have different rates of inflation associated with them.

For example, consider the following two options:

	Option (i)	*Option (ii)*
	£	£
Costs:		
Materials	8,000	3,500
Labour	2,000	6,000
Overheads	2,000	2,000
Total	12,000	11,500

As option (ii) is cheaper, it would be selected.

Assume, however, that in the following year rates of inflation will be as follows:

	%
Material	Nil
Labour	25
Overheads	10

Forecasts for the next year would become:

	Option (i) £	*Option (ii)* £
Materials	8,000	3,500
Labour	2,500	7,500
Overheads	2,200	2,200
	12,700	13,200

Option (ii), as a result of the differing rates of inflation, is now the less attractive of the two options. One should be aware that the actual issue here is price changes – not just inflation. As indicated above, the prices of many items has declined sharply in recent years. For example, a computing capability that thirty years ago would have cost millions of pounds can now be purchased in the high street for a few hundred pounds.

6 Uncertainty and planning

KEY POINT

If there were no uncertainty the control systems used to compare actual and budget performance would not be required.

Uncertainty is the risk element in planning. If there were no uncertainty the control systems used to compare actual and budget performance would not be required.

It is an accepted fact that the further into the future one tries to predict the more uncertain is the outcome. The reason for this is the variety of non-controllable events that could occur and thus impinge on the plans of the organisation.

Since planning also involves making choices it can be seen that it is not too different from decision-making in principle. Thus the techniques of probability estimates, random numbers and simulation modelling may be used in long-term planning. These will be considered later in this text.

7 Rolling budgets (or 'continuous budgets')

DEFINITION

'A **rolling budget** is a budget continuously updated by adding a further accounting period (month or quarter) when the earliest accounting period has expired. Beneficial where future costs and/or activities cannot be forecast reliably' (CIMA).

7.1 Rolling budget

If the budget interval is one quarter and the budget period is one year, then an initial budget is prepared for quarters 1 to 4. At the end of quarter 1 a budgetary control report is prepared comparing the actual results for quarter 1 with those budgeted for. At the same time, a budget for the following years quarter 1 is prepared and added to the budgets for quarters 2 to 4 to form the new master budget.

In this case, we have a one year rolling budget which is updated quarterly.

7.2 What distinguishes a rolling budget

Rolling budgets differ from flexible budgets in several ways:

- Flexible budgets are based on 'feedback control' which compares achievements for the month with budget targets which have been adjusted for unforeseen events beyond the control of the responsible manager
- Rolling budgets are 'feedforward control' which adjusts subsequent months targets for the changes in circumstances
- Rolling budgets tend to rise from a management philosophy which accepts that change is inevitable and forecasts are always imperfect
- Organisations that adopt rolling budgets tend to place less emphasis on budgetary control than those that do not. These forms instead will utilise additional control devices further

7.3 Advantages of rolling budgets

- Avoids wasting management effort in deriving detailed targets over long periods which will probably not happen. They can concentrate on short-term accuracy instead
- Force regular reappraisal of the budget to ensure it is up to date
- Ensures planning and control is based on the most up-to-date information available
- Avoids the de-motivational effects of unrealistic and unattainable budgets
- Overcomes the annual disruption of the budget round. There is always a budget covering the next few months
- Can be used to communicate changes in the organisation's strategy to management

7.4 Drawbacks of rolling budgets

- Increases the time and effort put into budgeting
- Constantly changing targets may make managers cynical or dispirited
- May lead to careless budgeting if managers know targets can always be changed later
- May slip into 'incremental budgeting' i.e. 'last month plus 5%' rather than be linked to strategic objectives
- May reduce control and increase bargaining if managers know they can hide poor performance behind changed targets.

Conclusion

A budget is a plan of action, normally expressed in financial terms. It provides a benchmark against which actual performance can be measured and therefore aids control of the organisation. Methods used in budgeting include flexible budgets, ZBB, incremental budgeting and rolling budgets. Inflation must be considered when preparing budgets.

SELF-TEST QUESTIONS

The practice of budgeting

1 What is a principal budget factor? (4.2)

2 Define zero-based budgeting. (4.3)

3 What are the benefits of zero based budgeting? (4.5)

4 Define incremental budgeting. (4.6)

5 Distinguish the information required for zero-based budgeting and incremental budgeting. (4.7)

6 Why is long-range planning important for successful budgeting? (4.8)

EXAM-TYPE QUESTIONS

The following two questions contain material that might feature in an examination question on budgeting. However, be aware that they are pitched at a basic level and more developed questions are given in the following two chapters.

Question 1: SKC

In 20X7, Stavros Kiriakides & Co. Ltd (SKC) of Wembley, England entered into an agreement with the Uganda Air Force for the shipment of essential supplies into Uganda. SKC paid £100,000 for 1,000 kg. of cargo space on each of twelve monthly flights in a UAF C-130 aircraft from Stansted airport to Entebbe airport. The cargo was to be sold to various government agencies in Uganda for cash (£ UK) by SKC's Uganda agent. Apart from the fee paid to the UAF, SKC's fixed administrative costs for the operation were expected to be £10,000 per year.

SKC's Uganda agent forecast that he could sell the following volumes of essential supplies in 20X8:

Whisky	1,000 cases
Long life milk	300 cases
Toilet paper	400 cases

The UK purchase cost charged to SKL and Uganda selling price charged by SKL of the three products were:

£ per case	*Whisky*	*Long life milk*	*Toilet paper*
UK purchase price	1,200	100	80
Uganda selling price	1,800	400	200

The weight per case of the three products was:

Whisky	60 kg.
Long life milk	20
Toilet paper	10

Note: the Whisky is contained in glass bottles.

Required:

Identify the mix of products carried during 20X8 that would maximise SKL's profit from the operation. Prepare a 20X8 budget statement for SKL. Suggest something that might be done with one or more or the products to improve the profitability of the operation. **(20 marks)**

Question 2: Budget

You are given the following information about a company's costs in the past two quarters.

QUARTER	*1*	*2*
Production (Units)	10,000	15,000
Sales (Units)	9,000	15,000
Costs (£'000)		
Direct material		
A	50	75
B	40	60
Production labour	180	230
Factory overheads	80	95
Depreciation	14	14
Administration	30	30
Selling expenses	29	35

For accounting purposes, the company values inventory of units at a constant standard cost.

In Quarter 3:

- Sales and production will be 18,000 units.
- Material A will rise in price by 20% relative to earlier quarters.
- Production wages will rise by 12.5% relative to earlier quarters.
- The selling price per unit will remain constant at £40.
- Expenses are all paid in the month in which they are incurred.
- Sales are all on 2 months' credit terms. 70% of sales are paid for on the due date while the remaining 30% are paid for one month after the due date.

Required:

(a) Prepare a budget profit statement for Quarter 3. **(10 marks)**

(b) Prepare a budget cash flow statement for Quarter 3. **(10 marks)**

(Total: 20 marks)

For the answers to these questions, see the 'Answers' section at the end of the book.

Chapter 15
BUDGETARY PLANNING

CHAPTER CONTENTS

This chapter explores the quantitative techniques that are used in the construction of budgets.

Objectives

When you have studied this chapter you should be able to do the following.

- Identify quantitative aids which may be used in budgetary planning and control.
- Discuss and evaluate methods for the analysis of costs into fixed and variable components.
- Give examples to demonstrate the use of forecasting techniques in the budgetary planning process.
- Explain the use of forecasting techniques in the budgetary planning process.
- Describe the use of learning curve theory in budgetary planning and control.
- Implement learning curve theory.
- Identify factors which may cause uncertainty in the setting of budgets and in the budgetary control process.
- Identify the effects of flexible budgeting in reducing uncertainty in budgeting.
- Illustrate the use of probabilities in budgetary planning and comment on the relevance of the information thus obtained.
- Explain the use of computer based models in accommodating uncertainty in budgeting and in promoting 'what-if' analysis.

1 Introduction

KEY POINT

It must be recognised that the environment is not static, and what was relevant in the past may not be relevant in the future.

The use of cost and revenue structures described in the previous chapter rests on being able to predict costs and revenues associated with a given level of activity. Such data is not always available from traditional cost-volume-profit analysis, and alternative approaches may be used. In this process historical information provides valuable guidance, but it must be recognised that the environment is not static, and what was relevant in the past may not be relevant in the future.

Practical use of certain of these techniques involves a style and level of numeracy that some readers may be uncomfortable with. This is not critical given that computer spreadsheet modelling has tended to displace traditional mathematics in many areas of management technique. For example, a spreadsheet model can develop a 'line of nearest fit' on a data series without recourse to regression analysis on the part of the accountant.

Current indications are that the examiner is unlikely to set questions that require full use of some of the more developed mathematical techniques discussed below. However, you are advised to read the relevant material in order to make yourself familiar with possible applications for those techniques.

2 Cost prediction

2.1 Alternative approaches

Any exercise in business planning or budgeting will involve the prediction of what costs will be at specified levels of activity.

KEY POINT

Five main approaches to cost prediction may be identified:

- the engineering approach
- the account analysis approach
- the high-low method
- scatter charts
- regression analysis.

Five main approaches to cost prediction may be identified:

- the engineering approach
- the account analysis approach
- the high-low method
- scatter charts
- regression analysis.

You should be familiar with these ideas from your earlier studies. The general concept involved may be illustrated by the following simple example:

The following simple example serves as a point of departure.

Example

Details of Widget production costs were as follows:

	Widgets output	*£ production costs*
April	500	6,000
May	600	7,000

Required:

(a) Calculate the variable cost per Widget

(b) Calculate the fixed costs per month

(c) Calculate what production costs will be in June if output is 550 Widgets.

Solution

A simple 'time series regression analysis' suggests that

(a) the variable cost per Widget is £10 (that is £1,000 increase in costs / 100 Widget increase in output)

(b) the fixed costs per month are £1,000 (£6,000 total costs in May less £5,000 variable costs in May (500 Widgets x £10))

(c) and hence production costs in June will be £6,500 (£1,000 fixed costs plus £5,500 variable costs).

KEY POINT

The linear model of cost behaviour is y = a + bx

where y = total costs
x = activity level
a = fixed costs
b = unit variable (or marginal) cost

In this basic model the assumption is made that the linear model of cost behaviour is valid, and therefore the relation between costs, y, and activity, x, is in the form:

$y = a + bx$

where y = total costs
x = activity level
a = fixed costs
b = unit variable (or marginal) cost

In this case - x is output in units, a is £1,000 and b is £10. One can use the model to 'interpolate' what costs will be at levels of activity are between 500 and 600 units or 'extrapolate' what costs will be at output levels of below 500 or above 600 units.

Let us turn our attention to the five alternative approaches to cost prediction specified above. Be aware that the approaches are not mutually exclusive and some cost prediction exercises may draw on several of them at the same time.

2.2 The engineering approach

KEY POINT

This approach is based on building up a complete specification of all inputs required to produce given levels of output.

This approach is based on building up a complete specification of all inputs (e.g. materials, labour, overheads) required to produce given levels of output. This approach is therefore based on technical specification, which is then costed out using expected input prices.

This approach works reasonably well in a single product or start-up situation - indeed in the latter it may be the only feasible approach. However, it is difficult to apply in a multi-product situation, especially where there are joint costs, or the exact output mix is not known.

2.3 The account analysis approach

KEY POINT

This approach uses the information contained in the ledger accounts. These are analysed and categorised as either fixed or variable (or semi-variable).

Rather than using the technical information, this approach uses the information contained in the ledger accounts. These are analysed and categorised as either fixed or variable (or semi-variable). Thus, for example, material purchase accounts would represent variable costs, office salaries a fixed cost. Since the ledger accounts are not designed for use in this way, some reorganisation and reclassification of accounts may be required.

Students should note that this is the approach implicit in many examination questions.

The problems with this approach are several:

- Inspection does not always indicate the true nature of costs. For example, today factory wages would normally be a fixed cost, with only overtime and/or bonuses as the variable element.
- Accounts are by their nature summaries, and often contain transactions of different categories.
- It rests on historic information with the problems noted above.
- One must adopt a model of cost behaviour which may be over-simplified. For example, in the Widget exercise above, how likely is it that costs fall into the simple fixed and variable categories that the model specifies?.

2.4 High-low method

The high-low method of identifying fixed costs and variable costs should be familiar to you from your earlier studies. It is also touched on in Chapter 6 (Short-term decision-making). This method uses two sets of historical data for total costs at two different volumes or levels of activity (a high volume level and a low volume level). It is assumed that these two sets of data are fully representative of fixed and variable costs. The difference between the total costs at the two activity levels must therefore be the variable costs of the difference in activity between the two levels. Where a number of observations of cost at different activity levels are possible then, the highest and lowest levels of activity are adopted as the reference points.

In an examination, you might be expected to apply the high-low method without the requirement to do so being specifically stated in the examination question. This is a technique you are expected to be thoroughly familiar with.

Example

A company has established that its total costs for 16,000 standard hours of output each month is £760,000 and its total costs for 20,000 standard hours each month is £862,000. What would be an estimate of fixed and variable costs using the high-low method?

Solution

	£
Total cost of 20,000 standard hours	862,000
Total cost of 16,000 standard hours	760,000
Variable cost of 4,000 standard hours	102,000
Variable cost per standard hour (£102,000/4,000)	£25.50

	£
Total cost of 20,000 standard hours	862,000
Variable cost of 20,000 standard hours (× £25.50)	510,000
Fixed costs each month	352,000

3 Regression

Regression is the practice of expressing the relationship between variables in the form of a mathematical relationship or equation. The Widget production example at the start of this chapter involved an element of 'regression analysis'. The mathematics we used to determine the equation for costs in the form $y = a + bx$ was essentially an exercise in regression analysis.

Regression analysis involves adopting a model for cost behaviour and then expressing the relationship between costs and activity in the form of that model. The simplest assumption is that costs have a 'linear' relationship with activity – a fixed cost component plus a variable cost per unit component. We saw that in our Widget production example.

3.1 Linear correlation

Let us say we have a number of observations for cost and output over a large number of periods, and these observations are plotted (each as an 'x') on a graph as follows:

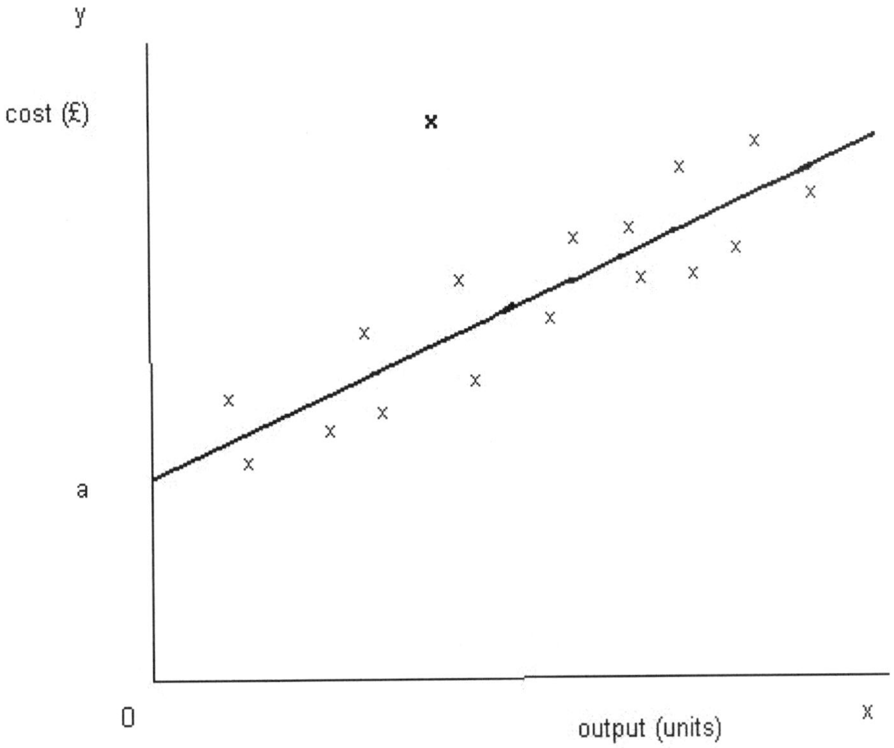

KEY POINT

Linear regression assumes that the relationship between variables can be represented in the form of a straight line graph using the equation y = a + bx.

A 'line of nearest fit' can be inserted along the various observations and this line may be adopted as the relationship between cost and output. It takes the y = a +bx form that we considered earlier. That is, it assumes a linear relationship between costs and output. The line departs the vertical axis at 'a' and rises by 'b' for each additional unit of x. It should be noted that not all of the observations are entirely consistent with this model Notably, one observation (plotted in bold) is well away from and above the line. This observation is what is commonly described as an 'outlier'.

Outlier observations are frequently encountered in both business and science. There is always the isolated case which is 'the exception to the rule' and it is not always possible to explain such cases away in terms of the model that is being used. That said, so long as one is satisfied that they are just isolated cases then they do not necessarily invalidate the model.

In a given case, one can establish values for a and b using methodologies with varying levels of mathematical refinement. One approach is simply to draw the line of nearest fit 'by eye' on a graph (on graph paper or computer chart). More mathematically sophisticated approaches are possible, but they do not always improve greatly on the results that can be achieved by simple means. Once one has a line of nearest fit in the form y = a + bx then that line can be used to predict costs at postulated levels of output.

Of course, that line is only an approximate model and most actual results are not quite on the line. However, so long as the actual results are close to and evenly distributed around the line, then we have a usable forecast model.

3.2 Other approaches to regression analysis

The relationship between cost and output need not always be strictly linear and a model can be developed to accommodate a curvilinear or exponential relationship.

Example

A total of ten observations are taken of output (units) and cost (£) at varying levels of output. Ranked in order of output levels these observations are :

Units	Costs (actual)
40	120
60	155
80	185
100	220
120	225
140	250
160	250
180	295
200	300
220	300

KEY POINT

Where the relationship between variables is curvilinear then that can be represented graphically using the equation $y = a + bx^n$.

These may be plotted on a graph with output on the horizontal axis and costs on the vertical axis. The relationship between output and cost is clearly not linear. Costs rise with output but the rise appears to diminish as output increases. The line of nearest fit is a curve with its slope diminishing as we move to the right (i.e. as output increases).

This curve can be plotted on either graph paper (using a flexi-strip, or just by eye) or on a computer chart. Either way, it appears that the curve may most closely be represented by the equation:

$y = 50 + 10x^{0.6}$, where y is costs and x is output.

The actual observations and the 'modelled equivalents' are:

Units	Costs (actual)	Costs (model)
40	120	141
60	155	167
80	185	189
100	220	208
120	225	227
140	250	244
160	250	260
180	295	276
200	300	290
220	300	304

On a graph these appear:

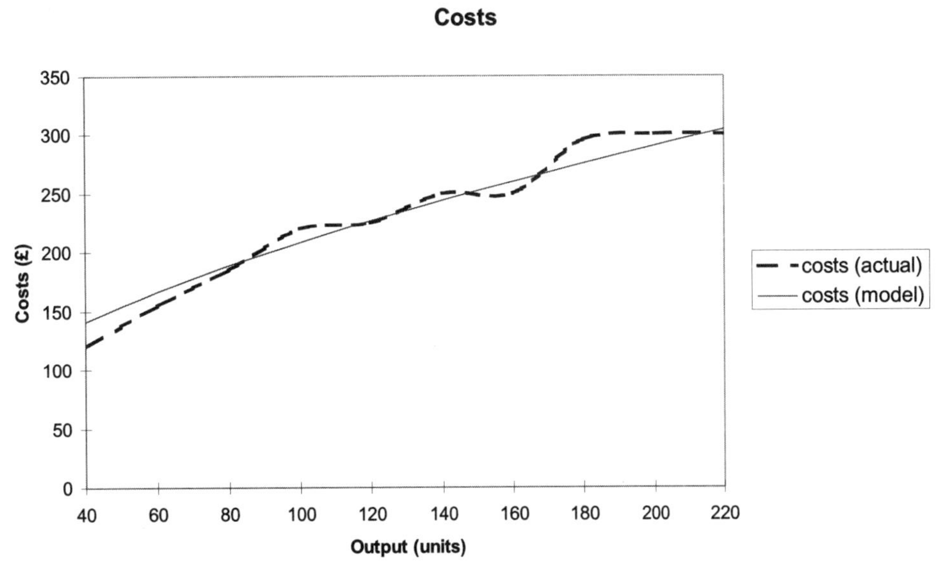

So, if we are asked to extrapolate from this model to predict what costs would be at a 250 unit level of output, then the answer would be:

$Y = 50 + 10x^{(2500.6)} = 325$

Be aware that the model is unlikely to produce a perfect forecast of what costs will be at postulated levels of output – but models never do produce perfect forecasts. A mathematical model is always a simple representation of a complex reality. That said, it gives a reasonable representation of what might be expected to happen.

4 Time series

4.1 The concept

KEY POINT

A time series is the name given to a set of observations taken at equal intervals of time. The observations can be plotted against time to give an overall picture of what is happening.

KEY POINT

The horizontal axis is always the time axis.

A time series is the name given to a set of observations taken at equal intervals of time e.g. daily, weekly, monthly etc. The observations can be plotted against time to give an overall picture of what is happening. **The horizontal axis is always the time axis.**

Examples of time series are total annual exports, monthly unemployment figures, daily average temperatures etc.

Example

The following data relates to the production (in tonnes) of floggels by the North West Engineering Co. These are the quarterly totals taken over four years from 20X2 to 20X5.

	1st Qtr	*2nd Qtr*	*3rd Qtr*	*4th Qtr*
20X2	91	90	94	93
20X3	98	99	97	95
20X4	107	102	106	110
20X5	123	131	128	130

This time series will now be graphed so that an overall picture can be gained of what is happening to the company's production figures.

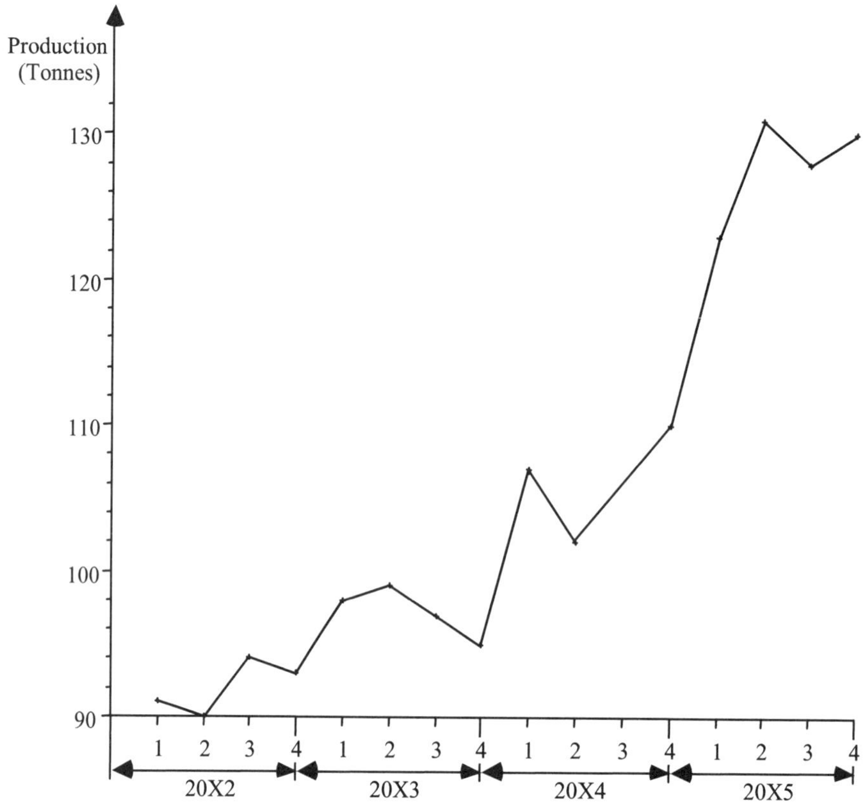

Note: that each point must be plotted at the **end** of the relevant quarter.

The graph shows clearly how the production of floggels has increased over the four-year time period. This is particularly true during the last year considered.

4.2 Variations in observations

KEY POINT

A time series is influenced by a number of factors, the most important of these being:

- long-term trends
- cyclical variations
- seasonal variation
- residual or random variations.

A time series is influenced by a number of factors, the most important of these being:

(a) **Long-term trends**

This is the way in which the graph of a time series appears to be moving over a long interval of time when the short-term fluctuations have been smoothed out. The rise or fall is due to factors which only change slowly e.g.

- increase or decrease in population
- technological improvements
- competition from abroad.

(b) **Cyclical variations**

This is the wave-like appearance of a time series graph when taken over a number of years. Generally, it is due to the influence of booms and slumps in industry. The distance in time from one peak to the next is often approximately 5 to 7 years.

(c) **Seasonal variation**

This is a regular rise and fall over specified intervals of time. The interval of time can be any length – hours, days, weeks etc, and the variations are of a periodic type with a fairly definite period e.g.

- rises in the number of goods sold before Christmas and at sale times
- rises in the demand for gas and electricity at certain times during the day

- rises in the number of customers using a restaurant at lunch-time and dinner time.

These are referred to under the general heading of 'seasonal' variations as a common example is the steady rise and fall of, for example, sales over the four seasons of the year.

However, as can be seen from the examples, the term is also used to cover regular variations over other short periods of time.

They should not be confused with cyclical variations (paragraph b) which are long-term fluctuations with an interval between successive peaks greater than one year.

(d) **Residual or random variations**

This covers any other variation which cannot be ascribed to (a), (b) or (c) above. This is taken as happening entirely at random due to unpredictable causes e.g.

- strikes
- fires
- sudden changes in taxes.

Not all time series will contain all four elements. For example, not all sales figures show seasonal variations.

4.3 A time series graph

Let us consider the following simple case:

Year	**q1**	**q2**	**q3**	**q4**
2001	25	20	23	37
2002	29	21	27	49
2003	42	29	36	64
2004	50	30	41	86

It is clear from this tabulation that Unit sales are on a rising trend throughout the four year period under review, but that there are pronounced seasonal variations around that trend. Sales appear to surge in quarter 4 (October to December) and then bottom out in quarter 2 (April to June) each year. The Unit might be a product used mainly in winter – e.g. skis or overcoats.

If we plot the sixteen observations on a time series graph, then it is possible to develop a line through those observations which represents the trend. We can construct the trend line using any of the methodologies we considered earlier in this chapter – high-low, line of nearest fit iteration or regression.

The time series graph now appears:

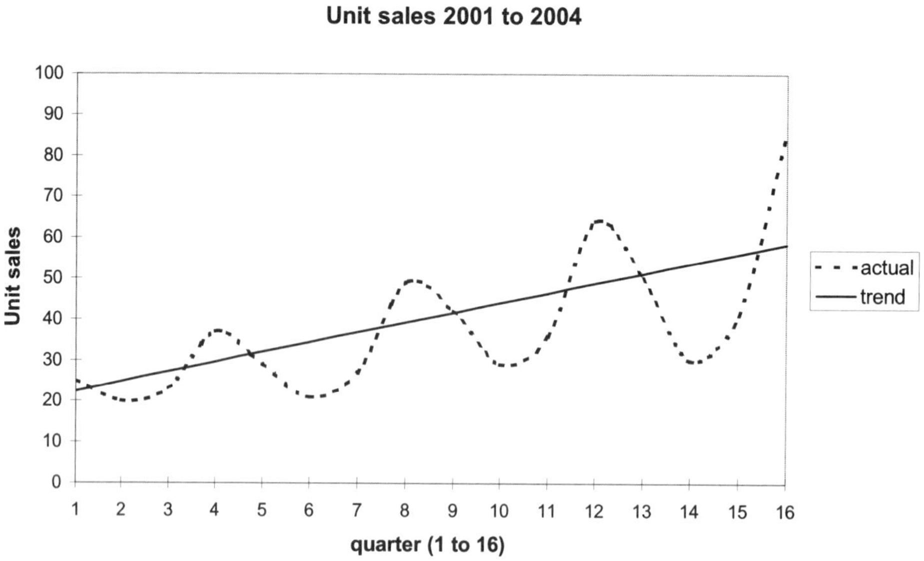

KEY POINT

In a time series model, the trend is a "de-seasonalised" representation of how the variable is moving over time.

In this case we have proceeded on the assumption that the trend is a straight line. That line follows the equation:

y = 20 + 2.4x. where y is unit sales and x is the quarter (2001 quarter 1 being x = 1)

That is, unit sales each quarter are 20 plus an additional 2.4 each quarter. Be aware that we are adopting the simplest possible model here. The trend might be represented by a curve if that were judged appropriate.

What we want to do is construct a full time series model for Unit sales in order to enable us to predict what unit sales will be in each quarter for 2005. How do we do this?

Time series analysis seeks to extract a model of activity over time from a series of past observations. We have already analysed our unit sales observations to determine the trend for unit sales (y = 20 + 2.4x). We now need to take that analysis further in order to develop a model that incorporates season variations. We will exclude cyclical variations from this model (since they are unlikely to have any impact over only four years) and random variations will appear of their own accord (see below).

There are two variations in the approaches to time series modelling that are possible.

4.4 The additive model

KEY POINT

An additive model assumes that seasonal variations are constant fixed amounts.

This approach proceeds on the assumption that seasonal variations are fixed and constant amounts above or below the trend. Such seasonal variations may be determined from our unit sales case study as follows:

Quarter	Actual	Trend	Variance	Quarter
1	25	22.4	2.6	**1.1**
2	20	24.8	-4.8	**1.2**
3	23	27.2	-4.2	**1.3**
4	37	29.6	7.4	**1.4**
5	29	32.0	-3.0	**2.1**
6	21	34.4	-13.4	**2.2**
7	27	36.8	-9.8	**2.3**
8	49	39.2	9.8	**2.4**
9	42	41.6	0.4	**3.1**

10	29	44.0	-15.0	**3.2**
11	36	46.4	-10.4	**3.3**
12	64	48.8	15.2	**3.4**
13	50	51.2	-1.2	**4.1**
14	30	53.6	-23.6	**4.2**
15	41	56.0	-15.0	**4.3**
16	86	58.4	27.6	**4.4**

The variance in each quarter is the difference between the actual observation and the trend at that quarter. Thus, we have 16 variances – four for each quarter. We can calculate the average variance for each quarter as follows:

Quarter	**Average variance**
q1	-0.30
q2	-14.20
q3	-9.85
q4	15.00

This is done on the basis of simple arithmetic averages. For example, the average for quarter 1 is:

(+2.6 –3.0 +0.4 –1.2) / 4 = – 0.30

And so, we have our time series additive model:

Trend is y = 20 + 2.4x

With Seasonal variations as follows:

Quarter 1 –0.30, Quarter 2 –14.20, Quarter 3 -9.85, Quarter 4 +15.0

The model does not fully account for all our observations in the period 2001 to 2004. For example, take 2001 quarter 4. The model predicts that units sales should be 44.6.

(that is 20 + (2.4 × 4) + 15), yet the actual was 37. There is a difference of 7.6 and in terms of our model this can only be explained as a 'random variation'. Random variations have not been built into our model and any difference between a modelled figure and an actual figure is taken to be a random variation.

We can now use our model to produce a forecast for unit sales in 2005:

Quarter	**Trend**	**Forecast**	**Quarter**
17	60.8	60.5	**5.1**
18	63.2	49.0	**5.2**
19	65.6	55.8	**5.3**
20	68.0	83.0	**5.4**

We know the trend figures and we just add or subtract the seasonal variations to these in order to produce a forecast for each quarter.

Is our additive model a good one? In this case, possibly not. One obvious observation is that our forecast Unit sales for 2005 quarter 4 is below that for 2004 quarter 4. That discrepancy could be caused by a random variation in the 2004 observation – but it could also indicate that the model does not accurately represent what is happening in this case. Can the seasonal variations be meaningfully treated as fixed lump sums which do not change over time? Maybe not. So, let us consider a different approach.

4.5 The multiplicative model

This approach proceeds on the assumption that seasonal variations are proportionate amounts (or percentages) above or below the trend. Such seasonal variations may, once again, be determined from our unit sales case study as follows:

Quarter	Actual	Trend	Variance	Quarter
1	25	22.4	11.607%	**1.1**
2	20	24.8	-19.355%	**1.2**
3	23	27.2	-15.441%	**1.3**
4	37	29.6	25.000%	**1.4**
5	29	32.0	-9.375%	**2.1**
6	21	34.4	-38.953%	**2.2**
7	27	36.8	-26.630%	**2.3**
8	49	39.2	25.000%	**2.4**
9	42	41.6	0.962%	**3.1**
10	29	44.0	-34.091%	**3.2**
11	36	46.4	-22.414%	**3.3**
12	64	48.8	31.148%	**3.4**
13	50	51.2	-2.344%	**4.1**
14	30	53.6	-44.030%	**4.2**
15	41	56.0	-26.786%	**4.3**
16	86	58.4	47.260%	**4.4**

In this case, the individual variances from trend are expressed as percentages rather than lump sums. Once again we can average the variances for each of the quarters to give us a seasonal variation:

Quarter	Average variance
q1	0.212%
q2	-34.107%
q3	-22.818%
q4	32.102%

KEY POINT

The multiplicative model assumes that seasonal variations are a given proportion (or percentage) of trend.

In the case of quarter 1, the average seasonal variance is:

(+11.607% -9.375% +0.962% -2.344%) / 4 = 0.212%

That might be expressed as an 'index figure' of 1.00212, or 100.2. It predicts that in quarter 1 the actual unit sales will be 0.212% above trend (or above 'de-seasonalised' figures).

And so, we have our time series multiplicative model:

Trend is y = 20 + 2.4x

With seasonal variations as follows:

Quarter 1 +0.2%, Quarter 2 –34.1%, Quarter 3 –22.8%, Quarter 4 +32.1%

As with the additive model, differences between 'modelled' figures and actual observations for any one quarter are explained away as 'random variations'.

We can now use our model to predict what unit sales will be in 2005:

Quarter	Trend	Forecast	Quarter
17	60.8	62.1	**5.1**
18	63.2	41.6	**5.2**
19	65.6	50.6	**5.3**
20	68.0	89.8	**5.4**

At first inspection, this forecast looks a little more realistic than the one produced earlier using an additive model. For one thing, the quarter 4 figure for 2005 is above the corresponding one for 2004 – which is what we would expect.

ACTIVITY 1

The overhead costs of RP Limited have been found to be accurately represented by the formula:

$$y = £10,000 + £0.25x$$

where y is monthly overhead cost and x is the activity level measured in Units. Monthly activity levels in terms of Units may be represented by the following tome series model:

$$x = 100,000 + 30b$$

Where x is the de-seasonalised activity level and be represents the month number. In month 240, the seasonal index value is 108.

Calculate the overhead costs for month 240.

Feedback to this activity is at the end of the chapter.

4.6 Choice of time series model

The management accountant often has to judge what is the most appropriate form of model to use in a business planning exercise. Should the trend be a straight line, or should it be curved? Should a multiplicative or an additive model be used? What methodology should be used to determine the equation for the trend line?

There are no right answers to these questions and the accountant usually has to use his/her judgement as to what is appropriate in any given situation. However, some advice can be offered. The essential features of the additive and multiplicative models may be compared as follows:

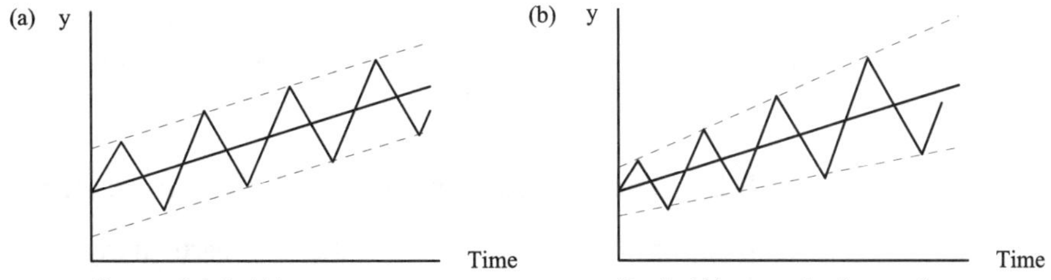

Constant band width.
Use additive model.

Band width proportional to trend.
Use multiplicative model.

KEY POINT

The selection or design of an appropriate model for any particular exercise will involve a substantial element of judgement. There is often no absolutely right approach.

If the seasonal variations appear to be getting larger in absolute terms over time, then it is probably most appropriate to use a multiplicative model.

If comparison of 'modelled figures' (those predicted by applying the model to each of the actual quarters) with actual figures appears to throw up large random variations, then that may point to a defect in the model that is being used. Take the figures we calculated above in our discussion of the additive model.

Quarter	Actual	Model	Random variations
1	25	22.1	2.9
2	20	10.6	9.4
3	23	17.4	5.7
4	37	44.6	-7.6
5	29	31.7	-2.7
6	21	20.2	0.8
7	27	27.0	0.1
8	49	54.2	-5.2
9	42	41.3	0.7
10	29	29.8	-0.8
11	36	36.6	-0.5
12	64	63.8	0.2
13	50	50.9	-0.9
14	30	39.4	-9.4
15	41	46.2	-5.2
16	86	73.4	12.6
		Total:	0.0

The random variations appear to be very large indeed relative to the model. For example, in quarter 2 the random variation is 89% of the model. That is too large for the model to be entirely satisfactory.

One suspects that the model would need some refinement – possibly a curved trendline and multiplicative seasonal indexation – before it would be acceptable in practice.

As an aside, note that the random variations add up to nil. This is mathematically inevitable and provides a useful check on the accuracy of workings.

5 The learning curve phenomenon

5.1 Background

Accountants are often said to assume that, within the relevant range of activity, costs display linear characteristics so that the variable cost per unit and the total fixed cost remain unchanged and can be depicted as lines (rather than curves) on a break-even chart. This section considers the learning curve phenomenon where the linear assumption is dropped.

5.2 The phenomenon stated and illustrated

It has been observed in some industries, particularly where skilled labour predominates, that as more of the same units are produced, there is a reduction in the time taken to manufacture them so that a learning process occurs when production on a new item is commenced. Eventually the learning process will end and a steady state is reached.

Experience has shown that in certain industries, or for certain types of activity, where the work force begins work on something new and gains experience over time, the time to produce additional units of output or to complete certain tasks gets less each time. The reduction in labour times to do the work can be predicted with reasonable accuracy using a mathematical model. This model is called the learning curve, or the learning curve phenomenon.

The learning curve phenomenon states that each time the number of units produced is doubled, the cumulative average time per unit is reduced by a constant percentage amount.

If this constant reduction is 20%, this is referred to as an 80% learning curve. Where an 80% learning curve applies, then each time that total output to date is doubled, the average time to complete a unit, for all units completed to date, is 80% of what it was before.

Similarly, if the constant rate of reduction in the average time is 10%, a 90% learning curve applies. with a 90% learning curve, then each time that total output to date is doubled, the average time to complete a unit, for all units completed to date, is 90% of what it was before.

KEY POINT

The learning curve phenomenon states that each time the number of units produced is doubled, the cumulative average time per unit is reduced by a constant percentage.

Suppose that it has taken 400 direct labour hours to manufacture the first unit of a new product. It is anticipated that a 75% learning curve will be experienced. A table can be drawn up with the following headings and calculations:

(1) Cumulative number of units	*(2)* Cumulative average time per unit	*(1) × (2)* Cumulative total hours
1	400	400
2	300 (75% of 400)	600
4	225 (75% of 300)	900

The first two columns form the basis for the calculations as the cumulative total hours in the third column are obtained by multiplying together the figures in columns (1) and (2). As the output doubles the cumulative average time per unit is 75% of the previous figure. Therefore, if one unit has been produced already taking 400 hours, the production of one more similar unit will only take (600 – 400) i.e. 200 hours in the situation of a 75% learning curve. Once two units have been produced, and the learning process continues, the production of two more units will take only (900 – 600) i.e. 300 hours. This represents 150 hours per unit.

ACTIVITY 2

Determine the cumulative total hours for 8 units and hence determine the total time to make the last four units.

If labour and production overheads cost £20 per hour and direct materials cost £4,000 per unit, what would be the cost of making units 5 – 8?

Feedback to this activity is at the end of the chapter.

ACTIVITY 3

A boat-building firm has just started making a new type of boat. The direct material costs for a boat are £5,000 and the time required to produce the first boat was 1,000 hours. The cost of labour and overheads is £15 per hour. To date, only two boats of this type have been made.

It is expected that an 80% learning curve will apply. A large customer has asked for a quotation for 6 boats. How much should the firm charge for these 6 boats if it wishes to make a profit margin of 20% on cost?

Feedback to this activity is at the end of the chapter

5.3 Learning curve equation

KEY POINT

The learning curve describing the cumulative average time per unit plotted against cumulative number of units can be represented by an equation of the form:

$y = ax^{-b}$ *or* $y = \frac{a}{x^b}$

where y = cumulative average time
a = time for producing the first unit
x = cumulative number of units
b = index of learning (0<b<1)

The index of learning, b = $\frac{\text{logarithm of the inverse of the learning rate(in decimal form)}}{\text{Logarithm of 2}}$

The learning curve describing the cumulative average time per unit plotted against cumulative number of units can be represented by an equation of the form:

$$y = ax^{-b} \text{ or } y = \frac{a}{x^b}$$

where	y	=	cumulative average time
	a	=	time for producing the first unit
	x	=	cumulative number of units
	b	=	index of learning (0<b<1)

$$\text{The index of learning, b} = \frac{\text{logarithm of the inverse of the learning rate (in decimal form)}}{\text{logarithm of 2}}$$

Therefore, for a 75% learning curve the index of learning is given by:

$$b = \frac{\log \frac{1}{0.75}}{\log 2}$$

$$= \frac{\log 1.333}{\log 2}$$

$$= \frac{0.1249}{0.3010}$$

= 0.415 = index of learning for a 75% learning curve

The following is a calculational check using the figures in the previous illustration, where one unit had taken 400 hours and a cumulative of four units of production is assumed:

$$y = ax^{-b}$$

where	y	=	cumulative average time per unit		
	a	=	400		
	x	=	4		
	b	=	0.415		
	y	=	$400 \times 4^{-0.415}$	=	225.01 hours

This can be evaluated on a scientific calculator as follows:

(a) Enter 4

(b) Press [x^y]

(c) Enter 0.415

(d) Press [±], [=], [×]

(e) Enter 400

(f) Press [=]

This gives y = 225.01 (2 dp)

(NB: on some calculators, the first [=] may not be necessary.)

Therefore, the cumulative average time per unit when a total of four units are produced is 225 hours (as previously determined).

For a cumulative production of three units, one unit having been produced in 400 units, the calculations would be as follows:

$$y = 400 \times (3)^{-0.415}$$
$$= 253.5 \text{ (the cumulative average time per unit)}$$

The cumulative total time for three units would be 760.5 hours (3 × 253.5).

ACTIVITY 4

If the learning curve rate is 85%, what is the value of b in the learning curve model $y = ax^{-b}$?

Feedback to this activity is at the end of the chapter.

Pricing example

The following worked example illustrates that the benefit of the learning curve relates to labour *and* labour-related costs, but *not* to the cost of materials.

A company wishes to determine the minimum price it should charge a customer for a special order. The customer has requested a quotation for ten machines; he might subsequently place an order for a further ten. Material costs are £30 per machine. It is estimated that the first batch of ten machines will take 100 hours to manufacture and an 80% learning curve is expected to apply. Labour plus variable overhead costs amount to £3 per hour. Setting-up costs are £1,000 regardless of the number of machines made.

(a) What is the minimum price the company should quote for the initial order if there is no guarantee of further orders?

(b) What is the minimum price for the follow-on order?

(c) What would be the minimum price if both orders were placed together?

(d) Having completed the initial orders for a total of twenty machines (price at the minimum levels recommended in (a) and (b)), the company thinks that there would be a ready market for this type of machine if it brought the unit selling price down to £45. At this price, what would be the profit on the first 140 'mass-production' models (i.e., after the first twenty machines) assuming that marketing costs totalled £250?

Initial order

If there is no guarantee of a follow-up order, the setting-up costs must be recovered on the initial order. Costs are, therefore, as follows:

	£
Material (10 × £30)	300
Labour and variable overhead (100 × £3)	300
Setting-up cost	1,000
Total	£1,600
Minimum price each (£1,600 ÷ 10)	£160

Follow-on order

The setting-up costs have been recovered on the initial order. Output is doubled; therefore, average time for each group of ten machines is reduced to

100×0.8
$= 80$ hours

i.e. cumulative time for twenty machines	=	160 hours
∴ Time for second group of ten	=	time for first 20 – time for first 10
	=	160 – 100
	=	60 hours

Costs are therefore

	£
Material (10 × £30)	300
Labour and variable overhead (60 × £3)	180
Total	£480
Minimum price each	£48

Both orders together

Total costs are:

	£
Material	600
Labour (160 hours)	480
Setting-up cost	1,000
Total	£2,080
Minimum price each	£104

This is, of course, the mean of the two previous prices: cumulative costs are the same but they are recorded evenly over twenty units instead of most of the cost being 'loaded' onto the first ten units.

The time spent on the first 140 mass production models is calculated as follows:

Working in units of 10 machines, $y = ax^{-b}$ where $a = 100$

$$b = \frac{\log \frac{1}{0.8}}{\log 2}$$

$= 0.3219$

Average time/unit for first 2 units (i.e. first 20 machines)

	=	$100 \times 2^{-0.3219}$
	=	80 hours
Total time for first 2 units	=	80×2
	=	160 hours (as before)

Average time per unit for first 16 units (i.e. first 160 machines)

	=	$100 \times 16^{-0.3219}$
	=	40.96 hours
Total time for first 16 units	=	40.96×16
	=	655.36 hours

Hence total time for units 3 to 16 (i.e. the 140 mass-produced units)
= (655.36 – 160) hours
= 495.36 hours

Cost of first 140 mass-production models

	£
Material (140 × £30)	4,200
Labour and variable overhead (495.36 × £3)	1,486
Marketing	250
Total cost	5,936
Revenue	6,300
Profit	£364

6 Uncertainty and budgeting

Since budgets are predictions and plans for the future non-controllable events will make the outcome of particular actions uncertain.

There are a number of factors which contribute to the uncertainty surrounding the budget setting and budgetary control process.

Some of the factors may be internal to the organisation but not controllable in the short-term. These would include productivity and efficiency factors which may be controlled in the longer-term by re-training and investment.

However many of the factors are external to the organisation for example:

- sales may be lower due to recession
- customers may be lost due to lack of goods due to lower productivity
- inflation
- government fiscal policy
- natural disasters
- changes in supplier costs and terms of supply.

7 Flexible budgets

7.1 The concept

DEFINITION

A **flexible budget** is one which, by recognising the distinction between fixed and variable costs, is designed to change in response to changes in output.

KEY POINT

The concept of responsibility accounting requires the use of flexible budgets for control purposes.

The concept of responsibility accounting requires the use of flexible budgets for control purposes. Many of the costs under a manager's control are variable and will therefore change if the level of activity is different from that in the budget. It would be unreasonable to criticise a manager for incurring higher costs if these were a result of a higher than planned volume of activity. Conversely, if the level of activity is low, costs can be expected to fall and the original budget must be amended to reflect this.

A variance report based on a flexible budget therefore compares actual costs with the costs budgeted for the level of activity actually achieved. It does not explain any change in budgeted volume, which should be reported on separately.

7.2 Flexible budgeting

The key points to note are:

- A fixed budget is set at the beginning of the period, based on estimated production. This is the original budget.
- This is then **flexed** to correspond with the actual level of activity.
- The result is compared with actual costs, and differences (variances) are reported to the managers responsible.

Example

Bug Ltd manufactures one uniform product only, and activity levels in the assembly department vary widely from month to month. The following statement shows the departmental overhead budget based on an average level of activity of 20,000 units production per four-week period and the actual results for four weeks in October.

	Budget average for four-week period	*Actual for 1 to 28 October*
	£	£
Indirect labour - variable	20,000	19,540
Consumables - variable	800	1,000
Other variable overheads	4,200	3,660
Depreciation - fixed	10,000	10,000
Other fixed overheads	5,000	5,000
	40,000	39,200
Production (units)	20,000	17,600

You are required:

(a) to prepare a columnar flexible four-week budget at 16,000, 20,000 and 24,000 unit levels of production;

(b) to prepare two performance reports based on production of 17,600 units by the department in October, comparing actual with:

(i) average four-week budget; and

(ii) flexible four-week budget for 17,600 units of production;

(c) to state which comparison ((b) (i) or (b) (ii)) would be the more helpful in assessing the foreman's effectiveness and why; and

(d) to sketch a graph of how the flexible budget total behaves over the 16,000 to 24,000 unit range of production.

Solution

(a) Production level	*16,000 units*	*20,000 units*	*24,000 units*
	£	£	£
Variable costs:			
Indirect labour	16,000	20,000	24,000
Consumables	640	800	960
Other overheads	3,360	4,200	5,040
	20,000	25,000	30,000

Fixed costs:			
Depreciation	10,000	10,000	10,000
Other overheads	5,000	5,000	5,000
	35,000	40,000	45,000

(b) (i)

	Average four-week budget	*Actual results*	*Variances fav./(adv.)*
	£	£	£
Indirect labour	20,000	19,540	460
Consumables	800	1,000	(200)
Other variable overheads	4,200	3,660	540
Depreciation	10,000	10,000	-
Other fixed overheads	5,000	5,000	-
	40,000	39,200	800

(ii)

	Flexed four-week budget	*Actual results*	*Variances fav./(adv.)*
Sales (units)	17,600	17,600	-
	£	£	£
Indirect labour	17,600	19,540	(1,940)
Consumables	704	1,000	(296)
Other variable overheads	3,696	3,660	36
Depreciation	10,000	10,000	-
Other fixed overheads	5,000	5,000	-
	37,000	39,200	(2,200)

(c) The flexed budget provides more useful data for comparison because:

(i) the fixed original budget makes no distinction between fixed and variable costs;

(ii) hence no data is available concerning the appropriate level of costs at the actual production level;

(iii) this would lead to the conclusion that the foreman had done well, when in fact costs had not fallen nearly as much as anticipated for the actual production;

(iv) responsibility for the production shortfall is not known.

(d) Graph of costs in the production range 16,000 to 24,000 units

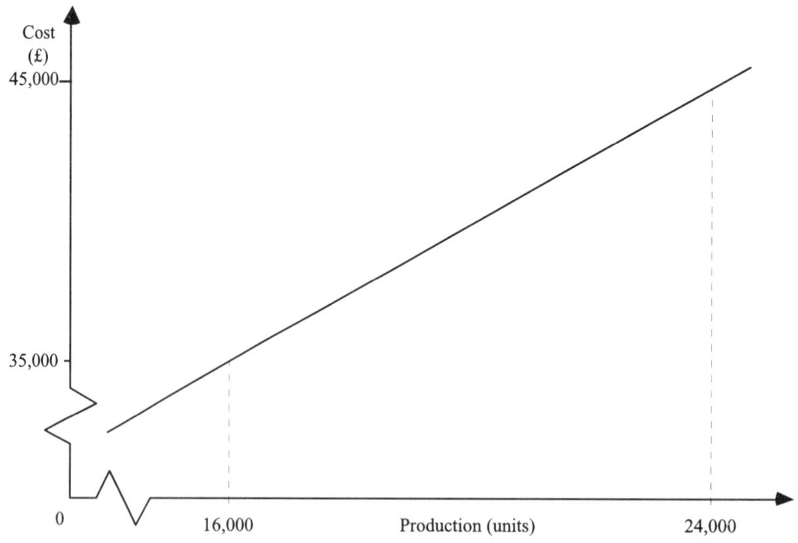

7.3 Flexible budgeting and management attitudes

The nature of cost behaviour patterns is not changed according to whether fixed or flexible budgets are used. What is changed is the way in which management view costs.

Example

The Alic Co Ltd has many small customers. Work measurement of the debtors' ledger shows that one clerk can handle 2,000 customer accounts. The company employs 30 clerks on the debtors' ledger at a salary of £3,600 each. The outlook for next year is of a decline in the number of customers from 59,900 to 56,300. However, management decides not to reduce the number of clerks.

Show the effect of this decision if debtors' ledger clerks' salaries are treated as:

(a) variable expenses per customer per year
(b) fixed overhead.

Solution

		£
(a)	Allowed expense $56{,}300 \times \dfrac{£3{,}600}{2{,}000}$	101,340
	Actual expenditure $30 \times £3{,}600$	108,000
	Adverse variance	6,660 A

		£
(b)	Allowed expense	108,000
	Actual expenditure	108,000
		Nil

Neither approach says whether the management decision was right. Approach (a), however, does give the cost of that decision.

Consequently the way costs are classified can influence the way management views costs, and ultimately the decisions that are made.

ACTIVITY 4

A company's production overhead budget is based on the principle that each unit of production incurs variable overhead cost of £5.40 and that each month fixed production overhead of £6,750 is incurred.

During June the budgeted output was 460 units and actual output was 455 units.

Calculate the allowed expense for June.

Feedback to this activity is at the end of the chapter.

8 Probabilities

8.1 Introduction

We now turn to the use of probabilities to assist the budgeting process. This involves fairly straightforward applications of simple probabilities and the use of expected values.

Example

Consider the following example.

The following information and estimates were available for the management of Z Ltd.

For the year ahead the following cost and demand estimates have been made:

Unit variable costs:

Pessimistic	Probability	0.15	£7.00 per unit
Most likely	Probability	0.65	£6.50 per unit
Optimistic	Probability	0.20	£6.20 per unit

Demand estimates at various prices (units):

			Price per unit	
			£13.50	*£14.50*
Pessimistic	Probability	0.3	45,000	35,000
Most likely	Probability	0.5	60,000	55,000
Optimistic	Probability	0.2	70,000	68,000

(Unit variable costs and demand estimates are statistically independent.)

You are required to calculate the expected contribution at each selling price.

Solution

Expected contribution = expected demand × expected contribution per unit.

Expected variable costs per unit = $£7 \times 0.15 + £6.50 \times 0.65 + £6.20 \times 0.20$
= £6.515 per unit

Selling price = £13.50

Expected contribution per unit = £13.50 - £6.515 = £6.985

Expected demand = $45 \times 0.3 + 60 \times 0.5 + 70 \times 0.2$ = 57,500 units

∴ Expected contribution = £401,637.50

Selling price = £14.50

Expected contribution per unit = £14.50 - £6.515 = £7.985

Expected demand = $35 \times 0.3 + 55 \times 0.5 + 68 \times 0.2$ = 51,600 units

∴ Expected contribution = £412,026

Further example

E Ltd manufactures a hedge-trimming device which has been sold at £16 per unit for a number of years. The selling price is to be reviewed and the following information is available on costs and likely demand.

The standard variable cost of manufacture is £10 per unit and an analysis of the cost variances for the past 20 months shows the following pattern which the production manager expects to continue in the future.

Adverse variances of +10% of standard variable cost occurred in ten of the months.

Nil variances occurred in six of the months.

Favourable variances of –5% of standard variable cost occurred in four of the months.

Monthly data

Fixed costs have been £4 per unit on an average sales level of 20,000 units but these costs are expected to rise in the future and the following estimates have been made for the total fixed cost:

		£
Optimistic estimate	(Probability 0.3)	82,000
Most likely estimate	(Probability 0.5)	85,000
Pessimistic estimate	(Probability 0.2)	90,000

The demand estimates at the two new selling prices being considered are as follows:

If the selling price per unit is		£17	£18
demand would be:			
Optimistic estimate	(Probability 0.2)	21,000 units	19,000 units
Most likely estimate	(Probability 0.5)	19,000 units	17,500 units
Pessimistic estimate	(Probability 0.3)	16,500 units	15,500 units

It can be assumed that all estimates and probabilities are independent.

You are required

(a) to advise management, based on the information given above, whether they should alter the selling price and, if so, the price you would recommend;

(b) to calculate the expected profit at the price you recommend.

Solution

(a) ***Step 1***

Calculate the expected variable cost per unit.

			Probability	*Expected VC*
		£		£
10 + 10%	=	11.00	0.5	5.50
10	=	10.00	0.3	3.00
10 – 5%	=	9.50	0.2	1.90
				10.40

Step 2

Calculate the expected demand at £17 and £18.

Demand	*£17 Probability*	*Expected demand*	*Demand*	*£18 Probability*	*Expected demand*
21,000	0.2	4,200	19,000	0.2	3,800
19,000	0.5	9,500	17,500	0.5	8,750
16,500	0.3	4,950	15,500	0.3	4,650
		18,650			17,200

Step 3

Calculate the expected contribution at each of the selling prices.

*(**Note:** since **not** altering the selling price is an option to be considered, the contribution at the present selling price of £16 should be calculated.)*

	£	£	£
Selling price per unit	16.00	17.00	18.00
Variable cost per unit	10.40	10.40	10.40
Contribution per unit	5.60	6.60	7.60
Expected demand in units	20,000	18,650	17,200
Total contribution	112,000	123,090	130,720

Recommendation: increase selling price to £18 per unit.

(b) Expected profit

	£
Contribution	130,720
Fixed costs (see below)	85,100
Profit	45,620

Fixed cost calculation:

Estimate £	*Probability*	*Expected value* £
82,000	0.3	24,600
85,000	0.5	42,500
90,000	0.2	18,000
		85,100

Conclusion

There are several alternative approaches to predicting costs, including the engineering approach, the account analysis approach, the high-low method, scatter charts and regression analysis. The analysis of a time series may provide information that can be used in forecasting. In industries that use skilled labour, a learning curve effect on the time taken for production may be identified. Flexible budgets reflect the distinction between fixed and variable costs in order to make the comparison of actual and budget results most meaningful.

SELF-TEST QUESTIONS

Cost prediction

1 What is the equation of a straight line? (2.1)

Time series

2 What is time series analysis? (4.1)

3 What is a seasonal variation? (4.2)

4 What distinguishes the additive from the multiplicative time series model? (4.5) (4.5)

The learning curve phenomenon

5 How does the learning process affect production times? (5)

Flexible budgets

6 What is a flexible budget? (7.1-7.2)

EXAM-TYPE QUESTIONS

Question 1: RT plc

RT plc operates a rail link between a city centre and an airport. The following information has been extracted from its records.

Number of passengers carried

Quarter	*Year 1*	*Year 2*
1	15,620	34,100
2	15,640	29,920
3	16,950	29,550
4	34,840	56,680

The trend equation for the number of passengers carried has been found to be:

$$x = 10{,}000 + 4{,}200q$$

where x is passenger numbers and q is time period (with year 1, quarter 1 having the value q = 1).

It has been determined that the relationships between individual operating costs (y) and the number of passengers carried (x) are as follows:

Premises:	$y = 260{,}000$
Premises staff:	$y = 65{,}000 + 0.5x$
Power:	$y = 13{,}000 + 4x$
Traincrew:	$y = 32{,}000 + 3x$
Sundries:	$y = 9{,}100 + x$

Required:

(a) Develop a multiplicative time series model and use it to predict the number of passengers to be carried in year 3, quarter 3 (that is, quarter 11 for the purposes of the trend equation).

(b) Explain why the equation for Traincrew costs might be in the form it is.

(c) Use the model you developed in answer to (a) in order to predict the value of each item of cost and cost in total in year 3, quarter 3.

(d) Explain why there may be differences between your predicted passenger numbers/costs and the actual numbers/costs for year 3, quarter 3.

(e) Discuss the proposition that RT plc should use non-financial performance measures in order to assess the effectiveness of its service and suggest any such measures that you consider appropriate. **(25 marks)**

Question 2: DKS

DKS manufactures a product called the Unit. One batch of Units is produced and sold each quarter. It is not possible to hold stocks of Units for any significant period.

At a batch size of 12,000 Units, the variable cost of a Unit is £15. Variable costs are all labour-related and Unit production involves an 80 per cent learning curve. Market research indicates that demand per quarter for Units relates as follows to the selling price per Unit:

Selling price per Unit	Sales of Units
£	
25	11,750
30	11,500
35	8,750
40	7,500
45	6,000

There is a complete discontinuity between the batches as regards learning curve effects.

You may assume that the variable cost per Unit (*h*) on an 80 per cent learning curve may be obtained from the following formula, where *B* is the batch size and *a* is a constant:

$h = a/B^{0.322}$

Required:

Calculate the optimum batch size for Unit production.

Question 3: Learning Curve Theory

'The learning curve is a simple mathematical model but its application to management accounting problems requires careful thought.'

Required:

Having regard to the above statement:

(a) explain the 'cumulative average-time' model commonly used to represent learning curve effects.

(b) sketch two diagrams to illustrate, in regard to a new product, the relative impacts of 70 per cent, 80 per cent and 90 per cent learning curves on:

(i) cumulative average hours per unit,

(ii) cumulative hours taken.

(c) explain the use of learning curve theory in budgeting and budgetary control; explain the difficulties that the management accountant may encounter in such use.

For the answer to this question, see the 'Answers' section at the end of the book.

FEEDBACK TO ACTIVITY 1

Trend activity = (100,000) + (30 x 240) = 107,200

Seasonalised activity = 107,200 x 1.08 = 115,776

Costs = £10,000 + (£0.25 x 115,776) = £38,944 (or, say £39,000).

FEEDBACK TO ACTIVITY 2

Cumulative number of units	*Cumulative average time per unit*	*Cumulative total hours*
8	168.75 (75% of 225)	1,350

Therefore time for last 4 items = 1,350 – 900 = 450 hours.

Cost = (4 x £4,000) for direct materials and (450 x £20) for labour and overheads, giving a total cost of £25,000 for the four units.

FEEDBACK TO ACTIVITY 3

Number made to date	Cumulative average time per unit hours	Total time to date hours
1	1,000	
2	800	1,600
4	640	
8	512	4,096
Time for units 3 – 8		2,496

Costs and pricing

		£
Materials	(6 x £5,000)	30,000
Labour and overhead	(2,496 x £15)	37,440
Total cost		67,440
Profit mark-up	(20%)	13,488
Total price		80,928
Price per boat	(£80,928/6)	£13,488

This price might be rounded to £13,500.

FEEDBACK TO ACTIVITY 4

$$b = \frac{\log(1/0.85)}{\log 2} = \frac{\log 1.1765}{\log 2}$$

$$b = \frac{0.0706}{0.3010} = 0.234$$

FEEDBACK TO ACTIVITY 5

(455 units × £5.40) + £6,750 = £9,207

Chapter 16
BUDGETARY CONTROL

CHAPTER CONTENTS

This chapter concludes our exploration of budgeting with a critical review of various aspects of budgeting practice. Particular attention is given to the relationship between budgeting and the behaviour of people in the organisation.

Objectives

When you have studied this chapter you should be able to do the following.

- Identify the factors which affect human behaviour in budgetary planning and control.
- Compare and contrast ways in which alternative management styles may affect the operation of budgetary planning and control systems.
- Explain budgeting as a bargaining process between people.
- Explain the conflict between personal and corporate aspirations and its impact on budgeting.
- Explain the application of contingency theory to the budgeting process.
- Discuss the impact of political, social, economic and technological change on budgeting.
- Critically review the use of budgetary planning and control.
- Enumerate and evaluate the strengths and weaknesses of alternative budget models such as fixed and flexible, rolling, activity based, zero-based and incremental.
- Identify the effects on staff and management of the operation of budgetary planning and control.
- Identify and appraise current developments in budgeting.

1 Introduction

KEY POINT

If budgetary control is to be successful, attention must be paid to behavioural aspects i.e. the effect of the system on people in the organisation and *vice versa*.

If budgetary control is to be successful, attention must be paid to behavioural aspects i.e. the effect of the system on people in the organisation and *vice versa.* Poor performance and results are more often due to the method of implementation and subsequent operation of a system, with a failure to allow properly for the human side of the enterprise, than to the system itself. The management needs to be fully committed to the budgeting system, and through leadership and education lower levels of management in the organisation should be similarly committed and motivated.

Budgets are one important way of influencing the behaviour of managers within an organisation. There are very few, if any, decisions and actions that a manager in an organisation can take which do not have some financial effect and which will not subsequently be reflected in a comparison between budgeted and actual results. This all-embracing nature of budgets is probably the most important advantage that a budgetary system has over most other systems in a typical organisation.

2 Behavioural aspects of budgeting

2.1 Roles of budgets

Budgets can take on a number of different roles in any organisation and each has important behavioural implications. The following main roles can be identified in many organisations:

(a) **Authorisation**

KEY POINT

There is a tendency in an underspend situation, when approaching the end of the financial year, to spend money when it is not really necessary to do so.

Once a budget has been agreed, it is not interpreted by many managers merely as an authorisation to 'spend up to the budget' but rather as an authorisation to 'spend the budget', otherwise there is a real fear that the following year's budget will be cut. Therefore, there is a tendency in an underspend situation, when approaching the end of the financial year, to spend money when it is not really necessary to do so.

(b) **Planning**

The budgeting system provides a formal, co-ordinated approach to short-term planning throughout the organisation. Each manager has a framework in which to plan for his own area of responsibility. Without budgeting it is difficult to imagine an alternative system, affecting all parts of an organisation, in which such planning could take place.

(c) **Forecasting**

KEY POINT

Budgetary slack is a common phenomenon in practice.

Short-term budgets covering the next one or two years may provide the basis for making forecasts beyond that period e.g. in appraising a project with a five year life, data may be extracted from the budgets and used to make forecasts for another three years. The danger with this approach is that, if the budgets are incorrect, the extrapolations beyond the budget period are also likely to be wrong and the financial analysis of the project may be unsound. The budgets could be incorrect because 'slack' has been built into them. Budgetary slack is a common phenomenon in practice. It involves building 'padding' into a cost or expense budget to allow some leeway in actual performance; in a revenue budget it involves a deliberate understatement of budgeted sales or other revenue.

(d) **Communicating and co-ordinating**

A budgeting system encourages good communications and co-ordination in an organisation. Information about objectives, strategies and policies has to be communicated down from top management and all the individual budgets in an organisation need to be co-ordinated in order to arrive at the master budget.

(e) **Motivation**

KEY POINT

Agreed budgets should motivate individual managers towards their achievement, which in turn should assist the organisation in attaining its longer-term objectives.

Agreed budgets should motivate individual managers towards their achievement, which in turn should assist the organisation in attaining its longer-term objectives. Motivational effects and the concept of budget difficulty are dealt with later.

(f) **Evaluation of performance**

KEY POINT

A comparison between the predetermined budget and the actual results is the most common way in which an individual manager's performance is judged on a regular basis.

A comparison between the predetermined budget and the actual results is the most common way in which an individual manager's performance is judged on a regular basis. The way this appraisal is made and how deviations are dealt with may influence how the individual manager behaves in the future. This role is also the subject of further discussion later.

The various roles identified for budgets may not all prevail at the same time, and some may assume greater importance than others. This will depend on each individual organisation and its operational environment. Some of the roles are indeed likely to conflict with others.

2.2 Problems associated with implementing budgetary control

- There may be a general fear and misunderstanding about the purpose of budgetary control. It is often regarded as a penny-pinching exercise rather than recognised as a tool of management at all levels in an organisation structure. If this tends to be the attitude, a carefully planned campaign of education and understanding should be undertaken. Managers should be encouraged to discover what is in the budgetary control system for them.
- Employees may become united against management and devote their energies to finding excuses for not meeting targets. Targets that are realistic, and are seen by the employees as being realistic, are what is required. Good communications involving consultation and participation should help to minimise this problem.
- One of the key roles in any organisation is at the supervisor/foreman level where the continual interface between management and employees exists. The leadership and motivational function of a supervisor or foreman is very important if the work is to be done and targets are to be achieved.
- The breaking down of an organisation into many sub-areas of managerial responsibility can lead to sub-optimisation problems as far as the whole company is concerned i.e. the optimisation of an individual manager's department or section at the expense of the organisation overall. Such dysfunctional behaviour should be minimised. It reflects a lack of goal congruence.
- If budgets are built up from the base of the organisation, with individual departmental budgets providing the input to the overall master budget, the tendency to incorporate slack into budgets needs to be carefully monitored.
- Some desirable projects could be lost because they were not foreseen and therefore not budgeted for. The system needs to be flexible enough to avoid this problem.

All of these problems really relate to criticisms of the manner in which budgetary control systems tend to be operated, rather than of budgetary control *per se*.

2.3 Motivating effect of budgets

KEY POINT

Managers do not usually work to their full potential if they know that a lower level of performance will still meet the budget. If the budget is too difficult, because it is based on idealistic levels of performance, managers become discouraged at what they regard as an unattainable standard.

Empirical evidence suggests that if a budget is set such that it does not contain a suitable element of targetry (i.e. difficulty), then actual performance should be a little better than the budget but it will not be optimised. In other words, managers do not usually work to their full potential if they know that a lower level of performance will still meet the budget (and they are evaluated on the basis of a favourable result compared with the budget). On the other hand, if the budget is too difficult, because it is based on idealistic levels of performance, managers become discouraged at what they regard as an unattainable standard. The effect of such demotivation is that actual performance falls short of what might reasonably have been expected. The aim should be to agree a budget that falls between these two extremes and therefore incorporates just the right degree of difficulty which will lead to the optimal level of performance. At this level the budget should be challenging enough to motivate a manager to optimise on his performance without being too ambitious. The right level of difficulty is that element of targetry which is acceptable to that individual manager. This level of acceptability will differ from manager to manager, as each individual behaves and reacts in a different way in similar circumstances. This concept of budget difficulty can be demonstrated diagrammatically as follows:

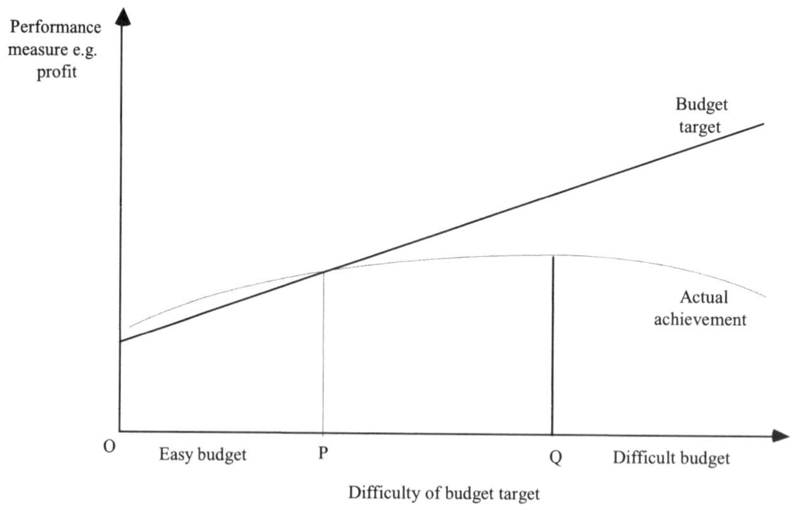

A budget set at the point where OP represents the degree of difficulty or targetry in it is referred to as an 'expectations budget' as budget and actual are likely to coincide. However, a relatively easy-to-achieve budget is likely to lead to a sub-optimal actual performance. In order to achieve a higher actual performance a more difficult budget needs to be set (an 'aspirations budget'). A budget set at the point where OQ represents the degree of difficulty or targetry in it should lead to optimal performance (highest point on the 'actual' performance curve). However, it should be noted that this would give rise to an adverse variance compared with budget. Senior management's interpretation of the reaction to such a variance needs to be carefully considered if the individual manager is not to react adversely in the future to not achieving the budgeted performance. It is in the overall company's best interest to optimise an individual manager's actual performance.

How the degree of difficulty, OQ, is determined is not at all easy in practice because it involves a knowledge of how each individual manager will react and behave. Attempts to quantify the degree of difficulty using work study assessments are a highly simplified approach to a very complex problem.

Furthermore, attempts to use the budget as a motivating tool in the manner described may in fact lead to the need for two budgets: one which is the summation of what all the individual managers have agreed to achieve (with the different degrees of budget difficulty incorporated into them) and a second which recognises that actual performance is likely to fall short of aspiration and is, therefore, a more realistic basis for planning purposes e.g. placing capital expenditure contracts (budgets used for forecasting purposes).

2.4 Evaluation of managerial performance

In the previous section the motivating effect of budgets was considered, but it should be remembered that the budgets by themselves have a limited motivational effect. It is the reward structure that is linked to achieving the budget requirements, or lack of reward for non-achievement, which provides the real underlying motivational potential of budgets. The rewards need not be directly financial but could be in terms of future prospects of promotion.

A manager will need to regard the reward as being worthwhile if his behaviour is to be influenced so that he strives actively towards the achievement of the budget.

It has already been mentioned in an earlier section that it is a common practice to attempt to assess the performance of a manager by a comparison of budgeted and actual results for his area of responsibility in the organisation. The choice of which particular measures to use is important to ensure that the individual manager sees the attainment of his targets as worthwhile for himself and at the same time in the best interests of the organisation as a whole. In practice, conflicts can and often do arise between individual managers' personal objectives and those of the organisation as a whole.

The way in which the information in budget reports is used in the assessment of managerial performance has to be considered. Different degrees of emphasis on the results of budget versus actual comparisons can lead to different attitudes and feelings among managers. There is a need to achieve the correct balance between, on the one extreme, an over-emphasis on results leading to pressure and feelings of injustice from the system and on the other, too little stress on results leading to a budget irrelevancy attitude and low morale.

For many years, the standard text on behavioural issues in accounting was 'Accounting and Human Behaviour' by A.G. Hopwood (1974).

Hopwood reported on his research in this area. He studied the manufacturing division of a US steelworks involving a sample of more then two hundred managers with cost centre responsibility. He identified the following three distinct styles of using budget/actual cost information in the evaluation of managerial performance.

KEY POINT

Budget constrained style

Here the primary emphasis is on the evaluation of a manager's performance in terms of meeting the budget in the short-term.

Profit conscious style

The performance of a manager is measured in terms of his ability to increase the overall effectiveness of his area of responsibility in the context of meeting the longer term objectives of the organisation.

Non-accounting style

A manager's evaluation is not based on budgetary information.

(a) **Budget constrained style**

Here the primary emphasis is on the evaluation of a manager's performance in terms of meeting the budget in the short-term.

(b) **Profit conscious style**

The performance of a manager is measured in terms of his ability to increase the overall effectiveness of his area of responsibility in the context of meeting the longer term objectives of the organisation. At cost centre levels of responsibility the reduction of long-run average costs could be seen as achieving this. Short-term budgetary information needs to be used with care and in a flexible way to achieve this purpose.

(c) **Non-accounting style**

A manager's evaluation is not based on budgetary information. Accounting information plays a relatively unimportant role in such a style. Other, non-accounting performance indicators are as important as the budget information.

A brief summary of the major effects that these three styles had on managers now follows.

The *budget constrained* style resulted in a great involvement in costs and cost information and a high degree of job-related pressure and tension. The latter often led to the manipulation of data for inclusion in accounting reports. Relations with both colleagues and the manager's superior were poor.

The *profit conscious* style showed good relations with colleagues and superiors. There was still a high involvement with costs but less job-related pressure. Consequently, the manipulation of accounting data was reduced.

The *non-accounting* style showed very similar effects to the profit conscious style except for the much lower impact of costs and cost information on the manager. Hopwood found some evidence that better managerial performance was being achieved where a profit conscious or non-accounting style was in use. Poor performance was often associated with a budget constrained style.

Subsequent studies involving profit centre managers in the UK coal mining industry undertaken by DT Otley (published 1978) did not always mirror Hopwood's earlier results. One particular area of difference was that the UK study showed a closer link between the budget constrained style and good performance.

The manager evaluated on a rather tight budget constrained basis tended to meet the budget more closely than if it was evaluated in a less rigid way.

The results of these studies by Hopwood and Otley can be reconciled in terms that each took place in a different organisational environment. The US study involved highly interdependent cost centres in a highly integrated production function; the UK study involved largely independent profit centres. Any generalisations about evaluation styles must take into account the contingent variables associated with differing organisational structures.

2.5 Participation in the setting of budgets

KEY POINT

The Theory X view is based on the assumptions that people in work environments are basically lazy and dislike work and any responsibility associated with it. They are motivated by money to meet their basic needs.

Theory Y is a participative theory of management, assuming that people in a work environment do seek more responsibility and do not have to be so tightly controlled.

In some organisations budgets are set by higher levels of management and then communicated to the lower levels of management to whose areas of responsibility they relate. Thus, such budgets are seen by those lower-level managers as being imposed upon them by their superiors in the organisational hierarchy without their being allowed to participate in the budget-setting process and therefore without their being able directly to influence the budget figures. This approach to involvement in the budgetary system is consistent with Douglas McGregor's Theory X view of how people behave in organisations. The Theory X view is based on the assumptions that people in work environments are basically lazy and dislike work and any responsibility associated with it. They are motivated by money to meet their basic needs. Therefore, the Theory X style of management is authoritarian, based on direction and control down through the organisation and typified by a host of rules and regulations.

The other end of the spectrum is described by McGregor as Theory Y. This is a participative theory of management, assuming that people in a work environment do seek more responsibility and do not have to be so tightly controlled.

Therefore, it is in organisations where a Theory Y style of management predominates that one is more likely to come across a fully participative approach to the setting of budgets.

The general argument is that the more individual managers are allowed to participate i.e. to influence the budgets for which they are held responsible, the more likely it is that they will accept the targets in the budgets and strive actively towards the attainment of those targets. In this way actual performances should be increased by the motivational impact of budgets. An important point to recognise is the difference between *actual* and *perceived* participation. It is the extent to which an individual manager *perceives* that he has influenced the budget that is crucial in that manager's acceptance of it.

KEY POINT

If budgets are used both in a motivational role and for the evaluation of managerial performance, then a serious conflict can arise.

There are limitations on the extent of the effectiveness of participation in the budget-setting process. If budgets are used both in a motivational role and for the evaluation of managerial performance, then a serious conflict can arise. A manager through participation may be able to influence the very budget upon which he is subsequently evaluated. By lowering the standard in the budget he has biased the budget and he may then appear to attain a better actual performance in any comparison with it. There is evidence to show that this tends to occur where a manager is actively seeking progression in an organisation. The effects of this sort of bias can be minimised by careful control, at the budget setting stage, over any changes in the budget from one year to the next which are not due to external factors.

Some people in organisations, by the very nature of the make-up of their personality, do not wish to participate in the wider aspects of their jobs. They prefer an authoritarian style of leadership and do not strive for independence. Participative approaches to budget-setting will be very limited in their effect in such circumstances. Participation will be less effective in organisational situations where a manager or employee feels that he has little scope to influence the actual results for the budgeted area of responsibility. The lower down in the organisation structure the budget holder is, the more constrained is he by factors imposed from above. For example, objectives, strategies and policies, as well as the sales forecast and budget, limit the extent that a subordinate manager in the production function has for real participation in the setting of the budget for his area of responsibility.

2.6 Budget bias

Budget bias, or budget 'slack as it is sometimes referred to, has been encountered earlier in this text.

Briefly to recap, it is the common process of building room for manoeuvre when setting a budget by overstating the level of budgeted expenditure or by understating the level of budgeted sales. The following are possible reasons for the creation of the bias:

- It should lead to the most favourable result when actual is compared with budget. Such a result should lead to the optimisation of personal gain for the individual manager.
- Where reward structures are based on comparisons of actual with budgeted results, bias can help to influence the outcome.
- In an uncertain business environment it is a way of relieving some of the pressures of a tight situation. The bias will allow some leeway if things do not go according to plan. An example at the factory floor level of this is where workers deliberately do not show how quickly a job can be completed when they are being closely studied by work study (time-and-motion) personnel. The standard time that results will leave the workers with room to manoeuvre in the case of non-standard or different work or where through more general dissatisfaction they do not want to work flat out.
- Some people may see the creation of bias in a budget as a way of 'legally' beating the system. Human behaviour generally in other fields tends to follow such an approach e.g. the legal avoidance of tax is a way of getting round the (tax) system. Therefore, a manager may regard the creation of bias as a desirable personal objective and success in achieving it as motivational towards the best actual performance.

Budget bias can sometimes be in the opposite direction to that which has been described already. A manager in the marketing function may bias his budget in an optimistic way by overstating budgeted sales. This could be due to a desire to please senior management by showing an optimistic forecasted sales trend. Alternatively, a manager whose performance has been weak previously may wish to show a promising situation in order to gain approval by his superiors. The short-term approval will usually be at the risk of future disapproval if the optimistic result is not reflected in the actual results.

Finally there is the question 'Is budget bias or slack good or bad?' It depends how the budget is used. If the bias has the effect of motivating a manager to his best actual performance, there would appear to be a good reason for its existence. However, if budgets are used to make forecasts and consequent major decisions then, to the extent that the budgets are biased, there will be errors in the forecasts being made beyond the budget period. Erroneous decisions may then be made. If budgets are to be made in this way the bias needs to be removed from any budgets before the forecasts are made.

2.7 Contingency theory and its relevance to budgeting

There has been a general approach over the years in both academic and professional circles to identify one universally acceptable and ideal system of management accounting – both from a technical or mechanistic viewpoint and from an organisational/institutional angle.

More recently there has been some move towards what has come to be known as a contingency theory for management accounting (explored in Chapter 4 of this text) and this has specific relevance to budgeting. The contingency approach adopts the view that there is no one optimal system of management accounting to meet the needs of all types of organisation in all circumstances. An appropriate model needs to be developed for each different situation rather than a general model (based on a scientific management or behavioural approach) being universally imposed on an organisation.

Much of the discussion concerning behavioural aspects of budgeting can be considered in the light of contingency theory. For example, the budget constrained management style reported by some academics such as Hopwood is probably a feature of certain types of organisation where a very structured approach to management is inappropriate because of the fluidity and uncertainty inherent in the type of business that is undertaken. The contingent variables that are found in such cases make a very rigorous system of budgetary control inappropriate.

However, where the business has a high degree of certainty then the associated organisation may be able to place greater reliance on budgeting systems. The relationship between systems and circumstances is what contingency theory is all about.

2.8 Management by objectives

In a previous section it was argued that budgets should be agreed rather than imposed from above. At the same time it is necessary to achieve *goal congruence* i.e. to ensure that individual managers are working towards the same or complementary targets and that their personal aims do not conflict with those of the organisation. Management by objectives (MBO), used in conjunction with systems of long-range planning and budgetary control, can help to achieve these aims and minimise the conflicts between individuals' and organisational goals.

MBO found much favour in the 1970s and early 1980s but the term itself is encountered rather less frequently nowadays. However, it can be argued that the balanced scorecard and benchmarking are all related concepts – being attempts to link performance measurement to shareholder value.

KEY POINT

MBO is an attempt formally to relate plans and targets to individual managers in the structure and thereby to achieve goal congruence.

Corporate objectives and other aspects of corporate planning relate to the whole organisation, and the budgeting process involves the setting of budgets for areas of responsibility in the organisation. Both these aspects of planning can be seen to relate to physical attributes of an organisation, whereas MBO is an attempt formally to relate plans and targets to individual managers in the structure and thereby to achieve goal congruence. The procedure is as follows:

- Top management agree on long-term corporate objectives, strategy and goals for the organisation.
  - The existing organisation structure is revised as necessary and up-to-date organisation charts are produced which illustrate job titles, responsibilities and relative positions. Job descriptions would provide fuller details of these aspects.
  - Each senior manager is required to establish key tasks associated with the successful running of his own area of responsibility and agree quantifiable targets for the period under review (e.g. the following twelve months) for each key task. These targets are established in a participative process involving consultation between the manager and his immediate superior. Just how far down through the levels of management the MBO system is operated will vary from organisation to organisation, but it is essentially a system which relates to the more senior management levels in all functions. If this approach is successful, MBO can be extended to the next subordinate level of management.

  The targets which are set and agreed should be such that they provide a challenge to the individual manager, but they should not be so difficult or idealistic as to have a demotivating influence. The concept is the same as that already described in terms of 'budget difficulty'.

- Periodically (e.g. quarterly) actual results are compared with the agreed targets and some form of performance appraisal interview takes place. This is a formal interview, involving the manager and his immediate superior, when results and actions are fully discussed.
- At the end of each period organisational goals are reviewed as a consequence of the actual results that have been achieved. This is essentially a stage that relates the MBO system back to the whole organisation.

If a system of MBO is to operate successfully, as with any system there must be commitment to it at all levels of management. It is usual to appoint an MBO co-ordinator – a senior manager whose role it is to receive copies of all targets that have been agreed and to provide the basic monitoring framework. At senior management levels the attainment of targets often depends not only on what happens in an individual manager's own department or function, but on other parts of the organisation. The MBO co-ordinator is responsible for ensuring that managers in the different departments and functions are aware of these overlaps, and tries to ensure that the required level of co-operation is attained.

As senior managers are involved, an MBO system is often directly (or more usually indirectly) related to a reward structure. Such a reward structure encompasses promotion and career advancement as well as salary review.

One of the major problems associated with the operation of a system of MBO is that of sustaining the motivational impact on senior managers year after year. If each year a manager is expected to set targets which better those for the previous year, then there may be a tendency to hold 'a little in reserve' for next time. This is why a number of large organisations operating MBO do so for a limited number of years in order to obtain the maximum out of the system, then discontinue it and perhaps re-introduce it several years later when again there may be some benefits to be gained from its operation.

2.9 Important behaviourists and researchers and their ideas

In the last forty to fifty years a number of management writers have contributed significantly to the understanding of the behaviour of people within a business environment. This section deals in outline with some of these:

(a) **Douglas McGregor** (*The Human Side of the Enterprise*, 1960) developed his well-known views on leadership styles that could be attributed to management. An outline of his Theory X and Theory Y styles appears above.

KEY POINT

Rensis Likert identified four management systems or different styles of management:

- Exploitive-authoritative
- Benevolent-authoritative
- Consultative
- Participative.

(b) **Rensis Likert** (*The Human Organisation*, 1967) identified four management systems or different styles of management:

(i) **System 1: exploitive-authoritative**

Rules and regulations are communicated down through the organisation from a powerful top management.

(ii) **System 2: benevolent-authoritative**

This differs from System 1 in that there is more delegation to lower levels of management.

(iii) **System 3: consultative**

There is some discussion between superior and subordinate before the rules and orders are set. Delegation is more pronounced.

KEY POINT

Abraham Maslow is famous for his identification of a hierarchy of needs. Five such needs were identified as human motivators:

- Self-actualisation
- Esteem
- Belonging
- Safety

Physiological.

(iv) **System 4: participative**

A fully participative style, and where a high degree of goal congruence is likely.

This model tends to be consistent with that of McGregor, in the sense that Theory X and System 1 have similar characteristics and, at the other extreme, Theory Y and System 4 emphasise similar attitudes towards people.

(c) **Abraham Maslow** (*Motivation and Personality*, 1960) is famous for his identification of a hierarchy of needs. Five such needs were identified as human motivators. These are illustrated in the following pyramid:

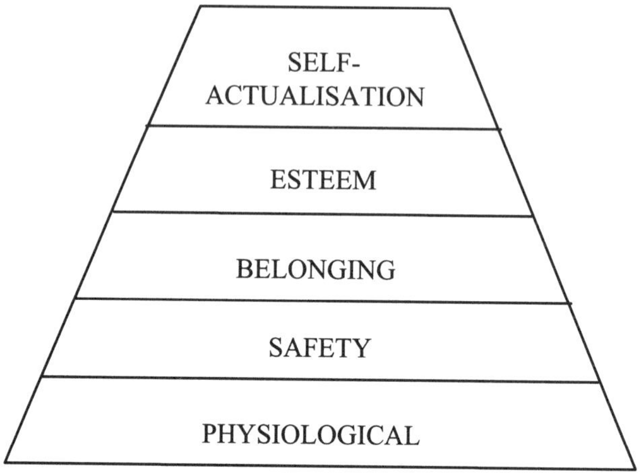

Maslow argued that basically physiological needs (food, clothing, housing etc) need to be met as a prerequisite. The next level, that of safety needs, comprises more than physical security in its widest sense (including continued supply of food, clothing, housing etc) and would include emotional aspects. Having met the personal needs of the lowest two levels of the hierarchy, the individual would want to satisfy belonging needs (i.e. to the work or social group). Esteem needs are a desire to be recognised and valued by the group and oneself. When all four lower needs have been largely satisfied, the highest level is that of self-actualisation or self-fulfilment, perhaps best described as being able to 'do one's own thing'.

Money largely meets the needs at the lower levels of the hierarchy but not at the higher levels. As each need is largely satisfied, the individual moves up to the next level of needs and different motivators.

(d) **Frederick Herzberg** (*The Motivation to Work* 1959): his analysis identified job satisfiers or motivators and, on the other hand, 'hygiene factors'.

Satisfiers, such as achievement, recognition, interesting and challenging work, responsibility and advancement, are the true motivators because they are the vital ingredients of job satisfaction. The way to foster motivators is through schemes associated with job enlargement or job enrichment. It is the job satisfiers that meet the higher needs in Maslow's hierarchy.

Hygiene or environmental factors, such as supervision, pay and working conditions, are essentially ingredients but are not themselves motivators. If they do not exist, people are dissatisfied. Hygiene factors can be related to the needs recognised by Maslow towards the bottom of the hierarchy.

(e) **R Blake and J Mouton** (*The Managerial Grid* 1961) provided a basis on which to assess, in quantitative terms, managerial style. Using a two-dimensional grid, with a nine-point scale on each axis, they classify a manager. One axis relates to a manager's 'concern for people' and the other to his 'concern for the task (the job)'.

Ideally a manager should have a (9,9) position on the grid with a high degree of concern for both people and the task.

(f) **Anthony Hopwood** (*An Accounting System and Managerial Behaviour* 1977) carried out research in the US on the way that budgetary information is used in a large organisation. He identified three styles of evaluation – 'budget constrained', 'profit conscious' and 'non-accounting'. These have been dealt with more fully above.

(g) **David Otley** (*Budget Use and Managerial Performance* 1978) repeated a similar study to Hopwood in the UK and obtained somewhat different results. Again, earlier sections have dealt with this in more detail.

The work of the behaviourists, like McGregor, Likert, Maslow and Herzberg, contrast strongly with that of the earlier management theorists who concentrated on the scientific management approach. Foremost among this group is F W Taylor who is generally accredited as being 'the father of work study'. Work measurement and method study are typical of the scientific approach to people in the work environment.

3 Budgeting as a bargaining process

3.1 Background

Whenever people are allowed to actively participate in the budget setting process there will always be negotiation and bargaining between those involved. There are two aspects to this in the budgeting arena:

- allocation of resources
- performance appraisal

although it is often difficult to separate them in practice.

3.2 Resource allocation

Every organisation has resource constraints. Indeed much of the planning and budgeting cycle is concerned with making the best use of limited resources. Individual resources may be limited in the short term due to world economic situations, or it may be that there is a financial constraint which limits the organisation's ability to obtain resources which are available.

KEY POINT

The idea behind ZBB is that budgets are set through an impartial scientific process which is not amenable to politics, bargaining and negotiation.

In both cases individual managers when preparing their individual budgets are competing with each other for the limited resources available. This can be seen most clearly in the context of capital budgets, where financial restrictions limit the investment projects to be undertaken. It can also be seen where zero-based budgeting (ZBB) is being used and individual decision packages are evaluated on a cost/benefit analysis. The idea behind ZBB is that budgets are set through an impartial scientific process which is not amenable to politics, bargaining and negotiation.

3.3 Performance appraisal

As has been seen earlier in this text, budgets may be used as a basis for appraising a manager's performance. For this purpose a manager will discuss their draft budget with their superior. The manager may be forced to amend this budget following such negotiations and the result of the amendment may make the achievement of the budget target harder.

Since the manager will be appraised on the basis of his/her ability to achieve the target, the negotiations and bargaining between the manager and their superior are a serious matter.

4 Aspiration levels and budgeting

An aspiration level is personal to an individual and represents a level of efficiency which the individual believes they are capable of achieving.

In an ideal situation the goals of the organisation will equate to those of the individual responsible for their achievement. This it is argued will lead to motivational benefits with the likelihood that the targets will be achieved.

However, for the motivational effect to work, the target set must be achievable but not being too easy.

KEY POINT

If the level of the budget is too easy to achieve the individual may see it as demeaning, and not make any effort to achieve it. This has a de-motivating effect and is worse than having no target at all.

If the level of the budget is too easy to achieve the individual may see it as demeaning, and not make any effort to achieve it. This has a de-motivating effect and is worse than having no target at all.

Therefore it is necessary to identify the aspiration level of the individual before setting the budget. The budget should then take account of this aspiration level so as to ensure goal congruence and encourage motivational aspects.

5 Budgeting and change

There are four aspects of change which may affect the budgeting process:

- political change
- social change
- economic change
- technological change.

Political change

A change in government policy, for example fiscal policy, may affect the demand for an organisation's products, and/or the costs incurred in providing them. Any such changes will affect both short-term and long-term planning. This is one reason why planning is a continuous process.

Social change

Changes in social responsibilities and people's attitude towards them affect every organisation. In recent years there has been much more concern about social responsibilities, some of which are now recognised by law. All of these factors may impinge on the plans of the organisation.

Economic change

When there is a change in the economic climate from boom through to recession the demands upon people's income become more focused. Money tends to be spent on necessary goods with little left for 'luxury goods' and savings. The lack of savings deters investment with the result that plans have to be modified if they are to be realistic targets.

Technological change

When plans are made they are based upon the use of certain methods and equipment. As technology advances the older methods are proven to be inefficient with the result that decisions are taken to update the operation. As a consequence the aspects of the budgets and plans which related to the old method are no longer relevant. Revised plans must now be drawn up on the basis of the new technology.

6 Fixed and flexible budgets

DEFINITION

A **fixed budget** is a budget which shows income/costs for a single level of activity.

6.1 Introduction

You should be familiar with the mechanics of these types of budget from your earlier reading. In this section we shall consider only their relative strengths and weaknesses.

KEY POINT

A fixed budget makes no attempt to separate the costs into those which are fixed and those which are variable. However a fixed budget is particularly suitable for controlling costs which are unrelated to activity. An example would be Research and Development expenditure.

6.2 Fixed budgets

A fixed budget makes no attempt to separate the costs into those which are fixed and those which are variable. It is therefore unsuitable for use as a basis of comparison with actual costs where such costs are known to vary with activity **and** the level of activity differs from that budgeted.

However a fixed budget is particularly suitable for controlling costs which are unrelated to activity. These are usually indirect costs and usually the aim is to limit expenditure on these items. An example would be Research and Development expenditure.

ACTIVITY 1

Identify another functional area where expenditure control is important.

Feedback to this activity is at the end of the chapter.

6.3 Flexible budgets

DEFINITION

A **flexible budget** is a budget which shows costs/revenues for different levels of activity by recognising the behaviour of each cost.

The flexible budget is suitable for use as a comparison with actual costs incurred when the activity level differs from that budgeted. Such budgets can therefore be used to measure efficiency but are not suitable as a means of capping expenditure.

7 Rolling budgets

7.1 Introduction

Budgets are deemed by many organisations to be unchangeable and sacrosanct. The reasons are twofold:

- How committed would management be to the budget preparation process if they knew that senior management accepted that their budgets would need to be adjusted before the end of the budget term?
- The comparison of the original master budget with annual revenues and costs is a useful one - even if the organisation operated under very changed conditions from that originally planned. Also the use of 'revision variances' can be used to bridge the gap and produce meaningful management performance reports.

However there are circumstances in which management may consider that the initial master budget is inadequate as a forecast of future outturn and/or as a control benchmark, and where alternative measures are required. For example, the environmental suppositions upon which strategic and budget planning are based may prove to be very unlike those conditions encountered during the budget term.

If change in the budget is required the options available to management are:

- to continue with the original budget, making allowances as necessary
- to adapt the original budget to reflect the changed circumstances
- to adopt a 'rolling budget' or forecast revision approach
- to re-budget from scratch.

The decision is liable to rely partly upon the degree of error from the budgeted assumptions, and partly upon the ways management use the budget e.g. as authority to spend, or limits on spending.

If environmental states are not considerably different from those budgeted for, it may be pragmatic to retain the original budget and expect middle and junior managers to **adapt to the changed situation within the structure of the original budget**. This policy would maintain the integrity of the budgeting procedures and most likely be a practical and economic approach.

If the different states evolved around only one or two assumptions (such as interest rates and a certain material input inflation), it might be wise and feasible to **adapt the master budget to the new situation**, particularly if the budgetary data are held in a sophisticated computer financial model. As the revised budget would be based on the original budget it is more likely to be accepted by managers who would appreciate the need to reflect new conditions.

Rolling budgets (and forecast revisions) are more likely to be practised as a matter of routine managerial philosophy, rather than as a response to a particular or unexpected situation.

The bigger the divergence of actual conditions from those budgeted the more logical would be the decision to recognise the inadequacy of the original budget and the need to rebudget. Failure to do so might cause managers to waste limited resources or to use them inappropriately.

The many consequences of changing the annual budget can be reduced to a few major considerations:

- a weakening of the importance placed on the budget system
- increased time spent by managers on budget preparation
- the problem of gaining budget acceptance
- the lack of clear financial objectives
- the lack of meaningful management performance measures.

7.2 Preparation of rolling budgets

KEY POINT

A rolling budget can be defined as "a budget continuously updated by adding a further period, say a month or quarter and deducting the earliest period.

A rolling budget can be defined as "a budget continuously updated by adding a further period, say a month or quarter and deducting the earliest period. Beneficial where future costs and/or activities cannot be forecast reliably".

A typical rolling budget might be prepared as follows:

- A budget is prepared for the coming year (say January - December) broken down into suitable, say quarterly, control periods.
- At the end of the first control period (31 March) a comparison is made of that period's results against the budget. The conclusions drawn from this analysis are used to update the budgets for the remaining control periods and to add a budget for a further three months, so that the company once again has budgets available for the coming year (this time April - March).
- The planning process is repeated at the end of each three-month control period.

The budgeting options available to management who face a dynamic business environment have been discussed above. The views outlined there suggest that rolling budgets are not essential if an organisation is undergoing rapid change, although there may be advantages for a company adopting this approach to budgeting. These include the following:

- Budgets are more realistic and achievable since they are continuously revised to reflect changing circumstances.
- The **annual** disruption associated with the preparation of an annual budget is removed.
- The pressures (and stress) placed on managers to achieve unrealistic budget targets are eased.
- Variance feedback is more meaningful.
- It tends to reduce budgetary bias.
- It reduces the rigidity of the budget system and builds contingency and innovation into the preparation/feedback stages of the control system.
- The assessment of objectives and plans is continuous rather than being a one-off exercise.
- Without some form of budget revision, operational management may continue to invest and recruit etc, with the belief that management strategy holds firm.
- It might help to increase management commitment to the budget.
- The arbitrary and artificial distinction drawn between one financial year and the next is removed, since budgets always extend for a year ahead.

However the problems likely to be encountered with rolling budgets include the following:

- If it is difficult to plan ahead accurately (and it always is!) when once a year managers spend a **lot** of time and effort on the task, how likely is it that managers can do the same forecasts more accurately every month or quarter when they are involved in other responsibilities?
- There is a danger that the rolling budget will become the last budget 'plus or minus a bit' and will be representative of absolutely nothing in terms of corporate objectives and meaningless for performance control purposes.
- Managers will be faced with a greater work load and additional staff may be required.
- Managers may devote insufficient attention to preparing budgets which they know will shortly be revised.
- The organisation might be required to operate annual budgets (such as enterprises operating in the public sector).

In conclusion it is worth noting that the relatively recent development of sophisticated computer budgeting models has increased the use of rolling budgets and similar concepts in organisations. Often figures are now revised by computers with minimal intervention by managers.

8 Activity based budgets

8.1 Introduction

The preparation of activity based budgets was compared with traditional budgets earlier in this text (see Chapter 4), so the idea is only referred to here. The critical thing with ABB is that costs are grouped according to their purpose rather than according to their nature.

For example the budget of a local authority street cleaning department may be presented under alternative sets of headings – traditional and activity based:

Traditional

Item of cost	£
Wages	140,000
Materials	28,000
Vehicle hire	35,000
Equipment hire	18,000
Total	221,000

Activity based

Activity	£	*Number of activities*
Street sweeping	84,000	4,000
School cleaning	68,000	800
Park cleaning	39,000	130
Graffiti removal	30,000	150
Total	221,000	

8.2 Activity based budgets

KEY POINT

The use of an activity based approach will assist in the comparison of costs with the activities which they achieve.

The use of an activity based approach will assist in the comparison of costs with the activities which they achieve. This should lead to a greater accuracy in the costs predicted and thus better management control. For example, if a proposal is made to increase the number of street sweepings in the period by 25% (from 4,000 to 5,000) then an ABB gives some indication of what the cost impact of this will be.

ABB reflects one modern development in budgeting and financial control. The focus has moved from inputs to the process to outputs from it. This involves a more intelligent and proactive approach to budgeting.

9 Zero-based budgets v incremental budgets

9.1 Introduction

The techniques of zero-based and incremental budgeting were considered earlier in this text. The brief discussion that follows compares the two approaches from a behavioural angle.

9.2 Zero-based budgeting

KEY POINT

Zero-based budgeting requires that every activity be justified.

Zero-based budgeting requires that every activity be justified. It thus forces managers to examine the business and identify any unnecessary or inefficient activities. This form of budgeting is very costly in terms of management time, and can if care is not taken lead to short-term cost savings which are detrimental in the long-term. However, with care it can lead to improved efficiency.

The critical thing about ZBB is that it starts from objectives and works back to departmental costs. The organisation decides what its objectives there and then it assembles a set of 'decision packages' (being units of activity) which is calculated to achieve these objectives in the most cost effective manner. In doing this it cuts across departmental boundaries.

Those packages which are adopted are assembled under departmental headings and the departmental budgets then just emerge.

ZBB is particularly applicable to service functions within a commercial business or the not-for-profit sector.

From a behavioural point of view, ZBB is a top down approach to budgeting. It implies that scientific means can be used to prepare a plan for the whole organisation and the departmental budgets emerge from this process, without being promoted by the departments themselves.

9.3 Incremental budgeting

KEY POINT

Incremental budgeting

This system is based on the previous year's activity, which are then adjusted for volume and price effects.

This system is based on the previous year's activity, which are then adjusted for volume and price effects. This system is used by many organisations on the grounds that it is a cheap method of budgeting. However, it often reflects the political realities of organisations – particularly local authorities. The departments and their managements are powerful entities and one cannot marginalise them in the planning process.

The disadvantage of the incremental budgeting method is that inefficiencies are not identified, in fact they may be built-in to the following year's target, a feature which is often known as budgetary slack.

Conclusion

Budgets are an important way of influencing the behaviour of managers within an organisation. However, if budgets are used for both motivational purposes and for control, then a serious conflict can arise. Differing styles of management will take varying approaches to participation in the setting of budgets.

SELF-TEST QUESTIONS

Behavioural aspects of budgeting

1 Identify the roles of budgets. (2.1)

2 Explain the motivating effect of budgets. (2.3)

3 Explain why participation in the budget setting process is important. (2.5)

4 Explain budget bias (slack). (2.6)

Budgeting as a bargaining process

5 Explain how budgeting is a bargaining process. (3)

Aspiration levels and budgeting

6 What is an aspiration level? (4)

Fixed and flexible budgets

7 Distinguish between fixed and flexible budgets. (6)

Rolling budgets

8 What is a rolling budget? (7.1)

Zero-based budgets v incremental budgets

9 Distinguish between zero based and incremental budgeting. (9.2-9.3)

EXAM-TYPE QUESTION

Flexible budgeting

It is common practice to flex a budget linearly according to the volume of production, using labour or machine hours as a proxy, yet this often results in a budget which is inaccurate and is thus less useful for control purposes.

Required:

(a) Explain why inaccuracies may result from the procedures commonly used to flex a budget. **(7 marks)**

(b) Explain how these inaccuracies detract from effective control. **(4 marks)**

(c) Discuss alternative ways of budgeting which might improve both accuracy and control. **(6 marks)**

(Total: 17 marks)

For the answer to this question, see the 'Answers' section at the end of the book.

FEEDBACK TO ACTIVITY 1

There are many possible answers here, e.g. Audit Costs or Management salaries.

Chapter 17
STRATEGIC PLANNING AND CONTROL

CHAPTER CONTENTS

This chapter explores the role that strategic planning plays in a business operation and the link between plans and the control function.

Objectives

When you have studied this chapter you should be able to do the following.

- Compare strategic with operational planning and control.
- Explain how organisational survival in the long-term necessitates consideration of life cycle issues.
- Identify the role of corporate planning in clarifying corporate objectives, making strategic decisions and checking progress towards the objectives.
- Explain the structure of corporate planning.
- Discuss the combining of strategic planning with freewheeling opportunism in a fast changing business environment.
- Comment on the potential conflict between strategic plans and short-term localised decisions.
- Explain the principles of SWOT analysis.
- Explain how SWOT analysis may assist in the planning process.
- Comment on the benefits and difficulties of benchmarking performance with best practice organisations.
- Explain how risk and uncertainty play an especially important role in long-term strategic planning that relies upon forecasts of exogenous variables.
- Explain aspects of strategic management in the context of multinational companies.

1 Introduction

1.1 The nature and purpose of planning

KEY POINT

Corporate planning is essentially a long run activity which seeks to determine the direction in which the firm should be moving in the future.

Corporate planning should be the starting point for business planning. It is essentially a long run activity which seeks to determine the direction in which the firm should be moving in the future. A frequently asked question in formulating the corporate plan is 'Where do we see ourselves in ten years time?' To answer this successfully the firm must consider:

- what it wants to achieve (its objectives)
- how it intends to get there (its strategy)
- what resources will be required (its operating plans)
- how well it is doing in comparison to the plan (control).

These areas are discussed in the following sections.

2 Corporate planning

2.1 Objectives

KEY POINT

Objectives are simply statements of what the firm wishes to achieve.

Objectives are simply statements of what the firm wishes to achieve. Traditionally it was assumed that all firms were only interested in the maximisation of profit (or the wealth of their shareholders). Nowadays it is recognised that for many firms profit is but one of the many objectives pursued. Examples include:

- maximisation of sales (whilst earning a 'reasonable' level of profit)
- growth (in sales, asset value, number of employees etc)
- survival
- research and development leadership
- quality of service
- contented workforce
- respect for the environment.

Many of these non-profit goals can in fact be categorised as:

- surrogates for profit (e.g. quality of service)
- necessary constraints on profit (e.g. quality of service)
- 'sub-optimal' objectives that benefit individual parties in the firm rather than the firm as a whole (e.g. managers might try to maximise sales as this would bring them greater personal rewards than maximising profit).

A variety of objectives can therefore be suggested for the firm and it is up to the individual company to make its own decisions. For corporate planning purposes it is essential that the objectives chosen are quantified and have a timescale attached to them. A statement such as to maximise profits and increase sales would be of little use in corporate planning terms. The following would be far more helpful:

(i) achieve a growth in EPS of 5% per annum over the coming ten year period

(ii) obtain a turnover of £x million within six years

(iii) launch at least two new products per year etc.

Some objectives may be difficult to quantify (e.g. contented workforce) but if no attempt is made there will be no yardstick against which to compare actual performance.

2.2 Strategy

KEY POINT

Strategy is the overall approach that the company will adopt to meet its chosen objectives.

Strategy is the overall approach that the company will adopt to meet its chosen objectives.

Strategy formulation usually involves:

- an analysis of the environment in which the firm operates, a review of the strengths and weaknesses of the company and a consideration of the threats and opportunities facing it;
- the results of the firm's existing operations are then projected forward and compared with stated objectives;
- any differences between projected performance and objectives are referred to as 'gaps'.

To bridge these gaps the firm will either change its objectives (because they are too optimistic) or attempt to change the firm's direction to improve performance. This change of direction is strategy formulation. The term 'SWOT analysis' is used to describe this activity. SWOT (strengths, weaknesses, opportunities, threats) analysis is explored further later in this chapter.

Formulation of strategy is largely a creative process, whereby the firm will consider the products it makes and the markets it serves. Policies are usually developed to represent the firm's strategy and cover basic areas such as:

- product development policy (e.g. new products, discontinuation of old products)
- market development (continue in existing markets, develop new ones)
- technology
- growth (i.e. internally generated growth, or growth by acquisition).

These policies are sometimes known as 'missions', set out in 'mission statements'.

KEY POINT

Long and short-term plans are both a means of communicating targets but they differ in terms of their style and sources of information.

2.3 Distinguishing long-term and short-term planning

Long and short-term plans are both a means of communicating targets but they differ in terms of their style and sources of information.

These may be tabulated as:

	Long-term	*Short-term*
Depth of information	Broad	Detailed
Source of information	External and internal	Internal
Style of information	Quantitative and descriptive	Quantitative

KEY POINT

Long-term planning is usually concerned with a 5 year time horizon and tends to be strategic in dimension, whereas short-term plans (or budgets) are often constructed for a 1 year time horizon and tend to be operational in dimension.

Long-term planning is usually concerned with a 5 year time horizon and tends to be strategic in dimension, whereas short-term plans (or budgets) are often constructed for a 1 year time horizon and tend to be operational in dimension.

2.4 Relevant costs for long-term planning

The basic principles of relevant costs are no different to those you have learned earlier in this text, but the longer time horizon may make some costs relevant for long-term planning which would not be relevant in a shorter time period.

Any costs which give rise to future cash flows within the planning period are relevant costs. These may include costs which are fixed in the short term but which become controllable within the horizon of the long-term plan. Examples would include rents payable under lease agreements which terminate in the planning period.

Again the length of the time horizon may introduce a greater number of opportunities which do not exist within a shorter timescale. Where such opportunities arise this could change or introduce opportunity costs which do not exist in the short term. An example would be new products becoming possible because of technological developments and staff training.

2.5 Operating plans

Strategic plans are essentially long term. Operating plans are the short-term tactics of the organisation. A strategic plan might call for expansion in a particular market, whereas the operating plan will detail how the extra products are to be made and how much is to be spent on advertising. A military analogy is useful here – strategy is how to organise to win the war, operating plans (or tactics) are how to fight individual battles.

Basically budgets are operating plans expressed in financial terms.

2.6 Control

It is not enough merely to make plans and implement them. The results of the plans have to be compared against stated objectives to assess the firm's performance. Action can then be taken to remedy any shortfalls in performance.

This is an essential activity as it highlights any weakness in the firm's corporate plan or its execution. Plans must be continually reviewed because as the environment changes so plans and objectives will need revision. Corporate planning is not a **once-in-every-ten-years activity,** but an **on-going process** which must react quickly to the changing circumstances of the firm.

2.7 Diagram of planning activities

The following diagram shows the relationships between planning and budgeting.

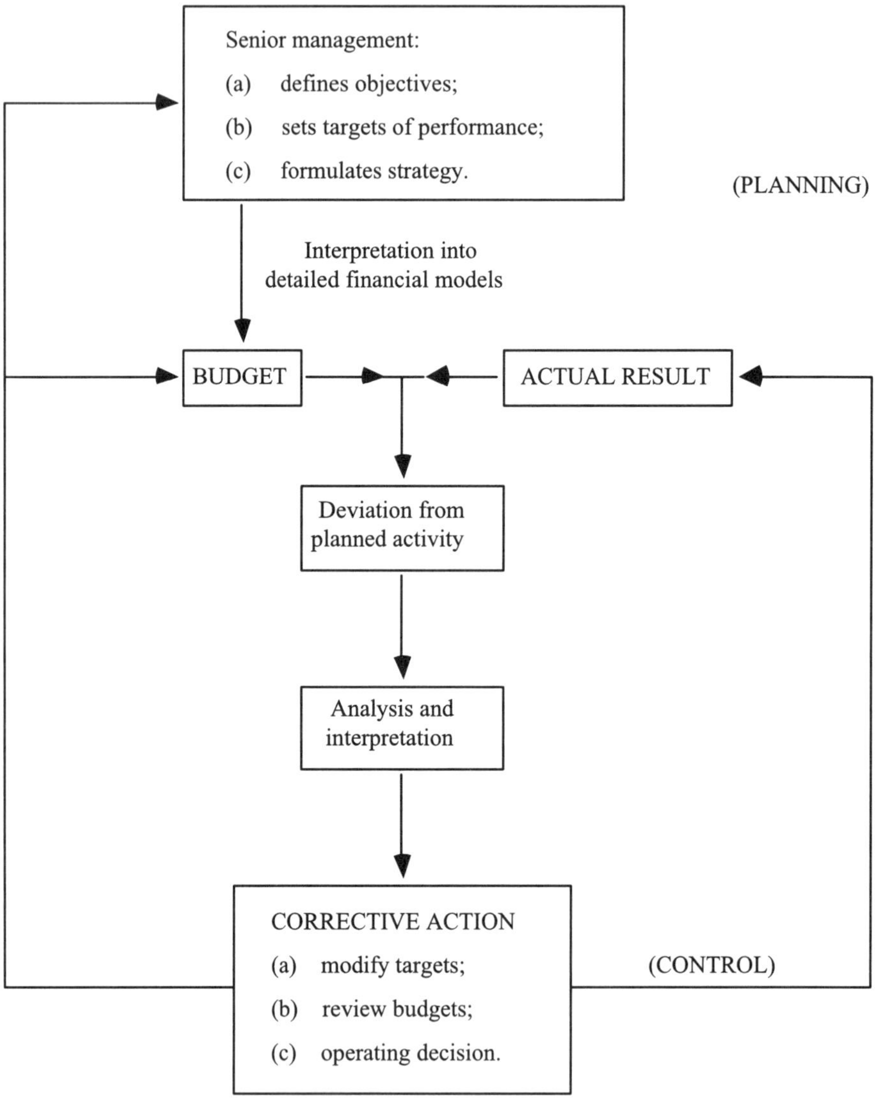

3 Product life cycles

KEY POINT

All products pass through a life cycle – starting with infancy, then passing through youth, maturity and finally reaching senility.

One issue that features in strategy is that of the product life cycle. The idea is that all products pass through a life cycle – starting with infancy, then passing through youth, maturity and finally reaching senility. Various aspects of how a product is handled relate to management's understanding of its current position in its life cycle.

In its infancy, a product will incur high development costs and will enjoy only limited customer acceptance. Pricing policy may have to reflect the need to develop customer acceptance and expand market share – consequently little profit may be expected from an infant product. An current example of this may be digital terrestrial television (DTV), introduced to the UK in 1999. The UK's first main supplier (ONdigital (later ITV Digital) – a member of the Carlton TV group) collapsed in 2002. However, the service was taken over by Freeview (a joint venture of BBC and Sky TV) and it is rapidly becoming the largest provider of multi-channel TV in the UK. DTV has certain advantages relative to its cable and satellite rivals – relating to cheapness, flexibility and political sensitivity. DTV is probably a product idea whose time will come.

As a product moves through youth and maturity, demand grows and measures taken to develop the product and its market share in infancy begin to earn a reward. A mature product may require little by way of development and may become a 'cash cow' in the strategic sense. The profits earned from such products may be used to finance the development costs of new infant products.

Eventually, a product becomes senile. This may happen because fashions change, customer needs change or technology moves on. There is still money to be made in a senile product. For example, the Douglas aircraft company was still making money from sales of parts for its DC3 aircraft 40 years after the aircraft went out of production. Until the early 1990s, new steam engines were still being made at a factory in China and sold to customers in South America for use on high altitude railways – where diesel engines could not operate effectively.

An obsolete product may survive in obscure market niches. Such products require no development costs and the surviving supplier is likely to enjoy high market share and high profit margins. That apart, in many market sectors one often encounters deeply conservative customers who will not readily accept new products or technologies. Well into the 1990s there were still buyers in the UK who would place special orders for old-style VW beetle cars which manufactured in Mexico.

A current example of life cycle end is in the photography market.

"Eastman Kodak yesterday said it would cut up to 6,000 jobs (9% of its workforce) as it tries to adjust to the growth in digital cameras, which has devastated the market for traditional films. Kodak has been desparately scrambling to diversify its business."

The Guardian, 24 July 2003

Eastman Kodak has been world market leader in the manufacture of photographic and cine film for over 100 years. However, that is a market which is now going into rapid decline. Digital photography became available to the average individual only in the late 1990s and it has spawned opportunities and growth for many new products and services – eg PCs, scanners, image software, camera memory chips and so on.

An understanding of product life cycles is an essential element in strategic planning. This is particularly so in the modern business environment where product life cycles are shortening and product customisation is tending to increase. The relevance of the product life cycle for management accounting purposes was encountered earlier in this text.

4 Internal control systems

4.1 Background

Control system theory has been encountered several times already in this text. At this point, we need only consider those aspects of control systems that are applicable to strategy.

DEFINITION

Organisational control is the process of ensuring that an organisation is pursuing actions and strategies which will enable it to achieve its goals.

One aspect of control is the assessment of actual performance against planned performance, and reacting to the results shown. To be effective, the internal control system must be designed to:

- provide quick, accurate reports of deviations from planned performance
- produce reports which are phrased in the same terms as the plan
- report to the correct level within the organisation
- reflect the needs of the organisation.

These issues were addressed earlier in this text in the context of information management.

4.2 Feedforward and feedback control

All performance measurements are part of a feedforward/feedback control model (an idea considered earlier in this text) where progress against plans, budgets, targets and standards is monitored by the analysis of significant variances and the use of different performance measures across various dimensions.

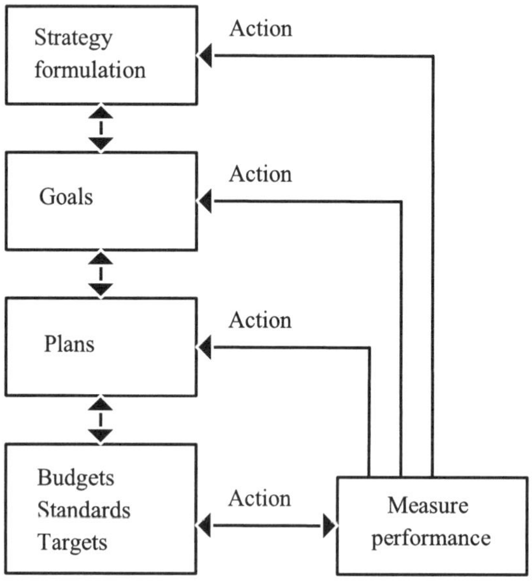

Feedforward/feedback control model

KEY POINT

A feedback control measures the outputs of a process and then provides information regarding corrective action to the process or the inputs, after the outputs have been produced.

Feedforward control will inform management of deviations from programme in time for them to take corrective action.

A feedback control measures the outputs of a process and then provides information regarding corrective action to the process or the inputs, after the outputs have been produced. In most management problems, because of time lags in implementing the corrective process, this is not good enough. For example if the chief accountant is informed in September that the administration department has overspent against budget due to a purchase in June, there is nothing that can be done.

Feedforward control will inform management of deviations from programme in time for them to take corrective action. This method is used to overcome the time lag problems often encountered by feedback systems, and also where future control is needed, for example in chemical and petrochemical process systems.

Feedforward systems monitor the inputs into the process to ascertain whether the inputs are as planned; if they are not, the inputs, or perhaps the process, are changed in order to ensure the desired results. In the above example, the administration department would have to submit an estimate for the item they wish to purchase. The organisation would then have to decide whether to refuse the request or change the budget in order to allow the purchase to be made without contriving budget restrictions.

4.3 Characteristics of operational planning and control

KEY POINT

Operational plans are the short-term element of the company's overall plan.

DEFINITION

Operational planning and control can be defined as planning and controlling the effective and efficient performance of specific tasks.

Operational plans are the short-term element of the company's overall plan. They are concerned with the day to day running of the company in the immediate future and usually cover a period of one year.

Operational planning and control can be defined as planning and controlling the effective and efficient performance of specific tasks. It therefore differs from management planning and control in focusing on one task at a time, whereas management planning and control focuses on resource requirements for the whole range of tasks.

A further difference is that management planning and control is essentially a matter of exercising management judgement, with some scientific forecasting and evaluation methods available to assist, while operational planning and control is in general far more scientific.

At the operational level, problems tend to be repetitive: general rules can often, therefore, be laid down as to how to respond to a given situation, though there are of course exceptions requiring management judgement. Anthony uses the terms 'programmable' and 'non-programmable' control: most management control is non-programmable while most operational control is of the programmable type.

Programmable control is applicable where the optimum relation between inputs and outputs can be established in advance and where rules can therefore be used to decide the action which will be most efficient in a given set of circumstances.

Examples are: inventory control, where stock levels can be decided when the storage cost, cost of losing an order etc, are known; the determination of the optimum mix under a set of constraints, which can be solved by linear programming techniques; production scheduling in automated plants. As new techniques are developed, more activities become susceptible to programmable control and the usefulness of computers is enhanced.

Because of the shorter time-scale involved, forecasting at the operational level can be more accurate than at the management or strategic planning levels, and actual data can be quickly obtained for comparison with the forecast or target. Continuous feedback is therefore possible as in the diagram below:

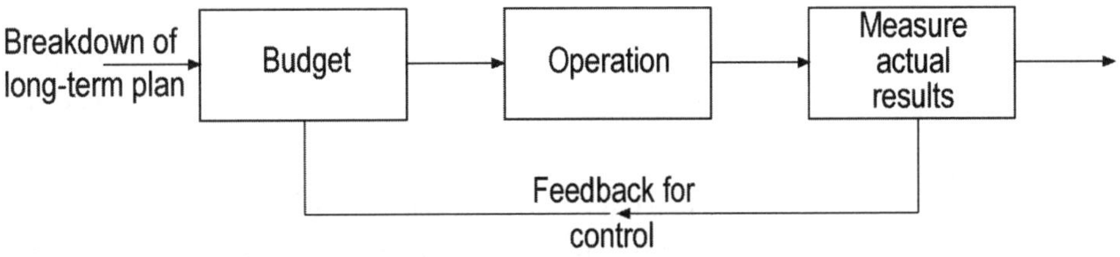

Contrast this with strategic or management control where, because plans are long term, results may never be available for comparison with targets because plans may never be fully implemented. Only progress towards targets can be measured. Even if results could be measured they would come too late for effective corrective action to be taken. Because operational control does not suffer from such difficulties, it is considerably easier.

KEY POINT

A computer can be used for comparing results with targets and analysing variances, but it cannot explain the variances.

A good operational control system should require a minimum of management intervention. The principle of management by exception can be applied, the manager intervening only when deviations from the plan are revealed. Nevertheless, success is dependent on good management - a good information system alone will not solve all the problems. Intervention, when it is necessary, must be done promptly to prevent any further deviations, and it takes a good manager to recognise the warning signs early enough. In addition it is only the manager who can take account of human factors - morale, motivation etc. A computer can be used for comparing results with targets and analysing variances, but it cannot explain the variances.

5 Benchmarking

5.1 Inter-firm comparisons – Benchmarking measures

Benchmarking has already been encountered in the context of performance evaluation and not-for-profit organisations. Benchmarking is also relevant in the context of strategy formulation.

KEY POINT

An inter-firm comparison helps to put the company's resources and performance into perspective and reflects the fact that it is the relative position of a company which matters in assessing its capabilities.

An inter-firm comparison helps to put the company's resources and performance into perspective and reflects the fact that it is the relative position of a company which matters in assessing its capabilities. The performance of different organisations, subsidiaries or investment centres can be compared ('benchmarked') by calculating suitable financial or non-financial ratios for each of them to ascertain which are better or worse than the average. Comparative analysis can also be usefully applied to any value activity which underpins the competitive strategy of an organisation, an industry or a nation.

To find out the level of investment in fixed assets of competitors, the business can use physical observation, information from trade press or trade association announcements, supplier press releases as well as their externally published financial statements, to build a clear picture of the relative scale, capacity, age and cost for each competitor. The method of operating these assets, in terms of hours and shift patterns, can be established by observation, discussions with suppliers and customers or by asking existing or ex-employees of the particular competitor. If the method of operating can be ascertained it should enable a combination of internal personnel management and industrial engineering managers to work out the likely relative differences in labour costs. The rates of pay and conditions can generally be found with reference to nationally negotiated agreements, local and national press advertising for employees, trade and employment associations and recruitment consultants. When this cost is used alongside an intelligent assessment of how many employees would be needed by the competitor in each area, given their equipment etc, a good idea of the labour costs can be obtained.

Another difference which should be noted is the nature of the competitors' costs as well as their relative levels. Where a competitor has a lower level of committed fixed costs, e.g. lower fixed labour costs due to a larger proportion of temporary workers, it may be able to respond more quickly to a downturn in demand by rapidly laying off the temporary staff. Equally, in a tight labour market and with rising sales, it may have to increase its pay levels to attract new workers.

In some industries, one part of the competitor analysis is surprisingly direct. Each new competitive product is purchased on a regular basis and then systematically taken apart, so that each component can be identified as well as the processes used to put the parts together. The respective areas of the business will then assess the costs associated with each element so that a complete product cost can be found for the competitive product.

A comparison of similar value activities e.g. cost structures, between organisations is useful when the strategic context is taken into consideration. For example, a straight comparison of resource deployment between two competitive organisations may reveal quite different situations in the labour cost as a percentage of the total cost. The conclusions drawn from this, however, depend upon circumstances. If the firms are competing largely on the basis of price, then differentials in these costs could be crucial. In contrast, the additional use of labour by one organisation may be an essential support for the special services provided which differentiate that organisation from its competitors.

One danger of inter-firm analysis is that the company may overlook the fact that the whole industry is performing badly, and is losing out competitively to other countries with better resources or even other industries which can satisfy customers' needs in different ways. Therefore, if an industry comparison is performed it should make some assessment of how the resources utilisation compares with other countries and industries. This can be done by obtaining a measurement of stock turnover or yield from raw materials.

5.2 Obtaining information for benchmarking

Benchmarking against competitors involves the gathering of a range of information about them. Financial information will generally be reasonably easy to obtain, from published accounts, financial press etc. Some product information may be obtained by acquiring their products and examining them in detail to ascertain the components used and their construction ('reverse engineering'). Literature will also be available in the form of brochures, trade journals etc.

However, most non-financial information, concerning competitors' processes, customer and supplier relationships, customer satisfaction etc, will not be so readily available.

To overcome this problem, benchmarking exercises are generally carried out with organisations taken from within the same group of companies (intra-group benchmarking) or from similar but non-competing industries (inter-industry benchmarking).

Benchmarking and associated performance evaluation practice lies squarely within the domain of 'strategic management accounting' (see Chapter 4). Such practice expands the scope of information used as part of the management accounting process far beyond what was considered normal until very recently.

5.3 Example of R&D indices

A typical analysis of the R&D expenditure of UK companies could take the following approach. Comparisons could be made with previous years, between industry sectors and also with international competitors. Some examples of the data that might result are as follows:

(a) **Change on previous year**

	% increase in spend
All industry	12
Aerospace	27
Chemicals	7
Food	2
Leisure	46
Service industries	5

(b) **Inter-industry comparisons**

	R&D per employee (£000)	**R&D / Sales (%)**
Aerospace	2.32	3.33
Chemicals	2.72	3.29
Food	1.01	1.22
Leisure	0.22	0.37
Service industries	2.59	2.65

(c) **International comparisons of R&D per employee (£000)**

	UK	USA	Germany
All industry	1.53	3.73	4.32
Aerospace	2.34	2.42	17.48
Chemicals	3.02	4.96	5.57
Leisure	0.21	4.85	n/a
Service industries	5.82	n/a	1.89

(d) **International comparisons of R&D/Sales (%)**

	UK	USA	Germany	Japan
All industry	1.69	3.80	5.09	3.71
Aerospace	3.34	4.20	23.78	n/a
Chemicals	3.56	4.50	5.79	3.88
Leisure	0.36	6.80	n/a	3.62
Service industries	4.51	n/a	2.75	n/a

The evidence seems to be that UK firms are not doing enough to match the efforts of their main competitors in other countries.

6 Behavioural issues

6.1 Management and behavioural aspects of strategic planning and control

The whole concept of strategic planning explored above implies a certain top down approach. In the context of budgeting it has been seen that organisations can adopt a top down approach whereby a master budget is first prepared which is split into subsidiary departmental budgets or a bottom up approach whereby departmental budgets are first prepared and then aggregated to form a master budget. This dichotomy applies also in strategic planning.

KEY POINT

The idea of divisional autonomy is that individual managers operate their business units as if they were independent businesses – seeking and exploiting local opportunities as they arise.

Even in the era of divisional autonomy and employee empowerment it is difficult to imagine that a rigorous strategic planning regime could be associated with a bottom up management culture. There is a potential for conflict here. The idea of divisional autonomy is that individual managers operate their business units as if they were independent businesses – seeking and exploiting local opportunities as they arise. Managers are rewarded in some manner which reflects the results they achieve. This is particularly critical in the modern economic context where product life cycles are short and the business environment changes very often and quickly.

One can suggest a list of measures that might be adopted to reconcile the different priorities in a variety of different circumstances. However, it is not always productive to try to express all and any situations in the form of a neat code of rules – particularly in a creative area like strategy.

6.2 Short-term freewheeling opportunism

Opponents of structured long-term strategic planning argue that in instigating explicit long-term strategy managers are putting their organisations into what is effectively a strait-jacket, resulting in a serious loss of flexibility rendering difficult the exploitation of opportunities on a more free-wheeling basis. The arguments imply certain weaknesses in the disciplined approach, such as its inflexibility, forecasting inaccuracy, complexity and bureaucratic nature.

The characteristics of **free-wheeling opportunism** are as follows.

- Essentially it concentrates on finding, evaluating and exploiting short-term product-market opportunities instead of adhering to the rigidity of a predetermined strategy.
- It encourages a non-corporate philosophy, and managers who have vested interests will try to exert pressure for the acceptance of their own ideas even if they are incompatible with existing corporate aims.

- It is perceived by some managers to be dynamic, exciting and innovative. Furthermore because of its unstructured approach, strategy arising from it is seen to bear the stamp of individual managers.

7 The arguments against long-term strategy

(a) **Setting corporate objectives**

A criticism frequently levelled at the practice of spelling out corporate objectives is that the exercise descends into the formulation of empty platitudes which offer no positive directional indicators for decision-making. Those executives responsible for decision-making need to know not merely the overall direction in which the organisation is supposed to be heading, but also which evaluative standards to apply in order to judge competitive strategies, with the standards expressed in meaningful terms such as market share and sales volume. Corporate strategy can be viewed from so many different angles and interests that it may be necessary to apply a whole range of evaluative standards, some of which may be in conflict, for instance, a strengthening of liquid resources may be accompanied by a lower return on capital employed. An individual measure will have to be weighted according to its significance in the problem situation under review, although it is not possible to carry out such evaluation with any sort of mathematical precision.

(b) **The difficulties of forecasting accurately**

The development of a forecasting capability, and the development of models which relate environmental changes to corporate performance are significant aspects of strategic planning. While the general level of practice concerning environmental issues is still quite primitive, the state of the art is rapidly advancing.

There are difficult problems associated with trying to accurately forecast for the long-term.

- The fact that it is a long-term period.
- The complexity of the environment that needs to be forecast.
- The rapidity and novelty of environmental change.
- The interrelationships between the environmental variables involved.
- The limitations of the data available.
- The amount and complexity of the calculations involved.

(c) **Short-term pressures**

The pressures on management are for short-term results and ostensibly strategy is concerned with the long term e.g. 'What should we be doing now to help us reach the position we want to be in, in five years time.' Often it is difficult to motivate managers by setting long-term expectations.

(d) **Rigidity**

Operational managers are frequently reluctant to specify their planning assumptions because the situations which their plans are designed to meet may change so rapidly that they can be made to look foolish. Even if a plan is reasonably accurate, the situation might change for reasons other than those forecast. Executives are often held prisoners by the rigidity of the planning process, because plans have to be set out in detail long before the period to which they apply.

The rigidity of the long-term plan, particularly in regard to the rationing and scheduling of resources, may also place the company in a position where it is unable to react to short-term unforeseen opportunities, or serious short-term crisis.

(e) **Stifling initiative**

If adherence to the strategy becomes all-important, it discounts flair and creativity. Operational managers can generate enthusiasm or dampen down potential trouble spots and quick action may be required to avert trouble or improve a situation by actions outside the strategy. If operational managers then have to defend their actions against criticisms of acting '**outside the plan**', irrespective of the resultant benefits, they are likely to become apathetic and indifferent.

(f) **The cost**

The strategic planning process can be costly, involving the use of specialists, sometimes a specialist department, and taking up management time. The process generates its own bureaucracy and associated paper or electronic data flow. Personal authorities are, to a greater or lesser extent, replaced by written guidelines.

(g) **Lacks dynamism**

The process might be inhibitive in that it programmes activities and events and removes the excitement and exhilaration of spontaneity and the unexpected.

(h) **Why start now?**

A general attitude particularly shown by managers in small growing companies is that they have managed quite successfully in the past without formalised strategic planning systems. So why start now?

(i) **Management distrust of techniques**

The strategic planning process involves the use of management techniques, not least forecasting, modelling, cost analysis and operational research. This can produce adverse reactions for two reasons. Firstly, senior management may distrust 'laboratory techniques untested in their ambit of activity', and secondly they might distrust the recommendations of younger specialist people who are 'on balance heavy on academic learning but light on practical experience'.

(j) **The clash of personal and corporate loyalties**

The adoption of corporate strategy requires a tacit acceptance by everyone that the interests of departments, activities and individuals are subordinate to the corporate interests. Department managers are required to consider the contribution to corporate profits or the reduction in corporate costs of any decision. They should not allow their decisions to be limited by short-term departmental parameters.

It is only natural that managers should seek personal advancement. As a company is the primary vehicle by which this can be achieved, a cleavage of loyalty may occur. A problem of strategic planning is identifying those areas where there may be a clash of interests and loyalties, and in assessing where an individual has allowed vested interests to dominate decisions.

8 SWOT analysis

8.1 Background

DEFINITION

'A critical assessment of the strengths and weaknesses, opportunities and threats (**SWOT analysis**) in relation to the internal and environmental factors affecting an entity in order to establish its condition prior to the preparation of the long-term plan.

To assist in closing the gap between its predicted and desired performance (note: the planning gap is considered in Chapter 9), the organisation's strengths, weaknesses, opportunities and threats need to be ascertained. The work involved draws on the data obtained about objectives, current position, extrapolated position, gaps and environmental forecasts, and is sometimes called **corporate appraisal**.

The factors involved in SWOT analysis are wide ranging and include decision variables which strengthen or constrain the operational powers of the company, such as the size of its markets, the competitive forces in the markets, opportunities for new products, availability of skilled labour, control of vital raw materials and access to additional capital.

KEY POINT

To assist in closing the gap between its predicted and desired performance, the organisation's strengths, weaknesses, opportunities and threats need to be ascertained, sometimes called **corporate appraisal**.

8.2 Competence and competitive profile

The appraisal process will raise serious questions and may produce surprises. The findings need to be compiled into a presentation format which will take the form of what Ansoff refers to as a **Competence and Competitive Profile**. If correctly formatted and presented, the document will be a succinct summary of the appraisal and will concentrate management's attention on main areas for resolution. The company profile provides details of current and projected corporate resources in terms of capacity, location, costs, operational flexibility, relevant details of past operational performances and trends, by activities, divisions and cost centres, as well as a survey of the major influences and pressure points impacting on the operational environment, such as target markets, market shares, competitive activities, product mix, technological factors, economic trends and assumptions.

Many analytical tools have been developed over recent years to aid this process. They include:

- financial ratio analysis
- product-market matrix displays
- product-life cycle analysis.

Here we consider the overall corporate appraisal without delving into all the individual techniques that might aid its process. The following table adapted from Ansoff's **Corporate Strategy** shows how a company's skills, facilities etc, can be analysed both in relation to competitors in its own industry and more widely. Ansoff suggests that in assigning the relative ratings some companies might use a simple two-valued strength or weakness classification. Others would prefer to rank the capabilities as outstanding, average or weak.

	Facilities	Personnel	Organisational Skills	Management skills
Finance & general management	Data processing equipment.	Depth of GM and Fin. skills to cope easily.	Divisional structure. Planning & control.	Investment management control. Centralised. Decentralised.
Research & Development	Special equipment test facilities.	Special technical skills.	Product development industrial & consumer products.	Cost-performance optimisation.
Operations	Machine shop automated products.	Machine operation. Close tolerance work.	Mass production. Batch & jobbing. Quality control.	Tight scheduling. Cost control.
Marketing	Warehousing. Retailing.	Types of selling expertise.	Direct sales. Retail. Industrial service.	Industrial marketing. Consumer marketing.

The competence profile will serve three separate uses for assessment.

(a) **Assessment of internal strengths and weaknesses**

The competence profile can be used to assess the company's internal resources and to determine the areas in which the company is either very good or very poor. The facts and figures required for the assessment would be obtained from the company's Position Audit.

(b) **Assessment of competitiveness**

A part of the appraisal will conduct a competence profile of each of the company's main competitors. Superposition of the company's competence profile with the respective competitive profiles measures the company's competitiveness and determines those areas where the company excels or is deficient.

(c) **Assessment of external opportunities and threats**

Another part of the appraisal will conduct a competence profile of the company's industry and outside industries. Superposition of these profiles measures the attractiveness, or otherwise, of the company's present industry and other industries. It will also measure the company's 'fit' with its existing industry, and its 'fit' with other industries thus indicating the chances of a successful entry.

All of these assessments should incorporate an allowance for the risks and uncertainties that are associated with exogenous variables. The SWOT analysis can be used as the basis for identifying the objectives and goals of the organisation. For example, objectives should be adopted which can draw on the identified strengths of the organisation. Conversely, objectives may be avoided which are likely to be frustrated by identified weaknesses.

9 Multinational companies

A multinational company is normally considered to be one that undertakes a substantial proportion of its business in countries other than that in which it is domiciled. Typically, it takes the form of a central corporation with subsidiaries in each of the countries in which it operates. Well known examples include Ford, Shell, Nestle, General Motors, Toyota and Microsoft.

By the early 1990s, 37,000 multinational companies with annual sales of $5.5bn controlled about one third of the world's private sector assets. The advent of these multinationals is associated with the apparent globalisation of the world economy. Various factors have contributed to this development, but one factor is critical. Increases in the scale of technology (in terms of cost, risk and complexity) have rendered even the largest national markets too small to be meaningful economic units on a stand-alone basis. Companies must expand internationally to support the technological development that is needed to remain competitive in many fields.

The strategic process in a multinational company must take account of certain special features. These include:

- **Process specialisation.** There may be a cost advantage in locating certain types of activity in certain countries. For example, a labour intensive operation may be best placed in a low wage area. Many companies (and not just traditional multinationals) have recently relocated customer service desks and telephone call centres to India. Some areas of IT support have been similarly moved.

- **Product specialisation.** In spite of globalisation and the concept of 'world products', particular countries have characteristic tastes that the multinational must cater to. For example, electrical goods sold in the UK are usually fitted internally with colour coded wires. Those same goods, when sold in Scandinavia, have to be fitted with white wires – even though those wires are barely visible from outside. This reflects national differences in product taste.

- **International trade issues**. The economics of a multinational operation may be highly sensitive to issues such as exchange rate fluctuations. For example, in the 1980s many car manufacturers (Nissan, Toyota and Peugeot to name but three) built car assembly facilities in the UK to serve the whole of Europe – because the UK was perceived as a low cost area. The UK's non adoption of the Euro and the appreciation of the Pound in the late 90s suddenly made the UK a high cost area. For a time, the viability of several high-profile plants (e.g. the Nissan plant at Sunderland) was brought into question.
- **Political sensitivities**. The multinational company operates across state boundaries and must be acutely aware of associated risk factors. In the 1970s the government of the Shah of Iran was regarded as a model of stability for the Middle East. Many multinational companies became involved in projects and business ventures in Iran. The sudden collapse of the Shah's government in 1979 resulted the wholesale repudiation of private and public debt and the appropriation of foreign owned assets by the new Islamic government.
- **Administrative issues.** A multinational company will find that even its own internal transactions are vulnerable to exchange rate movements, currency exchange controls and the existence (or absence) of international tax treaties. For example, if a multinational domiciled in country A tries to repatriate profits earned by its subsidiary in country B then it may find that those profits are taxed twice – once in A and again in B.

A detailed examination of strategic planning for multinational operations goes beyond the scope of this text. However, the above issues are important to most businesses considering extending operations outside their home countries.

It is important to note that many observers perceive the concept of the monolithic multinational company to have become dated.

"At the end of the 19th century, the vast majority of international transactions were organized through the market. By the last quarter of the 20th century multinational companies replaced the market as the primary mode of organization of the international economy. Economic transactions were internalized as trade and investment were brought within the organizational hierarchy of the corporation.

Alliances represent another shift in the organization of international transactions – from organizational hierarchies to networks; from mass to flexible production; from large integrated organizations to horizontal networks of economic units".

Stephen J Kobrin, 'Globalization and multinationals', 1997

The modern trend in international business seems to be away from the old multinational corporations and towards networks and alliances. Strategic planning for the latter is another issue altogether.

10 Environmental accounting

This chapter closes with a reference to the practice of 'environmental management accounting'. This is a topic that seems to vary in profile over time.

The link between business operations and the environment is one which is periodically highlighted by events such as the Bhopal chemical leak, the Exxon Valdez oil spill and the Brent Spa disaster. Industrial activity can impose costs on the environment which are external to the finances of the activities themselves. A company which pollutes the atmosphere around its plants may experience no direct cost arising from that pollution but many local residents and other businesses may suffer as a result of it.

Protest organisations such as the Eco-Warriors, Friends of the Earth and Greenpeace actively publicise such environmental costs and seek to draw attention to those responsible through protest, demonstration and boycott.

Environmental awareness has been reinforced through recent international agreements on relevant issues such as The Montreal Protocol, the Rio Declaration and The Kyoto Protocol.

Environmental management accounting is the practice of identifying and reporting the full impact on the environment of business activities. Thus, decision makers within a business are made aware of the impact on the environment of the activities they are responsible for and can decide whether or not to modify their plans having regard to this. EMA may be defined as 'using monetary and physical information for internal management use'.

Environmental awareness may influence management decisions in a number of areas ranging from long term strategic planning through to short term product costing decisions. For example, a business may decide not to place orders with a supplier known to harm the local environment it operates in or to exploit child labour. Such decisions are not wholly selfless. A business that is known to ignore the environmental impact of its activities may become unpopular.

An unpopular business may encounter problems in a number of areas ranging from difficulty in obtaining planning permissions through to outright customer boycotts.

One example of environment-friendly action taken by a business was the adoption of bio-degradable packaging by McDonalds. They were using plastic packaging which was causing a litter problem and a hazard to wildlife in many areas near their outlets. McDonalds responded (at some cost) by substituting paper packaging which degrades quickly once used.

Obviously, a business like that of McDonalds had to be sensitive to the impact of its operations on the environment. EMA seeks to report to management the full range of impacts that its activities are having on the environment. How it responds to such reports will usually involve an element of judgement.

The concept of environmental accounting is not new and terms such as 'environmental audit' and 'environmental activity-based accounting' are in wide use. Indeed, environmental awareness can be a central element in Life Cycle Costing and Total Quality Management.

Conclusion

Corporate planning is an ongoing activity that seeks to determine the future direction of the company. SWOT analysis is one technique that may be used in planning. Once the overall objectives have been set, long term strategies and short term operating plans can be developed. The product lifecycle concept means that businesses cannot rely on current revenue generating products to continue indefinitely and must therefore plan to replace those revenues. Plans are evaluated by means of control systems. The feedback obtained from these systems will be used to revise the operational activities of the company and/or the plan.

SELF-TEST QUESTIONS

Introduction

1 What are the four main elements in corporate planning? (1.1)

Corporate planning

2 What is the distinction between long and short-term planning? (2.3)

Product life cycles

3 What is a product life cycle and what is its relevance to planning? (3)

The arguments against long-term strategy

4 List the arguments against long-term strategy formulation. (7)

SWOT analysis

5 Explain the nature and purpose of SWOT analysis. (8)

EXAM-TYPE QUESTION

Strengths and weaknesses

In ascertaining an organisation's strengths and weaknesses, management often concentrate on certain key areas. You are required to specify and describe five possible key areas and explain the way that an assessment of this type may be conducted. **(25 marks)**

For the answer to this question, see the 'Answers' section at the end of the book.

Chapter 18
PRICING 1

CHAPTER CONTENTS

This chapter explores the role of product pricing in maximising shareholder value. In particular, it considers the manner in which management accounting technique contributes to pricing decisions.

Objectives

When you have studied this chapter you should be able to do the following.

- Identify and discuss market situations which influence the pricing policy adopted by an organisation.
- Explain and discuss the variables (including price) which influence demand for a product or service.
- Explain the price elasticity of demand.
- Manipulate data in order to determine an optimum price/output level.
- Calculate prices using full cost and marginal cost as the pricing base.
- Compare the use of full cost pricing and marginal cost pricing as planning and decision-making aids.

1 Introduction

Several factors underlie all pricing decisions and effective decisions will be based on a careful consideration of the following:

(a) **Organisational goals**. If a goal of cash maximisation is assumed, then the setting of selling prices must be seen as a means of achieving this end.

(b) **Product mix**. If the organisation produces a range of different products, it is faced with the problem of setting selling prices for each individual product in such a manner as to obtain the optimum product mix i.e. that mix which will maximise cash inflows generated from the sale of all products.

(c) **Price/demand relationships** (demand curves). For most products, there exists a relationship between selling price and the quantity demanded at that price. Customers will usually have an alternative source of supply and will be driven away by a selling price that is set too high, or, for instance in the case of certain luxury goods such as perfumes, jewellery and wines, by a selling price that is set too low. Product quality will also tend to influence the price and demand relationship.

A knowledge of the price elasticity of demand (i.e., the responsiveness of changes in demand to changes in price) is therefore vital in the selling price decision.

(d) **Competitors and markets**. An organisation's competitors will usually react in some way to changes made to the selling price structure. In practice, therefore, price adjustments may be heavily influenced by expectations of competitor reaction.

(e) **Product life cycle**. During the life of an individual product, several stages are apparent: introduction, growth, maturity, saturation and decline. The duration of each stage of the life cycle varies according to the type of product, but the concept is nevertheless important as each stage is likely to influence the firm's pricing policy. The sales pricing mechanism is sometimes used to 'control' the life cycle of a product.

(f) **Marketing strategy**. Selling prices should be set with reference to overall marketing strategy. Product design and quality, advertising and promotion, distribution methods etc, are likely to influence the sales pricing decision.

For example, by concentrating on advertising or packaging, a firm may be able to set higher prices for its product or, conversely, lower prices might be necessary in order to distribute the product through a supermarket chain.

(g) **Cost**. In the long run, all operating costs must be fully covered by sales revenue. However, as will be seen later, over-emphasis on cost in the short-run may result in sub-optimal decisions.

2 Demand and its determinants

2.1 Introduction

DEFINITION

Demand is the quantity of a good which consumers want, and are willing and able to pay for.

If you think about how you decide which goods to buy, you will realise that there are many factors entering into the decision.

2.2 Group demand

KEY POINT

If you think about how you decide which goods to buy, you will realise that there are many factors entering into the decision.

It is sometimes argued that the choices made by people are too unpredictable to form the basis of any realistic measurement of demand. This may be true of the actions of individuals, but it is a remarkable fact that if a sufficiently large group is examined, there is a sufficient degree of constancy for measurements and predictions to be made with a reasonable degree of accuracy. For example, you may be offered a choice of several breakfast cereals each morning and it would be difficult to predict which particular one to choose on any specific day. However, when a thousand people are observed over a period of time it may be possible to predict that, on average, a quarter will choose one brand, a fifth another and so on. If information of this type is available you can then estimate the size of weekly or monthly demand for the various types of breakfast cereal. In the same way, you can estimate the number of heart attacks likely to be suffered by people living in an area during a year, or the likely number of young people taking A-level examinations who will pass and qualify for higher education. This consistency of large numbers over a given period of time allows sufficient information to be gathered to provide the foundation for the study of economics.

People, of course, change and demand changes. The main influences bringing about changes in the demand for goods and services can be classified as follows:

2.3 Price

KEY POINT

For each of the goods, the higher the price, the less likely people are to buy it.

This is probably the most significant factor. For each of the goods, the higher the price, the less likely people are to buy it. Price is one of the most important elements of micro-economics and it will be discussed in considerable detail in the following sections.

However, the influence that any one manufacturer has over price depends on circumstances. Products such as crude oil and grain are traded on world markets. Those world markets establish 'going' world prices that no one supplier can influence. The individual supplier can sell as much or as little as he can produce at the going price. Traditionally, manufactured goods are differentiated (or 'branded') and traded through segmented markets where the individual supplier's unit sales vary inversely with the unit selling price he sets.

Some observers claim that the development of 'world products' may move more products towards the position of having going world prices. Conversely, other observers perceive that shorter product life cycles and greater product differentiation may move more products away from having going world prices.

2.4 Income

KEY POINT

In general, the more people earn, the more they will buy.

In general, the more people earn, the more they will buy. If someone is quite well-off, they are more likely to buy a certain pair of shoes (*ceteris paribus*), whereas if they are poor, they will not. Note the use of *ceteris paribus* here. We must say that 'all other things being equal' they will buy the shoes. An example of all other things **not** being equal would be if the weather suddenly changes. If it starts snowing heavily and they are wearing sandals, they may buy the shoes irrespective of how rich or poor they are.

KEY POINT

The demand for most goods increases as income rises, and these goods are known as normal goods.

The demand for most goods increases as income rises, and these goods are known as normal goods.

Do note, however, that people will not necessarily buy more of **all** goods as their incomes rise. Some goods are known as inferior goods, such as terrestrial analogue televisions. They are cheap goods which people might buy when on a low income, but as their incomes rise, they switch to more attractive alternatives (in this case, digital satellite televisions).

DEFINITIONS

For normal goods, demand rises as consumers' income rises, and vice versa. For inferior goods, demand **falls** as income rises, and vice versa.

Two or more goods are defined as substitutes if they are interchangeable in giving consumers utility. Substitution is a matter of degree i.e. all goods are substitutes, but some are closer than others.

If good A and good B are **substitutes**, a **rise** in the price of one will cause a **rise** in demand for the other, and vice versa.

2.5 The price of substitute goods

For example, margarine is a substitute for butter. Other goods, such as milk, have few, if any, substitutes. If something has a substitute, you will probably compare the price of the substitute with the price of the good you are thinking of buying. Butter is more expensive than margarine, so, apart from the health considerations, you may decide to buy margarine. On the other hand, milk has very few substitutes, so your decision to buy it will not depend heavily on the price of other products.

If the price of a substitute rises, then demand for the good in question will also rise.

Suppose the price of margarine rose. Even if it is still cheaper than butter, some people will decide that the difference in price is so small that they would rather buy butter. Demand for margarine will fall, while that for butter will rise.

Conversely, if the price of a substitute falls, then demand for the good in question will also fall, as people switch to the substitute.

2.6 The price of complements

DEFINITION

Complements are goods which must be used together.

KEY POINT

The price of a good's complements is very important when considering whether or not to buy it.

For example, a compact disc player is no good without any compact discs. The price of a good's complements is very important when considering whether or not to buy it. You may be able to afford the player, but if you will not be able to buy any compact discs, there is little point in the purchase. A common marketing ploy is to price a product fairly low, but to set the prices of its complements very high. The low price attracts the customers, who are not aware of the amount they will ultimately have to pay to use the product. For example, a high performance laser printer can be bought for as little as £75 but replacement ink cartridges for the printer may cost £50.

DEFINITION

If good A and good B are complements, a rise in the price of one will cause a fall in demand for the other, and vice versa.

If the price of a **complement** rises, then demand for the good in question will **fall**.

Suppose the price of compact discs rose. Fewer people would be able to afford them, so fewer people would find it worth their while to buy the compact disc players. Demand for the compact discs will fall, as will demand for the players.

Conversely, if the price of a complement falls, demand for the good will rise.

2.7 Taste

This is an all-embracing term. Taste is influenced by many different things. Advertising may make something popular or unpopular. You may decide not to buy butter purely on health grounds, having been made aware of its high cholesterol levels. Or fashion may induce you to buy a new pair of shoes even if you don't really need them and cannot afford them. The weather is a major factor. People will buy more umbrellas when it is raining and more ice creams when it is hot.

Of all the factors influencing demand, taste is the most difficult one to quantify.

2.8 Market size

Clearly, the size of total demand depends on the number of people who are aware of the good's existence, who are able to obtain it and who are likely to want it. Market size can, therefore, be altered by changes in the size and structures of the population. If the birth rate falls in an area, this will have a long-term effect on the total population size and will have a more immediate effect in reducing the number of babies hence influencing the demand for prams, equipment and clothing designed for babies. It will, of course, also affect the demand for school places, for schoolteachers and for people to train teachers.

2.9 Advertising

This may be regarded as a subsidiary influence affecting market size, but it can also be seen as a factor important in itself. In general, it is not only the volume and quality of advertising that can influence demand for a product but also the amount of advertising in comparison with that for competing products. Advertisers cannot often increase total consumption; more often they transfer it from one good to another. Some research indicates that there may be a direct relationship between the proportion of advertising carried out for a product within a market and the proportion of total market sales going to that product.

2.10 Segmentation in the market

One critical assumption in the foregoing is that all customers must pay the same price for a given good. However, this is rarely the case. Many markets can be segmented in some manner which allows different customers to be charged different prices. The advantages of this to the supplier are apparent when the following simple example is considered.

A company sells units (variable cost being £10 per unit) and market demand for units is as follows at alternative selling prices:

Units demanded	*Unit price*
100	£20
40	£30

If the company has to sell all the units at the same price, then it is apparent that contribution will be maximised at unit price £20 where demand is 100 units and contribution is £1,000 (that is 100 units × £10 contribution per unit). However, if it adopts this price then 40 of the customers will pay a price which is £10 per unit less than that they would have been prepared to pay – given that they pay £20 per unit when they would have been prepared to pay £30 per unit.

What if it is possible to segment the market and charge the 40 keenest customers a price of £30 and the remaining 60 customers a price of £20?

In this case a total contribution of £1,400 contribution will be generated (that is 40 units × £20 contribution per unit plus 60 units at £10 contribution per unit).

In effect, we are pricing along the demand function and extracting from customers what each is prepared to pay – not a single, uniform price. This practice is known as 'price discrimination'.

Price discrimination is surprisingly widespread. For example:

- richer people are usually willing to pay more. It is possible to charge higher prices in shops that are frequented mainly by rich people such as Harrods in London
- attaching some minor loss of flexibility to lower price sales will often allow the less keen customers to be charged lower prices. Public transport is a common example of this. Passengers travelling on a train from London to Newcastle all consume the same good but will be paying fares ranging from £140 (standard ticket) to £30 (pre-booked well in advance and available only on less popular services)
- geographic barriers may allow customers in one region to be charged a different price to those in another region; for some years cars were sold at higher prices in the UK market than those charged in neighbouring countries. This was sustainable because few British customers were willing to take the trouble to buy outside the UK.

Pricing is one of the most powerful weapons in the armoury of business management. Cost reduction programmes and strategic initiatives can take years to implement, but selling prices can be changed overnight. If a business understands its demand structure then it is usually able to squeeze far more revenue out of a market than is otherwise the case.

3 Calculating price elasticity of demand

3.1 The formulae for price elasticity of demand

DEFINITION

Price elasticity of demand is the degree of sensitivity of demand for a good to changes in price of that good.

We have already discussed the different influences on demand; one of the most important was price. It is useful to be able to analyse in numerical terms the effect on demand of a change in price. We do this using price elasticity of demand (often shortened to 'elasticity of demand' or PED).

Price elasticity can be defined in a number of ways. One possible formula is:

KEY POINT

$$\text{PED} = \frac{\text{Percentage change in quantity demanded}}{\text{Percentage change in price}}$$

$$\text{PED} = \frac{\text{Percentage change in quantity demanded}}{\text{Percentage change in price}}$$

ACTIVITY 1

If PED for a certain good currently equals -2, how will sales be affected if price rises by 10%?

Feedback to this activity is at the end of the chapter.

3.2 An alternative presentation

An alternative presentation of the formula is suitable for calculations involving a straight-line demand curve, and is illustrated on the following page:

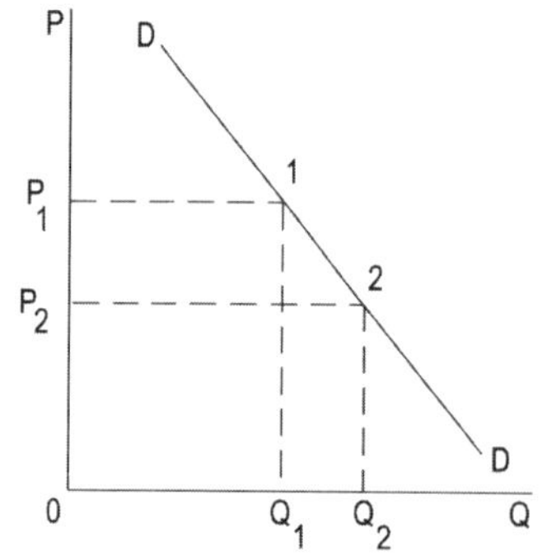

$$PED = \frac{\frac{Q_2 - Q_1}{Q_1} \times 100}{\frac{P_2 - P_1}{P_1} \times 100}$$

This equation calculates the elasticity at point 1 on the demand curve. The changes in quantity and price are expressed as a percentage of the quantity and price at point 1.

We will use an example to demonstrate how the equation works and how it relates to the first equation.

Example

A firm faces the following demand curve:

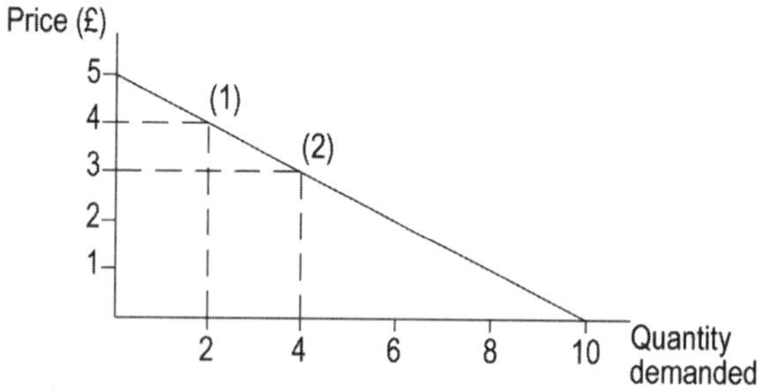

Figure 1

We want to work out the price elasticity of demand at point 1. The first step is to select any other point on the line to act as a reference point, point 2. Here we have chosen a point one step down the line from point 1, but on a straight-line demand curve any other point would give the same result.

The price and quantity at point 1 are P_1 and Q_1 respectively. So $P_1 = 4$ and $Q_1 = 2$. Similarly, price and quantity at point 2 are P_2 and Q_2 respectively. So $P_2 = 3$ and $Q_2 = 4$.

Applying the equation above:

$$PED = \frac{\frac{4-2}{2} \times 100}{\frac{3-4}{4} \times 100}$$

$$= \frac{\frac{2}{2} \times 100}{\frac{-1}{4} \times 100} = \frac{100}{-25} = -4.$$

So price elasticity of demand at point 1 is -4.

We can relate this to the formula which was given in terms of percentages. Consider quantity first. The move from point 1 to point 2 on the demand curve represents an increase in quantity of 2 units, from 2 to 4. In fact, quantity has gone up by 100%. This is reflected in the above calculation by the fraction $\frac{2}{2}$ = 1 or 100%.

Moving on to the price, a similar reasoning applies. The move from point 1 to point 2 represents a **decrease** in price of £1, from £4 to £3. Price has fallen by 25%. This is reflected by the fraction $\frac{-1}{4}$ = -25%.

Again, note the minus sign, which is there because price has **fallen**. Quantity demanded **rose**, so its change is **positive**. When we bring the two together in the fraction, the result is a negative number. The same would happen if price rose, giving a positive change, but quantity demanded fell, giving a negative change. Since for most goods price and quantity demanded move in opposite directions, most goods will have a negative price elasticity of demand.

So the second equation is simply a different form of the first equation. They are both measuring the response of quantity demanded to a price change, and they both measure the changes in the variables in terms of percentages.

ACTIVITY **2**

Explain in layman's terms what a price elasticity of –4 means.

Feedback to this activity is at the end of the chapter.

3.3 Notes on PED

- As mentioned above, PED for most goods is negative, so we often ignore the minus sign when talking about PED. For example, we could say that the price elasticity of demand at point 1 is 4, when strictly speaking it is -4.
- PED is different at different points of a demand curve, even if that 'curve' is a straight line. The next section will go into this more deeply.

3.4 The meaning of elasticity and inelasticity

It is important to understand what 'elastic' and 'inelastic' mean, rather than simply assign numbers to price elasticity.

If you return to the formulae, you should be able to see that when PED is greater than 1, a certain (percentage) change in price will give rise to a **greater** (percentage) change in quantity demanded. For example, the first activity in this chapter showed that a PED of 2 means that a 10% rise in price will induce a 20% fall in quantity demanded. In other words, demand is very responsive to price changes.

Conversely, when PED is less than 1, a given percentage change in price will result in a **smaller** percentage change in demand, so demand is **not** responsive to price changes, and when PED equals 1, the percentage change in quantity demanded equals the percentage change in price.

When PED>1, demand is relatively elastic and the quantity demanded is very responsive to price changes. When PED<1, demand is relatively inelastic and the quantity demanded is not very responsive to price changes.

KEY POINT

If demand is said to be inelastic, it means that the consequent demand change will be proportionately smaller than the price change.

Note that if demand is said to be inelastic, this does not mean that there will be no change in quantity demanded when the price changes, it means that the consequent demand change will be proportionately smaller than the price change. If demand does not change at all after a price change, demand is said to be perfectly inelastic, and this is a special case as will be seen below.

3.5 PED and revenue

When demand is elastic, total revenue rises as price falls. This is because the quantity demanded is very responsive to price changes. A fall in the price gives rise to a **more** than proportionate rise in the quantity demanded. The net effect is that revenue (= price × quantity) rises.

Conversely, when demand is inelastic, total revenue falls as price falls. Here a fall in price causes a **less** than proportionate rise in quantity demanded, the result being a net fall in total revenue.

Equally, when demand is elastic, total revenue falls when price rises; and when demand is inelastic, total revenue rises when price rises.

It would therefore be very useful to a producer to know whether he is at an elastic or inelastic part of his demand curve. This will enable him to predict the effect on revenue of raising or lowering his price.

4 Profit and profit maximisation

4.1 The downward sloping demand function

The downward sloping demand function reflects one of the most basic concepts of business economics. That is, that there is an inverse relationship between unit selling price and unit sales volume. As one rises, the other falls.

By associating the demand function with an understanding of cost behaviour within a business it is possible to produce a model which allows a profit-maximising unit selling price and output level to be predicted. This model may feature in the solution of a variety of problems in the areas of product pricing, budgeting, project appraisal and divisional transfer pricing.

The algebra and geometry of the demand function may be illustrated by the following simple example. A business manufactures and sells units. At a unit selling price of €10, no units are demanded, but demand increases by 2,000 units for each €1 reduction in the unit selling price.

In figure 1, the demand can be seen to run from 10 on the vertical (y) axis to 20,000 on the horizontal (x) axis. The algebraic equation for this demand function is:

$$y = 10 - x/2,000$$

It is obvious that revenue is nil at both ends of this line and it is also apparent (see figure 2) that revenue is maximised at €50,000 half way along its length, where y = 5 and x = 10,000.

KEY POINT

A marginal revenue (MR) function can be derived from the demand line. This MR function represents the change in total revenue associated with one unit increments of movement along the demand function.

A marginal revenue (MR) function can be derived from the demand line. This MR function represents the change in total revenue associated with one unit increments of movement along the demand function. The MR function will depart the vertical axis at 10, because the first unit demanded will increase total revenues by the amount of its unit selling price. The MR function will cut the horizontal axis at 10,000. This is so because total revenues increase as sales increase from 0 to 10,000 units but thereafter start to decline.

When demand reaches 20,000 units then the value of y on the MR function must be –10. This is so because at demand level 19,999 units, selling price is €0.0005 (calculated by substituting x = 19,999 in the demand function equation) and total revenue is €10. Moving from demand 19,999 to demand 20,000 results in a €10 loss of total revenue. Therefore, the MR associated with the 20,000th unit is –€10.

In figure 1, the MR function can be seen to run from 10 on the y axis to 10,000 on the horizontal axis. The algebraic equation for the MR function is:

$$Y = 10 - x/1{,}000$$

Figure 1 - demand structure

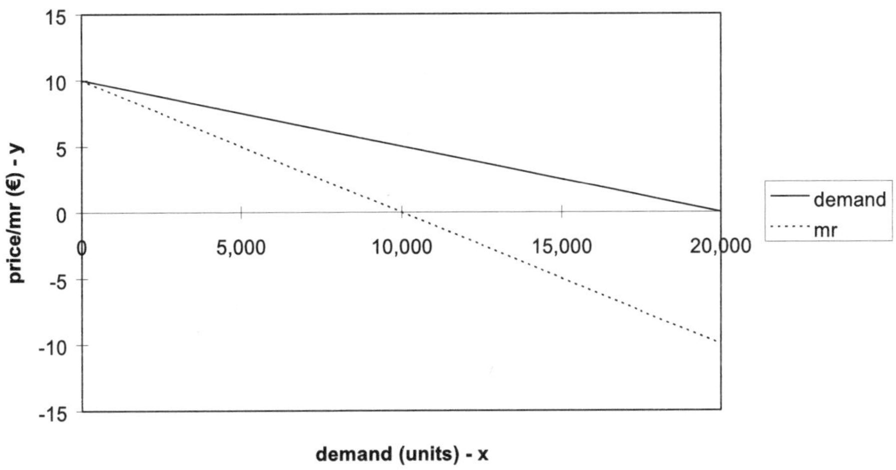

The total revenue associated with any given level of demand is equal to the unit selling price multiplied by that level of demand. We know that unit selling price falls by €1 for every additional 2,000 units sold. Hence if we take y as total revenue and x as unit sales then the relationship between total revenue and unit sales may be represented by the following equation:

$$y = (10 - x/2000)x, \text{ or } y = 10x - x^2/2{,}000$$

This may be represented graphically as follows:

Figure 2 - revenue structure

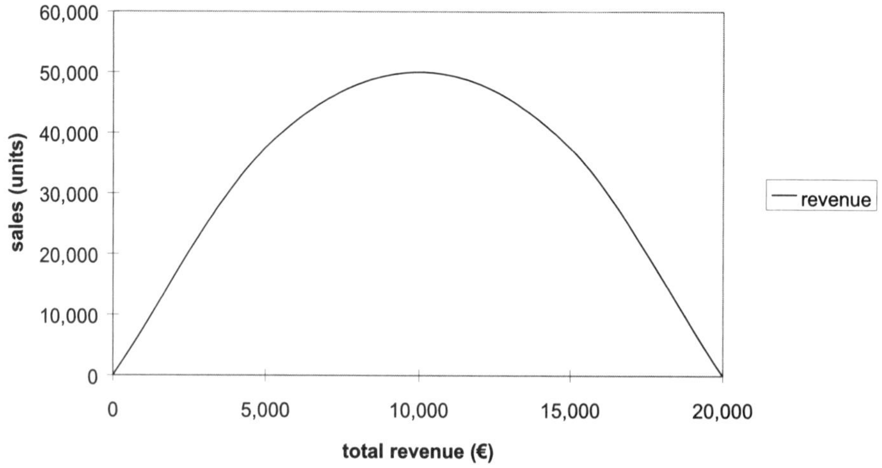

4.2 Profit maximisation

Let us now add information concerning cost structure to our simple example. Let us say that the marginal or variable cost of producing one unit is €5.

The profit achieved at any given level of output is revenue less costs. If we take y as total profit and x as unit sales then the profit structure of the operation may be represented by the following algebraic function:

$$y = 10x - x^2/2{,}000 - 5x, \text{ or}$$

$$y = 5x - x^2/2{,}000$$

This relationship is represented graphically in figure 3.

Figure 3 - profit structure

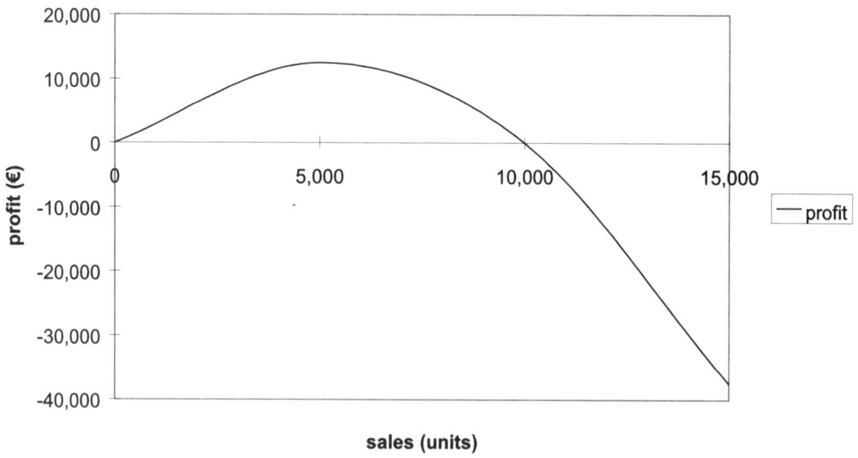

It can be seen that profit is maximised at a level of sales 5,000 units, having an associated unit selling price of €7.50. This last figure is determined by substituting 5,000 for x in the demand function equation. Maximum profit is €12,500 (5,000 units x €2.50 contribution per unit).

This is a graphical determination of the profit maximising level of output. The same figure can be calculated algebraically with varying levels of mathematical refinement.

- Profit is maximised where Marginal Revenue = Marginal Cost

  $10 - x/1{,}000 = 5$

  $5 = x/1{,}000$

  $x = 5{,}000$.

- The demand function is $y = 10 - x/2{,}000$.

  So at the profit maximising point where $x = 5{,}000$,

  Price $= y = 10 - (5{,}000/2{,}000) = 10 - 2.5 = 7.5$.

ACTIVITY 3

A business has fixed costs per month of £250,000 and variable costs of £8 per unit. It sells just one product for which it is a monopoly supplier, and the total monthly demand for the product will vary according to the price charged. A demand curve for the product has been estimated as $P = 80 - x/300$.

What would be the profit-maximising price for the product, and what would be the total profit each month?

Feedback to this activity is at the end of the chapter.

5 Cost plus pricing

5.1 Introduction

KEY POINT

Three main influences on the setting of a selling price, *costs, customers and competitors.*

A common method of pricing in practice is *'cost plus' pricing* and quite often prices are not calculated by reference to marginal costs, but rather *full absorption cost plus pricing* is adopted.

Despite the theoretical superiority of the approach to pricing dealt with so far, it suffers from one major weakness. It is unlikely that perfect information of cost and revenue functions can be obtained. To get information of this nature is likely to be a costly and unreliable process, and therefore such calculations become virtually impossible. Commercial firms have to turn to other methods to determine selling prices. Whilst one might consider three main influences on the setting of a selling price, *costs, customers and competitors,* it is usually the first of these that represents the starting point for pricing decisions. A common method of pricing in practice is *'cost plus' pricing* and quite often prices are not calculated by reference to marginal costs, but rather *full absorption cost plus pricing* is adopted.

5.2 The principles behind full-cost plus pricing

The main principles which are used to explain its use are as follows:

(a) The absorption of indirect costs over the firm's products will ensure that the indirect costs are all recouped in the sales of the products: this will be valid where all products can be sold at a price which covers their direct and absorbed costs and at the quantities assumed in the absorption base computations. This 'break-even' emphasis is consistent with risk aversion and satisficing objectives, rather than profit maximisation.

(b) The firm cannot afford to sell at less than full cost: the firm cannot survive in the long-term replacing its capital and incurring further amounts of fixed costs unless prices cover both variable and fixed elements. However, in the short-term the contribution to be gained from selling at less than full cost may exceed that from a full cost policy, particularly where sales volumes are price sensitive e.g. contribution from 1,000 units at 50p above direct variable cost will yield £500 which was unobtainable at the full cost price and is preferred to zero sales.

(c) The firm will be able to earn a reasonable rate of return: this is valid if the market will bear the price. It may be sensible pricing strategy to avoid new entrants to the market.

(d) The pricing system is simple and cheap to operate: whilst this is valid it is important to consider the loss of profit from failure to maximise contribution by recognising market factors.

KEY POINT

Many contracts (particularly government) are full cost plus based.

(e) The system ensures that control is exercised over the firm's pricing so that no products are under or over priced: this is consistent with the needs of decentralised control in a large organisation, and standardisation as a mechanism for ensuring a satisfactory level of profit.

(f) Many contracts (particularly government) are full cost plus based.

The general structure

	£
Direct product/job cost	X
Absorption of overheads	
Variable overheads	X
Fixed production overheads	X
Non-production overheads	X
Total cost	X
Profit margin (%)	X
Selling price	X

Example

Highwater Ltd has developed a new product, the grendle, and wishes to determine an appropriate selling price. Two possible levels of production/sales are being considered, 500 units and 800 units per month.

Each grendle requires 4 metres of material X at a basic price of £5 per metre. A bulk discount of 7.5% can be obtained for orders over 2,500 metres. Highwater will order each month's requirements at the beginning of the month.

The work is to be done in two departments:

Department A - employs skilled operators paid at £6.50 per hour. Each unit of output requires 4 direct labour hours in this department.

Department B - employs semi-skilled operators paid at £5 per hour. Each unit of output requires 1.5 hours in this department.

Overtime in each department is paid at time and a half. No premium for overtime is included in standard manufacturing overhead.

Standard manufacturing overhead per direct labour hour is as follows:

	Department A	*Department B*
	£	£
Variable	2.50	3
Fixed	8	6

Fixed overhead absorption rates are based on budgeted labour capacities of 12,000 hours (dept A) and 8,000 hours (dept B). The departments are currently working at 80% and 60% capacities for Departments A and B respectively. There is no prospect of employing additional labour in the near future.

Current pricing practice of Highwater is to add the following margins on full costs in arriving at selling price:

Department A – 20% Department B – 15% Direct materials – 5%

Calculate the price per grendle under the normal pricing practices of Highwater

(i) for each activity level, using the information above

(ii) if the production was to be for a one-off order of 800 units only, and an 80% learning curve is expected to operate in department A. The first 100 units are expected to take a total of 650 hours.

Solution

(i)

	Activity level 500 units	*Activity level* 800 units
	£	£
Direct material @ £20/unit	10,000	16,000
Less: Discount (7.5%)		(1,200)
	10,000	14,800
Add: Margin mark-up (5%)	500	740
	10,500	15,540
Conversion costs:		
Department A (@£(6.50 + 2.50 + 8) = £17 per hr)		
2,000 hours	34,000	
3,200 hours		54,400
Overtime pm (800 hrs (W) @ £3.25)		2,600
Add: Margin mark up (20%)	6,800	11,400
Department B (@£(5 + 3 + 6) = £14 per hr)		
750 hours	10,500	
1,200 hours		16,800
Add: Margin mark up (15%)	1,575	2,520
	£63,375	£103,260
Price per grendle	£126.75	£129.08

Working

Dept A is currently working at 80% capacity = 80% × 12,000 = 9,600 hrs. Of the 3,200 hours required for the grendle, 2,400 will be worked within normal capacity and 800 hours in overtime.

(ii) The revised labour time in Department A is calculated using the learning curve percentage, and can be done using a formula or by tabulation. The latter is demonstrated here:

Tabulation

Cumulative production		*Cumulative average time per unit*	*Cumulative total time*	
100		6.50	650	(given in question)
200	× 0.8 =	5.20	1040	
400	× 0.8 =	4.16	1664	
800	× 0.8 =	3.328	2,662.4	say 2,662 hrs

The revised price per grendle is thus:

	£	£
Total price per (i)		103,260
Less: Basic Dept A cost savings (3,200 - 2,662) × £17	9,146	
Overtime savings (800 - 262) × £3.25	1,748.50	
	10,894.50 × 1.2	(13,073)
		90,187

Price per grendle = £112.73

5.3 Modification to cost plus price

KEY POINT

The firm's master budget will be a primary source of absorption rates for overheads.

The firm's master budget has a special role in cost plus pricing. This budget will be a primary source of absorption rates for overheads. Profit margin data from the master budget could take several forms:

- target profit % of sales from master budget profit and loss account
- target return on capital employed taken from master budget and applied to the capital employed by the product.

Historical data based on the firm's previous experience in operating in various markets may provide an indication of the rate of return/mark-up which could be earned. An analysis of the profitability of other firms operating in a market into which the firm was about to enter would give an indication of the likely return to be earned.

5.4 Possible determinants of the 'plus element'

Market factors may affect the size of the 'plus element' and it would probably be more accurate to use the term 'modified cost plus' to describe the way in which cost plus pricing is used in practice. Although the 'plus element' is apparently derived from the cost base of the formula, the following are examples of situations which could influence the margins selected.

(a) **The size of mark-up may be altered to take into account the stage of the product life**

The capacity of a product to withstand a large mark-up may need to be reviewed during the early introductory stages to enable it to become established and during its later stages as it attracts competition or enters a period of decline through obsolescence.

(b) **The type of customer**

The size of the mark-up may be affected in situations where prices relate to individual customers. Examples would relate to the preparation of a quotation for a contract for an individual customer where the mark-up could depend more on knowledge of the competition and longer term considerations such as repeat orders.

(c) **The reduction of unit profit mark-up for bulk customers**

This latter practice can be incorporated into a standard cost-plus procedure, whilst still retaining its apparent integrity, by the use of discounts whose purpose is to discriminate between different groups of purchasers with different capacities to pay.

(d) **The nature of the market**

Differing mark-ups may be used for differing product groups or business segments to reflect differing degrees of competition facing different products or product groups. Thus, rather than using one target mark-up determined from a master budget, a variety of mark-up rates could be pre-determined and applied within the firm.

5.5 Limitations of full cost plus pricing

The general limitations of the full cost plus approach are as follows:

- The firm may either over-price or under-price its products in relation to the optimal price which maximises profit, if it fails to recognise formally the impact of price elasticity of demand in its pricing policy.
- In both multi-product and single-product firms, the arbitrary nature of absorption costing can generate differing rates of overhead absorption according to the bases of cost allocation used between cost centres, and activity measures used for determining absorption rates. Levels of activity used in the absorption rates and profit mark-up are based on budgeted volumes of activity. However, the volume of activity may itself depend on product prices and the final price is thus indeterminable unless one presupposes a volume.
- Absorption costing fails to distinguish between incremental fixed costs, relevant to pricing and output decisions, and committed fixed costs irrelevant to those decisions.
- Being based on budgeted data, the cost information including the recovery rates may soon be out-of-date. Also, the use of fixed percentages in the formula gives an impression of accuracy which may mislead the decision marker. For many pricing situations the use of the full cost formula is too inflexible and too restrictive in its total cost recovery goal.

5.6 Marginal cost plus pricing

KEY POINT

The principle behind marginal cost plus pricing is that the marginal cost can be clearly identified with the unit, thus justifying the price being charged.

The principle behind marginal cost plus pricing is that the marginal cost can be clearly identified with the unit, thus justifying the price being charged.

The logic is that only marginal cost is decision relevant – and that pricing decisions should therefore be linked to marginal cost rather than full cost. The latter contains a lot of absorbed fixed overheads which are not decision relevant.

However, marginal cost pricing must be considered either as a short-term or incremental pricing policy because it does not consider the impact of fixed costs (other than as part of the 'plus' factor).

5.7 Benefits and problems of marginal cost plus pricing

KEY POINT

The use of marginal cost plus pricing as a long-term policy may lead to a failure to recover fixed costs.

Marginal cost plus pricing is useful because, subject to a deliberate pricing policy, it shows the minimum price to be charged without incurring a loss. In some circumstances it may be necessary and advisable to sell at a price which is only a little above marginal cost, for example to enter a market or to make use of idle capacity. In these circumstances a price which yields a positive contribution is better than no sale.

The use of marginal cost plus pricing however, as a long-term policy may lead to a failure to recover fixed costs. Effectively fixed costs are part of the 'plus' factor but managers may view the 'plus' as being profit. If the fixed costs are high they will represent a significant proportion of the 'plus' and in the long run this cannot be ignored.

6 Cost based pricing and profit maximisation

Both full cost and marginal cost based pricing methods ignore the relationship between sales price and demand, however it is argued that marginal cost based pricing is more sensitive to demand than full cost based pricing.

The reason for this is that marginal costs can be traced to the unit and therefore must be related to its value and consequently its selling price. The inclusion of fixed costs on a per unit basis is arbitrary. It is based on budgeted expenditure and activity levels and a chosen basis of overhead absorption. This does not necessarily reflect the value of the resources used and therefore may have no relationship to the selling price/demand function.

Conclusion

In this chapter the two basic techniques of pricing have been considered. Market based pricing uses supply and demand analysis whereas cost based pricing may use either full or marginal cost as its starting point.

SELF-TEST QUESTIONS

Calculating price elasticity of demand

1 Define price elasticity of demand and state its simple formula. (3.1)

2 Is price elasticity of demand usually positive or negative? (3.2)

3 If price elasticity of demand is –2 and price rises by 10%, by how much will quantity demanded fall? (3)

4 If demand for a product is relatively elastic and the price of that product rises, what will happen to the firm's total revenue? (3)

Profit and profit maximisation

5 At what point of output will a firm maximise its profits? (4.2)

6 How far should a firm expand output? (4.2)

Cost plus pricing

7 Distinguish between full cost and marginal cost plus pricing. (5.2, 5.6)

EXAM-TYPE QUESTIONS

Question 1: Widgets

A manufacturing company producing widgets has weekly fixed costs of £900 and variable costs of £$(10x + x^2)$ where x is the quantity produced. The manufacturing company's capacity is about 70 units.

The demand function for this product is given by P = £$(120 - x)$ where £P = unit price and x = quantity sold.

Required:

(a) Find the level of production at which revenue is maximised. **(4 marks)**

(b) Find any break-even points. **(6 marks)**

(c) Sketch a graph of revenue and profit for the range of values $0 < x < 70$. **(4 marks)**

(d) Recommend how many widgets the manufacturing company should produce, justifying your answer. **(6 marks)**

(Total: 20 marks)

Question 2: Nantderyn Products

(a) Nantderyn Products has two main products, Exco and Wyeco, which have unit costs of £12 and £24 respectively. The company uses a mark-up of $33\frac{1}{3}$% in establishing its selling prices and the current prices are thus £16 and £32. With these prices, in the year which is just ending, the company expects to make a profit of £300,000 from having produced and sold 15,000 units of Exco and 30,000 units of Wyeco. This programme will have used all the available processing time in the finishing department. Each unit of Exco requires an hour of processing time in this department and every unit of Wyeco correspondingly requires half an hour.

Fixed overhead was £360,000 for the year and this has been charged to the products on the basis of the total processing hours used. All other costs may be assumed variable in relation to processing hours. In the current year it is estimated that £60,000 of the fixed overhead will be absorbed by Exco and £300,000 by Wyeco. With the existing selling prices it is considered that the potential annual demand for Exco is 20,000 units and that for Wyeco, 40,000 units.

You are required to comment critically on the product mix adopted by Nantderyn Products. Calculate what would have been the optimal plan given that there was no intention of changing the selling prices. **(8 marks)**

(b) For the forthcoming year increased capacity has been installed in the finishing department so that this will no longer be a constraint for any feasible sales programme. Annual fixed overhead will be increased to £400,000 as a consequence of this expansion of facilities, but variable costs per unit are unchanged.

A study commissioned by the sales director estimates the effect that alterations to the selling prices would have on the sales that could be achieved. The following table has been prepared:

	Exco		*Wyeco*	
Price	£13.50	£18.50	£29.00	£35.00
Demand	30,000	10,000	60,000	20,000

It is thought reasonable to assume that the price/demand relationship is linear.

Assuming that the company is now willing to abandon its cost plus pricing practices, if these can be shown to be deficient, **you are required** to calculate the optimal selling price for each product and the optimal output levels for these prices. State clearly any assumptions that you find it necessary to make.

(8 marks)

(c) 'The paradox is that, while cost plus pricing is devoid of any theoretical justification, it is widely used in practice.'

Discuss possible justifications for this use. **(6 marks)**

(Total: 22 marks)

Question 3: XYZ

XYZ is the only manufacturer of a product called the X. The variable cost of producing the X is €1.50 at all levels of output.

During recent months the X has been sold at a unit price of around €6.25. Various small adjustments (up and down) have been made to this price in an attempt to find a profit maximising selling price.

XYZ's Commercial Manager has recently commissioned a study by a firm of marketing consultants "to investigate the demand structure for the X and to calculate the elasticity of demand for the X".

The consultants have reported back that at a unit price of €10 there is no demand for Xs but that demand increases by 40Xs with each 1c that the unit price is reduced below €10. They have also reported that "when demand is at around half its theoretical maximum the elasticity of demand is around 1".

Upon receiving this report the Commercial Manager makes the following statement. "Recent experience gained in adjusting the unit selling price of the X suggests that the product has quite an elastic demand structure. Small changes in unit selling price seem to produce far larger proportionate changes in demand. I do not accept that elasticity of demand for the X can be 1."

Required:

(a) Write a memorandum to the Commercial Manager reconciling the consultants' report with his own observations on the elasticity of demand for the X.

(10 marks)

(b) Calculate the profit maximising unit selling price for the X (accurate to the nearest cent) and calculate the elasticity of demand for the X at that price.

(10 marks)

(Total: 20 marks)

For the answers to these questions, see the 'Answers' section at the end of the book.

FEEDBACK TO ACTIVITY 1

Use the formula, PED = (percentage change in quantity demanded) / (percentage change in price).

Here, –2 = (percentage change in quantity demanded) / +10%

So –2 × 10% = –20% = percentage change in quantity demanded.

In other words, quantity will **fall** by 20%. Note the minus sign, which is important. The PED given in the question was negative and this fed through to give a negative change in quantity demanded; in other words, a **fall.** This accords with all the previous work: price rose, so demand fell.

FEEDBACK TO ACTIVITY 2

Return to the previous activity if you are unsure. There, an elasticity of -2 meant that when price rose by 10%, demand fell by 20% i.e. by twice as much as the price rise. So an elasticity of -4 means that if price changes by a certain percentage, quantity demanded will change by four times as much. The minus sign indicates that if price goes up (has a positive change) quantity will fall (have a negative change), and vice versa. For example, if price rises by 10%, quantity demanded will fall by 40%.

FEEDBACK TO ACTIVITY 3

TR = 80x – x^2/300

So MR = 80 – (2x/300) = 10 – x/150.

- TC = 250,000 + 8x

  So MC = 8

- Profit is maximised where MR = MC

  80 – x/300 = 8

  72 = x/150

  x = 10,800.

- The demand function is P = 80 – x/300.

  So at the profit maximising point where x = 10,800,

  Price = 80 – 10,800/300 = 80 – 36 = 44.

- At a price of £44 and with variable costs of £8 per unit, total contribution = 10,800 × (£44 - £8) = £388,800. Deducting fixed costs of £250,000 gives a monthly profit of £138,800.

Chapter 19
PRICING 2

CHAPTER CONTENTS

This chapter explores specific aspects of price determination, including the use of ABC and strategic concepts.

Objectives

When you have studied this chapter you should be able to do the following.

- Calculate prices using activity based costing in the estimation of the cost element.
- Contrast and discuss the implications of prices using the activity based costing technique with those using volume related methods in assigning costs to products.
- Take informed pricing decisions in the context of special orders and new products.
- Discuss pricing policy in the context of skimming, penetration and differential pricing.
- Explain the problems of pricing in the context of short life products.
- Explain the operation of target pricing in achieving a desired market share.

1 Activity based approaches to cost based pricing

1.1 Introduction

The technique of activity based costing (ABC) was examined in an earlier chapter. It was seen that ABC involves attributing overhead costs to individual products on the basis of cost drivers relating to the activities that the costs relate to.

Here we examine the use of ABC as a basis for pricing, by use of an example which will start by revising the technique.

Example

Trimake Ltd makes three main products, using broadly the same production methods and equipment for each. A conventional product costing system is used at present, although an activity based costing (ABC) system is being considered. Details of the three products for a typical period are:

	Hours per unit		*Materials*	*Volumes*
	Labour hours	*Machine hours*	*per unit* £	*Units*
Product X	½	1 ½	20	750
Product Y	1 ½	1	12	1,250
Product Z	1	3	25	7,000

Direct labour costs £6 per hour and production overheads are absorbed on a machine hour basis. The rate for the period is £28 per machine hour.

(a) **You are required** to calculate the cost per unit for each product using conventional methods.

Further analysis shows that the total of production overheads can be divided as follows:

	%
Costs relating to set-ups	35
Costs relating to machinery	20
Costs relating to materials handling	15
Costs relating to inspection	30
Total production overhead	100

The following total activity volumes are associated with the product line for the period as a whole.

Total activities for the period

	Number of set-ups	*Number of movements of materials*	*Number of inspections*
Product X	75	12	150
Product Y	115	21	180
Product Z	480	87	670
	670	120	1,000

You are required:

(b) to calculate the cost per unit for each product using ABC principles.

Solution to example

(a) **Conventional cost per unit**

Tutorial note*:* There is less to this than meets the eye; two hourly rates are given, for labour and for overheads, standard times are supplied and thus unit costs can be found. A sub-total of direct costs may speed up (b) a little.

	X	*Y*	*Z*
	£	£	£
Materials	20	12	25
Labour (£6/hour)	3	9	6
Direct cost	23	21	31
Production overheads (£28/hour)	42	28	84
Total production cost/unit	65	49	115

(b) **ABC cost per unit**

Tutorial note*:* Each step required has been given its own sub-heading to make the procedure clear. The basic principle is to find an overhead cost per unit of activity for each element of overhead cost. In some cases it might then be possible to find an overhead cost per unit directly. Here it is probably easier to split overheads between each product type first and then find a cost per unit as shown.

(i) **Total overheads**

Using the production and unit overhead cost information from (a):

Total overheads for a period

= (750 × £42) + (1,250 × £28) + (7,000 × £84) = £654,500.

(ii) **Total machine hours**

Product	*Hours/unit*	*Production*	*Total hours*
X	1½	750	1,125
Y	1	1,250	1,250
Z	3	7,000	21,000
Total machine hours			23,375

Both the total and the split by product will be used subsequently.

(iii) **Analysis of total overheads and cost per unit of activity**

Type of overhead	*%*	*Total overhead* £	*Level of activity*	*Cost/unit of activity* £
Set-ups	35	229,075	670	341.903
Machining	20	130,900	23,375	5.60
Materials handling	15	98,175	120	818.125
Inspection	30	196,350	1,000	196.35
	100	654,500		

(***Note:*** It is worth retaining the cost per set-up figure in the memory of your calculator; the memory can be used for the other unit costs in turn.)

(iv) **Total overheads by product and per unit**

(***Note:*** This makes use of the table of total activities for the period, where it is important not to confuse rows and columns and costs per unit of activity just found.)

	Product X		*Product Y*			*Product Z*	
Overhead	*Activity*	*Cost* £	*Activity*	*Cost* £	*Activity*	*Cost* £	*Total* £
Set-ups	75	25,643	115	39,319	480	164,113	229,075
Machining	1,125	6,300	1,250	7,000	21,000	117,600	130,900
M Handling	12	9,817	21	17,181	87	71,177	98,175
Inspection	150	29,453	180	35,343	670	131,554	196,350
Total o/h cost		71,213		98,843		484,444	654,500
Units		750		1,250		7,000	
Cost per unit		£94.95		£79.07		£69.21	

(***Note:*** A little rounding has been done here.

- The unit costs could be rounded to £95, £79 and £69.
- Total costs could be split in the ratios of activities rather than finding cost per unit of activity.)

(v) **Cost per unit**

	X	*Y*	*Z*
	£	£	£
Direct costs (from (a))	23.00	21.00	31.00
Overheads (from (iv))	94.95	79.07	69.21
	117.95	100.07	100.21

1.2 Activity based and volume based costs compared

A comparison of the results from the above example shows the following costs per unit:

Product	*Volume approach* £/unit	*Activity based approach* £/unit	*Volume based*
X	750	118	65
Y	1250	100	49
Z	7000	100	115

It can be seen that the costs per unit are not the same for each method. It is argued that the activity-based approach should be used because it reflects the cost of the activities involved in the production of the product.

This is illustrated here with product Z being a major product line which may take longer to make than X or Y, but once production has started the process is simple to administer. Products X and Y are relatively minor products but still require a fair amount of administrative time by the production department, i.e. involve a fair amount of 'hassle'. This is explained by the following table of 'activities per 1,000 units produced'.

	Set-ups	*Materials movements*	*Inspections*
X	100	16	200
Y	92	17	144
Z	69	12	96

This table highlights the problem.

- Product Z has fewer set-ups, material movements and inspections per 1,000 units than X or Y.
- As a consequence product Z's overhead cost per unit for these three elements has fallen.
- The machining overhead cost per unit for Z is still two or three times greater than for products X or Y.
- The machining overhead is only 20% of the total overhead.
- The overall result is Z's fall in production overhead cost per unit and the rise in those figures for X and Y.

1.3 Cost based pricing and activity based costing

For the purposes of illustration a pricing policy of 25% on cost will be applied to the above example. If this 25% mark-up is applied to the volume based costs the resulting selling prices are as follows:

	£/unit
X	81.25
Y	61.25
Z	143.75

In the case of products X and Y, these prices compared to unit costs on an activity cost basis yield losses of £36.75 and £38.75 per unit respectively. On an activity cost basis the selling prices would be £147.50 and £125 respectively.

With regard to product Z the selling price calculated yields greater than 25% mark up on activity based cost. The danger with this is that the price may be uncompetitive, as it does not accurately reflect the resources used.

2 Special orders and new products

2.1 Introduction

KEY POINT

Special orders are often accepted to utilise spare capacity and new products are often priced differently to establish them in the market place.

Special orders are often accepted to utilise spare capacity and new products are often priced differently to establish them in the market place. The following illustration identifies some of the key aspects of short-term pricing decisions.

2.2 Illustration of costs relevant to short-term pricing decisions

Earlier in this text examples were given of pricing decisions where the relevant costs of various resources were considered. The following illustration uses the same principles but in a slightly different context.

The Snipe Company is an electronics company having eight product lines. Income data for one of the products for the year just ended is as follows:

	£m	£m
Sales – 200,000 units @ average price of £100		20
Variable costs:		
Direct materials @ £35	7	
Direct labour @ £10	2	
Variable factory overhead @ £5	1	
Sales commission = 15% of selling price (£15)	3	
Other variable costs @ £5	1	
Total variable costs @ £70		14
Contribution		6
Fixed costs:		
Discretionary	3	
Committed	2	
		5
Operating income		1

Consider the following situations:

(a) The electronics industry had severe price competition throughout the year. Near the end of the year, Albacone Co, which was experimenting with various components in its regular product line, offered £80 each for 3,000 units. The latter would have been in addition to the 200,000 units actually sold. Acceptance of the special order by Snipe would not affect regular sales. The salesman hoped that the order might provide entrance into a new application so he told John Hooper, the product manager, that he would accept half his regular commission rate if the order were accepted. Hooper pondered for a day, but he was afraid of the precedent that might be set by cutting the price. He said 'the price is below our full costs of £95 per unit. I think we should quote a full price, or Albacone Co will expect favoured treatment again and again if we continue to do business with them'. If Hooper had accepted the offer, what would operating income have been?

(b) The Gall Company had offered to supply a key part (MIA) for £20 each. One MIA is used in every finished unit. The Snipe Company had made these parts for variable costs of £18 plus some additional fixed costs of £200,000 for supervision and other items. What would operating income have been if Snipe purchased rather than made the parts? Assume that discretionary costs for supervision and other items would have been avoided if the parts were purchased.

(c) The company could have purchased the MIA parts for £20 each and used the vacated space for the manufacture of a different electronics component on a sub-contracting basis for Hewlett-Packard, a much larger company. Assume that 40,000 special components could have been made for Hewlett-Packard (and sold in addition to the 200,000 units sold through regular channels) at a unit variable cost of £150, exclusive of parts. MIA parts would be needed for these components as well as for the regular production. No sales commission would have to be paid. All the fixed costs pertaining to the MIA parts would have continued, including the supervisory costs, because they related mainly to the facilities used. What would operating income have been if Snipe had made and sold the components to Hewlett-Packard for £170 per unit and bought the MIA parts?

Solution to illustration

(a) Analysis of special order:

	Per unit	*3,000 units*	*3,000 units*
	£	£000	£000
Additional sales	80		240
Variable costs (excluding commission)	55	165	
Commission $(15\% \times \frac{1}{2} \times 240)$		18	
			183
Contribution			57

Note that variable costs, except for commission, are affected by physical units of volume, not pounds revenue.

Operating income would have been £1,000,000 plus £57,000, or £1,057,000, if the order had been accepted. In a sense, the decision to reject the offer means that Snipe is willing to invest £57,000 in immediate gains forgone (an opportunity cost) to preserve the long-run selling price structure.

(b)

	Make £000	Purchase £000
Purchase cost @ £20		4,000
Variable costs @ £18	3,600	
Avoidable discretionary costs	200	
Total relevant costs	3,800	4,000

Operating income would have fallen by £200,000, or from £1,000,000 to £800,000, if Snipe had purchased the parts.

(c)

	£000	£000	£000
Sales would increase by 40,000 units @ £170			6,800
Additional costs to the company as a whole:			
Variable costs exclusive of MIA parts would increase by 40,000 units @ £150		6,000	
Effects on overall costs of MIA parts:			
Cost of 240,000 parts purchased @ £20	4,800		
Less: Savings from not making 200,000 parts @ £18 (only the variable costs are relevant because fixed costs continue)	3,600		
Additional cost of parts		1,200	7,200
Disadvantage of making components for Hewlett-Packard			(400)

Operating income would decline by £400,000 from £1,000,000 to £600,000.

2.3 Pricing in limiting factor situations

KEY POINT

When there is a factor limiting production, opportunity cost (contribution per key factor) may be taken into account in price fixing.

When there is a factor limiting production, opportunity cost (contribution per key factor) may be taken into account in price fixing.

Consider the following example.

Example

A company has the following budget based on orders from the home market:

	£	£
Sales (2,000 units)		10,000
Cost of sales:		
Direct material	1,000	
Direct labour	4,000	
Variable overhead	1,000	
Fixed overhead	3,000	
		9,000
		1,000

At this level of output, the company has spare capacity and it is therefore planning to develop export markets. It believes that it will be able to sell an additional 750 units – the limit of its production due to a shortage of raw materials. No additional fixed costs would be incurred and selling prices and variable costs per unit would be the same as for the home market.

Before launching its export campaign, however, the company is approached by a homebuyer who wishes to purchase 200 deluxe models, which use twice as much material as the standard model. What is the minimum price that should be charged if this order is accepted?

Solution

If the company accepts the deluxe order, it will lose export sales due to the shortage of materials. On export sales the contribution per unit would be:

	£	£
Selling price		5
Direct material	0.50	
Direct labour	2.00	
Variable overhead	0.50	
		3
Contribution		2
Contribution per £1 of raw material (£2.00 ÷ £0.50)		£4

Each deluxe model uses £1 of raw material. In order to be no worse off by accepting this order, therefore, the company must obtain a contribution of at least £4 per unit – the opportunity cost of the raw material. The minimum price to be charged is therefore:

	£
Direct material	1.00
Direct labour	2.00
Variable overhead	0.50
	3.50
Required contribution	4.00
Selling price per unit	7.50

If 200 deluxe models are made sales in the export market will fall by 400 to 350.

Check	*Deluxe order rejected*		*Deluxe order accepted*			
		Export sales		*Export sales*		*Deluxe sales*
	£	£	£	£	£	£
Sales						
(750 @ £5)		3,750				
(200 @ £7.50)						1,500
(350 @ £5)				1,750		
Direct material (£0.50/£1)	375		175		200	
Direct labour (£2)	1,500		700		400	
Variable overhead (£0.50)	375		175		100	
		2,250		1,050		700
Contribution		1,500		700		800

Therefore, if it charges the minimum price recommended for the deluxe model, the company will obtain the same contribution as if it rejected the order and concentrated on the export market.

In practice, of course, the company will take other considerations into account e.g. the deluxe order is definite, export sales are speculative, more labour is required if the company concentrates on exports, there may be additional selling costs or other fixed costs associated with exporting.

3 Pricing strategy

3.1 Introduction

KEY POINT

Most new products are simply developments of older ones or substitutes for something that already exists.

It must be remembered that pricing decisions are not made in a vacuum and there are very few completely new products. Most new products are simply developments of older ones or substitutes for something that already exists.

There is, therefore, a background, or an expected price range, within which a new product will fit. This can sometimes give a completely new product development an enormous opportunity for profit. For example, when the ballpoint pen first appeared, it was offered to the public as a competitor to good quality fountain pens, which were then selling for around £1.50. The ballpoint pen sold at around this price until competitors discovered that it cost only a few pence to make, whereupon the price tumbled. For some time, however, the ballpoint continued with its fountain pen image being sold as a long lasting holder for which re-fills were supplied. Later the cheap throwaway ballpoint became more general.

Occasionally, there are completely new products that create new markets. In this case price tends to follow supply costs. These costs can be expected to fall as mass markets develop, as production becomes more reliable and as initial research, development and fixed equipment costs are recovered. One such product has been the small electronic calculator. Until the development of microprocessors, a calculator was a piece of office equipment outside the price range of most individuals. Early electric calculators were unreliable and prone to breakdown and initially they were expensive.

The microprocessor made possible a cheap, efficient and reliable piece of equipment of value to any individual. There was no price background for such an item because nothing like this had previously existed. Prices were established by a combination of competition and falling supply costs – a good example of the working of a free market economy.

For more normal products the supplier is operating in a known market with a price history. Decisions may be taken with some knowledge of the likely demand within a given possible price range.

3.2 Charging the 'going rate'

There are situations where the producer is satisfied that he can sell a satisfactory quantity at a satisfactory profit at a price which is in line with prices of similar goods or services. The existence of such a situation depends on the nature and strength of competition, especially price competition in the market. The Hall & Hitch survey produced strong evidence for people charging what they felt was 'the fair price'.

KEY POINT

Firms are more likely to charge the 'going rate' under the following conditions:

- When the quality or some other feature of a product or a service is more important than price and the price elasticity of demand at the ruling price is largely inelastic
- When it is believed that a fixed price has become established for a particular product
- When price competition will simply reduce revenue for all suppliers without giving additional profits or any other significant market advantage to any individual supplier.

Firms are more likely to charge the 'going rate' under the following conditions:

- When the quality or some other feature of a product or a service is more important than price and the price elasticity of demand at the ruling price is largely inelastic. Examples include local hairdressing services, daily and local newspapers, beer and cigarettes.
- When it is believed that a fixed price has become established for a particular product and identified with that product in the market. Inflation, metrication and the economic upheavals of the 1970s and 1980s upset most of these identities, of which one of the best known examples was probably that of the 6d (2½p) bar of chocolate which lasted for a long period in the 1950s and early 1960s. Fixed prices of this type tend to be associated with 'oligopolies'.
- When price competition will simply reduce revenue for all suppliers without giving additional profits or any other significant market advantage to any individual supplier. This position is associated with oligopolies and with what may be called, perhaps, local oligopolies where local supply is dominated by a small number of traders who are content to retain their local market share. Formal market sharing agreements or collusive behaviour are not necessary under these conditions. Self-interest builds up a form of custom and practice which all established suppliers observe as long as there is no internal or external threat to market stability. It is also likely that all suppliers will share similar cost conditions and will act together to avoid competing for factors and to preserve stable factor costs – including wages.

3.3 The price strategy

KEY POINT

The price strategy to be adopted for any particular product is part of the total marketing strategy for the product. This, in turn, is part of the firm's total production strategy.

The price strategy to be adopted for any particular product is part of the total marketing strategy for the product. This, in turn, is part of the firm's total production strategy. Firms will adopt very different behaviour patterns for different products and markets.

For example, breaking into a market requires different tactics from those needed when defending an established market position from new entrants or possible new entrants to the market.

Similarly, the approach to a new market area in which there has been substantial recent investment and which, it is hoped, will expand, will be very different from one to an old area expected to be in decline and where a decision has already been made not to renew investment.

Failure to recognise a change in market demand and in supply conditions such as the arrival of new and more attractive substitutes can lead to expensive errors involving more than just mistakes in pricing.

It is desirable for the business manager to keep an open mind in his approach to the place of prices in the total marketing strategy, but at the same time to recognise clearly the economic forces operating in the market area.

3.4 Market penetration

KEY POINT

Market penetration

This relates to the attempt to break into a market and to establish that market share which, it has been calculated, will enable the firm to achieve its revenue and profit targets.

This relates to the attempt to break into a market and to establish that market share which, it has been calculated, will enable the firm to achieve its revenue and profit targets.

Whether the market is an established one which the firm hopes to break open or a new and developing one, the most likely price strategy is to set price as low as possible and substantially below the ruling price of competitors without being so low that the product is thought to be inferior. To achieve this in an established market the firm is likely to need the benefit of a production or marketing innovation thought to give a special advantage.

Once the target market share has been achieved the next stage in the total strategy is likely to be to build up distributor and customer loyalty i.e. to reduce the product's price elasticity of demand (make the demand curve steeper). By reducing the relative attraction of substitutes it will also influence the cross elasticity of demand with rival products. This is unlikely to be achieved solely through price changes. There will also have to be changes in advertising, in policies over distribution margins and services and possibly over the availability of services and even of packaging. At this stage there may be a greater emphasis on price stability and stress on quality and availability.

This, of course, assumes that successful penetration is now leading to consolidation of the market share and probably an improvement in profitability.

3.5 Market skimming

This is also associated with the launching of a new product but represents a rather different approach – perhaps where the extent of market appeal is uncertain and the firm has not yet committed itself to a major investment programme in the project and its production. The supplier may also be the main or an important supplier of substitutes so that a successful launch will involve a major switch in production investment. Failure will not be too expensive if care is taken.

KEY POINT

Market skimming

The skimming approach involves setting a relatively high price stressing the attractions of new features likely to appeal to those with a genuine interest in the product or its associated attractions.

The skimming approach involves setting a relatively high price stressing the attractions of new features likely to appeal to those with a genuine interest in the product or its associated attractions. Reaction and support is thus solicited from the 'top end' of the particular market. If the launch is successful in this 'cream skimming' exercise, and when the decision has been taken to invest in the necessary new production resources so that larger scale production becomes possible, then the appeal of the new product can be enlarged through a shift in advertising and a reduction in price. The price reduction can be made in stages to coincide with supply side increases as new resources come into use.

One of the conditions necessary for market skimming is the existence of technical barriers to entry into the market. It must be difficult for competitors to come up with a similar product quickly with which they can undercut the price. Such policies are common in 'high-tech' fields which is why one saw calculators, personal computers, domestic stereo sets and videos initially sold at a high price but now those same products are sold for a fraction of their launch price. The same can be said of computer software, although in all of these cases the product life cycle has an influence on longer-term pricing policy.

3.6 Differential pricing

KEY POINT

Price discrimination, market segmentation and differential pricing are variations on a basic theme of charging different prices to different customers for the same goods or services.

Price discrimination, market segmentation and differential pricing are variations on a basic theme. That theme is the practice of charging different prices to different customers for the same goods or services. The basic mathematics of this practice were discussed in the previous chapter.

Differential pricing may be used whenever it is possible to differentiate the product or its market. There are many ways of differentiating sales. Common techniques are to differentiate:

- by product version
- by time
- by place
- by market segment.

One sector that uses many of these techniques is public transport. Rail and air companies differentiate their product by separating First Class and Economy Class travel accommodation. Further differentiation is then applied by time with higher prices being charged to travel at busy periods. Off-peak time travel is then further differentiated by market segment with special prices for students, family tickets etc. Cheaper prices are charged to customers who reserve seats well in advance on specific trains or flights.

4 Pricing of short-life products

4.1 Introduction

Short-life products require special pricing considerations. Any costs which are product specific (fixed and variable) must be recovered within the short life of the product.

4.2 Short-life pricing policies

When there is likely to be a high level of demand e.g. annual diaries, then prices can be relatively low, but where demand is limited prices will have to be set at a high level so as to ensure cost recovery. This is a form of skimming policy but perhaps without the subsequent price reduction.

5 Target pricing

5.1 Introduction

KEY POINT

Target pricing is a term which implies that the firm has a sufficient knowledge of the conditions of the market for its product and for the production factors which it uses to be able to set a price which it calculates will achieve a desired target.

Target pricing is a term which implies that the firm has a sufficient knowledge of the conditions of the market for its product and for the production factors which it uses to be able to set a price which it calculates will achieve a desired target.

Possible targets might include the following:

(a) **Short or long run profit maximisation**

In practice these are not normally considered to be specific targets and are not usually regarded as being within the scope of target pricing.

(b) **Sales maximisation**

This may be regarded in a similar light to that of profit maximisation. Strictly it does not represent a specific target.

KEY POINT

Achievement of an overall target may envisage successive sub-targets and successive price changes in the pursuit of a total strategy.

(c) **A desired rate of return on capital invested in a product**

This is, perhaps, the most common target, chiefly because investment decisions are based on comparisons of future returns and on estimates of attainable returns. Managers will, therefore, seek to achieve the projections made when the decision was being reached. The techniques and knowledge required to achieve a target rate of return are not too far distant from those required for profit maximisation but greater attention is likely to be paid to the time dimension. Thus, achievement of an overall target may envisage successive sub-targets and successive price changes in the pursuit of a total strategy. For example, a low price may be set initially to break into a market and to secure distribution channels. A higher price may then be charged as the product gains acceptance and demand becomes less price elastic – and shelf space and retailer support is gained. The manager is operating in a dynamic environment and must adapt his tactics as the strategy develops. The setting of an initial low price to achieve a desired level of market acceptance is known as **penetration pricing.**

The important point is that there is a constant awareness of the price/quantity/cost set of relationships and the greater the knowledge of these the more precise the price calculation can become. The manager is seeking that combination of marginal cost, marginal revenue, price and cross elasticity of demand that will achieve the desired target rate of return on the amount invested.

(d) **Market share**

This is rarely an end in itself. More often it is the necessary pre-condition for the firm to achieve the price and cost combination it desires.

The position, say, of being an acknowledged brand leader may ensure a given amount of shelf-space and selling attention from distribution channels and may give a degree of control over price and perhaps allow the firm to be the price leader in a period of changing costs.

(e) **Achieve a given rate of growth**

Growth may be an important objective of the firm but because of the costs and risks of obtaining capital, a steady growth rate is desired because this can be obtained from available capital funds. An objective of growth at a particular rate is also likely to require the achievement of a profit rate considered acceptable to the finance markets.

The firm cannot go to the capital market for additional finance unless it can prove to that market that it has achieved a satisfactory rate of profit on its existing capital. What is 'satisfactory' depends on a range of influences and conditions at any particular time.

(f) **Keep out competitors**

This involves the use of price as a barrier to the entry of market competitors. This may mean that some degree of monopoly profit may be sacrificed in the desire to keep price below the level at which it would become profitable for a new firm to enter the market. An example of this policy is seen in the market for UK air passengers (in which less orthodox marketing strategies are also alleged to take place).

5.2 Target costing and value analysis

Target costing combines the twin disciplines of cost estimation and value analysis and this is discussed as an introduction to target costing. The essential idea is that where the price of a product is determined by the market place, costs have to be reduced to enable the product to be sold at that price. That gives the target cost and value analysis is used to help the business achieve that target cost.

5.3 Value analysis

KEY POINT

Value analysis is basically a form of **cost reduction** i.e. a method of improving profitability by reducing costs without necessarily increasing prices.

Value analysis is basically a form of *cost reduction* i.e. a method of improving profitability by reducing costs without necessarily increasing prices. It is thus particularly useful to manufacturers or suppliers who are unable to fix their own price because of, for example, a competitive market. However, the use of value analysis in all circumstances should be considered, as it should be obvious that any failure to reduce costs will result in sub-optimisation of profitability.

Value analysis resulted from a realisation by manufacturers that they were incorporating features into their product that the user of the product did not require and was not prepared to pay for. For instance, few manufacturers of bath taps are prepared to produce taps in solid gold, as the demand for such expensive taps is very limited – most people are quite satisfied with brass. In the same way, other not so obvious but equally *useless*, features can be incorporated into products. Value analysis takes a critical look at each feature of a product, questioning its need and its use, and eliminating any unjustifiable features.

It is useful to distinguish two types of value – utility value and esteem value.

KEY POINT

Utility value is the value an item has because of the uses to which it can be put. **Esteem value** is the value put on an item because of its beauty, craftsmanship etc.

Utility value is the value an item has because of the uses to which it can be put. *Esteem value* is the value put on an item because of its beauty, craftsmanship etc. The difference may be illustrated by reference to furniture. An individual who requires something to sit on may be satisfied with a crudely made three-legged stool, or even a tree stump. He will be prepared to pay a very low sum of money for this. He may be prepared, however, to pay a great deal more money for a well-made fashionable reclining leather chair. Both serve the same basic purposes – a seat – but while a tree stump only has utility value, the leather reclining chair has esteem value as well. Value analysis is basically concerned with those products for which no esteem value is paid. In these circumstances there is little need for craftsmanship and beauty, and it may be possible to reduce costs by excluding such unnecessary features.

5.4 The value analysis method

Value analysis is concerned with five basic areas:

Step 1

Establish the precise requirements of the customer. By a process of judicious enquiry it should be possible to discover precisely why customers want an item, whether the item has any esteem value etc. Only in this way can the manufacturer be certain that each function incorporated into the product contributes some value to it.

Step 2

Establish and evaluate alternative ways of achieving the requirements of the customers. There may be methods of producing the item that have not been considered e.g. replacing metal panels with plastic. Each alternative method must be costed out in units of:

(i) **Materials** – amount required, acceptable level of wastage (can it be improved?), alternative, cheaper materials.

(ii) **Labour** – can the cost be reduced by eliminating operations or changing production methods?

(iii) **Other factors** – can new, cheaper processes be found? Would a cheaper finish be acceptable?

Step 3

Authorise any proposals put forward as a result of (b). The assessment in (b) may be carried out by middle management and, if so, it will require ratification by top management before implementation.

Step 4

Implementation of proposals.

Step 5

Evaluate feedback from new proposals to establish the benefits from the change.

Several benefits will result from value analysis. In the first place, many customers will be impressed by the interest shown in their requirements and this will lead to increased sales. In addition, a firm that adopts this approach is likely to attract better staff, due both to the prospects for an outlet for their ideas and the higher morale resulting from the team approach. Of course, there are the economic and financial benefits arising from the elimination of unnecessary complexity and the better use of resources.

5.5 Target costing

KEY POINT

The main theme behind target costing is not finding what a new product does cost but what it should cost.

Target costing, as with several other effective new developments in management accounting, has come from Japan where manufacturers such as Sony and Toyota feel that it is responsible for those firms improving their market share. The main theme behind target costing is not finding what a new product does cost but what it should cost.

The starting point for target costing is an estimate of a selling price for a new product that will enable a firm to capture a required share of the market. The next step is to reduce this figure by the firm's required level of profit. This will take into account the return required on any new investment and on working capital requirements. This will produce a target cost figure for product designers to meet. The cost reduction process usually described as value analysis then tries to provide a product that meets that target cost.

The idea is that various permutations of product design, specification and manufacturing process can be tried and a combination of features determined that can deliver required value to the customer at minimum cost.

Illustration

The following illustration of the application of target costing is based upon the two-part exam questions referred to above:

ABC Ltd makes and sells two products, X and Y. Both products are manufactured through two consecutive processes - assembly and finishing. Raw material is input at the commencement of the assembly process. An activity based costing approach is used in the absorption of product specific conversion costs.

The following estimated information is available for the period ending 31 December 20X5:

	Product X	*Product Y*
Production/sales (units)	12,000	7,200
Selling price per unit	£75	£90
Direct material cost per unit	£20	£20
ABC variable conversion cost per unit		
- assembly	£20	£28
- finishing	£12	£24
Product specific fixed costs	£170,000	£90,000
Company fixed costs	£50,000	

ABC Ltd uses a minimum C/S ratio target of 25% when assessing the viability of a product. In addition, management wish to achieve an overall net profit margin of 12% on sales in this period in order to meet return on capital targets.

Explain how target costing may be used in achieving the required returns and suggest specific areas of investigation.

Solution

The information provided will give the following estimated product and company results:

	Product X	*Product Y*		*Company*	
Per unit	£	£	£	£	£
Selling price		75		90	
Less: variable costs					
materials	20		20		
conversion costs	32	(52)	52	(72)	
Contribution		23		18	
Contribution: sales ratio		*30.7%*		*20%*	
Total for period					
Sales		900,000		648,000	1,548,000
Contribution (sales × cont/unit)		276,000		129,600	
Product specific fixed costs		(170,000)		(90,000)	
		106,000		39,600	145,600
Company fixed costs					(50,000)
Net profit					95,600
Net profit margin on sales					*6.2%*

The company is falling considerably short of its 12% net profit margin target. If sales quantities and prices are to remain unchanged, costs must be reduced if the required return is to be reached.

Product Y is falling short of the C/S ratio target. Cost reduction exercises must be concentrated particularly on this product if its production is to continue to be seen to be worthwhile.

The design specification for each product and the production methods should be examined for potential areas of cost reduction that will not compromise the quality of the products. For example:

- can any materials be eliminated, e.g. cut down on packing materials?
- can a cheaper material be substituted without affecting quality?
- can part-assembled components be bought in to save on assembly time?
- can the incidence of the cost drivers be reduced, in particular for product Y?
- is there some degree of overlap between the product-related fixed costs that could be eliminated by combining service departments or resources?

Conclusion

In this chapter we have considered the application of activity based costing to pricing and some of the practical issues surrounding pricing policies, which will be part of the total marketing strategy for each product.

SELF-TEST QUESTIONS

Activity based approaches to cost based pricing

1 Explain the principle of activity based costing. (1.1)

Pricing strategy

2 Explain market penetration. (3.4)

3 Explain market skimming. (3.5)

4 Explain differential pricing. (3.6)

Pricing of short-life products

5 Explain the problems of pricing short-life products. (4)

Target pricing

6 Explain target pricing. (5)

7 Explain value analysis. (5.3)

8 Explain target costing. (5.5)

EXAM-TYPE QUESTION

Distortions

"It is now fairly widely accepted that conventional cost accounting distorts management's view of business through unrepresentative overhead allocation and inappropriate product costing.

This is because the traditional approach usually absorbs overhead costs across products and orders solely on the basis of the direct labour involved in their manufacture. And as direct labour as a proportion of total manufacturing cost continues to fall, this leads to more and more distortion and misrepresentation of the impact of particular products on total overhead costs."

(From an article in the Financial Times, *2 March 1990)*

You are required to discuss the above and to suggest what approaches are being adopted by management accountants to overcome such criticism.

(15 marks)

For the answer to this question, see the 'Answers' section at the end of the book.

Chapter 20
TRANSFER PRICING 1

CHAPTER CONTENTS

This chapter considers the means by which a divisionalised organisation charges one of its divisions for goods and services provided by another division.

Objectives

When you have studied this chapter you should be able to do the following.

- Describe the organisation structure in which transfer pricing may be required.
- Explain divisional autonomy, divisional performance measurement and corporate profit maximisation and their link with transfer pricing.
- Formulate the "general rule" for transfer pricing and explain its application.
- Describe, illustrate and evaluate the use of market price as the transfer price.
- Assess where an adjusted market price will be appropriate for transfer business.
- Assess the impact of market price methods on divisional autonomy, performance measurement and corporate profit maximisation.
- Calculate an appropriate transfer price from given data.

1 Introduction

KEY POINT

'Decentralisation' could be defined as:

delegating authority to make decisions

or

devolving responsibility for profit.

In order to approach the difficulties of managing a large organisation a structure based on several autonomous decision-making units is often created. 'Decentralisation' as this is called could be defined as:

delegating authority to make decisions

or

devolving responsibility for profit.

The second of these two definitions might be called divisionalisation rather than decentralisation, but the distinction is a fine one. Decentralisation can result in the creation of various types of unit for which definitions are set out below.

2 Creating centres and divisions – decentralisation

2.1 Basic concepts

(a) **Cost centre**

DEFINITION

A **cost centre** is a production or service location, function, activity or item of equipment whose costs may be attributed to cost units.

A **cost centre** is a production or service location, function, activity or item of equipment whose costs may be attributed to cost units.

The manager of a segment of a business that is termed a cost centre has responsibility for certain costs and his performance and that of the business segment will be assessed by the extent to which those costs have been controlled. Typical cost centres might be the various central service departments such as maintenance, research and development or personnel, but the status of these departments can be changed using a transfer pricing policy.

DEFINITIONS

A **revenue centre** is a centre devoted to raising revenue with no responsibility for production e.g. a sales centre. Often used in a not-for-profit organisation.

A **profit centre** is a part of a business accountable for costs and revenues. It may be called a business centre, business unit or strategic business unit.

An **investment centre** is a profit centre whose performance is measured by its return on capital employed.

(b) **Revenue centre**

A revenue centre is a centre devoted to raising revenue with no responsibility for production e.g., a sales centre. Often used in a not-for-profit organisation.

(c) **Profit centre**

A profit centre is a part of a business accountable for costs and revenues. It may be called a business centre, business unit or strategic business unit.

(d) **Investment centre**

An investment centre is a profit centre whose performance is measured by its return on capital employed.

When talking about a divisionalised or decentralised structure one thinks in terms of an organisation that has been split into investment centres. However, the degree of responsibility for and control over costs, revenues and investments may vary and therefore the validity of certain performance assessment measures may also vary.

2.2 Reasons for decentralising

The benefits of and reasons for decentralising are discussed further below.

KEY POINT

The process of decentralisation breaks an organisation up into more manageable units, this enables decision-making to proceed quickly and effectively.

Size – the process of decentralisation breaks an organisation up into more manageable units, this enables decision-making to proceed quickly and effectively and, in theory, a closer control to be maintained on the day to day running of a business's activities.

Need for specialists – as a business grows the nature of its activities often becomes more complex so that the entrepreneur/chief executive has to rely on experts to run particular segments of the business.

Motivation – if managers are made to feel responsible for a particular part of a business then it is generally found that their efforts within that part of the business are improved and, as a consequence the business prospers. Some form of incentive may be needed to reinforce this philosophy, which has many advocates amongst 'behaviourists' of management accounting.

Uncertainty – with ever-changing market conditions, decisions cannot be pre-planned or centrally planned. It is important to have local managers who are closer in touch with each particular part of the business environment to be in a position to respond quickly as problems arise.

Geographical – decentralisation often refers to the delegation of responsibilities at a single location, an office or a factory. However, it is important for a business to get close to markets and to sources of supply and to have a responsible manager in those far-flung locations.

Fiscal – later in this chapter, transfer pricing stresses the efforts made by governments to prevent companies taking advantage of local favourable tax regimes. Nevertheless, this still remains a reason for decentralisation and even within the UK there are tax incentives for operating in areas such as Belfast, Scunthorpe or parts of Lanarkshire designated as Enterprise Zones.

Training – it is claimed that a divisional structure can provide a training ground for future members of top management enabling budding chief executives to acquire the required business skills in an environment that provides a stern, but not impossible, test. These managers are given a sense of independence that should allow them to flourish.

Releasing top management – in order to survive and expand time has to be found and efforts made by top management for strategic planning. Delegation of responsibility for mundane matters makes such time available and efforts possible.

2.3 Problems of decentralisation

Whilst it is generally agreed that some degree of decentralisation is essential for the efficient running of a large business there are some inherent difficulties.

KEY POINT

The danger arises that divisional managers will make decisions which, whilst in the best interests of their divisions, are not in the best interest of the company as a whole.

Lack of goal congruence – having set up a number of autonomous divisions run by managers all keen to show themselves as potential main board members, the danger arises that divisional managers will make decisions which, whilst in the best interests of their divisions, are not in the best interest of the company as a whole. This lack of 'goal congruence' leads to 'sub-optimal' or 'dysfunctional' decisions that, in part, are a result of the inevitable interdependence of divisions. It is often suggested that a necessary condition for successful decentralisation is for:

- the business to have very separate activities
- divisions to be independent of each other
- central management to be able to control divisions to avoid the problems of lack of goal congruence.

However, it is unlikely that these conditions will ever apply since a decentralised structure will either have arisen as a result of splitting up a business that formerly acted as one unit or else by a company taking over businesses with whom it traded.

Cost – the benefits of a large centralised structure result from the possibility of achieving economies of scale. One centralised buying department can achieve more favourable terms and requires fewer staff than if each division has its own buying function. Many examples such as this can be identified indicating that a decentralised organisation may be more costly to operate than a centralised one. Large companies overcome these problems by setting up centralised services, such as accounts departments, but there are problems of controllability and acceptability of these centralised services. One particular example of a cost of decentralisation that has been identified is a loss of 'managerial talent' who might be able to run a division without extending themselves to their full potential.

KEY POINT

Efficient cash management can be achieved much more effectively if all cash balances are centrally controlled.

There is one company asset that is often put under central control whatever the incentive for decentralisation, and that is cash. Efficient cash management can be achieved much more effectively if all cash balances are centrally controlled. If 'head office' has one single bank account with a nil balance the company will incur no interest charges. But if one division has a balance of £50,000 in hand in one bank and another division has an overdraft of £50,000 in a different bank then there will be a net interest cost.

Loss of central control – with decentralisation top management loses some element of control to managers of independent, autonomous divisions. An effective system of divisional reporting should overcome this problem, but there is always likely to be some decisions made that main board directors feel are inappropriate. An additional problem is the attitudes of senior management and particularly chief executives who set up decentralised structures but then are unwilling to let loose the reins, still wishing to have complete day to day control of all aspects of the business.

KEY POINT

In order for effective control of divisions a suitable reporting system producing the key figures that top management need must be installed, understood and operated conscientiously.

Need for divisional reporting – whilst an efficient information system is important in any organisation, it is even more important in decentralised firms. In order for effective control of divisions a suitable reporting system producing the key figures that top management need must be installed, understood and operated conscientiously. The information is needed to help in decisions over divisions and to monitor divisional performance and motivate the staff.

3 Transfer pricing

3.1 Background

The principles to be applied when setting a transfer pricing policy are frequently the subject of discursive and computational questions in management accounting examinations. It is essential that you understand why such a policy is needed, the methods of arriving at an appropriate transfer price for a given set of circumstances, and the problems that can arise with inappropriate prices. These are all covered in this chapter, with numerical examples that are computationally straightforward, but are important illustrations of the principles involved.

Chapter 21 examines the more involved numerical approaches in a more theoretical context.

3.2 The need for a transfer pricing policy

At this point it should be noted that aspects of divisional organisation have already been encountered in the context of performance evaluation (Chapter 10). At this point you may care to refer back to the relevant sections of text.

KEY POINT

A transfer pricing policy is needed if goods or services are passed between divisions.

The transfer price does affect the profit of each division separately and, therefore, can affect the level of motivation of each divisional manager.

One condition for successful decentralisation is that the various divisions should be more or less independent of each other.

However, in practice, this is unlikely to be the case and a certain amount of inter-divisional trading will take place. A transfer pricing policy is needed if goods or services are passed between divisions.

It might appear that the credit to the supplying division is merely offset by an equal debit to the receiving division and that therefore, as far as the whole organisation is concerned, it has a net zero effect. This is true in terms of the physical application of a transfer pricing system once it has been decided upon and implemented. However, there are important behavioural and organisational elements associated with transfer pricing and the choice of which method to adopt. The transfer price does affect the profit of each division separately and, therefore, can affect the level of motivation of each divisional manager.

3.3 Criteria for judging a transfer pricing policy

KEY POINT

There are four specific criteria that a good transfer pricing policy should meet:

- provide motivation for divisional managers
- allow divisional autonomy and independence to be maintained
- allow divisional performance to be assessed objectively
- ensure that divisional managers make decisions that are in the best interests of the divisions and also of the company as a whole.

Adopting a transfer pricing policy will result in:

- total corporate profit to be divided up between divisional profit centres, it may result in a cost centre being converted into a profit centre (e.g. if centralised services charge other divisions for the work that they do)
- information becoming available for divisional decision-making (particularly over whether or not to accept an internal transfer and the level of activity required)
- information being made available to help assess the performance of divisions and divisional managers (for instance allowing the performance of former cost centres to be compared with outside, specialist, profit-making firms in the same field).

The rules for the operation of a transfer pricing policy are the same as for any policy in a decentralised organisation. A system should be reasonably easy to operate and understand as well as being flexible in terms of a changing organisational structure. In addition, there are four specific criteria that a good transfer pricing policy should meet:

- it should provide **motivation** for divisional managers
- it should allow divisional **autonomy** and **independence** to be maintained
- it should allow divisional performance to be **assessed objectively**

This final feature is usually referred to as **goal congruence** and is perhaps the most important of the four.

- it should ensure that divisional managers make **decisions** that are **in the best interests** of the divisions and also of the company as a whole.
- This final feature is usually referred to as **goal congruence** and is perhaps the most important of the four.

3.4 Divisional autonomy

Divisional autonomy is the term used to describe the power given to divisional managers to implement decisions for the benefit of their division.

3.5 Divisional performance measurement

In a divisionalised structure with inter-divisional trading, the use of transfer prices means that the division will be treated as either a profit centre or an investment centre.

The evaluation of a profit centre is achieved by comparing actual and target levels of profit, whereas in an investment centre performance is measured relative to the level of investment using either Return on Capital Employed (ROCE) or Residual Income (RI).

3.6 Goal congruence

This is the term used to describe the achievement of common goals. In the context of divisionalised structures goal congruence exists when the maximisation of divisional profits causes corporate profits to be maximised.

3.7 Transfer pricing policies

Ideally the transfer pricing policy used would encourage divisional autonomy, allow divisional performance to be measured fairly and would lead to goal congruence. In reality, however this is often unlikely to be achieved with conflict arising between these objectives.

If divisional autonomy is maintained it is likely that some decisions will be sub-optimal to the company as a whole. If corporate profit maximisation is achieved, this may only be possible by making some decisions centrally thus reducing divisional autonomy and invalidating divisional performance measurement.

4 Setting transfer prices

4.1 Introduction to different methods

KEY POINT

There are three main types of transfer price:
- cost-based prices
- market-based prices
- negotiated prices.

There are three main types of transfer price:

- cost-based prices
- market-based prices
- negotiated prices.

The first of these uses a cost-plus approach to transfer pricing, the second uses intermediate market price and the third could be regarded as a particular form of bargaining. Each method will be discussed in turn. However, there are several variations on these that are of greater or lesser importance:

- **Using marginal cost and marginal revenue data** – much loved by academics and often tested in exams but rarely used in practice due to the lack of information.
- **Using dual prices** – the use of two prices to encourage or discourage a transfer, possibly by ensuring that each division makes a satisfactory profit from a desirable transfer (it can overcome some of the problems that may arise from the previous – MC & MR – method).

- **Incorporating opportunity costs** – this method, discussed briefly later, may simply provide support for cost-based or market-based methods under the relevant circumstances. However the term could also encompass the use of output from linear programming formulations to help arrive at transfer prices when divisions have limited production capacity.

4.2 Using opportunity costs

KEY POINT

The general rule is that the transfer price should be equal to the opportunity cost of both the buyer and the seller.

The general rule is that the transfer price should be equal to the opportunity cost of both the buyer and the seller. However, finding a practical means of achieving this objective is problematic.

Consequently both buyer and seller will be indifferent between trading internally or externally. Thus both should trade internally and this will maximise the use of organisational resources.

5 The central problem with transfer pricing

Transfer pricing is a critical issue in a wide range of business problems and situations. We will explore these as we proceed through this and the next chapter. However, it is useful to set the whole matter in context at this point by explaining the central difficulty with transfer pricing using a simple example.

Example

AB Ltd has two divisions – A and B. A makes the Unit (marginal cost £5) and B makes the Product (marginal cost £3 plus one Unit). The Unit can be sold to outside customers for £10 and the Product can be sold to outside customers for £12.

Let us appraise three alternative transfer pricing systems for the Unit in two different sets of circumstances. The alternative systems are as follows:

(1) Market price – that will be £10 per Unit under all circumstances

(2) Marginal cost – that will be £5 under all circumstances

(3) Opportunity cost – that depends on the circumstances

First set of circumstances – no production capacity constraint in A

Is the sale of 1 Product good for the business as a whole? Clearly it is. The marginal cost to AB of 1 Product is £8 (£5 in A and £3 in B) and the selling price is £12 – giving a positive contribution per Product of £4.

But, will each of the three alternative systems induce the production/sale of a Product?

Using a transfer pricing system based on market price will give the following result for division B:

	£
Transfer price from A	(10)
Marginal cost in B	(3)
Selling price	12
Contribution	(1)

The manager of Division B might decline to produce/sell the product because it has a negative impact on his own divisional profit. AB as a whole benefits from the sale, but B does not benefit. If the manager is only concerned with his/her own divisional profit then the transfer price system may induce 'dysfunctional behaviour'.

Using a transfer pricing system based on Marginal cost would avoid this problem. The B manager would correctly perceive the marginal cost of 1 Product to be only £8 (£5 transfer from A plus £3 B marginal cost) and the sale would generate a £4 positive contribution.

Using a transfer pricing system based on opportunity cost would also give the correct result. The opportunity cost of the Unit being transferred is £5 – being its marginal cost only, in this set of circumstances.

To summarise:

When there are no constraints on the transferor division, the impact of the three alternative transfer price systems are:

- Market price induces incorrect behaviour
- Marginal cost induces correct behaviour
- Opportunity cost induces correct behaviour

Second set of circumstances – production capacity constraint in A

We now consider the case where there is a production capacity constraint in A and the transfer of each Unit to B involves loss of the outside sale of that Unit.

Is the sale of 1 Product good for the business as a whole? Clearly not. The marginal cost to AB of 1 Product is still £8 (£5 in A and £3 in B) and the selling price is still £12. But transferring the Unit now also involves foregoing £5 contribution from the lost outside sale of that Unit. The net cash flow impact on AB as a whole of making and selling a product is £1 negative.

Will each of the three alternative systems induce or prevent the production/sale of a Product?

Using a transfer pricing system based on market price will give the same result for Division B as in the first set of circumstances.

	£
Transfer price from A	(10)
Marginal cost in B	(3)
Selling Price	12
Contribution	(1)

The manager of Division B will decline to produce/sell the product because it has a negative impact on his own divisional profit. In this set of circumstances, such action is acceptable since the manager is acting in the interests of both his own division and AB as a whole.

Using a transfer pricing system based on marginal cost would now cause a problem. The B manager would perceive the marginal cost of a product to be only £8 (£5 transfer from A plus £3 B marginal cost) and the sale would generate a £4 positive contribution for Division B. The fact that Division A would experience a £5 contribution loss by having to forego outside sale of the Unit does not matter to the Division B manager. The manager of B might insist on the Unit transfer being made and the Product made and sold.

Using a transfer pricing system based on opportunity cost would still give the correct result. The opportunity cost of the Unit being transferred is £10 – being its marginal cost of production plus the £5 contribution foregone.

To summarise:

When there are constraints on the transferor division, the impact of the three alternative transfer price systems are:

- Market price induces correct behaviour
- Marginal cost induces incorrect behaviour
- Opportunity cost induces correct behaviour

General conclusion

Market price and marginal cost are extreme possibilities for transfer pricing systems. They set the upper and lower limits for what is possible. The transferee manager will never agree to transfer at more than market price and the transferor manager will never agree to transfer at less than marginal cost. However, we have seen that neither of these alternatives can be relied on to induce correct behaviour from the point of view of the organisation as a whole.

Opportunity cost offers the theoretical advantage of always inducing correct behaviour from the point of view of the organisation as a whole. However, it has a practical disadvantage. It is not a given amount of money – it varies depending on the circumstances. In practice it can be very difficult to adopt a transfer pricing system whereby a whole range of internal and external circumstances have to be assessed in order to determine what the actual price is for a given transfer.

That sets the scene for the discussion that follows.

6 Simple market based methods of transfer pricing

6.1 Introduction

Where the product (or service) that is subject to internal transfer could be sold to other outside organisations by the supplying division and, similarly, where the product could be purchased from other outside organisations by the receiving division, a competitive market exists and a market price will have been established under normal supply and demand conditions. Such a market price would be a very suitable basis on which to make inter-divisional transfers. It would be easy to operate provided the source of the market price was clearly stated.

KEY POINT

In many situations the use of a market price as a transfer price will not lead to any divergence between divisional and company goals.

It would allow each division to remain autonomous, so that the profit of the division would not be affected by any decision to buy/sell externally or to trade internally. The resultant profits would be determined in an objective way. In many situations the use of a market price as a transfer price will not lead to any divergence between divisional and company goals – but see the example considered immediately above. However, there is a particular problem when there is spare capacity. This is dealt with in the next section.

Market prices are sometimes adjusted downwards for use as transfer prices, to recognise the benefits or savings from internal trading.

Such a reduction might relate to:

- lower packaging and advertising costs for goods sold internally in comparison with outside sales
- the benefits derived from purchases and sales in large volumes (where bulk discounts might be expected)
- the advantages of having an exclusive supplies contract.

An adjusted market price should encourage internal trading because it should lead to higher divisional profits than buying or selling in the open market.

6.2 Problems with market-based transfer prices

Before adopting a market-based transfer pricing policy, the inherent dangers must be recognised and, where possible, steps taken to overcome these problems.

- There may be **no intermediate market price**. The product or service might not be readily available on the open market (an example might be a partly completed car being transferred from one division to another).
- The market price might **not** be **independent**. This would occur if the transferring division was in the position of a monopolist both within the company and in the outside market.
- Difficulty in agreeing a **source of market prices**. Debates will occur over the size, quality, timing and location of internal transfers compared with a range of published prices.
- The need to adjust prices for **different volumes**. Prices quoted may well not relate to the levels of transfers that are likely to take place. In the same way, the extent of reductions due to saved selling costs will be difficult to estimate.
- Published **prices may be fictitious**. This is a variation on the previous problem but is typified by those products for which it is customary for a seller to publish a price then the buyer to negotiate a lower figure.

In a situation where there is spare capacity in the supplying division, the use of a market-based transfer price will not ensure that the divisional managers will be motivated individually to take independent action which is in the best interests of the whole company. This is because the manager of a receiving division may see his divisional profits fall as a result of a move to utilise spare capacity, even though it would benefit the overall profits of the company. A comprehensive example follows to illustrate this situation, and it will be referred to again in a later section.

Example

Kwaree Ltd, producing a range of minerals, is organised into two trading groups – one group handles wholesale business and the other deals with sales to retailers.

One of its products is a moulding clay. The wholesale group extracts the clay and sells it to external wholesale customers as well as to the retail group. The production capacity is 2,000 tonnes per month, but at present sales are limited to 1,000 tonnes wholesale and 600 tonnes retail.

The transfer price agreed is £180 per tonne, in line with the existing external wholesale trade price.

The retail group produces 100 bags of refined clay from each tonne of moulding clay, which it sells at £4 per bag. It would sell a further 40,000 bags if the retail trade price were reduced to £3.20 per bag.

Other data relevant to the operation are:

	Wholesale group	*Retail group*
Variable cost per tonne	£70	£60
Fixed cost per month	£100,000	£40,000

You are required to prepare estimated profit statements for the current month for each group and for Kwaree Ltd as a whole when producing at:

(a) 80% capacity

(b) 100% capacity, utilising the extra sales to supply the retail trade.

Solution

(a) **Wholesale group at 80% capacity**

Estimated profit statement for the current month

Transfer price: £180 per tonne

Wholesale group operating at 80% capacity.

	Wholesale group	*Retail group*	*Kwaree Ltd*
	£000	£000	£000
Sales outside the company:			
1,000 tonnes @ £180/tonne	180		180
60,000 bags @ £4/bag		240	240
Internal transfer of 600 tonnes	108	(108)	Nil
Less: Costs:			
Variable			
1,600 tonnes @ £70/tonne	(112)		(112)
600 tonnes @ £60/tonne		(36)	(36)
Fixed	(100)	(40)	(140)
Profit	76	56	132

(b) **Wholesale group at 100% capacity**

Estimated profit statement for the current month

Transfer price: £180 per tonne

Wholesale group operating at 100% capacity.

	Wholesale group	*Retail group*	*Kwaree Ltd*
	£000	£000	£000
Sales outside the company:			
1,000 tonnes @ £180/tonne	180		180
100,000 bags @ £3.20/bag		320	320
Internal transfer of 1,000 tonnes	180	(180)	Nil
Less: Costs:			
Variable			
2,000 tonnes @ £70/tonne	(140)		(140)
1,000 tonnes @ £60/tonne		(60)	(60)
Fixed	(100)	(40)	(140)
Profit	120	40	160

If it is assumed that the group (divisional) managers of Kwaree Ltd are being measured in terms of the profitability of their divisions, then the effect on divisional profits of utilising the spare capacity in the wholesale group can be summarised as follows:

	Profits in Wholesale group	*Profits in Retail group*	*Profits in Kwaree Ltd*
	£000	£000	£000
80% capacity	76	56	132
100% capacity	120	40	160
Increase/(decrease)	44	(16)	28

As a result of utilising spare capacity the profits of Kwaree would increase by £28,000. However, the wholesale group profits would increase by £44,000, whereas the manager of the retail group would see his division's profits fall by £16,000.

This fall is caused by the reduction in the selling price per bag of the moulding clay, affecting all the sales of the retail group and not only the additional sales. The manager of the retail group, acting independently, is unlikely to accept a decision to increase his production and sales if, as a result, the profit on which he is assessed is likely to decline. The action which he sees to be most beneficial for the retail group, for which he is responsible, is not the action which is in the best interests of the whole company. This is an example of sub-optimisation. Ideally the transfer price should be such that the profits of wholesale and retail groups and the company would all increase as a result of moving from the 80% to 100% capacity. Transfer price bases which would give rise to this situation are identified in the next section.

KEY POINT

It may be possible to establish the identity of a substitute product that is freely available and does have a market price that could be used as the basis for the transfer price.

Where the goods produced by the supplying division are only transferred internally to the receiving division, so that there is no existing market price, it may be possible to establish the identity of a substitute product that is freely available and does have a market price that could be used as the basis for the transfer price. The problems are associated with determining whether the other product is a valid substitute and, if so, what is the appropriate market price. –

6.3 Optimal transfer price – net marginal revenue

A transfer price must be adopted which will encourage the higher level of transfer to take place - since Kwaree Ltd then makes an additional £28,000 profit. At the moment it will not occur since the Retail Group can see its profits fall. The only way to encourage the Retail Group to increase its purchases from the Wholesale Group is to reduce the transfer price. Marginal cost and marginal revenue considerations will be used (strictly incremental costs and revenues).

As a result of increasing output:

	£000
Retail Group's revenue increases by (320 – 240)	80
Retail Group's own variable costs rise by (60 – 36)	24
'Net marginal revenue' (£'000)	56

This must be compared with the cost that the Wholesale Group charges for these extra 400 tonnes. This cost is currently (400 × £180) = £72,000, hence the fall in Retail profit by £16,000.

The transfer cost of these 400 tonnes must fall to no more than £56,000 or (£56,000 ÷ 400) **£140 per tonne**.

Note: it is not sufficient to simply determine a new transfer price at which the retail group's profit at full capacity is higher than that at 80% **under the old transfer price**. Once a price is set, the manager of the retail group will pick the operating level that gives him **maximum** profit. Thus the new transfer price must ensure that the profits operating at 100% capacity exceed those when operating at 80% capacity **both under the new transfer price**.

If the Wholesale Group is considered the transfer price must be at least £70 per tonne (its own variable production cost per tonne). Although this range of £70 - £140 per tonne has been calculated by reference to the incremental sales (of 400 tonnes) the transfer price will apply to all transfers. As a consequence some care must be taken over where in the range (£70 - £140) the final price is set, since the two Groups must make enough contribution to cover their fixed costs. A transfer price at the top end of the range will prove more equitable, such as **£135 per tonne**.

6.4 Demonstration of goal congruence

If a transfer price of £135 per tonne is adopted both divisions will see their profits increased by increasing output, and this is in the best interests of the company as a whole. **Goal congruence** is achieved. The two profit statements, at 80% and 100% capacity, with a transfer price of £135 are shown below.

(a) **80% capacity, transfer price £135**

	Wholesale group £000	*Retail group* £000	*Kwaree Ltd* £000
Outside sales			
1,000 @ £180	180	-	180
60,000 @ £4	-	240	240
Internal transfer			
600 @ £135	81	(81)	-
Variable costs			
1,600 @ £70	(112)		(112)
600 @ £60		(36)	(36)
Fixed costs	(100)	(40)	(140)
Profit (£'000)	49	83	132

(b) **100% capacity, transfer price £135**

	Wholesale group £000	*Retail group* £000	*Kwaree Ltd* £000
Outside sales			
1,000 @ £180	180	-	180
100,000 @ £3.20	-	320	320
Internal transfer			
1,000 @ £135	135	(135)	-
Variable costs			
2,000 @ £70	(140)	-	(140)
1,000 @ £60	-	(60)	(60)
Fixed costs	(100)	(40)	(140)
Profit (£'000)	75	85	160

(c) **Benefits from increasing output**

Wholesale group £000	*Retail group* £000	*Kwaree Ltd* £000
26	2	28

Whilst noting the fact that this new transfer price 'works', a few points are worth making.

- If this problem was observed by top management and the transfer pricing policy changed as a result, the manager of the wholesale division would need to be reassured that his performance would be compared with earlier periods under the revised transfer price and he would not be penalised for the reduced profit that came from the change.

- The Wholesale Group can see two markets, external and internal, in which different prices prevail. The reason why the two prices are permitted is because wholesale sales cannot be increased at present. The manager of the Wholesale Group would wish to make initial sales outside then transfer the balance internally. However this makes no difference to overall sales and profit.

Conclusion

Decentralisation enables businesses to make decisions more quickly and effectively. However, when goods are passed between divisions, a central transfer price policy is needed to ensure divisional profits are not distorted in a way which can reduce the profit of the organisation as a whole. The three main types of transfer price are: cost based, market based and negotiated. The general rule is that the transfer price should be equal to the opportunity cost of both the buyer and the seller.

SELF-TEST QUESTIONS

Creating centres and divisions – decentralisation

1 For what reasons might an organisation decentralise? (2.2)

Simple market based methods of transfer pricing

2 If a firm uses a market-based transfer price, what justification would it have in reducing the price below market price? (6.1)

3 What are the problems of using market-based transfer prices? (6.2)

EXAM-TYPE QUESTION

Transfer pricing

CD plc is organised on a divisional basis. Two of the divisions are the Components division and the Products division. The Components division produces d, e and f. The components are sold at the same price to a wide variety of customers including Products division. The Products division uses one unit of component d, e and f respectively in products X, Y and Z.

Recently, Products division has been forced to work below capacity because of limits in the supply of components from Components division. CD's chief executive has therefore directed Components division to sell all its output to Products division.

Price, cost and output data for Components division are as follows:

Components	d	e	f
Unit selling price	20	20	30
Unit variable cost (excluding transfers)	7	12	10
Period fixed cost	50,000	100,000	75,000

Components division has a maximum output capacity of 50,000 units of which each component must number at least 10,000.

Price cost and output data for Products division are as follows:

Products	X	Y	Z
Unit selling price	56	60	60
Unit variable cost	10	10	16
Period fixed cost	100,000	100,000	200,000

Products division has been forced to operate below capacity because of a lack of components coming from Components division. Products division is able to sell all the output it can produce at the current selling price.

Required:

(a) Assuming all components are supplied to Products division, calculate the different component and product output mixes that would maximise the profit of: (i) Components division, (ii) Products division and (iii) CD as a whole.

(15 marks)

(b) Comment on the effectiveness of the transfer pricing system used by CD plc and on the merits of preventing Components division from selling outside the company. **(10 marks)**

(Total: 25 marks)

For the answer to this question, see the 'Answers' section at the end of the book.

Chapter 21
TRANSFER PRICING 2

CHAPTER CONTENTS

This chapter explores aspects of transfer pricing using models of business economics and also considers certain specific issues relevant to transfer pricing.

Objectives

When you have studied this chapter you should be able to do the following.

- Describe the alternative cost-based approaches to transfer pricing.
- Identify the circumstances in which marginal cost should be used as the transfer price and determine its impact on divisional autonomy, performance measurement and corporate profit maximisation.
- Illustrate methods by which a share of fixed costs may be included in the transfer price.
- Comment on these methods and their impact on divisional autonomy, performance measurement and corporate profit maximisation.
- Discuss the advantages that may be claimed for the use of standard cost rather than actual cost when setting transfer prices.
- Explain the relevance of opportunity cost in transfer pricing.
- List the information which must be centrally available in order that the profit maximising transfer policy may be implemented between divisions where intermediate products are in short supply.
- Illustrate the formulation of the quantitative model for a range of limiting factors from which the corporate profit maximising transfer policy may be calculated.
- Analyse the concept of shadow price in setting transfer prices for intermediate products that are in short supply.
- Illustrate the corporate profit maximising transfer policy where a single intermediate resource is in short supply and a limited external source is available and explain the information that must be available centrally in order that the transfer policy may be formulated.
- Explain and demonstrate the issues that require consideration when setting transfer prices in multinational companies.

1 Introduction

KEY POINT

The prime objective is to maximise the profit of the company as a whole. The second objective is to achieve goal congruence.

As with pricing decisions for external sales, so for transfer pricing optimal policies can be reached using marginal cost and marginal revenue considerations. The prime objective is to maximise the profit of the company as a whole, therefore corporate marginal cost must equal corporate marginal revenue. The second objective is to achieve goal congruence. Therefore the levels of activity and selling prices that achieve maximum corporate profit should also achieve maximum profit levels for each division. It has been suggested by some observers that in trying to simultaneously achieve both of these objectives one may be attempting to reconcile the irreconcilable. However, the management can only try to come as close to perfection as is possible.

Various models have been developed, some of considerable complexity, to determine appropriate transfer pricing policies and practices in particular sets of circumstances. Such circumstances relate to the nature of intermediate markets for units being transferred and constraints at various points in the production process. Several of these models are considered below, but be aware that they are primarily of academic interest and experience suggests that knowledge of them is unlikely to be tested in any depth in the examination.

2 Marginal analysis

2.1 Background

Throughout these calculations, which have their roots in basic business economics it is important to look at problems practically - from the point of view of each of the divisional managers in turn. Remember that the transfer price represents additional costs to the buying division and additional revenue to the selling division. The precise approach depends upon the nature of the outside intermediate market for the product or service being transferred between divisions within a company. Problems will be considered where there is:

- no intermediate market
- a perfect intermediate market
- an imperfect intermediate market.

Where the transferred items have no market outside of the company then there is said to be 'no intermediate market'. Where there is a going market price outside of the company for the transferred items and the company has no influence over that price then there is said to be 'a perfect intermediate market'. Where the transferor division faces a downward sloping demand function for sales of the transferred items outside the company then there is said to be 'an imperfect intermediate market'.

The approach to be adopted also depends upon the precise circumstances and the way in which information is presented. Questions in exams have been seen that require a tabular approach or an algebraic approach. In each case describing a problem graphically may help with the solution.

2.2 No intermediate market

Mention has already been made of the fact that market-based approaches to transfer pricing will not be possible if, for one reason or another, no intermediate market for the item being transferred exists. Care must still be taken in choosing an appropriate transfer price in order to achieve goal congruence. Essentially the approach to finding a suitable transfer price is to:

- find the level of activity at which the company's profit is maximised
- pick a transfer price that ensures that each division's profit is maximised at that level.

KEY POINT

The approach to finding a suitable transfer price is to:

- find the level of activity at which the company's profit is maximised
- pick a transfer price that ensures that each division's profit is maximised at that level.

Example

Pollock Ltd manufactures a machine in its Bedford factory, the engines for which are made in a separate factory at Alicedale. Because of the specialised nature of the equipment, there is no outside market for the engines. Set out below are figures for costs and revenues for a range of activity levels for the two factories.

Annual production £000	Total cost in Alicedale £000	Total cost in Bedford £000	Total revenue £000
1,000	150	250	500
2,000	180	260	900
3,000	240	280	1,200
4,000	330	310	1,400
5,000	450	350	1,500

You are required to determine a suitable range for the transfer price. (Bedford's total cost figures exclude any transfer price from Alicedale.)

Solution

The level of activity that maximises the overall company profit can be seen by simply tabulating total costs and total revenue, alternatively by looking at the company's marginal costs and marginal revenues (once again 'incremental' would be more appropriate than 'marginal').

Annual production	Total cost £000	Total revenue £000	Profit £000	Marginal cost (MC_C) £000	Marginal Revenue (MR) £000
1,000	400	500	100	400	500
2,000	440	900	460	40	400
3,000	520	1,200	680	80	300
4,000	640	1,400	760	120	200
5,000	800	1,500	700	160	100

The table shows that profit is maximised at an annual production level of 4,000 units. The final two columns show that as output increases up to 4,000 units marginal revenue always exceeds marginal cost. However, once a level of 4,000 units is reached, there is no point increasing output to 5,000 units since the additional costs (£160,000) exceed the additional revenue (£100,000). (With these discrete activity levels a point may not be reached where marginal cost and marginal revenue are equal, nor should attempts be made to interpolate such a point.) Although the optimal activity level has been found (4,000 units), it is not yet clear what transfer price will encourage each division to produce, transfer, accept and sell this quantity.

The optimal transfer price can be found by modifying the final two columns of the table above showing marginal costs and marginal revenues.

Annual production	Company's marginal cost (MC_C) £000	Company's marginal revenue (MR) £000	Alicedale's marginal cost (MC_A) £000	Bedford's marginal cost (MC_B) £000	Bedford's net marginal Revenue (NM_B) £000
1,000	400	500	150	250	250
2,000	40	400	30	10	390
3,000	80	300	60	20	280
4,000	120	200	90	30	170
5,000	160	100	120	40	60

This second table shows separate marginal (or incremental) costs for Alicedale and Bedford. The final column shows Bedford's net marginal revenue. This has been calculated as Bedford's (the company's) marginal revenue minus Bedford's marginal costs. The optimal activity level can be found by spotting the final point that Bedford's net marginal revenue exceeds Alicedale's marginal cost (once again it is at 4,000 units).

To find the transfer price that encourages both factories to adopt this level of activity remember the significance of the transfer price.

Transfer price = Alicedale's income i.e. Alicedale's marginal revenue

Transfer price = Bedford's additional costs i.e. Bedford's additional marginal cost

When this is linked to the idea that profit is maximised when marginal cost and marginal revenue are equal the result is reached that, for goal congruence:

Transfer price = Alicedale's marginal cost at 4,000 units

Transfer price = Bedford's net marginal revenue at 4,000 units

In the case of these discrete cost and revenue figures the transfer price must be sufficiently high to encourage Alicedale to produce up to 4,000 units (> £90,000 per 1,000 units) but not so high that the factory considers producing more than 4,000 (< £120,000). At the same time it must be sufficiently low to encourage Bedford to accept up to 4,000 units (< £170,000 per 1,000 units) but not so low that Bedford would wish to accept more than 4,000 (> £60,000). Looking at all four of these, the range of transfer prices that would encourage both divisions to adopt the output level that maximises total corporate profit, 4,000 units, is given by:

$$£90 < \frac{\text{transfer price}}{\text{per engine}} < £120$$

Precisely where the transfer price is set in this range depends upon how total corporate profit is to be divided between the two factories.

If division A transfers an item to division B for which there is no intermediate market, the optimal activity level for the company as a whole, Q*, is found by:

either equating $MC_C = MR$

or equating $MC_A = NMR_B$

(where $MC_A + MC_B = MC_C$ and $MR - MC_B = NMR_B$)

The optimal transfer price is equal to MC_A at Q* and also equal to NMR_B at Q*.

The fact that in this case both divisions' profits are maximised at 4,000 units by a transfer price in the range £90 to £120 per unit can be seen by tabulating Alicedale's and Bedford's profits given a transfer price, say of £100.

Annual Production	*Alicedale's cost* £000	*Transfer Price* £000	*Bedford's net revenue* £000	*Alicedale's profit* £000	*Bedford's profit* £000
1,000	150	100	250	(50)	150
2,000	180	200	640	20	440
3,000	240	300	920	60	620
4,000	330	400	1,090	70	690
5,000	450	500	1,150	50	650

2.3 Perfect intermediate market

The case of a transferred item with a perfect intermediate market is used to illustrate 'The Central Problem with Transfer Pricing' in Chapter 20. At this point you may want to refer back to the case.

The central problem is that, in the circumstances specified, the use of the outside market price as a transfer price is likely to induce sub-optimal behaviour in the transferee division. In the example given it was seen that use of the market price as a transfer price caused bee production to be 25 units below optimum and company profit on bee sales to be £62.50 below the maximum attainable.

The analysis shown in that chapter does not consider the contribution generated by division A. On the critical assumption that A's production of the aye is not subject to some capacity constraint then the full picture may be shown in the analysis tabulated below.

Although A may sell ayes to outside customers, it is assumed that these sales are not affected in terms of unit volume or price by transfers to division B. In this case, the unit transfer price of £15 is sub-optimal. AB's opportunity cost in using 1 aye in bee production is only £10 and that is the theoretically correct transfer price.

Profit maximising output and unit selling price

(250 units of the bee and £55 unit selling price)

	div. A	*div. B*	*total AB*
Sales		13,750	13,750
Transfers	3,750	-3,750	0
Costs	-2,500	-5,000	-7,500
Profit	1,250	5,000	6,250

Transfer price induced output and unit selling price

(225 units of the bee and £57.50 unit selling price)

	div. A	*div. B*	*total AB*
Sales		12,938	12,938
Transfers	3,375	–3,375	0
Costs	–2,250	–4,500	–6,750
Profit	1,125	5,063	6,188

Division A sales to outside customers are ignored because they are assumed to be the same in both cases.

However, it all depends on the precise circumstances. If division A does have a production capacity constraint (that is, its sales are constrained by its production capacity) then moving from 250 units bee production to 225 units bee production may be optimal. The 25 units of aye no longer required for bee production can be sold to outside customers. In this case, the £15 transfer price is a genuine opportunity cost to AB.

If one allows for the outside sale of 25 surplus ayes to outside customers in the above analysis, then the position is as follows:

Transfer price induced output and unit selling price

(225 units of the bee and £57.50 unit selling price)

	div. A	*div. B*	*total AB*
sales	375	12,938	13,313
transfers	3,375	–3,375	0
costs	–2,500	–4,500	–7,000
profit	1,250	5,063	6,313

In this particular circumstance, the transfer price of £15 includes a £5 opportunity cost of contribution on outside sales of 1 aye foregone by producing 1 bee. The marginal cost of producing one bee is £35 (both actual and perceived by B). The transfer of ayes at market price induces the correct behaviour on the part of the decision-maker in division B.

This is fortunate because where there is a perfect intermediate market then it may be difficult to use anything other than the market price as the transfer price. In this case, if the transfer price is set at less than £15 then A will not voluntarily transfer to B whereas if the transfer price is set at more than £15 then B will buy its ayes from an outside supplier for £15.

KEY POINT

The general rule is that transfer price should be at marginal cost plus opportunity cost (if any) in order to induce optimum use of resources.

The general conclusion from this is that setting transfer prices can be a very difficult exercise and so much depends on the precise circumstances of the case. However, the general rule is that transfer price should be at marginal cost plus opportunity cost (if any) in order to induce optimum use of resources.

2.4 Imperfect intermediate market

This situation can become extremely complicated. The transferor division faces a downward sloping demand function for the transferred item and this creates several difficulties.

Let us return to the Pollock/Alicedale/Bedford case considered above. Now a product, such as Pollock's engines, can be transferred within the company or sold outside. The important difference now is the nature of the intermediate market. Alicedale can sell its engines outside at a price over which it has some control. The problem can be described diagrammatically.

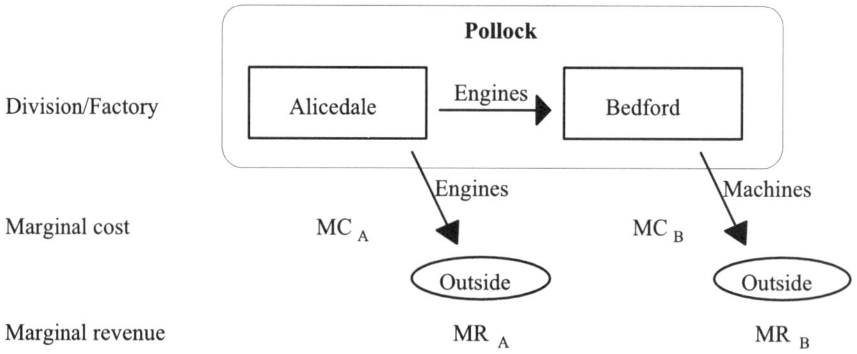

The decisions required are:

- how much should Alicedale produce
- how much should Alicedale sell outside

- how much should Alicedale transfer and Bedford accept
- what should the transfer price be
- what should the selling price be?

The problem is analogous to price discrimination. What should A produce and what should be sold in the two markets (intermediate and, via B, final)?

The method of solution is the same. If sales of engines by A in the intermediate market are denoted by a and sales of machines in the final market by B (which require engines in them) are b, then total production of engines must be a + b.

The company's profit is maximised, as usual, when marginal cost and marginal revenue are equal.

More specifically in this case when the marginal cost of making (a + b) engines is equal to the marginal revenue from sales of a engines and is also equal to the **net marginal revenue** from sales of b machines, or:

Profit is maximised when: $MC_A(a + b) = MR_A(a) = NMR_B(b)$

Example

Supposing that marginal cost functions and demand curves for Pollock's engines and motors were:

Marginal cost of Alicedale's engines, MC_A	=	20	+	0.03Q
Marginal cost of Bedford's converting the engines into machines, MC_B	=	30	+	0.01Q
Demand curve for engines, P_A	=	400	–	0.04Q
Demand curve for machines, P_B	=	600	–	0.05Q

(where costs and prices are in £'s and Q is annual level of production or sales in units).

You are required to determine Pollock's optimal pricing and output policy and a suitable transfer price for engines to achieve goal congruence.

Author's note

This is a complex problem and its solution is pitched at a certain level and style of numeracy. Nevertheless, it follows the basic logic explored above. It is probably the most demanding Example in this text.

Solution

Step 1

Find expressions for (net) marginal revenue.

A's revenue $R_A = P_A \times Q = 400Q - 0.04Q^2$

$\therefore \quad MR_A = \frac{dR_A}{dQ} = 400 - 0.08Q$

B's revenue $R_B = P_B \times Q = 600Q - 0.05Q^2$

$\therefore \quad MR_B = \frac{dR_B}{dQ} = 600 - 0.1Q$

Finally $NMR_B = MR_B - MC_B$ = (600 – 0.1Q) – (30 + 0.01Q)

= 570 – 0.11Q

(Take care with the signs.)

Step 2

Redraft MC_A, MR_A and NMR_B, with A selling a units, B selling b units, A producing (a + b) units, rather than just Q.

$MC_A = 20 + 0.03(a + b)$; $MR_A = 400 - 0.08a$; $NMR_B = 570 - 0.11b$

Step 3

Take (any) two pairs, equate and solve simultaneously.

MC_A & MR_A	20	+ 0.03a	+	0.03b	=	400 – 0.08a
MR_A & NMR_B	400	– 0.08a			=	570 – 0.11b

Rearranging:

(1)	0.11a	+	0.03b	=	380
(2)	–0.08a	+	0.11b	=	170
8 × (1)	0.88a	+	0.24b	=	3,040
11 × (2)	–0.88a	+	1.21b	=	1,870
Add			1.45b	=	4,910

b =4,910 ÷ 1.45 = 3,386.207

Substitute in (1)	0.11a	+	0.03 × 3,386.207	=	380
	0.11a	=	380 – 101.586	=	278.41
	a	=	278.41 ÷ 0.11	=	2,531.03

Step 4

Find the transfer price.

The transfer price to encourage A to make 5,917, sell 2,531, transfer 3,386 and for B to accept 3,386 will be:

MC_A (5,917) and also MR_A (2,531) and also NMR_B (3,386)

(It helps to find all three, they should be the same.)

MC_A	=	20 + 0.03Q	=	20 + 0.03 × 5,917	= £197.51
MR_A	=	400 – 0.08Q	=	400 – 0.08 × 2,531	= £197.52
NMR_B	=	570 – 0.11Q	=	570 – 0.11 × 3,386	= £197.54

The slight difference is the result of having rounded the values of a and b. If unrounded figures are used £197.52 proves to be the most appropriate figure.

The transfer price for engines should be £197.52.

Step 5

Find the selling price for engines and machines. (Remember to go back to the original demand curves.)

Engines: P_A = 400 – 0.04Q = 400 – 0.04 × 2,531 = **£298.76**

Machines: P_B = 600 – 0.05Q = 600 – 0.05 × 3,386 = **£430.70**

3 Capacity constraints, limiting factors etc

3.1 Background

KEY POINT

The transfer pricing problem can be complicated at several levels by the introduction of capacity constraints and limiting factors.

The transfer pricing problem can be complicated at several levels by the introduction of capacity constraints and limiting factors. One can develop models of immense complexity to accommodate such issues. However, it is possible to illustrate the general issue with the following simple example.

Example

A company AB consists of two divisions – A and B. A produces the aye and B produces the bee. Each bee requires one aye as a component. The aye can be sold on the external market. Extracts from the external demand and cost structures for the aye and the bee are shown in the tabulation below. It is apparent that we are dealing with a situation where we have an imperfect market for an intermediate product (the aye).

Division A			**Division B**	
units aye	**mc**	**mr**	**units bee**	**"net" mr**
1	19	40	1	35.00
2	18	37	2	33.50
3	17	34	3	32.00
4	15	31	4	30.50
5	14	28	5	29.00
6	15	25	6	27.50
7	16	22	7	26.00
8	18	19	8	24.50
9	20	16	9	23.00
10	23	13	10	21.50
11	27	10	11	20.00
12	32	7	12	18.50
13	37	4	13	17.00

Key:

mc – marginal cost in A
mr – marginal revenue from external sales of the aye
"net mr" – marginal revenue less marginal costs in B from sales of the bee

In the absence of any constraints, the optimum output can be determined as follows:

units aye	**mc**	**allocation**	**mr/"net mr"**
1	19	aye	40.00
2	18	aye	37.00
3	17	bee	35.00
4	15	aye	34.00
5	14	bee	33.50
6	15	bee	32.00
7	16	aye	31.00
8	18	bee	30.50
9	20	bee	29.00
10	23	aye	28.00
11	27	bee	27.50
12	32	(bee)	(26.00)

The first unit of aye produced gives an mr of 40 if it is sold direct to outside customers and a net mr of 35 if it transferred to B and incorporated in a bee. The first aye should be sold outside.

The second unit of aye produced gives an mr of 37 if it is sold direct to outside customers and a net mr of 35 if transferred to B. The second aye should be sold outside.

The third unit of aye produced gives an mr of 34 if it is sold direct to outside customers and a net mr of 35 if transferred to B. The third aye should be transferred to B.

And so on. You can follow this logic all the way down to the twelfth aye – at which point mc is greater then either mr or net mr. It is uneconomic to produce the twelfth aye. A total of eleven ayes and six bees should be produced.

Inspection of the above workings suggests that the theoretical optimum transfer price of an aye is between 27 and 27.50. This is so in the sense that such a transfer price will induce production and transfers which will maximise the total profit of AB. If the transfer price were less that 27 then the eleventh aye would not be produced – since its mc is 27. If the transfer price were greater than 27.50 then Division B would not produce the sixth bee (since its net mr is 27.50) and Division A would not produce the eleventh aye.

The situation here is complex – but one thing is apparent. There is no automatic reason why the manager of Division A should adopt the optimum transfer price if he is trying to maximise the profit of his own division.

Let us say that there is a capacity constraint of 6 units of aye. Then it is clear that optimum production will be six ayes and three bees. The theoretically correct transfer price in this case is between 31 and 32. A TP of 31.50 would not induce A to sell a fourth aye externally and would induce B to sell a third bee. This will induce both divisions to produce and transfer the right quantities. Again, there is no automatic reason why the correct transfer price and product output will be achieved if the manager of Division A acts to maximise the profit of his own division.

One thought here is that the central management of AB should intervene in order to impose an optimum transfer price. There are three problems with this:

- The information requirement (related to cost and demand structures) needed to do this is formidable in practical situations. Consideration of the example reveals the complexity of the information requirement.
- The optimum transfer price is linked to marginal cost – and this will not produce an equitable distribution of profit between the divisions
- Once central management intervenes in this way, the whole idea of divisional autonomy is eroded.

KEY POINT

The shadow price of a resource is the contribution that is obtained when one extra unit of a constraint is made available.

One further term that can be introduced is that of the shadow price or opportunity cost. The shadow price of a resource is the contribution that is obtained when one extra unit of a constraint is made available. In ranking the alternative uses of successive ayes produced, we are effectively using this concept. When we consider moving from the sixth to the seventh aye – the marginal contribution generated by selling it on the external market is 15 (that is mr of 31 less mc of 16) and the opportunity cost of that use is 14.50 (that is mr on the fourth bee of 30.50 less mc of 16).

One can pursue this general theme by considering ever more complex cases and ever more sophisticated mathematical models. However, these are probably of more interest to the academic theorist than the practising accountant. In management accounting textbooks this area is often described as 'the economics of transfer pricing.

4 Cost-based transfer prices

4.1 Background

The following cost-related transfer prices will be considered in this section:

- total cost
- variable cost
- fixed charge plus a variable charge per unit
- apportionment of contribution.

KEY POINT

In all cases the use of standard rather than actual cost ensures that the cost of inefficiency is reflected in the producing division's results, rather than being passed on via the transfer price to the receiving division.

In all cases the use of standard rather than actual cost ensures that the cost of inefficiency is reflected in the producing division's results, rather than being passed on via the transfer price to the receiving division.

4.2 Total cost plus

KEY POINT

Total cost plus

This approach involves the determination of the total cost per unit for the supplying division.

This approach involves the determination of the total cost per unit for the supplying division. This cost would include both fixed and variable elements. Such a total cost per unit would then be used to evaluate **each** unit of product internally transferred.

There is a fundamental problem with a transfer price based on an absorbed total cost, in that its use in a decision-making context by the manager of the receiving division can lead to action that is not optimal in terms of profit for the company. The reason for this is that, although the total cost is made up of fixed and variable cost elements relating to the supplying division, the one transfer price per unit is regarded by the receiving division manager as variable. This is understandable because the manager in the receiving division is always charged an amount equal to:

Number of units of product × Transfer price per unit

In other words, the receiving division manager recognises the cost behaviour of the transfer price he is charged as having the exact qualities of a truly variable cost i.e. varying directly with the quantity (of units transferred).

The receiving division manager, making decisions for his own area of responsibility and thinking primarily of optimising the profits of his own division, is likely to treat the transfer price as a variable item in the analysis. The danger is that in situations where the receiving division has spare production capacity, the manager may make the decision not to accept business at a lower selling price than usual, because it would apparently not make a profit or even a contribution for that division. However, for the company as a whole the special price does exceed the variable costs and in the short-term it would be worthwhile to accept the business.

The following example illustrates this situation.

Example

A company has two divisions – P and Q. Division P manufactures a product that it transfers to Division Q at a transfer price equal to the total cost of manufacture in Division P. Division Q incorporates each unit transferred from Division P into a product that it manufactures and sells.

Divisions P and Q currently have spare production capacity. Cost and selling price data are as follows:

	Division P *£/unit*	*Division Q* *£/unit*
Variable cost	3	
Fixed cost	2	
	—	
Total cost (= Transfer price)	£5	5
Variable cost	—	6
Fixed cost		3
		—
Total cost		14
Profit		1
		—
Selling price		£15
		—

If an opportunity arose for Division Q to sell the same product for £12 per unit, without affecting its normal existing business and its selling price of £15 per unit on that business, the manager of Division Q would reject it, as the divisional profit would fall. The total cost per unit of £14 would exceed the selling price of £12. However, the manager may apply a contribution approach and argue that the additional business, to utilise spare capacity in the short-term, is worthwhile because it would still make a divisional contribution. His calculations would be based on:

	£/unit	*£/unit*
Selling price		12
Less: 'Variable' costs to the division:		
Transfer price	5	
Variable cost	6	
	—	11
		—
Contribution to Division Q		£1
		—

Using the same set of data, but now assuming that the additional units could only be sold at a price of £10 each, the manager of Division Q would reject the business on both grounds i.e. a reduction of divisional profit and the fact that the business apparently does not even produce a contribution for the division. However, it would be in the best interests of the overall company, in terms of short-term profit, if the additional business were accepted, even at a selling price of £10 per unit, as the following demonstrates:

	£/unit	*£/unit*
Selling price		10
Less: Variable costs in:		
Division P	3	
Division Q	6	
	—	9
		—
Overall company contribution		£1
		—

The foregoing illustrations are based on the following major assumptions:

- the variable cost per unit and the total fixed costs of both divisions remain unchanged at all levels of activity under consideration
- the additional business at the special selling price doesn't affect existing business at the existing selling price

- the manager of the receiving division regards the total cost of the transfer price as a variable cost as far as his autonomous decision-making process is concerned
- divisional managers are being assessed in terms of the profitability of their areas of responsibility.

As far as making optimal decisions is concerned, a transfer price based on total cost is to be avoided. In addition, if transfers are made on this basis, the manager of the producing division will not be making a profit on goods traded internally (but neither will he be making a loss), so it will be difficult for profitability to provide an objective measure of the performance of the producing division and its manager. It is for this reason that 'full cost plus' is sometimes used, adding some profit for the producing division but exacerbating the decision-making problems.

4.3 Variable cost plus

KEY POINT

If the producing division transfers units at a price equal to its own variable cost of manufacture, the producing division manager is unlikely to show a profit on or even a contribution from that business.

If the producing division transfers units at a price equal to its own variable cost of manufacture, the producing division manager is unlikely to show a profit on or even a contribution from that business. Again, an objective measure of performance based on profitability would not be achieved. Such a basis would not be motivational as far as the producing division manager is concerned.

The use of variable cost as a basis for setting the transfer price would mean that the receiving division manager would be provided with the most meaningful cost information as far as decision-making in his division is concerned. There should be no

sub-optimisation, so that decisions made should be in the best interest of the division **and** the overall company.

Once again variable cost might just be the starting point for setting a transfer price and a contribution margin added for the producing division.

4.4 Fixed charge plus a variable charge per unit

KEY POINT

Fixed charge plus a variable charge per unit

This represents a two-part transfer price – a fixed amount per period, which is charged irrespective of the number of units transferred, plus an amount that represents a fixed rate per unit.

In effect this represents a two-part transfer price – a fixed amount per period, which is charged irrespective of the number of units transferred, plus an amount that represents a fixed rate per unit. This concept is similar to the way in which domestic consumers are charged for electricity, gas and the use of the telephone. Alternatively it could be viewed as a form of 'management charge'. An element of profit could be included in the two-part tariff to give the producing division manager the necessary motivation.

The advantage of this type of transfer pricing structure is that it will generally encourage the receiving division to accept more units from the producing division as long as the extra revenue is greater than the extra cost involved. It would be logical to base the fixed element in the charge on the fixed costs arising in the producing division, and to restrict it to any limit on the availability of capacity to supply the receiving division. The variable element would then approximate to the variable or marginal cost of manufacture (possibly plus a profit mark-up). The application of this type of transfer price would also avoid the problem that arose in the earlier example Kwaree Ltd.

If in Kwaree Ltd the transfer price were set as follows:

£50,000 fixed charge **plus** £96.66 per tonne transferred,

then the resultant profits for each division and the company as a whole when the wholesale group is working at:

(i) 80% capacity; and

(ii) 100% capacity

could be summarised as follows:

	Profit in Wholesale group £000	*Profit in Retail group* £000	*Profit in Kwaree Ltd* £000
Wholesale group working at:			
(i) 80% capacity	76	56	132
(ii) 100% capacity	86.66	73.34	160

The following points should be observed:

- The resultant profits for each group and the overall company are exactly the same, when working at 80% capacity, as those when the market price was applied in the original example. Therefore, the divisional managers would be indifferent, in terms of resultant profit, between the application of the market price or the two-part transfer price. The price of £96.66 is in the range £70 - £140. Profit has been split more evenly.
- The fixed charge of £50,000 per period represents 50% of the total fixed costs of the wholesale group, on the argument that up to 50% of its capacity could be used to produce moulding clay for the wholesale group.
- The profits on both the wholesale **and** the retail group, as well as those for the company as a whole, would increase if the divisional managers decided to utilise the spare capacity and work at 100% capacity. They would be motivated to move to the optimal production levels automatically. It should be recalled that in the original application of the market price as a transfer price, moving from 80% to 100% capacity would have resulted in a fall in the profits of the retail group.

4.5 Apportionment of contribution

Another suggestion for establishing transfer prices is based on working out the total contribution made by the company on goods subject to internal transfer, and then applying some logical but arbitrary method of apportionment of this contribution between the two divisions involved. For example, it might be agreed that each division was to make the same contribution margin ratio (P/V ratio) on the goods subject to internal transfer.

This can be illustrated by again using the basic data from Kwaree Ltd. Assuming the 100% level of activity, a transfer price can be established such that each group makes the same contribution margin ratio on tonnes of moulding clay subject to internal transfer, as follows:

	Kwaree Ltd £000	*Less: Outside sales by wholesale group* £000	*Tonnes subject to internal transfer* £000
Outside sales	500	180	320
Internal transfer less variable costs	200	70	130
Contribution	300	110	190
Contribution margin ratio (190 ÷ 320)			59.4%

The objective is then to set a transfer price such that each group makes a contribution margin ratio of 59.4% on the tonnes subject to internal transfer:

	Tonnes subject to internal transfer	*Internal transfer* *Wholesale group*	*Retail group*
	£000	£000	£000
Outside sales	320	-	320
Internal transfer		T	(T)
Less: Variable costs	130	70	60
Contribution	190	A	B

Contribution margin ratio 59.4%

Wholesale Group ratio = Retail Group ratio

$$\frac{T - 70}{T} = \frac{320 - T - 60}{320}$$

$$\therefore 320T - 22{,}400 = 260T - T^2$$

$$\therefore T^2 + 60T - 22{,}400 = 0$$

$$\therefore T = 122.6 \text{ (or } - 182.6)$$

$$= £122.6/\text{tonne}$$

The application of this approach will involve determining a range of transfer prices at different levels of prices, as in Kwaree Ltd, because to sell more the retail group has to reduce its selling price. It is a cost-related basis because the variable costs arising in each division are critical figures in the determination of the transfer price.

The transfer price is still in the required range.

5 Further considerations

5.1 Negotiated prices

KEY POINT

In any practical application of transfer pricing there is usually going to be some element of negotiation between the two divisional managers involved.

In any practical application of transfer pricing there is usually going to be some element of negotiation between the two divisional managers involved. Such negotiation may be loosely based on a market price or on costs, because it is difficult to negotiate in a complete vacuum. Empirical evidence has suggested that, where divisional managers are left to negotiate freely, market prices and costs do figure in the exercise. However, in addition the strengths and weaknesses of individual managers in a bargaining situation will play a role.

The problem with negotiated prices is when the two divisional managers cannot agree: they then have to seek a decision from higher central management on what transfer price to charge. This conflicts with one of the main criteria set out for transfer prices i.e. that the divisions should remain as autonomous decision-making units. Management theory suggests that decisions should always be made at the lowest appropriate level in an organisation structure.

The following four principles have been recommended:

- Prices of all transfers in and out of a profit centre should be determined by negotiation between buyers and sellers.
- Negotiators should have access to full data on alternative sources and markets and to public and private information about market prices.
- Buyers and sellers should be completely free to deal outside the company.

- Negotiators should be fully informed on the significance of the transaction in relation to the profitability of the company as a whole.

If these principles are followed goal congruence should be achieved.

5.2 Dual prices (two prices)

KEY POINT

Another approach to transfer pricing is the use of dual prices i.e., one price for crediting the supplying division and another (usually lower) price for debiting the receiving division.

Another approach to transfer pricing is the use of dual prices i.e. one price for crediting the supplying division and another (usually lower) price for debiting the receiving division. The inter-divisional profit would have to be removed when combining the results of the two divisions. This is intended to represent a motivational approach to transfer pricing but the problem is that both divisions would appear favourably, in terms of profit, from the application of this approach. One then questions the objectivity of profit as a measure of performance in these circumstances.

5.3 A general rule for transfer pricing

The following general rule has been put forward for setting transfer prices.

KEY POINT

Transfer price per unit = Standard variable cost in the producing division **plus** the opportunity cost to the company as a whole of supplying the unit internally.

Transfer price per unit = Standard variable cost in the producing division **plus** the opportunity cost to the company as a whole of supplying the unit internally

The opportunity cost will be either the contribution forgone by selling one unit internally rather than externally, or the contribution forgone by not using the same facilities in the producing division for their next best alternative use. This issue is discussed above.

The application of this general rule means that the transfer price equals:

- the standard variable cost of the producing division, if there is no outside market for the units manufactured and no alternative use for the facilities in that division
- the market price, if there is an outside market for the units manufactured in the producing division and no alternative more profitable use for the facilities in that division.

5.4 Taxation and International Issues

It has not gone unnoticed by the Inland Revenue and other Tax Authorities that companies can use transfer pricing policies to divert profits to subsidiaries based in countries with more favourable tax regimes. Raising the transfer price of goods going from country A division to country B division has the effect of moving corporate profit from country B to country A. This might be advantageous if A has lower tax rates than B. The first UK tax legislation to curb this practice was set up in 1951.

KEY POINT

The anti-avoidance legislation provides that if a transaction exists such as the importing of goods from a foreign division or subsidiary at too high a price or the export at too low a price (thus transferring profits abroad), the Revenue can treat the transaction as having taken place at a fair 'arms length' price.

The anti-avoidance legislation provides that if a transaction exists such as the importing of goods from a foreign division or subsidiary at too high a price or the export at too low a price (thus transferring profits abroad), the Revenue can treat the transaction as having taken place at a fair 'arms length' price.

Similar legislation exists in the USA where the IRS appears to some observers to be trying to take matters one stage further by forcing companies to adopt transfer pricing policies that could be held to be based on unsound accounting principles in order to ensure that profits do not get diverted outside the USA.

Exchange control systems are now quite rare in the developed world but they are still commonly encountered in other areas. The UK had an exchange control system from 1939 to 1979 and it was still being enforced aggressively in the 1970s. A typical exchange control system involves official permission being required to convert local currency into foreign currency. Such permission may be granted selectively in line with current limits and policies. A division in country B may earn profits but be unable to remit them to the parent company in country A because of exchange control restrictions on payment of dividends. Such profits give rise to 'blocked funds'. The only use for blocked funds is to develop the business in B further or to buy goods in B for export.

The transfer price system can be used as a means of evading exchange control systems. Raising the price of goods transferred to the B subsidiary will result in release of some of those blocked funds given that permission will usually be granted to pay for imported goods. However, the exchange control authorities in country B will usually be aware of the possibility of evasion and will scrutinise transfer prices used in cases of doubt.

Transfer prices can be used as a means of asset stripping a division which is about to be divested, closed or expropriated. This tactic was sometimes used by overseas owners of facilities that were being nationalised by African governments in the 1960s. Again, extreme caution should be exercised over the use of such tactics because of the kind of scrutiny they can attract.

Where a transfer takes place between divisions in different currency areas, then a choice has to be made over what currency should be used for the transfer price. In fact, such a choice exists in any transfer pricing situation. All sorts of subtle advantages might be claimed for the use of particular currencies, but if the purpose is to avoid uncertainty then the use of widely traded international currency such as the Euro is to be preferred for the pricing of international transfers.

There are conventions in some industries concerning currency denomination of internal transactions. For example, business in the oil industry is overwhelmingly US$ denominated – a historic thing arising from the traditional American domination of the trade in oil and the engineering sector that supports it. So, internal transfers within oil companies are frequently US$ denominated even if neither the transferor or transferee division is US based.

Conclusion

The primary objective of setting transfer prices is to maximise the profit of the company as a whole. The price should also provide motivation for divisional managers. The situation may be complicated by capacity constraints and limiting factors. Some element of negotiation between the managers involved will usually be required. Legislation exists to prevent companies avoiding taxation by means of transfer prices.

SELF-TEST QUESTIONS

Marginal analysis

1 What are the two essential steps to finding a suitable transfer price when no external market exists for the intermediate product? (2.2)

2 What is meant by net marginal revenue? (2.4)

3 How are the optimal levels of activity found when an imperfect intermediate market exists? (2.4)

Further considerations

4 State four recommended principles when setting transfer prices by negotiation. (5.1)

5 State a general rule for fixing the correct value of transfer prices. (5.3)

6 What does relevant tax legislation allow the IR to do if transfers are not made at a fair 'arms length' price? (5.4)

EXAM-TYPE QUESTIONS

Question 1: Quoin

(a) Quoin Ltd, an abrasives manufacturer, has two divisions. Division M manufactures abrasive grain, an intermediate product, which it can sell either to division D (where it is incorporated into coated-grain final products) or on the open market (where there is perfect competition). In order to maintain a sufficient element of divisional autonomy, division D is allowed to buy abrasive grain in the open market if it so wishes. There are no extra costs of buying or selling in the open market as compared with buying and selling between the divisions.

You are required to demonstrate and explain the optimal transfer pricing policy that will maximise the profits of Quoin as a whole, showing how this profit would accrue to the two divisions. **(15 marks)**

(b) Son of Quoin Ltd has three divisions. Division S supplies grain to divisions X and Y (in lots of 100 tons) which each utilise in the preparation of their own final products. There is no other market for the special grain.

Division S has the following cost structure:

Special grain				
Tonnage produced	400	500	600	700
Total cost (£'000)	400	420	450	485

Divisions X and Y can generate total net revenues (after meeting their own respective independent processing costs) as follows in relation to the tonnage of special grain processed:

Division X						
Tonnage processed			100	200	300	400
Total net revenue (£'000)			120	180	220	240
Division Y						
Tonnage processed	100	200	300	400	500	600
Total net revenue (£'000)	120	240	360	420	460	480

You are required to show the price at which the special grain should be transferred from division S to divisions X and Y, stating your reasons **(10 marks)**

(Total: 25 marks)

Question 2: Drums

L Ltd and M Ltd are subsidiaries of the same group of companies.

L Ltd produces a branded product sold in drums at a price of £20 per drum.

Its direct product costs per drum are as follows:

- Raw material from M Ltd at a transfer price of £9 for 25 litres.
- Other products and services from outside the group at a cost of £3.

L Ltd's fixed costs are £40,000 per month. These costs include process labour whose costs will not alter until L Ltd's output reaches twice its present level.

A market research study has indicated that L Ltd's market could increase by 80% in volume if it were to reduce its price by 20%.

M Ltd produces a fairly basic product that can be converted into a wide range of end products. It sells one-third of its output to L Ltd and the remainder to customers outside the group.

M Ltd's production capacity is 1,000 kilolitres per month, but competition is keen and it budgets to sell no more than 750 kilolitres per month for the year ending 31 December 20X0.

Its variable costs are £200 per kilolitre and its fixed costs are £60,000 per month.

The current policy of the group is to use market prices, where known, as the transfer price between its subsidiaries. This is the basis of the transfer price between M Ltd and L Ltd.

Required:

(a) Calculate the monthly profit position for each of L Ltd and M Ltd if the sales of L Ltd are:

(i) at their present level; and

(ii) at the higher potential level indicated by the market research, subject to a cut in price of 20%. **(10 marks)**

(b) (i) Explain why the use of a market price as the transfer price produces difficulties under the conditions outlined in (a) (ii) above. **(3 marks)**

(ii) Explain briefly, as chief accountant of the group, what factors you would consider in arriving at a proposal to overcome these difficulties. **(7 marks)**

(c) Recommend, with supporting calculations, what transfer prices you would propose.

(5 marks)
(Total: 25 marks)

For the answers to these questions, see the 'Answers' section at the end of the book.

Answers to exam-type questions

CHAPTER 1

EXAM-TYPE QUESTION

Strategic planning

A definition of long-term planning is 'the formulation, evaluation and selection of strategies, involving a review of the objectives of an organisation, the environment in which it is to operate, and an assessment of the strengths, weaknesses, opportunities etc, for the purpose of preparing a long-term strategic plan of action which will attain the objectives set'.

Strategic management provides the necessary organisational setting. McNamee describes this as 'that type of management through which an organisation tries to obtain a good fit with its environment'.

The case for abolition

- Strategic planning has a high opportunity cost. Board level management are intimately involved (they could be involved with the business operationally e.g. by selling).
- There is no statutory requirement for strategic planning.
- Any plans of action which are formulated using detailed quantitative techniques are likely to be rendered useless by drastic changes in the business environment. One can't plan for chaotic and turbulent change, since plans quickly become outdated and useless.
- Corporate entrepreneurial agility could be hindered by the shackles of fixed corporate planning.
- Critics of strategic planning have argued that the process tends to treat all businesses in the same way, as profit seekers. This may stifle managerial style.

The benefits of strategic planning

(a) Effective strategic planning is substantially dependent on a detailed knowledge of the environment.

  (i) The remote environment (e.g. the European economies)

  (ii) The immediate environment of the industry, as described by variables such as:

  - power structure
  - number of players
  - length and intensity of distribution channels
  - customer and supplier behaviour
  - various stakeholder interests and intents.

  Companies have found – from their strategic planning – the best ways to distribute resources. The decentralised SBU (strategic business unit) is a good example of this philosophy. Significantly, companies in adopting such structures are likely to enjoy competitive advantage.

  The flexibility implied by strategic planning is important. There is no single 'best' way of carrying it out.

Qualitative plans are more likely to succeed than the more fragile quantitative plans mentioned above. The former may be employed to identify key strategic variables and to define important management issues. The plans are also more likely to enable a unidirectional approach to be taken by the company.

(b) Strategic management accounting systems may be developed (to run in parallel with strategic planning) as decision–making aids.

(c) The sense of strategic direction, as represented by goals, and their resultant (probably largely qualitatively expressed) strategies, may be significant in acting as a set of codified rules for management to follow at an operational level.

A company-specific strategic planning system will result in substantial competitive advantage.

Note: aspects of this answer may seem more familiar when you have read further chapters in this text.

CHAPTER **2**

EXAM-TYPE QUESTION

Management accounting criteria

Tutorial notes: part (a) is fairly easy. Note there are seven criteria each requiring an explanation and an illustration. Fourteen separate parts for 14 marks. Remember to attempt each of these parts.

Part (b) is only worth 3 marks. Therefore attempt to make three distinctive points in your answer.

Overall a question requiring little technical knowledge. A little common sense, plus a good command of the English language, is all that is required.

(a) **Verifiability**

This means that managerial accounting information can be confirmed by reference to documentation and schedules maintained by the company. This is especially important when information is being used to aid decision making - the decision-maker will want to be in a position to check the information being made available to him. It is also important that the calculations used in planning and forecasting can be checked and that the subsequent control information based on these plans (budgets) can be verified. Proper documentation is essential to verification. Verifiability can be illustrated by reference to the stock records that would be used in valuing material issues for cost control.

Objectivity

It is highly unlikely that management accounting information will contain no subjective bias. However, efforts should be made to ensure that such bias is kept within acceptable limits and is appreciated during the planning and decision-making process. An example of the need for objectivity would be the setting of standard costs for labour or materials.

Timeliness

It is essential that information is produced and communicated to the management in time for it to be used. Delays in data gathering, processing or communication can transform potentially vital information into worthless waste paper. An example would be material price variances which should be reported at the time of purchase, not usage.

Comparability

Most information does not 'stand on its own'. It must be in a form which enables it to be compared with either data from previous periods or with some planned (budgeted) data. This is especially important for control purposes. A good example is the use of flexible budgets to ensure that the actual results are compared with the budgeted results for that level of activity. It is also very useful to use percentages instead of absolute values to enhance comparability.

Reliability

This means that the management accounting information should be processed and presented in such a way that the user can safely use the information while planning, controlling or making decisions. For example, analysis using a computerised system is likely to be more reliable than when using a manual system.

Understandability

Management must receive information in a style and format it finds readily comprehensible. This means that the management accountant must be aware of the recipient's knowledge of technical accounting terms, numeracy/literacy levels and his personal characteristics. An example would be the use of graphs and charts instead of tables of figures for (say) CVP analysis. Information which cannot be understood is at best useless and at worst 'dangerous', resulting in poor planning and decision-making and incorrect use of control devices.

Relevance

This is the primary criterion to be met by management accounting information. The information provided should be that which is required for the manager to plan, control or make decisions in the current environment. Information which is relevant in one environment, at a particular time, may not be relevant as the environment changes. An example would be information based on marginal costing principles, giving the contribution per unit, instead of total absorbed costs, for decisions relating to changes in activity level. This data may not be relevant to decisions on product pricing.

(b) Several of the criteria could be in conflict e.g. relevant data is not always verifiable or easily understood. The major conflict is likely to be, however, between timeliness and some (or all) of the other criteria. For example, it may be possible to improve the understandability of the information but not within the period when it is considered to be timely. Some objectivity may be lost in an effort to get the information out in time. The management accountant will have to balance the criteria to find the optimal practical position, which is not necessarily the optimal theoretical position for information.

CHAPTER 3 EXAM-TYPE QUESTIONS

Question 1: AB Ltd

To : Managing Director

From : Management Accountant

System controls fall under three headings:

Physical access controls

The main risk is that an unauthorised user gains access to a PC on the Head Office network. This would give him access to files held on all the other PCs in the network. A variation on this is that an additional PC could be 'plugged into' the network. The Subsidiary Office stand alone PCs are rather less vulnerable to this since each of them would have to be accessed individually.

Also, the equipment is vulnerable to fire and catastrophic breakdown.

Appropriate measures include:

- installation of password routines when computers are booted up, with rigorous enforcement of password discipline
- storing of data files on external discs (rather than internal hard discs) which are held in locked, fireproof cabinets. Duplicate copies of these discs might be maintained at alternative locations
- physical access controls, with door locks activated by swipe cards or PIN numbers.

Software controls

In a network system, many users have potential access to all the files held on that system. Large numbers of individual users might gain access to far more information than they need for their own personal duties. In addition, a network system is particularly vulnerable to virus contamination.

Appropriate measures include:

- password control activated upon logging onto the system, menus on each PC should be customised to give access to only those parts of the system required by the individual user
- access to some database information may be restricted on a hierarchical basis whereby some users can only read files, some can read and update files and others can read, update and erase files.
- barring the use of office PCs for any form of private work which involves using files brought in from outside the office, installing appropriate virus check software.

Data controls

Data should be loaded on the system in a manner which minimises the possibility of error or fraud. Practical measures include:

- data should be captured using sequentially pre-numbered forms (paper or screen) such that the source of any data can be identified
- authorities should be required for transactions above certain limits.

Question 2: Information for decision-making

(a) The characteristics of decision-making vary at different levels of the management hierarchy. The types of decisions taken by the junior managers are quite different to those taken by middle managers or senior managers. One way of classifying the different types of decisions is:

- strategic decisions
- tactical decisions
- operational decisions.

(i) **Strategic decisions**

These are long-term decisions (usually over three years or longer), taken by senior managers at the top hierarchy of management. They include such decisions as the geographical markets in which the company should operate, new products the company should launch, the type of organisation structure the company should have and so on.

(ii) **Tactical decisions**

These decisions relate to the shorter term (usually up to one year) and are taken by the middle managers of the organisation. Examples of tactical decisions are pricing policies the company should adopt, methods of promotion the company should use etc.

(iii) **Operational decisions**

These are day-to-day decisions taken by junior level managers. These decisions include the quantity of raw materials to be purchased, the number of workers that are required, the level of discounts to be given etc.

Another classification for the different types of decisions was given by Herbert Simon. He classified decisions as programmed decisions and non-programmed decisions. Programmed decisions are those taken in repetitive situations, where clearly defined rules and procedures are in place. Non-programmed decisions are usually 'one-off decisions', where there are no set procedures to guide the decision-maker.

Strategic decisions taken by the higher levels of management are regarded as non-programmed decisions, while the operational decisions taken by junior managers are regarded as programmed decisions. The tactical decisions taken by middle management could fall into either category, depending on the nature of the decisions.

(b) The management accountant must tailor the information to the type of decision being taken. For example, in the case of strategic decisions, the information presented tends to be both quantitative and external in nature. Since these decisions relate to the long term, the feedback tends to be quarterly or over longer periods.

The type of information provided for tactical decisions could be internal and/or external and could also be both quantitative and qualitative, depending on the nature of the decision. Since the time horizon for such decisions is up to a year, the feedback tends to be on a monthly basis.

The information provided for the day-to-day operational decisions is quite detailed and both quantitative and internal in nature. Since this information relates to day-to-day decisions, the feedback is very frequent, usually daily or weekly.

(c) Take the situation of a multi-national company, considering the setting up of a new factory in a third world country. This would be an example of a strategic decision taken at the highest management level. The type of information that should be supplied to the decision makers is:

- The economic conditions and political stability of the country.
- The rate of exchange and details of exchange control restrictions.
- The attitude of the host government to foreign multi-nationals.
- The availability of labour, rates of pay, trade union restrictions.
- Details of market surveys.

- Full details of capital costs, detailed cash flow forecasts and budgeted profit and loss accounts.
- An appraisal of the investment using DCF techniques.
- A sensitivity analysis of the key variables that would affect the project.
- Information on the methods of raising finance etc.

This list is not exhaustive. As can be seen from above, a large amount of the information supplied would be external and qualitative in nature.

CHAPTER 4

EXAM-TYPE QUESTIONS

Question 1: Limitation of traditional management accounting

(a) The traditional management accounting techniques for performance measurement are based around budgetary control and standard costing and the associated variances. The budgets are normally prepared annually and the standards are applied to all products of a particular type.

The move towards more flexibility, a readiness to meet customer requirements, smaller batches and continuous improvements results in a wider range of products or 'jobs' geared to customers' specifications with an associated variation in cost, making it difficult to apply a single standard cost. If a single standard were used in this context to calculate variances, these variances would be partly attributable to changes in product specification.

The effect of advanced manufacturing technology is that a greater emphasis is placed on machines and much less emphasis on direct labour. This has two major implications. Firstly the traditional direct labour efficiency variance is of limited use and secondly the method for calculation of unit cost needs to be amended.

The increased emphasis on quality contradicts assumptions made by traditional management accounting, which assumes that products should be made as reliable as is 'cost-effective'. This has been shown to be a short-sighted approach. In the long run, an emphasis on total quality, not only of products but of services to customers and services within the organisation not only increases sales but enormously reduces many costs associated with re-working and correcting errors.

Overall the traditional performance measures may, therefore, be misleading in the new manufacturing environment.

(b) Activity based costing is being introduced in order to identify more accurately the activities or 'cost drivers' which are causing costs to be incurred. The advantage of this technique is that not only can standard costs be adapted more quickly to custom-made products or batches made to customers' specifications, but also they can be quickly updated for changes in methods of manufacture.

If management accountants are to produce meaningful performance reports in the future, they should be concerned not only with comparing results against budgets but also against alternative methods of working. For example, they should be comparing the costs of traditional stock-holding policies against new techniques such as 'just-in-time'.

They should also be concerned with non-financial measures of performance, particularly those associated with quality, such as statistical control charts and reject rates.

Ultimately, management accountants are judged by the usefulness of the information which is given to management. They should be aiming to 'own' the information system of a company so that they can present integrated reports involving financial and non-financial factors. In order to do this, they must become very familiar with their firm's technical operations.

Question 2: ABC terms

(a) Activity based costing is a method of costing which is based on the principle that activities cause costs to be incurred not products. Costs are attributed to activities and the performance of those activities is then linked to products.

A cost driver is the factor which causes costs to be incurred (e.g. placing an order, setting up a machine).

(b) (i) Cost per set-up $\frac{£4,355}{1+6+2+8} = \frac{£4,355}{17} = \mathbf{£256}$

Cost per order $\frac{£1,920}{1+4+1+4} = \frac{£1,920}{10} = \mathbf{£192}$

Cost per handling of materials $\frac{£7,580}{2+10+3+12} = \frac{£7,580}{27} = \mathbf{£281}$

Cost per spare part $\frac{£8,600}{2+5+1+4} = \frac{£8,600}{12} = \mathbf{£717}$

Cost per machine hour (No. of m/c hours = 125 + 1,250 + 600 + 10,500)

$= \frac{£37,424}{12,475} = \mathbf{£3.00/hr}$

Costs are then attributed to products using the cost driver rates calculated above, for example:

Product A requires one machine set-up, therefore 1 × £256 = £256

Product B requires six machine set-ups, therefore 6 × £256 = £1,536

and so on.

Product	*A*	*B*	*C*	*D*
	£	£	£	£
Activities:				
Set-ups	256	1,536	512	2,048
Orders	192	768	192	768
Handling	562	2,810	843	3,372
Spare parts	1,434	3,585	717	2,868
Machine time	375	3,750	1,800	31,500
	2,819	12,449	4,064	40,556
No. of units	500	5,000	600	7,000
Cost per unit	£5.64	£2.49	£6.77	£5.79

The costs are then totalled and divided by the number of units to give the cost per unit for each product.

(ii) The activity based costing approach attributes more costs to products A, B and C and less to product D than the traditional method of accounting for overhead costs. The activity based costing method gives a more accurate cost by relating it to the resources used to manufacture each product, consequently these costs are more useful for decision-making than those provided by the traditional method.

CHAPTER 5 EXAM-TYPE QUESTIONS

Question 1: IT

The question has two distinct requirements:

- describing the main features of computerised financial planning packages
- giving **your views** on the quotation given in the question.

Your views on the quotation should concentrate on the word 'revolutionised' in the context of budget preparation. This will make for a more interesting answer.

Computerised financial planning packages are mathematical statements of the relationships among all operating and financial activities, as well as other major internal and external factors that may affect decisions. These packages come in varying degrees of sophistication. The most rudimentary merely produce standard financial statements and supporting schedules from specific company data input. They are packages applicable to companies in general. At the other end of the package spectrum are special purpose-built models designed for the specific company in question. Such models would include interactive capabilities, integrate detailed activities of all sub-units of an organisation and permit probabilistic analysis.

The most obvious application for computerised financial planning packages is in the preparation of budgets. The quotation states that the packages have 'revolutionised the process of budget preparation'. Whether they have revolutionised or merely 'helped' is a subjective argument, but nobody can deny that they have made a difference. The packages can make computations, based on data input such as product selling prices, variable cost, type of expense etc, very quickly and produce a number of different statements from the database. The packages will also greatly assist in budget revisions and assessment of the effects (financial) resulting from the various courses of action that may be open to management. Statistical techniques such as sensitivity analysis may also be easily incorporated into the budget preparation.

Any management accountant will confirm that these packages have helped in tasks which are time-consuming when undertaken manually, but to say 'revolutionised' may undermine the prior and current abilities of the professional accountant.

As recently as 10 years ago, some professional accountants maintained that IT had changed nothing fundamental in the nature of accounting. These people said, for example, that the computer spreadsheet was nothing more than an electronic version of the columnar analysis paper used by generations of accountants. This view is far less widely accepted today.

In the pre-computer era, budgeting was essentially an exercise in arithmetic. Nowadays, the arithmetic is all automated and this gives the opportunity for a far greater depth in analysis and option appraisal. In short, IT may have made the accountant's task a far more intelligent one.

Question 2: Quality assurance

In general terms, the suggestions made by the MD reflect a mistaken view of quality and how it is assured. His emphasis is 'reactive' rather than 'pro-active', is 'feedback' based rather than 'feedforward', and is concerned with quality control rather than quality assurance.

(a) Specifically:

- His initial statement that 'something drastic has to be done about quality' does not seem to be based on any kind of systematic analysis or measurement. Nor does it suggest that the MD understands the meaning of quality, which according to Crosby is 'conformity to requirements'.
- His statement that 'quality is the responsibility of your department' ignores the fact that quality is the responsibility of all staff at all stages, in all departments and at all levels.
- The 'tougher line' suggests a punishment-oriented approach which contradicts the advice of Deming 'to drive out fear', and to seek co-operation.
- 'Raising quality standards' without targeting particular areas, and without understanding why such quality improvement is necessary, is likely to be a costly and unproductive exercise.
- 'Increasing inspection rates' and 'giving greater authority to quality control inspectors' reinforces the 'control' approach, and the 'specialist' emphasis discussed earlier.

(b) An alternative approach involves viewing quality control as part of a more strategic approach to quality - quality assurance. This requires:

- An analysis of existing quality performance and problems. Such an analysis should involve all levels and all departments, and should concern itself with the customers, with the competition, and with suppliers as well as the activities of the firm itself. Crosby advocates the creation of 'quality committees' composed of members drawn from different departments.
- Calculating the 'cost of quality', which involves measuring the costs of not 'getting it right first time', and includes 'prevention costs', 'appraisal costs', and 'failure costs'. Such an analysis should identify a sizeable potential cost saving (or to quote Crosby 'quality is free').
- The careful selection and monitoring of suppliers, perhaps involving an 'active' rather than a passive relationship.
- The design of the product, to ensure an appropriate level of quality.
- The installation of quality information systems which measure and feedback quality performance to those involved, and which can serve as the basis for targets.
- Quality improvement, perhaps involving the creation of quality circles.
- Quality staff, which involves investment in recruitment, selection, training, development, appraisal and reward.

In conclusion, such an approach is essentially long term, and requires a shift in thinking about quality at all levels. The essential ingredient in this cultural shift is a 'right first time' mentality which encompasses all activities that impinge on quality. In short, the MD and other staff need to be educated in 'total quality management'.

CHAPTER 6 EXAM-TYPE QUESTIONS

Question 1: JK Ltd

(a)

			Product		
	J	*K*	*L*	*M*	*Total*
	£000	£000	£000	£000	£000
Sales	200	400	200	200	1,000
Variable costs	140	80	210	140	570
Contribution	60	320	(10)	60	430

(b) Calculate the contribution/sales ratios and plot each product starting with the product having the greatest C/S ratio.

J	*K*	*L*	*M*
30%	80%	(5%)	30%

Contribution – Sales Graph

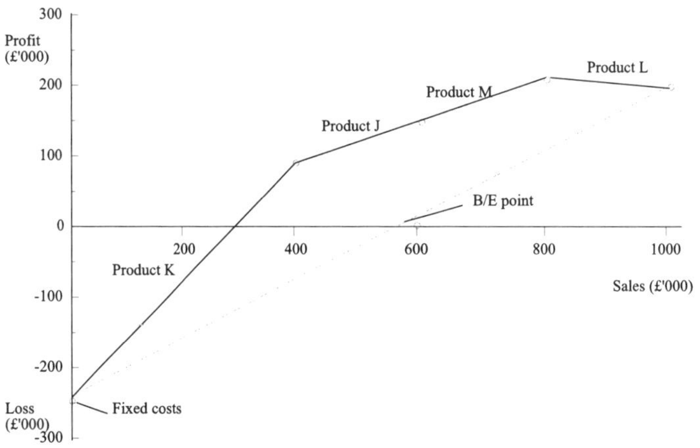

(c) The products are plotted in the order of their c/s ratios. The steeper the line for an individual product the greater the c/s ratio for that product. Thus it can be seen that product K provides the greatest contribution with respect to sales value.

It can be seen from the graph that product L should be dropped as it provides negative contribution.

The break-even point can be calculated using the c/s ratio of the mix. This can also be approximately seen from the graph.

$$\text{B/E} = \frac{\text{Fixed costs}}{\text{c/s ratio of the mix}}$$

$$= \frac{240,000}{430/1,000}$$

$$= £558,140$$

(d) The overall ratio could be improved by:

- increasing the selling prices
- decreasing the sales of products J, L or M
- automating the process. This would increase fixed costs but would reduce variable costs thus increasing contribution.

Question 2: A company

To: The board of directors

From: The management accountant

Date: X-X-20XX

Subject: Desirability of closing the factory for a year

In the forthcoming year (20X1) our alternatives are:

(1) Continue operating

	£
Sales	49,500
Total cost	59,500
Loss	(10,000)

(2) Close down for 20X1 and re-open in 20X2.

	£
(a) Unavoidable fixed cost	11,000
(b) Redundancy payment	7,500
(c) Necessary maintenance	1,000
(d) Re-opening cost	4,000
	23,500

This is more than twice the loss incurred if we continue at 50% capacity and I would suggest continuing production.

(3) The anticipated result for 20X2 would be

	£
Sales	90,000
Total cost	79,750
Profit	10,250

Finally assuming the consultant's forecast is correct and we carry on producing, the cumulative position at the end of year 20X2 would be a small profit of £250 without the trauma of closing down.

Workings

(W1) Since direct labour and direct material increase from zero by equal increments of cost for each 20% change in volume they must be entirely variable. The increments for activity changes on production, administration and selling overhead do not account for all the cost and these must therefore include a fixed proportion.

Production capacity	*40%*	*60%*	*Increment for 20%*	*Fixed*
	£	£	£	£
Direct material	16,000	24,000	8,000	-
Direct wages	12,000	18,000	6,000	-
Production overhead	11,400	12,600	1,200	9,000
Administration	5,800	6,200	400	5,000
Selling and distribution	6,200	6,800	600	5,000
Total			16,200	19,000

Allowance for 50% = $\frac{50}{20} \times 16{,}200 + 19{,}000 = £59{,}500$

or

				£
Direct material	=	$\frac{50}{20} \times 8{,}000$	=	20,000
Direct wage	=	$\frac{50}{20} \times 6{,}000$	=	15,000
Production overhead	=	$\left(\frac{50}{20} \times 1{,}200\right) + 9{,}000$	=	12,000
Administration	=	$\frac{50}{20} \times 400 + 5{,}000$	=	6,000
Selling	=	$\frac{50}{20} \times 600 + 5{,}000$	=	6,500
Total cost				59,500
Revenue at 50%				49,500
Loss at 50% activity				(10,000)

(W2) Second year

Total cost =	$\frac{75}{20} \times 16{,}200 + 19{,}000$ =	79,750
Revenue at 75% activity		90,000
Profit at 75% activity		10,250

Question 3: Choice of contracts

(a)

	North East		South Coast	
	£	£	£	£
Contract price		288,000		352,000
(1) Material X: stock	19,440			
(2) Material X: firm orders	27,360			
(3) Material X: not yet ordered	60,000			
(4) Material Y			49,600	
(5) Material Z			71,200	
(6) Labour	86,000		110,000	
(8) Staff accommodation and travel	6,800		5,600	
(9) Penalty clause			28,000	
(10) Loss of plant hire income			6,000	
		199,600		270,400
Profit		88,400		81,600

The company should undertake the North-east contract. It is better than the Southcoast contract by £6,800 (£88,400 - £81,600).

(b) ***Notes***

(1) Material X can be used in place of another material which the company uses. The value of material X for this purpose is 90% × £21,600 = £19,440. If the company undertakes the North-east contract it will not be able to obtain this saving. This is an opportunity cost.

(2) Although the material has not been received yet the company is committed to the purchase. Its treatment is the same therefore as if it was already in stock. The value is 90% × £30,400 = £27,360.

(3) The future cost of material X not yet ordered is relevant.

(4) The original cost of material Y is a sunk cost and is therefore not relevant. If the material was to be sold now its value would be 24,800 × 2 × 85% = £42,160, i.e. twice the purchase price less 15%, however, if the material is kept it can be used on other contracts, thus saving the company from future purchases. The second option is the better. The relevant cost of material Y is 2 × 24,800 = £49,600. If the company uses material Y on the South coast contract, it will eventually have to buy an extra £49,600 of Y for use on other contracts.

(5) The future cost of material Z is an incremental cost and is relevant.

(6) As the labour is to be sub-contracted it is a variable cost and is relevant.

(7) Site management is a fixed cost and will be incurred whichever contract is undertaken (and indeed if neither is undertaken), and is therefore not relevant.

(8) It is assumed that the staff accommodation and travel is specific to the contracts and will only be incurred if the contracts are undertaken.

(9) If the South-coast contract is undertaken the company has to pay a £28,000 penalty for withdrawing from the North-east contract. This is a relevant cost with regard to the South-coast contract.

(10) The depreciation on plant is not a cash flow. It is therefore not relevant. The opportunity cost of lost plant hire is relevant, however.

(11) It is assumed that the notional interest has no cash flow implications.

(12) It is assumed that the HQ costs are not specific to particular contracts.

CHAPTER 7 EXAM-TYPE QUESTION

Ski runs

General workings

	Skiers
Good season	60,000
Moderate season	25,000
Poor season	4,000
Expected	29,200

(a)

Low investment

	c/f	*disc. factor*	*PV*
year 0	–440000	1.000	–440000
1	106000	0.893	94643
2	106000	0.797	84503
3	106000	0.712	75449
4	86000	0.636	54655
5	106000	0.567	60147
6	106000	0.507	53703
7	106000	0.452	47949
8	86000	0.404	34734
9	106000	0.361	38225
10	106000	0.322	34129
		NPV (a)	138136

(b)

High investment

	c/f	*disc factor*	*PV*
Year 0	–850000	1.000	–850000
1	194400	0.893	173571
2	194400	0.797	154974
3	194400	0.712	138370
4	134400	0.636	85414
5	194400	0.567	110308
6	194400	0.507	98489
7	194400	0.452	87937
8	134400	0.404	54282
9	194400	0.361	70103
10	194400	0.322	62592
		NPV (b)	186039

Given that the high investment strategy yields the highest NPV, all other things being equal, it is preferred.

(c) In the worst case scenario, seasons follow the pattern PPPMMMMGGG. The result is:

Worst case results

Low investment

	c/f	*disc. factor*	*PV*
year 0	–440000	1.000	–440000
1	–20000	0.893	–17857
2	–20000	0.797	–15944
3	–20000	0.712	–14236
4	65000	0.636	41309
5	85000	0.567	48231
6	85000	0.507	43064
7	85000	0.452	38450
8	240000	0.404	96932
9	260000	0.361	93759
10	260000	0.322	83713
		NPV (c)	–42580

High investment

	c/f	*disc. factor*	*PV*
Year 0	–850000	1.000	–850000
1	18000	0.893	16071
2	18000	0.797	14349
3	18000	0.712	12812
4	105000	0.636	66729
5	165000	0.567	93625
6	165000	0.507	83594
7	165000	0.452	74638
8	350000	0.404	141359
9	410000	0.361	147850
10	410000	0.322	132009
		NPV (c)	–66962

(d) In the best case scenario, the seasons follow the pattern GGGMMMMPPP, with results as follows:

Best case results

Low investment

	c/f	*disc factor.*	*PV*
year 0	-440000	1.000	–440000
1	260000	0.893	232143
2	260000	0.797	207270
3	260000	0.712	185063
4	65000	0.636	41309
5	85000	0.567	48231
6	85000	0.507	43064
7	85000	0.452	38450
8	–40000	0.404	–16155
9	–20000	0.361	–7212
10	–20000	0.322	–6439
		NPV (d)	325722

High investment

	c/f	*disc. factor*	*PV*
Year 0	–850000	1.000	–850000
1	410000	0.893	366071
2	410000	0.797	326849
3	410000	0.712	291830
4	105000	0.636	66729
5	165000	0.567	93625
6	165000	0.507	83594
7	165000	0.452	74638
8	–42000	0.404	–16963
9	18000	0.361	6491
10	18000	0.322	5796
		NPV (d)	448661

(e) A diagram may be constructed based on these figures:

	Worst	**Best**
Low inv.	–42580	325722
High inv.	–66962	448661

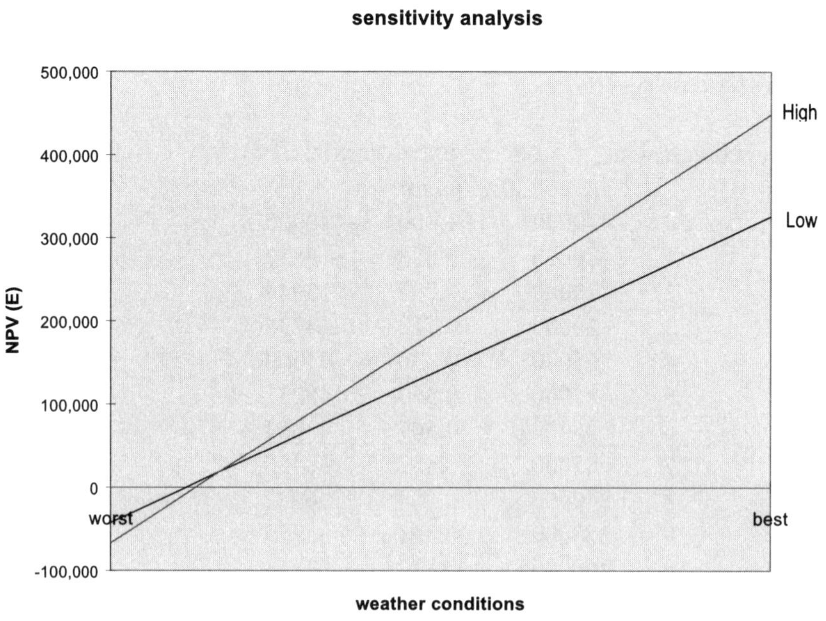

(f) On the basis of a purely quantitative analysis, the high investment strategy offers the following advantages:

- at the expected outcome it has a higher NPV
- it is only in a very limited range of adverse outcomes that it offers an inferior NPV to the low investment strategy, and even then it is only by a small margin
- over most possible outcomes it offers a superior NPV to the low investment strategy – and in the more favourable range of outcomes the margin between the two becomes quite large

The downside to this reasoning is that the high investment strategy involves a much larger financial commitment. The sequence of seasons is not the only risk factor. For example, environmental campaigners have recently been campaigning to have skiing banned in parts of Scotland because it damages the fragile topsoil. Such an outcome would result in a total failure of the project – and one might wish to be in a position to minimise one's losses in a way that the low investment strategy would allow.

CHAPTER 8 EXAM-TYPE QUESTIONS

Question 1: Homeworker Ltd

(a) **Increased production availability**

Present production	4,752 hours ÷ 36 machine hours	= 132 batches
Buying out A		
Production capacity	4,752 hours ÷ 26 machine hours	= 182.77 batches
	INCREASE	= 38.46%
Buying out B		
Production capacity	4,752 hours ÷ 22 machine hours	= 216 batches
	INCREASE	= 63.64%

Buying out C		
Production capacity	4,752 hours ÷ 24 machine hours	= 198 batches
	INCREASE	= 50%

(b) **Financial implications**

*(**Tutorial note:** assuming a risk neutral attitude, the appropriate cost price for the bought out components is the 'expected' purchase price.)*

Expected purchase price:
Component A 96 (0.25) + 85 (0.5) + 54 (0.25) = £80
Component B 176 (0.25) + 158 (0.5) + 148 (0.25) = £160
Component C 149 (0.25) + 127 (0.5) + 97 (0.25) = £125

Contribution possibilities:

	Present position	*Buy out Component A*	*Buy out Component B*	*Buy out Component C*
Number of batches	132	182.8	198*	198
	£	£	£	£
Per batch:				
Variable cost A	32	80	32	32
Variable cost B	54	54	160	54
Variable cost C	58	58	58	125
Variable cost D + E	16	16	16	16
Assembly costs	40	40	40	40
	200	248	306	267
Selling price	600	600	600	600
Contribution	400	352	294	333
Total contribution	52,800	64,346	58,212	65,934

* Only a 50% increase in demand next period.

Decision: Buy out C to maximise contribution.

Tutorial note: an incremental approach would have been equally satisfactory.

(c) **Revised profit statement**

	Per batch	*Total (198 batches)*
	£	£
Sales	600	118,800
Variable cost (as per part (b))	267	52,866
Contribution	333	65,934
Fixed costs (316 × 132 batches)		41,712
Profit		24,222

(d) **Other factors to consider to avoid risk**

- **Component prices**. The expected price for Component C is £125. It could be as high as £149. There appears to be no incentive for General Machines Ltd to keep down costs.
- **Dealing with risk**. The use of expected values is only one way of dealing with risk. A calculation of the worst possible outcome may have suggested a different choice.
- **Uncertainty of sales estimate**. The sales estimate was assumed to be certain. A range of probabilities should have been used.
- Would fixed costs remain constant with a 50% increase in output?
- There will be an added risk in obtaining an essential component from only one outside supplier.

Tutorial note: only three factors are required. You should choose the three considered most pertinent to the question.

Question 2: Test marketing

(a)

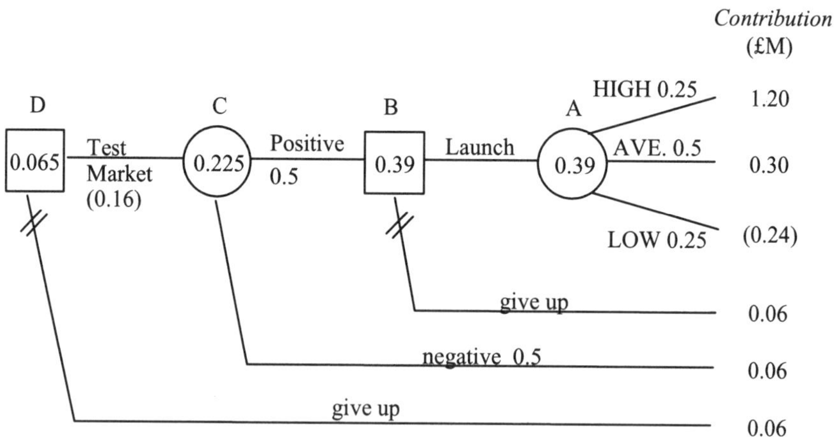

Notes:

(i) The values by the events and the double bars should be ignored at this stage as they belong to the answer to part (b).

(ii) Monetary amounts have been shown 'gross' and the cost inserted at that point in the tree where it becomes payable.

(b) The tree is evaluated as follows, in £m

At A, EMV	=	$(0.25 \times 1.2) + (0.5 \times 0.3) - (0.25 \times 0.24)$
	=	0.39
At B, EMV for 'launch'	=	0.39
EMV for 'give up'	=	0.06

$\therefore$ choose 'launch' and insert its EMV by the decision point and block off the other branch.

At C, EMV	=	$(0.5 \times 0.39) + (0.5 \times 0.06)$
	=	0.225

At D, EMV of 'test market'	=	0.225 – 0.16
	=	0.065
EMV of 'give up'	=	0.06

∴ choose 'test market' and block off the other branch.

The optimum strategy is to test the market and if it proves positive, to carry out the national launch. The net EMV of this policy is £0.065m or £65,000.

Notes:

(i) In the evaluation, do **not** eliminate probability branches as the decision-maker has no control over which branch is taken.

(ii) The optimum strategy must state which branch is to be taken at **each** decision point.

(c) Possible limitations of the method are:

- There is difficulty in estimating the relevant cash flows and their probabilities.
- In practice there are likely to be a whole range of possible outcomes at each stage, rather than the two or three shown in this example.
- The EMV may not be the best criterion. A possible reason for this is that being an average, the EMV assumes that losses are permissible as well as gains, provided they have a relatively low probability. In practice, management may not be prepared to gamble on making a loss, which might ruin the firm.

CHAPTER 9

EXAM-TYPE QUESTION

Corporate mission

To: The Managing Director

From: The Management Accountant

Subject: Corporate mission statements

The meaning of corporate mission

The corporate mission embodies the overall purposes of an organisation. A corporate mission statement is formulated to express the company's philosophy and should answer fundamental questions such as: Why does the company exist? Who will be served by and benefit from the company? What products or services will be provided? The majority of mission statements are presented using general, rather than detailed, concepts.

Corporate mission and strategic planning

In order to prepare an effective strategic plan, the management must first address the organisation's mission. There is a certain amount of controversy regarding the point in the planning process at which the mission statement is best formulated. One view is that the mission statement is of such a fundamental nature that the strategic plan cannot be prepared without reference to it. Another view, expressed by Argenti, is diametrically opposed. He postulates that the mission statement is the end result of the strategic planning process. These opinions demonstrate how difficult it can be to differentiate between an organisation's mission and its objectives. The *mission* is a wide-ranging statement which presents the organisation's *raison d'être* in terms of its ability to satisfy some of society's needs whilst its *objectives* are the company's broad goals.

Areas to be covered

The mission statement is likely to be formulated by the company's board of directors. Although it will not be quantitative in nature it will usually highlight several areas:

- the kinds of products and services the company aims to provide
- the customers to be served
- the markets in which the company anticipates operating
- an overview of the company philosophy and the broad expression of its policies
- the company's attitude towards matters encompassing social obligations
- the manner in which management wishes the firm to be perceived by the public.

Benefits from developing a mission statement

The usefulness of a mission statement may be summarised as follows:

- All staff will gain an understanding of the firm's purpose and philosophy.
- Expectations and attitudes within the firm will be expressed in terms of a long-range vision.
- The organisation will benefit from a unanimity of purpose which should result in decisions advantageous to the purposes of the company.
- The boundaries within which the company operates will be clearly laid down. This will assist in developing co-ordinated plans.
- An unambiguous statement regarding the overall direction of the company should lead to enhanced allocation of resources.

Conclusion

The company would gain several benefits from the formulation of a mission statement. It would greatly assist the decision-makers and those responsible for implementing the firm's policies. The mission statement also has an important role to play in helping management focus on fundamental issues in terms of strategic planning and will ensure that strategic plans do not conflict with the basic purpose of the organisation.

CHAPTER 10

EXAM-TYPE QUESTIONS

Question 1: Theta Ltd

(a) **ROI using Alpha's basis**

	£000
(i) Profit	225
Capital employed:	
Fixed assets (at cost)	1,000
Net current assets	250
	1,250

$$ROI = \frac{225}{1,250} \times 100 = 18.0\%$$

(ii) Profit	225
Add: Savings less depreciation $(35{,}000 - \frac{120{,}000}{6})$	15
	240
Capital employed:	
Fixed assets (at cost)	1,000
Add: Purchases (at cost)	120
	1,120
Net current assets	250
	1,370

$$ROI = \frac{240}{1{,}370} \times 100 = 17.52\%$$

(iii) Profit as stated	225
Less: Contribution lost	30
	195
Add: Depreciation not charged	20
	215
Capital employed:	
Fixed assets (at cost)	1,000
Less: Disposals (at cost)	200
	800
Net current assets	250
	1,050

$$ROI = \frac{215}{1{,}050} \times 100 = 20.48\%$$

Note: as the net current assets are average for the year the inflow of £20,000 realised on the sale of the asset has not been included. Similarly in (ii) above it is assumed that the machine was purchased out of additional funds and not from existing cash resources (a common assumption in this style of question).

	£000
(iv) Profit	225
Add: Reduction in cost	4
	229
Capital employed:	
Fixed assets (at cost)	1,000
Net current assets	250
	1,250

$$ROI = \frac{229}{1{,}250} \times 100 = 18.3\%$$

Note: the reduction in creditors is offset by bank overdraft therefore no change in 'net' current assets. Overdraft interest ignored.

		£000
(v)	Profit	225
	Less: Lost contribution	6
		219
	Capital employed:	
	Fixed assets	1,000
	Net current assets (£250,000 – £25,000)	225
		1,225

$$\text{ROI} = \frac{219}{1,225} \times 100 = 17.9\%$$

(b) **ROI using Theta's basis**

All profit figures are as computed in part (a). Capital employed must be recomputed on basis of original cost less depreciation for fixed assets.

		£000
(i)	Profit	225
	Capital employed:	
	Fixed assets (£1,000,000 – £475,000)	525
	Net current assets	250
		775

$$\text{ROI} = \frac{225}{775} \times 100 = 29.03\%$$

		£000
(ii)	Profit	240
	Capital employed:	
	Existing fixed assets	525
	Addition (£120,000 – £20,000)	100
		625
	Net current assets	250
		875

$$\text{ROI} = \frac{240}{875} \times 100 = 27.42\%$$

(iii) Profit		215
Capital employed:		
Existing fixed assets		525
Net sales at book value	£000	
Original cost	200	
Accumulated depreciation	200	-
		525
Net current assets		250
		775

$$ROI = \frac{215}{775} \times 100 = 27.74\%$$

(iv) Profit	229
Capital employed:	
Fixed assets	525
Net current assets	250
	775

$$ROI = \frac{229}{775} \times 100 = 29.54\%$$

(v) Profit	219
Capital employed:	
Fixed assets	525
Net current assets	225
	750

$$ROI = \frac{219}{750} \times 100 = 29.2\%$$

Summary

	(a) %	*(b)* %
(i)	18.0	29.0
(ii)	17.5	27.4
(iii)	20.5	27.7
(iv)	18.3	29.5
(v)	17.9	29.2

(c) **Goal congruence**

Goal congruence is the state that exists in a control system which leads individuals or groups to take actions which are both in their self-interest and also in the best interest of the entity.

(i) **Transaction A**

Theta uses ROCE for assessing performance of subsidiaries. The implementation of transaction A reduced this ratio from 29.0% to 27.4% and from this point of view was incorrect.

Alpha uses the same ratio but a different base. Even here, however, there is a deterioration from 18.0% to 17.5%.

In answering parts (a) and (b) the cost of capital of 14% has not been utilised. From a decision-making point of view it may be informative to discount the annual cash flows of £35,000 in order to see how it relates to capital cost.

(ii) **Transaction B**

The calculation for this transaction indicates that from the view of Theta there is a decline from 29.0% to 27.7%, whilst from the view of Alpha there is a rise from 18.0% to 20.5%. The movements are opposite, indicative of a lack of goal congruence. Without computation, it seems questionable whether selling for £20,000 a machine which is producing annual cash flows of £30,000 is good management.

Question 2: Hawlit Ltd

(a) **ROI and Residual income**

		Annual and expected net income at the following annual investment levels											
		£0.35m		*£0.40m*		*£0.45m*		*£0.50m*		*£0.55m*		*£0.60m*	
Price/ gallon £	*Prob*	£000	*EV* £000	£000	*EV* £000	£000	*EV* £000	£000	*EV* £000	£000	*EV* £000	£000	*EV* £000
1.20	0.1	55	5.5	60	6.0	68	6.8	72	7.2	74	7.4	75	7.5
1.25	0.1	52	5.2	58	5.8	63	6.3	68	6.8	67	6.7	64	6.4
1.30	0.4	46	18.4	52	20.8	55	22.0	58	23.2	56	22.4	53	21.2
1.40	0.3	40	12.0	46	13.8	47	14.1	49	14.7	43	12.9	40	12.0
1.50	0.1	30	3.0	35	3.5	35	3.5	34	3.4	30	3.0	25	2.5
	1.0		44.1		49.9		52.7		55.3		52.4		49.6

Annual investment level £000	*Expected annual net income* £000	*Minimum required return on investment (10% pa)* £000	*Residual income* £000	*ROI* %
350	44.1	35.0	9.1	12.6
400	49.9	40.0	9.9	12.5
450	52.7	45.0	7.7	11.7
500	55.3	50.0	5.3	11.1
550	52.4	55.0	(2.6)	9.5
600	49.6	60.0	(10.4)	8.3

Notes:

(1) Residual income = expected annual net income less minimum required return on investment.

(2) ROI = expected annual net income as a percentage of investment.

(b) **Optimal investment level**

On the basis of giving the highest level of residual income (£9,900) an investment level of £400,000 pa is the optimum.

The annual investment levels given are in steps of £50,000 and, in stating an optimum, any levels between these steps have not been considered. Further information would be required to determine a more 'precise' optimal level.

Residual income is chosen as the basis for determining the optimal level as it takes account of the absolute surplus of income after deducting the minimum required return on the investment. The maximisation of profit is assumed to be a major objective of the company, that is the maximisation of an absolute sum.

(c) **Residual income and return on investment (ROI) as measures of performance**

Residual income and return on investment are just two approaches to the measurement of performance. The problem of measuring performance is considerably magnified in a company which has an organisation structure in which different segments or parts have been clearly defined. The management in each section should have clearly specified responsibilities and, therefore, there is a need to be able to assess segment performance.

Traditionally ROI has been considered the best measure of performance. It is an all-embracing ratio that relates net income to the level of investment. It is generally easily understood by all levels of management. It can be used as a basis for comparison with investment opportunities both inside and outside the company.

As the key ratio in a company it can be sub-divided into a series of secondary ratios as part of an analysis. The first stage in such a breakdown can be illustrated:

$$\text{ROI} = \frac{\text{Net income}}{\text{Investment}}$$

$$= \frac{\text{Net income}}{\text{Sales}} \times \frac{\text{Sales}}{\text{Investment}}$$

Such a sub-analysis assists management in making appropriate decisions and assessing their effect on ROI, which may well be the subject of a target or objective.

The use of ROI as a measure of performance focuses the attention of management on the key factors of net income and the level of investment. A profit maximisation objective for the company is assumed.

Briefly, the problems or limitations of ROI are very much associated with the measurement of net income and investment. The value that has to be placed on fixed assets is a particular problem. If valid comparisons are to be made, should it be based on historical cost, depreciated book value or on replacement cost? Furthermore, in a divisional organisation structure the apportionment of costs and assets between the different parts of the organisation has to be considered. This applies where there are shared facilities.

In a divisional structure, each segment will have a different ROI which will not necessarily tally with the overall company ROI. Where a division has a ROI in excess of the company's, the manager will not be motivated to accept a project which gives a lower ROI than his division currently attains although that return is above the company's ROI target. If the project was accepted the divisional manager would see his measure of performance fall, yet it would be in the best interests of the company as a whole to accept the project. (It was because of this type of conflict that the General Electric Company in the USA introduced the concept of residual income in the 1950s.)

ROI is a relative measure of performance (net income being related to investment), whereas residual income is an absolute measure, being the net income less the minimum required return on the investment. It is the return over and above the minimum required. A comparison can be made between the IRR and NPV approaches in capital budgeting, which are relative and absolute measures of projects respectively, and ROI and residual income in performance measurement.

The conflict, already mentioned, where the divisional and the overall company ROI do not tally can be overcome if a residual income approach is adopted rather than a ROI one. A project yielding at least the overall company's ROI will increase the division's residual income.

ROI, as a measure of performance, is widely used in practice. It relates net income and investment in an easily understood concept. The bases of measuring cost and investment need to be considered and consistently applied where ROI is used for comparison purposes. In a divisional organisation structure particularly, the residual income approach overcomes a lot of the conflict that can arise between divisional goals and overall company goals.

CHAPTER 11 EXAM-TYPE QUESTION

New manufacturing environment

(a) The traditional management accounting performance measures are best suited to a stable environment which is programmable. These measures include budgetary control measures and standard costing. Standards and budgets are often based on past performance – on the assumption that what has happened in the past is a good guide to what might happen in the future.

With the increase in competition in world markets and the increasing rate of technological change, manufacturing has had to become more flexible in order to survive. Rather than being able to have long batch runs of the same product, companies have to place an emphasis on tailoring customised products and producing in small quantities. Quality of product and service has become vital.

Traditional management accounting measures do not provide any impression of flexibility or quality. For example, a traditional costing system provides little information concerning the cost of quality in both its financial and non-financial forms. Such a system does not therefore provide the information needed by management in order to control this critical area in the business operation.

It is therefore true to say that the modern business environment requires a more comprehensive approach to performance measurement than that provided by a traditional accounting system.

(b) One of the major developments in management accounting in recent years has been the development of performance measurement systems which are not based solely on simple financial metrics.

A modern performance measurement system seeks to develop a range of indicators which relate to the strategic objectives and mission of the business. In particular, measures should be adopted which relate to :

The customer perspective, specific measures being:

- Market share
- Customer turnover
- New customer acquisition
- Image and reputation (possibly worked using a points score system)

The internal business perspective:

- Number of product innovations
- Production cycle time (time between customer order and delivery)
- Quality measures including reject rates and customer returns

The learning and growth perspective:

- Employee training and ability (employee numbers achieving particular competencies)
- IT system capability
- Staff motivation and empowerment (possibly worked using benchmark or points score systems.

The critical thing is that these indicators should be aligned with the strategic objectives of the business – to ensure that managers are motivated to move towards the maximisation of shareholder value.

CHAPTER **12**

EXAM-TYPE QUESTION

A college

Tutorial notes: the flow diagram is not difficult, but the time allowance for 3 marks does present problems. However, time spent on ensuring that a correct picture of the cost apportionments is depicted will not only gain these marks but help a great deal in answering part (b). Part (b) is basically an arithmetic exercise. Good use of the flow diagram will help in breaking this down into a series of apportionments. The model answer uses a 'step' approach. Students should adopt this approach. Any attempt to apportion all the costs in a single table is likely to fail. There is no one answer for part (c). Use your commonsense and make brief general statements.

(a)

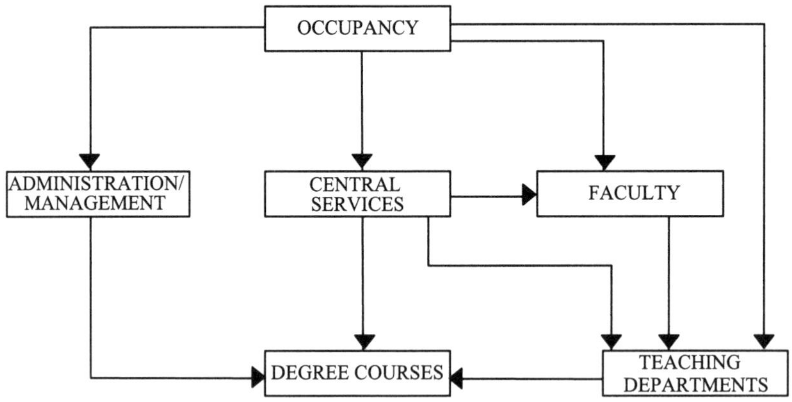

(b) ***Step 1***

Apportion occupancy costs: $\frac{£1,500,000}{37,500 \text{ sq ft}} = £40$ per sq ft

	£000
Administration/Management	280
Central Services	120
Faculty	300
Teaching Departments	800
	1,500

Step 2

Apportion central services costs:

$\frac{£1,000,000 + £120,000}{\text{External Costs } £1,600,000}$ 70p per £ of external cost

	£000
Faculty	168
Teaching Departments	560
Degree Courses	392
	1,120

Step 3

Apportion teaching department costs (includes 100% of Faculty costs) and Administration/Management costs, to degree courses.

Teaching department: £800,000 + £560,000 + (£300,000 + £168,000 + £700,000) + £5,525,000 = £8,053,000

Administration/management: £280,000 + £1,775,000 = £2,055,000.

Total degree courses costs: £8,053,000 + £2,055,000 + £392,000 = £10,500,000.

Average College cost per student = $\frac{£10,500,000}{2,500 \text{ students}} = £4,200$

Step 4

Analyse £10,500,000 by degree course (in round £000).

	Business Studies £000	*Mechanical Engineering* £000	*Catering Studies* £000
Teaching department	242	201	564
Administration/management	51	103	82
Central services (based on external costs)	22	34	22
	315	338	668
Average cost per graduate	£3,938	£6,760	£5,567

(c) The average cost per graduate will differ from one degree course to another for several reasons, the most obvious of which is the very different nature of the courses.

The engineering and catering courses will require much greater use of expensive machinery and equipment, which in turn will need more room. In addition these courses will probably require much greater lecturer input than on the business studies courses. The much lower staff/student ratio will push up the teaching costs per student.

Another factor to be considered is the variability in the student numbers. This variable is unlikely to have an impact on many of the College costs, which are mainly fixed in nature. For example, if in the following year intake is up to sixty on the mechanical engineering degree, with a similar level of costs, the average cost per student would fall to nearly that being reported for a catering studies student.

These average cost figures must be interpreted with great care by the management. They give a 'rough' guide to the relative cost of degree courses but the arbitrary apportionments render them very nearly useless for decision-making. For decision-making, incremental costs are required.

CHAPTER 13 EXAM-TYPE QUESTIONS

Question 1: FPE 1

(a) Base case:

ROCE is 9.4%, CCP is 45 days, innovations are 4

Office manager's proposal

in 20X8 ROCE is lifted to 10.1% and CCP is reduced to 12 days

in 20X9 ROCE will be around 9.4% and CCP will be around 36 days

This proposal might be attractive to several of the executives since it would secure their bonuses in 20X8 and contribute to the achievement of bonuses in 20X9.

Production manager's proposal

Immediate implementation of the proposal would only cause ROCE to drop in 20X8. Implementation at the start of 20X9 would cause ROCE to drop to 9.2% and would tend to depress ROCE below its current level for some years thereafter.

The proposal would not be popular with the executives.

Design manager

Again, immediate implementation would achieve a negative result. Implementation at the start of 20X9 would reduce ROCE to 9.3%, increase CCP to 50 days and increase innovations to 5 in that year.

The design manager and possibly the CE might favour this proposal – but it is unlikely that the other executives would.

(b) **Office manager's proposal**

The stock reduction would result in an immediate cash inflow of £160k, an annual cash inflow of £16.5k being forgone over 10 years and a cash inflow of £160k being forgone at year 10.

The NPV of these items is negative. The proposal should be rejected.

Deferring payment of the invoice incurs an interest charge of 1.11%. Annualised, this is 33%. The proposal should be rejected.

Production manager's proposal

The annual depreciation charge is £(400,000 – 40,000)/8 years = £45,000. Operating profit will increase by £25,000 each year, so the annual operating cash flow will be £25,000 + £45,000 = £70,000.

Acquisition of the new equipment would result in an immediate cash outflow of £400k, an annual cash inflow of £70,000 for 8 years and a cash inflow of £40,000 at year 8.

The NPV of these items is £24,000 positive. The proposal should be accepted.

Design manager's proposal

Implementation of the proposal would result in an immediate cash outflow of £263,000 in respect of equipment and working capital, and annual cash inflow of £30k over ten years and an inflow of £163,000 at year 10 from liquidation of working capital.

The NPV of these items is £14,000 positive. The proposal should be accepted.

CCP calculation

$$\text{Debtor days} = \frac{1{,}035{,}000}{6{,}900{,}000} \times 365 = 54.75$$

$$\text{Days stock} = \frac{530{,}000}{(6{,}900{,}000 - 450{,}000)} \times 365 = 30$$

$$\text{Days creditors} = \frac{320{,}000}{2{,}920{,}000} \times 365 = 40$$

CCP = 55 + 30 – 40 = 45

Cash outflow – designer

Increase in sales	$\frac{20}{450} \times 6{,}900$	= 307
Increase in debtors	$307 \times \frac{6}{12}$	= 154
Increase in stocks	$(530 - 320) \times \frac{20}{450}$	= 9
Investment		= 100

Total £263k

Fixed cost of production

Since the increment for 20% for production overhead is £1,200 and at production capacity at 40% overhead is 11,400, at 20% capacity it will be 11,400 – 1,200 = 10,200 and at 0% it will be 10,200 – 1,200 = 9,000. This 9,000 must therefore be a fixed cost.

The same principle applies to admin and selling/distribution.

Question 2: FPE 2

(a) ROCE is a relative performance measure which does not allow for the cost of capital engaged in a business operation. RI is an absolute measure, calculated by deducting a charge for the full cost of capital from operating profit.

Neither measure is 'perfect' but RI does offer certain advantages. When alternative investments are being considered then a decision influenced by RI is more likely to be satisfactory than one influenced by ROCE. This is so because a very small investment may yield a high ROCE – but nevertheless be inferior to a larger project which yields a lower ROCE but a higher RI.

Over the long term, when business policy is guided by ROCE then the result may be that an organisation is whittled down to a small, high-earning core. There are many well-documented cases where businesses guided by ROCE have virtually liquidated themselves in pursuing this metric.

On the other hand, ROCE is a relative measure that allows a ready comparison of divisions which are very different in size. The use of ROCE is probably safest when accompanied by the use of a package of measures.

One problem with RI (and EVA, its modern variant) is that the management accountant has to determine the cost of capital to be used in calculating it. This can be a difficult and subjective area.

(b) The basic purpose of a business performance indicator is to measure the progress that the business has made towards achievement of its objectives. Given the complex nature of business planning and development, those objectives are usually several in number and complex in nature.

A simple financial metric such as ROCE is unlikely to give a full impression of business performance on its own.

Hence, Rapier propose the use of a package of measures for FPE. The use of non-financial measures allows a business to be guided towards long term, strategic objectives. In the case of FPE, 'innovation numbers' reflects the priority that must be given to overcoming resistance to new technologies.

CHAPTER 14 EXAM-TYPE QUESTIONS

Question 1: SKC

The preparation of the budget involves the identification and manipulation of two limiting factors – cargo space and market demand.

Consider each of the three products in turn:

	contribution per case	*contribution per kilo*
	£	
Whisky	600	10
Long Life Milk	300	15
Toilet Paper	120	12

The ranking of the products is therefore

First	Long Life Milk
Second	Toilet Paper
Third	Whisky

The available 12,000kg of cargo space should therefore be allocated as follows:

Long Life Milk	-	6,000kg (300 cases)
Toilet Paper	-	4,000kg (400 cases)
Whisky	-	2,000kg (33$^1/_3$ cases)

The annual budget for the operation may therefore be shown as follows :

	Long Life Milk	*Toilet Paper*	*Whisky*	*Total*
				£
Sales	120,000	80,000	60,000	260,000
Purchases	30,000	32,000	40,000	102,000
Contribution				158,000
Shipment costs				(100,000)
Selling expenses				(10,000)
Profit				48,000

In practice, this would probably be broken down into monthly budget intervals.

Limiting factors are typically short-term things. Products can be redesigned to make less use of a limiting factor. New sources of a scarce material or labour skill can be accessed. Limiting factor analysis is essentially a short-term planning technique.

In this case, the whisky could be put in plastic bottles which would considerably reduce the weight of a case. It is doubtful that the clientele in Uganda would perceive great loss of value in this – but it would make the operation more profitable by allowing greater quantities of whisky to be carried.

Question 2: Budget

Applying a linear regression approach to the figures supplied, the cost structure forecast for Quarter 3 is as follows:

	Unit vc	*Quarter fc*
material A	6.00	
material B	4.00	
production labour	11.25	90,000
factory overheads	3.00	50,000
depreciation		14,000
administration		30,000
selling expenses	1.00	20,000
total	25.25	204,000

Note that selling expenses seem to vary with units sold rather than units produced.

(a) The budget profit statement for Quarter 3 is:

sales revenue	720,000
costs:	
materials	180,000
wages	292,500
factory overheads	104,000

depreciation	14,000
administration	30,000
selling expenses	38,000
profit	61,500

(b) The budget cash flow statement for Quarter 3 is:

cash inflow:	
Q2 month 1	60,000
Q2 month 2	200,000
Q2 month 3	200,000
Q3 month 1	168,000
cash outflow:	
materials	180,000
wages	292,500
factory overheads	104,000
administration	30,000
selling expenses	38,000
net cash flow	–16,500

70% of month 1 sales from Quarter 2 will be paid during Quarter 2. The other 30% of those sales will be paid in Quarter 3. Q2 month 1 sales therefore give rise to a £60,000 (that is 5,000 units × £40 × 30%) cash inflow in Quarter 3. The same logic is applied to sales in later months.

CHAPTER 15

EXAM-TYPE QUESTIONS

Question 1: RT plc

(a) The simplest possible multiplicative model for passenger numbers is based on:

A = T × S (Actual = Trend × Seasonal variation %)

On that basis, trend passengers for quarter 3 in both years 1 and 2:

Q3 : x = 10,000 + 12,600 = 22,600

Q7 : x = 10,000 + 29,400 = 39,400

Comparing trend with actual for both figures

Q3, A = 16,950 and T = 22,600, hence S = 75% (that is 16,950/22,600)

Q7, A = 29,550 and T = 39,400, hence S = 75% (that is 29,550/39,400)

So, it appears that the quarter 3 seasonal variation is 75% of trend and we can exclude the possibility of any random variations.

The trend passenger number for quarter 3, year 3 is:

Q11 : x = 10,000 + 46,200 = 56,200

Applying the 75% season variation gives a predicted passenger number of 42,150.

(b) The equation indicates a semi-variable cost. The train driver is paid the same regardless of how many or how few passengers are carried. But, ticket inspectors and catering assistants probably have to be increased in number with increased passengers.

(c)

	£
Premises	260,000
Premises staff	86,075

Power	181,600
Traincrew	158,450
Sundries	51,250
Total	737,375

(d) The model we are using assumes a simple, linear trend in passenger numbers and with uniform seasonal variations throughout. As with any mathematical model, this is a simplified representation of a complex reality. It is highly likely that there will be random variations throughout the period under review and the trend may change.

The projected costs assume constant price levels and simple linear relationships between costs and passenger numbers. Again, these assumptions are probably over-simplified.

That said, use of the model gives a usable forecast. The result may be imperfect, but forecasts never are perfect.

(e) Any public transport operator has to be sensitive to the quality of service it provides. If the quality is poor or declining then it will probably experience a loss of passenger numbers in the future as travellers find alternative means of making the journey – e.g. taxi, bus or private car.

RT should investigate the key factors that determine passenger perception of service quality and devise appropriate forward looking performance indicators:

Service punctuality

- % of trains arriving within 5 minutes of scheduled time
- % of scheduled service cancelled
- % of services that break down en-route or crash

Service safety

- number and % of passengers suffering accidents at platforms and on trains
- number and % of passengers suffering assault or robbery while en-route
- number and % of passengers reporting damage to or soiling of clothes/luggage while en-route

Facility reliability

- number of ticket machines out of service for more than normal allowance in period
- number of signalling and communication failures in period
- number of public toilets reported out of order in period

Question 2: DKS

When B = 12,000, h = £15 – therefore:

15 = a / 12,000 0.322

15 = a / 20.5824

a = 15 × 20.5824 = 308.7

(***Note:*** students should ensure that they have a calculator with logarithm, root and power functions – and that they know how to use it)

Now, a is known it is possible to calculate h for different batch sizes and from that it is possible to determine total variable costs at different batch sizes.

Batch size units	VC per unit	VC total £
11,750	15.10*	177,425
11,500	15.21	174,915
8,750	16.60	145,250
7,500	17.45	130,875
6,000	18.75	112,500

Workings

308.7 / 11,750 0.322 = 15.10; 15.10 × 11,750 = 177,425

From this, the contribution generated by different batch sizes can be calculated.

Batch size	Sales revenues	VCs	Profit £
11,750	293,750	177,425	116,325
11,500	345,000	174,915	170,085*
8,750	306,250	145,250	161,000
7,500	300,000	130,875	169,125
6,000	270,000	112,500	157,500

*Optimum

It can be seen that the optimum batch size is 11,500 units

Question 3 : Learning Curve Theory

(a) The `cumulative average time' (CAT) model commonly used to represent the learning curve effects is demonstrated below for a 80 per cent learning curve:

Units made	Cumulative avg. hrs per unit	Total hours taken	Incremental hours
1	100.0	100.0	0.0
2	80.0	160.0	60.0
4	64.0	256.0	96.0
8	51.2	409.6	153.6

The CAT model assumes that the cumulative average time required to produce a unit of production is reduced by a constant proportion of the previous cumulative average time, every time the output doubles.

In the above example, unit 1 requires 100 hours, but units 1 and 2 require only 160 hours (that is, 100 hours × 80%), unit 2 being produced in 60 hours due to labour becoming more adept and better organised. Units 3 and 4 require only a further 96 hours.

This situation may be modelled mathematically by the equation

y = axn

where Y = cumulative average hours per unit, x = cumulative demand, and a and n are constants.

(b) Assuming 100 hours is required for the first unit produced, then the impact of different learning curve values on CAT per unit is:

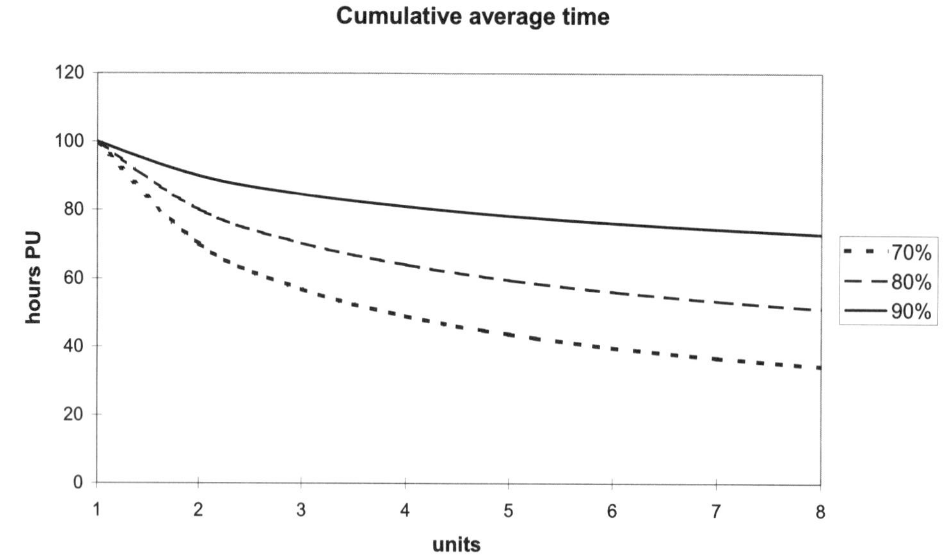

Assuming 100 hours is required for the first unit, the impact of different learning curve values on CT total is:

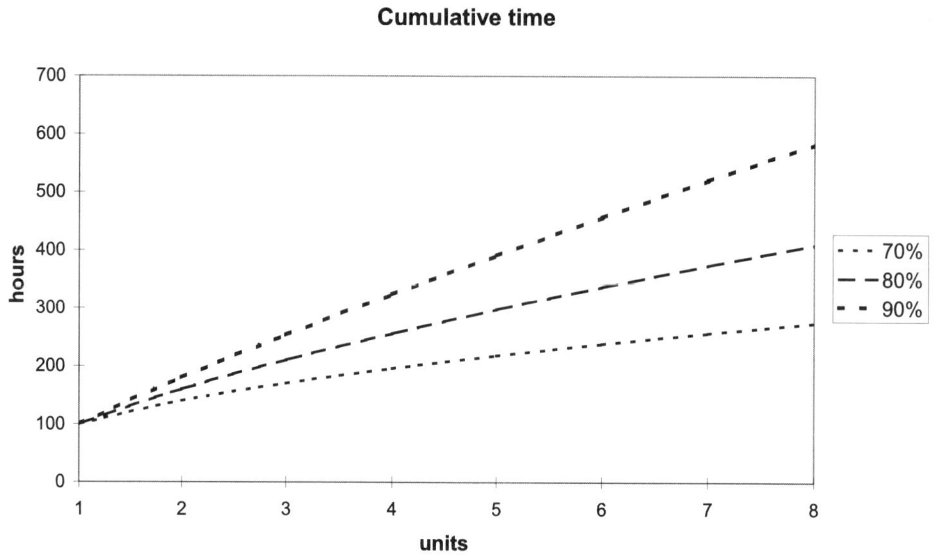

(c) Budgeting, budgetary control and project evaluation all involve the preparation of accurate meaningful projections of production capacity and operating costs. Learning curve theory may be deployed in the preparation of such projections.

In particular, the learning curve theory may be used when repetitive manual tasks are introduced into a production process. Under these circumstances, application of this theory may result in more accurate prediction of labour time, labour costs, variable overhead costs that are driven by labour usage, and possibly material usage savings. Furthermore, if absorption costing is used, then this theory will enable the relationship between fixed overhead recovery and production rate to be accurately included in the budgeting process.

For budgetary control to be effective, the variances calculated must be based on realistic targets. A constant standard for labour, materials and variable overhead variances is not appropriate when the learning curve effect is present. By incorporating the learning curve theory into the targets, meaningful variances may be calculated and used in budgetary control.

Problems may be experienced in obtaining data on the rate of the learning curve until significant production has taken place. High labour turnover and changes in motivation levels may have significant effects upon the learning process. If there are extensive periods of time between batches of a particular product then the learning effect may be lost. The learning curve does not model long-term behaviour when there are no further productivity gains due to the learning process.

CHAPTER 16 EXAM-TYPE QUESTION

Flexible budgeting

(a) For the sake of convenience, it is common practice for all the variable elements in the budget to be flexed according to the **same** activity indicator. This technique assumes the same linear relationship between the activity indicator, and all the variable elements that are being flexed. This can result in inaccuracies in the flexed budget. In the case of raw materials, for example, this technique would assume that there were no economies of scale such as bulk discounts etc. Furthermore this technique ignores external factors, which can also have an effect on the actual costs.

In flexible budgeting, we also assume that fixed costs remain unchanged. This assumption too has to be questioned, since fixed costs usually rise in steps as output increases and are rarely constant in the longer term.

Due to the above inaccuracies, a flexible budget may not indicate the actual total costs.

(b) For reasons indicated in (a) above, since a flexed budget may not necessarily indicate the actual total costs, it would have limitations in its application as a control tool. For example, inaccurate figures in the flexed budget, which result in significant variances, could waste a lot of management time and expense in investigating what is in fact an incorrect figure. By the same token, variances which do not appear to be significant, may in fact be significant and management would be misled into not investigating such variances.

(c) One way of overcoming some of the above inaccuracies is by the use of planning and operational budgets. In this technique, we compare the actual results with the revised budget results that take into account the actual conditions. This technique groups the variances into two broad categories, which are planning variances and operational variances. To compute the operational variances, we compare the actual figures with the ex-post standard or budget figures i.e. the operational variance is simply the difference between the actual figures and the revised budget figures.

To compute the planning variances, we compare the ex-post standard or budget with the ex-ante standard or budget i.e. the planning variance is simply the difference between the 'original budget' and the 'revised budget'.

Such a system would make budget comparisons more meaningful and direct management attention 'correctly', to those areas that require attention.

CHAPTER 17 EXAM-TYPE QUESTION

Strengths and weaknesses

When conducting a survey of the strengths and weaknesses of an organisation, invariably there is a tendency for management to concentrate on certain aspects of the operation. This is not to say however, that the extent of the survey will be identical in each area on every occasion. Neither does it imply that other areas of investigation should automatically be eliminated. A strengths and weaknesses appraisal is part of the work of a position audit.

(a) **Financial resources**

As with internal appraisal, this consists of constructing a series of accounting ratios to measure profitability, growth and liquidity, and then comparing them with earlier results and also with results of other firms in similar circumstances. Such an exercise will indicate the firm's strengths and weaknesses both in terms of former occasions and current competitiveness.

(b) **Profitability**

This involves a series of analyses each with the aim of identifying the organisation's operational position. For example, it might include an analysis of sales and profit involving sales mix, pricing strategy, discount facilities, and an assessment of the returns on total assets employed. Costs obviously have important implications for profitability and therefore, determination of operational costs and internal efficiency is also required.

(c) **Effectiveness of functional departments within the organisation**

This is normally done by defining the specialist knowledge available, specialist activities undertaken, the significant factors on which the company depends, including the areas of vulnerability.

During the exercise these issues will be raised in connection with all the functional activities and in addition, it is necessary to ascertain specific details for each function. For example, the plant utilisation rate, the proportion of bad debts, the extent of production delays due to failure of supplies etc.

(d) **Product range**

Frequently companies have an extensive product range which needs frequent reviewing to ensure that it is well balanced and relevant to current market needs. This involves the determination of the profit contribution of each product in relationship to the resources it utilises. It is also necessary to pay particular attention to market trends to ascertain whether in the product mix, certain products need upgrading whilst others require phasing out. In addition, there is the need to establish the position regarding the introduction of new products, both in terms of frequency and timing, to ensure the company's competitive position is maintained. All these various activities add up to an extensive marketing research assignment.

(e) **Human resources of the organisation**

Any such appraisal must ensure that personnel are suitably motivated and adequate facilities are available for appropriate staff development. One technique which many companies have adopted in one form or another, is management by objectives (MBO). This includes establishing key tasks for a job, agreed performance standards and providing suitable encouragement for such standards to be achieved and is followed by a subsequent stage in which a review is conducted involving the managers and their superiors to compare actual performance against the standards agreed. It also provides from time to time, an assessment of the potential of each manager.

Whatever form of management style the organisation uses it is essential that a thorough assessment of the human resources of the organisation is carried out with the main purpose of ensuring that the manpower resources of the company match both the current technical and social skills requirements, and also those that it is anticipated will be required in the future.

In addition, it is necessary to ensure that the organisational structure is the most suitable for present day needs. With rapid technological, economic, political and sociological changes, an organisation can rapidly become out of date. Conducting frequent organisational appraisals should avoid this happening.

Therefore, it can be seen that an appraisal of the firm's strengths and weaknesses is a considerable task with a notable contribution required from the accountant. The exercise involves considerable analysis and invariably leads to certain criticisms of the existing arrangements. Such criticisms, even if only implied, may not always be readily acceptable but must be carried out, and carried out authentically, if the company is to obtain the maximum benefit from an appraisal of its strengths and weaknesses.

CHAPTER 18 EXAM-TYPE QUESTIONS

Question 1: Widgets

(a) Revenue = price × quantity

$= (120 - x)x = 120x - x^2$

Differentiating with respect to x:

$$\frac{dR}{dx} = 120 - 2x = 0 \text{ at a turning point}$$

$$\therefore 120 = 2x$$

$$x = \frac{120}{2} = 60 \text{ widgets}$$

To check it's a maximum

$$\frac{d^2R}{dx^2} = -2 \text{ negative } \therefore \text{ maximum}$$

Revenue will be maximised when 60 widgets are sold.

(b) The company will break-even when:

revenue = costs

i.e. profit = 0

Profit = revenue – costs

$P = 120x - x^2 - (10x + x^2 + 900)$

$P = -2x^2 + 110x - 900 = 0$ at break-even points

This is a quadratic equation with:

$a = -2,\ b = 110,\ c = -900$

$$x = \frac{-b \pm \sqrt{b^2 - 4ac}}{2a}$$

$$= \frac{-110 \pm \sqrt{110^2 - 4(-2)(-900)}}{2(-2)}$$

$$= \frac{-110 \pm \sqrt{4,900}}{-4} = \frac{-110 \pm 70}{-4}$$

$\therefore x =$ **10** or **45**

(c) **Graph showing profit (*P*) and revenue (*R*) functions: 0 < *x* < 70**

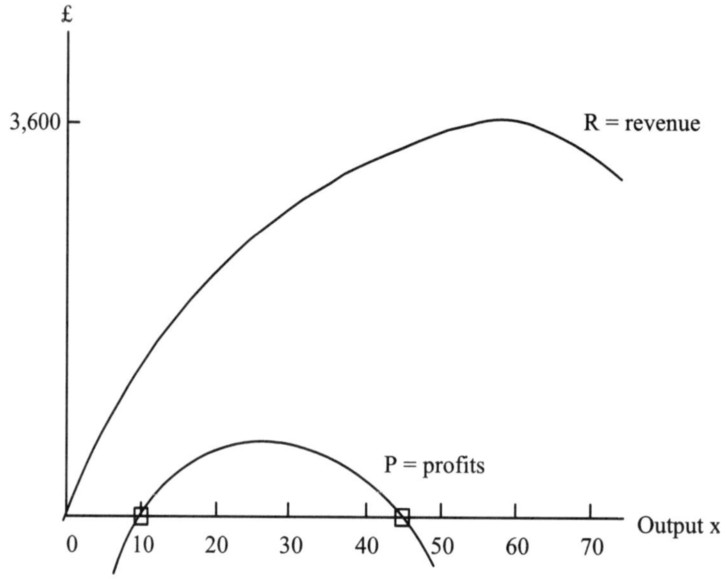

$R = 120x - x^2$. This passes through (0, 0)

and has a maximum at (60, £3,600)

$P = -2x^2 + 110x - 900$. This equals 0 when $x = 10$ and 45

(d) To find the profit maximisation point:

$$\frac{dP}{dx} = -4x + 110 = 0$$

$$\therefore \quad 4x = 110$$

$$x = \frac{110}{4} = 27.5 \text{ widgets}$$

$$\frac{d^2P}{dx^2} = -4 \text{ negative } \therefore \text{ maximum}$$

Profit at this point $= -2\,(27.5)^2 + 110\,(27.5) - 900$

$= £612.50$

The manufacturing company would be advised to produce 28 widgets a week, as this production level maximises profits.

Question 2: Nantderyn Products

Tutorial notes:

(1) Overall it is not difficult to achieve more than half marks on this question.

(2) Part (a) is a straightforward 'limiting factor' question with no special problems.

(3) Part (b) is not difficult if and only if you appreciate the need for differential calculus and the matching of marginal revenues and marginal costs.

(4) Part (c) is quite easy, but you should ensure that you give a full answer.

(a) **Cost-plus pricing**

	Exco		*Wyeco*	
	£		£	
Total costs per unit	12		24	
Fixed costs per unit	4	$\left(\frac{£60{,}000}{15{,}000}\right)$	10	$\left(\frac{£300{,}000}{30{,}000}\right)$
Variable costs per unit	8		14	
Selling price per unit	16		32	
Contribution per unit	£8		£18	
Processing time per unit	1 hour		0.5 hour	
Contribution per processing hour	£8		£36	
Ranking	2		1	
Maximum demand	20,000 units		40,000 units	
Use of processing hours	10,000 hours		20,000 hours	
(Total available = (15,000 × 1 hour + 30,000 × 0.5 hour))				
Units produced	10,000 units		40,000 units	
Contribution achieved	£80,000		£720,000	

Total contribution of £800,000 is £140,000 in excess of current contribution of £660,000 (15,000 × £8 + 30,000 × £18).

The fixed costs are assumed to be unchanged and are therefore irrelevant.

(b) **Optimal pricing policy**

(i) **Exco**

The table provided indicates that an increase of 25p in selling price results in a fall in demand of 1,000 units. Therefore, an increase of 10 × 25p on top of the £18.50 selling price would eliminate demand. This would be at £21.00 per unit. The selling price can therefore be represented by:

SP = 21.00 – 0.25x where x = demand in 000s of units

and total sales revenue R = $21.00x - 0.25x^2$

The marginal revenue (MR) can be calculated by using differential calculus:

MR = $21.00 - 0.50x$

Optimal sales level is where MR = marginal cost.

$$8 = 21.00 - 0.50x$$

$$x = 26$$

Therefore, a price resulting in demand for 26,000 units is achieved with a selling price of £(21.00 – 0.25 × 26) = £14.50.

(ii) **Wyeco**

Applying the same concepts as for Exco:

Increase in SP of 15p results in fall in demand of 1,000 units.

Selling price, P	=	$38.00 - 0.15x$
Total sales revenue, R	=	$38.00x - 0.15x^2$
MR	=	$38.00 - 0.30x$
Marginal cost	=	14
14	=	$38.00 - 0.30x$
x	=	80,000 units
∴ Selling price	=	£(38.00 – 0.15 × 80) = £26.00

Tutorial note: the recommended selling price for Wyeco is outside the range of the sales director's estimates and must therefore be reviewed to ensure that it is feasible. Moreover, many students may have thought that they had the wrong answer because the recommendation is not between £29.00 and £35.00.

(c) **Why cost-plus pricing is used**

Several reasons can be advanced in favour of computing target selling prices by means of cost-plus formulae, even if the prices are later modified.

Firstly, the decision-maker is faced with a host of uncertainties. The use of cost-plus formulae enables the decision-maker to absorb some of these uncertainties and come up with a price that will be acceptable given the constraints at hand.

Secondly, cost may be viewed as a base from which the price-setter moves, guarding against the possibility of setting the price too low and incurring losses. Cost-plus pricing will not guarantee against loss-making: for instance, there are problems of volume estimating. However, these will point the price-setter in the right direction.

A third explanation of the popularity of cost-based pricing is that estimates of the company's own costs may help the decision-maker to predict either competitors' costs or a competitive price. For example, if a company is operating in an industry where a 30% mark-up is the norm, then the company may be able to assume that this pattern will hold for new products and thereby either to predict competitors' prices or to price in such a way as to gain quick acceptance of a new product line.

The main reason is that the information is rarely (if ever) available to allow an approach based on marginal cost and marginal revenue.

Question 3: XYZ

(a) Elasticity of demand varies along the whole length of a linear demand function. It is infinity at the point it leaves the vertical axis, nil at the point where it reaches the horizontal axis and 1 at exactly half way along its length.

It is the proportion change in demand divided by the associated proportion change in price.

If y is price and x is demand then this may be stated algebraically as follows :

Elasticity = (dx/x)/(dy/y), or Elasticity = (dx/dy).(y/x)

The demand function has the following equation:

y = 10 – x/4,000, or y = 10 – 0.00025x

It follows that dy/dx = –0.00025 and dx/dy = –4,000

Where y = 6.25 we know that x = 15,000 (by substituting 6.25 for x in the demand function equation). Hence the elasticity of demand is:

4,000 . (6.25/15,000) = 1.67

The elasticity of demand at unit selling price €6.25 is 1.67. At half its theoretical maximum demand (that is, 20,000 units at unit selling price €5) elasticity is 1. The two observations do not conflict.

(b) The mr function is:

y = 10 – 0.0005x

So, if mc is €1.50 it follows that profit is maximised at 17,000 unit sales and a unit selling price of €5.75.

At this point, elasticity of demand is:

4,000 . (5.75/17,000) = 1.35

CHAPTER **19**

EXAM-TYPE QUESTION

Distortions

Overhead absorption is the technique of attributing departmental overhead costs to a cost unit.

Traditionally the basis of overhead absorption was the number of labour hours expected within the budget period and this was then used to calculate an absorption rate per labour hour. This was then used to attribute costs to the cost unit on the basis of the number of labour hours used to produce the cost unit.

Alternative bases of apportionment exist such as the number of machine hours or a percentage of particular elements of prime cost incurred in respect of the cost unit. If the method of manufacture is machine intensive for example, it is more realistic to absorb the overhead cost on the basis of the number of machine hours instead of the number of labour hours.

A further development is to divide the overhead cost into those costs which are labour related and those which are machine hour related and apply a separate absorption rate to each part of the overhead cost. This use of multiple rates is similar to the principles of activity based costing.

Activity based costing is based on the principle that activities cause costs and therefore the use of activities should be the basis of attributing costs to cost units. Costs are identified with particular activities and the performance of those activities is linked with products. The activity is known as the cost driver and the costs associated with that activity are then attributed to cost units using a cost driver rate. This then more accurately reflects the usage of the activity by the product.

CHAPTER **20** EXAM-TYPE QUESTION

Transfer pricing

(a) (i) The Components divisional contribution per Unit is:

X – 13, Y – 8, Z – 20

Hence, the divisional profit maximising mix is 10,000X, 10,000Y and 30,000Z.

(ii) The Products divisional contribution per Unit is:

X – 26, Y – 30, Z – 14

Hence, the divisional profit maximising mix is 10,000X, 30,000Y and 10,000Z.

(iii) The company contribution per Unit is:

X – 39, Y – 38, Z – 34

Hence, the divisional profit maximising mix is 30,000X, 10,000Y and 10,000Z.

(b) A perfect transfer pricing system has to satisfy three criteria:

- It has to give a fair impression of divisional profit.
- It has to avoid distorting the decision making process.
- It has to be cheap and simple to operate.

CD's transfer pricing system probably satisfies the first and last requirements. However, it clearly does not satisfy the second requirement. For one thing, who decides which components are to be prioritised? If the decision rests with either of the two Divisional managers then a sub-optimal product mix will result.

One possibility if outside sales are allowed is that product Z could be discontinued and all product f sold to outside customers. The marginal impact of this measure would be as follows (if 10,000 Units of f / Z were formerly in production):

Sales of f to outside customers	+300,000
Sales of Z to outside customers	–600,000
Products division variable costs	+160,000
Products division fixed costs	+200,000
Net	+ 60,000

So, CD's existing transfer pricing policy appears defective in several respects.

CHAPTER **21** EXAM-TYPE QUESTIONS

Question 1: Quoin

(a) Perfect intermediate market

Under these conditions the transfer price has to be the intermediate market price (otherwise no transfers will take place). If the grain-manufacturing division, M, has increasing marginal cost and the final product division, D, has decreasing net marginal revenue (marginal revenue – marginal cost) then the problem can be shown graphically as follows.

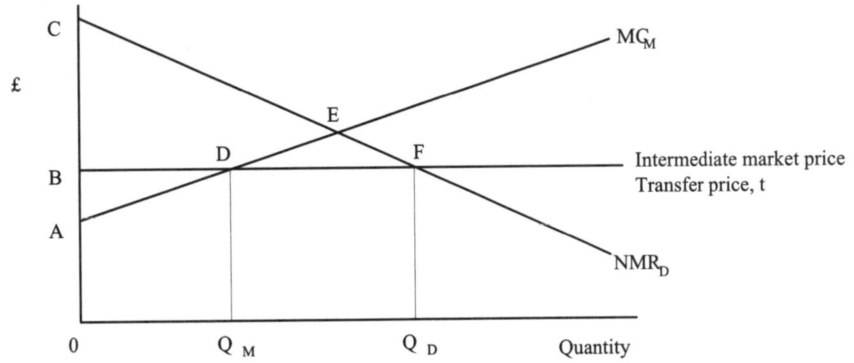

Division M should manufacture up to the point where its marginal cost and the intermediate market price are equal (Q_M). Division D should manufacture up to the point where its net marginal revenue and the intermediate market price are equal (Q_D). In this case D will have to purchase additional grain ($Q_D - Q_M$) from outside. Given its activity level (Q_D) division D can determine the selling price needed to generate that demand. Once the transfer price, output levels and sales prices have been found, profit can be calculated for each division, in this case being:

	D	*M*	*Group*
	£	£	£
Outside sales	S	-	S
Internal transfers	(T)	T	-
Outside purchases	(U)	-	(U)
Divisional production and selling costs	(V)	(W)	(X)
Profit	Y	Z	Y + Z

Tutorial note: It is possible to see how contributions (but not profit) accrue to the divisions from the graph.

D's contribution can be found by comparing NMR_D and t; it is the area CBF.

M's contribution is seen from MC_M and t; it is the area ABD.

In the case of the diagram shown it is hoped that division M has considerably smaller fixed costs than division D or else a two part transfer pricing policy will be needed of a fixed cost per unit, t, plus a fixed cost per period.

(b) **Two selling divisions**

Although the question states that there is no intermediate market, the problem is identical to one in which one of the final markets (X's or Y's) is treated as an imperfect intermediate market for S.

The marginal cost of producing grain has to be compared with the net marginal revenue from sales as tabulated below.

Production Division S			*Selling Division X*			*Selling Division Y*		
Qty (tons)	MC_S £000		*Qty* (tons)	NMR_X £000		*Qty* (tons)	NMR_Y £000	
400	400	(1–4)	100	120	(1)	100	120	(2)
500	20	(5)	200	60	(5)	200	120	(3)
600	30	(6)	300	40	(7)	300	120	(4)
700	35	(7)	400	20		400	60	(6)
800	40	(8)*				500	40	(8)*

900	60	600	20
1,000	80		

The table shows incremental costs and revenues rather than strictly marginal costs and revenues. It is worth Son of Quoin increasing output provided the incremental net marginal revenue is greater than (not less than) marginal cost. Determining this requires a little care and makes use of the numbers in brackets.

(1–4) If S produces 400 tons its cost is £400,000 and they should be sold wherever net marginal revenue is highest. This is achieved by selling 100 tons in X and 300 in Y earning net incremental revenue of £480,000.

(5) The next 100 tons (up to 500) cost S an extra £20,000. If sold through X they would take X's sales up to 200 tons and revenue up by £60,000; if sold through Y they would take Y's sales up to 400 tons and also increase revenue by £60,000. The sales are shown going through X.

(6) The next 100 tons increases S's output to 600 tons at an additional cost of £30,000. If sold through X net revenue would now go up by £40,000; if sold through Y net revenue rises by £60,000. Therefore sales are made through Y and at this stage S has produced 600 tons, X has sold 200 tons and Y sold 400 tons.

(7) S's additional costs are £35,000; sales could either be through X or Y, both earn an extra £40,000; X has again been chosen. Now S has produced 700, X sold 300, Y sold 400.

(8)* The final 100 tons produced by S costs an extra £40,000. If sold through X (X's sales rising to 400) they would only earn £20,000; if sold through Y (Y's sales rising to 500) they would earn £40,000. Son of Quoin would be indifferent over this last batch; it has been included for lovers of MC = MR.

The transfer price must encourage S to produce 800 tons, and no more; X to accept 300 tons, and no more; and Y to accept 500 tons, and no more.

To assure S's production level:	£40,000	≤	transfer price per 100 tons	≤	£60,000
To assure X's production level:	£20,000	≤	transfer price per 100 tons	≤	£40,000
To assure Y's production level:	£20,000	≤	transfer price per 100 tons	≤	£40,000

In this case, rather than there being a range of transfer prices, only one price satisfies all three conditions. The transfer price must be **£400 per ton**.

Question 2: Drums

Tutorial note: This is a very typical transfer pricing question that has arisen in various very similar guises over the years. Part (a) asks for the profits of 2 divisions with the present transfer pricing policy at different levels of output. Part (b) requires a discussion of why dysfunctional decisions may arise and then asks you to explain how this could be solved. Part (c) asks you to follow your own advice and suggest an improved transfer price (at which point many different answers will be acceptable.

(a) ***Note:*** many different layouts are possible. Shown below is one of the simpler ones.

(i) **Current output level**

M Ltd's output 750 kl (500kl to external customers; 250kl to L)

M's contribution per kl	£
Price £$\frac{9}{25}$ × 1,000 =	360
Variable costs	200
	£160

L's contribution per drum		£	£
Price			20
Variable costs:	External	3	
	Internal	9	12
			£8

M's current output 250kl ÷ 25l per drum = 10,000 drums

Profit statements (£000) - current output

M Ltd		**L Ltd**	
Contribution: external 500kl @ £160 =	80	Contribution 10,000 drums @ £8 =	80
Internal 250kl @ £160 =	40	Fixed costs	40
	120		
Fixed costs	60		
Profit	60	Profit	40

Note: Group profit = 60 + 40 = 100

(ii) **Higher output level**

M Ltd's output = 750kl + (250 × 0.80) = 950kl
M's contribution per kl – as above £160
L Ltd's output 10,000 × 180% = 18,000 drums

L's contribution per drum, price £20 × 80% =	£16
Variable costs (as above)	£12
	£4

Profit statements (£000)

Higher output

M Ltd		**L Ltd**	
Contribution: external	80	Contribution 18,000 @ £4	72
internal (450 @ £160)	72		
	152		
Fixed cost	60	Fixed cost	40
Profit	92	Profit	32

Note: Group profit = 92 + 32 = 124

(b) (i) The use of market price as a transfer price is likely to cause friction between the divisions because M Ltd make higher profit at the higher output whereas L Ltd's profit is greater at the lower output. Clearly, therefore, the market price does not represent the opportunity cost of the transferred units.

(ii) There are three major stages in setting a transfer price, each requiring consideration of different factors:

Stage 1 - identify the output level that will maximise company profit. This will require consideration of all possible price v output combinations, and the effect of differing volumes on cost.

Stage 2 - identify the opportunity cost of the units demanded for internal transfer, when operating at the company's optimum output. Factors to consider might include: external demand; external market price; marginal production costs; and whether scarce resources are utilised.

This will establish the transfer price that is required in order to achieve goal congruence.

Stage 3 - consider whether the transfer price based on opportunity cost is likely to give a fair share of profit to both divisions. If not, possible solutions might be: 2 part tariff; full cost plus pricing; dual pricing.

(c) From (a) company profit is greater at the higher output level (£124,000 against £100,000). We therefore need to establish the opportunity cost of the 450kl being demanded by L Ltd.

M Ltd has sufficient capacity to supply all 450kl to L, without affecting its supply of 500kl to its external customers. Therefore, since there is no mention of scarce resources, opportunity cost is M's variable cost of £200 per kl.

The next problem is whether a transfer price of £200 per kl will be fair to K Ltd and L Ltd. L Ltd will presumably be delighted in this reduction as it will significantly increase their profit. From K Ltd's view, however, it will be quite unacceptable to transfer at marginal cost - why should they do all that work and earn no contribution?

Solutions to consider might be:

(i) 2 part tariff (i.e. MC +)

(ii) full cost +

(iii) dual pricing.

A fourth alternative in this case, would be to set the transfer price at a level so that both divisions benefit by operating at the higher output level.

Minimum acceptable to M Ltd

	£
Minimum contribution required on internal sales (as (a))	40,000
At higher output, variable costs on these sales will be 450 @ £200	90,000
∴ Minimum acceptable internal revenue	£130,000

÷ 450kl = £288.89 per kl

Maximum acceptable to L Ltd	£
Minimum contribution required (as (a))	(80,000)
Sales revenue will be 18,000 @ £16	288,000
Variable costs (excluding transfers) will be 18,000 @ £3	(54,000)
∴ Maximum acceptable for transferred costs	£154,000

154,000 ÷ 450kl = £342.22 per kl

∴ Recommend transfer price of say £315 per kl

Index

T

U

V

W

Z

FTC Foulks Lynch
A **Kaplan Professional** Company

STUDY TEXT REVIEW FORM
ACCA Paper 3.3

Thank you for choosing the official text for your ACCA professional qualification. As we are constantly striving to improve our products, we would be grateful if you could provide us with feedback about how useful you found this publication.

Name: ....

Address: ....

....

Email: ....

Why did you decide to purchase this Study Text?

- Have used them in the past ☐
- Recommended by lecturer ☐
- Recommended by friend ☐
- Saw advertising ☐
- Other (please specify)..

How do you study?

- At a college ☐
- On a distance learning course ☐
- Home study ☐
- Other (please specify)..

Within our ACCA range we also offer Exam Kits and Pocket Notes. Is there any other type of service/publication that you would like to see as part of the range?

- CD Rom with additional questions and answers ☐
- A booklet that would help you master exam skills and techniques ☐
- Space on our website that would answer your technical questions and queries ☐
- Other (please specify)..

During the past six month do you recall seeing/receiving any of the following?

- Our advertisement in *Student Accountant* magazine? ☐
- Our advertisement in any other magazine? (please specify) ☐

....

- Our leaflet/brochure or a letter through the post? ☐
- Other (please specify)..

Overall opinion of this Study Text

	Excellent	*Adequate*	*Poor*
Introductory pages	☐	☐	☐
Syllabus coverage	☐	☐	☐
Clarity of explanations	☐	☐	☐
Clarity of definitions and key terms	☐	☐	☐
Diagrams	☐	☐	☐
Activities	☐	☐	☐
Self-test questions	☐	☐	☐
Practice questions	☐	☐	☐
Answers to practice questions	☐	☐	☐
Layout	☐	☐	☐
Index	☐	☐	☐

If you have further comments/suggestions or have spotted any errors, please write them on the next page.

Please return this form to: Veronica Wastell, Publisher, FTC Foulks Lynch, Swift House, Market Place, Wokingham, Berkshire, RG40 1AP, United Kingdom

Other comments/suggestions and errors

ftc
FTC Foulks Lynch
A **Kaplan Professional** Company

ACCA Order Form

Swift House, Market Place, Wokingham, Berkshire RG40 1AP, UK
Tel: +44 (0) 118 989 0629 Fax: +44 (0) 118 979 7455
Order online: www.financial-training.com
Email: publishing@financial-training.com

Examination Date: Dec 04 ☐ Jun 05 ☐ (please tick the exam you intend to take)	Study Text £23.00	Exam Kit £13.00	Pocket Notes £7.00
Part 1			
1.1 Preparing Financial Statements (UK)	☐	☐	☐
1.1 Preparing Financial Statements (International)	☐	☐	☐
1.2 Financial Information for Management	☐	☐	☐
1.3 Managing People	☐	☐	☐
Part 2			
2.1 Information Systems	☐	☐	☐
2.2 Corporate & Business Law	☐	☐	☐
2.2 Corporate & Business Law (Global)	☐	☐	☐
2.2 Corporate & Business Law (Scottish)	☐		
2.3 Business Taxation – FA 2004	☐	☐	☐
2.4 Financial Management & Control	☐	☐	☐
2.5 Financial Reporting (UK)	☐	☐	☐
2.5 Financial Reporting (International)	☐	☐	☐
2.6 Audit & Internal Review (UK)	☐	☐	☐
2.6 Audit & Internal Review (International)	☐	☐	☐
Part 3			
3.1 Audit & Assurance Services (UK)	☐	☐	☐
3.1 Audit & Assurance Services (International)	☐	☐	☐
3.2 Advanced Taxation – FA 2004	☐	☐	☐
3.3 Performance Management	☐	☐	☐
3.4 Business Information Management	☐	☐	☐
3.5 Strategic Business Planning & Development	☐	☐	☐
3.6 Advanced Corporate Reporting (UK)	☐	☐	☐
3.6 Advanced Corporate Reporting (International)	☐	☐	☐
3.7 Strategic Financial Management	☐	☐	☐
Research and Analysis Project Guide (supporting Oxford Brookes University BSc (Hons) in Applied Accounting)	£20 ☐		
Postage, Packaging and Delivery (per item): **Note**: Maximum postage charged for UK orders is £15		**TOTAL**	

Study Texts and Exam Kits	First	Each Extra	**Pocket Notes**	First	Each Extra
UK	£5.00	£2.00	UK	£2.00	£1.00
Europe (incl Republic of Ireland and Channel Isles)	£7.00	£4.00	Europe (incl Republic of Ireland and Channel Isles)	£3.00	£2.00
Rest of World	£22.00	£8.00	Rest of World	£8.00	£5.00

Product Sub Total £.................. **Postage & Packaging £.................** **Order Total £....................** **(Payments in UK £ Sterling)**

Customer Details

☐ Mr ☐ Mrs ☐ Ms ☐ Miss Other ....

Initials:.................................. Surname: ....

Address: ....

....

....

Postcode: ....

Delivery Address – if different from above

Address: ....

....

Postcode: ....

Telephone: ....

Email: ....

Fax: ....

Delivery please allow: United Kingdom – 5 working days
Europe – 8 working days
Rest of World – 10 working days

Payment

1 I enclose Cheque/Postal Order/Bankers Draft for £.....................................
Please make cheques payable to '**The Financial Training Company Ltd**'.

2 Charge MasterCard/Visa/Switch/Delta no:

Valid from: Expiry date:

Issue no:
(Switch only)

Signature: .... Date: ....

Declaration

I agree to pay as indicated on this form and understand that The Financial Training Company's Terms and Conditions apply (available on request).

Signature: .... Date: ....

Notes: All orders over 1kg will be fully tracked & insured. Signature required on receipt of order. Delivery times subject to stock availability. A telephone number or email address is required for orders that are to be delivered to a PO Box number.

ACCA
Official Publisher

Distance Learning Courses include VAT and all materials. Add postage & packing – applicable to both Distance Learning options (for rates see below).		**Distance Learning**		**Distance Learning** (excluding Official ACCA Study Text applicable for the December 2004 and June 2005 examinations sittings only)	
		£	✓	£	✓
Part 1					
1.1	Preparing Financial Statements (UK)	104		80	
1.1	Preparing Financial Statements (International)	104		80	
1.2	Financial Information for Management	104		80	
1.3	Managing People	104		80	
Part 2					
2.1	Information Systems	104		80	
2.2	Corporate & Business Law	104		80	
2.3	Business Taxation (FA 2003)	104		80	
2.4	Financial Management and Control	104		80	
2.5	Financial Reporting (UK)	104		80	
2.5	Financial Reporting (International)	104		80	
2.6	Audit & Internal Review (UK)	104		80	
2.6	Audit & Internal Review (International)	104		80	
Part 3 Options					
3.1	Audit & Assurance Services (UK)	104		80	
3.1	Audit & Assurance Services (International)	104		80	
3.2	Advanced Taxation (Finance Act 2003)	104		80	
3.3	Performance Management	104		80	
3.4	Business Information Management	104		80	
Part 3 Core					
3.5	Strategic Business Planning & Development	104		80	
3.6	Advanced Corporate Reporting (UK)	104		80	
3.6	Advanced Corporate Reporting (International)	104		80	
3.7	Strategic Financial Management	104		80	

FEES	£
Postage & Packing	£
Total	£

POSTAGE & PACKING

Distance Learning (per paper):

UK & NI £6, Europe & Channel Islands £15, Rest of World £40

DISTANCE LEARNING TERMS AND CONDITIONS OF ENROLMENT:

1. Full payment of fees or employer's authorisation is required prior to despatch of materials.
2. Where an employer's authorisation is received, the full fees are payable within 30 days of the invoice date. The employer is responsible for the payment of fees due in all circumstances including termination of employment or cancellation of course. FTC Foulks Lynch reserves the right to charge interest on overdue accounts.
3. A deferral to the following exam sitting can be processed subject to a deferral fee of £25 if notified in writing. If new study materials are required due to syllabus changes or changes in Finance Acts, they will have to be paid for in addition to the deferral fee.
4. No cancellation or refund can be made after materials have been despatched.
5. Courses are not transferable between students.
6. Distance Learning fees include VAT and all materials but exclude any taxes or duties imposed by countries outside the UK.

METHODS OF PAYMENT:

☐ Please invoice my employer (details completed overleaf).

☐ I enclose a cheque made payable to The Financial Training Company Ltd for £ ____________

Payments will only be accepted in UK Sterling.

☐ Please charge my Credit/Debit Card Number for the fees indicated above.

Expiry ☐☐☐☐ Solo/Switch Issue No ☐☐ Security Code ☐☐☐

I agree to the terms and conditions of enrolment which I have read.

Student Signature ______________________________ Date ________________